# FAITH ON THE FRONTIER

# FAITH ON THE FRONTIER

*A Life of J.H. Oldham*

KEITH CLEMENTS

T&T CLARK • EDINBURGH

WCC PUBLICATIONS • GENEVA

Published jointly by

T&T CLARK LTD
59 GEORGE STREET
EDINBURGH EH2 2LQ
SCOTLAND
www.tandtclark.co.uk

and

WCC PUBLICATIONS
PO BOX 2100
1211 GENEVA 2
SWITZERLAND
www.wcc.coe.org



T&T Clark ISBN 0 567 08690 9
WCC ISBN 2 8254 1289 9

British Library Cataloguing-in-Publication Data
A catalogue record for this book is available from the British Library

Typeset by Waverley Typesetters, Galashiels
Printed and bound in Great Britain by Page Bros, Norwich

*To my many friends in the ecumenical movement*
*who, consciously or not, owe gratitude to*
*J.H. Oldham*

# Contents

## Part III
## MISSION AND THE CORRIDORS OF COLONIAL POWER



## Part IV
## CHURCH, COMMUNITY AND STATE



## Part V
## CRISIS, WAR AND SOCIETY 1938–45



## Part VI
## STILL "A PERFECTLY MAD ADVENTURE"

# *List of Illustrations*

# Foreword

It is a privilege and pleasure for me to contribute a foreword to this long-awaited and distinguished biography of Joseph Houldsworth Oldham (affectionately known as Joe Oldham) by Keith Clements. Dr Clements has already given an adequate introduction to Joe Oldham in his preface and prologue, completed by his epilogue. I would only like to indicate some of the moments when Oldham touched my life in the ecumenical movement as an example of the immense impact he had on so many of us throughout this "century of extremes", as historians call it.

I participated in the first assembly of the World Council of Churches in 1948 as one of the hundred youth delegates. We were supposed to have our meetings separately on the four sections. I chose the third on "The Church and the Disorder of Society", and at Amsterdam I chaired the group dealing with this theme. So I read the essays of Oldham on "Technics and Civilisation" and especially on "A Responsible Society". This phrase became a leitmotiv of the assembly and of my own life.

After the assembly, I joined the staff of the British Student Christian Movement with responsibility for the overseas department, concerned with mission (Oldham had been secretary for the Student Volunteer Missionary Union in 1896–97), international affairs, the care of overseas students and student relief. To prepare myself I read a book Oldham had written in 1916 on *The World and the Gospel.* His concluding words have remained with me throughout my pastoral and ecumenical ministry:

> God does not call us to withdraw from the world, but believing in Him and abiding in Him to press into its living heart, to open our eyes to all its truth, to sound the depths of its need and to meet and overcome its sin. Only in doing this can we know what the love of God is . . . It is only in attempting to apply the law of Christ to the whole of our social and national life and in seeking to evangelize the whole world that we shall become rooted and grounded in love . . .

It was also at that time that I acquired Oldham's classic *Devotional Diary*, published in 1947 in its fifteenth edition, and I encouraged students to use it, as I still do. At the time Oldham's *Real Life Is Meeting* (1942) not only introduced me to Martin Buber's *I and Thou* and all his other writings, but enabled me to develop an ecumenical style of living and acting. This was intensified by reflecting on what he himself called his "testimony", *Life Is Commitment* (1953).

On the eve of my joining the staff of the Methodist Missionary Society in London in 1961, with responsibility for West Africa and the West Indies, I came across another of Oldham's books, written with his colleague Ms B.D. Gibson on *The Remaking of Man in Africa* (1931), which still makes refreshing reading. But even more challenging was his *Christianity and the Race Problem* (1924), which was very relevant, especially in Oldham's declaration: "When Christians find in the world a state of affairs that is not in accord with the truth they have learned from Christ, their concern is not that it should be explained but that it should be ended. In that temper we must approach everything in the relations between races that cannot be reconciled with the Christian ideal." At that period I was involved with a group at the Institute for Race Relations in London, struggling with these issues, and we often went to Oldham's old haunt, the Athenaeum, for special encounters and a meal.

Early in 1967, I rejoined the staff of the World Council of Churches as director of the Commission of World Mission and Evangelism, formerly the International Missionary Council of which Oldham was the first secretary. I was also editor of the *International Review of Mission*, which Oldham founded. One of my first acts was to read his editorials and articles from 1912. This exercise was both enlightening and encouraging. By 1969, just before Oldham died, we were able to launch the Programme to Combat Racism, and our major emphases were "Mission on Six Continents" and "The Church for Others".

Even though we did not have a chance to engage in long conversations, due to his deafness, Oldham was my model in all my ministry since 1948, and not least during the time (1972–84) that I was general secretary of the World Council of Churches. This testimony is confirmed by reading Keith Clements' very thorough, faithful and excellently arranged and written biography of Joe Oldham, whom my old chief, Wilhelm Visser 't Hooft described as the one to whom the ecumenical movement owed more than to any other of its pioneers.

PHILIP POTTER

# Preface

A book on J.H. Oldham, one of the greatest ecumenical pioneers of the 20th century, ought by rights to have appeared long before now. That it has not done so in the thirty years since his death is not due to lack of effort on anyone's part. When Oldham had still a few years to live Kathleen Bliss, his close friend and collaborator for over twenty years, secured his reluctant agreement to her attempting his biography. With her characteristic energy and thoroughness Kathleen Bliss set about gathering an archive of Joe Oldham's papers and letters. Oldham himself was not the most reliable keeper of his own documents, and on one occasion Kathleen Bliss was alarmed to find him in his garden cheerfully constructing a bonfire out of several piles of them. Oldham's somewhat cavalier indifference to a biography was of a piece with his characteristic self-effacement. Never having sought the limelight during his life, he considered that the next generation would have far more important tasks to undertake than that of reconstructing his particular career.

Kathleen Bliss's work continued and intensified after Joe Oldham's death in 1969, and by the 1980s she had not only assembled a considerable archive from Oldham himself and from other sources, but had also made a start on the actual writing. Her efforts however were overtaken by illness. On the eve of her death in September 1989, she made clear her dearest wish that the work which she had begun should be taken up and completed by another. She had appointed Duncan Forrester, for some years her colleague in the University of Sussex, and subsequently professor of Christian ethics and practical theology at New College, Edinburgh, as her literary executor. The Oldham Archive was transferred to the library of New College, and Duncan Forrester was entrusted with the responsibility of ensuring the completion of the project.

In 1990 Duncan Forrester approached me with a view to taking on this task. I readily accepted, knowing full well that it would be full of interest but perhaps not quite as aware how demanding it would also prove. It has been my main literary preoccupation for the past seven years, during which time I have been working, first, at the international affairs desk of the Council of Churches for Britain and Ireland (CCBI) and then, since September 1997, as general secretary of the Conference of European Churches based in Geneva. Compared with my previous existence in largely academic life, opportunities for sustained research and writing were few. The work, being extra-mural to my primary commitments, has been done as much in late-night sessions, in conference-centre bedrooms and on intercity trains commuting between Bristol and London, as in libraries and in the study. Nevertheless, to have kept such close company with Joe Oldham while wrestling with the practicalities of ecumenical life today has been an overwhelmingly great and inspiring privilege.

This book is *a* life, and does not claim to be *the* life, of J.H. Oldham. Quite simply, Oldham lived so long, and did, wrote and thought so much, that a fully comprehensive and definitive account would not be possible within the covers of a single volume of manageable size. Time and again I had to concede that a particular topic merited far fuller treatment, and would have to await yet more detailed research, than I myself could afford. In no area was this more apparent than in Oldham's dealings with colonial policy in Africa, and it is encouraging to note that this is attracting the attention of a new generation of scholars whose work we must await with interest. Nevertheless, I hope that the book as it stands will contribute to a fresh awareness of Oldham and his significance, especially for the ecumenical movement which today is in urgent need of recovering its own "memory".

What has transpired in the pages that follow owes much to many other people. First and foremost, of course, to Kathleen Bliss herself belongs the immeasurable credit for initiating the project, assembling the archive which has been so crucial, and beginning the writing. In terms of actual content, approximately 44 per cent of the first six chapters incorporates her draft text. The rest of the writing is mine. Overall therefore this is not the book that she would have written (and doubtless in her forthright way much pungent comment would have been scribbled in the margins), but without her it would not have appeared. I hope that in some measure at least it may be thought worthy of her aspirations to do justice to the one whom she admired so greatly, and a fulfilment of the hopes she herself did not live to see realized.

Second, to Duncan Forrester who drew me into the project, I owe more than I can say for his continual interest, support and encouragement, not to mention patience, over these years. It has been a pleasure to be associated with New College, Edinburgh, as an honorary fellow and to benefit from many of its facilities. But the most delightful aspect of the relationship has been the warm hospitality in the Murrayfield home of Duncan and Margaret Forrester on the numerous visits to Edinburgh which the work entailed.

It is one thing to have an archive, but quite another to have an archive which is properly sorted, classified and indexed so as to be of maximum usefulness to the researcher. In 1993 Dr William Naphy (now of the department of history, University of Aberdeen) was employed on the archive with this in view. Not only did he create an excellent annotated index, but he also offered a number of highly perceptive comments on certain of the contents, for which I have been grateful. Dr Naphy also surveyed materials in the Public Record Office and Lambeth Palace library.

That archival work was greatly assisted by a fund specially created by the Evangelical Church of Germany with contributions from seven of its *Landkirchen* (Evangelisch-lutherische Kirche in Bayern, Evangelisch-lutherische Landeskirche Hannover, Evangelische Kirche in Hessen and Nassau, Nordelbische Evangelisch-lutherische Kirche, Evangelische Kirche in Rheinland, Evangelische Kirche of Westfalen, Evangelische Landeskirche in Württemberg), to support the Oldham biographical project, under the initiative in particular of Bishop Dr Heinz Joachim Held. Other costs incurred have similarly been met from this fund. The reason why it is in Germany, in particular, that a debt of gratitude should be felt towards J.H. Oldham, will, I trust, emerge in the book itself. Here, my own appreciation for the support of Bishop Held and the German churches must be recorded. The writing of the central chapters was undertaken during a period of special study leave in the summer of 1997 granted me by the CCBI prior to my moving to Geneva. I am grateful both to the CCBI for this and, again, to the German Church fund which underwrote part of this study period.

Much is owed to many other individuals. I was especially glad to be able to interview at length some who knew Joe Oldham personally: the Very Revd Eric Fenn and Mrs Fenn; the late Bishop Lesslie Newbigin and Mrs Helen Newbigin; Dr Daniel Jenkins; and Prof. Kenneth Grayston. Others with whom I have conversed or corresponded on their recollections are Dr Paul Abrecht, Prof. Eberhard Bethge and Dr Renate Bethge, the Revd Rupert Bliss, Lady Deborah Cassidi (daughter of Kathleen Bliss), the late Revd Clifford Cleal, the late Prof. Donald Mackinnon, the late Canon David Paton, Prof. Ronald Preston, Dr Marjorie Reeves and Dr Philip Potter who has also kindly written the foreword. In addition, among Kathleen Bliss's papers in the archive were found a number of letters from people who had written to her with their reminiscences and who should therefore also be noted here, in particular the Revd James Dougall, Mrs Muriel Duncan, Prof. Donald MacKay, the Very Revd Alan Richardson, and Dr Monica Wilson.

Other scholars have been of great assistance at several points. Two unpublished pieces of work should especially be mentioned. First, there is the Ph.D. thesis of Warham Lance Martin, "Joseph Houldsworth Oldham: His Thought and Its Development" (University of St Andrews 1967). I was glad to make use of the bibliography which Dr Martin had constructed and, with his ready concurrence, to adapt and at some points amend it for the bibliography included in this work. Second, I much appreciate Dr Daphne Hampson's willingness to allow me to consult her D.Phil. thesis "The British Responses to the German Church Struggle 1933–1939" (University of Oxford

1973) which by turns corroborated and corrected the picture which I had gained of Oldham's dealings with Nazi Germany. Others to whom I am grateful for comments, additional information or indication of important sources are Dr David Bebbington, Dr Andrew Chandler, Dr Ruth Franzen, Prof. Adrian Hastings, Dr Eleanor Jackson, Dr Marjorie Reeves, Sir William Taylor and Prof. Charles West.

Librarians and archivists are indispensable in work of this kind. At New College, Edinburgh, the former librarian Dr Murray Simpson and his successor Mrs Pamela Gilchrist, with their staff, gave readily of their time in helping me make best use of the Oldham Archive. Martha L. Smalley of the Yale University Divinity Library helped me in some vital detective work on the Oldham–Mott correspondence, not least in obtaining a full copy of Oldham's remarkable letter of 5 August 1914, the use of which is hereby gratefully acknowledged. Brenda Hough and Sarah Duffield at the Church of England Record Centre traced several important items from the early days of the British Council of Churches. Mr Matthew Steggle, archives assistant at Trinity College, Oxford, provided valuable information on the college's scene in Oldham's undergraduate days as well as supplying the college photographs which are gratefully included in the volume. Similar help has been provided by Dr Pauline Adams, librarian of Somerville College, Oxford. In Geneva, I have benefited greatly from the assistance of the librarian of the World Council of Churches, M. Pierre Beffa and also the staff of the photographic services section. The staffs of the Selly Oak Colleges library and the India Office library have been most helpful, and no acknowledgments would be complete without mention of that unsurpassed treasure-trove in London, the British Library and its staff.

Use of the following photographs is by permission of the British Library: p.7 (Bombay) shelfmark 752/15(19); p.42 (Lahore) shelfmark 406/1(16); p.45 (S.K. Datta) MSS Eur F 178/83. Acknowledgment is made for use of photographs on other pages as follows: pp.12, 309: New College Library, Edinburgh; pp.17, 25: Trinity College, Oxford; p.53: Somerville College, Oxford; p.191: Council of the National YMCAs of India; p.370: St Deiniol's Library, Hawarden; p.404: Revd Rupert Bliss and family; p.454: SCM Press; p.463: The family of the late Bishop Lesslie Newbigin; all other photographs: WCC Photographic Archive, Geneva.

Final acknowledgments must include those who have helped in all kinds of practical ways, from computer-problem-solving and manuscript-preparation to hunting for sources and photographs, beginning with my wife Margaret who in addition must at times have felt she was married to Joe Oldham as well as me, and including friends and colleagues such as Richard Bingle, Colin Davey, Robin Gurney, Francoise Maxian, Gillian Paterson and Irmhild Reichen-Young, and not forgetting of course the staff of the World Council of Churches' Publications Department. I apologize for overlooking any others who deserve mention: perhaps I can cover myself with a general word of thanks to all, not forgetting the anonymous fellow-passenger sitting behind me on the London–Bristol intercity train who, evidently fixated on the screen of my lap-top computer, tapped me on the shoulder to say, "Hey, you've spelt 'disappointed' wrong."

In conclusion, a personal word is appropriate on what I have discovered of my own relation to Joe Oldham. When Duncan Forrester invited me to undertake the task, I was probably typical of many in my generation who knew of J.H. Oldham and his importance in a general kind of way. I had even quoted him from time to time. The more deeply I went into his life and thought, however, the more I realized just how much I was already indebted to him, and how many aspects of ecumenical life and Christian social thinking which I took for granted in fact owed their genesis to him. Moreover, I became aware that much of his influence, more than I realized, had been transmitted to me through two figures, both now departed, whom I am fortunate to count among my chief mentors in theology and ministry. Alec Vidler, my first theological teacher in Cambridge, had worked closely with Oldham during and immediately after the second world war. Clifford Cleal, my senior minister in my first Baptist pastorate in Cheshire, had collaborated with him as a staff person in the early years of the British Council of Churches. I was indeed blessed to have been able to absorb, if unconsciously, some of the Oldham inheritance in this way. But with the passing of the generations, a more conscious retrieval of the legacy is necessary and to that end this work is gratefully dedicated.

KEITH CLEMENTS
*Geneva, summer 1999*

# *Prologue: The Sundial*

IN the grounds of the Ecumenical Centre in Geneva, home to the World Council of Churches and kindred bodies, stands a small sundial. Engraved on its face are the words:

TO THE MEMORY OF
JOSEPH H. OLDHAM 1874–1969
MISSIONARY STATESMAN FOREMOST PIONEER OF WCC
FRIEND OF AFRICA

The sundial is so unobtrusive that even many of the people who work at the Ecumenical Centre seem hardly to notice it. If they do, they are unlikely to give it more than a glance as they hurry past, for the words themselves have become worn with time and weather. By design and default, all of this adds to the aptness of a memorial to one who for all his achievements was remarkably self-effacing. He did not court publicity, preferring to work mostly behind the scenes, and for much of his working life had to endure the silent world of deafness.

But the words engraved on the sundial speak of great matters and achievements, any one of which would be enough for a normal biography. Moreover, as this account will show, even to describe him as missionary statesman, foremost pioneer of the World Council of Churches and friend of Africa, is to tell but half the tale. To comprehend adequately such a life and its significance is an unusual challenge both to the writer and the reader.

Precisely because such a life was so full, the danger is that the story will become a sheer catalogue of events and writings, simply an enlarged version of the subject's engagement diaries, and the person himself in all his individuality will be lost. Right at the beginning, therefore, it is useful to present a vignette of the person to be met throughout these pages, as he was remembered by those who knew him and worked with him.

Joe Oldham was usually spoken of as a Scot, and he possessed many characteristics which others (certainly the English) tend to think of as Scottish: caution, tenacity, reserve, individuality and industry. He was of medium height, spare in physique, keen-faced and with clear blue eyes, balding by middle age. He was brisk in movement, a fair rugby player in youth and a strong walker, for whom the Scottish hills were an almost lifelong source of refreshment. His speech had a roughened 'r' and was enriched by many Scottish words and phrases. He was proud of Scotland's history and culture: for reading aloud he turned most frequently to Burns and Scott, Stevenson and Buchan. He found it useful on occasion to keep his distance from typically English dissensions and to refer to himself as an "outsider".

Nevertheless like some others of his generation, he thought of himself as a Scot who was not thereby debarred from being English. No author took precedence with him over Shakespeare, no game excited him as much as cricket; he enjoyed English jokes, he believed in English institutions. Part of his sense of dual nationality was his church allegiance. When in 1920 he made his home in England he immediately became a regular communicant at the parish church in the village of Chipstead on the edge of London's green belt where he and his wife Mary lived for about thirty years. But he had left Scotland as an elder of the Free Church of Scotland. For him, as for others who moved from Scotland, a higher value was placed on belonging to the church of one's community or place than to one form or another of church order. Their Chipstead home, incidentally, was the Dial House, so called because there too was a sundial set on the flagstones, a well-remembered feature for their many guests from all over the world and from all walks of life. The Geneva memorial therefore also recalls that English garden which Joe and Mary Oldham lovingly cared for with their hands and where they also took time to be still.

Working unobtrusively behind the scenes did not mean that Joe Oldham preferred solitude to company. "Real life is meeting" became almost a catchphrase associated with him during the 1940s. He was never so effective as when he brought people together in small groups to hammer out an issue together, or as when he sought to get to know someone in one-to-one conversation, preferably over lunch in a London club, having read that person's book or House-of-Lords speech some days previously. Anyone with more than the scantiest awareness of who Oldham was loves to cite what is almost universally regarded as his motto: "Find out where power lies and then take it to lunch at the Athenaeum." Unfortunately, this book will not be able to substantiate that Joe Oldham himself ever actually said this. But the fact that it *was* said so often about him is testimony to how he was regarded, generally with affection and amusement as well as admiration, by his contemporaries.

His is not an easy character to sum up. "A wily saint", says one; "that canny Scot", says another; "the silently omniscient (or omnipresent) Scotsman", say others. Another who knew him well says simply, "that great man of God"; yet another, "a modern prophet". In the pages that follow, let J.H. Oldham as far as possible speak for himself.

PART I

# TO BE A MISSIONARY

CHAPTER I

# *The Cradle: India, Scotland and Evangelicalism*

JOSEPH HOULDSWORTH OLDHAM was born in India on 10 October 1874, the eldest child of Captain George Wingate Oldham and his wife Eliza – "Lillah" as she was generally known. In a mission church in Girgaum, a hot and noisy part of Bombay, he was baptized and given the Christian name of his paternal grandfather and his mother's maiden name.

George Oldham[1] had by then been in India for fourteen years, steadily and successfully pursuing his career as a military engineer employed in public works, especially railways. His early life, however, had not run so smoothly. He was born in Dublin in 1840, the third son to an English merchant, Joseph Oldham, and his wife Christina. Christina was the daughter of Andrew Wingate, a Glasgow merchant, and while George was still an infant the Oldhams moved out of Glasgow so that his father might take up a partnership in the Wingate business. Christina Oldham died when George was only 3 years old, and just four years later Joseph died too. George's brothers both died when he was 10. He was left with a younger sister, born shortly before his mother's death, and a half-sister, Sarah, the child of his father's brief second marriage. Thereafter George's family life was to be provided, with generosity and warmth, in the homes of his stepmother and uncles and aunts. In his teens he was sent south for schooling at Wimbledon, and while there became closely attached to his uncle Sir George Wingate, whose house at Tichfield in Hampshire became a second home to him. George Wingate had had a distinguished career as an engineer officer in the East India Company, and it was doubtless under his influence that George Oldham was directed towards a similar course. In 1857 George entered Addiscombe, the military college of the East India Company,

[1] See H.W. Oldham, *Lt-Col. G.W. Oldham R.E.: A Memoir*, London, Morgan & Scott, 1927, on which this chapter draws extensively.

and did well enough to qualify for a commission in the Engineers and to receive further officer training at Chatham.

In May 1860, aged 20, he embarked for India. It was a very significant year in which to arrive in the country. The previous year had seen the catastrophe of the Great Mutiny, and already drastic changes in British administration were being enacted by parliament. The East India Company, which for some 250 years had operated as an autonomous body under charter from the British government, growing from a purely trading enterprise into a formidable administrative machine over the territory it controlled, was effectively abolished and all its rights and responsibilities transferred directly to the crown. The governor was now called viceroy; Queen Victoria would be proclaimed empress of India in 1876. The army itself, hitherto in effect the private army of the Company, was of course directly affected by these changes and by lessons learnt (as regards imperial interests) from the Mutiny. The proportion of Indian to British troops was reduced, and Indian recruits were now to be mainly from those communities which had proved most loyal to their British commanders during the uprising. Artillery and other "scientific" military specialities were to be firmly in the hands of the British. Politically, British rule was to be somewhat more circumspect, if more thorough in its methods. The frenetic pace of Westernization pursued by Lord Dalhousie during his governorship in the late 1850s was brought under control. The policy of "lapse", whereby territories of princes with no natural heirs would on their death automatically be ceded to British rule, was discontinued, and in fact a new phase began in which Indian princes were courted as client rulers by the crown and proved to be an elite corps of support for the British Raj. Anti-Western religious feeling, on the part of both Muslims and Hindus, was recognized to have been a key factor behind the Mutiny, and Western missionaries were implicitly cautioned against becoming over-zealous in their work: education rather than evangelism became its primary expression.

Young Lieutenant Oldham was assigned to the Corps of Engineers in Bombay. The first months in India, demanding enough for any new subaltern, must have been made even more so by the reorganization of the army and the new tasks being given to it. After postings to Poona and Mhow, he was assigned to work on the Bombay harbour defences, and at the same time his East India Company Engineers were amalgamated with the Royal Engineers in which he received a Queen's commission. With the boom in Indian cotton, Bombay was rapidly expanding as a port and commercial centre, and new defence batteries on islands in the harbour were considered essential.

It was, however, in the area of public works that British energy in post-Mutiny India was most marked, and above all in the great programme of railway-construction. If nothing else, the Mutiny had underlined the significance of rapid communications, and a reduced army would need railways and metalled roads. The advantages for the commercial development and physical unification of India were in any case clear enough (not to mention the profits to British manufacturers who supplied the entire outlay of track, locomotives

*Bombay, late 19th century*

and rolling-stock). The railways were also to prove their worth in the great famines of 1876–78 and later. In 1859 there had been just 432 miles of track. By 1869 there were 5,000. By the end of the century, there would be 25,000 miles. It was to the early phase of this huge expansion that George Oldham's talents were now to be devoted. In 1865 he was posted to Nagpur as a consulting engineer officer to the railway department. With other such colleagues he had a comprehensive range of duties, from deciding on the routes of new lines and approval of designs to estimates of costs of construction and periodic inspection of all track and bridges for safety requirements. In 1867 he had the satisfaction of seeing the first train steam into Nagpur amid great public excitement.

Lieutenant Oldham must have seemed a typical young officer of the "best" type: highly competent and diligent at his work, and a popular figure at the balls, parties and hunting expeditions in his spare time. Like most of his peers, such contact as he did have with Indians themselves would have been in a purely official capacity. He never learned an Indian language. The British in India were increasingly drawing themselves into a self-contained life apart from the "natives". Long gone were the early days of the East India Company when not a few of the traders and officials, relatively isolated in their new, strange yet alluring environment, "went Indian" to the extent of speaking the local language, wearing Indian dress, and taking an Indian mistress if not an Indian wife. During the first half of the 19th century several new factors in the British presence worked against such experiments. The increasing size of the British community, gradually joined by more British women, itself encouraged social self-containment. But in addition, particularly under the rising evangelical influence even among East India Company officials, there was the increasingly moralistic dismissal of the Indian ethos. Into this already growing sense of distance, the Mutiny of 1859 and its brutal suppression injected a fundamental, mutual mistrust from which India never recovered during the "long afternoon" of empire. One historian has commented on this period:

> The wall that insulated white *sahib* society from the natives suddenly loomed impervious to any but a handful of princes and landed gentry, and even they complained of feeling mistrusted, eternally suspect outsiders. New towns and suburbs, called civil lines and camps, were now built for British officials and their wives, with grand "bungalows" on wide, tree-lined streets and spacious roads through which a regiment of troops could gallop swiftly, if needed, to put down any "trouble". The post-Mutiny separation of "races" brought a boom to the overseas market for British brides, now that fear of the treachery of Indian "housekeepers" made most young servants of the crown prefer the comfort and security of a British spouse to the availability of a native mistress . . . The British Club emerged as the insular nucleus of European society, and it was to retain its mid-Victorian mannerisms and morality on Indian soil long after Edwardian attitudes and fresh ideas liberated London from the narrow formalism and rigidity of such inhibiting mores. Distrust, frustration and fear fed upon one another throughout the era of crown rule . . .[2]

This was the world which George Oldham inhabited, as a person of his time, probably unquestioningly. It is doubtful if he was a rabid "imperialist" such as came towards the end of the century when, faced with a succession of crises and rivalries, the British empire required a concerted ideology to justify itself. Most probably, like many others, George Oldham simply accepted British rule of India as a fact and, on that basis, believed that it ought to be exercised as dutifully, competently and fairly as possible.

George Oldham completed eight years of competent government service and relatively comfortable bachelor existence in India, and returned to England for his first leave in October 1868. En route homeward in Egypt he took time to see the nearly-completed Suez Canal, which was to affect British India still further by reducing so drastically the sea-distance. But changes were also in store for Oldham himself on his home leave, in ways he could barely have imagined, and he was to return to India a rather different person.

First of all, while attending the wedding of one of Sir George Wingate's daughters, he fell in love at first sight with Lillah Houldsworth, a niece of Lady Wingate and younger daughter of John Houldsworth of Glasgow.

Second, he experienced a profound religious conversion. It began with reflections at the death-bed of an uncle in Scotland and was triggered into full life by a sermon he heard some weeks after his uncle's death, when attending church with his bereaved aunt at Kilcreggan. The preacher was Henry Batchelor,

[2] S. Wolpert, *A New History of India*, 3rd ed., Oxford, Oxford Univ. Press, 1989, p.245.

a Congregational minister from Glasgow, and his text was Hebrews 7:25: "Wherefore He is able to save them to the uttermost that come unto God by Him, seeing He ever liveth to make intercession for them." It was the preacher's emphasis upon the *risen, living* Christ which struck George Oldham as nothing had done before, and he always spoke of this day as the beginning of his Christian life. Not long afterwards in October 1869 his diary made its first ever reference to God: "At Crofton – church morning and afternoon. Took the sacrament for the first time. May God keep me in the way of life!"[3]

Meanwhile his courtship of Lillah Houldsworth progressed. Already of similar and deep religious conviction, she eventually consented to marry him. The wedding took place in June 1870 in an Episcopalian church in Glasgow, and soon after the couple were on board ship for India.

George Oldham resumed his railway engineering work, and within weeks was promoted captain. The Oldhams first made their home on Malabar Hill, a fashionable residential area favoured for its airy situation and magnificent views. George Oldham's day now included early morning and household prayer and Bible study as well as his army duties. Very quickly he also began making new friends – unusually, Indian as well as European – within the Christian community. "The Christian society here", he wrote, "is so very agreeable – all denominations work so well together."[4] Significantly, it was to a church in the heat and dust of Girgaum in the city that he and Lillah devoted themselves. George Oldham's faith emphasized "peace in the Holy Ghost" in contrast to a life of strenuous spiritual effort.[5] It would be easy, at this remove, to imagine a figure of unctuous piety. But all the written accounts and reminiscences speak of a man whose faith, centred on a joyful, personal relationship with the living Christ, flowed out naturally in a genuine, loving concern for people as individuals irrespective of their religious, social or racial background. The genuineness of that faith and commitment, his wife's no less than his own, was demonstrated when after two and half years the Oldhams left the breezy avenues of Malabar for the noise and smells of Girgaum itself, to share the mission bungalow with T.K. Weatherhead, pastor of the Girgaum church. It was asked of George Oldham whether he ought not to have stayed on in Malabar Hill to witness to his new faith in that polite but indifferent society. His reply was that he had not dropped his former friends nor refused invitations to their houses, "but that he must be free to speak of Christ, and in so doing found that he ceased to be invited".[6]

Not that George Oldham was now short of company. He enjoyed many close friendships not only with missionaries but with Indian Christians, especially Manekji Mody, a Parsee convert whose conversion led to his being cast out by his own people. When in 1877 T.K. Weatherhead and his wife moved to the CMS mission house, it was at the Oldhams' invitation that Mody

[3] Oldham, p.29.
[4] *Ibid.*, p.36.
[5] *Ibid.*, p.39.
[6] *Ibid.*, p.40.

moved into the bungalow with them – a far cry indeed from the conventional European attitude to relationships with Indians. When the Oldhams went on home leave in 1875, they took Mody with them and placed him in a missionary college for two years' study. On Mody's return – with an English wife – he began a full-time ministry of preaching and teaching in Bombay.

This was the atmosphere into which the Oldhams' first son was born in Girgaum, in 1874: of sincere and joyful evangelical piety, of discipline and diligence in work where the highest standards were aimed at, and of openness in friendship to people of all sorts and conditions, set in a teeming city of great human need at every level. "Joey", as his mother called, him was a healthy child, and life at Girgaum was full of interest and unmarred by any tragedy. The family spent 1875–76 on home leave in Scotland, where the next son, George, was born. The third son, Harry, arrived soon after their return to Bombay. Lillah Oldham kept a notebook in which she recorded her children's spiritual progress. She watches anxiously for signs that they have the relationship with God which she earnestly tries to inculcate by teaching them to pray, and Joey – by turns strongly antipathetic to the discipline and fluent in the use of its phraseology – delights her by announcing that "he wants to grow up to be God's man and not fight Georgie".[7]

For a while George Oldham continued his Christian activities with ever-increasing zeal, adding to his concerns the formation of the Bombay YMCA in 1875. But his government duties grew more onerous. In 1878 he was promoted major, and the following year was appointed acting consulting engineer and under-secretary for railways to the Bombay government, with a seat on the legislative council. The famine of 1876–78 and the Afghan war of 1879–80 threw even greater pressure on the railways, and Major Oldham had to concede a curtailment of his religious activities. Meanwhile another concern was looming. Health was always a natural preoccupation for the British in India, and the welfare of Lillah Oldham, having borne three children in almost as many years, was causing particular concern. The Oldhams' next home leave was due in 1881, and it was decided that, for the mother and children at least, this would be goodbye to India. The family returned to Britain in the spring. George Oldham returned to India briefly, having resolved to retire from the army with the rank of Lieutenant Colonel – twenty years' service assured him of a comfortable pension at that rank. He was only 41 years old, and in many ways in an enviable position to start a new career. He rejoined his family in Scotland on the last day of 1881 – the family now rejoicing in the addition of a new-born daughter, Lallah.

George Oldham already had an inkling of where his future course might lie, for he had proven gifts in preaching and teaching. Moreover, opportunities were awaiting a man of his deep religious conviction, practical aptitudes and

[7] Bliss MS, p.6 (Kathleen Bliss's draft of earlier chapters of her projected book on Oldham, which is incorporated or drawn into the first six chapters of this book).

willingness to cooperate with others. The late 1870s and early 1880s were years of agricultural depression, of failing businesses and high unemployment. These hard times were accompanied by a revival of evangelical Christianity, particularly in Scotland where the American evangelists Dwight L. Moody and Ira D. Sankey had made their first big impact during 1873–74. George Oldham soon made contact with groups in and around Ayr such as the YMCA, the Ayrshire Christian Union and the Ayr Working Men's Christian Union. Soon his gift for expounding the Bible in simple language placed him in great demand, and he had no doubt that this indeed was his new vocation. He became an outstanding lay evangelist spending his time, when not with his family, on missions to towns and villages, conducting meetings, visiting in homes and cooperating with churches and organizations of all denominations. People commented that he always seemed to leave behind more harmony than he found (which cannot be said of all such itinerant ministries). Moreover in 1887 at the invitation of the Church Missionary Society he joined a group of missioners sent out to India and Ceylon (as it then was) for a preaching tour intended to encourage indigenous Christians and to evangelize among English-speaking Indians and Ceylonese.

After short stays at Ayr and Birnam the family settled at Crieff, set amidst the beautiful Perthshire hills. Among its advantages was the excellent boys' school, Morrison's Academy. George and Lillah Oldham were not the sort of evangelical pietists who simply wanted to prepare their offspring for heaven. With their belief that children were an inheritance from the Lord, and that human good is to be developed and offered back to God, was an underlining of the typically Scottish belief in the importance of education. Joe, with his father's sharp features and bright eyes, was showing signs of more than usual intelligence. Yet another child, Jack, was born at Crieff in 1885.

Nearly everything seemed set fair for the Oldham family at Crieff. The older boys were doing well at school, sustained by a devoted, disciplined and cultured home life where expectations of achievement were high. George Oldham, supported whole-heartedly by his wife, was finding fulfilment in his new vocation as evangelist, and she too found equal joy both in the surrounding scenery and in local church work in Sunday school and mothers' meeting. The one dark cloud, always on the horizon, was her physical weakness. A heavy cold proved fatal and she died in March 1890. George Oldham made no secret of the bitterness of his loss, but the faith in the triumph of Christ over death to which he had been a convert more than twenty years ago now showed itself both in quiet confidence for himself and in an even deeper, tender solicitude for his five children. He knew that if he now had a vocation, it was to be a total commitment to their welfare. He set himself to make a new home life for them, aided by his half-sister Sarah who came to keep house. He gave up his evangelistic missions and all engagements that would take him away from home. Later he told his sons that he resolved to fulfil towards them the role that their mother had played in their religious upbringing and he certainly succeeded in making this enjoyable.

*J.H. Oldham's father, George Wingate Oldham*

George Oldham also continued to be concerned that they should have the best possible education and that raised an immediate problem. Joe, the eldest, was 15 when his mother died and was *Dux* – star pupil – of Morrison's Academy that summer. Where next? The choice made was for Edinburgh Academy for the three eldest boys, and that autumn the family moved to Walker Street, Edinburgh, a few minutes' walk from the city's world-famous Princes Street.

Scarcely had they settled in their new home when another tragedy struck in the summer of 1891. Lallah, 10 years old and a great favourite with her brothers, and her father's chief consolation, was taken ill with peritonitis and died. Death had the effect of drawing the family very close together and Jack, now so much the youngest, drew a true picture when he said: "Our family is like a rope with Joe first, then me, then George and Harry and Father beside us cheering us on." This role their father continued to perform throughout his life. During their school days all their concerns were followed with the greatest interest and he had a practical care for their clothing and the long-remembered "stout boots" they all had to wear. The older boys had bicycles, and outings and holidays were planned and greatly enjoyed. "Let the walkers go ahead," said Aunt Sarah on one of these expeditions; "*and* the talkers", muttered the silent brother George, with a glance at Joe who had a reputation for argument. Very likely it was on one of these outings that Joe manifested his sharpness of observation in a detail of natural history in a highland glen, which he recalled many years later when arguing that "emotions which have all the appearance of being instinctive may have their real origin in experiences that are socially transmitted". He records:

> While we were standing with our bicycles, three or four young birds flew across from a neighbouring tree and perched on the handle-bars. For two or three minutes they were as happy as could be. Then the mother bird returned to the tree, and quite obviously told them that they were in grave danger. They immediately took alarm and flew away.[8]

There was certainly plenty to talk about in an intelligent family that took an interest in what was going on in the world. This was the time, in any case, when debate on public and political affairs – notably inaugurated by Gladstone's Midlothian speech of 1879 – was bursting into fashion at all levels in society, not least through the growth of the popular press. No doubt the Academy buzzed with debate about the "Newcastle Programme" put out by the Liberals in 1891, with its proposal to disestablish the Church of Scotland and Church of Wales. The family's political colour was mildly Tory and Joe drew a caricature of Mr Gladstone to help his youngest brother in identification.

Edinburgh Academy was one of Scotland's finest schools. To be *Dux* there, as Joe Oldham was in 1892, was a distinction in itself and a promise of further academic honours. For such a bright student the choice of a career was now the leading question. His father and several of his relations on both sides of the family were soldiers and administrators. The Wingates, whom Joe later referred to as "the cousins we saw most of when we were young", were a formidable and distinguished band in both walks of life. Joe used subsequently to say that he might have made a general; but his choice while at Edinburgh fell on administrative service, presumably in India. Entrance to the higher grades of the civil service was hotly contested by competitive examination and Oxford was the recognized route for some of the ablest entrants. In October 1892 therefore, shortly before his 18th birthday, Joe Oldham bid farewell to Edinburgh and home and entered Trinity College, Oxford.

George Oldham must have watched his firstborn depart from Waverley station with a mixture of pride and anxiety. Oxford, he knew, could offer the greatest opportunities for worthy advancement – but also, from his evangelical point of view, worldly allurements. He entered in his diary an earnest prayer that it would not be the latter. He could not know, then, that for Joe Oxford was to be the opening up of a path of spiritual discovery and Christian vocation

[8] J.H. Oldham, *Christianity and the Race Problem*, London, SCM, 1924, p.33.

as surprising as the turn his own life had taken when on home leave twenty-three years before, and with eventual results that would literally encompass the world. Nor was he to be disappointed in his other sons. George was to follow his father into the Royal Engineers, becoming a colonel decorated with the DSO. Harry went as a missionary to China and Jack entered the ministry of the United Free Church of Scotland. In their father, all of them had been given a role-model of dedication to work for the public good and the upbuilding of the church, enlivened by an awareness of life far beyond the shores of Britain, yet imbued with a deep and loving loyalty to family and friends, regardless of race. For Joe, future author of *Christianity and the Race Problem*, as for his brothers, this had perhaps been the most decisive and enduring education of all.

CHAPTER 2

# *The Student: Oxford 1892–96*

## Oxford in the 1890s

In comparison with Edinburgh, Oxford in the 1890s wore the atmosphere of a country town. "Beautiful as youth and venerable as age, she lies in a purple cup of the low hills . . . Her sombre domes, her dreaming spires rise above the tinted haze, which hangs about her like a delicate drapery and hides from the traveller's gaze the grey walls and purple shadows, the groves and cloisters of Academe."[1] So one travelogue at the end of the last horse-drawn century waxed eloquent on the view from Headington Hill. Today, when the city is as well-known for manufacturing cars as for producing scholars, it is hard to believe that in those days grass grew down the middle of the High Street during the long summer vacation. To the north of the university area there were spreading the imposing lines of brick-built houses along the Woodstock and Banbury Roads, but the eastbound walker across Magdalen Bridge and along the Iffley Road would be out in the fields within minutes.

Even in the 1890s, however, the air of isolated, dreamy changelessness was deceptive. The university was undergoing far-reaching changes, driven partly by internally felt needs for reform, and partly by the demands of society for an educated leadership more adequate to the responsibilities of professional and public life, at home and in the empire overseas. Oxford in the 1890s was certainly a far cry from that of half a century earlier, the Oxford of John Henry Newman and the Tractarian movement. Then, the university had been virtually a cloistered preserve of the Church of England, concerned with the moral at least as much as the intellectual development of its pupils. Fellows (senior, teaching members) of the colleges almost entirely comprised unmarried men in holy orders, and only members of the Church of England could take degrees.

[1] C. Headlam, *The Story of Oxford*, London, Dent, 1907, p.2.

By the 1890s much internal argument, two government commissions and acts of parliament had produced an Oxford much changed and still changing. Religious tests for both undergraduates and fellows had been abolished, though all students still had to take a divinity examination regardless of what main subject they were studying, and attendance at college chapel was compulsory. Subjects taught for the degree were diversifying, and fellows were increasingly lay in background and secular in their academic interests. The social ethos of students remained predominantly middle and upper-middle class but one significant development, albeit very small at first, was making its presence felt – the arrival of women students, signalled by the founding of Lady Margaret Hall and Somerville College in 1879, and St Hugh's and St Hilda's soon after. On the one hand, by today's standards students lived under a heavily disciplinarian regime exercised *in loco parentis* by the colleges and the university proctors: no patronizing of public houses, no smoking while wearing academic dress, a virtual curfew well before midnight. On the other hand, students were increasingly organizing their own extracurricular activities, ranging from rowing and cricket, college literary and debating societies, to university political clubs.

Oldham's college, Trinity, founded in the 16th century, had acquired a sense of its own tradition. Its most famous undergraduate of the 19th century was John Henry Newman. Not that Trinity reflected Newman's later religious leanings and convictions or those of the Tractarians generally, but the college awarded him an honorary fellowship in his old age, long after his conversion to Rome. By the end of the century there was claimed to be a famed "Trinity ethos", denoting "considerable classical attainments, and certain theological susceptibilities".[2] There had been an expansion of student numbers in the 1880s, but overall it was still a relatively small college. When Joe Oldham matriculated in October 1892, he was one of just forty-nine freshmen. The president of the College was H.G. Woods, later to be the Master of the Temple, London.

Oldham entered Trinity as a commoner, a student not financially supported by a college scholarship. Trinity's classical bent suited his ambitions for as an aspiring colonial administrator he had come to read "Greats", or *Literae Humaniores.* Greats was, and some would argue still is, the Oxford education *par excellence*: following a year or more of Latin and Greek language studies, a concentration on the history and philosophy of ancient Greece and Rome combined with reflection on the treatment of the perennial philosophical questions by contemporary thinkers. By the later 19th century such a programme was being justified as more than erudite cultivation for its own sake. It was being seen as the proper tuition for those destined for government and administration – and especially for those who were going to carry the burden of empire.[3] Study of the Greek city-state and of how Rome managed –

[2] H.E.D. Blakiston, "Trinity College", in A. Clark, ed., *The Colleges of Oxford*, London, Methuen, 1891, p.345.

[3] See R. Symonds, *Oxford and Empire: The Last Lost Cause?*, London, Macmillan, 1986, for a wide-ranging survey of the Oxford commitment, academically and socially, to British imperialism.

*Joe Oldham aged 18, Oxford, summer 1893*

or mismanaged – her empire would, it was argued, provide the best instruction on sensible and just imperial rule in the present. As far as contemporary philosophy was concerned, Oxford's main thrust in the later 19th century was provided by the idealism of F.H. Bradley, T.H. Green and Edward Caird.

## Oldham the freshman: culture and conversion

The Trinity College photograph taken in 1893, towards the end of Oldham's first academic year, shows him as a dapper figure, physically slight alongside most of his peers, wearing a straw boater with a plain silk ribbon, and sporting a rudimentary moustache. In the group taken in his final term in 1896 he is more soberly dressed in dark suit and mortar-board – and without the moustache. Certainly the Oldham who graduated in 1896 was in important respects a rather different person from the freshman of 1892, and we must now trace the steps he took and the influences upon him.

Joe Oldham the freshman showed himself to be eminently sociable with those who shared his background and interests in cultivated conversation. He quickly made friends with four others of his year who with him styled themselves the Trinity Quintette. They met on Saturday nights and starting from some literary topic branched off into philosophy or any other avenue that took their fancy. One of the Quintette was Temple Gairdner, also a Scot, who became one of Oldham's closest Oxford friends and of whom more will be heard presently. At one of the earliest meetings Oldham himself read a paper on Boswell. One wonders whether, when fifty years later several of his "Moot" meetings took place in Oxford, Oldham recalled these early experiences of lively debate in an intimate circle of collaborators. Certainly this typically

"Oxbridge" style of informal yet serious exploration with others was to become one of the chief forms of study he promoted. During that first Michaelmas term, however, Oldham's life was to be changed from a quite different quarter, and he was to be drawn into a larger circle, overlapping to some extent with the Quintette but inspired by decidedly other concerns. He met, and irrevocably became part of, the evangelical student world.

Joe Oldham, we have seen, had been nurtured in a devoutly evangelical home and revered his father, who epitomized lay evangelistic enthusiasm. Before leaving Edinburgh, however, he had not come to any definite decision in the matter of his own religious commitment. For his part Colonel Oldham, while maintaining a pattern of domestic piety, had wisely not brought any undue pressure on his sons to "accept Christ". That pressure, if it existed, was maintained in his prayers and his personal example. Joe, like many before and since, evidently left home for the university world still open to persuasion. The critically persuasive moment came sooner than either he or his father probably expected.

In the autumn of 1892 the famous American evangelist Dwight L. Moody was making his last tour of England and included Oxford in his itinerary. Evangelicals in both the university and the city arranged a week-long series of evening meetings in the corn exchange and town hall, with large blocks of seats reserved for undergraduates. Moody was now an old and somewhat tired man, no longer quite the figure who had caused such a sensation in his earlier campaigns in Britain during 1873–75 and 1881–84. But during the second of those visits he had proved himself – somewhat to his own surprise and in the face of some initial opposition from the boorish element among undergraduates – capable of gaining a significant hearing at Cambridge and Oxford. So it now proved again at Oxford, and for one freshman in particular. Joe Oldham attended one of the meetings, and late that night wrote to his father:

[Trinity College]
Oxford
Nov. 14th 1892

Dearest Father,

I have news tonight that will give you more pleasure than anything I have yet written. I went to-night to Moody's meeting and have given myself definitely to Jesus Christ. I and a fellow Mather went to the meeting in the corn exchange which was crowded out – about 200 undergraduates among the audience. After the meeting we went to the after-meeting in the town hall, as did most of the audience. Moody said a few words and then said (I think without expecting an answer) "Who is willing to break with sin to-night?" A fellow in the choir immediately jumped up and called out "I will". Another undergrad in the body of the hall followed him at once and at least half-a-dozen more got up and called out "I will too"; Mather was among their number. I didn't, as I did not want to be too hasty in deciding. After the meeting Alvarez came round and asked Mather to come round to his rooms and I asked to go too. Alvarez talked with us and we both prayed and gave ourselves to Jesus. Pray for me as I am afraid I will find it very difficult. . . .

I ask you again to pray for both Mather and me.
Your loving son
Joe Oldham

P.S. The college Bible reading is to be held in my rooms on Monday. I have joined the University Total Abstinence Society, of which there is a branch at Trinity.[4]

Two features stand out from this letter. First, it is clear that Oldham was already associating with evangelical student circles prior to Moody's meeting. T.E. Alvarez (not a Trinity man) was president of the Oxford Inter-Collegiate Christian Union that year. That he was already personally known to Oldham beforehand is implied by the unadorned reference to "Alvarez" as though his father would have known of him from earlier correspondence. Evidently, Moody's appeal was the final factor in eliciting from Joe Oldham a step he had been seriously pondering for some time under encouragement from the evangelical student fraternity. Indeed his own description of having given himself "definitely" to Christ more than hints that what had taken place was the confirmation of a faith to which by upbringing, interest and current influences he already felt inclined.

Second, there is no doubting that Oldham knew he had taken a decisive step of commitment, which at the same time was but the begetter of further challenges. There is no indication in the letter of having gone through a soul-shattering conviction of sin and repentance, nor an overwhelming emotional experience of any kind. It was, rather, an act of considered, thoughtful commitment. In fact Moody's typical preaching eschewed the overwrought emotional histrionics of some evangelists and concentrated on presenting in fairly matter-of-fact and homespun language, the claims of the love of God in Christ for whole-hearted, grateful acceptance and obedience: "[B]ecause [Christ] died for me, I love him. Because he died for me, I will serve him. I will work for him, I will give him my very life."[5] Nor had Moody that night called for acceptance of any particular dogma, rather the challenge was the very existential one to "break with sin". It was the call to a consecrated commitment which Oldham answered – and one which he admits he would find "very difficult" to follow through. Whether the difficulties to which he alludes were those of intellectual problems facing belief, or the strain of maintaining a new-found religious commitment amid the conformist pressures of college life and friendships, we cannot know. But he was clearly aware of the biblical warning against starting to build a tower without calculating the cost, or of going out to meet an enemy with inadequate forces. What is unmistakable, right there at the start of the Christian life he was to follow for his remaining 77 years, was the fusion of commitment with thoughtfulness.

[4] [OA] (J.H. Oldham archive produced by Kathleen Bliss and now in the library of New College, Edinburgh).

[5] J.F. Findlay, Jr, *Dwight L. Moody, American Evangelist 1837–1899*, Chicago, Univ. of Chicago Press, 1969, p.248.

## Oxford religion and evangelicalism

Oxford throughout the century had been almost synonymous with the trends and controversies within the Church of England from the Tractarian movement onwards. But by the last quarter of the century the relationship between the university and religious life was changing significantly. The assumed role of the university and its colleges as being themselves the prime movers of religious influence (and Anglican influence at that) was steadily being eroded despite the continuance of compulsory chapel attendance and examinations in divinity, not to mention a conspicuously entrenched presence of clerical dons. The abolition of religious tests for admission to degrees and fellowships, and the appearance on the scene of Nonconformist theological colleges (Mansfield for Congregationalists in 1886, Manchester for Unitarians in 1888) were just two of the factors which, in an increasingly secular atmosphere, were weakening the old mutual embrace of Oxford and the Church of England.

In any case, in response to the secular trend and, inevitably aiding and abetting it, the centres of gravity of active Christianity in Oxford were shifting away from official college religion to other and newer sites. St Stephen's House and Pusey House were established during 1883–84 as centres for Anglo-Catholic teaching, worship and pastoral care among undergraduates. At the other end of the ecclesiastical scale, evangelicalism was likewise striking vigorous roots in certain of the city's churches and in college Christian unions, largely independently of the college chapels and their clergy. Student evangelicalism was never numerically as strong in Oxford as in Cambridge but it had undeniable, indeed exuberant, vigour. Bands of undergraduates, twenty abreast and arm-in-arm, could be met marching up the High Street chanting "Hallelujah!" as a refrain to some ditty learnt at the Keswick Convention, "to let the glory out!"[6] College Bible readings and daily prayer-meetings were the order of the evangelical day, and every Sunday evening there was an open-air evangelistic meeting at the Martyrs' Memorial in St Giles. It was right into the midstream of this raw, muscular devotion that Joe Oldham was brought by his decision at Moody's meeting.

The father-figure of Oxford evangelicalism in the later 19th century was Canon Alfred Christopher, an associate secretary of the Church Missionary Society who moved to Oxford in 1859 on his appointment as rector of St Aldate's in the centre of the city. During his long tenure, lasting until 1905, St Aldate's became the main focus for evangelical influence among undergraduates.[7] Christopher kept open house on Saturday evenings for Bible expositions and extempore prayer, and held prayer breakfasts on behalf of foreign missions when several hundred undergraduates and city church people would be

[6] C.E. Padwicke, *Temple Gairdner of Cairo*, London, SPCK, 1929.

[7] See V.H.H. Green, *Religion at Oxford and Cambridge*, London, SCM, 1964, ch. II, "The Oxford Evangelicals". For Christopher's career as a whole, see J.S. Reynolds, *Canon Christopher of St Aldate's, Oxford*, Abingdon, Abbey, 1967.

addressed by prominent missionaries on furlough. A staunch ally appeared on the scene in 1879 in the person of Francis Chavasse, rector of St Peter-le-Bailey. Among his enterprises was the Greek Testament class for undergraduates, which was attended by Oldham and drew attendances of a hundred at a time.[8] Ultimately, however, the most decisive evangelical development in Oxford was the founding in 1879 of the Oxford Inter-Collegiate Christian Union (OICCU). While supported and counselled by such as Christopher and Chavasse, it was not only *for* students but led by them. With a branch in each college, this was the engine behind the daily prayer meetings, college Bible studies and open-air services.

## "These narrow young desperadoes": Oldham's circle

Albeit in his undemonstrative way Joe Oldham joined whole-heartedly in Christian Union activity at college and university level – and at home, too. During his first Christmas vacation he took his brother George to a meeting of evangelical students in Edinburgh, and the following term he attended a joint Oxford and Cambridge meeting. For Sunday worship in Oxford, he and his immediate circle appear to have attended St Peter-le-Bailey for Chavasse's ministry at least as much as the somewhat more popular services of Canon Christopher at St Aldate's.[9] Was this because Chavasse, the provider of instruction in the Greek New Testament, was on a somewhat higher intellectual plane than Christopher? Such allegiances of undergraduates to particular pulpits were probably less significant, however, than the immediate circles of friendships within which Christian commitment was sustained and enriched. For Joe Oldham these relationships were very important indeed.

Among Oldham's Christian friends there stood first and foremost Temple Gairdner who was also, as has been seen, a member of the Trinity Quintette. Older than Oldham by a few years, Gairdner was the son of Dr (later Sir) William Gairdner, professor of medicine at Glasgow University. Dr Gairdner was Unitarian by inclination but Temple, under his mother's influence, firmly embraced orthodox Christian beliefs and joined the Church of Scotland. Unusually artistic by nature, and a very talented musician, Temple Gairdner was also a deeply emotional individual "swept by agonies and ecstasies" yet in whom also "the philosopher with his balancing wisdom intervened and righted the ship just when it seemed she must be over".[10] His religious experience was more mystical, more solitary in its cultivation, than the standard evangelical variety. Like Oldham, Gairdner was reading Greats. This, together with their common Scottish cultural and religious background and their evangelicalism, provided the setting for an intimate friendship described by Gairdner as

[8] Green, pp.217–19.
[9] Reynolds, p.279.
[10] Padwicke, p.12.

"unbroken fellowship", while Oldham called Gairdner "my oldest and closest friend at Oxford".[11] Oldham's own value-judgments in assessing character are revealed in his recollection of Gairdner:

> In the matter of making friends with uninteresting people, and that not as from above, but as really seeing in them something that the rest of us could not see, Temple Gairdner was incomparably the biggest Christian I have known.[12]

Also in the circle were Paget Wilkes, a dynamic character who had been converted at a service in Ipswich by the famous Baptist preacher and Keswick speaker F.B. Meyer and described by Oldham as "an old-style evangelical Keswick movement enthusiast – quite a character and a very good sort"; Alek Fraser, another Trinity Scotsman, much given to practical joking and who was destined to become Oldham's brother-in-law; and R.J. Wright. In their final year at Oxford, 1895–96, Oldham, Gairdner, Wilkes and Wright shared lodgings together in Pembroke Street. Gairdner was president of OICCU that year, and Wright later recalled:

> I stood a little in awe of men so very evangelically disposed. Gairdner was for his years a capital controversialist . . . Wilkes was a very racy, lively talker, and Oldham a careful, restrained talker. It was good to listen to the three. We were all four reading for Greats and busy with philosophy. I think it was Oldham who said that Wilkes and I were the "extremes" and he and Gairdner "the means". Gairdner's bent was towards philosophy. He was full of it. He revelled in metaphysics.[13]

Oldham for his part seems to have been less infected with enthusiasm for the contemporary philosophy taught at Oxford, whether that of Spencer and Mill or the idealists such as Bradley and Green, or Edward Caird of Balliol. His mind was to be set alight much more by the personalism he met some years later in Germany.

Even within the ardent and mutually supportive atmosphere of the Christian Union, to be avowedly and openly evangelical at Oxford was not an easy ride. The aesthetes regarded piety with distaste; the boorish hearties sometimes physically attacked them. For such as Gairdner it was an effort to maintain a foot each in the camps of both culture and piety – it was deemed necessary on occasion for him to veil the nudity of his classical statuettes in his room so as not to offend his more puritanical visitors. Underlying each moment of every day was an almost terrifyingly single-minded devotion to Christ and, above all, to winning others to the same faith. Some found this commitment redolent of the most ardent and austere religious orders of the middle ages:

> These narrow young desperadoes had some claim to the term *pauperes Christi*, for in the evangelistic fury in which they lived every possible penny must be saved from personal expenditure to buy a Bible or pay for a fraction of a missionary. When W.E.S. Holland bought a luncheon basket at a railway station it was felt that he had

[11] Bliss MS, p.14.
[12] Quoted in Padwicke, p.36.
[13] *Ibid.*, p.43.

all but given away his cause. A sandwich and a glass of milk was lunch enough for one who might save the rest of the luncheon-basket price for evangelistic funds.[14]

Moreover, the circle of intimates to which Oldham belonged quickly became united in a yet more specific evangelical cause. On 26 April 1893, just after he had returned to Oxford for the start of the summer term, Oldham wrote to his father:

> What would you say if I signed the enclosed? Do not think that the thought of doing so is a new one. Munro's address at a Thursday morning missionary meeting at the beginning of last term set me thinking, and I have prayed about the matter more or less regularly since. Wilkes has been at me lately and urged me to come to a decision.[15]

The "enclosed" was a copy of the membership declaration of the Student Volunteer Missionary Union, founded the previous year and which Wilkes had already joined: "It is my purpose if God permit, to become a foreign missionary." We will shortly examine more closely the development of this movement in North America and Britain, in which Oldham was to play such a leading role in his early career. For the moment all that lay beyond this horizon, which was dominated by the urgent need for personal decision. His letter to Colonel Oldham continued:

> I do not *feel* as if I should like to be a missionary in the very least, but, according to the author of "A Christian's Secret of a Happy Life", feelings don't matter at all and it is altogether a question of the *will* in the Christian life. Well, my *will* is on God's side and I want to keep his commandments, and one of his commandments is "Go into all the world and preach the gospel to every creature." Again, there is the verse, "Ye are not your own, ye are bought with a price", and if God calls I must obey in spite of natural disinclination. We have to put our will over on God's side and trust him to bring our feelings in harmony with our will. Is not this right? I have for some months thought that I should like to be a foreign missionary, but it has been a hard struggle to come to a definite decision. There is a sentence of Robert Wilde's which has helped me a good deal – "If the command in Matt. xxviii.19 is too general to apply to you, the promise in verse 20 is too general to apply to you also."
>
> Dear Father, please tell me what you think about it, and pray that I may not be influenced by *men*'s opinion either way in this or any other matter, but be guided by God.

Colonel Oldham may well have felt that Joe had already answered his own questions in this appeal. Once more, there is revealed an unusual degree of sober thoughtfulness tempering what might otherwise have been a sheer youthful fancy, blossoming in the hot-house of missionary ardour then sweeping the student world.

Encouraged by his father, Joe Oldham did sign the declaration. It was probably the last time he consulted his father on a major matter – and as the letter shows Joe was not wanting a simple directive from him but rather support

[14] *Ibid.*, p.16.
[15] [OA].

and counsel in how to make such a decision. Having made it, Oldham was bound together with Wilkes, Gairdner and Fraser in the band of student missionary volunteers, regarded by some as the elite corps of university evangelicals. The "declaration" was to them a promise as binding as a monk's vows. Each of them, albeit in very different ways and contexts, was to make good that commitment in the ensuing years.

For the moment, they knew that much spiritual training was necessary for such an arduous vocation. They not only met together regularly in Oxford, but that summer of 1893 the Oxford volunteers formed a party attending the annual Keswick convention, now in its 18th year and by then one of the most important forces in British revivalism. Largely Anglican in its constituency but with some Church of Scotland, Free Church and Brethren participation also, Keswick was the most prominent channel of the "holiness" stream of piety which flowed into British evangelicalism in the second half of the century. The holiness movement stemmed from a variety of sources: the Mildmay conferences organized by the Anglican clergyman William Pennefather in the 1870s; the teaching of Americans such as Robert and Hannah Pearsall Smith; Brethren and earlier Methodist teaching on sanctification; and some Quaker emphases on inwardness and spiritual illumination. Essentially, holiness teaching claimed that through an act of utter trust in the all-sufficiency of God, perfect sanctification could be realized and experienced by the believer. Spiritual "effort" was a sign of lack of maturity in the faith. Through the true "rest of faith", spiritual struggle is left behind and the power of the Holy Spirit takes complete control of the individual. Wilful sin is no longer possible. With this emphasis upon the possibility of complete personal sanctification went pre-millennial eschatological views, that is, the belief that the return of Christ would precede his thousand-year reign on earth and might happen any time. On his return the Lord would expect to find a spiritually pure company of believers ready to meet him in the air. That view of the second coming naturally also lent urgency to the missionary task. By the 1890s over 2,000 were attending the annual Keswick gatherings.

Student evangelicals and missionary volunteers found the Keswick ethos congenial for a number of reasons, quite apart from its theological emphasis. Sitting loose to denominational differences and stressing rather the spiritual unity of all believers in Christ, it rang true to the non-denominational character of the Christian unions. Like much of later 19th-century revivalism as a whole, it was also a decidedly middle-class phenomenon catering for the well-educated who could afford one or more weeks' annual break in the Lake District. The very setting amid the landscape associated with Wordsworthian poetry was also significant: there were real affinities between the holiness piety which looked increasingly inwards to the cultivation of the soul's life with God, and the romantic spirit at large in its rejection of rationalism and industrialism.[16] In

[16] Cf. D.W. Bebbington, *Evangelicalism in Modern Britain. A History from the 1730s to the 1980s*, London, Unwin Hyman, 1989, ch. 5.

*Trinity College, Oxford, summer 1896. Oldham, wearing mortar-board, is 2nd row, 3rd from right. Next left, bare-headed, is Temple Gairdner. Alek Fraser is front row, 8th from left.*

both, too, there was a rejection of dogmas as secondary to the life of the spirit. Keswick, for all its biblical stress, emphasized doctrine (conservative or other) much less than prayer, personal ethics and evangelistic zeal.[17]

At Keswick in 1893 student volunteers from several universities camped together and held their own meetings. They puzzled some of the regulars at the convention, and amused local youths who hung over the walls close by their tents. The Oxford tent was much the smallest and its occupants made an appeal to "good evangelical parents" at the convention not to send all their sons to Cambridge (itself an interesting comment on the social constituency of Keswick). A number of women students from Oxford also attended as members of the convention, among them Alek Fraser's sister Mary, a student at Somerville College. The Cambridge contingent was far larger, as were those from the medical schools of Edinburgh and London. But as well as what took place in public, for Gairdner and Oldham Keswick 1893 became memorable for a very private spiritual experience. At one of the early meetings, the campers were challenged "to choose out one uncomely characteristic and claim in Jesus' name to have it forth". Gairdner chose to name cowardice, physical and moral, as his besetting weakness, and bravery as his deepest petition. His biographer recounts what ensued:

> On the morning of the third day a silent transaction took place. He went out by the lake with his friend J.H. Oldham, his prayer for bravery still burdening his spirit. Suddenly he burst out, "Look here! If we are not right, let's get it right!" They knelt there in the fields. "We did not rise," says Gairdner, "till we had claimed light through Christ and received it. 'Twas God's intervention. I had prayed for *bravery* and suddenly I felt that I would not mind being beaten for Christ. Then I knew that I was right with God, my prayer was answered."[18]

This does not tell us quite what was going on in Oldham's own soul, but clearly it was a shared experience of deeper consecration and submission to God's will and promise, and what emerged was an even greater dedication to the missionary cause. Each in Oldham's closest circle was to fulfil that commitment in later life. Gairdner took his passions, his questions and his deep cultural interests to Cairo in a highly colourful and at times controversial ministry until his early death in 1928.[19] Paget Wilkes worked as energetically in Japan as he had raced around Oxford[20] and died in 1934. Alek Fraser became an outstanding educationist, described by a recent historian as "perhaps the greatest colonial headmaster of his time"[21] yet never lost his adolescent sense of humour (though frequently losing his temper). After working in Uganda, he was principal successively of Trinity College, Kandy (Ceylon), and of Achimota College on the Gold Coast.

[17] *Ibid.*, pp.166–69.
[18] Padwicke, p.30.
[19] See Padwicke for Gairdner's whole career.
[20] See I.R.G. Steward, *Dynamic. Paget Wilkes of Japan*, London, Marshall, Morgan & Scott, 1957.
[21] Symonds, p.250.

The outflow of missionary volunteers from the British universities was by then a well-established pattern. David Livingstone's famous address in the Senate House at Cambridge in 1857 in which, in the words of one hearer, he "remarkably combined an encomium for missions both Catholic and Protestant with an appeal to the universities for hands", resulted almost at once in the Universities' Mission to Central Africa (UMCA). By 1880 the Cambridge Mission to Delhi and the Oxford Mission to Calcutta were also active as missions making a special claim on Anglican undergraduates. Other missionary societies made forays into the universities looking for recruits. But the most successful recruiting agencies were the students themselves – as Oldham had experienced with Paget Wilkes. Evangelicals were particularly successful in the medical schools. The most famous rallying-cry of all rang out from Cambridge in 1882 when, as a result of Moody's mission there, the captain of the university cricket eleven C.T. Studd and the stroke of the Cambridge boat Stanley Smith publicly decided for Christ and soon after declared their resolve to go out as missionaries with the China Inland Mission. They were quickly joined by three other Cambridge men and two army officers. The "Cambridge Seven", the name by which the group entered evangelical legend, caused a sensation in Cambridge and elsewhere in Britain, inspiring both further recruitment to missionary service and growth in the Christian Unions themselves. Young Christianity had found a cause, a channel for bounding energies: to "burn out for Christ" in the world which both within and beyond the growing British empire, was opening up to exploration and adventure.[22]

The formation of the Student Volunteer Union (SVU) in Britain in 1892, however, following upon the parent body's founding in the United States in 1888, marked the opening of a new phase in the story. From its modest beginnings it was to result in a new flood of recruits to the foreign mission field. Some might put its success down to the simple rigour of its declaration; or to its bold, even grandiose, Watchword "the evangelization of the world in this generation"; or to the fact that it was seeking to provide a stable organization in which evangelicals and those of a different churchly stamp could meet in a common purpose. Probably all three were significant factors. What none could foresee at the time was that the SVU was soon to develop a significance well beyond its own immediate, declared aims and purposes, and to become one of the most vital stimuli in what later generations would call the ecumenical movement. In the summer of 1893, as he returned from Keswick to Edinburgh and prepared for the start of his second academic year at Oxford, Joe Oldham was as unaware of all this as anyone else. He was simply another volunteer for missionary service, and a deeply committed worker for the Christian Union in Oxford. But events were already conspiring to make him and the student movement important to each other in a unique way.

[22] *Ibid.*, ch. II, "The Missionaries", comments extensively on Oldham's generation at Oxford.

## Enter John R. Mott[23]

It was early in the summer of 1894. Paget Wilkes came round to Oldham's rooms and asked if he could help in showing round Oxford an American who, but for his letter of introduction, was a total stranger. The visitor was John R. Mott, intercollegiate secretary of the Young Men's Christian Association (YMCA) in the USA, and chairman of the Student Volunteer Union in the USA. He was nine years senior to Oldham who later recalled: "It was Mott's first visit to Oxford and we walked him round the Parks while he plied us with questions about the university which we could not answer. He revealed to me what a babe I was. I was in his company for most of that weekend. Although we did not see much of one another for some years, it was the start of a lifelong friendship."[24] That last remark might be judged something of an under-statement, for this meeting marked the start of one of the most crucial relation-ships of Oldham's life – and indeed for the modern ecumenical movement. In encountering Mott, Oldham was meeting one who was already emerging as the most significant leader on the world scene of Christian student life, who was to become one of the key figures of the ecumenical movement in the first half of the 20th century, and with whom much of his own most creative work until middle life was to be done. For the sake of an adequate perspective on the start of this relationship and Oldham's early career, some further background must now be given on the story of the birth of the Student Volunteer Union, on Mott's growing stature within it, and on the interconnections between student evangelicalism in Britain and North America.[25]

Once again, it is a story which involves Dwight L. Moody but also, at least as importantly, the YMCA with which he was closely associated. The Young Men's Christian Association originated in London in 1844. Impressed by this example, a group of Americans set up a parallel organization in Boston in 1851. Intended as a means of pastoral care and evangelization among young men in business and commerce, the YMCA flourished and spread in the expanding towns of the east coast and mid-west, drawing support from virtually all the main Protestant denominations. Moody, who was born in Massachusetts in 1837, was converted in Congregationalism but owed much of his nurture to the YMCA – one might say that as a young salesman in the shoe trade, he was its typical protégé. Living in Chicago from the age of 22, he threw himself into YMCA work with the same energy he brought to the shoe trade, and in 1860

[23] For Mott's whole career see C.H. Hopkins, *John R. Mott 1865–1955: A Biography*, Geneva, WCC, and Grand Rapids, Eerdmans, 1979.

[24] Bliss MS, p.22. In Hopkins, pp.90f. there is some unclarity about the date of this first meeting with Oldham. Hopkins refers to a first visit by Mott to Europe in the summer of 1891, which appears to have included a three-day stay in Oxford when he met Oldham. But if Mott did visit Oxford that year he could not have met Oldham, who did not go up to Oxford until the following year. Either the year Hopkins gives for this first visit to Oxford by Mott is incorrect, or Mott's visit in 1894 was not his first. But Oldham is quite certain in the Bliss MS that the 1894 visit was Mott's first.

[25] See Findlay, *op. cit.*, on Moody's involvement, and R. Rouse, *The World's Student Christian Federation*, London, SCM, 1948.

he left his secular trade entirely for religious work, both under YMCA auspices and his own enterprises.

The latter included a congregation he established in one of the poorer areas of the city. It was in the 1860s that there began his wider, itinerant evangelistic ministry in partnership with the singer Ira D. Sankey. In 1867 he made his first visit to Britain, travelling widely and making important contacts with like-minded evangelicals, especially YMCA officials. But his fame as an evangelist, even at home, did not really begin until his revival campaign in Britain of 1873–75.

Moody carried over into his evangelistic work the YMCA ethos of unifying Christians of all traditions in the cause of the gospel. He hoped "to see the day when all bickering, division and party feeling will cease, and Roman Catholics will see eye to eye with Protestants in this work. Let us advance in a solid column – Roman Catholics, Protestants, Episcopalians, Presbyterians, Methodists, against the ranks of Satan's emissaries."[26] It may be queried how far in practice Moody was accepting and respectful of sacramentalist rather than evangelical churches[27] and therefore whether such revivalism was a genuine precursor of later "ecumenism". But the fact is that many of the younger generation who were touched by Moody in Britain and America found themselves caught up into a movement which put the highest value on working together to win the world for Christ in a way which transcended denominational loyalties. It was in this ethos that much of the future ecumenical leadership was bred.

Nowhere was this to be more true than in student circles, even though at first any connection between Moody the revivalist and the supposedly more sophisticated college scene seemed most unlikely. Moody, the self-taught lay evangelist, for some years consciously eschewed any particular attention to the student world. But his surprising success with British students in 1882–83, especially at Cambridge, encouraged both him and others to consider what potential impact might lie in that direction. In fact Moody had already been developing an interest in education, though not at university level, and in 1878 founded the Mount Hermon boys' and girls' schools at Northfield, his birthplace in Massachusetts. Soon afterwards, summer conferences were being held there too, along lines similar to the Keswick meetings and with a strong emphasis on reconsecration. Meanwhile, important developments were taking place within the YMCA and student Christian activity in the USA. Many college and university Christian groups were in fact affiliates of the YMCA or campus branches of the movement. For a time no special status or distinctive approach was thought necessary by the YMCA for student members. For instance, collegiate members of the YMCA were expected to attend the annual convention instead of holding a separate meeting of their own. But such was the growth of the college scene, and of Christian groups within it, that by the

[26] Findlay, p.248.

[27] See J.H.S. Kent, *Holding the Fort: Studies in Victorian Revivalism*, London, Epworth, 1978, p.134.

early 1880s the demand was growing for a special student department of the YMCA.

Foremost among the advocates of the Student cause was a YMCA staff member, Luther Wishard, who shrewdly saw the need to win Moody's own sympathy and support. Moody was finally persuaded to host a summer conference specifically for students at Mount Hermon in 1886, and it was an overwhelming success thanks in large measure to Moody's personal impact on the participants. But, quite apart from the expected emphasis on reconsecration and evangelism, Wishard and his collaborators had a particular agenda in view for this and subsequent events: the capture of students and the YMCA itself for the foreign missionary cause. In a way which took Moody himself by surprise, this became the most prominent theme of the conference. A number of foreign missions activists and overseas participants had been invited, and their impact was dramatic. Before the conference closed, nearly a hundred students – the "Mount Hermon Hundred" – pledged themselves to work in foreign missions after graduating. Deputations were formed there which toured American campuses urging others to join and make similar pledges. By the time of the next conference in 1887, over 2,000 had been recruited into the movement. This was effectively the birth of the Student Volunteer Movement although it was not formally constituted as such until 1888.

The Cambridge experience of 1882 had been repeated on a vastly magnified scale. The link with Cambridge was more than just a parallel, however, and involved more than the effect of Moody in both locations. As part of the preparatory work for the conference, the YMCA organizers had invited over J.E.K. Studd, brother of C.T. Studd the leader of the Cambridge Seven, and himself a famous cricketer, to tour the campuses. What was even more remarkable was the growth of close trans-Atlantic connections in the succeeding Northfield student conferences. Sixteen students from Britain attended Mount Hermon in 1888, and fourteen the following year. In fact for the remainder of the century there was a continual interchange of students between Britain and the United States for intercollegiate missionary conferences.

It was at this point that the whole burgeoning Christian student scene in the USA was taken hold of by the visionary zeal, dynamic organizational ability, oratorical gifts and sheer force of personality of John R. Mott. Joe Oldham was not the only one to feel "a babe" on a first meeting with this larger-than-life character: solidly six feet tall, with an arrestingly open and alert face topped with reddish hair standing straight up, and a manner of speaking which made *everything* sound of decisive importance. Even in the pictures of him Mott appears to be asking the photographer, "And what are you going to do with *your* life?" Not that people normally spoke of Mott as intimidating. As Oldham and Wilkes discovered that day in Oxford, it was the intensity of real interest he took in everyone and everything he met, which was out of the ordinary.

Mott was born in 1865 and brought up within Methodism. At Cornell University, where he studied law and history, he quickly became a leader in the Christian Association (the college YMCA). In 1886 J.E.K. Studd visited Cornell on his tour of campuses in preparation for the first student conference at Mount Hermon. Meeting personally with Studd proved to be a decisive spiritual turning point for Mott, who thereupon delved ever more deeply into the New Testament with its call to single-minded pursuit of the kingdom of God regardless of cost, and he experienced something akin to a second conversion of "entire sanctification" as taught by the holiness movement. That summer Mott attended the first Mount Hermon student conference as Cornell's representative, and was personally challenged by Luther Wishard to face the call of foreign missions. He was among the Mount Hermon Hundred who answered the call. Mott had entered Cornell with a view to a career in law or politics. Now he saw his future in some form of Christian ministry. Ever a voracious reader, while he continued his course in law and history he widened his reading to embrace biblical studies, theology and German.

His gifts as a speaker and organizer were not lost on the YMCA staff. Mount Hermon 1886 had consolidated the case for a special student department of the YMCA, and in 1888 Mott was appointed the inter-collegiate secretary for the United States, travelling many thousands of miles each year to visit campuses, conducting evangelistic meetings and building up local leadership. That same year the Student Volunteer Movement for Foreign Missions was formally constituted, and Mott was appointed its travelling secretary, a post which naturally went in tandem with his YMCA work. In fact the SVM drew together a number of student organizations in the USA and Canada. Mott insisted, for example, that women students no less than men should be fully involved, and so the YWCA as well as the YMCA was a constituent body from the beginning.

Mott threw himself into the YMCA and SVM work with boundless energy. But he also made his own the vision, first glimpsed by such as Wishard, of a united movement of Christian students not confined to North America, but embracing the whole Christian world and dedicated to reaching the rest of the globe. The trans-Atlantic connection, it has been noted, was vital in the early Mount Hermon conferences. What Mott and others were soon seeking was nothing less than a worldwide Christian student body, linking all national intercollegiate unions, and dedicated to the task of world evangelization. This dream was to be realized in the formation of the World Student Christian Federation (WSCF) at Vadstena in Sweden in 1895, and one of Mott's main purposes in visiting Britain and Europe in 1894 was to further preparation for this event. What he wanted to know from Oldham and Wilkes, was what part Oxford might play in such a worldwide enterprise.

The nine years from the first Mount Hermon conference in 1886 to the formation of the WSCF in 1895 were thus crucial ones in the development of international Christian unity at the student level. Oldham was maturing as a student precisely at the time when, if the movement was going to make progress, people capable of a large vision and also of sound organizational and communication skills were going to be needed at both national and international levels. Mott on his travels was ever the talent-spotter, looking for potential leaders, and he did not forget the quietly-spoken yet sharp-witted young Scotsman who guided him around Oxford that weekend in 1894. Perhaps the most remarkable point about Mott's own career was that, despite all his talents, he did not swerve from his chosen path of Christian service. As Oldham himself was later to say of him, he was in every respect a man "cast in a large mould".[28] He was offered and declined a fellowship in philosophy. Yale University would make strenuous efforts to get him as president of its large and prestigious divinity school. President Woodrow Wilson would offer him the post of US ambassador to China. Mott refused to leave the plough to which he had put his hand in 1888.

During the summer vacation of 1894 the Oxford Volunteers went to Keswick again, joining the record student attendance of over 200. And Mott was one of the main speakers. In a series of addresses to the students he carried his audience before him and issued two challenges. One was to evangelism. This he said was a worldwide task, not only for them in the future and overseas, but here and now and in the colleges. Evangelism was personal work: "Remember, one man is a big audience." The second challenge was to work for reconciliation between Christians isolated in separate groups. Students could use the proposed Federation as a means to that end.[29]

One of Mott's outstanding gifts was his ability not only to enthuse his hearers by appeal to their emotions, or even to their wills, but also to convince them of the necessity and possibility of sound organization and adequate funding. This recognition in fact lay at the heart of the change in much Christian and voluntary work during the 1880s and 1890s. Previously, evangelistic enterprise had relied heavily upon the charisma of founding figures and the personal loyalty to them of supporters and funders. This was the case with Moody himself. What Mott and his generation were seeking was a form of organization which would be capable of generating its own loyalty and resources through the commitment of those who shared its aims and values. This would put a very high premium on corporate strategy and planning, and likewise on the leadership and organizational qualities at national and local level.

Mott therefore persuaded the students at Keswick in 1894 to pledge financial support for the appointment of a travelling secretary to consolidate the work in the colleges of Britain as a whole. He used his influence with the small executive committee to look ahead to the appointment of a common secretariat for the Volunteers and the Inter-Varsity Christian Union, the new umbrella organization for all the student Christian Unions in the country. Further, Mott advised them to move away from Keswick to another site so as to broaden their appeal beyond their evangelical origins to other groups. Mott, for all his own indebtedness to the holiness movement, probably found the Keswick atmosphere somewhat precious by comparison with the Mount Hermon conferences. Even Moody, biblically conservative though he was, felt quite happy with the presence of more liberal speakers at Northfield such as Henry

[28] Bliss MS, p.23.
[29] *Ibid.*, p.21.

Drummond. At Northfield it was at least open for discussion that literal pre-millennialism might not be the *only* way of interpreting the "second coming" of Christ, and that the urgency of "the evangelization of the world in this generation" might have other theological groundings.

## Oldham, student evangelicalism and the future

Whether or not Mott deserves to be called a "manipulator", in a certain sense, of young people from a Christian background[30] could be discussed at length. But clearly he facilitated student Christian life to take on a distinct identity and responsibility of its own, which was to be crucial in the next stage of the modern ecumenical movement. Two other questions are probably more important. The first concerns the whole strategy of channelling student energies into the foreign missions cause, on the scale of the Mount Hermon conferences and the ensuing Volunteer Movement. Was there a price to be paid for this, in terms of a diversion of energy from a mission of critical challenge to society at home, in North America, Britain and Europe? The second concerns the weight that was being placed on the student constituency in the vision of the Christian future. It was natural, at the time, to perceive in the growing student population of the world the future leadership in church and society, and therefore to regard it as the key constituency both to evangelize and to train for Christian leadership. The future of the whole world, it seemed, lay in colleges and universities. In many respects the strategy was to be successful in terms of the impact on students themselves, and it has become a commonplace to note how many of the leading men and women in the later ecumenical movement were nurtured in student Christian circles around the turn of the century. Less often, however, has it been noted that this emphasis inevitably loaded the ecumenical movement, and particularly its leadership, with a distinct class bias. Both these questions, it will be seen in later chapters, were to arise as implicit challenges in J.H. Oldham's later work.

Joe Oldham returned early to Oxford for his third academic year to put in the "week's work for God before the term began" that Mott had suggested. After all, said the Oxford contingent, "the rowing men collar their chaps before the term starts". Oldham was secretary of OICCU that year, and this was to provide his fellow students with the final proof of his competence as well as commitment. It seems certain that he met Mott again in 1895 as one of a group working on the plans for the Federation which Mott was canvassing in a long series of visits to universities around the world. And that summer, Oldham was elected by the students as the joint general secretary of both the Student Volunteers and the Inter-Varsity Christian Union, to take effect on his graduation from Oxford in 1896.

Meanwhile, there was a final year of study in Greats to complete. Oldham finished with a second-class degree, as did Temple Gairdner. A "first" had been

[30] Cf. Kent, p.160, n.26.

confidently predicted of Gairdner when he came up to Trinity, and mutterings of criticism were heard from the Gairdner household in Glasgow about the distractions which over-preoccupation with religious activities had entailed. Oldham seems neither to have been surprised nor disappointed by his own result. There were to be many occasions ahead when the first-class quality of his mind would be shown.

From a contemporary perspective, an obvious point to remark on is the apparent divergence between the strenuous evangelicalism of this student circle, and the breadth of ecumenism with which Oldham was later to become identified as a leader. Depending on the commentator's own loyalties, the apparent contrast can be seen as either a fall from grace, or as a fortunate and maturing development. To press either case, however, is somewhat to misread both 19th-century evangelicalism and the later Oldham. Agreed, many of the Oxford evangelicals in later life disowned what they came to regard as the strident and arrogant excesses of youth – but were also prepared still to defend and value the place that sure conviction and dedication play in moving human affairs along, and in providing the foundation on which the rest of character can be built. Temple Gairdner in later years wrote revealingly to his own son who was being troubled by an intrusive kind of evangelism promoted by people who "see a few things clearly, and other things not at all . . . Everything will be black and white with them; no shading of any sort. And their vocabulary will be to match. *But* . . . these people have to be reckoned with. Was I not in the midst of them, and one of them at Oxford? And as I look round the world I see everywhere that it is *these men* (perhaps mellowed and developed now) who are doing the big things in the world – the big things for mankind, and God, and the kingdom of Christ: A.G. Fraser, J.H. Oldham, W.E.S. Holland, to take only those known to yourself."[31]

There is also the danger of anachronistically reading back into the late century certain polarizations and dichotomies which, hardened in later controversies, did not dominate that scene even if some of the issues were known to be important. Terms such as "modernist" or "fundamentalist" were not yet known, nor was "ecumenical" yet used as descriptive of an interest or commitment, nor were "liberal" and "evangelical" yet assumed to be mutually exclusive. That Moody could invite Henry Drummond, a leading liberal preacher, to Northfield as a personal friend will no doubt surprise many. No less striking was the massive support which Canon Christopher of St Aldate's received from clergy of all persuasions in Oxford, including prominent Anglo-Catholics, when he had recourse to the courts in a libel action.

Most important of all, as far as J.H. Oldham himself is concerned, it would be a serious distortion to imagine that his student evangelicalism was a phase he merely "outgrew". His last theological book, written some sixty-five years after deciding to give himself "definitely to Jesus Christ" at Moody's meeting, had the title *Life Is Commitment.* During the second world war, while wrestling

[31] Padwicke, p.20.

with the need for the churches to re-engage with society and to work for a new world order, he could still write: "To save society we have to begin by saving persons. Nothing can supersede, or take the place, of the evangelistic and pastoral ministries of the Church, reinforced by the insights that general and medical psychology can supply."[32] When in his most substantial book *Christianity and the Race Problem* he famously described Christianity as "not primarily a philosophy but a crusade"[33] he was echoing the vital note of social campaigning which had been sounded in classic evangelicalism from Wilberforce onwards. And throughout his adult life nothing was as important in the Oldham domestic routine than prayers at the breakfast table, nor was any of his publications more widely appreciated than his manual of daily prayer.[34] When, therefore, in 1937 he returned to Oxford as one of the main organizers of the world conference on "Church, Community and State", he would by no means have felt a complete stranger to the student who had walked those same streets more than forty years before.

[32] *Real Life is Meeting* Christian News-Letter Books no. 14, London, Sheldon, 1942, p.23.
[33] *Christianity and the Race Problem*, London, SCM, 1924, p.26.
[34] *A Devotional Diary*, London, SCM, 1925.

CHAPTER 3

# *The Student Volunteer: Aldersgate Street and India 1896–1901*

A single aim dominated Joe Oldham when he graduated from Oxford in the summer of 1896: to fulfil his sense of calling to be a student missionary volunteer. This aim was to be realized when he sailed for India in the autumn of 1897. The year between leaving Oxford and that passage to India was spent in London as the joint general secretary of the British College Christian Union and the Student Missionary Volunteer Union. In effect, staying very much within the student world, it was a continuation of his Oxford life. Even while in India he was relating closely to students, but it was while there that he was stimulated to his first truly independent and critical reflections on the missionary task and its methods.

Oldham's career at this stage contrasts notably with that of J.R. Mott whose progress to leadership in the North American student world was, as described in the preceding chapter, truly meteoric. But Oldham was not looking to be anything other than a missionary. Even his appointment to the joint secretaryship of the student Christian bodies was hardly a remarkable portent of future significance. He was following what was already becoming a well-established pattern whereby recent graduates took up the post for just twelve months or so, and the work it involved was for the most part fairly humdrum. He was however coming into the work at a vital point in the development of student evangelicalism.

### Consolidation and enterprise: the Christian Unions and the Student Volunteer Movement 1895–97[1]

The Student Volunteer Missionary Union (SVMU) had been founded in 1892, but there did not as yet exist a national organization linking all evangelical

[1] Much of the background material in this chapter draws on Tissington Tatlow, *The Story of the Student Christian Movement of Great Britain and Ireland*, London, SCM, 1933.

student groups. The only semblance of such a body was the annual student camp at Keswick, and the annual joint meetings of the Oxford and Cambridge Christian Unions. In 1893, however, the decision was taken at Keswick to form an Inter-Varsity Christian Union – renamed in 1894 the British College Christian Union (BCCU). The relationship between the SVMU and BCCU was inevitably and deliberately intimate from the start. Their constituencies were identical, the goal of each body presupposed the other's, they shared the same office in Aldersgate Street, London, and to a considerable extent were served by the same staff. A crucial role in cementing the early partnership of the two bodies was played by Donald Fraser, a former medical student at Glasgow University, who in 1893 was appointed travelling secretary of the SVMU in succession to C.H. Polhill Turner. Fraser's contribution was twofold. He intensified the appeal for missionary volunteers, and he saw the need for the extension and organization of Christian Unions throughout the British university scene (being a non-Oxbridge Scot doubtless helped here). Very quickly he realized that if the latter was to take place then the BCCU, no less than the SVMU, needed its own travelling secretary. In 1894 Fraser took up that post, the SVMU appointing Frank Anderson of Oxford in his place. Meanwhile, the two bodies shared the same general secretary in a succession of one-year appointments: L.B. Butcher, Crayden Edmunds, and in 1896 J.H. Oldham who in turn was succeeded by H.C. Duncan. By then it had become clear that a more permanent arrangement was called for. Provision of an adequate secretariat had been one of the key points urged upon the students by J.R. Mott at Keswick in 1894.

The student evangelical scene was maturing fast. The outstanding sign of this, and an immense stimulus to further advance, was the international students' missionary conference which opened in Liverpool on new year's day 1896. By any standards it was a remarkable achievement of vision and organization – five days of meetings, prayer sessions, Bible studies and the like, attended by nearly a thousand delegates. The majority were from seventy-four British universities and colleges, but twenty nationalities were represented. Much of the stimulus for the venture had come from America, where Donald Fraser had attended a similar conference in Detroit in 1894. The Liverpool conference however was held not for its own inspirational sake, but with a deliberate strategy in view. Fraser and other student leaders had over the past two years been disturbed to find the British churches either unaware of or unresponsive to the growing missionary interest in the colleges. In some cases the missionary societies themselves were unable to make use of student volunteers because of lack of funds. The conference was therefore aimed not simply at rousing yet more students to missionary zeal, but at awakening the *churches* to an appreciation of the rising tide of missionary interest and commitment in the student world. The climax of the gathering came in a service of consecration, in which the conference adopted the Watchword of the American Volunteer Movement by affirming a commitment to "the evangelization of the world in this generation". Hardly less impressive than the conference itself was its handsomely produced report *Make Jesus King*, bound in hard covers and 328 pages in length.[2]

The Liverpool conference met during Oldham's last year at Oxford. Nowhere in Oldham's extant papers however is there any reference to his attending the event. Nor is there in the conference records any list of participants by name. It is difficult to imagine him *not* being present, and therefore one may conjecture that he was among the six stated as attending from Trinity College, Oxford. In any case, whether he had actually attended or not, Liverpool was to set the agenda for much of Oldham's year at the joint secretary's desk, 1896–97.

## Aldersgate Street: the general secretary's desk

J.H. Oldham was in fact the first full-time general secretary of the SVMU, his predecessor Crayden Edmunds having been only part-time. Both the setting and the content of the work were unpretentious. The office at 93 Aldersgate Street was a single room with a large desk, a cupboard, two tables and any number of packing cases overflowing with "literature". His colleagues required of their general secretary parcels and parcels of study syllabuses, books, copies of the two magazines *The Student Volunteer* and *News from the Colleges*, and – especially – the Liverpool conference report *Make Jesus King* which quickly went into a second edition and was sold out within the year. "I was", wrote Oldham, "my own secretary, stenographer and office boy, ending each day by carrying an armful of parcels to Aldersgate Street Post Office."[3]

Tied to the London office by such duties, Oldham registered and corresponded with the rapidly proliferating Bible study groups in the college Christian unions. Group Bible study is today a commonplace of church life but in the 1890s it was relatively new, and it was a student invention. Mott encouraged it wherever he went and a number of study guides were written to meet student needs. Oldham's own contribution in this year was a pamphlet on aims and organization, based on his and others' experience of the pitfalls of amateur study. In *The Bible Study Department of the College Christian Union* can be seen the Oldham of the future, the past-master of group leadership with his careful preparation both of himself and of the participants.

The Liverpool conference had generated a surge of interest and financial support, which required and enabled the SVMU to strengthen its administration. Oldham as general secretary worked with a five-person committee: three travelling secretaries touring the colleges extending and sustaining the enthusiasm engendered by the conference, an education secretary and one commissioned to penetrate the more difficult terrain of the theological colleges. The appointment of an education secretary was to be particularly significant, and the holder of this post, Donald Thornton, proved to be a catalytic figure. His *Africa Waiting* was the first of a long series of study textbooks published by the SVMU and later by the United Council for Missionary Education. Equally

[2] London, Student Volunteer Missionary Union, 1896.

[3] Letter of JHO to K. Bliss, 11 Sept. 1962 [OA].

significant was Ruth Rouse, another member of the committee destined to be an outstanding ecumenical leader and scholar, who edited *The Student Volunteer*.

If nothing else, this year at the Aldersgate Street office gave Oldham vital administrative experience, including that of working cooperatively with strong-minded people (both men and women), which was to stand him in good stead later on. One task which fell to Oldham was to look for an alternative site for the summer conference, as Mott had advocated. This he found at Curbar in Derbyshire. The move from Keswick was hotly debated on the committee and only consented to when a statement of loyalty to evangelical principles had been accepted. Some years later the move to neutral as well as less expensive ground had the effect Mott hoped for. The High Anglican communities of Kelham and Mirfield would never have sent students to Keswick.

It is true that, as Kathleen Bliss comments,[4] this year for Oldham was essentially a time of waiting to go abroad, and that while the student movement was ecumenical in the sense of having in it members of many churches it gave him no experience of the sort of problems that were later to loom so large. Cocooned as it was in the evangelical tradition, the movement among students attracted little interest in the churches: no bishop protested when the committee reaffirmed the practice of closing the summer conference with a communion service, nobody raised an alarm when Oldham and others commended the critical study of the Bible to students who had time for it.

On the other hand, during the year this very fact of the problematic relationship among the student movement, the churches and overseas missions, came to the fore in a quite dramatic development which must have made Oldham ponder, even at this early stage, on the capacities of the churches to respond to the wider world scene. As mentioned earlier, the Liverpool conference had concluded by adopting the goal of "the evangelization of the world in this generation". It had been presented to the conference only after vigorous debate in the organizing committee, but its adoption was unanimous and forthright. In the months following the conference, the executive committee became increasingly concerned that, despite the immediate interest aroused by the event and the continuing demand for *Make Jesus King*, the British churches as such were not displaying any more noticeable zeal for the worldwide missionary task. Urged on by Donald Thornton in particular, at Christmas 1896 the committee decided to throw down the gauntlet to the churches and challenge *them* to adopt the Watchword as their own. A memorial, 1,600 words long, was drawn up. "Evangelization" was carefully distinguished both from "conversion" on the one hand, and a mere hurried presentation of the truth of Christ on the other:

> We understand it to mean that the Gospel should be preached intelligibly and intelligently to every soul in such a manner that the responsibility for its acceptance shall no longer rest upon the Christian Church, but upon each man for himself.

[4] Bliss MS, p.26.

> Hence the Watchword is perfectly in harmony with the leavening influences, educational, medical and pastoral, now in operation in the mission-field.[5]

The memorial culminated in the appeal itself:

> We venture to ask you, who are called to the holy office of guiding the counsels and action of the Church, to recognize our Watchword as expressive of the present duty of the Church, and to ACCEPT IT AS YOUR MISSIONARY POLICY. We beseech you to enlarge your borders, and to direct your plans with a view to carrying the Gospel to all men speedily. In the name of a thousand volunteers, we entreat you to use your influence, by voice and pen, to rouse the Church to a realization of the present crisis, and to claim her sons and daughters, and her wealth to send them forth, and thus redeem the shame of centuries.[6]

The memorial was signed by the executive and the secretaries, Oldham's name among them. It was a bold gesture for such a small and relatively inexperienced group – as indeed the Liverpool conference itself had been. Yet they also acted astutely, taking soundings among prominent church leaders beforehand and gaining the personal support of a number, including the archbishop of Canterbury, Frederick Temple. The appeal did indeed go to the churches during the course of 1897. None rejected it, but most tended to pass it on to their missionary societies who not surprisingly were already whole-heartedly in agreement. The student volunteers had to confess to disappointment. "Mission", having become the delegated task of the societies, was evidently an extra to the life of the churches themselves.

Overall, for Oldham himself the most important outcome of the year was to establish him in the twin student movements. A few years later, on his unexpectedly early return from India, this was to prove vital in providing him with a ready-made base. Alongside that base was the family. Home life was very happy during this year. While Oldham was still at Oxford his father and Aunt Sarah moved from Edinburgh to London and made a home for him and his youngest brother Jack, in Kensington Park Road, Notting Hill. The house became a meeting place for students who came not only to enjoy the traditional warm hospitality but to seek George Oldham's advice and help. Colonel Oldham joined Trinity Presbyterian Church and continued his evangelistic activities.

## The call to India

During the Liverpool conference a cablegram had arrived from India: "Asia's crisis demands thousands of mountain-moving volunteers." John R. Mott was on a world tour, visiting and strengthening college YMCAs where they existed and encouraging their formation where as yet there were none. The Indian section of his journey was especially creative; accompanied by Amos Wilder

[5] Tatlow, p.98.
[6] *Ibid.*, p.100.

*Lahore in the 1890s*

who was working there at the time, Mott addressed student conferences in Bombay, Lahore, Lucknow, Calcutta and Madras. The groundwork for these visits had been laid by prominent members of the American and British volunteer movements already in the field. The aftermath of the tour was to be equally important. Mott listened carefully to the assessments of their needs for further personnel and leadership, and made his own shrewd judgments which he turned into suggestions on finally reaching home again. He had already sent out hand-picked, very able Americans to staff the YMCAs in Bombay, Madras and Calcutta, and also in China and Japan.[7]

Early in 1897 Oldham received and accepted an invitation from the Scottish National Council of YMCAs to work as YMCA secretary in Lahore. Mott very

[7] Letter of JHO, *op. cit.*

likely had an indirect hand in this appointment, at least to the extent of prodding the Scottish YMCA to help with the Indian effort. At the same time, Oldham had no direct dealing with Mott about the assignment – or indeed about anything else during his Indian episode – although he saw a good deal of Mott's able lieutenants in India.

Having thus been commandeered by the Scottish YMCA, during the summer of 1897 as his departure date approached Oldham was required to spend some time in Scotland speaking at missionary gatherings. At the end of July came the annual student conference at its new venue, Curbar in Derbyshire. Oldham himself addressed the closing devotional meeting, basing his talk on 2 Corinthians 5:9: "So whether we are at home or away, we make it our aim to please him." "We must", said Oldham, "do little things as if they were great things, because of the majesty of Christ; and we must do great things as if they were little things, because of his Almighty power."[8] In September he was back in Scotland, addressing the YMCA conference in Glasgow.

In October, aged 23, he sailed for India, the country of his birth which he had last seen at the age of 7.

### India: "A very happy chapter in my life"

That was how Oldham described his three and a half years in India. He also said that he was in India for too short a time to achieve anything. The evidence, though scanty, does not wholly confirm this. What is clear is that this was not only a happy but a profoundly transforming chapter of experience for Oldham himself. The seeds of his critical awareness of Christianity's problematic identification with Western domination of the world, which was to be such a feature of his mature thought, can already be seen germinating in the quarterly newsletters he wrote home to his YMCA supporters in Scotland.

British rule in India in the 1890s was fast approaching its zenith of achievement: the efficiency of government, the success of the railways and road-building schemes, the spread of education at every level, were apparent for all to see. But the nationalist forces were also stirring, stimulated in part by the very same education brought by the British. The Indian National Congress, albeit a cautious and moderate movement at first, had been formed in 1885, tolerated in a dismissive kind of way by the government. The combined strengths and weaknesses of British rule were perhaps epitomized in Lord Curzon, viceroy 1895–1905:

> He had integrity, vigour, imagination and a sense of history. He was proud of his country as of himself, he served India in his own manner with unremitting toil. In everything administrative he excelled; in anything requiring any understanding he lacked and failed. He could relieve famine and extend irrigation, build railways and encourage commerce, reorganize the frontier and overhaul the educational machine,

[8] *The Christian*, 5 Aug. 1897, SCM archives, Selly Oak, UK.

> exhort princes and uphold racial justice. He could preach the gospel of imperial service and match precept with practice. But he could not understand the Indian mind, appreciate its feelings or sympathize with its aspirations.[9]

That last sentence could never have been said of Oldham. When he arrived at Lahore station he was met by a student, S.K. Datta. It was the beginning of a close and intimate friendship which lasted many years. Datta was to become, in Oldham's view, the leading Indian Christian of the time, and was appointed to the legislative assembly to represent the Indian Christian community. For the moment Datta's significance lay, through personal friendship, in providing Oldham with precisely that avenue into the Indian mind, its feelings and aspirations, which the likes of Curzon were denied. In fact, with the sole exception of the woman he was to marry, Oldham's most intimate associates in India were all Indians. True friendship is not contrived but takes what is on offer from the other, and for Oldham this was the natural way to act as a Christian. His own parents' custom in Bombay, of welcoming Indians no less than Europeans into their home, may well have been a formative example. Thirteen years later, at the Edinburgh world missionary conference, there would be a poignant plea from V.S. Azariah, later to be the first Indian bishop of the Anglican communion, who in talking about the barrier which often separated missionaries from their Indian co-workers, cried out: "Through all the ages to come the Indian Church will rise up in gratitude to attest the heroism and self-denying labour of the missionary body. You have given your goods to feed the poor. You have given your bodies to be burned. We also ask for *love.* Give us FRIENDS."[10] As few others, Oldham knew what that meant.

The last decade of the century was a testing time for the capacity of Europeans to accept Indians as friends and colleagues, on a basis of genuine equality and mutual respect, and in the Punjab it was perhaps particularly so. The Punjab (today of course in Pakistan) was the last Indian province to be annexed by the British, in 1849. For that reason, coming under the British Raj so late in the day it was subjected to an administration unusually efficient and paternalistic in one – a "pampered province".[11] Its position so close to the north-west frontier made its imperial guardians even more watchful, and its administrative handling had to be much more delicate than in many other provinces. Another factor was the religious mix of the population: a Muslim majority, followed by Hindus and a small Sikh minority. Communal politics had not yet arrived, but social development, more educational opportunities and the prospects of rising standards of living were beginning to make adherents of the different religions watchful of one another in the search for material

[9] P. Spear, "India, 1840–1905", in *The New Cambridge Modern History*, vol. XI, ed. F.H. Hinsley, Cambridge, Cambridge Univ. Press, 1967, p.435.

[10] Quoted in Ruth Rouse and Stephen Neill, eds, *A History of the Ecumenical Movement 1517–1948*, London, SPCK, 1967, p.359.

[11] Shyamala Bhatia, *Social Change and Politics in the Punjab 1848–1910*, New Delhi, Entry Publications PVT, 1987, p.40.

S.K. Datta

betterment. Education was a particularly powerful motor of social change. Both government and missionaries opened educational institutions in the Punjab. At the higher level, Punjab University College was started in 1869–70 and became a university in 1882. By 1892 it had six arts colleges attached to it, together with a medical and a law college. Five of these colleges were in Lahore itself. Oldham himself wrote of Lahore: "It is the capital of the Punjab and the headquarters of its government. Hundreds of young men are employed as clerks in Government offices. Lahore is also a great educational centre . . . Here are gathered for a few years, young men from almost every village in the province. They are at the most impressionable time of life . . . they will soon be scattered far and wide; many of them will hold positions of responsibility and influence."[12]

Oldham was of course underlining the significance of the students as a mission field. Yet it was precisely with those who were educated, or being educated, in the European way that Anglo–Indian relationships were becoming most difficult. In 1836 Macaulay had written: "We must at present do our best to form a class who may be interpreters between us and the millions whom we govern, a class of persons, Indian in blood and colour, but English in taste, in opinions, in morals and in intellect."[13] Superficially, this dream was being

[12] Bliss MS, pp.28f.

[13] *Minute on Education*, quoted in Bhatia, p.116.

realized in the colleges, but beneath the surface it was proving disruptive in a number of directions. For one thing, to be educated in the European way would mean acquiring at least a modicum of rationality and critical ability – and then why should not those reasoning, critical faculties be turned to examine the very imperial system itself, and to articulate the felt grievances and injustices of the Indians? Further, those who were Western-educated might well be thereby qualified to work in government service and find a measure of fulfilment (though the competition for such employment was growing ever more severe). But those who, having been educated, felt critical of their Indian upbringing, its customs and religious beliefs, now all too frequently found that a Western education and even a university degree did not themselves provide a passport into Western society. They remained the ruled under the rulers. As Shyamala Bhatia describes it:

> The Western educated Punjabi elite was groping in the dark. On the one hand these men were misfits in their own society and on the other hand the English society did not accept them. The handful of Englishmen in India kept themselves aloof and did not allow these Indians into the sacred precincts of their social life.
>
> Social isolation and economic deprivation, along with non-existence of any means of expression created an atmosphere of tension and frustration.[14]

Sociologically speaking, Christianity had arrived as a vital and complicating factor in all this. The first real missionary agency was the American Presbyterian Mission at Ludhiana, established in 1835. British officials lent their support to missions after annexation in 1849. The Punjab, it was felt, would be fertile soil for the gospel, especially among the Sikhs whom Westerners claimed to find the "least bigoted". Schools and colleges, as elsewhere in India, were soon central to the missionary enterprise in the Punjab. Though always a tiny minority, in relative terms, the Christian population was expanding quite impressively by the end of the century. In 1881 there were just 3,912 Punjabi Christians. In the next decade there was a 410 per cent increase to 19,750. By 1910 this figure had doubled to 38,513.[15] Over the years the Christian mission had by turns varied its targeting of groups, from the aristocratic strata to lowest caste people. By the close of the century, it was especially among those coming under Western educational influence that missionary hopes were highest.

Yet, again, it was in just this group that British–Indian sensitivities were most complex and acute. In some ways the entry of Christianity heightened these tensions. Even more than just Western education, should not acceptance of the Westerners' religion ensure acceptance into European society? The answer coming from Indian Christians was by no means clear. In any case, while Christianity was arriving at a time when the traditional religions were relatively somnolent, and were perceived by many educated Indians as inadequate to their needs, the crisis with which Christianity faced those religions in turn helped to stimulate their revival.

[14] *Ibid.*, pp.116f.
[15] *Ibid.*, p.115.

It was into this web of uneasy relationships that J.H. Oldham arrived as "the Scottish YMCA missionary to the young men of India" in the autumn of 1897. No doubt he had many plans and ideas in his mind. But perhaps more than he realized, his missionary work actually began, and was embodied in, the handshake with S.K. Datta amid the dust and steam at Lahore station.

## The YMCA secretary

Higher education was expanding rapidly throughout India, and the student YMCAs were therefore highly strategic points in the Christian mission. Even in Christian-run colleges Christians remained a small minority, yet the YMCA had made considerable progress with students in colleges and high schools, and with young men in employment. In some of the main cities the YMCA was acquiring an impressive amount of plant and personnel. In Calcutta for instance the association had just taken over and adapted a disused hospital for its rapidly growing work under its secretary J.N. Farquhar, later to become a distinguished Sanskrit scholar and writer on Hinduism. In Madras the association had fine new buildings and, with the exception of its versatile and energetic secretary Sherwood Eddy, its management was almost entirely in Indian hands.

It was far otherwise in Lahore, and Oldham must have felt he had been given the Cinderella of the Indian YMCAs. The association was small and weak, and the reading room – the main point of contact with non-Christians – had been closed. But there were deeply committed Christians like S.K. Datta – a convert through one of Mott's meetings the previous year – and it was with such that Oldham immediately began his work. From the first he believed that India could be evangelized (no exponent of the Watchword would add the words "if at all") only by Indians. But he did not think of Christian students merely as a means to evangelism; their own needs were his personal concern. Mott had urged the study of the Bible in groups, and Oldham took this up. They met weekly. He invited speakers on topics ranging from "St Paul on Athletics" to "Why I am a Christian" (by a former Muslim) and "Evangelizing the Punjab". Once a month the students themselves broached some problem of a more personal kind and they prayed for one another. Later Oldham took them through some of the books he was reading for his own theological self-education (B.F. Westcott's *The Gospel of Life*, for example – no easy meat). Oldham at this stage had no formal theological education. Perhaps because of this, his approach was not that of a teacher. Indeed, he was apt to pass humorous remarks about the pomposity of some of the university teachers. He sat with the students as a fellow-learner and as their friend. Practical tasks included visiting Christian families in the villages and delivering the association's newspaper to scores of government officials ("They will read it to improve their English," he commented). For non-Christians Oldham organized a series of public lectures on various aspects of Christianity and these maintained an average audience of 150 throughout a fairly long course in 1898–99. But few of those who showed this intellectual interest were prepared to study the Bible or to talk about religion.

Oldham regularly sent a quarterly newsletter on his work to the Scottish YMCA. He felt that it was not until after he had been a year in Lahore that the association was properly organized.[16] During his second year he was away for a great part, and "we were hardly strong enough to think of expansion". But it was with something like jubilation that Oldham wrote of the reopening of the reading room and the start of a social centre in 1899. It was an immediate success:

> I wish I could successfully picture to you the scene that would meet your eye if you were to walk into the association rooms on an ordinary afternoon . . . In the large central room you would find from 20 to 30 fellows. Round each of four little tables in different parts of the room would be sitting four men playing at Crokinole, the most popular game we have. It is played by shooting small wooden men with the finger, the aim being to get them to lie as near the centre as possible and to drive away the opponent's men . . . One or more couples might be seen at the large table playing chess or draughts. Three or four men would be seen standing at the newspaper stands reading the daily newspapers. Several others would be sitting in various parts of the room reading the weeklies and monthlies or talking with one another. Outside in the compound a number might be seen playing badminton. Nearly all the men would be Indians, most of them would be students; a good number would be Hindus or Mohammedans. Some would be wearing English clothes, others a more eastern garb. Several would have turbans, others little caps (it is not the Indian fashion to remove the headdress); others would be bare-headed, which would be an almost certain indication that they were Christians. All could speak and understand English; but if you were to listen to those who were playing games, you would hear a good deal of Hindustani, the excitement of the game leading men to drop into their mother tongue. Many of the men who entered the room would come in boldly as if they were quite at home. But you would see others coming in more shyly as if they were strangers. Then you might see one of the Christian men on reception duty rising and speaking a word of welcome to the stranger, and giving him a paper to read, or asking him to join in a game. Not all of even our active members, I fear, realize their privilege in being able to do a little act of kindness of this sort for Christ's sake; but the Christian men are more and more coming to do so.[17]

Some of his Scottish evangelical readers may well have asked what Oldham was doing playing games when he should have been saving souls. In fact, Oldham believed that it was precisely in this space for truly interpersonal relations, with its possibilities for friendship, that true evangelism could occur.

While his work centred on Lahore, Oldham extended his contacts to other colleges in the Punjab. In 1899 he took sixty students to camp in and around a mission bungalow at Beas and discuss the theme "Raising up a Student Movement for India". The camp was a fresh experience for the students, and greatly enjoyed. It was decided to found a district union of YMCAs for

[16] *Quarterly Paper*, no. 6, 20 April 1900 [OA].
[17] *Quarterly Paper*, no. 7, 7 June 1900 [OA].

continuing contact and to camp again the following year, holding all the proceedings in Hindustani. Oldham found a suitable site with the Presbyterian mission at Gujarat. Still more adventurously he took four young men to a regional meeting in Bombay – "1,200 miles, but well worth the trouble and expense". The leader was training leaders. Such simple actions as these were important steps in the formation of an articulate Christian laity, confident enough to stand up to missionary paternalism and to take, at times, an independent line on matters of church government, educational policy and national politics. Oldham was to see some of the fruits when he revisited India in rather different circumstances in 1923.

In 1900, partly on medical advice, Oldham accepted an invitation to work with the YMCA in Simla during the hot season. Simla was the hill station in the Himalayas to which government and business migrated from the oppressive summer heat of Lahore and Calcutta. "I expected to find a small and struggling association but I discovered that having found an energetic secretary in the Rev. J.H. Bateson it had launched out into a big and enterprising work."[18] Rooms had been rented in the centre of Simla; the lieutenant-governor addressed the meeting and there were already 240 members. The attendance at religious meetings however was "very poor," Oldham wrote, "only five or six at the Sunday Bible class . . . The only thing to be done . . . is to build up the association by steady persistent personal work. This will take time but I have no doubt that now the association has made a successful start on a large scale an intensive development will follow the extensive." The relation of "intensive" to "extensive" work in mission strategy was to occupy Oldham in years to come.

As a worker for the YMCA, how did Oldham view the churches themselves and their missionary role? The follow-up to the 1896 Liverpool conference – the attempt to get the British churches to adopt the SVM Watchword – had, after all, raised inescapably the question of inter-relationships among churches, missionary societies and the student movement. Oldham was quite clear in seeing that the YMCA was called to work evangelistically among non-Christians and educationally and pastorally among Christians, *and* in partnership with the churches. "The YMCA," he wrote, "has done much to develop voluntary work for Christ among Indian Christian young men, among whom there is a tendency to think that propagating the gospel is the work solely of missionaries and paid agents. But the Association is but the handmaid of the Church and it is only in loyalty to the churches and in co-operation with missionary societies that it can continue to do good work."[19]

But for Oldham in India the most critical question was the relation between the European Christian and the Indian. It was this theme which prompted his most independent and outspoken reflections, in which the germ of much of his later thinking and study is clearly recognizable. Crucial in the formation of

[18] *Quarterly Paper*, no. 8, 15 Sept. 1900 [OA].

[19] Bliss MS, pp.36f.

his outlook and actions was his experience of living in close daily touch with Indians, regarding them as friends and colleagues on an equal basis, from whom he had much to learn. Frank Anderson, Oldham's opposite number in Bombay who had also served as a secretary to the Student Volunteers before coming to India, had written:

> The material here is by no means plastic. While it may be safely asserted that the extent to which rationalism in one shape or another prevails among students in Western India is very great, yet we constantly meet with superficial efforts to support Zoroastrianism or Hinduism. The ambition to pass examinations, the craving for appointments, the desire for wealth, in short the attractions of the world, fill their horizons and God is left out of court.[20]

No doubt Anderson was better in personal relationships than this clinical-observer attitude seems to imply. Nevertheless, this is what he thought should be the message to Volunteers at home who might soon be following him. For his part, Oldham wrote to the same audience in rather different vein:

> If the missionary finds it difficult to make contact and gain a hearing, then he must look to himself to find the reason. The missionary is a foreigner, separated from Indians by barriers of custom, modes of thought and language, by racial prejudice, and by belonging to a conquering race.[21]

Being a foreigner and a member of a conquering race were disabilities which the missionary could not remove, but in 1900 Oldham was writing on "Foreignness: a hindrance to evangelism", stressing the actions that could help to bridge the gulf. He put first "a patient, thorough grammatical study of the language" and "courage to insist on being relieved from other work and given the necessary facilities for learning". He himself studied Urdu although he was working among English-speaking students. Next he put relations with Indian Christians:

> Every action, word and gesture is noted and interpreted. A missionary nods in a friendly way to an Indian Christian student . . . "He was too proud to shake hands." The treatment of Indians by many of our countrymen is contemptuous and insulting . . . Is any of us quite free from this overbearing spirit? It is a national failing, that faculty for despising everything and everybody but ourselves which Rudyard Kipling has been satirizing lately. One form of this national self-assertiveness shows itself in the desire to have things done always in our own way . . . The civil administrator does his duty if he is just and kindly; a missionary must be an Indian to Indians. This is the work of a lifetime . . . many prejudices still have to be overcome; natural tastes and predilections will have to be surrendered. The spirit that says "these petty differences are absurd, they are nothing" is fatal to missionary work. They are everything; the way we treat them makes the difference between winning men's hearts and remaining continually a foreigner to them.[22]

[20] *Ibid.*, pp.29f.
[21] *Ibid.*, p.30.
[22] *Ibid.*, p.31.

This recognition of the problematic nature of British–Indian relationships underscored for Oldham the value of the social side of the YMCA work. As he put it in another of his quarterly newsletters:

> It is only after one has been out here for a little time, and has got to know the men better, that one begins to realize how strong a prejudice there is against us foreigners. We know that there is a good deal of national prejudice among the European nations. Here the feeling is perhaps stronger; for there is a greater gulf between the East and the West than between the different nations of Europe. This natural feeling is very much intensified by the fact that in India we are the *ruling race*. There is constantly present a sense of the relation of conquerors and conquered. I am afraid that this is often encouraged by our overbearing manner, which I think is one of our national characteristics. This is, very naturally, galling to the Indian people, and especially to the student class, which is very much better educated and perhaps more high-spirited than other classes. It has always seemed to me that the fact that we are here not only as foreigners . . . but also as members of the conquering and governing race, is one of the peculiar difficulties of missionary work in India . . . When we speak we are met by prejudice. Men think that we have forced our Government upon them, and now we want to force our religion and so they brace themselves up to resist it. This is why I feel that the social side of the Association is so valuable. It makes men feel that we are their friends.[23]

With the benefit of hindsight a century later, Oldham might be held to be naively innocent if he imagined that nationalist prejudice might be overcome by playing draughts together. But equally, he was more sharply percipient of the problem than many of his generation, and was already beginning to recognize that the inter-racial relations within colonialism were not only the context of Christian mission but the *subject* which it should address. The crucial point was the formation of a genuinely Indian church, which was vital for the evangelization of India. Oldham down the years never lost sight of the importance, in all Christian activity and at whatever level, of personal relationships. The social work of the YMCA was itself evangelism:

> There, day by day, for three or four hours, one can mix freely with the men, and they can see one not merely as a religious teacher but as a *man*. I think that this is an immense privilege, and it is my earnest prayer, in which I would ask you to join, that as I mix with the men in games and in conversation, every word, every gesture, and every look may speak of Jesus Christ. If it be true, as I believe it is, that our unconscious influence is greater than that which we consciously exert, then the social life of the Association affords to all truly Christian men a most glorious opportunity of letting their light shine.[24]

The young student volunteer was quickly becoming a mature missionary, and clearly the Indian experience, though it was to be shorter than he had wished or expected, was to enable him to speak with genuine authority about

[23] *Quarterly Paper*, no. 6, 20 April 1900 [OA].
[24] Bliss MS, p.32.

missionary questions for decades to come. Meanwhile, another factor of lifelong significance entered Joe Oldham's life.

## Marriage: Mary Oldham, née Fraser

As mentioned in the preceding chapter, among the women students associated with the Christian Union at Oxford was Mary Fraser, sister of Oldham's close friend at Trinity, Alek Fraser. Reading modern languages at Somerville College, she was a year junior to Oldham, and one of the small group of women who came along to the summer conferences. Joe Oldham and Mary had obviously grown close to one another at Oxford and during the year following his graduation, but he had offered no formal proposal before embarking for India. In fact their engagement was to be very brief indeed, for one day in Lahore while Oldham was still turning over in his mind the wording of a formal letter of proposal, the home mail brought a letter from Alek Fraser with some surprising news: "We are all delighted that you and Mary are to be married."[25] A moment's resentment at the intrusion was succeeded by relief that he would not have to wait for a reply. Mary quickly made her preparations, stayed for a brief and happy few days with her future father-in-law in London, and was on her way. The wedding took place in the Anglican cathedral in Lahore on 24 October 1898, with – typically – another of Oldham's close Indian friends, Surandra Nath Chandu Lal, as best man.

Mary, like her bridegroom, had returned to the land of her birth. If she did not feel the same attachment for India in later years as did her husband the reason probably lay in her unhappy childhood. Her and Alek's father was in the Indian Civil Service, as governor of the Punjab and then of Bengal, the most volatile and (from the British point of view) difficult province. Andrew Fraser was dedicated to his work. In both provinces he made long and exacting tours. In manner he was quiet and reserved, but there is no doubt of his affection for his children. Misfortune, not neglect, caused the months of delay between his wife's death on tour with him and the breaking of the news to Mary, by then at boarding school in Scotland. She was desolated, but her intense loyalty to her father prevented her from telling him that the school he had chosen for her was a disaster and she was underfed, bullied and wretched. Her sole resource was her brother Alek whom she closely resembled and deeply loved.

In her husband, Mary had not only the ardent lover but the friend who protected her from the assaults of those who smell out the person who has been bullied and is vulnerable. Their married partnership was to last more than sixty years. Mary created wherever they lived a home of great beauty where her unfailing hospitality was extended to a never-ending stream of guests – colleagues and friends, unknown contacts who might prove useful in Oldham's work, colonial governors and visiting professors, Indians and Africans, writers whose work interested Oldham, promising young men and women needing

[25] *Ibid.*

*Mary Fraser, Oxford 1896/97*

advice or encouragement, children with parents abroad and needing long holidays; not to mention stray dogs, wounded birds and starving rabbits.

Mary had read German at Oxford and was an accomplished linguist. She taught herself shorthand and typing and acted as secretary in many confidential matters. Without her Oldham could never have overcome as he did the crippling deafness which overtook him in his late forties. Childlessness was to be their chief sorrow but they never suffered from that biting envy which renders some couples incapable of extending affection to other people's children. To nephews and nieces, and to their children in turn, Mary was the adored "Auntie Mag", while Uncle Joe, who could always switch off from work even for a brief time and read aloud, play cricket or throw off a Latin translation as though he were reading the newspaper, was a good companion.

Mary's presence in Lahore provided the opportunity for reopening friendships with women who had been in the student movement at home and were now working in women's education or in that nest of Indian female leadership, the YWCA. The hot weather season in 1900 with the YMCA in Simla was followed by a walking tour in the Kulu valley, accompanied by Agnes de Selincourt. They planned to go on with her to conduct one of the first ecumenical camps for Indian women. "We hope to be back in Lahore by the end of the month and are looking forward to the next winter's work," wrote Oldham from the Kulu on 15 September, and promised that his next letter would give an account of the district union conference and the beginning of the new season's work at Lahore. There were hopes of starting a "good library" for the association, and the donation of any books on any subject would be welcomed from Scotland, "except technical books now out of date and old sermons".[26]

## Farewell to India

But there was to be no new season's work. Joe Oldham was struck down by typhoid. So serious was the attack that for days he lay close to death, and indeed one night Mary was told by the doctor that he would not live to see the morning. The Oldhams were convinced that his survival and recovery were answers to the intense prayer by members of the association. Any immediate rejoicing however was premature. Mary herself succumbed to the illness. Both were left extremely weak and debilitated, and any thought of resuming work or even travelling to a suitable place for convalescence was out of the question for several weeks. All this news was received with great concern, though of course with equal relief that danger had passed, in the Scottish YMCA council.

The medical verdict was uncompromising. As soon as they were strong enough for the voyage the Oldhams must leave India and not return. Early in 1901 they embarked for Britain, still by no means fully fit. What had looked like the opening up of a new chapter in a happy and useful life, and in answer to the great missionary call, had ended abruptly and without any alternative in sight. But Joe Oldham's career was to be marked by successive stages and transfers from one form of work to another while maintaining a marked continuity of direction, and this was to be but the first instance of such a transition.

In terms of visible lasting achievements, Joe Oldham did not feel very sanguine about his three and a half years in India. Others however, mindful of his own emphasis on the importance of personal relationships and influence, were unreserved in their tributes. His colleague in Madras, Sherwood Eddy, who used to meet him on exchange visits and at the committees which established the Indian Student Christian Movement, wrote of his "spiritual consecration and the drive of his strong will – stubborn in the best sense, for all his quiet manner – and his mental maturity and well-balanced judgment".[27] The most significant comments were perhaps from the Indian Christians themselves and his closest friend in Lahore, S.K. Datta, saw another side: "He left no organization, nor bricks and mortar; but he builded greatly in the lives of a few men. Joe Oldham, a young YMCA secretary, will live for ever in the life of the Punjab."[28] And while Oldham might have left India, the Indian experience and what he had learned through it would never leave him.

[26] *Quarterly Paper*, no. 8, 15 Sept. 1900 [OA].
[27] Bliss MS, p.37.
[28] *Ibid.*

CHAPTER 4

# *Theological Student and Missions Educator, Edinburgh 1901–07*[1]

WHERE to live and what to do were still open questions when the Oldhams reached Colonel Oldham's home in London in April 1901. Certain objectives were, however, clear. The immediate priority for the couple was full recovery of health. Further, Joe Oldham, wherever his long-term future might lie, was feeling the need for an extended period of theological study. Both requirements pointed to Edinburgh: a familiar and healthy place, and moreover the location of New College which offered what was perhaps the best theological education in the British Isles. Their families provided sufficient means to relieve them of immediate financial anxieties, the college admitted Joe as a mature student to a shortened course of three years, and furnished rooms were engaged for the autumn. Then the couple left for a long recuperative holiday in Switzerland where (at that time) it was as cheap to live as at home.

## New College[2]

New College, standing impressively – as it still does – on the Mound close by Edinburgh Castle was indeed one of the most prestigious theological schools in the whole English-speaking world. Yet at that time it could confer no degrees. As an institution it was bound up with and symbolized the conflicts which had beset Scottish church life in the 19th century and which at the turn of the 20th century still had to run their full course. In 1843 there had taken place the Great Disruption, when about a third of ministers and parishes seceded from the Church of Scotland, largely over the issue of patronage. The "evangelical" party wished for greater freedom for parishes to choose their ministers, which

[1] This chapter is largely based on the Bliss MS supplemented by material from Tatlow, Warneck *et al.*, issues of the *Student Volunteer*, and other background material.

[2] See H. Watt, *New College Edinburgh: A Centenary History*, Edinburgh, Oliver & Boyd, 1946.

meant in practice the right to veto the nominee of the lay patron. Behind this conviction lay an impulse to minister more widely and effectively in a changing and progressively urbanized society, an attitude embodied in the dynamic evangelical leader Thomas Chalmers. Not that the evangelicals wished to "disestablish" the church; no less than the "moderates" who defended the status quo they believed in a national church, but they also strongly asserted the need for its spiritual and legal freedom if it was to fulfil its ministry to the whole nation.

The Free Church, as the secessionist body was known, therefore reproduced alongside the Church of Scotland a whole new set of institutions at every level, from parish churches and manses to a national assembly hall in Edinburgh – and three theological colleges in Edinburgh, Glasgow and Aberdeen respectively, of which New College in Edinburgh became the largest and most influential. That New College was quite separate from the university did not detract from the quality of its scholarship. At the end of the 19th century its principal, Robert Rainy, was the leading figure in the Free Church as a whole. During the late 1870s, in a bruising encounter with the Old Testament scholar William Robertson Smith of Aberdeen, Rainy had led the conservative reaction to higher criticism, but by the turn of the century the methods of historical scholarship were accepted and practised at New College no less than anywhere else in Britain. In 1900 names such as A.B. Davidson, professor of Old Testament and Hebrew, and Marcus Dods in New Testament studies, were of international status. Its student body was larger than that of any other British seminary, not least because of its intake from elsewhere in the British Isles and from overseas. In fact New College was often welcoming more students from abroad than were all other theological institutions in Britain put together.

That feature alone must have increased the attraction of New College for Joe Oldham. In any case the more evangelical ethos of the Free Church was congenial to him. In 1900 the name of the church was changed to the United Free Church, following the merger of the Free Church with a smaller secessionist body, the United Presbyterians – a move which was to result in an astonishing legal tangle in the church a few years later. Such ecclesiastical politicking had little interest for Oldham. For his three years at New College he devoted himself almost entirely to his studies, gaining a handful of prizes for Greek, Hebrew and New Testament and a number of mentions as "first in class". He was elected a president of the college's theological society for 1903–04. What might be read into this appointment is not entirely clear, given the views of a later member of the teaching staff who remarked that "he hoped New College would never again have a theological society as thriving as it had been in his own student days, for his experience was that it was when the teaching was at its dullest and least relevant, that the men most resorted to theological discussion to supplement what was lacking in the classroom . . ."[3]

[3] *Ibid.*, p.126.

That Oldham thought this true of some, at least, of the formal teaching is evident from his own confession that many a boring lecture gave him the chance of learning another twenty words of German from the vocabulary under his desk.

Oldham could not, however, isolate himself completely from the wider evangelical student world and especially the missionary Volunteer Movement in which he had already played such a central role. In fact it was while at New College that he produced for the British College Christian Union his most substantial publication to date, and the one by which he was first to become widely known. *Studies in the Teaching of Jesus* appeared in 1903[4] and was carefully designed to aid group Bible study on the synoptic gospels. It ran to just under 200 pages, and dealt with Jesus' teaching thematically – on God, the kingdom of God, the righteousness of the kingdom, Jesus' teaching on social questions, the development of the kingdom, the last things and so forth. Each section was concluded with a set of questions for group discussion. The style was simple, straightforward and not theologically academic though the footnotes give evidence of a wide range of sources – Bruce, Dods, Wendt and Harnack in particular. And while the author has no doubt of the authority of Jesus' teaching he also insists that at the same time "we have always to bear in mind that Jesus Himself is greater than His teaching. Mere words count for little; it is the personality behind them which gives them their force".[5] The book stood well the test of two decades, running to 34,000 copies by the time its ninth edition appeared (with minor alterations) in 1933.

Oldham was also still active as a speaker and Bible study leader at student gatherings. In 1904 he gave a Bible reading during the summer conference at Conishead, at the southern edge of the Lake District, on "The Organic Relation between the Missionary Command to Jesus' Teaching."[6] Even if, as some critical scholars had stated, the great commission of Matthew 28:18–20 had not been given by Jesus himself, Oldham argues, the universal missionary call would still be valid since it was rooted in Jesus' own conceptions of God and his kingdom, and his ethical ideals. To confess Jesus as Lord means confessing also that all things should be placed under his feet. Yet

> how much it has meant to the Church that He did utter it! It does not make the obligation more binding, but it shatters the excuses of our indolence and selfishness, and nerves our faltering faith. In the might of this commission weak men have time and again dared to summon the sleeping Church to the task of evangelization. Thousands of weary workers in the mission-field, worn by disease, crushed by disappointment, overwhelmed by their loneliness, have drawn from these words fresh encouragement: "Jesus willed it", they have said to themselves, and their hearts became brave again and their hands strong. Today when the march of history and the play of

[4] J.H. Oldham, *Studies in the Teaching of Jesus. As recorded in the Synoptic Gospels,* 1st ed., British College Christian Union, 1903; 2nd and subsequent eds to 9th, London, SCM, 1933.

[5] *Ibid.*, p.10.

[6] *Student Movement,* vol. VII, no. 1, Oct. 1904, pp.13–16.

> world-forces have forced on the Church the duty of evangelization with an urgency never known before, we shall be able to confront the superhuman task that lies before us only as we believe that Jesus said, "All authority . . . Go ye therefore . . ."

Only the one who had himself been worn by disease and smitten with disappointment at having to return from India could have said this so cogently. Nor was it an attitude of mere bravado. It was founded upon a thoroughly Christocentric faith in God's grace, as is shown by two articles on "The Death of Christ" written for *The Student Movement* in the same year. While his studies on the teaching of Jesus had drawn much from contemporary liberal Protestantism, there is no mistaking in these devotional pieces a starker – and more enthralling – note such as was already being sounded by P.T. Forsyth and was to become heard resoundingly in the neo-orthodoxy of two or three decades hence. Thus:

> There are many who think that the forgiving love of God is something so plain that we may believe in it apart from the revelation of the cross. Such a view is possible, so long as with our ordinary self-complacency we think of ourselves as not so very unworthy to be forgiven. But such a view was altogether impossible for St Paul . . . Forgiveness is something unbelievable, unthinkable. And when we find that we are forgiven, it is a humbling, surpassing, overwhelming revelation.[7]

Meanwhile, Oldham's clandestine German studies were not simply a distraction from dull lectures. Germany was proving an increasing attraction to the Oldhams, who holidayed there more than once during this period. Joe was no doubt tutored also by Mary who was already fluent in the language. There was, moreover, a well-established tradition of the more able theological students from Britain, especially from Scotland and the English Free Churches, completing their studies in Germany. It was not surprising therefore that at the end of his New College course Joe Oldham took this route. His choice was the University of Halle. He could not have foreseen that it was an opportune time at which to have concluded his course at New College, for it was in August 1904 that, after several unsuccessful contests in the Scottish courts, the tiny minority of Free Church dissenters from the union of 1900 – the "Wee Frees" – obtained a judgment in their favour from the House of Lords. Overnight, the Wee Frees became legal owners of all the Free Church property, including the theological colleges. New College had to vacate its premises for three years until, in 1907, a royal commission decided on a reasonable disposition of resources between the United Free Church and the continuing secessionists. Oldham at least was spared this further disruption.

## Halle and Gustav Warneck 1904–05

Halle stands on the sandy plain of Saxony about twenty miles north of Leipzig. Its university, founded in the late 17th century by the Elector Frederick of

[7] *Student Movement,* vol. VII, no. 2, Dec. 1904, p.59.

Saxony (later king of Prussia), closed by Napoleon after his victory over Prussia and reopened in 1815, was home to one of Germany's most famous Protestant theological faculties. Friedrich Schleiermacher, father figure of modern Protestant theology, had taught there. It had subsequently drawn a steady stream of English-speaking students. The theological ethos had originally been pietistic, but rationalist and critical scholarship now flourished there as well. For Joe Oldham, accompanied by Mary, the chief reason for choosing Halle was the presence there of Gustav Warneck, professor of theology of missions.

Gustav Warneck (1834–1910) is widely regarded as the father of the modern discipline of missiology. Coming from a Lutheran pietistic background, he was the first to see that the missionary enterprise of the church, if its effectiveness was to be sustained and increased, could not be just a matter of effort and enthusiasm. It had to be studied with scientific rigour, theologically, historically and sociologically. In 1874 he founded the journal *Allgemeine Missionszeitschrift* and – still a local pastor – in 1879 he set up the mission conference of Saxony followed within six years by the German Protestant committee on missions, the *Ausschuss*. His chair at Halle was the first in missions anywhere. Though he was an immensely erudite scholar with an encyclopaedic knowledge of the story of Christianity's expansion in both ancient and modern times (his achievements for missiology stand comparison with what Ernst Troeltsch did in establishing the sociology of Christianity), no less evident was the sharpness of his analysis in a long series of monographs. Chief among these were *Moderne Mission und Kultur* (1879), the historical study *Abriss eines Geschichte des Protestantismus* (1882–1910 in several editions), and – his *magnum opus* – the five volumes of *Evangelische Missionslehre* (1897–1903). Significantly, the first two of these titles were translated into English by Scotsmen.[8] Warneck had certainly visited Edinburgh at least once, as shown by his perceptive comments on the statue of David Livingstone there.[9] The interest in Warneck was therefore notably strong in Scotland, and in proceeding to Halle Oldham was not following some idiosyncratic whim but was going to sit at the feet of an already acknowledged authority.

Warneck's understanding of mission was on a grand scale: "I understand by missions the whole operations of Christendom directed towards the planting and organization of the Christian Church among non-Christians, that is, their Christianization. . . ."[10] Historically, he argued, a period of missionary activity comprises three stages. The first stage is that of the conversion of individuals

[8] *Modern Missions and Culture: Their Mutual Relations* was translated by Thomas Smith, professor of evangelistic theology at New College, Edinburgh, and published Edinburgh, James Gemmell, 1888. *Outline of a History of Protestant Missions from the Reformation to the Present Time* was translated by George Robson, published Edinburgh and London, Oliphant Anderson & Ferrier, 1901.

[9] *Modern Missions and Culture*, p.59: "It is a suggestive symbol that the statue of Dr Livingstone erected in Edinburgh represents the great traveller and missionary with the Bible in one hand, and the other resting on an axe. With these two great means of culture – to which the plough might have been added – the men have in fact set to work who have preached to East Africa in these last years, to erect for their noble countryman a living monument after his own heart."

[10] *Outline of a History*, p.xi.

and the gathering of comparatively small churches. The second is that of the organized cooperation of the converts, "the upbuilding of the churches, the leavening of the life of the people with the power of the Gospel and the extension of Christianity by assimilative incorporation". The third stage is that of "the Christianizing of the masses, which for the most part takes place in connection with means and motives not purely religious, with political and social movements, with the acceptance of Christianity on the part of leading men, and so on".[11] Warneck recognized that, chronologically, this third stage has often in fact been the first, with highly ambiguous consequences for the type of "Christianity" planted in the country in question. But it was Warneck's particular intellectual contribution, in viewing missions as an object of proper scientific study, to insist on seeing them as part of the wider human, historical scene rather than in pious isolation from secular forces.

It will already be evident from his three-stage understanding of the missionary process that Warneck – here rejecting the individualist elements in his pietist background – laid great emphasis on the formation, organization and upbuilding of the corporate life of the churches as fundamental to mission. That in itself was a timely marker laid down against much of contemporary evangelicalism which saw the evangelization of the world in terms of numbers of individual conversions and downplayed the significance of the church as a collective entity. It was, however, Warneck's understanding of the third stage – the Christianization of the masses – which generated most controversy at the time, and it is a debate which is not over yet. Mission, Warneck argued, cannot be considered complete until Christianity has really taken root in the life of the people as a whole – "a form of the new Christian spiritual life conformed to the whole national life of the people and which leads to its rebirth".[12] Warneck had in fact seen, very early on, that the modern missionary enterprise was in danger of simply conveying European and North American culture to the "non-Christian" peoples of the world, instead of allowing a truly indigenous Christianity to be formed, under indigenous Christian leadership. If this seems commonplace now, it was certainly not the case then.

However, Warneck's emphasis on a form of Christianity "conformed to the whole national life of the people" also contained a seed of ambiguity which proved highly divisive in later Protestant thought. In the great commission of Matthew 28:19 the risen Christ bids the eleven to "make disciples of all nations". What is the significance of "the nations" – *ta ethne* – in biblical thought? Much of contemporary evangelicalism simply regarded "a nation" as a grouping *out of which* disciples should be drawn. The actual Greek text of Matthew 28:19, however, reads more like "discipling the nations". Encouraged by this interpretation, Warneck and his followers viewed the biblical "nation" as a distinctive category, a corporate entity with a peculiar nature of its own, equal to that of any individual human being. Indeed, one might argue that here was

[11] *Ibid.*, p.2.

[12] Quoted in K. Müller *et al.*, *Mission Theology: An Introduction*, Nettertal, Steyler, 1987, p.79.

an ex-pietist merely transferring his former emphasis upon the unique nature of each individual person, to the unique nature of each "nation". Each nation then required a form of Christianity peculiar to its own ethos.

At the time, this was certainly a valuable corrective to any tendency of imposing, by design or default, Western culture on African or Asian peoples in the name of "Christianity". But an emphasis on the distinction and significance of the "nation" could take another turn. It could be used as a justification for a racist domination of one culture by another in the guise of "separate but equal development", as came to pass in the South African apartheid system. And, a few decades later in Warneck's own nation, the call for Christianity to be conformed to the national ethos took the highly sinister form of the programme of the so-called German Christians and their demands for an "Aryan" gospel to match the ethos of the Third Reich.

To condemn Warneck himself for the later misuse and abuse of such insights would be unjust. His position as the definitive initiator of missiology for modern Protestantism is unassailable, and, as one contemporary commentator puts it, he brought mission theory to such a high point and completion that later theological reflections on mission have been mere sketches only.[13] Nevertheless, some of his assertions must have shocked contemporary evangelicals, for example: "the facts of history are also an exegesis of the Bible and in the last analysis they have the final word when the theological interpretation remains a matter of dispute."[14] That sounds dangerously close to saying that whatever has happened in history to promote the spread of Christianity, by whatever means, is of God – which would itself contradict Warneck's own criticisms of the equation of Christian mission with Westernization. The problem lay in Warneck's view of the development of foreign missions as being parallel to the progress of secular society: they were different but they both were "a divine process of mission as education". Behind this notion of a divine will worked out equally through the church and through society lay the Lutheran doctrine of the two realms, or two swords, and led Warneck to see in trade and colonial expansion the same "divine mission of education" at work. But what would happen if and when the colonial powers, as happened in 1914, came to blows?

Whatever the arguments about the precise interpretation of Warneck's views, there can be no doubt that the encounter with Warneck marked a decisive intellectual watershed in Oldham's life. In meeting Warneck, the enthusiastic volunteer for overseas mission was confronted with the need to see mission in its wider social, cultural and political context, in other words *as an item in world history*, to be studied critically and objectively in relation to other world developments. Progressively, he found himself consciously in much more sympathy with the German missiological approach than with the Anglo-Saxon. Moreover, as has been seen in the previous chapter, Oldham's Indian experience

[13] Cf. *ibid.*, p.207.
[14] *Ibid.*, p.1 8.

had very quickly induced in him a critical attitude to much of the contemporary missionary ethos, and a conviction of the urgent necessity for indigenous Christian leadership and initiative. Much of Warneck's teaching therefore rang bells with him. The International Missionary Council, founded in 1921 largely under Oldham's influence, was to resemble in many respects the plans for an international missionary body which Warneck had suggested in 1888.

There was, however, one issue of particular sensitivity to Oldham on which Warneck had decided views: the Watchword of the Student Volunteer Movement – "this fascinating motto" as Warneck ironically described it.[15] Warneck regarded the call for the evangelization of the world in this generation as little more than an inspirational piece of rhetoric, the meaning of which became more confused with every attempt to explain it precisely. The main problem was its sheer impracticability if taken literally:

> If it is understood literally, that . . . the evangelization of the whole non-Christian world should be actually carried through in the life-time of those now living, then the realization of this phrase "within a generation", apart from all other probabilities, is rendered impossible by this, that within such a short space of time the crowd of languages which are spoken in the world where as yet no missionaries have been placed, cannot be mastered in a manner qualifying for the intelligible exposition of the fundamental truths of the Gospel.[16]

If on the other hand the motto is simply an appeal to the present generation to sacrifice all for the ultimate goal, then indeed it deserves to be taken universally to heart. But the Watchword itself is open to much misapprehension. Warneck hoped that the student movement, in so many respects a positive development, would drop the rhetorical phrase. Oldham, in fact, after his return to Britain was to play a key role in the discussions of a reassessment of the Watchword.

In Warneck, Oldham therefore met a mind with which he might well disagree on occasion, but one that nonetheless demanded a whole new scale of thinking about mission, both its theology and its stern practicalities in the real world. Following Oldham through the first decade of the century, we find his mind moving beyond the immediate devotional aspirations of the missionary volunteer – though these, it must be emphasized, were never lost to the life-long evangelical – towards a more inclusive understanding of mission within the total historical context. As such, it was also becoming a more critical understanding. It must have been shortly after his return from Halle that Oldham wrote two articles for the *Student Movement* on "Christianity and Asia". What, Oldham asks, is the implication of the increasing sense in the West that non-Christian societies such as Japan can produce as much moral insight and sensitivity as "Christian" nations? This presented a real challenge to Christianity – and hope might come from some unexpected directions. It could be, suggests Oldham, that it will be the peoples of Asia who will make

[15] *Outline of a History*, p.114.
[16] *Ibid.*

something far grander of Christianity than the European nations have succeeded in doing in the past nineteen centuries.[17] Deliverance for Christianity may come from the infusion of fresh blood into the body of Christ. Moreover, social relationships and national policy must be brought more into line with the principles of Christ "or we can hardly expect the peoples of Asia to think that the acceptance of Christianity will do them much good".[18] The student volunteer was beginning to think like a world mission-strategist and theologian.

The year in Halle had other important consequences for Joe Oldham. He had become competent in the German language, acquainted with German culture, on familiar terms with some of the country's leading theological thinkers and versed in their intellectual styles. This familiarity with the German scene was to become of enormous consequence later on, not only to his personal theological development but also to his ecumenical work and at two periods in particular: during the 1914–18 war when the plight of German missions in Africa and Asia became a crucial test of ecumenical integrity for British Christians, and during the 1930s when Christian witness in the face of Nazism was put on trial in the German church struggle.

## Return to Edinburgh: the missionary educator

Joe Oldham therefore returned to Scotland in 1905 with a fund of ideas. He had seen the practical value of missionary cooperation; he had begun to think about the larger questions of the relation of missions to the church and to society. He had now to find a base from which to work.

The assumed way forward was to become a minister of the United Free Church. The completion of his course at New College qualified him to act as assistant to a minister. Full ordination could only be conferred on those who, in addition to completing their college course, received a call from a congregation to take full ministerial charge. He made one or two applications – but did not regret their lack of success. "A stick-it minister" he called himself – the Scottish term for a minister failing to find a first charge. But two important assistantships were offered and accepted. The first and shorter was in Dundee; the second at Free St George's (now St George's West) Edinburgh, under the celebrated scholar and preacher Dr Alexander Whyte, who was to become principal of New College in 1909. In both congregations his main work was with young people, but towards the end of his time in St George's he was carrying a substantial part of the work of this large congregation. The work of the parochial ministry was therefore familiar to him, but it did not appeal as a life work. Any disappointment at not receiving a call to a full-time charge was still out-weighed by the fundamental frustration of having had to leave the mission field, and a number of the articles he wrote for magazines and the reports of his addresses at student conferences during this time strike the note

[17] "Christianity and Asia" (2nd article), *Student Movement*, vol. III, no. 5, Feb. 1906, p.106.
[18] *Ibid.*, p.107.

of patient obedience to the divine will. The commitment to furthering the cause of foreign missions remained as strong as ever. Although he refused a request to become chairman of the Student Volunteers on the ground that this office ought not to be held by someone who was debarred from serving abroad, he never lost and indeed he strengthened his links with the Student Christian Movement. In 1905 he was elected chairman of its theological colleges department, and this brought him into partnership with its secretary, Tissington Tatlow.

Tissington Tatlow (1876–1957) was an Anglican of Irish birth. Never himself a missionary, he was nevertheless a missionary enthusiast. He stayed for many years with the Student Christian Movement, becoming its general secretary in 1898 and in fact serving in many capacities, not least pressing the claims of missionary service on students and promoting missionary study in the colleges. He appears in those group photographs beloved of student societies and conferences, scarcely ageing from one decade to the next, his scrawny neck emerging from a wide hoop of dog-collar and surmounted by a small, balding head fronted by aquiline nose and precariously balanced glasses. A stage clergyman in appearance maybe, but he was a shrewd and energetic operator and exercised considerable influence in ecclesiastical high places. In 1906, Tatlow and E.J. Wigney, secretary of the Young Christians' Missionary Union, formed a group to work at the question of missionary study in the churches. Along with the (Anglican) Church Missionary Society, the Wesleyan, Baptist and Congregational missionary bodies were represented – and Oldham was recruited on behalf of the United Free Church.[19] The group effectively became an editorial board for producing missionary study guides for use in all the constituent churches. Oldham was therefore working in united Christian efforts both at a student level and in the churches generally. But theological colleges remained a particular concern.

Compared with many of the universities, theological colleges tended to be small, geographically isolated and monochrome in church allegiance. Oldham and Tatlow put great energy into organizing summer conferences and regional meetings for ordinands, advising on books, working out schemes of missionary study and passing information from college to college on activities by the students in practical social work. "There can be little question," they wrote to the colleges in the autumn of 1905, "that, amid the pressure of other studies, the thoughtful consideration of the great tasks the Church has to face is frequently too much neglected. The very difficulty of finding time for missionary and social study makes it important that it should be encouraged." Equally, for the reason stated, it was not always easy to gain the cooperation of college principals. Nevertheless this work was important in laying some foundations for ecumenical understanding among the future ministers of the churches (apart from the Roman Catholic Church).

[19] Tissington Tatlow, *The Story of the Student Christian Movement of Great Britain and Ireland*, London, SCM, 1933, p.106.

One matter repeatedly preoccupied the leadership of the Student Movement in the decade prior to 1914: the famous Watchword of the Missionary Volunteers adopted by the international student conference at Liverpool in 1896 and issued as a challenge to the British churches. Often reiterated at an international level by John R. Mott, for the next seven years it had been in constant use as the unifying slogan of the British movement and criticism of it would have seemed sacrilegious. Criticisms of it, however, began to be raised in about 1903, and by one Frank Lenwood in particular. In that year Oldham himself had given an address on the Watchword at the summer conference, and, according to Henry Hodgkin in his report to the committee, had given a rather different interpretation to that of Mott himself. Mott had stated: "The evangelization of the world in this generation means the preaching of the Gospel to those who are now living. To us who are responsible for the preaching, it means *in our life time. . . .*"[20] Within the Student Volunteer Movement, however, a divergence was now becoming apparent between those who considered this impossible, and those who thought it entirely possible.

For the next six years or so there would be constant discussion of the Watchword among the SVMU leadership. At the 1904 student quadrennial conference at Edinburgh Mott gave a powerful address on it, but this did not permanently quell the unease. The Student Movement executive committee called a special meeting on the subject in December 1906, inviting all former leaders to attend as well. Oldham could not be present himself but two letters he wrote to Tatlow were the basis of its discussion.

In his correspondence Oldham affirmed the immense service rendered by the Watchword, in calling young Christians and the churches to the urgency of mission by an imperative note of *now*, a kind of thunderbolt. "Therein lies its power." That power would however be weakened by the kind of abstruse semantic dispute that was now arising on whether the Watchword represented a "prophecy" or a "purpose":

> The crux of the whole matter lies in the word "evangelization", or to be more exact, the seeming necessity of defining the word "evangelization" imposed by the words "in this generation". If you hold strictly to the view that the Watchword is the expression of a purpose and not a prophecy, there is no necessity for defining "evangelization".[21]

Mott had asked for one missionary for every 50,000 people as being what evangelization meant. But against any such precise definition – and distortion – of the word "the whole soul of men like Warneck rises in indignant protest". Oldham proceeds to cite Warneck's pragmatic objections to this kind of supposed programming – the difficulty of adequate command of the languages, the resistance generated against foreigners, and so forth. The Watchword's unclarity on what evangelization meant had, unfortunately, generated a great

[20] *The Evangelization of the World in this Generation*, quoted in Tatlow, p.313.
[21] JHO letter to Tatlow 3 Dec. 1907 [OA].

deal of controversy within the colleges and the committee of the SVMU and had taken up a good deal of energy which might have been better employed in raising volunteers. Nevertheless, Oldham's final advice to the committee was that it would be best to leave the Watchword untouched lest its note of pressing and overwhelming urgency be lessened.

Tatlow gave an address on the Watchword at the 1908 quadrennial conference in Liverpool. A number of articles appeared subsequently in *Student Movement*. Discussion continued in desultory fashion until the 1914–18 war, during which time it became effectively forgotten. It was finally omitted from the new constitution of the Student Christian Movement in 1922 and, as Tatlow comments, no one objected. Nor, as far as we know, did Oldham himself object to its demise. He was probably shrewdly correct in his judgment that more intense debate on its meaning, or attempts to reword it, would have killed its spirit prematurely.

The fact was that from about 1905 onwards, issues other than the precise meaning of the Watchword were also challenging the Student Movement leadership. On the one hand, no one could doubt the rapid numerical growth of the movement, its reach into more and more branches of the student population and, at the national and international level, the confidence of its adult leadership which was prepared to take on the most august church hierarchies. This last feature was epitomized early in 1905 when J.R. Mott, accompanied by a somewhat diffident Tissington Tatlow, secured an interview with Archbishop Davidson at Lambeth Palace. Mott, given half a chance to penetrate the diplomatic pleasantries proffered by the busy archbishop, swept Davidson along with a *tour de force* of impassioned eloquence and clinched his support for the role of the Student Movement in recruiting for the ordained ministry.[22] On the other hand, questions were being raised about the proper course for this still-rising stream to follow. How far should Bible study take historical, critical methods into account? And should the focus of student groups be so narrowly upon Bible study anyway? The rise of interest in religion among students was clear, but many were also now asking how their faith related to the wider worlds of science and scholarship and, in particular, to the social movements and challenges of the day.[23] An increasing number of students admitted to finding little help from Bible study groups in facing the questions posed by their world.

At Easter 1908 the general committee decided to appoint a commission "to wait upon God to know His will regarding the Movement" and to review its policy and methods of work. It was at this point that Oldham was invited to become the missionary study secretary of the Student Movement, and that Tatlow was confirmed in office as permanent general secretary. The commission

[22] Tatlow, p.253.

[23] The early 1900s saw intensifying social and political debate in Britain, particularly regarding the rise of socialism as a party political force (the autumn election in 1906, when the Liberals won a landslide victory, also saw the first bloc of Labour MPs into the House of Commons). The debates about labour relations were increasingly aired within the churches too.

met for several days in Baslow at the end of October 1908. Its main findings included the observations that the Movement must stress allegiance to the church and, in addition to evangelism, tackle social issues.

Meanwhile, Oldham's pastoral work was taking him beyond purely student circles. His duties at St George's and its mission church at Fountainbridge (where he was in charge of the Sunday school) brought him into contact with a wider range of young people. He had a lasting influence on some of them through his Bible study classes. His study guide *Studies in the Teaching of Jesus*, originally intended for students, was becoming far more widely used. He was also helping to foster the growth of a Young People's Mission Study Movement under the aegis of the Foreign Mission Committee of the United Free Church. His association with this movement, which seemed so natural at the time, led to an event which took him decisively out of the parochial ministry.

The foreign mission committee was one of the most influential bodies in the United Free Church. Its work was the same as that of other missionary societies in Britain – appointing and supporting missionaries, recommending strategy, promoting interest among church members, and (of course) raising funds. In December 1906 this committee reported that the Young People's Mission Study Movement had grown sufficiently to justify "a defined and permanent place". A Mission Study Council was set up to register local groups, prepare suitable literature and train leaders. Dr George Robson – translator of Warneck's *History of Protestant Missions* – was to be its chairman, and Oldham was the sole and unanimously supported candidate for the secretaryship. The secretaryship was to be full-time and the committee was to include members of the foreign mission committee and of the parallel organization, the women's board of mission. Oldham resigned his assistantship at Free St George's (being subsequently elected an elder) and set up his office in Lady Stairs House, that picturesque old building on the Mound.

The next two years were very strenuous and Joe Oldham's health was still not robust. He was helped by the unfailing support of his chairman, George Robson, a person of great charm and outstanding ability, and by the happiness of his home. Joe and Mary had bought a pleasant house in Murrayfield, the suburb on the south-west side of Edinburgh commanding fine views of the Pentland Hills to the south (and today chiefly famous on the international scene as the site of the rugby football stadium). Mary's brother Alek Fraser, temporarily invalided home from Uganda with sleeping sickness, and his wife Bee made their home with them while Alek recovered his health and did some theological study at New College. Another long-term resident was S.K. Datta, Joe's great friend from Lahore, who came to study medicine at Edinburgh University and became a frequent participant in and speaker at student gatherings. Oldham's youngest brother Jack also lived with them during his vacations from Cambridge. Mary was endlessly hospitable and the presence of a faithful family friend, Anna, as cook and mainstay on the domestic front enabled her to give active support to Joe's work.

Immediately on his appointment as secretary of the Mission Study Council Oldham began to organize a summer school for potential leaders. Eighty came for a week in the summer of 1907. Very significantly, there were fifty visitors from other countries and churches to help them master a formidable programme – and also to observe for themselves how the techniques of a summer conference for students (in which Oldham had been adept for over a decade) could be adapted for adults from average congregations. The following year's summer school (1908) was even larger and visitors came not only from most of the major missionary societies in Great Britain but also from the United States and Europe. But the summer schools did not produce enough leaders to meet the demand in the congregations and Oldham organized a correspondence course for suitable leaders who could not get to the summer schools.

By the end of his first year in office 120 groups had registered, and the figure was 400 by the end of 1909. But the groups did not, as such, give young people the chance to exercise initiatives of their own. Oldham therefore set up in the autumn of 1907 two training institutes for young people, one in Edinburgh and the other in Glasgow. These broke quite new ground, as is evident from an account left by an observer present at Glasgow. The young people were to be trained to master the contents of the by no means simple study book for the year. Africa was the subject for one year, China for the next. For this they had the help not only of missionaries but of administrators and others whose interest in the country went wider than the missionary endeavour. The young people were also trained to present some aspect of the study to a congregation, by acting out their imagined reception by an apathetic congregation or an enthusiastic but ill-informed minister – what is now called role-play. By the end of the Glasgow Institute Oldham had, wrote this observer, a company of young people who could and did go out to congregations and "present the case for missions".

The other constituency of young people with whom Oldham was still in close touch was that of the theological students. In the Easter vacation of 1906 there was a missionary campaign at Stirling, at which Oldham spoke on "The World Outlook" and S.K. Datta on "Missionary Study Methods".[24] In April 1907 students from most of the Scottish theological colleges went on a missionary campaign to Inverness, addressing congregations and public meetings. Oldham planned a similar campaign for Aberdeen in the following spring, first taking Tatlow's advice that before he made any plans he should call on the local bishop of the Scottish Episcopal Church. This Oldham did, winning the bishop's warm support. No less than 138 students took part, addressing seventy congregations in and around Aberdeen. "The effect", wrote Oldham, "was tremendous: the appeal of students to educated youth was immediate." He might have added that the work was tremendously demanding as well, for he had no assistants and relied entirely on volunteers. They needed guidance and support and their efforts had to be coordinated. Days were spent

[24] See *Student Movement*, vol. IX, no. 2, Nov. 1906, Edinburgh, supplement p.2.

at his Edinburgh office, making plans, answering queries and receiving visitors, and many requests came to speak at meetings.[25]

The other half of Oldham's work was the production of study material for the groups. His own study book *The Teaching of Jesus*, as has been mentioned, remained in print till the mid-1930s. He could get from missionary sources particulars about mission work, but what he wanted the study groups to understand was something of the cultural, historical and social background. Most of the time left over from other activities went on reading, much of it done at home.

## Oldham the reader

To the end of his days Oldham was a voracious yet disciplined reader. The range and discrimination of his choice of books often provoked comment. "Who told you what to read in German?", Karl Barth asked on his first visit in 1930. The answer lay in the habits of a life-time. Oldham belonged to a circulating library and books came through the post – mostly novels, thrillers, travel books, popular books on science or biographies. These were for leisure reading, or to see if they were worth buying. For the purposes of his work Oldham bought books. Every mention of a likely book by a correspondent or a visitor was jotted down. He belonged to a club and here read the weeklies and quarterlies and took notes from their reviews, articles and correspondence (he confessed, however, to almost never bothering with the religious press). He easily remembered the names of interesting people and pounced on any book they published, perhaps years later. Government reports and the records of learned societies were also grist to his mill. On sea voyages he would aim to read for seven hours each day.

Oldham was one of those people who without the benefit, real or imaginary, of a rapid-reading course was naturally a very rapid reader, taking in the sense of whole paragraphs at a glance. He gave every book he bought a first reading which might take little more than an hour: if the book disappointed he had done with it. But every book that excited his interest was given what he called "a careful reading", and this involved marking with a carefully drawn pencil line any passage he might later wish to look back on or quote. Books which became seminal to his lifetime of developing thought were read many times. His library contained a good stock of works of reference but he ruthlessly discarded books in which he saw no further use or interest. This once occasioned the embarrassment of no less a person than Emil Brunner who, on his way to visit Oldham in London, not only picked up a second-hand copy of one of his own works on a stall in the Charing Cross Road but found it inscribed in his own hand to Oldham. "Oh", said Oldham momentarily taken aback when confronted with this discovery, "I didn't think it was one of your best, and I

[25] But see also Tatlow, p.247. He emphasizes the part played by A.W. Stevens, appointed by the Student Movement for three years as secretary for campaigns.

wouldn't part with any of *those*." The author admitted that his choice for sacrifice had been the right one.

### The missions educator

As well as collecting the material for his Scottish groups Oldham wrote the study books himself and saw them through the press. They had to be carefully aimed to suit congregations; but he had on the whole a more homogenous and better educated public than he would have found in England at the time. In 1908, 3,000 copies of the study book were sold. In addition he contracted with publishers for numbers of "background" books and sold them as "libraries". This venture however caused some financial worries. He wrote to Tatlow: "Last year we issued 100 sets of a special library on Africa and sold hardly more than half. This year we have issued 100 sets on China and you will see they are a remarkably good set of books offered on remarkably good terms. Would you think of taking fifty if we ordered another 100?"[26] Tatlow agreed: what Oldham was producing for congregations was suitable for students. He soon proposed to Oldham that since he was doing the work of mission study secretary for the Student Christian Movement this should be regularized as one-third of his time, carrying one-third of his salary. As mentioned earlier, this move was also in response to the critical need being felt in 1908 for greater organization and direction in the Student Movement.

Oldham's activities at this time may seem fairly desk-bound and at the level of the parish pump. However, from these beginnings of interchurch and interagency cooperation grew the United Council for Missionary Study, which could properly be called the first sustained effort by missionary societies to do something together in relation to their home constituencies. Mission secretaries began to meet regularly, to plan courses of study and, later, to publish books under a joint imprint. Moreover, combining as it did a grasp of the missionary vision on the largest possible scale, with an application to practical administrative and educational matters down to the smallest detail, it was a crucially important preparation for what was so soon to follow in Oldham's career.

At a large meeting held in Edinburgh on 7 June 1907 the provost proposed the founding of a laymen's missionary movement in Scotland, on lines already tried in the United States. The provost's motion was carried with enthusiasm and a few months later Kenneth Maclennan was appointed the movement's full-time secretary. This was but one more sign of an informed missionary enthusiasm both in the churches and among people in public life in Scotland, which accounts for the confidence of the churches there that they would be fully capable of entertaining in 1910 a large international missionary conference. It is in the preparation and execution of this event, and in its follow-up, that the story of J.H. Oldham and that of the modern ecumenical movement were to become decisively fused – and both were to take a great leap forward.

[26] Bliss MS, p.55.

PART II

# ECUMENICAL PATHFINDING

CHAPTER 5

# *Edinburgh 1910*

"THE World Missionary Conference, Edinburgh 1910, was the birthplace of the modern ecumenical movement."[1] So 20th-century church history passes its virtually unquestioned judgment on this event in which, as also in its aftermath, J.H. Oldham played such a crucial role. Conversely, the Edinburgh conference gave Oldham's career a decisive turn to the direction it was to pursue for the rest of his life. From now on, Oldham's career and much of the ecumenical story were to be inseparable.

The contours of Edinburgh 1910, however, need to be drawn rather carefully if its exact significance, both for the ecumenical movement and for Oldham himself, is not to be missed. Birth it may have been, but life begins before birth. There had been earlier international missionary conferences: in New York and London in 1854, Liverpool in 1860, London again in 1878 and 1888, and most spectacularly again in New York in 1900. This last one had been a vast concourse of missionaries and mission supporters. Meetings were held all over the city. Three thousand speeches were made. A mountainous collection of artefacts from hundreds of tribes and cultures was assembled and later moved to the Museum of Natural History. This and similar events had largely been inspirational and informative. Edinburgh however was to aim at developing a continuing, coordinated strategy among the missionary churches and agencies worldwide. Moreover, for this purpose it set in place a continuing structure, albeit rudimentary at first. It is *this* development which justly entitles Edinburgh 1910 to claim to be the birthplace of the modern ecumenical movement, insofar as it directly gave rise to the organizational pattern which eventually led to the formation of the World Council of Churches.

[1] K.S. Latourette, in R. Rouse and S.C. Neill, eds, *A History of the Ecumenical Movement 1517–1948*, London, SPCK, 1967, p.362.

It is also somewhat ironic that while the 1888 and 1900 conferences had been called ecumenical, the international committee responsible for Edinburgh 1910 deliberately rejected the inherited title "Third Ecumenical Conference", on the grounds that:

> to use the term "Ecumenical" is not only clumsy but misleading, since a real Ecumenical Conference would consider a wider range of subjects than is proposed at Edinburgh and would include some historical Christian churches which will not be represented there. "Ecumenical", moreover, is a technical and ecclesiastical term and suggests the professional and formal rather than the common living convictions of practical men and women who are working together for the evangelization of the world.[2]

"The common living convictions of practical men and women who are working together for the evangelization of the world": this was the real ethos and impulse of Edinburgh 1910. And if it was birth, it was the result of the long gestation of evangelical revival, in which most of the cooperating missionary societies had originated. It was above all an outflow of the late 19th century cross-denominational evangelicalism of the student movements, of which John R. Mott was now the indisputable world leader, and in which Joe Oldham had been nurtured and was continuing to work in Scotland. Thoughts, visions even, were expressed a number of times during the Edinburgh conference of a visible Christian unity going beyond more effective cooperation and in that sense too Edinburgh was maternal for much else that followed in the 20th century. But most of those who gathered there in the summer of 1910 did not see themselves as "beginning the ecumenical movement". They saw themselves as answering the challenge of winning the one world for the one Christ, and becoming one in that united, all-demanding, all-consuming venture.

Nor did Joe Oldham, when he became drawn into the preparatory work for the conference, imagine that this was going to prove *the* most decisive threshold of his career. The secretarial work for the planning committee seemed like an interesting but fortunately temporary interruption of his real work as a missions educator – work which was the next best thing to being an actual missionary again.

## The preparation committee: metamorphosis from national to international

The idea of a "third ecumenical missionary conference" first emerged in 1907 at the foreign missions conference of North America. John R. Mott immediately had his hand on the tiller and persuaded the meeting that, far from yet another "great popular convention" what was needed was a "thorough unhurried conference" of the leaders of mission boards in Europe and North America.[3]

[2] Bliss MS, p.62.

[3] C.H. Hopkins, *John R. Mott, 1865–1955: A Biography*, Geneva, WCC, and Grand Rapids, Eerdmans, 1979, p.343.

That same year came the invitation from Scotland for such a conference to be held in Edinburgh in the summer of 1910. The assumption in Scotland was that, as with the previous conferences, the host churches and missionary societies would issue the invitations, organize the hospitality, arrange the programme and foot a large part of the bill. Accordingly the Scottish missionary committees appointed some of the senior members, returned missionaries and other worthies and invited all missionary societies in Great Britain to send two delegates to preparatory meetings which, they decided, should take place in Scotland. A meeting was duly held and did little more than appoint an executive. George Robson had some difficulty in persuading this elderly body (most were in their 70s or even 80s) that a stripling of 33 might with advantage be coopted to their counsels. Oldham was shocked by what he saw. The committee was nominally British but to all intents and purposes Scottish since the meetings were invariably held in Edinburgh for just two hours in an afternoon and none of the London secretaries cared to attend. With his SCM experience Oldham was alarmed at the preparations for a "world" conference being made by an exclusively Scottish committee "consisting of fossils".[4] Oldham got Robson to move, with himself seconding, a motion that the meetings in future be held in York to give the Londoners a better chance to attend. Oldham later recalled: "It was defeated by 46 votes to two. I won't swear to the figure 46; I am certain about the two." As they walked away from the meeting Robson took Oldham's arm and said, "Don't be discouraged; we have not seen the end of this yet." "No," Oldham replied, "let us talk with Mott about this at Liverpool."[5]

"Liverpool" meant the next quadrennial conference of the Student Volunteer Movement, due in a few weeks' time in January 1908. Mott was making a special trans-Atlantic voyage to attend and speak. Robson and Oldham went down to Liverpool in the first week of January, and spent a long evening together with Mott in a hotel bedroom, and followed it up with a working breakfast. In Oldham's own words:

> It taught me a permanent lesson in regard to the ways in which history is made – ways that don't get into the history books. The vital decision on which everything that happened in subsequent years depended was taken in that bedroom. We explained to Mott how things stood. He was as shocked as we were. He said vehemently, "*Of course* an international conference must be internationally planned," and being a man of action he added, "The first thing I shall do when I reach America is to call a meeting of the secretaries of the foreign mission boards. I know that they will take the same view as we do and they will send a letter expressing it to the Scottish committee and offer to send a strong American representation to an international meeting this summer."[6]

[4] Letter of JHO to K. Bliss 11 Sept. 1962 [OA]. See also Oldham's later reminiscences of Edinburgh and its preparations in his "Reflections on Edinburgh, 1910", *Religion in Life*, vol. XXIX, summer 1960, pp.329–38.

[5] *Ibid.*

[6] *Ibid.*

*John R. Mott*

There is also evidence[7] that in fact Robson and Oldham actually brought to Liverpool and presented to Mott the draft of just such a letter as should be sent by the American secretaries to the Scottish committee. At any rate, Mott did meet with the foreign missions boards immediately on his arrival back in the United States. The meeting appointed a special committee to further American preparation for the Edinburgh conference. Within a week this group produced a lengthy document signed by Mott and Arthur Judson Brown as chairman, and dispatched to Edinburgh at the end of January. Edinburgh thus received the suggestion that an international committee should meet in the summer of 1908, and that a strong American delegation would attend. Scotland accepted. With considerable understatement of the role played by himself and Robson, half a century later Oldham commented:

> By Mott's action the planning of the Edinburgh Conference was transformed from a national to an international committee. If this change had not taken place, the developments of the last fifty years would have been quite different from what they were.[8]

[7] Bliss MS, pp.87f.

[8] Quoted in Hopkins, p.344. Cf. JHO, "John R. Mott", *The Ecumenical Review*, vol. VII, no. 3, April 1955, pp.256–59. This article is Oldham's tribute to his recently deceased colleague and friend, and sums up Oldham's whole appreciation of Mott. It is both generous and honest.

The international committee duly met at Wycliffe Hall, Oxford, for six days in July 1908. Oldham himself was there – but only, as it proved, through a set of fortuitous (or providential) circumstances. Scotland was entitled to four places on the committee, and Robson had been determined that Oldham should be one of the four. At the Scottish meeting which made the final decision on this, however, someone got up and reminded the committee that Principal Mackichan, one of the greatest of Scottish missionaries, was home on furlough and could not possibly be left out of such a party. This carried the day against Robson and Oldham's name was dropped. Oldham in later years commented: "It was a bit of a dunt after having put so much work into bringing about the Oxford meeting. But I was enabled to take it philosophically, or rather to accept it cheerfully as God's will for me, and I turned my attention to other things."[9] Then, two days before the committee was due to gather in Oxford, Oldham was informed that Dr Buchanan, honorary secretary of the Scottish committee, was ill. Would Oldham take his place? So Oldham went to Oxford, and not merely as a member of the international committee but as its secretary.

The international committee comprised five members from North America, including J.R. Mott, ten from Britain and three from the continent. Mott was unanimously elected chairman. The Americans already had definite and ambitious plans for the shape and purpose of the eventual conference, and under Mott's dynamic though careful leadership these were largely accepted. It was to be a conference of *delegates*, to be chosen by the participating missionary societies in proportion to the amount of their income that was spent abroad. The conference was therefore not to be mainly inspirational and informative but, so the committee claimed, to be distinguished from all previous missionary conferences by being "a united effort to subject the plans and methods of the whole missionary enterprise to searching investigation and to coordinate missionary experience from all parts of the world". This was to be done by eight *commissions*, to each of which would be assigned a specific area of current missionary concern which would be thoroughly investigated prior to the conference. Each commission would send in its report before the conference, to be thoroughly debated there. The eight subjects on which the commissions would focus were:

I carrying the gospel to all the non-Christian world
II the church in the mission-field
III education in relation to the Christianization of national life
IV the missionary message in relation to non-Christian religions
V the preparation of missionaries
VI the home base of missions
VII relation of missions to governments
VIII cooperation and the promotion of unity

[9] Letter to Bliss 11 Sept. 1962 [OA].

Not only the subjects, but the officers of the commissions were chosen there and then, and a list was drawn up of 160 suitable persons (almost entirely from Europe and North America) for their membership. It was to these people – not all of whom would be delegates – that the collection and collation of preparatory material from all over the world was to be entrusted. The commissions were an entirely new phenomenon. So important did they prove that Edinburgh was not only to mark the start of international conferences on this scale, but to set a pattern and a standard for conference preparatory work which operate in ecumenical circles to the present.

The conference itself was now less than two years away. Even today, in the age of jet travel, faxes and electronic mail, to organize such an event involving over a thousand participants from around the world, in that space of time, would be a daunting task. Mott, characteristically, simply took the measure of the challenge and called for adequate resourcing. A full-time secretary would obviously be essential, as also sufficient funding, though from which sources no one could be sure at present. When the decision to have a secretary was taken, Mott called Oldham to his room and told him that he had to take on the job, saying that it was also the unanimous decision of the committee. Oldham protested that it was impossible, since he had only recently taken on the job of promoting mission study in Scotland. Mott rejoined: "Look at it in this way. Suppose you *had* to do this new job, what arrangements could you make for your work in Scotland?" On reflection, Oldham admitted that he had just been given a promising young assistant (Kenneth Maclennan) who could probably keep things going for a couple of years, but already a third of Oldham's time was contracted to the SCM as mission study secretary. A letter accordingly went to Tissington Tatlow stressing the qualities which fitted Oldham for the task – "his missionary experience, his organizing ability and his spiritual resource". This was pushing at an open door, Tatlow already being an enthusiast for the conference and indeed one of the few functioning non-Scottish members of the old committee. He could hardly refuse to release Oldham, the only condition being that Oldham would give six weeks each year to the SCM, which he willingly did. Oldham, for his part, undertook the secretarial role still assuming that this would be no more than a two-year diversion from his mission education work.[10]

"If Mott master-minded Edinburgh 1910, . . . Oldham was its chief engineer. Their teamwork epitomized the fact of British and American missions being virtually a joint enterprise."[11] It was this Oxford meeting which in fact marked the real beginning of the close and intimate partnership between Oldham and Mott lasting over forty years. For his part, Oldham's first move was to take a holiday. By early September he was writing to Mott that he had settled down to the work of the conference.

[10] Hopkins, p.731, n. 12, refers to H.T. Hodgkins, missionary in China, writing to Mott in December 1908 suggesting JHO for the post – but this was in December 1908, several months after the Oxford meeting of the international committee.

[11] *Ibid.*, p.345.

**Starting work: the commissions**

Oldham's immediate task on appointment was to get the eight preparatory commissions started on their work. Each was to have a chairman from one of the three areas (North America, Europe and Great Britain), a vice-chairman from one of the other two areas and a membership from all three. Most of the 160 names for the commissions were decided at the international committee meeting at Oxford. The choice was not limited to delegates and there were some leading high church figures on the list. It fell mainly to Oldham to try and get them to serve. The most easily won were those who already knew the SCM and Tatlow, its general secretary: for example E.S. Talbot, bishop of Southwark, and Walter Frere, warden of the Community of the Resurrection at Mirfield. But by far the biggest catch was Charles Gore, bishop of Birmingham, as chairman of commission III, on education and national life. Gore (1853–1932) was not only the leading Anglo-Catholic but carried more weight in the Church of England than any other bishop at the time, and none played in national life a role that equalled his as a knowledgeable voice on education and social reform. In short, whatever the subject, be it the Apollinarian heresy or the education bill, when Gore spoke people listened. Oldham already had some acquaintance with him (and in fact they had in common an association with Trinity College, Oxford, where Gore had been a fellow some years before Oldham arrived as an undergraduate), having gone to solicit his support for the SCM in its early days. "What plans have you for these young men and women when they cease to be students?" Gore had asked. "None," said Oldham. "Then you have my support."

A crucial ground-rule had been laid down by the international committee for Edinburgh. It being a conference based on the principle of *cooperation*, matters of doctrine and church polity, issues which marked difference and division, would not be discussed. In relation to the commissions, Gore asked the question which others did not see: Would the commissions be bound by this same rule? And in fact was not commission VIII, on cooperation and unity, bound to breach the agreement? Oldham drafted a reply and circulated it. The Americans disagreed: how could commissions avoid discussing issues which came up as matters of fact in the reports they collected from overseas? Oldham judged that the differences between British and American points of view was not one of substance but a verbal misunderstanding: he carefully got the British committee's support before he sent his letter to Gore, and then followed it up with a personal visit. Their long talk, far into the night, established a firm mutual respect and understanding. This was but the first of many tactical problems with which Oldham had to deal, in addition to the purely administrative load on his shoulders.

The success of the commissions, Oldham realized, would depend on a speedy start. Although he wrote regularly – often weekly or more – to Mott he told him only a proportion of the anxieties he had in getting the commissions to meet in their own geographical areas and to consult with other areas on the questions to be sent out. Missionary societies and other agencies were consulted to find the most suitable recipients. Oldham drafted the covering letter to go with all the questions, making clear that those actually at work in the mission field could play a vital role in the deliberations of the conference. Fortunately most of those into whose hands the questions fell had not yet been battered by questionnaires and many took the encouragement of the commissions as an opportunity to say what had long been on their minds. But the questions had to travel out, and the answers back, and could do so no faster than the age of steam, on land or sea, would allow. Months passed and nothing came back. "I have not enough material for a magazine article, let alone a report," wrote one chairman, and there were many pleas for more time, or for reports to be published only after the conference, and even for the conference itself to be postponed for a year. When the answers began to flow in morale was restored but work intensified. Some of the material was collected together in America, some in Britain, some on the continent: all had to be copied and sent across the Atlantic. Oldham translated from German and French, reconciled the differing continental standpoints of chairmen and vice-chairmen, spent days at work with the commissions in turn. Mott, in their regular correspondence, sympathized with his problems but pressed for the fulfilment of the original programme – each report to summarize and comment on the material received and produce it as a single, narrative whole, printed and in the hands of delegates three weeks before the conference opened.

Mott was himself chairman of commission I, "Carrying the gospel to all the non-Christian world". It was perhaps fortunate for the long-term partnership between Mott and Oldham that early on a crisis occurred which tested and yet in due course strengthened their mutual trust. Without actually saying so, Mott tended to regard his commission as the most important one, and he took the international committee's ruling that chairmen should be responsible for the writing of the report to cover the formulating of the questions also. He viewed the British end of the commission as no more than advisory and told his vice-chairman, Robson, to accept his questions without change. This provoked a reaction in which Robson associated Oldham's name, and an even stronger reaction when it transpired that Mott *had* altered and added to his questions in the course of a visit to Julius Richter in Germany. It was a delicate situation for Oldham – his closest colleague in Edinburgh at odds with his crucial partner, and driving force of the whole enterprise, in North America. He dealt with it at the personal level, recognizing that under Mott's habitual display of unruffled confidence there might be a vulnerable heart. So he wrote a letter regretting that when Mott was so beset with other problems, and was shortly setting out on a long tour for the World Student Christian Federation, the matter of commission I should cause so much anxiety. Nothing he and Robson had said, he continued, meant any diminution in their trust and affection. "I did not need such reassurance," Mott replied, "and yet this renewed expression from you as a friend means very much indeed to me."

## Further trials: statistics, Anglicans and the Archbishop

The personal tensions caused by Mott's interpretation of his role were much less threatening than the conflict of opinion which arose during 1909 over the work of commission I, and which could have led to the withdrawal of some of the most significant Anglican figures from the preparatory work as a whole. Mott well understood – and indeed shared – the impatience of many other lay supporters of the missionary movement who wanted to get ahead and finish the task of ensuring that every man, woman and child in the world had at least the opportunity of hearing the Christian gospel. Their questions were thoroughly pragmatic: How far short of this goal were they? Where were "the unoccupied fields"? What was needed in money and manpower to finish the job? A small team was at work, based in the United States, collecting statistics and preparing an atlas of the missionary advance. Oldham for his part had not much faith in statistics, doubted the value of rapid expansion which would inevitably divert funds from consolidating work already begun and, as a true student of Gustav Warneck, preferred a study of the problems of culture and language in the communication of the Christian faith.

Commission I was "to consider missionary problems in relation to the non-Christian world". But which areas of the world were "non-Christian"? Many regions had clearly never been touched by any form of Christianity. But what, for example, of South America, where Roman Catholic advance had come with the Spanish and Portuguese conquests? To many evangelicals, especially in North America, vast sections of the Latin American population could only ambiguously be described as "Christian" if by that was meant a personal commitment to Christ as distinct from a mixture of nominal Catholicism and residual paganism. In February 1909 however it became clear that prominent figures in the Church of England were taking a very different view. Oldham received letters from three bishops, Charles Gore of Birmingham, H.H. Montgomery of the Society for the Propagation of the Gospel, and E.S. Talbot of Southwark. For them, the American statistical operation was violating the understanding that the world missionary conference would not include within its scope "missions or enterprises directed towards other Christian communions", and they gave notice of their intention to suspend their involvement if the matter could not be settled. Their main anxieties related both to South America and to the Near East. Oldham sought to reassure the bishops that the principle remained inviolate but that, in relation to South America, hard and fast lines were difficult to draw where "there is, I understand, a very large and neglected half-Christianized community, nominally Roman Catholic".[12] Nevertheless, said Oldham, "any mission work which is immediately and predominantly directed towards Christian communities will be excluded from the returns." Oldham reported the matter to

[12] JHO letter to Talbot 23 Feb. 1909 [OA].

Mott, describing the issue as "one of considerable moment, but I do not think it is really serious".[13] However, the very next day a short note arrived from Gore announcing the suspension of his membership of commission III.[14] No classification of missions would satisfy him which would leave South American missions, aimed at converting Roman Catholics "to some other kind of Christianity" within the purview of the conference. He put the matter another way: "I do not suppose that Roman Catholics would consent to join our Conference in any case. But I cannot write in the principles or methods of a Conference, if there is anything which would exclude them, supposing they were willing to join."

The immediate effect of Gore's action was to delay the sending out of the letter of enquiry from commission III. Oldham wrote again to Mott, reporting that the situation was more serious than at first thought. Gore resolutely refused to accept Oldham's explanations of the American reasons for inclusion of these statistics. The only concession Oldham could secure from the bishop was for him to delay making his suspension public for a month. Worse, and it was no idle threat, Gore suggested that twenty leading Anglicans would withdraw from the conference and the Church of England would to all intents and purposes be out of it. The reaction of the press to this, once it broke, would be obvious. The work of several of the other commissions would also founder, and the credibility of the whole enterprise was in jeopardy.

Mott was by now in Russia, making his first visit to Russian Orthodox students. Oldham could do little more than keep him informed by letter and telegram of the state of play. The nub of the problem lay in New York, where Arthur J. Brown, secretary of the American executive committee, was "startled" to receive a letter from Oldham and another from Robson reporting on the stormy scene in England. Brown immediately summoned the New York members of the executive committee and of commission I, including the sub-committee on statistics.[15] The Americans themselves were confused on the issue and divided on how to respond. Some favoured telegraphing Oldham "statistics should conform to conference basis". Others however felt that the literal carrying out of this policy "would involve many perplexities", and suggested that while the *basis of representation* at the conference should be confined to work among non-Christian peoples, the *statistical survey* "should be as comprehensive as possible for purposes of information, and that it should therefore include all forms of foreign missionary work wherever conducted". Fortunately, neither side felt led to press the case to a conclusion before a fuller consultation with the whole committee, including Mott, and bearing in mind that the British executive committee was due to meet on 25 March. Accordingly Brown cabled Oldham: "New York members Executive and Statistical Committee personally willing to conform to judgment of British Executive on Statistics. Confer Mott."

[13] *Ibid.*
[14] Gore letter to JHO 24 Feb. 1909 [OA].
[15] Brown letter to JHO 13 March 1909 [OA].

Oldham relayed the message on to Mott in St Petersburg[16] with the comment: "This is very encouraging and another illustration of God's goodness and of His great purpose for the Conference." The indication of flexibility from America, Oldham perceived, meant that the corner had almost certainly been turned as far as negotiations with the Anglicans were concerned. A meeting with the bishop of Southwark confirmed him in this view, followed by an overnight stay with Charles Gore. Both proved "extraordinarily cordial and friendly".[17] But some tricky negotiations still lay ahead.

By now, a decision had been taken in England, and welcomed in New York: Oldham should personally visit America as soon as possible. It would obviously have been advisable to meet with Mott before sailing westwards, but this was just not practicable. Instead, in his letter to Mott of 17 March Oldham stressed how significant it was that the participation of the Church of England should be assured: "It has never done anything of the kind before, and I think this marks an important event in the religious history of this country." Two essential points were to be identified. First, it was quite clear that any reference to work among Roman Catholics or other Christians must be excluded. Second, no surrender of conscientious conviction must be asked for from those cooperating in the conference, any more than had been the case in the Student Movement. On the basis of his conversations with Montgomery and Gore, Oldham was able to state: "If this principle is clearly defined and loyally adhered to, I do not think we need anticipate any difficulty from the High Church party."[18]

Oldham was anxious to tell Mott that his visit to America had nothing to do with the particular issue which had emerged, and there was no prospect of securing effective cooperation between the two sections on the various commissions unless he could confer personally with the members on the American side.[19] Nevertheless the passage to New York would hardly have been booked so quickly had not this immediate crisis arisen. Mott for his part wrote three letters from Russia counselling Oldham on how to approach the American committees tactfully, warning him to keep in mind that the withdrawal of any of the large American mission boards would be as serious as the withdrawal of the high-church Anglicans.

Oldham sailed in the last week in March, arriving in New York on 4 April. He discovered that the American executive committee had specially set up a three-day conference beginning in two days' time which, while gratifying in itself, gave little opportunity for personal talks beforehand with several of the key figures involved. However, the cordiality of the welcome and the hospitality extended to him quickly relieved all anxieties. Moreover, on the first evening of the conference another event took place involving his father-in-law, Sir Andrew Fraser, which greatly impressed him, as he wrote to Robson:

[16] JHO letter to Mott 15 March 1909 [OA].
[17] JHO letter to Mott 17 March 1909 [OA].
[18] *Ibid.*
[19] *Ibid.*

> Mr John S. Kennedy [the mayor of New York] gave a dinner in honour of Sir Andrew Fraser at the Metropolitan Club and invited about seventy people. The guests included some of the leading men of New York such as Mr Seth Lowe, Admiral Mahan, President Murray Butler, and a number of the most important business men. After dinner Sir Andrew made the best speech I have heard him deliver on the situation in India and closed with a few particularly telling words on the Gospel as the only power to save India and on the purpose of his visit to New York. Mr Brown then spoke on the world changes rendering a conference necessary and I was enabled to make a statement on the World Missionary Conference, which I believe made a deep impression. I have never been at a dinner at which it was possible to get so completely to the heart of things and I think the conviction of the Conference has been fully grasped by those who were at this representative gathering.[20]

Oldham's meeting with the American executive committee was long and painstaking and focused on the problem of the statistics. Substantially, the Americans came over to the British view. Even the two who had put so much work into compiling the statistics and preparing the atlas accepted with a good grace, reserving the right to publish rejected material elsewhere. The Americans passed to the British commission the difficult decision on precisely what should or should not be excluded. Oldham mailed a long typewritten report to Robson in Edinburgh and a hurriedly scribbled letter to Mott in Russia. In both, the relief was evident: "The difficulty is a real one for our American friends but the most cordial relations have been preserved;"[21] ". . . I believe we have been guided aright, and the most friendly and brotherly relationships have been preserved. Indeed the generous action of the American Committee in this matter will prove a great object lesson and greatly increase the spiritual power of the conference".[22] The outcome in fact owed much to Oldham's willingness to listen carefully and at length to the American anxieties, not just as a group but in one-to-one conversations, and to register the real pain that a number of them felt. This was ecumenical brick-laying, without which no grand construction would ever have materialized. But while on a visit to New Haven, Oldham was given some confidential information about another possibility which, if it were to be realized, would threaten the fabric of the whole Edinburgh enterprise: Mott was being approached by Yale University with a view to becoming its president. Not even Mott himself was aware of this at the time.[23]

[20] JHO letter to Robson 9 April 1909 [OA].

[21] *Ibid.*

[22] JHO letter to Mott 13 April 1909 [OA].

[23] Hopkins, p.347. Some variance will be found between the account of Oldham's visit to America (and its significance) given in the present study, and that given by Hopkins. Hopkins merely states that Oldham "came to America briefly to clarify some issues with the North American committee" without stating (except in the briefest possible way in a subsequent reference) what these issues were nor acknowledging the serious threat they posed to further preparations for the conference. He cites Mott's instructions to his junior colleague in New York, Hans Anderson, on "how to handle the visit", ordering that special efforts be made to "convert" Oldham from what Mott considered his mistaken views on YMCA foreign work and that he should be prevented from talking privately with members of the conference committee. If this accurately records Mott's state of mind it is rather revealing and not entirely flattering to him. Hopkins

Oldham arrived home early in May, and soon after spent a whole day with the British members of commission I, Charles Gore and E.S. Talbot attending for part of the time. Impressed by the generous attitude of the Americans, the British group set out in some detail the rules governing the use of statistics in relation to particular regions. Thus, for Turkey, Persia and Egypt for example, in view of the predominantly Muslim populations all statistics provided by foreign missionary agencies were to be included, as also for South-Eastern Europe. South American statistics however were to be excluded, except in relation to work "among aboriginal tribes not yet Christians and among non-Christian immigrants". Work among "the negro populations of North America, South America and the West Indies" was to be excluded. Work among Jews was to be included. Statistics of the Roman and Greek churches, since they had not been officially supplied to the commission, were to be included but placed in separate tables. The main objective to be born in mind was that of showing how much more work *still needed to be done* throughout the world, rather than a league-table of achievements by missionary agencies. Oldham wrote up these conclusions in detail for James Dennis in New York.[24]

The troubles caused by statistics seemed to be over, the Anglo-Catholics being satisfied by the new understanding and arrangements. But scarcely had word of the accord begun to circulate in Britain than it was attacked from another quarter – the evangelical. Leaders of the Wesleyan Missionary Society, the Baptist Missionary Society and the China Inland Mission took strong exception to what they saw as new restrictions being placed upon the conference. Oldham in return offered that careful explanations of the nature and purpose of each set of statistics, when published, should suffice. But the evangelical leaders were not easily persuaded. Oldham wrote to Mott – still in Russia – with renewed anxiety, confessing that but for the extreme pain it would cause the Americans he wished the statistics could be dropped entirely. And, albeit in as respectful a way as possible, his growing frustration surfaced:

> We are experiencing the great difficulty of arranging an international conference. The difficulties which have arisen could be adjusted if we had only one country to deal with, and those concerned could meet and confer. The difficulties are enormously increased when you are on the Continent and we have to deal with a Committee in America. For some weeks I have desired earnestly the opportunity of full conference with you.[25]

Robson for his part was overwhelmed with work and Oldham did not wish to burden him still further by seeking his counsel. While it may be true that

---

concludes: "Fortunately the problems were adjusted [*sic*] and Oldham returned home satisfied that a serious crisis had been averted". As the present study should have made clear, Oldham in fact succeeded in his determination to have personal conversations with members of the American committee, and if he returned "satisfied" it was not because he himself had been "converted" but that he had elicited highly significant concessions from the American statisticians.

[24] JHO letter to Dennis 8 May 1909 [OA].

[25] JHO letter to Mott 21 May 1909 [OA].

Oldham could not as yet appreciate Mott's immense capacity for work, it is not evident, either, that Mott fully realized how serious a burden was falling on the small Edinburgh team. Clearly Oldham felt that the statistical question which he himself was having to sort out was really the responsibility of Mott and his own commission. But this, and every other problem that seemed to snag at progress, he kept firmly within the framework of a providential faith: "I have no doubt that the enemy will endeavour to put every hindrance in our path or lessen the usefulness of the Conference, and the higher our aims, the greater will be the difficulties that we shall encounter. God has so markedly set His seal upon the work, however, that I believe that if we go forward in faith, He will bring us to the goal appointed."[26]

The evangelical missionary leaders were eventually mollified but "the enemy", to use Oldham's respectful phrase, seemed to have a predilection for using the Church of England in his nefarious designs. The question of Anglican involvement was much wider than that of the personal decisions of such as Gore and Talbot on whether to participate or not. It was a matter also of the corporate participation of the major Anglican missionary agencies. When the conference was first definitely announced in 1908, the principle was clearly enunciated that participation by churches or missionary bodies would be based on willingness for cooperation, not on doctrinal agreement nor on measures which would compromise sincerely held distinctives of belief or which would conflict with conscience. This modestly stated basis would certainly appeal to those who saw the prime need to evangelize the world as over-riding all other considerations. But there were also those who believed that cooperation and doctrinal agreement could *not* be sundered in this way, and that one could *only* cooperate on the basis of co-belief. What would the Anglican answer – or at least that of the Church of England – be to this?

There was not in fact one view. The Church Missionary Society (CMS), born of the evangelical revival, was certainly ready to cooperate in preparations for Edinburgh. The Society for the Propagation of the Gospel in Foreign Parts (SPG) was not: could it be persuaded? The difference between the two societies and the lack of cordiality between them was not simply that one was evangelical and the other high church, nor even that the SPG was much older and regarded the CMS as an interloper. Bishop H.H. Montgomery, general secretary of the SPG at the time, used frequently to say that the work of the Church of England beyond the parochial system was carried out by three agencies, each of which acted for the church in its given sphere: the Society for the Promotion of Christian Knowledge (SPCK) in the field of publications, the National Society in education, and the SPG in mission overseas. Substance was given to this view by the relation of the highest authorities in the church to these bodies. The standing committee of the National Society, for instance, met fortnightly for many decades and the archbishop of Canterbury was hardly ever absent

[26] Hopkins, p.351.

from the chair. When Montgomery was appointed general secretary of SPG he was summoned from his bishopric in Tasmania by a telegram signed by the archbishops of Canterbury and York and three other bishops, who had formed the appointing committee. Many of the same names appear on the committees of two or more of these societies. There is something to be said for Montgomery's assertion that the SPG only became high church because, after the founding of the CMS, evangelicals left the SPG; the other two bodies were not affected in the same way. Thus for the SPG it was not just an issue of holding Anglo-Catholic principles; it was that of assuming to be the authoritative voice of the Church of England in missionary affairs. Accordingly, Tissington Tatlow believed that if he and Oldham succeeded in getting the SPG to cooperate in Edinburgh they would have "collared" the Church of England.

While Montgomery himself was in fact personally well disposed towards the conference,[27] given the assurances that it would be "inter-" rather than "undenominational" in character, enlisting the SPG did not prove as simple as that. The SPG had sent an observer to Scotland for one of the mission study summer schools, and also a delegate to the student missionary conference in Liverpool in 1908, but the SPG standing committee rejected the invitation to take part in preparations for Edinburgh. However, *the* authoritative forum of church opinion was the floor of convocation. A proposed message of greeting to the conference, expressing "cordial sympathy", was introduced in the lower house of the Convocation of Canterbury in February 1910. It was vehemently opposed by a minority, consisting mainly of SPG supporters. Falling into the trap of thinking that it is better to say anything unanimously than to say something of substance with a minority against it, the house allowed itself to stand adjourned till the next day, when a compromise motion deleting all mention of "sympathy" was proposed. Thereupon Hensley Henson, at that time rector of St Margaret's, Westminster, and fast becoming known as one of the most independent-minded of English clerics, rose to his feet and made one of those devastating speeches for which he became famous: "They cut out the goodwill: they send the message. That is not sending a message of greeting but a circuitous mode of preferring an insult." He was warmly supported by many speakers and the debate usefully clarified to this representative body of clergy the actual aims of the conference. The original motion was passed by a large majority (73 to 14) and sent forthwith to the upper house where it obtained the unanimous support of the bishops and a strong commendation from Archbishop Randall Davidson in the chair.

Behind the archbishop's gesture lay another story which was to prove crucial for the Edinburgh conference. Such a conference taking place in Great Britain could hardly claim an intrinsic authority and spiritual weight without the declared support, and moreover the actual attendance, of the archbishop of

[27] Latourette, p.406.

Canterbury who was not only primate of all England but leader of the worldwide Anglican communion. As seen in the preceding chapter, Mott had made a great impression on Davidson at their meeting in Lambeth Palace in 1905 and there had followed some correspondence between the two. However, when on 5 July 1909 Mott, accompanied by Oldham, Tatlow, Prebendary Fox of the CMS and Bishop Montogomery of the SPG, visited him again to invite his participation at Edinburgh, the archbishop while responding warmly said he must "think it over". Months passed without any result of that thinking being made known. The caution for which Davidson was famous was all too evident. Oldham wrote to Lambeth Palace. Davidson replied, "I have been, and am, under continuous pressure. Surely I have done enough for you without coming?" The pressures were clear enough. Not only was the standing committee of the SPG calling for the brakes to be applied but the editorials and correspondence columns of the high church *Church Times* rang with accusations of the surrender of church principles to "undenominationalism". By his "enough" Davidson presumably meant his replies to many letters, and his careful, implicitly approving study of the involvement of other bishops in the Edinburgh preparations, not to mention his sincere acknowledgment of "the greatness of the work and the power and capacity of missionaries belonging to other churches who are taking part in these discussions". But, for a time at least, as with other archbishops before and since, the preservation of the unity of his church came at least as high on his agenda as these other matters. However, the decisive convocation vote of February 1910 and his own commendation made Davidson aware that he had reached a point of no return. He could hardly now, with integrity, stay away from an event to which he had personally and publicly given such moral support. He agreed to go to Edinburgh and, moreover, to give the opening address. That an archbishop of Canterbury, for the first time in history, should be prepared to address an international gathering of Christian representatives most of whom belonged to churches not in communion with his own, was in itself a landmark event. One would like to know more of the part that his chaplain, George Bell, himself destined for a crucial role as an ecumenical leader, may have played in the eventual making up of his mind.[28] Nor should be forgotten the ecumenical debt to the critical – in every sense – intervention of Hensley Henson.

The final months and weeks of preparation saw no let-up in effort and anxiety for Oldham and his Edinburgh team – or, for that matter, Mott. Distractions ranged from the persistent attempts by an Australian layman, H.E. Wootton, to commandeer the conference as a platform for his own scheme of world evangelization, to the sheer logistical nightmare of arranging the accommodation of over 1,200 visitors in hotels, boarding houses and private

[28] The only figure who would be able to enlighten us here is also the one who through self-effacement would be the least desirous of doing so – George Bell himself. Cf. the spare account of the Edinburgh episode as seen from Lambeth Palace in his *Randall Davidson*, Oxford, Oxford Univ. Press, 1935, Vol. I, pp.572–75.

homes all over the city. The conference itself was to be held in the assembly hall of the United Free Church, in the complex of buildings on the Mound that included New College. Mott enjoined well in advance that he and Oldham should stay for the duration of the conference in a hotel close to the site (and, equally insistently, that being a notoriously light sleeper he himself should have a room well away from the lift and other intrusive noises). But the over-riding concern was that the reports of the eight commissions should be completed, printed and in the hands of all the delegates before they set out for Edinburgh from all four corners of the world. As late as October 1909 Oldham was persuading Mott by letter that some quite drastic restructuring of the commission reports was desirable in order to make them more coherent and readable: "I may say that the situation is really quite serious, and looking at it from a merely human standpoint, I am many times tempted to take a gloomy view. But I have a deep confidence that God will enable us to pull through and that the work will be accomplished."[29]

It was both a necessity, and a sign of faith, that Oldham, Robson and Alexander Whyte took a break with a holiday in Switzerland after Christmas 1909. The reports were in fact completed, and dispatched some weeks before the opening date of the conference, 14 June. That in itself was perhaps the single most crucial factor in ensuring the successful running of a highly concentrated programme packed into little over a week. (Those used to attending more recent international conferences, and familiar with the experience of hurriedly scanning their papers between in-flight meals, may well envy their predecessors who had the leisure of ocean cruises or transcontinental rail journeys in which to prepare themselves.)

But as public interest in the conference built up, it also became clear that it could not be entirely given over to the discussion of the reports, and both Mott and Oldham wanted the best possible speakers for the evening meetings which would be widely reported in the press. The planning of these also caused some headaches, as certain of the participating societies were primarily anxious to hear their own lions roar; concessions to the loyalties of missions supporters had to be made, but they were few. In fact the evening meetings were to give a platform to that woefully under-represented minority, the leaders of indigenous churches. Only a handful of the societies, as it turned out, had included a Chinese or an Indian in their delegation, and no African was present. Oldham himself seems not to have noticed this lack in the lists of delegates until a letter from a British missionary in China, Nelson Bitton, warned him that the conference seemed likely to confirm nationally self-conscious young Chinese in their opinion that the Christian church was a foreign enterprise, directed from the West. A late flurry of activity resulted at least in getting a (then) little-known Indian, V.S. Azariah, included. As mentioned in an earlier chapter,[30] his plea for *friendship* from the missionary churches of the West was to prove the

[29] Letter of JHO to Mott 13 Oct. 1909 [OA].

[30] See ch. 3.

longest-remembered address of the entire conference. Azariah in fact was not only invited to Edinburgh. He joined the Oldhams, Mott, Robson and Mrs Alexander Whyte, among others, for a three-day retreat in the Yorkshire village of Goathland a week before the conference opened.

## Nine days in June[31]

On the evening of Monday 14 June 1910, the delegates streamed up to the Mound by the great castle, into the quadrangle of New College, past the forbidding statue of John Knox and into the assembly hall. The opening session had presented special problems; it had to be a great public occasion with an international dimension, yet able also to satisfy the religious expectancy of the delegates: all in an atmosphere charged with some tension, excitement among some and misgivings among others, and not a few people experiencing both emotions at once. In fact public formality and spiritual aspiration were combined superbly. Lord Balfour of Burleigh, president of the conference, called upon Alexander Whyte, principal of New College and Oldham's old chief, to inaugurate the proceedings with prayer. Silas McBee, American high Anglican, was to write that in that prayer "we heard the voice of Catholic Christianity". Balfour in his own opening remarks reiterated the undertaking that matters of doctrine would not be discussed, but went on to express "the hope . . . that unity, if it begins in the mission field, would not find its ending there." There was read out a message of greeting and encouragement from the new king, George V (his father, Edward VII, had died just days before), for which the gathering stood respectfully and then sang the national anthem. Messages were also read from the German colonial office and the former President of the United States, Theodore Roosevelt. Then Robert Speer, foremost American missionary leader, spoke with arresting power on Christ's great commission to follow him and witness to the ends of the earth.

The real impact of that evening, however, was made by another. Randall Davidson was no great orator, still less given to histrionics. But the archbishop of Canterbury's address that night, precisely by its simplicity allied to real conviction, made an unforgettable impression. He did not talk *about* Christian unity or cooperation, but embodied it in addressing his audience as "brothers and sisters in Christ". He stood there as the head of the established Church of England embodying what the majority of English Nonconformists greatly distrusted, but his commitment to the world mission of Christianity was as total and obvious as that of William Carey, the Baptist pioneer of modern Western missions who had himself called for a world conference of missionary societies – exactly a century earlier, in 1810. Davidson concluded with a plea to make missions central in the life of the church, and then:

[31] This section draws upon the vivid account by W.H. Temple Gairdner, *"Edinburgh 1910". An Account and Interpretation of the World Missionary Conference*, Edinburgh and London: Oliphant, Anderson & Ferrier for the World Missionary Conference, 1910.

Secure for that thought its true place, in our plans, our policy, our prayers; and then – why then, the issue is His, not ours. But it may well be said that, if that come true, there be some standing here tonight who shall not taste of death till they see the Kingdom of God come with power![32]

Temple Gairdner describes the impact of those words on the assembly in almost theophanic terms – "For one supreme moment, it seemed, GOD had stood forth nakedly revealed, and had spoken in HIM who first spoke those words and lives in the Divine glory".[33] In fact, like Lord Balfour, Davidson had articulated what a number were feeling: that while the conference's precise aims were carefully defined in terms of cooperation, and rightly so, scarcely imaginable possibilities might be burgeoning in the direction of more structured unity. So the appetite was quickened for the days of deliberation that were to follow. Oldham, for his part, must at least have breathed a sigh of satisfaction that all the efforts at getting the archbishop's participation had proved so decisively fruitful.

Next morning the proceedings began in earnest. Each day was given over to the presentation and discussion of a single commission report and, with the exception of Sunday when business was confined to the evening, followed a very similar pattern: a few minutes' opening worship, brief formal notices, then down to business (no time was spent either at beginning or end with votes of thanks and mutual compliments). The chairman of the respective commission presented his report and the floor was then open to debate, with a strict limit of seven minutes allowed to each speaker – and at the end of each day, when the vice-chairman of the commission was called to sum up, there was always a long queue of disappointed people whose names had not been called. Before leaving hotel or lodging each morning, every delegate received by special delivery a copy of the conference daily newspaper including the minutes of the previous day's proceedings so that these could be taken as read at the start of the new day's session. And over all the sessions on the reports – except for his own, the first – towered John Mott as chairman. Authority and strength were conveyed by his very demeanour and intent expression. From the chair, except for his closing summary speech he did not indulge in intervention except on procedural matters. But what he said never failed to impress, by that blend of firmness, courtesy and wry humour which is perhaps always the secret of the best chairing and in his case won both respect and affection (delegates relished his opening advice to speakers in the debates, that the best acoustic effect in the hall would be obtained by addressing one's remarks to the clock, "which might have certain other advantages as well", and his request that delegates "applaud *concisely*").

But while it was Mott whose personality was stamped so decisively on the conference, delegates as a whole were no less aware of how much was due to its

[32] *Ibid.*, p.43.
[33] *Ibid.*, p.44.

secretary. Temple Gairdner sketches vividly the impression made by his old Oxford friend:

> Just beneath [Mott] at the Committee Table, sat the General Secretary of the Conference, J.H. Oldham, a man strangely contrasted with the Chairman. Small of stature, and of unassuming face and mien, he slipped into or out of his place at the table, as one not merely unnoticed but not meriting notice. The Chairman, though he did not intervene in the discussions, at least gave the important closing address, and his voice was frequently and authoritatively heard; but the Secretary, from beginning to end, never opened his lips, save to give out formal notices. Why then was it that the first time he rose to give out a notice, the whole Conference applauded as though it would never cease? Some did so, perhaps, because they wanted to show their appreciation of a triumph of organization. But those that knew were aware that, more than any one other, the spirit that was at work in this very unobtrusive exterior had been at the back of that great Conference, not merely in respect of its organization and its methods, but also of its ideals, its aspirations, and its hopes.[34]

If the main impression conveyed to posterity is one of efficiency and fairness in the conduct of business and the welding of very different elements into something like a common mind, this was not the only impression left on the delegates themselves. The spiritual seriousness of the conference was manifest above all in the periods of worship integral to each day's programme – not only in the devotions of scripture, hymns and intercessory prayer with which each morning began, but in the thirty-minute period of largely silent intercessory prayer in the middle of each morning session. Oldham himself remembered as one of the highlights "the utter silence that fell when Father Walter Frere, standing there in his monk's robes, flung wide his arms and prayed . . . 'regard not our sins but the faith of thy Church and grant to her such peace and unity as may be in accordance with thy will'".[35]

As far as organization was concerned, no feature was more important than the role played by the stewards who, largely recruited from the Student Christian Movement, also brought a touch of youth and gaiety to the scene. They were Oldham's special responsibility and he remembered them with affection:

> They worked out their own system for allowing members of the conference to have interviews with the speakers: "Just take this ticket to the head of the stair", they would say, and the unsuspecting bearer would be introducing himself as worth two minutes or twenty by the colour of his ticket. I read them a lesson on discretion when they barred the door to the President of the conference [Lord Balfour of Burleigh] because he had forgotten his ticket, and I had my heart in my mouth when I could see that, behind the platform and in full view of the entire gathering, Neville Talbot was closing an argument with another steward by extending his ten fingers to the end of his nose.[36]

[34] *Ibid.*, p.65.
[35] Bliss MS, pp.79f.
[36] *Ibid.*, p.80.

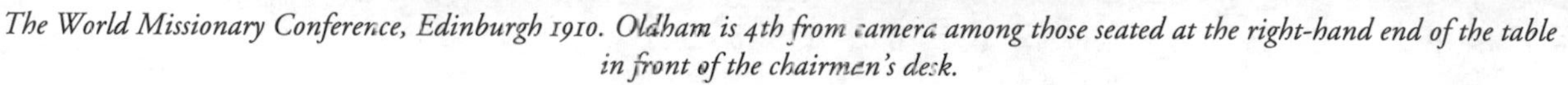

*The World Missionary Conference, Edinburgh 1910. Oldham is 4th from camera among those seated at the right-hand end of the table in front of the chairmen's desk.*

The 1914–18 war took its toll of these young men, but many went on to become leaders in the ecumenical movement or supporters of it in their own churches. Among them were William Temple, John Baillie and Walter Moberly, all of whom were to be future close associates of Oldham. Temple in later life "often testified that his first acquaintance with the world problems of the Church was made in 1910, in the Assembly Hall of the Church of Scotland".[37] The practice of sowing the seeds of future ecumenical commitment and leadership by the recruitment of young stewards has continued at almost every major ecumenical gathering since Edinburgh – although by now it has become a tradition that younger people should also be full participants in their own right.

It was perhaps as well that the stewards should have been sticklers for the rules rather than respecters of persons, for those attending comprised not only an unprecedented mix of confessional traditions but an unusual variety of ecclesiastical office, social standing and academic status. There were the good and the great like Bishops Charles Gore from England and Charles Brent from the Philippines. There were academics like the German missiologists Julius Richter and Johannes Warneck (son of the famous Gustav). There were colonial eminences like Lord Reay, ex-governor of Bombay and Sir Andrew Fraser, Oldham's father-in-law. But the mass of delegates were previously unknown to each other even by name. They included a good number of lay people (though few women among them) and it was from these, and from certain of the minority representing indigenous Asian Christians, that some of the most strikingly fresh and vital interventions were made from the floor. What is also significant is the strong presence of evangelicalism as represented, for example, by the China Inland Mission. The dichotomy between "ecumenical" and "evangelical" still lay in the future.

## "Cooperation and the promotion of unity" . . . and the future

"Cooperation and the promotion of unity" had, in the original schedule drawn up by the international committee at Oxford in 1908, been placed in the rearguard as the eighth and last of the commissions. In the actual programming of the conference, however, the actual order of presentations of the commissions was:

1 carrying the gospel to all the non-Christian world
2 the church on the mission-field
3 education in relation to the Christianization of national life
4 the missionary message in relation to the non-Christian religions
5 missions and governments
6 cooperation and the promotion of unity
7 the preparation of missionaries
8 the home base of missions

[37] F.A. Iremonger, *William Temple. Archbishop of Canterbury*, Oxford, Oxford Univ. Press, 1948, p.392.

On this programme the first four commissions occupied the conference each day in turn until Saturday 18 June. On Sunday the delegates, in Temple Gairdner's cheerful phrase, "rested the strenuous rest of an Edinburgh Sabbath". On Monday morning the conference reassembled to consider the report on missions and governments. In retrospect, some claimed to have seen it as auspicious that the next day was midsummer's day and thus the longest in the northern hemisphere, and it was this day which was devoted to the report on cooperation and the promotion of unity which brought with it the only resolution of the conference – the resolution which was to mark Edinburgh's vital place in the story of the modern ecumenical movement, and the next step in J.H. Oldham's own career. If for no other reason, this chronological detail is significant insofar as some summary accounts of the Edinburgh conference imply that the decision to set up a Continuation Committee was a hurried measure taken at the end of the gathering, and without a great deal of forethought. In fact, not only was the decision taken with two full days of the conference still to run, but a great deal of thinking, however discreet, had gone into the matter beforehand, and not least from Oldham himself. A number of the reports of other commissions had also raised the question of a means of greater and continuing cooperation in missions.

Very early in the preparations Oldham had recognized that the commission on cooperation and unity would almost certainly arouse fears, particularly in Britain. In the autumn of 1908, on behalf of the British committee, he wrote to Silas McBee, whom the international committee had invited to be chairman, asking whether he would be willing to step down in favour of Sir Andrew Fraser. McBee, an eirenic character and not one eager to be in the crossfire of any British controversy, accepted the vice-chairmanship graciously. "Your letter proves", he wrote to Oldham, "that you are the frank friend I took you to be." Sir Andrew was the wise diplomat: McBee and Oldham came to share a common expectancy about the possible outcome of the commission's work. Every other commission produced some evidence of the urgency of the need for more and closer cooperation on the mission field, but evidence of any matching sense of urgency in the societies at home was almost entirely lacking. "I recognize", Oldham wrote to McBee, "that on all human calculations the difficulties in the way of any important steps in advance are insuperable and decisive. But the issues are so great and the resources of God so incalculable that I think we ought prayerfully to wait on him to know whether it is his will to bring us to something to which we cannot at present imagine a way."[38]

The greatest concerted pressure for "advance" in this respect was coming from Germany. Julius Richter, secretary of the *Ausschuss*, prior to the conference pressed hard for a continuing agency of cooperation to be set up by the conference. The Germans were not only inspired by Warneck's vision: they had bitter and recent experience of the vulnerability of their missions to the hostile

[38] Bliss MS, p.40.

sanctions of other nations. Two of their missions – the Berlin and the Brandenburg – had suffered severe losses during the South African (Boer) war of 1899–1902 and all attempts to get the British government to consider paying compensation had failed. Surely, argued the Germans, missions in a position of strength should plead the cause of the weak. Furthermore, missionary societies had a great store of first-hand experience on such matters as the sale of spirits, the trade in opium, the Congo atrocities, the Melanesian labour trade and so forth. These were international matters and the missions could join in international negotiations and act alongside philanthropic organizations to influence governments. In January 1910 Richter had visited the American societies meeting in their committee of reference and counsel and persuaded them to approach the British societies suggesting the creation of some similar body in Britain. Such steps in Britain seemed essential to the establishment of any international body.

If what the Americans proposed to the British (and they did it by a personal visit) was along the lines that Richter suggested, the hesitant reception they elicited was not surprising. It looked as though the British societies would be the main ones called upon to put pressure on the British government on behalf either of foreign missions or of social causes to which their government was known to be indifferent or even hostile. By the time the Edinburgh conference met there was still no counterpart in Britain to the German *Ausschuss* or the American committee, nor was there any commitment to form one.

Oldham himself was by no means averse to the formation of some structured means of international cooperation, but the relations of missions and governments played no part in his thinking at this stage (it was to be a very different matter, as will be seen, during the 1914–18 war). It was the actual missionary task overseas on which his mind was focused. Nor did he envisage himself as playing any particular role in some such development. Far from it: his ruling assumption was that it would be Mott who would be instrumental in this. He wrote to Mott in the early autumn of 1909:

> I think you cannot fail to see what vast possibilities of cooperation are looming up before us, and if they are to be seized there must be someone to seize them. I believe that God may call you to some great and comprehensive work which will enable the Christian Church to make one great united special effort in the next twenty years which may perhaps be the only ones that remain for the Church of the West to be allowed to make a direct contribution to the progress of Christianity in some of the countries of the East. This matter is much in my prayers.[39]

Again, he wrote to Mott on 13 October 1909 that the time would be ripe immediately after the conference for a great, coordinated international effort in missions. "Many times the thought comes to me whether you might not find the climax of your life work in leading such a movement." Oldham's pursuit of Mott's sense of vocation was being lent urgency by his knowledge of the

[39] Bliss MS, p.83.

invitation to Mott of the Yale presidency. Mott replied: "Your reiterated references to the possibility of my coming into some special relation to the work of following up certain lines after the Conference have not been overlooked. I have been making them a matter of special prayer. It is possible that they may yet be the determining factor in leading me to decline the Yale position."[40] Whatever the precise determining factors proved to be, Mott within a few weeks did decline Yale.

It was not until halfway through the Tuesday morning session devoted to the commission's report that the actual resolution was moved by the commission's chairman Sir Andrew Fraser. It was

> That a Continuation Committee of the World Missionary Conference be appointed, international and representative in character, to carry out, on the lines of the Conference itself, which are inter-denominational and do not involve the idea of organic and ecclesiastical union, the following duties . . .[41]

These duties included maintaining in prominence the idea of the world missionary conference as a means of coordinating missionary work; furthering continued investigation of the missionary task; to consider a future world conference and make initial preparations; and to devise plans for maintaining the relationships established at Edinburgh. The list of duties concluded with three proposals for action by the Continuation Committee which, modest and mundane at first sight, were in the context of that time the most significant and challenging:

> (5) To place its services at the disposal of the Home Boards in any steps which they may be led to take . . . towards closer mutual counsel and practical cooperation. (6) To confer with the Societies and Boards as to the best method of working towards the formation of such a permanent International Missionary Committee as is suggested by the Commissions of the Conference and by various missionary bodies apart from the Conference. (7) And to take such steps as may seem desirable to carry out, by the formation of Special Committees or otherwise, any practical suggestions made in the Reports of the Commissions.[42]

The debate was as powerful as any during the conference. Speakers from the United States and Canada argued cogently that the experience of their own national interdenominational missions committees testified to what might be achieved on an even wider level. And no speech, either in that or any other session at Edinburgh, was more prophetic (in every sense) than that made by the Chinese delegate Cheng Ching-yi. In an earlier debate, another representative from China, the Anglican bishop of Hankow, had warned that unless the authorized church leadership in China made a concerted bid for unity, then a quite other but wholly indigenous leadership might take matters into their own hands. Cheng Ching-yi now elaborated these points and called

[40] Mott letter to JHO 21 Oct. 1909 [OA].
[41] Gairdner, p.187.
[42] *Ibid.*, p.188.

upon the Conference to seize the opportunity for definite action – "China, with all her imperfections, is a country that loves unity both in national and family life . . . The future China will largely depend on what is done now."[43] (The shock that occurred to the Western missionary enterprise in China forty years later might not have been so great if his words had been fully registered there and then.)

The debate was not one long avalanche of unquestioning enthusiasm for the proposal, and it had its moments of tension. A number of Anglican delegates, in particular, reiterated concerns about the integrity of doctrinal differences in the promotion of unity. The commission report had itself ventured to suggest that the ultimate goal was the realization of Christ's intention "that we should be one in a visible fellowship".[44] But what the commission had set out, and what the debate as a whole affirmed, was an understanding that the proposal for some form of Continuation Committee was both modest enough to allay the fears of those who were suspicious of a rush towards organic ecclesiastical union, and at the same time sufficiently concrete to encourage those who even now aspired towards such union as an *ultimate* goal. Thus it was that Edinburgh did have wider historical import for ecumenism than the missionary movement *per se*. In later life Charles Brent, soon to be a prime mover in the Faith and Order movement, identified a moment of prayer during an Anglican eucharist at Edinburgh as the occasion when he felt a personal call to work for visible unity. For his part, Oldham felt that Brent's speech announcing that he intended, on his return to America, to take immediate steps to bring into an existence an organ to examine faith and order questions, was the most memorable of all the utterances at Edinburgh.

Late in the afternoon the chairman rose. Was the conference ready to vote? A deep murmur of assent rang round the hall. Dr Wallace Williamson stood to ask whether provision was actually being made for the continuance of the Continuation Committee. George Robson gave an assurance that the point had not been overlooked, and it was agreed that this and other matters be left to the business committee (anticipation of this necessity was no doubt why the resolution had been presented with two more full days of the conference still to run). Sir Andrew Fraser waived his right of reply to the debate. Mott called for the ayes, and the house roared. He called for the noes, and received an equally eloquent silence. The motion was declared carried unanimously, and the mounting tension not just of that but the preceding days was released as with one voice the delegates rose in a spontaneous rendering of the doxology.

The two remaining sessions of the conference, on preparation of missionaries and the home base of missions, ran as smoothly as the earlier ones. When the delegates left Edinburgh, had they all fully realized what the resolution would now require of them at home? For most of the conference Oldham himself had little inkling as yet what it would all mean for him personally. He had been

[43] *Ibid.*, pp.184 and 185.
[44] *Ibid.*, p.204.

looking forward to resuming his missions education work in Scotland, or at any rate working full-time for the Foreign Mission Committee of the United Free Church. His name had twice been proposed as secretary to the committee, in 1909 and in 1910 just prior to the conference, but on both occasions the assembly had decided for another candidate by a narrow margin.[45] But at the Edinburgh conference, at the international level, he had acquired a tremendous reputation for reliability and efficiency, and that is always a mistake if one is looking for a quiet life.

[45] Cf. James Dougall letter to K. Bliss 24 Oct. 1969 [OA] citing Free Church general assembly records. The episode is also alluded to in E. Templeton's biography of Archie Craig, *God's February* (London, CCBI, 1991), p.16: "This was not because he was not thought the best man for the job, but because the Assembly reacted with hostility to the feeling that some of Oldham's supporters were acting as a caucus, and thought they had the appointment sewn up!" Oldham presumably was a willing nominee in both instances, but nowhere in his own records is there any mention of all this, let alone of his feelings at the outcome. Clearly, however, Oldham was remaining a powerful stimulus on the SCM scene while in Edinburgh, and had a lasting impact on Craig and others of his student generation.

CHAPTER 6

# *After Edinburgh: The Beginning of the Doing*

ON the final evening of the Edinburgh conference, J.R. Mott gave notice to the delegates that the conclusion of the gathering was only in one sense an end – the end of the planning. It was, he said, more significantly to be the beginning of the doing. That beginning was in fact already in process. The previous afternoon – the day following the momentous debate on the resolution from commission VIII – George Robson as chairman of the business committee had risen to bring the recommendations for the composition of the Continuation Committee.[1] Thirty-five names were proposed and endorsed: ten each from Great Britain, North America and the continent of Europe; one each from South Africa, Australasia, Japan, China and India. Of course, by (most) present-day standards it was overwhelmingly white, Western – and patriarchal (only two women were included). But it was the Continuation Committee of the conference itself, and that conference – by deliberate policy – had comprised representatives of the missionary organizations which were themselves, of course, largely white, Western and male-led. Joe Oldham never tired of emphasizing in later years that Edinburgh, for the first time in history, brought together *delegated* representatives of missionary bodies. That fact, on the one hand, invited the delegating bodies into the possibilities of real and hitherto untried commitments; on the other, it raised equally real questions of accountability on the part of the structures set up to fulfil those commitments. In its own historical context, it is this which sets Edinburgh in relief. Moreover, within its obvious limitations, the membership of the Continuation Committee did signify a real advance in interchurch relationships. The British slate of names, for example, included both E.S. Talbot, the Anglo-Catholic bishop of Southwark, and the Baptist layman Sir George Macalpine. At that time of continuing and often bitter Anglican–

[1] *World Missionary Conference, Edinburgh 1910, Vol. IX, History, Records and Addresses*, p.101.

Nonconformist rivalry, in how many other bodies could such figures have willingly sat together?

Prelates and academics from Britain, North America and Europe were well represented on the Continuation Committee. Others were obvious choices, such as George Robson from Scotland, Mott from America and Julius Richter of the German *Ausschuss*. And the Committee lost no time in getting to work, even before the conference ended. It held a brief meeting on the final afternoon (Thursday 23 June), three lengthy meetings the next day, and another prolonged meeting on Saturday 25 June by which time most of the other delegates were well on their way home. Certain decisions were taken at once. Mott (who else?) was elected chairman, and Oldham was appointed secretary, "to devote his whole time to the work".[2] Oldham's appointment, by virtue of his superlative organizational skills displayed before and during the conference, may appear to have been as obvious as Mott's, but other factors also played their part. A committee bringing together heavily academic Germans, cautious Anglo-Catholics, ardent evangelicals and activist Americans would need not only firm and fair chairing, but a continuous presence at the centre which could engender trust all round. The Germans, foremost in advocacy of a permanent international organization, told Oldham that his acceptance would allay their fears of being swamped by the larger forces of Britain and North America. Equally important to Oldham was the message from Walter Frere of Mirfield, that he would enjoy the confidence of Anglo-Catholics. Nor can it be doubted that the Americans, for their part, would welcome one who the previous year had taken such personal trouble to visit them and listen to them on their home ground during the controversy on statistics. Any thoughts of what might have been on offer had he been appointed to the Free Church foreign mission secretaryship evidently faded quickly from his mind.

During those long hours in Edinburgh, after an already gruelling conference, the Continuation Committee hammered out its working procedures. The committee would meet again next year, and thereafter biennially. There would also be an executive committee, meeting at least annually and comprising members from at least five countries. There would, moreover, be provision for special committees to be formed to work on particular subjects, and which could include persons not on the Continuation Committee. The messages of the conference would be circulated as soon as practicable to the church in Christian and non-Christian lands, and a letter would be sent to missionaries "conveying to them the deep appreciation of their contribution to the work of the Conference, and informing them of the plan and constitution of the Continuation Committee".[3]

It was the setting up of the special committees that chiefly engaged the Continuation Committee, for it was in these that the work of *continuation* – continuation of the coordinated study of the world missionary enterprise –

[2] *Ibid.*, p.135.
[3] *Ibid.*, p.136.

could, it was thought, be best achieved. No fewer than nine were proposed, their chairmen appointed and membership (at least provisionally) chosen. Their respective topics would be: unoccupied fields; formation of a board of study in Britain for the preparation of missionaries; training schools for missionaries; Christian education in the mission field; Christian literature; uniformity in statistical returns; the formation of an international committee of jurists to draw up a statement of the principles underlying the relations of missions to governments; missionary information in the secular press; exploration of the possibility of forming a body for dealing with questions arising between missions and governments. Such a list reads, at first, like a narrowing of the Edinburgh objectives from the visionary and theological to the pragmatic and mechanical. There was also some overlap between topics chosen. In part, these agendas were determined by the feasibility of committee members actually getting together, and geography as much as interest played a part in determining priorities. For his part, Oldham was already pondering further ways by which the cooperative initiative of Edinburgh might be pursued. Nor was he under any illusion that even the somewhat piecemeal programmes set for these committees would easily be fulfilled. He wrote:

> The work to be done along the various lines of action in view must needs be arduous; it demands prudence and patience as well as industry; but it is fraught with possibilities of incalculable gain to the missionary enterprise. The cooperation of many efficient and devoted workers in the cause of missions is being sought, and their united labours may, by the blessing of God, contribute materially to the realization of the vision which rose before the hope of the assembled Conference of a new era in the history of the missionary enterprise of the Church. But this will only be if the whole work is kept and carried forward under the guidance of the Holy Spirit and in His power.[4]

Oldham's immediate task was to see through the press the reports of the conference. Nine substantial volumes were produced – one for each commission report and a record of the plenary discussion on it, and a final volume, *History, Records and Addresses* which included an account by Oldham himself of the setting up of the Continuation Committee and its initial meetings. Fifteen thousand sets of the reports were sold in Britain alone,[5] itself a testimony to the interest aroused by the conference. In addition, for the popular market there soon appeared Temple Gairdner's compellingly written *"Edinburgh 1910"*,[6] capturing alike the essential spirit, the human touches and the dramatic moments. Mott, too, made a vital post-Edinburgh impact of his own through his book *The Decisive Hour of Christian Missions*.[7] Dictated at breakneck speed

[4] *Ibid.*, p.138.

[5] The reports were published in 1910 for the world missionary conference by Oliphant, Anderson & Ferrier (Edinburgh and London), and Fleming H. Revell Company (New York, Chicago and Toronto).

[6] W.H. Temple Gairdner, *"Edinburgh 1910": An Account and Interpretation of the World Missionary Conference*, Oliphant, Anderson & Ferrier for the World Missionary Conference, 1910.

[7] London, Church Missionary Society, 1910.

to two stenographers in Scotland just *before* the Edinburgh conference, it was in effect a running commentary on the report of commission I and appeared in print by the end of the summer.[8] It is the quintessential Mott.

But there still remained the question: what now? Vision and enthusiasm were bound to fade, but could the energy generated at least be transformed into realizable activity? The Continuation Committee members were separated by vast distances. There was £1,175 in the bank. There was Oldham himself, virtually without assistance, in Edinburgh. But it was Oldham's genius, then as always, to discern, first, what *could* be done; and then, out of the various possibilities, what *should* be done as a first priority, in order to move nearer the goal. He recognized that nothing could be done without the separate mission societies and boards. His aim would have to be to get them to agree to joint enterprises. That could not be done except by one who would follow up Edinburgh by personal visits to boards and secretaries, meetings with some of their committees, getting to know and be known by people and absorbing the different standpoints from which they viewed matters. This was to be the pattern of much of Oldham's life for the next few years, in visits to the European continent, North America and of course within Britain. It was important also to remain in closest possible contact with Mott, and not only by their frequent correspondence. In December 1910 Joe Oldham, this time accompanied by Mary, sailed for his second visit to the United States. He visited mission boards in Nashville, New York City and Toronto, and shared in the full evening report on Edinburgh to the annual meeting of the foreign missions conference of North America.[9] In January 1911, the Oldhams, accompanied by Mott and his wife and Silas McBee, sailed back to England on the second eastbound voyage of the *Lusitania*, the ship which four years later was to play such an ill-fated role in bringing American opinion into the war against Germany. Mott was to spend the next few months intensively touring Europe and the Levant on behalf of the WSCF.

There was as yet no permanent international committee, nor any plans for one. But the Continuation Committee had decided to meet again in 1911. Oldham might not be able to be fix his sights beyond it, but organizing *this* meeting was, *ipso facto*, an imperative for Oldham.[10] It was scheduled for 16–19 May at Auckland castle in the north of England, official residence of the bishops of Durham since the days when they were medieval prince-bishops. Auckland castle was (and still is) appropriately gaunt, if impressive. Oldham paid it a reconnoitring visit and wrote to Mott in some alarm. How would American delegates react to the lack of amenities; or delegates wanting to bring their wives cope with the interconnecting bedrooms? He need not have worried: it is scarcely possible to go wrong with a privately owned castle, especially when it

[8] C.H. Hopkins, *John R. Mott 1865–1955, A Biography*, WCC, Geneva, and Grand Rapids, Eerdmans, 1979, p.351.

[9] *Ibid.*, p.364.

[10] Cf. the Mott–Oldham correspondence 1910–11 [OA].

is warmed by the quality of hospitality that Bishop Handley C.G. Moule and his wife extended. Despite Mott's trekking seemingly everywhere from Utrecht and Basle to Cairo and Constantinople, Oldham was able to maintain an intensive correspondence with his chairman by letter and telegram and the preparations for the meeting progressed.

The meeting was a notable success, with one exception: none of the three oriental members could be present. It was a Western meeting, and at that a meeting of the home base of missions rather than of active missionaries "in the field". To that extent it was a diminution of the Edinburgh experience, but no less intensive and decisive in its accomplishment. In sixteen sessions, punctuated by daily matins and evensong in the castle chapel, Mott steered the committee through eighty-eight items of business. The constitution was adopted, and the work of the special committees clarified and reorganized. More important still was the concerted request from the members to Mott to disentangle himself from other commitments sufficiently to pay a series of visits to missions and churches in Asia. And for Oldham himself the most crucial decision – one which bears visible fruit down to the present day – was the agreement to launch a journal of mission studies.

## The *International Review of Missions*

There had been general agreement at Edinburgh and afterwards that some means of continuing contact was desirable among the delegates, and, more widely, those whom they represented in the missionary enterprise. There was talk of a "news sheet", which Mott had thought should be an occasional publication confined largely to "the necessary notices and records of proceedings of meetings and to a record of what we hear is being done in different parts of the world".[11] Oldham agreed, but was also turning over in his mind a more far-reaching possibility. In November 1910, shortly before sailing to America, he had written to Mott: "The thought of establishing an international missionary review, after I had banished it from my mind on account of the obvious practical difficulties, has recurred to me." He sketched some outline ideas for Mott to think over in preparation for a fuller discussion when they met, and, while careful not to overstate his case in advance, made clear his own excitement at the prospect: "I am often stirred as my mind dwells on the ends which I have outlined." Oldham had in mind a quarterly journal, akin to Warneck's *Allgemeine Missionszeitschrift* but with something also of the liberality and immediate contemporary interest of the *Hibbert Journal*. The journal, Oldham suggested, would contain matter which the Continuation Committee wished to communicate, together with articles not only from missionaries and administrators but also from scholars who could make a serious contribution to the scientific study of missions in their context. A wide range of books would be reviewed, and there would be an annual survey of the state of the

[11] Mott letter to JHO 21 Nov. 1910 [OA].

missionary enterprise. Although his memorandum dealt mainly with practical details, in his own mind he hoped for a spiritual end, and that the review might "give living and concrete expression to the idea which it is so vital that the Church should grasp, namely, the unity of the work of preaching the one gospel of the one God, who sent his only begotten son to save the one human race and gather it into one holy fellowship and brotherhood".[12] This, one might say, was the fullest "ecumenical" statement of Oldham's career thus far.

The committee accepted Oldham's proposals as they stood, and he was asked to edit the review on these lines, in the expectation that it would occupy a large part of his time. It certainly did. In May 1911 Oldham wrote to Tissington Tatlow excusing himself, for the first time in his life, from the Swanwick student summer conference and citing the paramount importance of getting the review started:

> The editing of the Review is recognized by everyone to be a job that will ultimately demand my entire strength, and I cannot be relieved of the Secretaryship for the present, as any change will probably destroy confidence. In addition to the larger requirements of the Review, there will be an immense amount of detail to attend to in making a start. I think I am bound to give my time exclusively to this great responsibility and cancel everything else.[13]

The first issue of the *International Review of Missions* (*IRM*) appeared in January 1912, and ran to 192 pages. It opened with fourteen pages of "editor's notes" by Oldham, setting out in fuller detail the aims and methods of the journal as agreed by the Continuation Committee. Its primary purpose, he reiterated, was "to further the facts and problems of missionary work among non-Christian peoples, and to contribute to the building up of a science of missions".[14] While it would be published in Britain, full coverage would be given to American and continental students of missions. It was intended as a tangible expression of the aims of the Continuation Committee, and its publication "may be regarded as the first effort of missionary societies and boards to undertake in international combination what it would hardly be possible for any one of them to do alone". Special importance would be given to study of the missionary message in relation to each of the non-Christian religions, beginning with Islam. The subject of unity and cooperation would be kept fully in view, together with the history of missions. The review would draw upon, and serve, both scholarship and practical missionary endeavour, for "in the Kingdom of God truth is apprehended, not by those who stand by as spectators, but by those who do and serve".

The contents of this first issue well exemplified Oldham's aims: "The Impressions of a Traveller Among Non-Christian Races" (James Bryce); "The Growth of the Church . . . among the Bataks" (Johannes Warneck – first of a

[12] JHO letter to Mott 19 Nov. 1910 [OA].
[13] JHO letter to Tatlow 22 May 1911 [OA].
[14] *IRM*, vol. 1, no. 1 Jan. 1912, p.1.

series on progress in various mission fields); "The Vital Forces of Christianity and Islam" (Temple Gairdner); "The Present Position and Problems of Christianity in Japan" (Tasuku Harada); "The Place of Women in the East" (Agnes de Selincourt); "The Special Preparation of Missionaries" (H.T. Hodgkin); "China and Education" (J.F. Goucher). There was also an important article by Mott on the work of the Continuation Committee, together with an extensive section of book reviews and a bibliography. It was well received and, the quality and range of the contents being maintained, the circulation of *IRM* increased steadily with each quarterly issue. It was indeed a solid and lasting ecumenical achievement owed almost entirely to Oldham's own vision and diligence.

Note has already been taken of Oldham's emphasis, post-Edinburgh, on the need for unity among the churches for the sake of mission. This however was not the only sign of a "prophet" in the making, if by prophetic is meant the discernment of a new direction of history being offered by the Spirit and an awareness of the challenges this poses. In his first editorial notes, Oldham picked up and underlined one of the most critical issues that had begun to find a voice – though not actually heard by everyone – at Edinburgh: "In many countries the problem of making Christianity indigenous, and of building up a strong, independent, self-supporting, self-propagating Church is even more pressing than that of securing more foreign missionaries." It was fifty-seven years later, and coincidentally the year of Oldham's death (1969), that the title of *IRM* was slightly but significantly changed by substituting *Mission* for *Missions.* One cannot help feeling that even in 1912 Oldham would not have demurred at that. Equally prophetic was his recognition that the relations of Christianity with Islam, and the significance of "the revolution which is in process in China" must receive serious attention.

The launching of *IRM* – the first truly ecumenical, international periodical – thus marked another definitive stage in the ecumenical movement, and in Oldham's own career as a major initiator in that movement. The sense of a coming of age, of a responsibility now lying in his own hands, was deepened by two deaths which he had cause to note in that first edition of *IRM*: that of Gustav Warneck, pioneer of mission studies as a genuine science and Oldham's own mentor in Halle; and, still more significant personally, that of George Robson, his senior colleague in Edinburgh and chairman of the business committee of the Edinburgh conference. It was to Robson's own initiative and encouragement, as has been seen in the previous chapter, that Oldham owed his involvement in the Edinburgh conference in the first place. Moreover, Oldham knew – as few others could have done – what the Edinburgh conference had owed to Robson in those hectic and at times traumatic months of preparation: "it was his unwearied labours for the Conference that, more than anything else, wore out his strength". And the wearing out of strength was a matter Joe Oldham was himself coming very close to appreciating.

In the course of 1912 Georgina Gollock, literature secretary of the Church Missionary Society, joined Oldham as assistant editor. She was to give many years of hard work and the benefit of an astringent and generous personality to this and other aspects of missionary cooperation. This assistance proved highly necessary to Oldham. Launching and editing *IRM* demanded time-consuming and sometimes anxious effort – on top of all his other work for the Continuation Committee. His health gave some concern. "I am rather run down," he confessed to Tatlow in May 1911, "and have never quite got over the strain of the Edinburgh Conference, as the result of having failed to take a sufficiently long break last summer."[15] Frequent visits to London from his home base in Edinburgh, journeys to the continent, speaking engagements (not least for the SCM) – all contributed to his sense of exhaustion. Yet his recuperative powers were enormous and he had the spiritual serenity which accepts bouts of ill-health and waits for them to pass. This was in some respects a bad period for him, yet it was never the prospect of having to face a particular strain which prostrated him, only the aftermath of having met it.

## Identifying a strategy

What Oldham lacked in physical and nervous stamina, Mott possessed in abundance. Mott could never have edited the *IRM* nor Oldham accomplished what Mott did on his stupendous, galvanic world tours. Early on in their post-Edinburgh partnership the need emerged for a quite clear and conscious differentiation in the respective roles of these two leaders. The May 1911 meeting of the Continuation Committee at Auckland castle had encouraged Mott to undertake a visit to Asia. The following year, Oldham was pressed very urgently by the secretaries of a number of British mission boards to accompany Mott for the two-month tour of China. Relations between missions and indigenous churches were – as the Chinese presence at Edinburgh had indicated – in a number of cases badly strained, and mission secretaries were convinced that new policies were demanded. Oldham's help in formulating and commending them was urged upon him to the point of his agreeing to take the proposition seriously.[16] Mott thought otherwise. The *IRM*, the Continuation Committee itself and its special committees needed Oldham. Mott pointed as an example to what could have been done for Korean Christians under severe restrictions by the Japanese occupation by a proper international committee on the relations of missions and governments, had it existed. Mott's letter of counsel was one of the longest and one of the frankest Oldham ever received from his American friend, and concluded "Thanking God for a friendship which enables me to write as fully as I have done in this letter without feeling that you will misunderstand."[17]

Oldham accepted the advice with good grace. He had hesitations (though he touched on them but lightly) on the score of health for so long and exacting

[15] JHO letter to Tatlow 22 May 1911 [OA].
[16] JHO letter to Mott 18 June 1912 [OA].
[17] Mott letter to JHO 15 July 1912 (handwritten) [OA].

a journey. He was also working flat out to make the *Review* the important journal it did become, and felt in sore need of assistance at the administrative level. He had already told Mott that "for two or three years the magazine will need every ounce of work that I can put into it" if its combination of geographical and thematic balance with scientific rigour was to be established. Yet he felt caught in a dilemma: "I doubt if I can succeed in this if there is much work to do in connection with the Continuation Committee. It is clear to me that my capacity to edit the Review would be almost halved if I were to cease to be Secretary of the Continuation Committee."[18] He hoped in vain for an assistant secretary to be appointed to the committee.[19]

It would be more than ten years before Oldham himself visited China. But meanwhile, by 1912 Mott and Oldham had thoroughly established a mutually trustful relationship which enabled each to speak openly to the other. Whether by frankness or encouragement, each of the hundred or so letters they exchanged during 1911–12 seemed to increase their degree of friendship. Nothing conveys more vividly what Mott meant to Oldham than the closing, poignant paragraph of Oldham's letter of late April 1912, written on return to Edinburgh from "a most delightful, restful and invigorating time in Italy":

> The terrible loss of the "Titanic" has filled our thoughts for the past week. When the first news came, I realized that I had no definite information regarding the boat by which you were returning to America, and I very anxiously scanned the list of passengers to see whether by any chance you were among the number.[20]

Mott had been in Europe since early in the year on a speaking tour to student unions. For his homeward voyage, with George Sherwood Eddy, he was in fact offered a passage on the *Titanic* but chose another sailing the same week. Later he confessed to Oldham that he "very nearly" took the *Titanic*.[21]

As regards the China visit, Oldham did as Mott suggested, turning his mind away from exotic visits he would have so much welcomed. He threw himself into the work of the *IRM* and the sub-committees of the Continuation Committee, and took whatever opportunity he could to widen his contacts, in the interests both of the journal and the committees. Some of these efforts were ecumenically pioneering and remarkable in their results. He reported to Mott:

> I had committee meetings in London last week and again this week. Instead of returning to Edinburgh for the weekend I decided to pay a visit to Münster . . . in order to come into touch with those who are editing the Roman Catholic scientific missionary journal which was started eighteen months ago. It is being edited with remarkable ability. Its attitude towards Protestant missions is something quite new, being marked by great courtesy and a genuine desire to get at the facts. I have seldom received so much kindness as I did during the three days I had in Germany, first at

[18] JHO letter to Mott 11 Dec. 1911 [OA].
[19] JHO letter to Mott 24 April 1912 [OA]. Oldham suggests Basil Hall as a possibility for an assistant.
[20] *Ibid.*
[21] Hopkins, p.386.

> Münster and then at Steyl, which is the headquarters of the largest German Roman Catholic missionary organization. There are quite a number of these Roman Catholic scholars who have a thorough knowledge of Protestant missionary work. I think we have made a mistake in not taking steps to follow more closely what they are doing and my chief object in going was to ascertain the sources from which information can be obtained.[22]

The members of the Continuation Committee and its sub-committees were beginning to understand and trust one another across the boundaries of culture and confession. They were unfettered by the necessity to wait upon the mandate of appointing bodies. But the committee was not really representative, appointed as it was by a conference long since dissolved. This had severe disadvantages: the societies could ignore or even repudiate it if they wished. Oldham himself, increasingly aware that the results of Edinburgh were in danger of being dissipated, saw the need for a properly constituted international committee to be formed as soon as possible, and in November 1911 expressed himself strongly on the point to Mott,[23] the difficulties and complexities notwithstanding. He hoped that the next meeting of the Continuation Committee to be held in September 1912 might tackle the matter decisively.

This meeting was held over five days at Lake Mohonk, New York. Met from their boats or trains by Mott and his assistants and conducted to a specially chartered steamer, the whole company sailed up the Hudson River talking all the way with the solemnity of a think-tank and the jollity of a Sunday school outing. By now there were ten sub-committees to review, some of them with solid achievement to report (of which more later). Eighty-six agenda items were dispatched under Mott's chairmanship. The careful preparations laid down by Oldham and endorsed by Mott, and the prior discussion between them, once more paid off in smooth progress and virtual unanimity. But the central issue remained unresolved: they could find no way to form a representative and permanent organ of international cooperation. Oldham had worked hard at the question exploring every possibility: the reluctant conclusion was that too many societies were unprepared to commit themselves, and the committee had to face frankly the fact of diminishing enthusiasm for such a permanent body.

This however was not the sum total of the Mohonk meeting. The matter of the difficult relations of missions to governments was referred to national organizations. More concretely, a strong letter was sent to the Japanese ambassador in Washington on the imprisonment of Korean Christians, including T.H. Yun who had been a delegate at Edinburgh. Letters were also sent to missionaries in Korea, and intercessory prayer was offered for all parties in the situation.[24] But centre-stage at Mohonk were Mott's plans for his visit to the Far East, which were discussed at length by the committee. As the

[22] Bliss MS, pp.91f.
[23] JHO letter to Mott 25 Nov. 1911 [OA].
[24] Hopkins, p.382.

committee members left for home – Oldham spending several days more in America contacting officers of boards and potential contributors to the *IRM* – Mott headed for Asia.

Mott fulfilled his plans in every particular between October 1912 and May 1913. For his part, Oldham's role was to continue struggling to bring together established mission boards which were locked into longstanding historical and doctrinal differences, patterns of denominational separateness. He was the confidant of board secretaries, but he knew it was useless to put pressure on them. In Asia Mott was venturing onto more creative frontiers, among missionaries in the field (some of whom were already putting the needs of their situation before the behests of their home boards) and, moreover, among the emerging leaders of indigenous churches to whom the divisive quarrels of the Reformation meant less than the needs of their own people. It was here, in Asia, that the pressure for missionary cooperation was to become the pressure for Christian unity and thus to supply much of the motive force for fulfilling Oldham's longer term hopes.

Mott's Asian tour thus forms a real part of the Oldham story, and a brief account is appropriate here.[25] The situation was ripe for Mott's action, but the man himself was all-important and shows Oldham's partner at the zenith of his powers. Before he left, Mott was able to tell the committee that anonymous friends had paid for all his travel and covered the cost of the many conferences which he had called into being and was to chair. He had read everything he could find and a special researcher supplemented his knowledge of each different situation. He went as an evangelist to students, holding meetings in dozens of universities and colleges. To missions and churches he went as the ambassador of the Edinburgh conference, sending ahead of his visit questions based upon its commissions. Local preparatory committees set up the twenty-one regional and national conferences he chaired in Ceylon, India, Burma, Malaya, China, Manchuria, Korea and Japan. It was, in effect, a re-run of Edinburgh on the road. But the outstanding feature of these "Continuation Committee conferences", even more important than the diffusion of the spirit of Edinburgh, was the part played in them by indigenous church leaders. They formed overall more than a third of all the participants. Most of the committees and councils which grew out of these conferences, either as new bodies or as existing ones reshaped, wrote into their constitutions an obligation to incorporate nationals as full members. These were the bodies which, in the then distant future, were to form the basis of a genuinely *international* missionary cooperation. Oldham kept in touch as much as possible with Mott during this period, for he saw the visit itself as the kind of concrete demonstration of what was possible through cooperation. He made a special request for an article from Mott on India, emphasizing this point and adding: "I do not think that the difficulty that was raised by one or two members of the Continuation

[25] See *ibid.*, pp.386–404.

Committee being compromised by such an article [because of its personal viewpoint] is really serious. We are learning now how much we lost after Bishop Auckland through an excess of timidity."[26]

Hopes of immediate progress towards a permanent international body may have failed at Mohonk, and Mott's trail-blazing tour to the East may have put some distance between pioneering excitement and the secretary's desk. But Oldham still believed deeply in the real potential still offered by the Continuation Committee. Much solid work continued, and not only in the form of the *IRM*. The ten sub-committees of the Continuation Committee were active. Not that they met, as such, more than rarely. The usual pattern was for three regional groups based in North America, Europe and Britain to take on specific responsibility for some part of the committee's work and to be in communication with the other regions by correspondence and personal visits. Chairmen and secretaries were volunteers: Oldham was still the only officer. He kept himself informed about all ten and acted as go-between when he travelled. In certain of them he played a considerable hand, notably the committees on education, on women's work, and on work among Muslims.

Most of these committees concentrated their efforts on some one problem among the many meriting attention – for example, the medical committee on training, the committee on the church in the mission field on the urgent problem of the relation of missions and churches in China and Japan; that on women's work on the education of women and girls. On rare occasions a committee made an effective protest – as when the education committee, through its British and continental members, caused the government of India to refrain from changing the relations of government to government-aided mission schools.

Oldham's experience with these committees taught him lessons vital for his future strategy. He found that general communications from the Continuation Committee to mission boards were ineffectual. "We took immense pains to send a letter to all Boards after the last meeting of the Continuation Committee" (he wrote to T.R.W. Lunt of the CMS) "and Hodgkin's board was the only one to acknowledge its receipt. I found that scarcely any of the secretaries were aware that they had received such a letter. I am somewhat strongly of the opinion that the sound thing is to approach Boards not with a general statement but with a concrete proposition calling for action. We shall not get them to believe in us by any abstract statement of our policy but by doing some one definite thing."[27] Action, where action was needed but was beyond the power of one society acting alone, seemed to be one of the keys to cooperation. The other, the importance of which Oldham had already begun to see in these pre-war years, was research.

Oldham found the value of research convincingly demonstrated, above all, by the committee on work among Muslims. This set up an enquiry into the

[26] JHO letter to Mott 10 Dec. 1912 [OA].
[27] Bliss MS, p.97.

advance and nature of Islam in Africa, where its rapid progress was causing considerable anxiety to some missions. The enquiry drew on the experience of missionaries, scholars and civil administrators, and Temple Gairdner was sent to Germany to visit universities and mission institutes specializing in the study of Islam. The committee's work (some of it published in the *IRM*) proved valuable to the missions concerned and Oldham could also report that "friendly relations of a new kind have been established with government officials in the English, French and German colonies in Africa and with the leaders of thought in regard to Islam on the continent, many of whom have been previously hostile to missionary work among Moslems".[28] Among those he mentions as taking part were two figures who were to become his close collaborators and personal friends, Prof. Westermann of Berlin and Sir Frederick Lugard, at that time governor-general of Nigeria. It is revealing, however, to note just why, as early as December 1911, in a letter to Mott[29] he was so enthusiastic about this project. Quite apart from the obvious importance of the issue to the missionaries and churches in the field, Oldham cites two reasons for it being given priority. First, it is "just the kind of survey that seems to me worth doing" because it was defined and concrete, and "It would seem to me sound policy for the Committee . . . to throw its weight into a definite piece of work without waiting to work out a world plan." Second, it "would at once give the Continentals a living part in the work of the Continuation Committee and allow scope for their special gifts". Oldham was by now, if not the wily saint, then certainly the shrewd politician.

## Beyond cooperation?

In June 1913, Oldham wrote a report on "The Progress of the Movement for co-operation in Missions", for the third meeting of the recently-formed Conference of Missionary Societies in Britain and Ireland (CMSBI). He concluded:

> No-one can take a broad view of history and of the present situation in the world without realizing that Protestantism has manifested weaknesses through its innumerable divisions and that these weaknesses make themselves felt in a specially acute form in the face of the tremendous constructive task to which the Church is called in the non-Christian world. It is not possible to go back to the unity which was broken up at the Reformation, but only to go forward towards a larger and higher unity which recognizes and is based upon the freedom of the Christian man. It is certain that no kind of cooperation will be accepted by the missionary societies except one which rests on the free acceptance of common ends. To seek co-operation along these lines, however, makes large demands on character. Behind all the consideration and discussion of co-operation, ennobling and filling even petty details with large and deep meaning, lies the question – a question of real and deep historical significance – whether there is among the leaders of the missionary movement the loftiness of Christian character, the statesmanship, the largeness of vision, the depth

[28] *Ibid.*, pp.97f.
[29] JHO letter to Mott 2 Dec. 1911 [OA].

> of sympathy, and the faith in God to enable them to achieve a living, rich, effective unity in which the gifts that God has bestowed upon each will find their highest expression, and the resources which He had entrusted to His church will be used to the uttermost for the speedy advancement of the Kingdom of God.[30]

Oldham's audience at Swanwick comprised board secretaries and leading members of most of the British missionary societies. Board secretaries had for a number of years been meeting together in London, but it was only with the stimulus of the Edinburgh conference that a properly representative body of missionary societies came into being with the CMSBI. With its inception missionary societies in Britain came into line with those on the continent and North America in having a permanent organ of cooperation, a step which greatly simplified Oldham's work for the Continuation Committee. Among other things the CMSBI took on the task of collecting from the societies their financial contributions to the Continuation Committee.

In his report, Oldham was going beyond talk of cooperation, to unity. Why was this so, when it was cooperation which formed the basis of participation in the CMSBI, and indeed the work of the Continuation Committee, and openings were already being found for the practice of it? No doubt he spoke out of personal conviction born of his own experience in India and his subsequent thinking about the nature of the church. But the immediate cause of his strongly worded plea for some new action by the societies was his knowledge that denominational barriers in the mission field were being breached not only by cooperative ventures sanctioned by some societies but by the utterances and actions of individuals. Even before the Edinburgh conference Silas McBee told Oldham that even Anglican bishops overseas sometimes said and did things which "it was as well should not be known at home". Such secrecy was neither desirable nor possible. If discontent with denominational restrictions was growing, the only real way forward was for something or somebody to make some move challenging denominational complacency at home. Were not the missionary societies in a position to take some step towards unity which would have the effect of liberating the churches from the constraints put upon their work overseas by their home-based divisions? He did not say what step, nor did anyone, it seems, act upon the challenge – for reasons which very soon became painfully obvious.

In fact, talk of unity rather than just cooperation quickly provoked strong reactions in some quarters. What is more, a tendency to exaggerate the influence of the Edinburgh conference on local events did the cause of cooperation no good. One or two of Mott's Asian conferences came under fire as the result of one visitor's interpretation of them in the British press. This visitor's prophecy of "an end to denominationalism" bore as little relation to what actually happened at the conferences as did the heated reassertions of uncompromising rigidity with which it was met. But nothing with which either Mott or Oldham

[30] Bliss MS, p.99.

had any direct connection caused such embarrassment for the Continuation Committee and for Oldham in particular as the fracas over the *Kikuyu conference.*

In June 1913, in the village of Kikuyu in British East Africa, a missionary conference was held by Anglicans, Presbyterians and other Protestants, under the leadership of the bishops of Mombasa (W.G. Peel) and Uganda (J.J. Willis). Proposals were made, and sent home to the mission boards, for a federation of the constituent churches on the basis of common acceptance of the Apostles' and Nicene Creeds, and the recognition of a common membership between the churches of the federation, with the right of receiving communion in any of them. The Anglo-Catholic reaction to these proposals, and to the conference itself, was vehement. In fact the Kikuyu proposals had first been discussed in 1907 and the resolutions of 1913 were (wrote Bishop Willis) "in almost every detail those already passed by a somewhat smaller conference in 1909". This movement towards two federations each involving the Church of Scotland Mission and the Church Missionary Society therefore owed nothing to the Edinburgh conference or to its Continuation Committee except perhaps an expectation in the minds of the actors that Edinburgh might have created a climate of opinion at home favourable to such endeavours. Prior to Kikuyu, in April 1913, Oldham himself was written to by a Church of Scotland missionary in Kenya, J.W. Arthur, who asked for "literature that would be helpful" and for advice on issues that might be brought up at the conference in June". But the letter arrived on Oldham's desk while he was on the continent, and by the time he read it there was no time to reply. Arthur, a medical man, quite unversed in theological warfare, later wrote to Oldham an enthusiastic letter about the conference itself: "... A wonderful time and full of inspiration. The unity was just wonderful". Oldham wrote swiftly back to warn him of difficulties in the Church of England "which is perhaps not altogether surprising when one considers how many points of view are represented in it".

In England the Anglo-Catholic attack on the Kikuyu proposals, initiated from Africa by Frank Weston, bishop of Zanzibar, was frequently abusive. Hensley Henson and others replied in kind. Edward Talbot, bishop of Winchester, was the member of the Continuation Committee most sharply under attack, and he tried both to condemn the proceedings at Kikuyu (which had included a joint service of holy communion) and to defend the Continuation Committee from accusations of propagating "undenominationalism". Whatever discussion of Kikuyu may have eventually taken place at the 1913 meeting of the committee (for which see later) was unminuted and no resolution referred directly to it. Oldham's anxiety was to defend the committee against the accusation made in at least two British newspapers that the committee had actually pronounced *against* the Kikuyu resolutions and indeed against Christian unity. It did not much matter to Oldham that Bishop Montgomery, pursued afresh by a now even larger band of anti-Edinburgh demonstrators among SPG supporters, should declare that "if he had known that *this* would be the result he would never have gone to Edinburgh at all"; but it mattered a great deal to him that among those who had had the highest hopes of Edinburgh and given it the most generous support, some should now think that the Continuation Committee was actually working against unity and masking its change of front. So his only intrusions into the press were letters correcting points of fact and insisting that the committee had not made any such condemnation since both condemnation and approval of any matter involving doctrine and church order were equally outside its sphere.

"Kikuyu" cast a long shadow over ecumenical relations in an important respect. Archbishop Davidson, who stood in the middle and received attacks from both sides, eventually gave an "opinion" that Nonconformists in the region might receive communion from Anglican chalices, but that Anglicans should not seek to receive communion from non-episcopally ordained ministers. Oldham, for the time being, made no more speeches on Christian unity and no more appeals for missionary statesmanship to take a lead in that direction: such talk would lead him closer to that dangerous boundary between practical action and "matters of doctrine and order" than the secretary of the Continuation Committee should go if his committee was to keep its own cohesion and to stay clear of the charge of meddling. The Mohonk meeting of the Continuation Committee in 1912 had already signalled its caution in deciding to continue its own existence and not make any proposals for a permanent, formally constituted body. Till then, Oldham had been eager to grasp the nettle and go forward to some representative international structure. But the societies were clearly not ready for it and he had to pull back. The question now was what, in the aftermath of Kikuyu and its accompanying controversies and accusations, the Continuation Committee would decide at its next meeting, to be held in mid-November 1913 at the Hague in the Netherlands.

As was expected, Mott reported on his Asian tour on the first morning of the meeting, and distributed a printed report on the twenty-one conferences he had held. It was a galvanizing vision of the reality of a world church, both potential and in the making. An immediate result was a resolution by the committee, passed unanimously, that the chairman specifically devote henceforth a large amount of his time and energy to the committee, to enable it to offer its services more effectively to the world mission of the church. Mott accepted. But what of the committee itself, its nature and role? The meeting laid down certain ground-rules which came to be known as the "Hague Principles", stating in summary that: "The only committees entitled to determine missionary policy are the Home Boards, the Missions and the Churches concerned. It believes however that the missionary policy in any particular area can be rightly determined only in view of the situation of that area as a whole, and in relation to other work which is being carried on."[31] It was also made plain that the committee was not related organically to or

[31] *Ibid.*, pp.105f.

responsible to its new counterparts in the east, though it anticipated a growing relationship of "mutual understanding and helpfulness".[32]

The Hague Principles thus achieved some clarity, but at the cost of satisfying the conservatism of the home boards. It was "two cheers for missionary imperialism and only one for indigenous churches".[33] If however they represented a victory for the ideal of cooperation rather than unity on a representative basis, they at least emphasized the *imperative* of that cooperation in crucial spheres. And Oldham believed it was necessary above all to win and keep the confidence of the home societies.

From one point of view therefore, for Oldham at least, the Hague meeting of the Continuation Committee represented yet another ebbing of the high tide of hope reached at Edinburgh. But at least the channel of cooperation remained navigable and clearly marked. There were other compensations. In particular, means were agreed upon for some relief, at long last, from the chronic burden of over-work which ever-multiplying demands were putting upon him. Kenneth Maclennan, who had worked so effectively with him on the concluding stages of preparation for the Edinburgh conference, was to leave the Laymen's Missionary Movement and join him as the colleague who would take over all the administration immediately and, in the longer term, assume responsibility for other areas of work. It must also have been encouraging for Oldham to receive from Mott, immediately following the meeting, a letter expressing "overflowing thankfulness to God for the many answers to prayer, and the joy of fellowship with you".[34] It was, in fact, to prove to have been the last meeting of the Continuation Committee.

## India and women's education

Oldham also received at the Hague a quite unexpected and very fruitful solution to a question which was engaging his enthusiastic attention at the time. Among the visitors to the meeting were the leaders of two of the most important women's missionary movements in the United States, Mrs Peabody and Mrs Montgomery. They were present when Oldham gave the report of the education committee. He had been working closely with the secretary of its British section, T.W. Lunt, on a scheme which had originated in Madras for the founding of an interdenominational university college for women. Oldham had seen that the endeavours of a local committee needed active support from the societies at home. He and Lunt had just held a conference for some British women educators interested in women's education in India (of whom two had visited a large number of girls' schools in India, on the committee's behalf) and some of the leading mission board secretaries. Oldham had experienced considerable difficulty in getting any coordination between the North American and the British sections of the education committee, and he told Lunt there was little

[32] Hopkins, p.408.
[33] Comment by K. Bliss, Bliss MS, p.106.
[34] Hopkins, p.408.

hope of American support for what was (owing to the almost exclusively British character of the original suggestion) a scheme for a college on British lines. "Americans," he wrote, "have almost exactly the same feeling about British education as we have about American."[35]

Mrs Peabody swept such obstacles aside. She revealed that she and Mrs Montgomery were on their way to India, representing five major women's missionary movements in the United States and Canada, to explore on their behalf the possibility of founding a university college for young women educated in American mission schools. She was enthusiastic for cooperation. Oldham was taken completely by surprise. He had evidently not given due attention to the independent line often taken by the women's missionary committees, even when they were auxiliaries of main mission boards. Adequate mission support for the college was now assured and as an added bonus he had a splendid example of Anglo-American missionary cooperation in his pocket. However, even that success in turn bred its own snags. Missionaries in North India soon started asking why Madras should be so favoured by the committee. Were not Bombay and other cities in at least equal need? Oldham sought to mollify them with explanations that the committee was only responding to requests for coordination from the local scene, and not taking initiatives of its own.[36]

## A home ministry

Joe Oldham continued to be closely involved on the student scene, both in Edinburgh and in Britain at large, during these years. William Temple was not the only future archbishop to come under his influence through the SCM: Geoffrey Fisher while at Oxford warmed both to him and John Mott.[37] Oldham chaired the student conference on foreign missions and social problems held in Liverpool in January 1912, and wrote a preparatory article for it. He warned that it was misleading to speak of a "Christian world" confronting the "non-Christian world", since many features of the so-called Christian countries were profoundly unChristian, especially in their social life which was "a denial of Christ".[38] It was an awareness which was to become instantly and far more acutely painful for him with the outbreak of war two years later. Looking back from that tragedy, it is even more significant that at Liverpool he was a prime mover in getting a telegram sent by the gathering to the German SCM, lamenting the tensions between Britain and Germany and praying deliverance from war: such a fratricidal conflict would set back the Christian cause in the world "for a generation".[39] Prophecy indeed.

[35] Quoted in Bliss MS, p.107.

[36] JHO letter to "Miss Latham", Ahmednagar, India, 28 May 1914 [OA].

[37] See E. Carpenter, *Archbishop Fisher – His Life and Times,* Norwich, Canterbury Press, 1991, p.13.

[38] Oldham, "The Liverpool Conference", *Student Movement,* XIV, 3 Dec. 1911, pp.50f.

[39] W.L. Martin, "Joseph Houldsworth Oldham: His Thought and Its Development", Ph.D. thesis, St Andrews University, 1967, pp. 57–59.

Nor did he address only students. In May 1912 he spoke to the wives of ministers of the Church of Scotland and the United Free Church on "Women and the Church in Scotland". Christians, he declared, could not but be in whole-hearted sympathy with the aspirations for a greater share in society by the working classes, which lay behind much of the present industrial unrest. The same applied to the rising women's movement for suffrage. The gospels show Christ, "the best friend that woman ever had", choosing women as his friends and companions and revealing to them some of the deepest things he had to teach. By his assertion of the infinite value of every human being he "opened up for women a life of freedom, service and endless possibility".

## On the eve of war

Oldham's approach to his work was always characterized by an awareness of the need for the long-term view, combined with a sense of the immediately practicable steps towards fulfilment of that goal. At the end of 1913 few could have known how little time was left for the gradualist approach which followed Edinburgh. After the Hague meeting, the Continuation Committee never met again. Like so much else, it was thrown into the maelstrom of the catastrophe that broke upon Europe in August 1914. Many of the bonds, including those of personal friendship, broke under the strain of conflicting loyalties in 1914–18. Such of the work of the committee as did continue did so within national groupings. But Oldham's own faith in the value of international cooperation had been clarified by his four years of work with the committee. He himself summarized the grounds for belief in cooperation. First, there was the practical value of consulting and planning together in a situation which was everywhere offering fresh problems to societies, many of which they could not solve in isolation. Second, the world was becoming internationally organized for science, trade and many other purposes, and missions found themselves in an international world too, their nearest neighbours in the mission field seldom belonging to the same nation or the same church. Third, and the strongest and most enduring reason though the least visible or calculable, it was the precursor of Christian unity.

Oldham may have had to soft-pedal that third note following the Kikuyu episode, but it remained deep in his head and his heart, as did the first two reasons. Moreover, as so often in Christian history, crisis became the bearer of opportunity. In a totally unforeseen way the tragedy of 1914–18, far from dashing the hopes engendered at Edinburgh, was to prove the context in which, eventually, there was forged the will for a permanent instrument of international, ecumenical cooperation in world mission.

CHAPTER 7

# *World Missions and World War 1914–18*

EVEN after more than eight decades the impact of the great conflict into which Europe was plunged in August 1914 is almost impossible to describe without resort to the superlatives of shock and horror. It is not simply the scale of suffering and death that still appals. It is the sense of contemporary shock at the very outbreak of war, a war between nations priding themselves on their civilization, their Christianity and their progressive ideals, that still transmits itself to us from sermons such as this in August 1914:

> Before we could realize what was happening, we found all the apparent solid ground beneath our feet breaking up, and ourselves standing in horror on the edge of the abyss. We would not be educated into seriousness, and now God has shocked us into it . . . It needs little foresight to see that as a result of this war ancient institutions will be shaken, much will be overthrown never to rise again, and a staggering blow will be dealt at our civilization.[1]

The sense of an event of earthquake proportions was typical both of the pulpit and of widespread public feeling in August 1914. Many recognized that Christianity itself would be on trial, however short or long the conflict might prove to be. For such as Joe Oldham, however, the sense of crisis was unequalled, for reasons obvious enough in view of his role in the movement which for the past four years had witnessed to claims to a unity transcending confession, nationality and race for the sake of bringing the one gospel to the one world. As he wrote during the first few weeks of the war:

> The World Missionary Conference in 1910 called the attention of the Christian Church to the critical importance of the next ten years in determining the spiritual evolution of mankind, and declared that if those years were wasted, "havoc may be

[1] Sermon by A.J. Nixon, quoted in K.W. Clements, "Baptists and the Outbreak of the First World War", *Baptist Quarterly*, vol. XXVI, April 1975, p.83.

> wrought that centuries are not able to repair." Deep as was the sense of the gravity of the issues, the Conference little dreamed that before the decade had half run its course Christian Europe would plunge into the abyss of war and spend in the work of destruction energies and resources that were meant to be used for the uplifting and enriching of mankind.[2]

The Continuation Committee of which he was the chief servant was itself deliberately representative of the international nature of this movement. Prominent German scholars and missionary leaders were members of it. Could it be a witness to unity in this crisis, and help the churches to meet it, or would it itself become overwhelmed by and part of the conflict? The challenge for Oldham would doubtless have been less daunting if he had been a citizen of a neutral country – an American, say, or a Swede. As it was, he belonged to one of the belligerent nations. Moreover, while he eschewed any form of jingoism or self-righteous belief in the total innocence of his country's cause, and while he recognized that Britain was not totally innocent of blame nor Germany wholly without a case, he did believe that at the end of the day the allies had more right on their side. The war, tragic and terrible product as it was of a sinful disorder affecting all the European countries and not just Germany, had to be fought to a successful conclusion for the sake of a better world to follow.

Oldham was thus not afraid to be known as a loyal "Englishman" (Scottish though he was), and *at the same time* as belonging to the universal church of Christ, of which the international missionary movement was a concrete and visible expression. The manner in which he tried to maintain both loyalties, distinctly yet in creative relation to each other, forms the dynamic for much of his story during these four years of war. That he was, largely, able to do so with integrity was an essential contribution to the ecumenical movement. The small craft which was continuing the spirit and plans of Edinburgh 1910, frail enough already, was all but broken to pieces by the reefs and breakers of war. Oldham managed to preserve enough of the timbers to begin fashioning a new vessel which set sail again in the calmer waters after 1918.

## The initial trauma: August and September 1914

On medical advice, at the beginning of July 1914 the Oldhams had begun what was intended as a long holiday, prior to the forthcoming meeting of the Continuation Committee scheduled for 17–24 September in Oxford. On Britain's declaration of war on Germany on 4 August Oldham hurried back to his desk in Edinburgh and consulted urgently with Kenneth Maclennan. The very next day he wrote to John Mott. The first five paragraphs merit quoting in full:[3]

[2] JHO, "The War and Missions", *IRM*, vol. III, no. 12 Oct. 1914, p.625.

[3] Letter to Mott 5 Aug. 1914 [Yale Divinity Library]. In C.H. Hopkins, *John R. Mott 1865–1955*, Geneva, WCC, and Grand Rapids, Eerdmans, 1979, short extracts from this letter are quoted (p.433) but it is incorrectly dated as 28 August 1914. Much of the significance of the letter as Oldham's *instantaneous* reaction to the war is thereby missed. Oldham did write to Mott on 28 August 1914 but largely on other matters.

It is impossible yet to take in the meaning of this terrible blow to all that we have been working for during the past few years. Our deepest need, I feel sure, is to continue to have faith in God, and to believe that not even human sin and madness can ultimately defeat His purpose of love for the world. So far as I have been able to think at all in the confusion of these terrible days, it seems to me that the service which the Continuation Committee may render at the present time is to seek to learn the purpose of God in what for the moment seems almost complete darkness, and to help the friends of missions throughout the world to lay to heart the lessons which He would teach.

I am sure that the first feeling in all our hearts must be one of penitence and contrition. We need not trouble about the distribution of responsibility. We need to get behind that to the fundamental fact that Christian Europe has departed so far from God and rejected so completely the rule of Christ that a catastrophe of this kind is possible. It may be that in God's sight the Christian nations were spiritually incapable of the tasks awaiting them in the non-Christian world, and that they had to be purified by the discipline of suffering. Everything will be lost if we fail in deep humility to learn the lessons which God desires to teach the Church. Unless we see how utterly God has been forgotten and denied in national life, nothing lies before us but a calamity which will set back the progress of the world for generations. If that lesson can be learned, there may come to the Church a moral rebirth and a fresh accession of moral energy which will outweigh the diminution of material resources which will be inevitable. It is on this thought, I believe, that we must try to focus the attention of Christian people.

We must also seek earnestly to maintain our faith in God's purpose, in which He taught us to believe at the Edinburgh Conference. It may have to be worked out more slowly than we thought, and it will certainly have to be worked out by far other ways than we had expected. We must not allow ourselves to think, however, that even so great a crime and folly as we are now witnessing can ultimately defeat His plans, if He can find men who will dare to believe in Him. It is certain, however, that so overwhelming a catastrophe cannot leave us where we were. If the missionary societies set themselves only to make the necessary adjustments on the plane of spiritual experience on which we are at present, nothing great can come out of it. We need to bow in deep humility before God, beseeching Him to show us things of which we had never dreamed, and to make us willing to be led along paths of which at present we have no conception. This surely is something which we must seek for ourselves, and endeavour to help others to seek.

Another thought that is much in our minds is that we must strive, even in this confusion of national interest, to maintain the international fellowship and love which we began to learn at Edinburgh. I have written personal letters of loving sympathy to our brethren on the continent, though I am doubtful whether those addressed to Germany will reach their destination.

Maclennan and I thought it right at once to issue a special number of the Paper of Intercession. I am sure that we ought not to lose a day in seeking to take a fresh hold of the things that God has taught us through the Edinburgh Conference: otherwise we may be swept away by the tide of antagonistic influences which is surging around us. I hope you will approve of what we have done . . .

The letter went on to deal with a number of immediate and practical issues being dealt with by Oldham and Maclennan, and concluded:

> I do not know how the events of the past few days will present themselves to your eyes in America. The universal feeling in this country is, I think, that our statesmen made every possible effort to maintain peace. Things have been so ordered that even the most ardent friends of peace are convinced that war has been inevitable in the defence of our vital interests and of international morality. The German treatment of Belgium has removed the last questions that existed, and the nation is united as it has never been before. I am glad to say that, on the whole, there is a remarkable absence of a jingo spirit and of feelings of bitterness and hatred. Many of us feel and pray as keenly for Germany as for our own land. Every nation in the world will suffer terribly from this catastrophe, but what the German people may have to bear in suffering and anxiety is almost unthinkable.
>
> May God cause light to arise in the darkness!

Some of the noble public sentiments with which Oldham identifies himself were, to say the least, put under severe strain as the war unfolded in unforeseen length and bitterness over the next four years. But this letter is not only remarkable: it is arguably the *most* remarkable Oldham ever wrote. The maturity of its grasp of both the immediate situation and its long-term consequences, and its discernment of priorities for the international missionary movement, all held within a deep theological discernment, make it a *locus classicus* of 20th-century prophecy.

Two days later, on 7 August, Oldham and Maclennan met in London with the hastily assembled committee of the Conference of Missionary Societies in Britain and Ireland (CMSBI). Much time was spent in prayer,[4] and two vital decisions were taken: the Continuation Committee meeting was postponed indefinitely, and Oldham and Maclennan offered their services to the CMSBI. Their offer was accepted and they became in effect joint secretaries of the organization. Mott was cabled on these decisions. Three days later came Mott's cable in reply, approving the action taken, and also announcing his hope still to travel to Europe in September.

The decision to fuse the secretaryship of the Continuation Committee with that of the CMSBI was intended not only as a means of consolidating resources under the likely exigencies of wartime. It was apparent, right from the beginning of the conflict, that the Continuation Committee could not hope to function as it had done so far. In order to carry out its aims, Oldham would need a base, of a different order but still carrying some weight with the missionary bodies. Meanwhile it was also apparent that Mott, being a citizen of the neutral United States, would be in a specially advantageous position of leadership, not least through networks of the YMCA and WSCF. The meeting in London on 7 August had recognized that the French and Dutch committees just would not have the resources available. Effectively, much of the work of the Continuation Committee was now to pass to the CMSBI and to the Foreign Missions Conference in the USA. Moreover, the British committee felt that all continental-based missionary work – including the German – would now be

[4] As stressed in letter of 5 Aug. 1914.

in imminent danger of collapse, and resolved to raise £20,000 – £25,000 as a "practical demonstration of the reality of Christian love and of its power to transcend national differences". Such was the strength of the feeling of Christian solidarity, even with the German mission bodies, at this early stage. The same attitude informed Oldham's letter of 28 August to Mott: "Each day that passes makes me feel more strongly that we have no time to lose in giving help to German missions. I think that probably already many of their missionaries must be in distress."

To such as Oldham, who in addition to his involvement with the international Christian scene had actually spent time in and learned much from Germany as a student, the pain of August 1914 was doubly great. He knew too much, and loved too much, of that country's great cultural heritage to be swept along with the tide of demonizing hatred of everything German which engulfed so much of the secular, and religious, press in the first autumn of the war. At the same time, he humbly and honestly believed that Britain had been left with no alternative but to go to war in fidelity to treaty obligations and in defence of the rights of small nations such as Belgium. It was a position he held with sadness and without rancour, though he was stirred to the depths by the evidence of a new-found unity and solidarity throughout British society. Oldham thus belonged to that sector of Christian opinion, along with such as William Temple and P.T. Forsyth, who believed that the war was a judgment upon all European society yet had to be seen through for the sake of justice. It was a position equally distinct from, on the one hand, the religious jingoism which saw the Kaiser as the sole anti-Christ; and on the other, the pacifism which saw all war, this no less than others, as inherently wrong and outcast to the Christian conscience. Each extreme could be as self-righteous as the other.

As editor of the *IRM*, Oldham had a printer's deadline to meet for the October issue, and decided to write an introductory article on "The War and Missions", feeling that the first issue of the *Review* to appear in wartime could hardly *not* carry any comment on what was now the burning issue of the hour. The article is basically a manifesto for recognizing the great crisis now facing the cause of world missions and their unity, and at the same time a call for a renewed faith in the long-term purposes of God: "The disaster may be in part retrieved; in the mercy of God good may be brought out of evil. But it belongs to the moral government of the world that men shall reap what they have sown. Europe cannot expect to escape the consequences of its sin." As to the root causes of the war, Oldham goes deep and wide:

> It is the product of a false and unchristian conception of the relations of men to one another. Of this conception the antagonisms of the western nations are only one expression. The same wrong attitude is seen in the racial prejudice and hatred which is one of the most sinister features of our time. It expresses itself in the industrial warfare and class alienation that disturb the life of all western nations. The whole commercial system of the West is based largely on the principle of securing advantages at the cost of some one else; and it is noteworthy that conflicting commercial interests have been one of the chief influences that have fostered national antagonisms.

The war thus sounds a call for repentance, not least to the church itself which might be inspired by the spectacle of new national unities to seek its own true unity. "For the present the struggle for national existence absorbs all thoughts; but it is not too soon to think what new edifice of ideas and hopes may be built on the ruins of the old."[5] The great task seen at Edinburgh may still be pursued, based on hope in God.

As with his letter to Mott of 5 August, this was a notable attempt to do full justice to the passions aroused by the conflict, yet maintaining an overarching perspective from the world missionary situation. His text is dated 8 September. He barely had time to inform Mott and some other members of the Continuation Committee. Mott and the American committee by cable counselled caution and asked that the article be deferred, but by then it was going through the press. Oldham was relieved and encouraged, especially, that Friedrich Würz of the Basel Mission (an agency of German as well as Swiss churches) and Karl Fries of Sweden were warmly approving. Oldham had clearly established his credentials as one able to speak, albeit in Britain, from a truly international position.

By the time the October *IRM* appeared, however, another critical development had taken place on the ecumenical scene. It was just after Oldham completed his article that there arrived in Britain and other countries the "Appeal to Evangelical Christians Abroad", signed by a large number of German Protestant church leaders, theologians and missionary representatives. It was a pained response to the widespread condemnation of Germany's part in starting hostilities – "a systematic network of lies, controlling the international telegraph service, is endeavouring in other lands to cast upon our people and its Government the guilt for the outbreak of this war, and has dared to dispute the inner right of us and our Empire to invoke the assistance of God". Germany had gone to war only as a desperate measure to defend her frontiers and land "from being ravaged by Asiatic barbarism".[6] In a clear reference to Britain it lamented that Germany's adversaries had then been joined "by those who by blood and history and faith are our brothers, with whom we felt ourselves in the common world-task more closely bound than with almost any other nation". It expressed horror at "unnameable" crimes committed against Germans living peaceably abroad, at the Tsar's proclamation of the war as a campaign against Teutonism and Protestantism, and at the involvement of "heathen Japan ... under the pretext of an alliance". Above all, the statement recoiled at the prospect of what the conflict would mean for missionary work:

> The mission fields which the World Missionary Conference in Edinburgh indicated as the most important in the present day – mid-Africa with its rivalry between Christendom and Islam for the black races, and eastern Asia remoulding its life – are

[5] "The War and Missions", pp.626, 630f., 634.
[6] *The Times*, 30 Sept. 1914.

now becoming the scenes of embittered struggles between peoples who bore in a special degree the responsibility for the fulfilment of the Great Commission in these lands.

Such celebrated names as professors Adolf Harnack and Adolf Deissman, and court-chaplain Ernst Dryander, were among the signatories. But, no less significantly, so also were those of leading figures in missions, including Julius Richter (a vice-chairman of the Edinburgh Continuation Committee) and Karl Axenfeld, secretary of the *Ausschuss.* In fact it emerged that Axenfeld was the main drafter, and that the whole initiative had indeed been prompted by the missionary leaders. (Moreover, it was the Edinburgh conference which the statement highlighted as the international point of reference, not the various peace movements which had been active since about 1908 and which at Constance, on the very eve of war, had set up the World Alliance for Promoting International Friendship through the Churches.)

Oldham's initial reaction to the Appeal verged on the indifferent. "It is an unfortunate document," he wrote to Mott on 15 September, "but I do not think it will do any real harm in this country, as people are inclined to treat it with good-humoured toleration." A more serious view was taken in Lambeth Palace. Archbishop Randall Davidson invited a small group, including Armitage Robinson (dean of Wells), Neville Talbot (bishop of Winchester), Scott Lidgett, W.H. Dickinson and Sir Claud Schuster, to meet with him on 11 September. Oldham was also invited, probably at the suggestion of Neville Talbot, and decided to attend. Oldham's own account of the meeting is vivid and revealing, and on several counts merits quoting:

> So far as I can see, the two largest problems immediately before us after the close of the war will be, how to save German missionary work from disaster, and how to keep German Christians within the international fellowship . . . After some discussion, the Archbishop stated his view of what should be said, and it met with so much approval from the others present, that he was asked to write it out at once . . . The result can probably best be described in the comment of the Bishop of Winchester, that it was "spirited". It is not what I should have written, but I am not sure that in the circumstances, it is not better to have something vigorous. The German mind at present appears to be absolutely closed to reason, and soft words would be thrown away. It will perhaps do no harm for them to know what Christian people in Great Britain feel about the war . . . I had to return to Edinburgh last night. I left one or two suggestions which, if they are accepted, will have the effect of adding to the friendliness of the document without weakening its "spirit".[7]

The statement was not in fact all the Archbishop's own work. As George Bell's account[8] makes clear, a central section dealing with the technicalities and history of the diplomatic efforts to prevent the war, and especially Britain's role

[7] JHO letter to Mott 15 Sept. 1914 [OA].

[8] See G.K.A. Bell, *Randall Davidson: Archbishop of Canterbury*, Vol. II, Oxford, Oxford Univ. Press, 1935, pp.740–43.

in these, had been drafted elsewhere (quite possibly by Bell himself, on the basis of Foreign Office briefing). Davidson's draft first spoke of the high regard with which the German signatories were held in British circles, especially in light of the Edinburgh conference experience. It then went on to express "amazement" that the signatories should "commit themselves to a statement of the political causes of the war, which departs so strangely from what seem to us to be the plain facts of this grave hour in European history . . ." It could only be supposed that the men who signed it were unaware of the obligations to which Britain was bound, and the story of the negotiations. "A violation of such promises on our part would have been the basest perfidy." Then towards the conclusion comes the heartfelt declaration:

> God knows what it means for us to be separated for a time by this great war from many with whom it has been our privilege – with whom we hope it will be our privilege again – to work for the setting forward of the Christian message among men. We unite wholeheartedly with our German brethren in deploring the disastrous consequences of the war, and in particular, its effect in diverting the energies and resources of the Christian nations from the great constructive tasks to which they were providentially called on behalf of the peoples of Asia and Africa.
>
> But there must be no mistake about our own position. Eagerly desirous of peace, foremost to the best of our power in furthering it, keen especially to promote the close fellowship of Germany and England, we have nevertheless been driven to declare that dear to us as peace is, the principles of truth and honour are yet more dear . . .

What cannot be known at this distance of time is whether the final version of the reply includes any of Oldham's suggestions for increasing its "friendliness", nor indeed what these suggestions were. Oldham's caution is shown in two further paragraphs of his account to Mott:

> I raised the question whether, in view of the obvious fact that the initiative in the German letter came from the missionary societies, the missionary societies should not be associated with the reply. The suggestion did not meet with much favour, the general view being that the signatures should be confined to the ecclesiastical big guns. I did not press the suggestion, as I thought that on the whole it might be better for our relations after the war if the missionary societies in Great Britain were to keep their hands free, so that when the proper time comes, they can take action on their own lines.
>
> The Archbishop asked if I would sign, but I told him that, as Secretary of an International Committee, I felt it my duty to keep out of anything that was exclusively British.

The statement eventually received forty-two signatories and, as with the German Appeal itself, received much publicity in the national and religious press. As well as the two archbishops, several other bishops (including London and Winchester) and prominent deans and professors, it was endorsed by many well-known Free Church leaders. The general reservation about missionary involvement notwithstanding, Eugene Stock of the Church Missionary Society also signed.

Was it just that Oldham was in two minds about the whole exercise? Perhaps, but more likely, as he stated to Mott earlier in his letter, he was primarily anxious to know just what went on in framing the reply, and to be on stand-by in case any disproportionately damaging response was being mooted. He had done enough to be helpful in the drafting – and enough to ensure he was not publicly identified with it in a way that might be obstructive to eventual relations with the Germans. And the fact that he had also stated to Mott his over-riding concerns for the protection of German missions and the keeping of the Germans within international Christian fellowship, made clear the solid grounds for this diplomatic tact.

To Mott himself, his trusted friend, Oldham could in any case make clear that he personally accepted the substance of the archbishop's reply, and that he found the present German temper totally irrational, especially in its anti-Britishness:

> The Christian leaders are among the most extreme Jingoes, and will not hear or speak of any fellowship with British Christians until the British Empire has been destroyed. I have a letter from one of my closest friends among the missionary leaders in Germany who says that, while nothing will affect his love for me personally, German Christians will refuse from henceforth any suggestion of common prayer from or with Christians in England. They deny absolutely the right of England to have any part or lot in missionary work.

Oldham, for his part, urged upon Mott that whenever the opportunity might arise, he should "assure our German brethren that in this office we strive to keep constantly before us the fact that we are the secretaries of an international committee, and that in everything which is done from this centre we are striving to preserve the strictest neutrality". That opportunity came sooner than Oldham expected. On 2 October he learnt by cable that Mott was on board the *Nieuw Amsterdam*, heading for Europe. Oldham wrote to await his arrival in Holland, and assured Mott of the prayers of friends in Britain as he visited Germany.[9]

From this point on, for the sake of clarity the story of Oldham's ecumenical work during 1914–18 is best separated into four concurrent strands. Each of them relates to a theme or an issue with which we have already seen him engaging, in one form or another, in the first two months of war. These are: his own theological reflections on the war and its significance for the world missionary movement; the dialogue with the German missionary leaders; the present difficulties and future prospects of German missions; and the future of the Continuation Committee itself. By the time Mott was on the seas, these had clearly emerged as the main challenges, and they were to preoccupy Oldham and his colleagues until, over four years later, an exhausted Europe greeted the Armistice.

[9] JHO letter to Mott 2 Oct. 1914 [OA].

## Reflection on war, gospel and missions

In his introductory article in the October 1914 *IRM* "The War and Missions", Oldham had been able to do little more than say that the depth of the crisis facing world mission had to be faced, and could be faced with a deepened and renewed faith in God. That in itself was worth saying just then, and many people welcomed it. Moreover, he offered not just commonplace piety. He had also been able to put down a marker that what the war was revealing was not just the evil mind of any one particular nation and its rulers, but rather a deep malaise infecting the whole of European society, and seen not least in economic exploitation and racial antagonism. The article presaged a significant way of combining a profound spirituality with a determination to widen the vision and sharpen the analysis of what was going on in the world.

Of course, the outbreak of war was marked not only by artillery barrages but by an almost deafening cacophony, from all quarters, militarist to pacifist, of voices declaiming on what was wrong with the world and what must be put right, and how. Oldham himself for a time turned to an interest in post-war reconstruction, as he conveyed in a letter to Mott on 26 January 1915. He was convinced that what was needed was "to move towards a state of society in which the conception of brotherhood, fellowship and cooperation fills a much larger place than it does at present". At the same time, he was worried that pure idealism and sentiment would not wash with the politicians who would actually be responsible for a post-war settlement. He was especially anxious that the demand for "disarmament" would count for little: "There is no movement that has suffered more from sentiment and lack of contact with actuality than the peace movement, and I think there is real ground for fearing lest the Christian churches lose the present opportunity by failure to recognize the essential elements of the situation." More will be achieved by concentrating on some definite, constructive policy: "to try to bring about a concert or league of the nations to defend one another against aggression from any quarter" – an idea being advocated for example by Norman Angell. Oldham, however, seems not to have pursued this particular idea any further. Other concerns, especially on the role of the churches, took its place.

Oldham's remarks about the impracticality of much of the peace movement probably stemmed from his experience during the first nine months or so of the war. He gravitated towards a small group centred around William Temple, then rector of St James', Piccadilly, which shared a concern both to deepen and moderate public discussion of the war, its causes, the proper Christian response and the likely needs of reconstruction afterwards. Its particular aim was to produce a series of pamphlets, *Papers for War-time*, and included Arthur Clutton Brock, B.H. Streeter, J. Arthur Thomson and – for a while – some pacifists like Henry Hodgkin, the Quaker medical missionary who was also a member of the Edinburgh Continuation Committee. Temple was editor of the series and wrote the first pamphlet. Problems arose, however, on reaching unanimity between the pacifist and non-pacifist members of the group. In late November

1914 the pacifists, mainly Quakers, amicably withdrew in order to allow both main Christian positions to be advocated more freely. The pacifists were mainly to give their energies to the Fellowship of Reconciliation, founded at Cambridge in January 1915. Oldham was party to the discussions and welcomed this development which at least enabled the *Papers for War-time* core group to clarify its ends, and the basis on which the pamphlets were published, as follows:

1) that Great Britain was in August morally bound to declare war and is no less bound to carry the war to a decisive issue;
2) that the War is none the less an outcome and a revelation of the un-Christian principles which have dominated the life of Western Christendom and of which both the Church and the nations have need to repent;
3) that followers of Christ, as members of the Church, are linked to one another in a fellowship which transcends all divisions of nationality or race;
4) that the Christian duties of love and forgiveness are as binding in time of war as in time of peace;
5) that Christians are bound to recognize the insufficiency of mere compulsion for overcoming evil, and to place supreme reliance upon spiritual forces and in particular upon the power and method of the Cross;
6) that only in proportion as Christian principles dictate the terms of settlement will a real and lasting peace be secured;
7) that it is the duty of the Church to make an altogether new effort and apply to all the relations of life its own positive ideal of brotherhood and fellowship;
8) that with God all things are possible.[10]

Oldham himself wrote two of the pamphlets. The first, written in late 1914 and appearing anonymously, was essentially an exposition of the above programme of the group and entitled "The Witness of the Church in the Present Crisis". The second, "The Church the Hope of the Future" was the thirty-sixth and last in the series, written in the early summer of 1915 and appearing over his own name. In it, Oldham allows himself to speak more openly in condemnation of Germany than at any time before or subsequently, and to Mott (and indeed to one or two of his German friends) he confided the reason he had written "in a hot fit" which he subsequently regretted: the sinking of the *Lusitania* on 7 May, with heavy loss of civilian life (including many Americans), had shocked him, as it did so many others, as a wilful, callous act of barbarity; likewise the use of asphyxiating gases by the Germans.[11] "The war", he writes in his paper, "was brought about by the temper, ambition and folly of Germany. But . . . it is not enough to know that Germany is responsible for the war. It is necessary to inquire further how Germany became what she is." Then follows a long exposition of his diagnosis that the war was but the culmination of selfish acquisitiveness infecting every part and every level of European society. Only a transformed church could redeem this fragmented

[10] This version is taken from that printed in the front of *The Church the Hope of the Future*, Papers for War-time, London: Oxford Univ. Press, 1915.

[11] JHO letter to Mott 30 July 1915 [OA].

and fragmenting social order. Again he returns to the importance of economic issues, and in one of his proposals for the future there are clearly seen emerging his later and dominant ideas on the role of the church, primarily through the laity, for transforming society:

> The existence within the State of a body of people whose entire energies are directed to the promotion of understanding and reconciliation would in itself be an enormous contribution to the health of the social organism ... It is not, of course, the business of the Church to frame political measures or economic theories. But behind political and economic questions there lie views of life with which the Church is very much concerned. If these are changed, the political and economic questions assume a new aspect ... It will not do for the Church to stand outside the organized life of the world and proclaim the Christian ideal. That life has to be brought into obedience to Christ, and this can be done only by Christian men taking the Christian ideal with them into the market-place and workshop and seeking to apply it to the social life around them. We need Christian thinkers who will approach political and economic questions with Christian presuppositions, and behind such men there must be a Church passionately concerned to see the Christian social ideal realized in practice and the will of God done on earth as it is in heaven.[12]

"The circulation of the pamphlets was never a large one; but the names of the writers ... secured their welcome among cultured Christians."[13] It is tempting to see in *Papers for War-time* the precursor of Oldham's own much more effective project in the next war, *The Christian News-Letter*. Oldham seems not to have regretted the ending of the series, and in any case he was soon to be wholly engaged in a much more extensive piece of writing which both took up and went far beyond his pamphleteering pieces. In October 1915 he was asked by the United Council for Missionary Education if he would write a book on missions in the light of the war. Excited yet daunted by the prospect, he wrote to Mott that the request chimed in with his own feeling of the past year that "some restatement of missionary aims and principles is essential if the Church is to maintain its missionary activities after the war".[14] But Oldham, typically, did not enter on the task lightly. He sought Mott's approval first, for it would mean a considerable allocation of his time and he was, after all, not paid to be a scholar but the servant of the Continuation Committee. It would also prevent him from fulfilling his hopes of making a visit to America the following summer. But the work would serve the proposes of the Continuation Committee and of the *IRM* – as well as clarifying his own mind on the overall objectives of the missionary movement in the future.

Oldham received all the support and encouragement he asked for, and for the next few months his energies were devoted to writing *The World and the Gospel*. It appeared, published by the United Council for Missionary Education, in July 1916, that month of unprecedented hopes and grief in Britain

[12] *The Church the Hope of the Future*, pp.3f., 14f.
[13] F.A. Iremonger, *William Temple. Archbishop of Canterbury*, Oxford, Oxford Univ. Press, 1948, p.178.
[14] JHO letter to Mott 26 Oct. 1915 [OA].

as the battle of the Somme raged. "This book is not concerned with the war, though but for the war I do not think it could have been written as it is," said Oldham. Nor, as he acknowledged, could it have been written but for his editorship of the *IRM* which throughout the war years continued to harvest the results of missionary research and thinking from many parts of the world.[15]

*The World and the Gospel* is an extraordinary book, ranging as it does in some 220 pages over theology, the situation in the worldwide mission fields, the state of the churches and society in the West, and the spiritual life – and all with a passion and vigour such as many had previously assumed could only come from John Mott. It can, in a real measure, be read as a reaffirmation of the Edinburgh conference vision for a world shaken by the war. Indeed, much of the book reiterates and carries forward the Edinburgh agenda and its methods of fact-finding, analysis and proposals for future action. At its core are surveys (and here the *IRM* was crucial) of the current scene in Asia and Africa (with special emphasis now on Islam). There are sections on the church in the mission field, and on the education of missionaries and of the whole church – the latter also containing a special chapter on inter-racial questions. The book opens, as would be expected, with the now familiar assertions of the war as a judgment, on the immediate responsibility of Germany but also the wider and deeper malaise of which that culpability was but one expression, and on the need to rediscover in the Christian gospel the resources for true human brotherhood and fellowship at every level of society.

But new elements in Oldham's thinking are also quite apparent. There is a greater recognition that human life throughout the world is becoming ever more interlinked and interdependent, and that much of social life is not just individual but corporate, and that ethical thinking must relate to collectivities:

> that large part of a man's life in which he acts not as an individual but as a member of a class, a business corporation, a trades union or a nation. Either this part of his life must be withdrawn from the control of Christ or it too must be consecrated, and the attempt must be made to apply the rule of Christ to the methods of industry and commerce and to national aims and policy. In the world as it now is we cannot be Christians in the full sense without setting ourselves to Christianize the social order.[16]

Still more to the point, reflecting on the widespread missionary experience that it is not what Christianity says it is but what it is actually seen to be doing that carries weight, Oldham states:

> The Christian protest against the unchristian forces in social and national life must be clearer, sharper and more patent than it has been in the past. It may be that Church as it was before the war could never have evangelized the world; that its witness had not the penetrating force necessary for so gigantic an undertaking; that before God could answer the prayers of His people some deep-seated evil had to be removed, however terrible the cost.

[15] In addition to the many specialist articles supplied by contributors, each January issue of *IRM* featured an article by Oldham himself, surveying trends in world missionary activity over the previous year.

[16] *The World and the Gospel*, p.15. Following quotations taken from pp.21, 21f., 22, 207, 209, 211 and 220.

This is arguably the most telling passage in the whole book, for it is in effect putting the severest question mark against the whole Western-led world missionary movement – including Edinburgh 1910 – and its assumptions hitherto. The real issues for the missionary movement, Oldham is virtually saying, begin at home, with the Western church in Western society; and to make this point explicit, in an extended footnote he refers to the alarming results of recent surveys into child poverty in England, commenting: "It may be doubted . . . whether a Church that was willing to tolerate a state of things that denied to a large section of our population the elementary conditions of health and happiness possessed the moral passion which would enable it to evangelize the world."

Not that Oldham was now advocating the diversion of the church "from its proper religious mission to projects of social and political reform, or that its primary concern is the amelioration of the conditions of our earthly existence". Quite the opposite: "The greatest need of our age is a deepened sense of the living reality and transcendent majesty of God." It is through faith in the gospel, expounded at great length by Oldham as centred on forgiveness and new life in Christ, that the means of reconciliation and new fellowship with God and with others is found, and the moral passion kindled to restore a broken world. The conclusion of the book is a trenchant appeal for a new spirituality in which faith and prayer are linked to action in society. To serve God in government or commerce can be as clear a call of God as any other vocation, "for the secular life is also God's, and if He is to be acknowledged and honoured in it, as he should be, His servants must be in the heart of it, meeting its difficulties, battling with its evils, bearing witness to His truth, proving that this earthly life is not sufficient in itself but has its meaning in that which lies beyond and above it". Moreover, if this is so, then because life has become so complex and organized, Christians belonging to the same profession need to meet together to learn how the Christian spirit should be expressed in their work:

> Why should there not be federations of Christian employers of labour to consider how industry can be conducted so as to promote the health and happiness of all engaged in it, and unions of Christian workmen for the purpose of finding out how labour can best promote the interests of the community? More important still, why should not employers and leaders of labour meet in frank conference in order that through prayer and the guidance of their common Master they may come to understand one another's point of view and to realize their fellowship in a common service?

No calling is secular, states Oldham: all lay people and professionals in their daily work need upholding by the prayers and fellowship of the church. "In a far greater degree than has yet been attempted, the Church must learn to hallow the secular life by shedding on its struggles and difficulties the light and healing of God's love." For that, the church must discover for itself what fellowship means, in prayer and holy communion. On the concluding pages of the book are found what can be regarded as the charter for the rest of Oldham's life work:

> What we need is to make larger ventures. God does not call us to withdraw from the world, but believing in Him and abiding in Him to press into its living heart, to open our eyes to all its truth, to sound the depths of its need and to meet and overcome its sin. Only in doing this can we know what the love of God is . . . The real life of the world alone can reveal its meaning. The deep in God's world answers to the deep in the heart of God. It is only by attempting to apply the law of Christ to the whole of our social and national life and in seeking to evangelize the whole world that we shall become rooted and grounded in love . . . and be filled with the entire fullness of God.

Kathleen Bliss summarizes the public impact of *The World and the Gospel*: "Published in 1916 at the darkest period of the first world war, it had the effect of lifting the sights of Christians beyond the horrors of the present to a renewed faith in God's call to mission."[17] Twenty-thousand copies were sold in Britain alone. Quite apart from its influence, from the biographical point of view it is a work of immense significance for an understanding of Oldham's lifelong career and the development of his theology. If a decisive point is to be located on the long trajectory he pursued from being a Keswick evangelical and student volunteer to organizing the research for the 1937 Oxford Life and Work conference and founding the Christian Frontier Council, it is surely here. He had been asked to write a book on the world missionary enterprise in the light of the war: he did so, but in the course of it moved to a new conception of mission itself. Crucial for him was the realization, due to the war, that the "Christian-nation" idea of the West was bankrupt, and that Western Christianity itself – that which was sending missionaries to the "mission fields" in their thousands – had all but lost its credibility and its moral authority for engaging in such an enterprise. The missionary task of evangelizing the whole world remained, and is asserted in *The World and the Gospel* as vigorously as ever. But what it *means* to evangelize is to be learned in the daily, secular life of Western society, in the call to Christianize social structures and economic life as much as to call individuals to personal faith. Virtually all Oldham's later emphases on mission, above all the focus on the laity in their secular vocations as the main agents of that mission, are to be found here. When he spoke, as he often did during 1914–18, about God being able to bring good out of evil, even out of the war, he was speaking not least of his own personal experience of a deepened and renewed perception of faith and mission.

## "Positive neutrality"? Dialogue with the Germans

Oldham had stated to Mott early in the war that one of his over-riding aims as secretary of the Continuation Committee would be to maintain, or restore as necessary, the relationships with the German missions within the international Christian fellowship. We have seen how, while personally supportive of the reply to the German "Appeal to Evangelical Christians Abroad" in September

[17] K. Bliss, "The Legacy of J.H. Oldham", *International Bulletin of Missionary Research*, Jan. 1984, p.20.

1914, he had declined to sign it in order to protect his distinctive role as servant of an international, as opposed to a British, committee. To maintain contact with the German partners on the Continuation Committee, and other mission representatives within the enemy nation, was of course not easy. But communication, if slow, was possible via colleagues in neutral countries, especially Scandinavia and the United States, but perhaps above all Switzerland – Friedrich Würz, director of the Basel Mission which was a major agency of the Lutheran and Reformed churches throughout the continent, was to be a crucial go-between and was himself a representative of the German viewpoint. The real problem was not correspondence, but mutual understanding. As had already emerged in September 1914 with the German Appeal and the British reply, Christian leaders in both nations were accepting of their respective governments' accounts of responsibility for the war, and heavily conditioned by their own national and patriotic perspectives. Oldham, very early in the war, had received from one German colleague (probably Axenfeld or Würz) both an assurance of personal regard and an outburst of bitter denunciation of the British attitude, political and Christian.

Oldham knew that only direct, personal contact with such colleagues could hope to counteract these feelings – yet this was impossible for the time being as far as he himself was concerned. He therefore greeted John Mott's arrival at the beginning of October 1914 with immense relief and hope. In fact, though the *Nieuw Amsterdam* was bound for Rotterdam it was briefly detained by the British navy at Plymouth on suspicion of carrying contraband, enabling a hurried visit by Mott to London.[18] Mott hastily travelled through Holland to Germany. He had much to do on behalf of the WSCF and YMCA, and had many meetings in Berlin with leading church officials, theologians and mission representatives including Julius Richter, Karl Axenfeld and Würz from Basel. He experienced at first hand the intensely nationalist emotions, and was able to communicate Oldham's desire for immediate aid to be given to German missions. For their part, the Germans conveyed a deep appreciation for his and Oldham's declarations of a neutral stance as far as the Continuation Committee was concerned. Grief for the first casualties among the German families he visited – and among the membership of the German SCM – also made its impact on Mott, as did the searing sight of the scores of wounded in a hospital to which he was taken. He returned to England for two weeks, reporting fully to Oldham and others, and then visited France before returning home to the United States.

The partnership between Oldham and Mott now grew to be important as never before, marked by the unceasing exchange of letters and cables, weekly or even more frequently, across the Atlantic. Together they constituted "the remnant-symbol" of the Continuation Committee.[19] They knew they would be carefully watched, especially on the German side. Each had to trust,

[18] See Hopkins.
[19] *Ibid.*, p.447.

encourage and be prepared at times tactfully to warn the other about how their actions might be seen and interpreted. They generally took each other's advice. In December 1915, for example, in conversation with Henry Hodgkin, Oldham learnt that Mott had become a member of the Fellowship of Reconciliation. Hodgkin, of course, was gratified at such a weighty recruit for the "peace" cause, and for a day or two Oldham thought little about it, as being Mott's own affair. However, on 13 December he wrote to Mott saying that the news had created "an unfortunate impression" wherever it had become known:

> The Fellowship of Reconciliation is regarded by those who do not belong to it as being in effect a "stop the war" organization. Hodgkin denies that this is so, but as no-one who is in favour of prosecuting the war would be allowed to join, it is difficult to see how it can be regarded as anything else. Moreover, it is in its origin a definitely British organization, and has practically no members in Germany and Austria. The consequence is that most people are inclined to interpret your having given your influential support to this organization as putting yourself on the side of the very small minority of Christian people in England who desire peace at any price.[20]

He continues shortly after:

> The word "reconciliation" more nearly than any other sums up what I most desire and hope for . . . Hodgkin is thinking primarily of love for the Germans, who are for the time being our enemies. Others of us feel that love demands consideration for the countless generations yet unborn and for those great peoples of the East who are struggling into a new and unknown future.

Probably, as Hopkins says, Mott and Oldham had a talk about it during his next visit to Britain in the summer of 1916. At any rate, Mott seems to have quietly withdrawn from the organization some time that year. Oldham for his part was just as willing to seek counsel from Mott. As we have seen, Oldham at first wondered whether in his paper "The Church the Hope of the Future" he had expressed himself too strongly on German culpability, overstepping the bounds of his international role, and even wrote to Mott on 30 July offering his resignation. Mott was evidently not interested in such a possibility.

In this same letter, Oldham speaks of the need for a "positive neutrality" – "the expression of a strong love which includes all within its sweep", "an ever-deepening willingness to serve all men, to understand their point of view and to put away as far as we can all barriers between us and them". In this he sees the hope of rebuilding the international ideal. By implication, he evidently feels, the Fellowship of Reconciliation line was effectively a *disengaged* neutrality which by taking an absolutist moral stance against war made it difficult for its adherents really to understand the underlying passions both motivating and aroused by the conflict. By means of a "positive neutrality" Oldham sought to make space for sharply conflicting passions and perspectives within an overall conviction that *final* truth lies in the love of God for all, rather than in the

[20] JHO letter to Mott 13 Dec. 1914 [OA].

here-and-now convictions of any one party (including the pacifist). Naturally, the stance of the two-men "remnant symbol" of the Continuation Committee could be more obviously seen to be neutral so long as Mott's country remained neutral, enabling his freedom of access to all belligerent parties. As we shall see, once that ceased with the United States' entry into the war in 1917 such a self-presentation became far more difficult.

Though he was to make one, or possibly two, efforts to meet some of the German mission leaders on neutral territory, for the duration of the war Oldham's own dialogue with such people could only be by letter. The material that has survived is mainly from two periods: roughly the first six or seven months of the war, and then from about mid-1917 to late 1918. It would be presumptuous to conclude that there had not been any correspondence in the intervening two years or so, but there were special factors rendering contacts urgently necessary in the two periods in question. It should also be borne in mind that throughout the war, one of the burning issues on the German side was the fate of the German missions in British territories, or in territories that had fallen to British forces, in Africa and Asia, and recurs persistently in the Oldham–German exchanges. It is, however, a matter of such importance and complexity that it merits treatment in its own right and is therefore dealt with mainly in the next section of this chapter.

In the first period, from the start of the war to early 1915, there was naturally a deep anxiety both in Germany and in Oldham's office to know one another's minds. Julius Richter wrote to Oldham on 9 November 1914 on behalf of the German *Ausschuss* lamenting the bitterness of the war but speaking with deep and warm affection towards Oldham himself, and protesting about the plight of the German missions. In his reply of 9 November, Oldham declared that both he and Kenneth Maclennan, as far as their work for the Continuation Committee was concerned, would remain emphatically neutral:

> This means that I regard myself as being as much the servant of German missions as those of any other country and as bound to further their interests as far as may lie in my power. It also means that I shall not in any public utterance, even apart from my work, say or write anything directed against Germany ... It will be our constant endeavour in everything that is done from this office to work in a region which is above and beyond the antagonisms of this present war.

At the same time, Oldham wished there to be no illusions on the German side that the mass of Christians in Britain, himself included, believed that Britain had any alternative but to fight and that the cause was just. While it may be thought that two contradictory loyalties are being expressed here, "I know it is possible for I find them in my own heart. It is this that occasions the deepest pain of the present trial. If I ever feel that wholehearted loyalty to the Church of Christ becomes impossible, I shall at once resign my office." It was clearly this sentiment which very nearly did lead to his resignation in 1915 following "The Church the Hope of the Future" when for a time at least he *did* feel he had committed himself to an utterance "directed against Germany".

Richter and his colleagues were greatly assured by Oldham's letter[21] and expressed appreciation. But by December feelings among Christians generally, in both countries, were hardening. In the same letter Richter objected strongly to a sermon by Alexander Whyte, principal of New College, Edinburgh, versions of which had reached Germany. Oldham was equally depressed by a recent meeting of the Committee on Christian Literature, at which a representative of the Tract Society maintained "that for the present any talk of cooperation with Germany was impossible, because it could not be supposed or admitted that their Christianity was the same kind of thing as ours, and that it was necessary for Christian people here publicly to dissociate themselves from German Christianity". Personally, Oldham told Mott, "I am convinced that the international outlook has the truth on its side and is bound to win in the end". For the moment it was fraught with dangers and difficulties, not least the risk that in both Germany and Britain "very little can be said without the risk of doing more harm than good". By the same post as Richter's letter came "a very pessimistic" one from Würz "who says that the feeling of bitterness in Germany against England is increasing in intensity". Further evidence of this was supplied by an article by Richter himself which appeared in the German mission journal and arrived on Oldham's desk on new year's eve. Oldham was alarmed by its tone, coming as it did from the vice-chairman of the Continuation Committee, and he feared a disastrous effect on relationships if it became publicly known. By contrast the British members of the committee, Oldham judged, had been careful and guarded in their utterances, and "will expect their German brethren should come some way to meet them". The year therefore ended gloomily, but not without hope: "We are cast back upon God. Only His grace can save the situation". Nor was Oldham asking Mott to make direct representations to Germany – "We must attack the problem in other and more indirect ways."[22]

One such way, Oldham decided, might be for himself to meet with some of the Germans in a neutral country. In January 1915 he began to plan a visit to France for a "holiday", whence he would travel on to Switzerland, turning up in Basel to meet with Würz. He would let Würz know he was coming, not stating his real object but hoping that Würz would realize what was in his mind and invite some of the colleagues from inside Germany for a discreet and informal meeting.[23] For whatever reasons, the plan did not materialize. In fact Oldham never managed to travel abroad at all during the war. A further planned visit to France in December 1916 was prevented by the authorities: "A hitch arose in connection with my passport. Some difficulty was raised about my correspondence with German missions. I am taking steps to have any misunderstanding regarding my attitude to the war cleared up."[24] Nor would the pressures on his time, or his health, allow him the hoped-for visits to America.

[21] JHO letter to Mott 15 Dec. 1914 [OA].
[22] JHO letter to Mott 31 Dec. 1914 [OA].
[23] JHO letter to Mott 18 Jan. 1915 [OA].
[24] JHO letter to Jane L. Latham 11 Dec. 1916 [OA].

Oldham's wish to visit Basel was greatly stimulated by the fact that in January 1915 he received from Würz a collection of several recent articles by Germans on Britain's stance in the war, together with a long letter from Würz himself. Würz, among other things, accused British public attitudes of insincerity and hypocrisy – exaggerating for example the significance of Belgian neutrality – and vehemently repeating the German case and the Christian support for it. Oldham replied to Würz on 15 January, pleading that, as a starting-point, on both sides people should not impute the worst motives to the others, and should pause to consider why it was that people whom they knew to be *good* could be so sharply divergent in view. "If the German case were as wholly evil as the bulk of people in Great Britain think it is, men like you and Richter would not be able to give it your wholehearted support ... Similarly if the British case were only what most Germans conceive it to be, many whom you know personally in England would certainly not be among its supporters." Christian people in both Germany and England must acknowledge that in neither country did most people want the war. Every good Englishman, and every good German, knows that the country he loves is not as the prevailing enemy opinion pictures it – "Love is a surer guide to truth than hate. Many of us in this country are trying to think of the Germany that Germans love. Let Germans also try to think of the England which Englishmen love." Then there is the fact of a common experience of suffering. "The suffering through which German missionaries are passing, and the whole German people, touches me profoundly. One is able to know what it means because our own people are passing through similar sufferings." On the religious level, the proper response, on both sides and at every level, must be penitence, which in fact is already leading to a new realization:

> I cannot help thinking that the war is teaching us to draw a clearer distinction ... between the Church of Christ and what we have been accustomed to speak of as Christian civilization. We have assumed that we had "a Christian civilization" which was something we could proudly offer to the non-Christian world. God is showing us how rotten that civilization is. We shall need in the future to be more humble, to be more ready to take up the cross, follow Christ and bear His reproach among men.

Oldham wrote to Würz again on 27 January 1915 on the subject of German missions in India. Meanwhile there had arrived a long letter from Karl Axenfeld, pleading that German and British Christians help each other to reach "as correct and just a judgment as possible" on their respective attitudes to the war (he stated that every Sunday in the pulpit he was trying to preach against hatred of England), while also, as Würz had done, protesting about British "hypocrisy" and "insincerity". He also injected into his letter a full dose of standard Lutheran eschatology which saw the cause of universal peace as being realizable at the end-time, while in the here-and-now conflict was only to be expected and was containable only by the actions of the state, not well-meaning attempts to bring about peace through "progress". Oldham wrote a very lengthy reply on 11 March, more or less on the lines of his response to Würz, again pleading that good people on each side should try to appreciate why the others loved their country as they did. He was also frank in acknowledging that some of the charges Axenfeld made were fair:

> You refer in your letter to many foolish things that have been said by Christian people in England since the war began. The charge is only too true. But which of us at such a time as this is really in a normal state of mind? And able to speak with complete sanity and self-control? . . . Foolish and unjust things have been said also in Germany and have caused pain in this country. We need to be patient with each other in these days of strain and remember with humility how weak and pitiful a thing our common human nature is.

So that just acknowledgment might be done to Axenfeld's corresponding intention as a German, Oldham prepared a translation of Axenfeld's letter in the hope that it might be published as one of the *Papers for War-time.* William Temple was enthusiastic for the idea, even allowing for the likely hostile public response to those passages berating English hypocrisy.[25] In the end, Axenfeld declined to give permission on the quite understandable ground of the likely exposure to what would probably have been the even greater hostility in his own country.

So ended this first period of attempted dialogue. At least if there was still bafflement on both sides, there had been efforts at mutual listening and understanding. For his part, Oldham's voice was more than just that of sweet reason. He was calling for an increased awareness, on all sides, of how *un*reasonable all parties to a conflict are apt to be, and a recognition that for the present it was unwise to press for instant "agreements", or even to try to convince the other side of one's rightness. It was this awareness of the necessity for the provisional view, in preparation for a new order, which enabled Oldham even in these early exchanges to make one of his most prescient statements on behalf of the *Papers for War-time* group:

> It will be clear to you that these principles determine our view with regard to the treatment of Germany in the event of a victory for the Allies. It is quite clear to us that any attempt to humiliate Germany or to impose on her unjust and crushing conditions of peace or to restrict her natural and legitimate aspirations is simply to sow the seeds of another war.[26]

Difficult as these exchanges proved, those which took place more than two years later, from mid-1917, were far more fraught and marked a nearly complete breach in relationships with the German mission leaders. On 6 April 1917 the United States entered the war, largely in response to Germany's unrestricted submarine warfare. One of President Woodrow Wilson's first diplomatic moves was to appoint a mission to visit Russia in order to encourage the provisional government both in pursuing the path towards democracy and in continuing the military struggle against Germany. The mission was led by Elihu Root, a

[25] In Iremonger, p.178, the reference is probably to this proposal.
[26] JHO letter to Axenfeld 11 March 1915 [OA].

renowned senator, former secretary of state and Nobel peace prize winner. It comprised several other prominent figures from public life, politics and the military – and John R. Mott. Mott's wide international standing and experience had already been recognized by the White House (he served on a joint high commission with Mexico in 1916), and his personal knowledge of Russia was felt to make him outstandingly fitted for this particular task. He accepted the invitation with relatively little hesitation. When Oldham read of the Root mission (as it was called) in the British press he was no less enthusiastic and wrote to Mott on 11 June commending his participation in it.

The Root mission spent several weeks in Russia (travelling mainly in the unfortunate Tsar's royal train), visiting government officials in Petrograd and Moscow and representatives of other sectors in society. Mott, on behalf of the YMCA, solicited the support of military officials for work among troops, and also had a number of meetings with Orthodox church leaders. If the results of the mission in diplomatic terms were meagre, for relations between the ecumenical leadership in the allied countries and the German Protestants they were spectacularly damaging. Even when allowance is made for the wisdom of hindsight, it is hard to understand how both Mott and Oldham, both usually so perceptive, could apparently have been so disingenuous about how Mott's involvement in the diplomatic mission of a belligerent nation would be viewed in Germany. It is just possible that in Germany little notice might have been taken of the visit as a whole, had not some fortuitous items of extra publicity occurred. But occur they did. One day in Petrograd Mott addressed a congress of Cossack officers. He was fulsome in his praise of the Cossack tradition and spirit, and just as stirring was his endorsement of their current attitude: "Your insistence that the way to bring about the desired peace is by an immediate offensive has the true ring."[27] Newspapers around the world picked up the story, including the enthusiastic reception Mott received and the unanimous passing of a resolution in favour of prosecuting the war (though this had been prepared before the mission's arrival).

In a German newspaper in Shanghai, Mott was reported as saying that the Cossacks were the hope of Russia and the Germans the enemy of civilization and democracy. German missionaries in turn reported this in correspondence home. Mott was later to protest vehemently against this distortion of his remarks, and to assert that his part in the Root mission was strictly religious. He may indeed have been misreported in Shanghai, but as Howard Hopkins states, his mission was "[i]n both fact and implication ... hardly neutral" – and this speech least of all. The damage was therefore done, and within Germany there was a violent reaction.

This however was not the only sore point being felt in Germany. The whole question of the fate of their missions in British or British-conquered territories had been a running sore to the Germans from the start of the war. Into it was now being rubbed the salt of the likely future of these missions after the war. In

[27] Hopkins, p.499.

late May 1917, coincident with the general assemblies of the Church of Scotland and the United Free Church of Scotland, the *Glasgow Herald* and *The Times* carried reports that after the end of the war German missions would be excluded from all British territories for many years. The matter was referred to at both assemblies. At the Church of Scotland assembly J.N. Ogilvie, a member of the Continuation Committee, gave vent to some intemperate remarks on the difficulty of reconciling German atrocities with the claims of German missions to be agents of the gospel. At the Free Church gathering, Oldham himself spoke on the subject. He acknowledged that the majority of German missionaries had taken the German view of the war, and that where the repatriation or internment of German missionaries had taken place, it had been a political necessity in view of the state of public feeling and the known attitudes of many of the personnel concerned. He also stated that on the whole and until quite recently the work of German missionaries had been entirely free of political motives and had been carried on out of sincere love of Christ.

Reports of all these interventions reached Germany, and in July Oldham received a letter from Friedrich Würz objecting strongly to Mott's actions, to Ogilvie's utterance and indeed to Oldham's own speech. Oldham's reply, dated 14 July, in the first place betrays some embarrassment at what Ogilvie had said about the unacceptability of German missions, but preferred that Ogilvie should reply for himself and forwarded a copy of Würz's letter to him. Concerning Oldham's own speech, Würz had fastened onto the qualifications which Oldham had made – "on the whole" and "until quite recently" – regarding the purely spiritual and non-political motives of German missionaries. The report which reached Würz had in fact omitted the word "unquestionably" from this sentence. What Oldham had intended as an essentially positive affirmation about the genuinely spiritual motivation of German missions, Würz and others had read as denigration. Oldham in turn argued strongly to Würz that it would have been impossible for him to have made an absolutely unconditional statement about the purity of motives of *all* German missionaries – yet because he had not done so Würz had read him as taking an essentially hostile line.

Such was the difficulty of communication in a situation both passionate and increasingly weary after three years of war. Quotations – of varying accuracy – from the British church scene were being widely circulated in the German journals during the summer of 1917. Oldham begged Würz "not to be misled in regard to the attitude of responsible missionary circles in Great Britain by isolated utterances" – in contrast to the considered positions, for example, of the CMSBI standing committee. There are signs that Würz was in fact seeking to defend Oldham himself from the worst vituperation being hurled around in Germany – there was no reference to Oldham in an article Würz had published in the July *Evangelisches Missions-Magazin*. As for Mott, in his letter to Würz Oldham stoutly defended his right to participate in the Root mission: "I feel sure that if there is to be reconciliation after the war it cannot be on the basis of asking any of us to suppress our honest convictions, but only on the ground that deeper than our radical differences on political questions is the unity that binds us together in Christ." And as he reminded Würz, he had never concealed his own deep commitments during the war, to the point of stating that had he been of military age he would gladly be serving in the forces of the crown.

All Oldham's efforts, however, could not prevent the German missionary leaders, in August 1917, issuing a formal "Declaration" condemning Ogilvie and Mott for words and actions inconsistent with their membership of the Continuation Committee.[28] They could no longer recognize Mott as chairman, calling on him to resign, and could no longer accept Ogilvie as a fellow member. Oldham was mentioned as having participated in the Free Church assembly, but otherwise escaped opprobrium. The "Declaration" was signed by Julius Richter on behalf of the *Ausschuss* and ten others, including the other three German members of the Continuation Committee (Bishop P. Hennig, Friedrich Würz and D.G. Haussleiter). What had for some time been a slow attrition of the ideals and vision of Edinburgh 1910 now seemed to have turned into a total collapse. It was certainly the lowest point reached in ecumenical relations during the war.

On 5 September Oldham forwarded an English translation of the German "Declaration" to Mott, who had just sent him an account of his Russian visit. He urged Mott not even to consider resigning. "There is no criticism of your position which does not affect mine," he wrote. To Würz, who had officially communicated the "Declaration" to him, Oldham repeated his view that the report of the United Free Church assembly had been seriously distorted. He continued:

> In the Declaration by the German members of the Continuation Committee the British missionary movement is charged with a denial of the supranational character of the Church of Christ. I am quite sure that this charge would be repudiated. For myself, I entirely subscribe to the resolution which was recently passed by the House of Laymen of the Province of Canterbury ... "that Christians owe their first and highest allegiance to the Catholic church which is the Body of Christ, and that they are bound to love all the disciples of Christ of whatever nationality as brethren". A firm adherence to this view does not, however, affect one's judgment of what political measures it is right and necessary to take in regard to German subjects in the emergency of war.[29]

The main reason why he himself has not resigned, states Oldham, is that in addition to its being an international fellowship – a feature necessarily much in abeyance since the war began – the Continuation Committee had been a practical means of promoting missionary work and that more had been done in this regard during the war even than prior to it. His letter ends with an expression of deep sympathy in the pain Würz must feel at the whole situation.

[28] "Erklärung", in *Evangelisches Missionszeitschrift*, 1917, pp.305–08.
[29] JHO letter to Würz 12 Sept. 1917 [OA].

Early in October, the standing committee of the CMSBI met and drew up a reply to the German "Declaration", comprising three short paragraphs.[30] The first stated their view that matters relating to the organization of the Continuation Committee could only be taken by the whole membership of the committee. The second was as follows:

> The Declaration contains statements and judgments with which the British members cannot agree; but it does not seem to them that discussion of these matters, at the present time, with those whose view of the whole situation is so divergent from their own, can conduce to an understanding, which can be arrived at only under renewed conditions of brotherly fellowship.

The third paragraph reiterated that in spite of these divergences, the British members were one with the German members "in affirming their loyalty to the principle of the supranational character of Christian Missions" in loyalty to Christ the King of all the earth, and that this was not inconsistent with acceptance of certain political measures of wartime.

Oldham sent the reply to Würz with a letter[31] enlarging on its three points, and adding a gloss to the third paragraph. The Germans had felt that the principle of "supranationality" of missions had been violated by the British treatment of German missionaries in British territories or British-held territories, and the seeming acquiescence of British Christians in these political measures. The point was indeed highly sensitive, and Oldham tells Würz:

> The German missionaries are Christian brethren, and we desire to recognize this without reserve. But they are not only Christians but also Germans, and are subject like other German citizens to the military and political measures which have to be taken under war conditions. I do not think that in the German discussion of the treatment of German missionaries there has been adequate recognition of this aspect of the situation.

It is a measure of how far trust and understanding had broken down, that on the German side the British view (fundamentally Oldham's own) that further discussion should wait until more suitable conditions prevailed at the end of the war was received as a wholly negative rejection of any further negotiation at all. Würz conveyed this to Oldham early in 1918. Oldham, of course, was simply expressing his lifelong view that there can be no substitute for personal encounter and dialogue "in God's time". Würz also returned to the issue of Mott's behaviour, arguing that his position as chairman put him in a different category from the other members. Oldham in his reply[32] went so far as to concede he had "made a case" here. Much of the rest of Oldham's reply deals with the question of supranationality, which the Germans still felt the British were dismissing in cavalier fashion and ignoring its bearing on the question of

[30] "Reply to German Declaration", typed copy attached to JHO letter to Mott 15 Oct. 1917 [OA].
[31] JHO letter to Würz 15 Oct. 1917 [OA].
[32] JHO letter to Würz 5 Feb. 1918 [OA].

German missions. Oldham pleads for both patience and realism, in a realm where the heavenly treasure is found in earthen vessels:

> No one longs more than I do for the restoration of Christian fellowship in life and work between those whom the war so deeply divided. But we cannot at a stroke sweep away the fundamental differences of judgments and feeling which the war has evoked. The restoration of fellowship and understanding must almost inevitably be a slow growth. It will require time. The bridges will have to be built stone by stone . . .
>
> I remember when I was in Germany some years ago and spoke on international relations, being taken to task for an idealism which ignored the practical realities of the situation. Similarly in the early days of the present war, when copies of *Papers for War-time* reached Germany, they were criticized on the ground that they contemplated a state of international relations which was impracticable in this hard and unregenerate world. Now it would seem that those who made these charges were themselves demanding the immediate application of an ideal principle without reference to the conditions in which we find ourselves.

We do have available a transcript of Würz's comments on Oldham's letter, made for the benefit of his German colleagues.[33] It welcomes Oldham's admission about Mott and, still more so, his affirmation of the supranationality of missions. However, he still expresses deep disappointment and amazement that German missionaries should be thought a permanent menace in British territories. This of course was not Oldham's view, which was that so long as public opinion and governmental policy were shaped by the passionate feelings of war, protest was unrealistic. What he would have wished was that Würz in turn might have realized that his own views were just as politically and nationally conditioned.

Further treatment on these exchanges will be given in the following section, on the specific matter of the German missions. What has clearly emerged is that the interpretation of "supranationality" became a key theological and ethical point of contention between the German and Anglo-Saxon members of the Continuation Committee. The Germans evidently wished it to mean that the missionary project and the work of the Continuation Committee should continue as if the war was not happening. Oldham, and Mott too, early in the war affirmed that the international nature of the Continuation Committee must be maintained. Oldham, as a citizen of a belligerent country, had realized the problem of maintaining his international commitment on behalf of the Continuation Committee, and his national commitment as a British citizen, and believed he could keep the two quite distinct, to the point of refraining from any anti-German public comment. By 1915 he was finding this extremely difficult: the outrage of the *Lusitania* and poison gas saw to that. Did it, then, finally prove impossible to be both a missionary internationalist and a loyal British citizen? Oldham resolved the matter with a view of the *time* needed to resolve differences and conflicts of view. He could not for the present jump out

[33] Handwritten translation of "Comments by Würz on Oldham", 7 March 1918 [OA].

of his British skin. And all he wished of his German partners was a recognition that they, in turn, did have a German skin even as Christians, and needed to be patient. For the moment, supranationalism had to mean not a denial of nationality, but a realistic recognition of the limitations it was imposing. "In God's time" things would change, and for the moment the watchword must be patience, and *honest* words and deeds, on all sides.

## The German missions

Of all the enterprises of the German Protestant churches, since the early 19th century none occasioned more justifiable pride than their foreign missions. Through such notable bodies as the Basel, Leipzig and Gossner missions they had spread far and wide in Africa, Asia and the Pacific. It is estimated that on the eve of the first world war they had nearly 1900 missionaries in the field, serving about 630,000 baptized Christians (and of course many others besides), and responsible for approximately 215,000 pupils in their schools.[34] They were therefore a major feature of the modern missionary enterprise, and cooperation between them and the British, American and Scandinavian societies was a prime focus of the ecumenical movement from the Edinburgh conference onwards. The outbreak of war had an immediate and near catastrophic effect on their work. Quite apart from the inevitable disruption in communication between the missions in the field and their home headquarters, most of the German missionary work was located in British territories, or in territories soon seized by British forces. Overnight, therefore, many of the German missionaries became aliens on enemy territory, and subject to British governmental measures dictated by the exigencies of war. Many were interned or repatriated. The fate of their missions became the single most contentious issue between the Germans and the "remnant symbol" of the Continuation Committee, and provided Oldham with his most demanding problem as an international secretary. What he was eventually able to achieve on behalf of the German missions, while limited if judged by idealistic standards, was arguably his most important achievement of the war years and provided a solid demonstration of the need, and possibility, of ecumenical cooperation.

First, as has been seen already, right at the start of the conflict Oldham stated that one of the greatest problems, after the end of the war if not before, would be "how to save German missionary work from disaster". Nor can there be any doubting his compassionate concern when, just over four years later, the war did end and he asked his readers to imagine the plight of the German missionaries:

> The missionaries who have been repatriated are men and women who have had their career cut short, who, in many instances, are face to face with the practical difficulty of earning a livelihood and who are facing the still severer trial of separation from the

[34] W.R. Hogg, *Ecumenical Foundations. A History of the International Missionary Council and its Nineteenth Century Background*, New York, Harper, 1952, p.167.

> work to which the best years of their life have been devoted and from those to whom they had become bound by ties of the deepest affection . . . Figures of native Christian communities bring before us in the aggregate hundreds of thousands of men and women deprived of the spiritual guides through whom they had learned of Christ and to whom they looked for enlightenment and consolation. Where schools have had to be closed it may mean for many hundreds the shutting of doors of opportunity into a larger and richer life.[35]

One of the earliest actions of the CMSBI standing committee after the outbreak of war was to set up a fund to subsidize the work of continental missions, including the German, since "the interruption of communications might easily lead to great temporary distress in many parts of the mission field".[36] It was a noble gesture but, on two counts, not particularly effective. The amount raised was disappointingly small. The British missionary societies were themselves faced with financial difficulties due to the war, and the rapidly hardening public feeling told against aiding any German enterprise, of whatever kind. Besides, the German mission bodies themselves wanted nothing to do with money, even Christian money, coming from perfidious Britain. Mott, on his visit to Germany in October 1914, found greater openness to the offer of financial help from the wider ecumenical fellowship, especially America, but even then a loan to be repaid after the war, not a gift, was preferred. Oldham for his part was sensitive to the likely feelings on the German side. The fund "was never intended to subsidize the missions of other countries in a way inconsistent with their self-respect".[37]

It was in West Africa that severe disruption of the German missions was first felt, although this varied according to place and circumstance. At first, the Basel Mission was allowed by Britain to continue its work in the Gold Coast (present-day Ghana), and likewise for a time the German missionaries remained active, though under certain restrictions, in the German colony of Togo which was quickly occupied by the British and French. In the Cameroon, however, which was invaded by British forces, there was considerable destruction of mission property – with evidence of some involvement by British troops – and all the German missionaries were deported. Women, children and ordained men were repatriated to Germany, while men of military age were detained in camps in Britain or elsewhere. The German anger at this treatment was intense, inflamed by accounts of the looting of mission property and stories – some told by the missionaries themselves on arrival in Germany – of the harsh conditions under which they were detained and made to travel. Richter, Axenfeld and Würz made their feelings plain to Oldham and Mott.

Oldham and the CMSBI-led committee on missions and governments considered the complaints carefully in February 1915, and Oldham kept Mott

[35] JHO, "German Missions", *IRM*, vol. VIII, no. 32, Oct. 1919, p.460. This article is the most comprehensive survey of the situation from this period.

[36] JHO letter to Mott 2 Oct. 1914 [OA].

[37] *Ibid.*

fully informed on their findings. Oldham left no one in any doubt that what was happening to the Germans was a disaster for the entire missionary enterprise and, thus far, the most tragic fruit of the war. At the same time, Oldham's enquiries led him to believe that the evidence of maltreatment of the Cameroon missionaries was often exaggerated or conflicting:

> The missionaries undoubtedly suffered some hardships, but these were for the most part inevitable under the circumstances. Some of them hardly seem to realize that it was not possible to provide an Atlantic liner to convey the Germans from Duala to Lagos. It also appears that the German missionaries themselves admitted in conversation that they received no small kindness from individual British officers, and they were certainly kindly entertained by the British missionaries in Nigeria. Not a word of all this appears in their official reports. It is only natural that what the missionaries have suffered should arouse very keen feeling in Germany, but the statements issued by the Basel Society are extremely unbalanced. The most vehement complaints are made about conditions to which missionaries in West Africa have occasionally to submit even under normal conditions and which were shared in common by the British troops themselves.[38]

Oldham's greater concern was how in this and other instances the wider missionary community could ensure the continuation of the work which the Germans were forced to leave, in addition to the efforts being made by indigenous preachers and other leaders. In the Cameroon itself American Presbyterians, already working there, gave assistance and were joined by the Paris Evangelical Society in 1917. In Togo, where all Germans were repatriated in 1916, the African pastors had to shoulder the work alone. In the Gold Coast, the Basel Mission was banned from 1916, and the United Free Church of Scotland, at the invitation of the governor, accepted responsibility for carrying on the work.

If to the non-German missionary bodies such efforts seemed like Christian brotherly solidarity in an hour of crisis, to many of the Germans themselves they seemed like a deliberate take-over: a further imperial annexation, in ecclesiastical form, and deeply humiliating. Nowhere was the hurt greater than in India, chief field for the Gossner and Basel Missions, and other German societies. At first the attitude of the British authorities to the German missions, renowned for their educational and philanthropic work, was reasonably friendly. Early in 1915 this changed and the missionaries, no less than other Germans in India, were treated as enemy aliens and interned or deported. Again, Oldham felt deeply for the Germans, but also called for some understanding of the British government's predicament in war time. He wrote to Würz on 27 January 1915, "without any desire to take sides", on the change in British policy. It must, he states, have been intolerable for the German missionaries to have read certain statements about Germany in the press without an opportunity to reply. But also, "there can be no doubt that German agents were at work in the country

[38] Cf. JHO letter to Mott 12 Feb. 1915 [OA].

endeavouring to stimulate revolt". The fact that Germany would reap advantage from trouble in India was hardly likely to be mentioned in the German press. Moreover there is no doubt, says Oldham, that *some* German missionaries had tried to spread "the truth" about the war. It is natural for any government at war to suppress strong criticisms – the more so when made by people of a hostile nation "and in a country where a Government rules over an easily excitable subject nation".[39]

The means of providing some replacement leadership for the German missions in India was greatly assisted by the existence of the National Missionary Council of India. At the meeting of the CMSBI standing committee in February 1915, Oldham tried to persuade his colleagues to recommend to the National Missionary Council that an experienced missionary be set free to attend to the plight of the German missions, and especially by personal contact to help remove misunderstandings. There were hesitations in the CMSBI over the likelihood of finding anyone suitably gifted and preferably of British background.[40] However, coordination did take place through the National Missionary Council, and much valuable help was given to the German missions. When the Gossner missionaries were removed from Bihar and Orissa in 1915, the Anglican bishop of Chota Nagpur, Foss Westcott, at the request of the government took charge of their work. In particular, the schools (over 300) were maintained under his supervision with the help of government grants. American Lutherans took over the work of the Schleswig-Holstein Society north of Madras. The Church of Sweden likewise helped with the work of the Leipzig Mission ... and so on. It was with the work of the Basel Mission that the National Missionary Council became most directly involved. Efforts to form a Swiss missionary society to take responsibility proved abortive, and so the National Missionary Council, with government permission, organized the linking up of different sections of the Basel work with the South India United Church, the London Missionary Society, the United Free Church of Scotland and other bodies.

With all such efforts, Oldham and his CMSBI colleagues took a keen and supportive interest, advising and suggesting, and in certain cases obtaining financial support for the National Missionary Council. But of course, vital as it was, it was no more than a holding operation. The really daunting questions concerned the long-term future. As has been seen, some time in the spring of 1917 reports began to circulate that after the war it would be government policy to exclude German missions from all British territories, at least for a very long time. In fact, Oldham had long foreseen that this issue would arise and would present perhaps the most serious challenge to the international missionary movement, and especially for its British representatives. Already on 14 December 1915 he had written to Mott:

[39] In addition, in relation to the Indian scene Oldham obtained information from Sir Andrew Fraser on reports of the behaviour of German nationals there. Cf. JHO letter to Mott 8 Sept. 1915 [OA].

[40] JHO letter to Mott 12 Feb. 1915 [OA].

I cannot exaggerate the concern which the best missionary leaders feel about the future of German missions . . . Not only are we concerned about the future of German missions in their relation to their contribution to the advancement of the Kingdom of God, but we are also deeply concerned as British citizens that a just solution of this question should be found . . . We shall find action being taken both on the German and British side all over the mission field, and it will need all the tact that those of us who are in contact with the larger interests possess to prevent mistakes being made through haste.

The context of this letter was a slight disagreement between Oldham and Mott over whether the British section of the special committee on surveys should press ahead with gathering information from India – and Oldham was stressing the urgent need for this. On the main issue, events proved him absolutely right. Not that Oldham was relying either on guesswork or prophetic inspiration, since through his own close contacts with the Foreign Office he was receiving strong clues on future government policy. On 12 October 1916, in a letter headed "Private & Confidential" (almost the only time his correspondence was so classified) he wrote to Mott:

It seems very unlikely that German missionaries will be permitted on the conclusion of the war to resume work in British territory. This fact will probably come as a shock to some of the friends of missions in North America, and it has caused deep regret to many in this country who know that the work of German Protestant missions has been carried on for the most part in a spirit of unselfish service and from a disinterested love to Christ. I believe, however, that I am expressing the mind of the Standing Committee of the Conference of British Missionary Societies when I say that I do not think it would be wise to make any protest against the decision of the Government if it should prove to be of the nature we expect.

Such protest would only complicate the situation even more, argued Oldham, and prejudice further relations. Rather, the aim must be how to save the work of German missions from complete disaster. Nor should it be assumed that the government's decision would be absolutely final. British missionary societies, for their part, would not be rushing to assume major further responsibilities, and would most likely consult with the CMSBI committee. There would also be the highly important ethical question of whether bodies of one denomination should take over communities hitherto nurtured in another tradition.

As was seen earlier, the British government's decision to exclude German missionaries from British territories after the war was made public during 1917. The violent German reaction to this news, and the apparent acquiescence of the British missionary bodies in it, were among the motivations to the production of the "Declaration" in the summer of that year. Würz and his German colleagues demanded to know where was the Christian protest from within Britain itself, at this denial of the principle of the supranational nature of missions. Oldham advised his German partners that the principle was one thing, the conditions and process of its realization another. Whatever the ideality of the principle, German missionaries could hardly be expected to be welcomed back to India and resume their teaching in schools, given the state of public opinion in Britain which, like it or not, was still coming to terms with 15,000 deaths of combatants and civilians by submarine warfare.[41]

The Germans did not, and could hardly, know that while he might not be stirring up vigorous protest, Oldham was in fact characteristically very busy behind the scenes. He was working towards an achievable solution with the British government which could – and eventually did – contribute to a restoration of much of the German work to German control in the post-war world. What proved helpful, paradoxically, was that the proposals for limiting access by all foreign nationals to British territories after the war seemed draconian to the point of indefensibility. First, there was proposed the exclusion from certain prescribed parts of the empire of all "enemy" organizations and individuals engaged in philanthropic, educational or medical work. Second, in certain parts of the empire, all foreigners engaged in such work would require licences. Third, if this last measure was thought unacceptable and discriminatory, the licence system would be extended to all British organizations as well.

Oldham had been prepared to concede to government the need to take extreme measures in wartime out of political necessity. What was now being proposed for peace time, however, would hardly be conducive to peace. He was particularly concerned about the dangers that would result to missionary freedom, first and foremost to missions of any non-British nationality. Since most of the problems that loomed for all mission bodies related to India, it was with the India Office that discussion would be most appropriate. The India Office had in fact given an assurance that before it settled any policy on missions it would consult with the relevant missionary societies. For the permanent under-secretary, Sir Arthur Hirtzell, this presented the forbidding prospect of having to negotiate with some forty different bodies. When Oldham went to see him on behalf of the CMSBI committee on war and missions, therefore, great was Hirtzell's amazement and relief as he exclaimed, "We can deal, then, with *one* body to represent all Protestant missionary societies!"[42] Oldham in fact found Hirtzell to be "a keen Christian" and "a warm friend" to missionary enterprise.

The fruit of these conversations was a conference between Foreign Office officials and missionary representatives at the India Office on 12 December 1917, at which the CMSBI presented its objections to the pending legislation. In a strategic move, Archbishop Randall Davidson had been invited to lead the delegation, and he spoke to great effect on the shortcomings of the measures. There would be great alarm if the British government were to impose on missionary and other humanitarian agencies restrictions which would not even be imposed on traders. The reaction in the United States would be particularly

[41] JHO letter to Würz 5 Feb. 1918 [OA].
[42] Hogg, p.178.

sharp. Moreover, there was the danger of similar counter-measures by other countries being imposed on British nationals working in their territories. He asked for a definite assertion of religious liberty in any government document dealing with the question, affirming that the missionaries would assist the government in working out a plan for securing loyalty on the part of the foreign missionary to the government of the country in question. He concluded with a powerful statement on the value of missions for the betterment of the empire. Oldham also spoke. It had been agreed beforehand among the missions delegation that they would not protest about the exclusions that had been made during the war, but concentrate on a positive approach to the future. The basis for dealing with all missions should be one of welcome, not restriction. To underline this, American societies should be admitted on the same terms as the British, and there should be opportunity for missionary societies from other countries to be received on the same terms, as negotiated by post-war international missionary organization.

The delegation was largely effective. It elicited from the government the so-called "Memorandum A" relating to Protestant work in India. It spoke appreciatively of missions, but still excluded enemy alien missionary bodies and personnel for an indefinite period. At the same time it provided for no restrictions to be imposed on British or American societies recommended to the government by either the CMSBI or the North American Foreign Missions Conference. Further, and most significantly, the government declared it would deal only with these two bodies and with the National Missionary Council in India. "Memorandum B" dealt with churches in communion with Rome. "Memorandum C" dealt with societies of neutral and allied countries not covered by "Memorandum A". All such missionaries were required to take out a permit and to cooperate loyally with the government.

An immediate consequence of this action was that the CMSBI was recognized as the representative agent for British Protestant missions, and the principle of ecumenical cooperation was thereby given a powerful boost. For Oldham himself the experience provided a further important outcome – a permanently valuable lesson in how church bodies should deal with government. Kathleen Bliss sums up what he had learnt, and in due course taught to others:

> Have as little to do with government as is strictly necessary and keep the distinctions clear. Missions have a spiritual task but . . . "the first duty of government is to govern", a maxim often ignored by protestors, to their own disadvantage. If you *have* to negotiate, act together, prepare and know your facts, be consistent in what you are asking, listen to how the government's spokespersons see things (and it will be a help if, in general, missions have been appreciative of any government actions that have been on the side of justice and the welfare of the governed). Lastly, know your officials and let those who have an underlying sympathy with the Christian cause do some of your work for you![43]

[43] Bliss, "The Legacy of J.H. Oldham", p.20.

At about the same time, the Basel Mission was informed through the British ambassador in Bern that its West African properties, already in government hands, were to be auctioned. Oldham managed to get a stay of execution, on the already agreed basis that no governmental action on missions would be taken without his being informed.

Of course none of this satisfied Würz and the other Germans who were demanding outright protest. Oldham was applying the art of the possible, on their behalf. He knew that it would seem in their eyes far too compromising. But he knew also that "God's time" would come, when what had been achieved now, modest though it was, would provide the basis for better things. On 3 December 1918, soon after the armistice, he again replied to a pained letter from Würz. Yes, the CMSBI had acquiesced in the decision of the British government on exclusion of German missionaries: given the long and terrible bitterness of the war, given what public opinion was both in Britain and Germany, this had to be accepted for the time being. The real test was to see that the work begun and established by the Germans was carried on – and the British societies were *not* expansionist in this regard. Nothing could take away the great record of achievement of the German missions. And then:

> To the great majority of Christians in Germany this will no doubt appear a statement of the whole case and they will draw the conclusion which inevitably follows . . . This can only lead to the growth of bitterness against Great Britain and British Christians and postpone still longer the day of reconciliation and understanding which it is our chief concern to bring about. We cannot expect from the rank and file or from those who are under the influence of strong and deep feeling a fair judgment of the issues. But may we not hope that there will be some men of large views with an understanding of life in its complex relations who will endeavour to keep before their minds not merely one set of facts and considerations isolated and abstracted from their living context, but the whole difficult and involved situation through which we have gradually to feel our way towards the light? In the presence and guidance of such men on both sides lies the hope of ultimate understanding.

Würz's reaction was to assume that no further dialogue with Oldham was possible – and with that Oldham would surely have agreed if by dialogue was meant further correspondence by letter. Oldham never tired of stressing that certain matters could only be dealt with by personal encounter and conversation, and for the day when that was possible he longed as eagerly as anyone else. It was left to another British member of the Continuation Committee, the pacifist Henry Hodgkin, with whom Oldham had had certain major disagreements on the Christian response to the war, to point this out to Würz early in 1918:

> . . . I am quite sure that it was not Oldham's intention to break off communication with you in any sense whatever, but simply to hold over the unravelling of the tangled skein until you can meet face to face and talk things out in brotherhood . . . I am confident that, when all that Oldham has done for the things about which you and I care is known to you and Richter and others, you will be deeply impressed, and

> thankful for the stand that he has taken and for the way in which he has been enabled to avert certain very grave dangers . . . [A]lthough I have had to differ from Oldham from time to time on certain points, I am bound to say that you could hardly have had anyone in this country who has done more than he has done. He has done what I, had I been in his position, never could have done, because my position has not been one in which I could have established confidential relationships with persons whose goodwill was necessary.[44]

## The Continuation Committee . . . and beyond

As noted in the preceding chapter, the status of the Continuation Committee was already problematical by the time war broke out in 1914. At the meeting at the Hague in 1913, it had been affirmed that the prime authority for joint action lay with the mission boards themselves. Yet the Continuation Committee had not, strictly, been set up by the boards but by the Edinburgh conference which with each succeeding year was ever more distant. Implementation of the principle of accountability largely rested with Oldham's personal capacity and commitment to consult with the boards and thus provide a means of continuing dialogue between them and the Continuation Committee. This, however, did not solve the basic problem: the need for a permanent international body appointed by, and continually renewed by, the constituent societies. Edinburgh had pointed towards that goal, but had only got as far as a Continuation Committee.

The advent of war both made the problem far more acute and eventually stimulated its solution. As was seen earlier in the chapter, almost the first step taken by Oldham was to ensure the transfer of his and Kenneth Maclennan's services to the CMSBI. At least here would be a group, a child of Edinburgh and representative in nature, albeit national and not international. But the CMSBI was also the body which assessed and collated British funding for international cooperation, and several of its members were also members of the Continuation Committee. Furthermore, a number of the special committees of the Continuation Committee had national sections, such as the committee on surveys, and on missions and governments, which had British sections. It could therefore be fairly claimed that the CMSBI, if it closely associated itself with and supported such groups, was in fact acting as a kind of delegate of the Continuation Committee. And what at first had been taken as an immediate emergency measure was before the end of the war seen to indicate the longer term way ahead: national cooperative bodies were seen as the key.

What is remarkable is how much in fact the Continuation Committee, albeit centred around the "remnant symbol" of Oldham, Mott and the CMSBI, did achieve during 1914–18.[45] Oldham once went so far as to claim it achieved even more than in the previous four years of its existence. The *IRM* continued to

[44] Hodgkin letter to Würz 17 Feb. 1919 [OA].
[45] Hogg.

appear every quarter with its high standards maintained, in itself a remarkable achievement for Oldham and his assistant Georgina Gollock, amid all the extra pressures of the time. (However, the note of loss cannot be missed, that after an article by Johannes Warneck in the October 1914 issue no further German contribution was to appear before January 1923, a gap of nearly nine years.) Betty Gibson joined the office staff in 1916, and at the end of that year Kenneth Maclennan moved to London for government service but was able to give a small amount of time to the CMSBI office. Through the machinery of cooperation between Oldham's office in Edinburgh and that of the CMSBI in London, not to mention the frequent journeys to London this entailed for Oldham, much of the Continuation Committee's agenda was carried on: Christian literature, relations with Muslims, the development of women's education in India (notably the college for Christian women in Madras), education of the mass movements in India, preparation of missionaries, and so forth. Some of these areas raised critical questions for discussion, in particular the so-called "conscience clause" question in Indian education. Nor, on the global level, was the cooperative advance limited to Britain-based initiatives and partnerships. In February 1916 there took place in Panama the congress on Christian work in Latin America – in effect an Edinburgh conference for Latin America. Oldham had been invited to attend, but could not leave Britain in the circumstances of the time. All these concerns, of course, were in addition to those major issues of the relations with the German missionary leaders and the fate of their missions in the field.

But the problem of the Continuation Committee itself and the need for a permanent, accountable organ of cooperation could not be displaced. In July 1915 Oldham first shared his growing concerns with Mott, pointing out that, partly as a result of the war, while the work of the Continuation Committee was officially in suspense, cooperation between missionary bodies was growing at *national* level, as with the CMSBI and the Conference of Foreign Mission Boards in North America. In his letter[46] Oldham had no quarrel with this tendency, and in fact stated that since the Lake Mohonk meeting [of the Continuation Committee in 1912] he had been of the opinion that "the international work must be built up on the basis of the national conferences". However, certain difficulties have to be anticipated, for example from the Anglicans in the light of the Archbishop's final opinion on intercommunion following the Kikuyu episode[47] – Oldham's implication is that the high Anglicans may prefer to remain on a Continuation Committee of steadily declining status and effective power, rather than be committed to a new and more determinedly representative body. At the same time there should be limits

[46] JHO letter to Mott 15 July 1915 [OA].

[47] Oldham is particularly concerned about the attitude of Bishop H.H. Montgomery, secretary of the SPG, who in response to the Kikuyu episode was saying that if he had known such would have been the post-Edinburgh developments he would not have associated with the conference. Oldham also expressed disappointment with the actions of the South African Anglicans who moved into German South-West Africa in the wake of the deportations of the German missionaries from there.

to the extent of efforts to keep the Anglicans on board, and in any case, Oldham suggests, a revolt from the younger end of the Church of England might ensue if the official policy was to break off relations or withdraw from cooperative work.

Four months later, Oldham was sounding a slightly different note.[48] His experience as a member of the Foreign Mission Committee of the United Free Church of Scotland had taught him the need for some such body as the Continuation Committee and for that body to have the full confidence of the mission boards. However, the main burden of his letter is that such a body – on the assumption that Britain wins the war – will mainly have to be the responsibility of Britain and the United States since it is from the Anglo-Saxon peoples that the bulk of the missionary effort is provided. It was not for nearly another two years that he returned to the subject. At its meeting in September 1917 the standing committee of the CMSBI had to deal with the German "Declaration" which called into question the whole credibility of the Continuation Committee. In addition, and more fundamental to the discussion, was the matter of providing joint support from British societies to the work of the China Continuation Committee and the India National Missionary Council. Oldham's own view, once again, was crystallizing in favour of the national bodies being the cornerstones of international cooperation. Certainly in Britain the missionary societies would have greater confidence in their own representation on a national body, and that national board in turn cooperating with other such bodies in a permanent international structure, rather than allowing the present undefined status of the Continuation Committee to continue or be replicated. Already the CMSBI commanded greater confidence from the British societies than did the Continuation Committee.

The CMSBI set aside two days in January 1918 to discuss the matter further and approved, with some revisions, a memorandum from Oldham setting out the fundamental principle that "the international missionary organization should in future be built on the national missionary organizations". It further proposed that the office of the new body be moved from Edinburgh to London. Perhaps that was specially symbolic – after all, the proposal itself marked a step beyond Edinburgh 1910 when the idea of such a scheme had been dismissed as impractical (the CMSBI did not even exist then). On 4 April, at its next meeting the standing committee was joined by Mott, then making another European tour. Part of Mott's brief, and that of his colleague Charles R. Watson, was specifically to attend this meeting on behalf of the corresponding body in the USA, the committee of reference and counsel of the Foreign Missions Conference, and to convey its own similar proposal. The group which met at the Bible House in London could not, of course, abolish the Continuation Committee. What it did resolve was that "a new international committee to deal with questions demanding immediate attention and to be called the Emergency Committee of Cooperating Missions should be created", its offices

[48] JHO letter to Mott 4 Nov. 1915 [OA].

to be in London. The Committee would comprise eight representatives from the Foreign Missions Conference, six from the CMSBI, and one each from any other country wishing representation. Mott was elected chairman, Oldham and Maclennan secretaries (the latter in a marginal, part-time capacity in view of his government service). The Emergency Committee would handle all governmental relations in which the societies were jointly concerned, consider means for aiding war-impaired missions, and act as a means of coordination in facing jointly the major problems all the societies shared in the transition from war to peace. The Continuation Committee would maintain for the time being its nominal existence, and under its auspices the *IRM* would continue to be published. The CMSBI and the Foreign Missions Conference would assume financial responsibility for the Emergency Committee.[49]

Within months the proposals had been formally ratified both by the CMSBI and the Foreign Missions Conference. As quickly, the Emergency Committee had its own letter-heading. What response, though, from other countries? From the Anglo-American standpoint what had been undertaken was an urgently needed measure to provide for the tasks that would soon be descending on the international missionary effort: not ideal but brilliantly and generously pragmatic. From elsewhere, it could seem like an almost brutal Anglo-American grabbing of the reins of power, if not the spoils of war. Oldham wrote to the appropriate secretaries in neutral countries, and to Würz. The Council of Danish Missions, through Count J. Moltke, while appreciating the reasons why America, Britain (and France) would wish to act quickly, declined to give an immediate answer on the grounds that for the present Danish concerns could be dealt with "in the ordinary way of transaction".[50] A similar reply came from Karl Fries on behalf of the Swedish missions, with the hope that as peace had now come (December 1918) the Continuation Committee itself might be able to resume its work.[51] Würz stated that Switzerland should stand aside from the Emergency Committee, and on behalf of the Germans (though no official reply seems to have been received from them) expressed serious doubts about the concept of the Emergency Committee itself, fearing that (though this was not its intention) it would lend itself to high-handed treatment of the dispossessed German missions.[52] As for the Continuation Committee, while the events of the summer of 1917 had severely shaken the confidence of the Germans in it, and while indeed it held its commission from a conference now eight years in the past, it was questionable whether "this was ground enough for setting aside the Continuation Committee so completely, and for hurrying on to the formation of a new committee which may have embarrassing consequences". By those consequences, Würz meant a continuing unjust treatment of the German missions. The mistrust was as deep as ever.

[49] Cf. Hogg.
[50] Moltke letter to JHO 5 Nov. 1918 [OA].
[51] Fries letter to JHO 4 Dec. 1918 [OA].
[52] Würz letter to JHO 2 Oct. 1918 [OA].

The formation of the emergency committee therefore in some eyes raised as many questions as it sought to answer. But at least there was now in place, in however provisional a form, a means of *action* by those who had the resources to act.

## Oldham at the end of the war

When the armistice came on 11 November 1918, Oldham was coming out of a four-week bout of exhaustion and influenza. Never able to take as much holiday as his doctor recommended during those four years, it was inevitable that the strain of his work – effectively between two offices in Edinburgh and London – should take its toll on his already fragile constitution. It had been a very long war, and could easily have been too long for Oldham. Early in 1918 the age of military call-up was raised to 50. Oldham was 43. As he had made clear, he had no compunction about military service in principle. If selected he would probably have been exempted on medical grounds, but he took the precaution of requesting from Mott a note stating the case, from the American standpoint, of the importance of his present work: "since at my age and with my present state of health I am no use for fighting purposes, I feel that the best national service I can render is in my present work."[53]

That last statement indicates another kind of toll which the war had taken. It had not, after all, been so easy to keep distinct his international vocation from his commitment as a loyal British citizen. The torpedo that sank the *Lusitania* had also dealt a heavy blow to his earlier stated intention never to speak a word against Germany in public. But what then happened if a word *did* have to be so spoken? At least Oldham had the honesty to recognize it, and be troubled by it, in 1915. By 1917 he was far less troubled, though he did drop more than a slight hint to Würz that Mott's participation on the Root mission to Russia did raise legitimate questions about the standing of the chairman of the Continuation Committee. As far as a genuinely international commitment was concerned, what remained the bottom line for Oldham was not the maintenance of an abstract principle about "supranationality" but the *practical* business of doing the best, within the grim realities of the war, to safeguard the work of the German missions. That is the touchstone of his integrity, even if for the present it was not so seen by the Germans themselves.

Nothing demonstrates more clearly what the war had taught Oldham than the brief exchange with Karl Fries of the Swedish missions, in December 1918. Fries conveyed what sounded like a very reasonable and generous offer from his colleagues, who hoped for a resumption of the Continuation Committee and its work:

> It is thought that the missionary leaders of the neutral countries might be able to carry out preparatory work to facilitate the restoration of the Continuation

[53] JHO letter to Mott 23 April 1918 [OA].

> Committee, by making a study of the points on which the missionary leaders of the belligerent countries of opposite camps differ and to try to pave the way towards mutual understanding.[54]

A meeting of missionary organizations in neutral countries was therefore proposed. Oldham's reply dated 19 December 1918 is both appreciative and yet, in the politest way possible, utterly dismissive:

> Everything will depend in efforts directed towards this end on their being made at the right time and in the right way. In the light of the experience of the past ten years, I am convinced that nothing will be achieved by correspondence. I have had constant experience of the difficulty if not impossibility of those who are separated by distance arriving at a common mind by correspondence even where there is no fundamental difference in the general outlook and the underlying assumptions. I therefore have personally very little hope from your plan of making a study of the points on which the missionary leaders of belligerent countries of opposite camps differ . . . My strong feeling is that the one means of bringing about understanding and reconciliation is personal intercourse.
>
> I do not doubt, that in the Providence of God, those of you who have not experienced the bitterness of the struggle will have your own contribution to make in His time and way to the growth of a new international fellowship. But it would be a mistake to assume too easily that Christians in neutral countries are in a specially favourable position to assume the initiative. It is eminently desirable that you should, through direct contact, understand the state of feeling in allied countries before any formal attempt is made to approach the missionary societies here with definite proposals.

Oldham was speaking now not as a bureaucratic functionary, nor as a missionary enthusiast and organizer, nor even as an educator, but as one with profound theological and human insight into the crisis of the hour. What he had wrought out of the bitterness of war was a rare blend of the long-term vision *and* of the need for practical, patient wisdom in its actual implementation. The relation between Mott and Oldham, so crucial during these dark years yet also in turn strengthened by them, has been likened to that of the Roman and the Greek – the man of action and the philosopher.[55] But it should be remembered that Greece included Pericles as well as Plato (just as Rome numbered Marcus Aurelius among its emperors). In his way, as much as Mott Oldham was a man of action: the quiet actions which prepare the ground for others to act together.

The year 1918 brought one further change to Oldham. In June 1918 the Continuation Committee offices moved from Edinburgh to London, at first into temporary accommodation in Victoria Street. At the same time a fund was started to purchase a permanent London headquarters for missionary cooperation in Britain, to be known as Edinburgh House. The location may therefore have moved from one city to another, but there would be a permanent

[54] Fries letter to JHO 4.12.18 [OA].
[55] Cf. Hogg, p.201.

reminder of the heritage to which the work was heir. London was to be the base from which Oldham would now operate nearly all his days. Chipstead in Surrey became Joe and Mary Oldham's home for the next thirty years.

In addition, once settled in England Joe Oldham became by default if not desire an adopted Anglican. He never consciously disowned his nurture in the United Free Church of Scotland. It was simply that for him denominational allegiances were not important. His father, Colonel Oldham, had moved back to Scotland in 1915. It is in fact noticeable how often during the following years Oldham was to select Scottish, or at any rate Presbyterian, pastors and theologians as his collaborators.

CHAPTER 8

# *A New Beginning 1918–25*

THOUGH so greatly longed-for, the silencing of the guns on the Western front at the eleventh hour of the eleventh day of the eleventh month in 1918 had come sooner than most had expected. It was in fact no more than a ceasefire asked for by Germany, her military capacity now virtually exhausted, starving under the allied blockade and beset by revolution. For the ceasefire to become a peace required negotiations and a treaty. The world knows that it was the Treaty of Versailles, signed in the summer of 1919, which settled the terms of the peace – and sowed some of the seeds for the second great conflict to come.

Seen through the lens of history after eight decades, such a significant event as the Paris peace conference seems to stand with a solid and fateful inevitability about it, both in its decisions and its consequences. At the time, however, nothing seemed inevitable and much seemed unclear in what was often, by many accounts, a somewhat chaotic process where neither the procedures nor the aims were always clear. Certainly, like the armistice itself, much seemed to happen quicker than many people expected. President Woodrow Wilson, whose "fourteen points" of peace aims delivered early in 1918 had eventually appealed to the Germans as a basis for seeking an armistice, arrived in Europe on 13 December. As leader of what was now the world's most powerful nation, whose intervention had finally tipped the military balance against Germany, he came as the harbinger of a new world order which would centre on a League of Nations. The conference proper opened on 18 January 1919. Twenty-five allied and associated nations were represented, under the presidency of Georges Clemenceau, the French prime minister and as such the bearer of his country's demands that Germany be both weakened and humbled so as never to threaten her neighbours again. The British delegation was led by Prime Minister David Lloyd George who had just won his "coupon" election, partly on the basis of a "make-Germany-pay" platform – though Lloyd George was also shrewd enough to see that such demands were likely to yield little if made of someone reduced to pauperdom. The Italians were led by Prime Minister Vittorio Emanuele Orlando, somewhat marginalized by the trio of the high-minded Wilson, the caustic-tongued Clemenceau and the mercurial Lloyd George. It was with these leaders, first in the "Council of Ten" and then later in the much more effective "Council of Four" comprising themselves alone, that the main decisions lay. However, such a group could not act in isolation from the plenary conference, nor from their government colleagues at home, nor from their own groups of staff advisers in Paris who were themselves subject to lobbying from all kinds of interested parties. There was *some* chance of affecting the provisions of the eventual treaty.

## The Versailles peace and German missions

Joe Oldham, as was seen in the previous chapter, had already acted in at least one case – that of the Basel Mission – to secure German missions property from confiscation and sale. It was clear that the real danger from such moves would come with the peace. Already there had been much talk of "making Germany pay" for the misery and suffering brought by a war which the outside world generally adjudged to have been at her instigation. Woodrow Wilson in his fourteen points had stipulated that the territories invaded by Germany must be "restored", and in offering the Germans an armistice the allies had stated that this meant that compensation would be made by Germany for all damage done to the civilian population of the Allies and their property by the aggression of Germany. How this compensation would be met, as well as the size of it, would of course be one of the main talking-points at Paris. And while another of Wilson's points was that all colonial questions and claims would be dealt with impartially, few doubted that after a conference where recompense was being sought – and from which Germany itself would be excluded until the treaty was ready in draft form – little if anything would remain of German overseas possessions. Joe Oldham, well in advance, was aware of this.[1] In such a setting the German missions, and especially their properties, seemed extremely vulnerable to inclusion in the spoils of war and as sources for reparations.

It became known that the Versailles treaty would provide for appropriation by the Allies of private property belonging to Germans to help pay the German debts to nationals of Allied governments. It was here that missions property was most vulnerable, and Oldham knew he must act. Once again, Oldham's approach was not to raise a public hue and cry on behalf of German missions. At a time when the whole tide of public opinion in Britain was for making Germany pay there would, to say the least, have been little sympathy for the cause. Rather, he entered into conversation with Foreign Office officials. The December 1917 conference had set an important precedent for relations between

[1] Oldham had some correspondence with Edwyn Bevan on the issue during 1917 [OA].

the government and the CMSBI standing committee, and thereby on the government side the positive benefits of missions had been fully acknowledged. Quite how Oldham built on this beginning is not known, but it was undoubtedly his influence which was behind article 438 of the Versailles treaty, whereby German missions property was specifically exempted from appropriations. The article in full reads:

> The Allied and Associated Powers agree that where Christian religious missions were being maintained by German societies or persons in territories belonging to them, or of which the government is entrusted to them in accordance with the present Treaty, the property which these missions or missionary societies possessed, including that of trading societies whose profits were devoted to the support of missions, shall continue to be devoted to missionary purposes. In order to ensure the due execution of this undertaking the Allied and Associated Councils will hand over such property to boards of trustees appointed or approved by the Governments and composed of persons holding the faith of the missions whose property is involved.
>
> The Allied and Associated Governments, while continuing to maintain full control as to the individuals by whom the missions are conducted, will safeguard the interests of such missions.
>
> Germany, taking note of the above undertaking, agrees to accept all arrangements made or to be made by the Allied or Associated Governments concerned for carrying on the work of the said missions or trading societies and waives all claims on their behalf.[2]

W.R. Hogg comments: "This single article in the peace treaty saved German missions from complete dissolution. It preserved almost intact Protestant mission property estimated to be worth from fifteen to twenty million dollars. What this article means for Protestant and Catholic missions alike need not be dwelt on here. It was, to say the least, cause for heartfelt thanksgiving."[3]

Safeguarding the German property would not by itself, however, secure the eventual return of German missionaries to their mission fields. Oldham and his colleagues, as was seen in the previous chapter, had managed to get the British government to enshrine certain safeguards on the freedom of mission work within its own territories, particularly in relation to India. To get the peace conference to introduce a like concern for *all* colonial settlements dealt with by the treaty, and to be observed by all the colonial powers concerned, seemed at first an undertaking of a wholly different magnitude. Oldham, however, perceived that the tool for achieving this lay already to hand, and was able to persuade his contacts in the Foreign Office to believe likewise. The Treaty of Berlin (1885), formulated at the height of the European imperial forays into Africa, and under Bismarck's leadership, had dealt with the large band of territories running across middle Africa from the Atlantic to the Indian Ocean. In addition to designating this a free-trade area and open to traders, explorers

[2] Cited in Oldham, *The Missionary Situation after the War*, London, Edinburgh House, 1920, pp.17f.

[3] W.R. Hogg, *Ecumenical Foundations. A History of the International Missionary Council and its Nineteenth Century Background*, New York, Harper, 1952.

and scientists alike, it specifically guaranteed religious freedom. Oldham seized upon this, suggesting that it could be applied to all African territories and indeed to elsewhere in the world also. With the backing of a unanimous resolution from the CMSBI standing committee he approached the Foreign Office with the plea that in any revision of the Treaty of Berlin at the peace conference, the relevant article (VI) should stand. Oldham's approach to the Foreign Office was sympathetically received and, while he received no definite promise, he had every reason to believe that he had been heeded. The Treaty of Berlin was in fact taken up into the Paris proceedings, and at St Germain-en-Laye on 10 September 1919, two months after the signing of the Versailles treaty itself, a convention revising the general act of Berlin was signed. What had been article VI now became article 11, dealing with the responsibility of the ruling powers in any African territory "to watch over the preservation of the native populations and to supervise the improvement of the conditions of their moral and material well-being", in particularly seeking the complete suppression of slavery. Then:

> They will protect and favour, without distinction of nationality or of religion, the religious, scientific or charitable institutions and undertakings created and organized by the nationals of the other Signatory Powers and States, Members of the League of Nations, which may adhere to the present convention, which aim at leading the natives in the path of progress and civilization . . .
>
> Freedom of conscience and the free exercise of all forms of religion are expressly guaranteed to all nationals of the Signatory Powers and to those under the jurisdiction of States, Members of the League of Nations, which may become parties to the present Convention. Similarly, missionaries shall have the right to enter into, and to travel and reside in, African territory with a view to prosecuting their calling.
>
> The application of the provisions of the two preceding paragraphs shall be subject only to such restrictions as may be necessary for the maintenance of public security and order, or as may result from the enforcement of the constitutional law of any of the Powers exercising authority in African territories.[4]

Oldham of course was not alone in his concern for the future of missions in the peace conference. The German missions leaders themselves requested that missions should only be dealt with by a separate and independent commission. A similar proposal came from the Danish, Dutch, Norwegian and Swedish committees (i.e. from neutral countries) for the World Alliance for Promoting International Friendship through the Churches. As was seen in the previous chapter, missions leaders from the neutral countries, Sweden in particular, had offered their services in conciliation – an offer to which Oldham was distinctly cool. Hogg comments ". . . Oldham's efforts probably served the missionary enterprise as well if not better than a post-Versailles meeting could have done".[5] The American missionary leadership was likewise deeply concerned. They had

[4] See also Hogg, pp.186f.
[5] Hogg, p.188.

conducted a country-by-country survey of the lands where German missions had operated, and also took detailed legal opinion. John Mott, Charles Watson and James L. Barton were dispatched to Paris to lobby for concessions favourable towards the German missions – only to find that the main work had already been done by Oldham with article 438. There is some uncertainty over what, if any, communication on the subject took place between Oldham and Mott before the latter reached Paris. Certainly Oldham wrote two letters to Mott[6] intended to intercept him on his arrival in Europe and brief him. Likewise with the provision on religious freedom and freedom for missions, Oldham had laid the crucial foundation with his plea on the Treaty of Berlin provision. However, what the Americans were able to assist in ensuring, to great effect, was that in each of the provisions for mandates over ex-German territories, the same provision as was stipulated for Africa as a whole in the revised Treaty of Berlin was now specifically stated in each mandate, not only for African territories but elsewhere in the world as well.

Nothing of what was achieved at Paris mollified in the least the German missionary leadership. A spate of articles appeared in missions literature concerning what appeared to them simply as another stage in the expropriation of German missions by allied missions and churches in collusion with their governments. Karl Axenfeld viewed article 438, not as the preservation but as the "outraging" of German missions, the most immoral demand ever made by any government.[7] The suspicions against Mott and Oldham actually grew in the time of peace. Not only, it was alleged, had they been quiescent when German missionaries were interned and deported, not only had they refused to protest effectively at the British government's exclusion policy, but now they had actually instigated this policy of "confiscation". The Germans were now placing more faith in the neutrals' attitude, and were encouraged by their wait-and-see approach regarding membership of the Emergency Committee. They also found more amenable the stance of the Society of Friends, and especially Henry Hodgkin, the British Quaker on the Continuation Committee. The whole ethos of the World Alliance for Promoting International Friendship through the Churches, now reviving after its faltering start on the eve of war in 1914, was much more congenial to the German missionary leadership. There, they felt, they found an ethos more willing to understand and sympathize than to judge and condemn. Five Germans attended the first meeting of the World Alliance in Oude Wassenaar in Holland in October 1919 and were able to meet a number of American and British missionary representatives including Neville Talbot, bishop of Winchester, and Louise Creighton, both British members of the Continuation Committee. The Germans were grateful for this opportunity but declared that they were unwilling to share in any specifically missionary gathering at an international level "until the most fundamental and outstanding differences between the German members and English and American members

[6] JHO letters to Mott 17 and 18 March 1919 [OA].
[7] Hogg, p.188.

– such as Dr John Mott, Mr Oldham and Dr Ogilvie – had been adjusted by thoroughgoing personal conferences".[8]

What did result from this immediate post-war period was a spate of new statements on the "supranationality" of missions. The World Alliance meeting in Holland produced one, as did the CMSBI standing committee a few weeks later, and likewise the Foreign Missions Conference in the United States in January 1920. By this time, to all intents and purposes the principle had been recognized in the Versailles treaty and accompanying conventions. With that, we may imagine, Oldham was well content to let matters take their course. And take their course they did. Before many years were out, a number of German missionaries were returning to their pre-1914 spheres of work. German Protestant and Catholic missions, for example, were back under German leadership in parts of India by 1925–27, and in East Africa likewise by the later 1920s. The whole issue, not to mention the war itself, had of course revealed the need for new Christian thinking on the still more basic questions of nationhood and national loyalty in relation to the universal nature of the gospel. Drawing upon what he had felt to be a matter of integrity during the war, yet recognizing the need now for a new world order, Oldham set out his own reflections on this in an essay of 1920, "Nationality and Missions":

> For the Christian nationality is not the ultimate loyalty. His highest allegiance is to the Christian fellowship. He cannot be indifferent to the claims of nationality, for the genius and tradition and spirit of the nation have made him what he is. He cannot divest himself of the duties of citizenship. The nation is a fact in the life of the world and we cannot set the fact aside as if it did not exist. There are many points at which the claims of national loyalty and of loyalty to humanity as a whole are difficult to reconcile and create perplexity for the Christian conscience. But there can be no doubt that our great need today in a world fevered and torn by national antagonisms is to be recalled to the simple and universal things, and to realize how much more fundamental are the things that unite men than those that divide them . . .[9]

Something very similar was to be said, seventeen years later, by the Oxford conference on "Church, Community and State".

## A painful reconciliation

The process of post-war reconciliation was intimately bound up with the task of establishing new machinery for international missionary cooperation. This was so for two reasons. First, the building of new relationships between the missionary leaders of the allied countries and of Germany, and the whole question of German missions, would obviously feature prominently on the agenda of any new body. Second, the vital question was whether, how and when the Germans themselves would be willing actually to participate in the

[8] Hogg, p.192.
[9] Oldham, "Nationality and Missions", *IRM*, vol. IX, no.35, July 1920, p.381.

new structure. For Oldham these were more than administrative or even tactical questions to be solved. He knew that to the Germans he himself was part of the problem thanks to his perceived behaviour during the war.

Despite his repeated wartime insistence that the deep Anglo-German differences could be bridged only through personal meeting, Oldham did not rush off to Germany at the earliest possible moment. The first British member of the old Continuation Committee who did meet with any of the Germans was Henry Hodgkin who, as has been seen, had been viewed by the Germans as much more sympathetic and understanding of their views. Hodgkin travelled to Holland in April 1919 and, with Dr Gunning of the Dutch missions, met with Würz, Axenfeld and Johannes Spiecker. Oldham meanwhile had work to do in getting the Emergency Committee into action. As has been seen, not only the Germans but the mission leaders in the neutral countries had proved very wary about joining in the Emergency Committee, and at its first meeting in London on 24 March 1919 only British and Americans, nine in number, were present. However, at its next meeting on 2–3 May, fourteen were present including representatives from the French, Dutch, Danish and Indian societies. Mott and Charles Watson reported on the latest developments at the Paris peace conference. Hodgkin and Gunning relayed what the Germans had told them at their recent meeting: their despondency over the plight of their missions, their continued hurt at the accusations of disloyalty among German missionaries in British territories at the start of the war, and their pain at what they took to be now permanent banishment from many of their mission fields. And why had the British missions not spoken out for supranationality? They were more impressed with the attitude of the neutrals, who had held back from joining the Emergency Committee until the views of the Germans had been sought. This meeting also requested that Oldham be released from his executive duties at the CMSBI so as to devote himself wholly to the international matters faced by the Emergency Committee – and to this the standing committee of the CMSBI agreed four weeks later.

The Treaty of Versailles was signed on 28 June 1919. Soon afterwards, a fraternal letter signed by a number of British missionary representatives was sent to the German friends of missions. While frankly stating the British view of the situation it assured them: "We need you, and you need us. We must seek every opportunity of coming together. We must try to believe in one another's motives . . . We hope in the future for full and free cooperation in this work."[10] Signatories included Louise Creighton, Henry Hodgkin, Kenneth Maclennan and Mary Oldham (but for some reason not her husband). On 19 August the German societies replied, asking for mutual confession of the fact that each country had deceived the other during the war, and stating that now, as then, German Christians still felt forced to defend the fatherland. And again, why no protests on behalf of the supranationality of missions? Why so little concern about deported and interned missionaries . . . ? But there was also the plea,

[10] Hogg, p.191.

"Please have confidence in us, and we will have confidence in you."[11] Tentative threads of relationship were beginning to be spun. Further strands were exchanged at the meeting of the World Alliance in Holland in October that year.

When would Oldham meet the Germans? At first it seemed that he might accompany Arthur J. Brown who, as chairman of the special committee on German missions appointed by the American section of the Emergency Committee, was to tour Holland, Germany, Belgium, France and Britain during the autumn. As well as attending the World Alliance meeting in Oud Wassenaar, he travelled to Berlin, meeting with the *Ausschuss* and many German leaders. Correspondence had shown, however, that it would be more diplomatic for him to visit on his own – at least, Oldham thought so. Brown was an enthusiast for the earliest possible return of German missions. Somewhat concerned, soon after Brown's European tour Oldham wrote to Mott with a warning that Brown had spent only one day in Britain (at the CMSBI standing committee) as against a whole week in Berlin, and could hardly appreciate the general feeling in Britain and France.[12] Meanwhile, in mid-November Oldham also managed to get to the continent, visiting France and Switzerland. At Zürich on 13 November, he at last met with Würz and others of the Basel Mission.[13] Plans to travel on to Tübingen and meet with Bishop Hennig did not materialize – the German railway service was suspended.

On his way home, Oldham reflected on his impressions and on the resolution from the World Alliance meeting, and on what Brown had told the CMSBI standing committee. As soon as he was back in his office on 18 November he cabled Mott: "Visit to Continent points to international missionary gathering next year preferably early June – Can you adjust your European programme accordingly – writing." His letter to Mott that same day indicates that while he had reservations about Brown's zeal for an instant restoration of the German missions, that point of view and the strength of feeling of the constituency behind it could not be ignored – as the resolutions at the Oude Wassenaar meeting of the World Alliance had shown:

> Dr Brown is quite clear that unless the missionary bodies arrange at an early date for an international missionary gathering their hand will be forced by the World Alliance. As the result of my conversations with friends in France and Switzerland, including Würz, I am convinced that it is desirable that an international missionary gathering should be held at an early date.[14]

In wresting the initiative from such a body as the World Alliance, however, Oldham was equally concerned to set a more inclusive agenda for any such meeting and not to allow it to be dominated by the German missions issue alone. The overall agenda should be that of missions in relation to governments,

[11] *Ibid.*, p.192.
[12] JHO letter to Mott 17 Nov. 1919 [OA].
[13] Hogg, p.154.
[14] JHO second letter to Mott 17 Nov. 1919 [OA].

with particular attention to two main subjects: the nature and extent of the freedom missions could expect from governments, and the obligations of missionaries of alien nationality to the governing power.[15] Within this framework German missions would obviously be given a high profile, but not to the exclusion of everything else, and Oldham believed it was vital to set discussion of even the most immediate and pressing problems within wider and more fundamental considerations.

Oldham was soon able to confer with Mott in more detail, for in mid-December he made his first post-war visit to the United States, accompanied by his wife and Betty Gibson. As well as the plans for the international missionary gathering, he and Mott discussed questions ranging from education and missions, to the relationships between the national missionary bodies in Britain and North America. Oldham attended the Student Volunteer convention, speaking on India and on the crisis in education on the mission field, and he also addressed the Foreign Missions Conference.

The Oldhams returned to England in the new year. By February 1920 the CMSBI standing committee had given its support to the international meeting plan, as had the committee of reference and counsel in America. It was therefore basically under these joint auspices – not that of the Emergency Committee – and supported by the French, Danish and Swedish societies that agreement was reached and planning begun for the international missionary meeting to be held at Crans, Switzerland, in June that year.

Meanwhile the Germans were objecting that large conferences of this type were inappropriate to what they felt were their needs of smaller and more intimate occasions, especially bearing in mind their outstanding grievances – to which had now been added that of the "war guilt" clause in the Versailles treaty. It was to meet this need that an informal meeting was arranged at Oegstgeest, near Leiden, on 16–17 April. Joe Oldham, Frank Lenwood, Kenneth Maclennan and Betty Gibson attended from the British side, with Bishop Hennig, Martin Schlunk, Friedrich Würz and Missionar Lutz from the Germans, with Hennig in the chair. Probably neither side were able to be quite as forthright as they would have wished, but "frankness prevailed".[16] It was revealed that the *Ausschuss* would not appoint official delegates to the Crans meeting, but that several Germans would probably attend in a personal capacity. Though strained, the meeting had fulfilled its purpose of at least creating a stage for further bridge-building. On the German side it began to dawn for the first time that, far from deserting the German missions, Oldham and others had been toiling on their behalf during the war. Shortly after the meeting, Oldham received a letter from Karl Fries saying: "It will please you to hear that I met a person the other day who had a letter from Pastor Schlunk expressing his great satisfaction at the discussion which he and the other German delegates had with you in Holland."[17] And years later, Schlunk himself said, "We

[15] *Ibid.*
[16] Hogg, p.159.
[17] *Ibid.*, p.160.

[Germans] had lacked communication. I was at Leiden. It was wonderful. Lenwood and I went home as if there had never been a war."[18]

Oldham therefore returned home much encouraged, whatever the continuing German misgivings, to prepare for the Crans meeting. One vital element in the preparation was his extensive paper *The Missionary Situation After the War.* In this Oldham surveyed such obvious and immediate problems as that of German missions and the Versailles treaty, but also deeper problems including that of education on the mission field – a question which he was about to investigate still more thoroughly[19] – and the claims for missionary freedom and the obligations of missions to governments. Perhaps the most searching section of his paper, however, was that on "The Attitude of the Missionary to Political Questions". Using as a case-study the very recent episode of the CMSBI protest about forced labour in Kenya, Oldham argued that missions have a duty to protest over human wrongs, although they may not be in a position to choose precisely between different political methods of righting those wrongs. In addition, the situation of missionaries who were nationals of the offending government was rather different from those who were aliens. The whole question, while sharpened by recent experiences, had in fact been on the agenda since Edinburgh. Oldham's paper became in effect the working document for much of the meeting, and ensured that the questions which Oldham had identified to Mott the previous November as being the most important, were indeed dealt with at length.

## The Crans meeting June 1920

The meeting took place 22–28 June 1920, in the Château of Crans overlooking Lake Geneva, home of Colonel and Madame van Berchem, missionary enthusiasts whose daughter had died after a short period of service in India. For Oldham it marked the truly new beginning of international missionary cooperation. "The views of the lake and of the mountains beyond, including Mont Blanc in the distance when the atmosphere was sufficiently clear, with their changing aspects and colours, were an unfailing source of delight. The lovely grounds afforded pleasant walks and opportunities of quiet intercourse. Bathing in the lake was a regular feature of each day's proceedings. But more even than the loveliness of the outward surroundings, the hospitality and kindness of the household under whose roof the Conference met helped to create an atmosphere which had from the first a sensible influence on its proceedings."[20] It was, technically, an independent, ad hoc meeting owing its standing to the support given it by the national organizations. Equally important however, those attending included the old Continuation Committee

[18] *Ibid.*

[19] Cf. Oldham, "The Crisis in Christian Education in the Mission Fields", in *Papers in Educational Problems in Mission Fields,* London IMC, 1921.

[20] See Oldham's account of Crans, "A New Beginning of International Missionary Co-operation", *IRM*, vol. IX, no. 36, Oct. 1920, pp.481ff.

*The new beginning: the International Missionary Conference, Crans, June 1920. Group includes: front row from left, 1st Bishop Hennig, 4th Georgina Gollock, 6th J.H. Oldham, 7th Bishop Roots (Chairman), 8th J.R. Mott, 9th Julius Richter, 11th Prof. Haussleiter, 12th Betty Gibson, 13th Mary Oldham; 3rd row, 1st from left, Frank Lenwood, 2nd from right (in dark glasses) Friedrich Würz. Colonel and Mrs van Berchem are in the left-hand window.*

and the recent Emergency Committee. The standing of such bodies could be as high or as low as any cared to make them, but of the significance of those actually attending there could be no doubt. As forecast at Leiden, a number of the Germans attended in a personal capacity: Hennig, Haussleiter, Richter and Würz, all members of the Continuation Committee. Mott was chairman of the business committee, Oldham was the secretary. Bishop Logan H. Roots of Hankow, China, was overall chairman – and that in itself was a healthy reminder to the Europeans that their own problems had to be set within a rekindled vision of the whole world.

Crans enabled honest exchanges, helped by Oldham's preparatory material. He had pointed out that one of the most important developments now having to be faced by mission agencies was the increasing role being taken by governments in education, where previously it had been missionaries providing virtually the whole of schooling. The conference, however, did not at this stage seem ready to take up this issue as seriously as Oldham wished. He "attempted to startle us with anticipations of the future, and failed – largely, I fancy, because we were too sluggish or preoccupied to give due weight to the facts he cited", said Frank Lenwood.[21] Discussion of the section on "The Attitude of the Missionary to Political Questions" was especially lively.[22] Much time was spent on German missions, resulting in a nine-point statement emphasizing the need for understanding on all sides, and for national bodies to work to hasten the return of the German missionaries to their fields.

The paramount task of Crans, however, was to tackle the need for a new, permanent international missionary structure. The Emergency Committee, clearly, was no more than a temporary device to keep the post-Edinburgh project afloat. Oldham had set out on paper a number of possibilities. The most practicable, in his view, was based on the maxim which had become ever firmer for him during the war years: that the national cooperative bodies should form the basis of an international organization for coordinating missionary policy. (This in turn went back to the "Hague principle" of 1913 which affirmed that the ultimately authoritative voices in determining international missionary policy were the mission boards themselves.) In what was to prove a prophetic statement, Oldham envisaged even this organization soon having to give place to "something that may represent the beginnings of a world league of churches".[23]

After lengthy discussion, the Crans delegates unanimously recommended that the national missionary organizations create an "International Missionary Committee" on the lines Oldham had set out. It would function as an international coordinating committee through its secretaries and biennial meetings. Between its regular meetings a "Committee of Reference" would act

[21] Cf. F. Lenwood, "The International Missionary Council at Lake Mohonk", *IRM*, vol. XI, no. 41, Jan. 1922, p.34.

[22] Oldham, "Notes of International Meeting at Crans", attached to JHO letter to Mott 2 Sept. 1920 [OA].

[23] Hogg, p.165.

for it. Its budget would be supplied by the national bodies (at the start, this effectively meant the Foreign Missions Conference and the CMSBI). It was also resolved that John Mott be its chairman and Joe Oldham its secretary. Further, A.L. Warnhuis, an American of Dutch descent working as a missionary in China, would be invited to become Oldham's associate. The thirteen members of the Continuation Committee present at Crans all agreed to transfer their responsibilities (and their funds) to the International Committee once it was properly constituted. Thus was a process of transition between Edinburgh and the new world effectively set in motion.

### North America 1921: education and race

The most important task immediately following Crans was to get its proposals circulated to all the national bodies and their constituent boards. This Oldham did in the second half of 1920. In view of the preponderant part, in every way, which the North American societies would play in the new organization, he went to America for the first three months of 1921, in order to confer with the boards. Once again Mary Oldham and Betty Gibson accompanied him. Gibson not only provided first-class secretarial and organizational support on such trips but also, incidentally, wrote her family copious letters, many of which have been preserved, and serve as excellent travelogues, as entertaining as they are informative, of the Oldhams abroad.

Oldham and Mott spent a good deal of time planning the first meeting of the new International Committee, scheduled for the autumn at Lake Mohonk, at which the responses from the national bodies to the Crans recommendations would be considered and final decisions on the new structure would be taken. Oldham's presence became doubly important because Mott himself was ill for much of these three months – most of their time together was spent at a hotel resort in Ashville, North Carolina – and a good deal of the weight of the preparatory work fell to Oldham: "Mr Oldham is spouting letters like a whale," Betty Gibson commented.[24] In addition, however, he and his companions took in more of the North American scene than on any of their previous visits. There was an important visit to Canada where, thanks to the strength of conservative Protestantism, missionary cooperation was viewed with much more caution than in either the United States or Britain. In Montreal and Toronto they discovered that the Student Volunteer Movement was regarded with suspicion by the churches and the mission boards, and in turn felt marginalized and unsure where to go. In Toronto, the Student Volunteer people "listened like lambs to the most radical of Mr Oldham's propositions and some of the local radicals were greatly amused".[25] Soon afterwards, on 19 March from New York, Oldham wrote to E.H. Clarke, the leader of the student movement in Toronto, with advice on tactics out of the wealth of his own experience. The

[24] B. Gibson letter to family 1 Feb. 1921 [OA].
[25] B. Gibson letter to family 4 Feb. 1921 [OA].

mission boards, says Oldham, whatever their limitations, are at least where a truly world outlook and commitment are to be found in Canada, and they must be won to the student cause. But this will take time, tact and patience. The only way is personal contact, mutual sharing of problems and anxieties.

More important still, from the point of view of Oldham's work over the next few years, was the party's encounter with the southern states and their black communities. They visited the well-known Tuskegee Normal and Industrial Institute for the Training of Coloured Young Men and Women and a number of other black educational establishments. Joe himself went on to St Louis, Indianapolis and Chicago. He was deeply stirred by what he met in the black face of America, and above all by the leaders of the black education movements themselves. In great excitement, on 11 February he wrote home to Lionel Curtis, founder of the Round Table, an exponent of a truly inter-racial commonwealth ideal for the British empire, and newly-elected Fellow of All Souls, Oxford:

> I have just completed a week's visit to Tuskegee and Calhoun. It has been my first intimate contact with leaders of the Negro race . . .
>
> What strikes one most in contrast with national and racial situations elsewhere is the extraordinary sanity of outlook of the Negro leaders and the absence of any kind of sourness of disposition notwithstanding the discriminating disabilities of which they are daily reminded. They exhibit restraint and balance of judgment, a power of recognizing and reckoning with facts, patience in working towards a far distant goal, a concentration of their energies on constructive efforts and a cheerful optimism to which I know no parallel. This is no doubt partly due to the magnificent tradition established by Booker Washington, but it is so general and widespread (though of course by no means universal) that one cannot help recognizing in it the expression of very admirable and valuable racial qualities. The Indian situation would be much more hopeful than it is if Indians possessed a larger measure of these gifts.
>
> I have met two or three men from Africa, and in particular have had two or three long talks with a man from Rhodesia who has been for ten years in the United States, and after taking a two years post-graduate course at Chicago University is now on the staff at Tuskegee. He wants to go back to Rhodesia to help in the uplift of his own people . . . It may be long in coming but sooner or later we shall have the same situation in Africa that we are facing in India . . . The African students studying in the United States have formed an African Students' association, embracing all African students studying in America . . . The striking thing to me is how all these men have an African consciousness; their loyalty and interest is not Liberian or Rhodesian or Gold Coast, but African. The man to whom I have especially referred is a better educated man than the average missionary. The number of educated Africans at present is small, but they can hold their own with the European just as the Indian can do.

Oldham a few years later would not be speaking of "racial qualities" in such an unexamined way. But clearly these encounters were already revelatory to him, and the prophetic imagination was stirring: above all in a new, dawning consciousness of *Africa.*

The Oldhams were back home just before the end of March. One of the first things Oldham did on his return was to write to Mott with a strong plea for the *concentration* of the training of missionaries in one centre, preferably New York, where all available resources could be brought to bear instead of being dissipated among scattered institutions. While still in America, he had confided to Mott that he thought the quality of present leadership in the Student Volunteer Movement left much to be desired.[26] As will be seen, both the education of missionaries and the place of education in the missionary task were to become dominant concerns for Oldham during the 1920s, and what he had seen in America greatly fuelled this concern. Moreover, it was also already apparent that the post-war scene was both demanding and enabling new secretarial responsibilities for Oldham. It was therefore fortunate that Arnold Warnshuis was able to join Oldham's office at the new British missionary headquarters, Edinburgh House in London, in mid-June 1921. Warnshuis was to prove himself an extremely able administrator. One of the first experiences awaiting him was a visit to Berlin with Oldham and Lenwood to make first-hand contact with the German missions and their problems. In 1924 Warnshuis transferred to New York so that the international missionary movement also had a coordinating office there. Others were crucially important to Oldham in the London office. Betty Gibson was a graduate in both French and German and provided much help in translating material. Marion Hunter, a voluntary assistant, collated a great deal of documentation. Georgina Gollock continued in her forthright and forceful way to steer each successive number of the *IRM* through the press until 1927, and was succeeded by Marion Underhill, an Oxford graduate who had served in India for eighteen years and had worked with Gollock since 1923. Only with such an efficient, able and committed team in London could Oldham himself have provided such confident leadership including successively longer spells away from the office on his travels abroad.

## Lake Mohonk, October 1921

So to the Lake Mohonk meeting, in the first week of October 1921. This mountain resort had been the scene of the second meeting of the Continuation Committee nine years before, in many ways another world now. But equally there was continuity, for what was about to be launched at this meeting was indeed that which Oldham and Mott had been envisaging since Edinburgh – and indeed, had first been envisaged by Johannes Warneck in a plan publicized in 1888. There were sixty-one participants, preponderantly European but with notable participation from Asia with such as S.K. Datta – Oldham's friend from his YMCA days in Lahore – representing the new National Missionary Council of India, Dr Ma Saw Sa (a woman) from Burma, Y.Y. Tsu from Shanghai and two from Japan. Conspicuous by their absence, however, were the Germans. The *Ausschuss* and the German continental missions conference meeting at Bremen had ruled that there could be no German participation so long as German missions were barred from allied lands. Julius Richter, for one,

[26] JHO letter to Mott 15 Feb. 1921 [OA].

was deeply unhappy with this rigidity from some of his colleagues, and shortly after the Bremen meeting wrote to Oldham: "Is it not a fundamental Christian principle that differences between Christians, however deep and great, are to be resolved within the Christian fellowship and not as a precedent condition to it?"[27] Oldham, Lenwood and Warnshuis had at their meeting in Berlin in June pressed strongly for the Germans to come to Mohonk but, after vigorous discussion, their position remained unaltered.

At Lake Mohonk, eleven years after Edinburgh, the structure and aims of a permanent body were at last agreed. Built into its constitution was the Hague principle of 1913, and the Edinburgh premise that its brief did not include ecclesiastical or doctrinal questions. Its theological basis was simply that of the duty of Christians to witness to the gospel of Jesus Christ and the call to unity in that task. Its functions were spelled out as:

- to stimulate thinking and investigation on missionary questions,
- to make the results available for all missionary societies and missions,
- to help to coordinate the activities of the national missionary organizations of the different countries and of the societies they represent,
- to help bring about united action where necessary in missionary matters,
- to help unite Christian public opinion in support of freedom of conscience and religion and of missionary liberty,
- to help unite the Christian forces of the world in seeking justice in international and inter-racial relations,
- to be responsible for the publication of the *International Review of Missions* and such other publications as in the judgment of the Council may contribute to the study of missionary questions,
- to call a world missionary conference if and when this should be deemed desirable.

One further change, small but significant: "Council" was substituted for "Committee" in order to underline where the seat of decision-making authority lay, in the national bodies and their constituent boards, not in an autonomous committee. So was born the *International Missionary Council* (IMC).

The Mohonk meeting took no further executive action but a number of resolutions were passed: on the need to enquire further into relations and partnership with indigenous church leadership; on missionary freedom, especially regarding German missions – on which an important bridge-building statement was passed that in general German missionaries on allied territory had not been guilty of disloyalty – and the hope that they would be represented at the next meeting; and on recommendations for work by the officers. Mott was asked to pay attention to the Middle East and Islam. Oldham, for his part, was named again as editor of *IRM* with Georgina Gollock as his assistant and

[27] Hogg, p.204, n.2.

Arnshuis as business manager. The Council also encouraged him to visit India to consult with the National Missionary Council. What is more, this time the education issue which he had raised in *The Missionary Situation after the War* and on which he had attempted to focus attention at Crans the previous year, was accepted as a priority for the Council, perhaps because he had secured in Dr Paul Monroe a notable ally to speak in support, and Oldham was encouraged to pursue his studies on the subject. Without designating personal responsibility for each item, the Council also set out an agenda for the secretaries including: labour conditions in Portuguese Africa, the growth of industrialism in Asia and elsewhere, and – to be especially important for Oldham – race relations in America and the West Indies and their bearing on missions in Africa. The work on financial relief for German missions, and on lobbying with the British and other governments for the return of the missions staff to their former mission fields, was obviously a priority. The CMSBI clearly had to take the lead here and appointed Oldham joint secretary of a committee on government relations. Constant reference had to be made back to article 438 of the peace treaty. Negotiations were slow, but a major breakthrough came in 1923 when the British government adopted a policy in the colonies and protectorates of placing no restrictions upon alien missionary societies "recognized" by the CMSBI or the Foreign Missions Conference. The CMSBI liaised with the *Ausschuss* on which societies should be so recommended.[28]

## What is the IMC for?

The IMC committee, conducting interim business, met in England in July 1922; at Atlantic City in the United States in January 1925 (when the decision to hold a world conference at Jerusalem in 1928 was taken); and at Rättvik in Sweden in July 1926. The IMC as a whole met once prior to the Jerusalem conference, at Oxford in July 1923. As almost always happens when new instruments are set up, especially ecumenical ones, a good deal of the officers' time was soon preoccupied with the basis and aims of the IMC. The 1920s saw increased theological controversy in Britain and America with increasing polarization between "conservative" and "liberal" attitudes, and this was reflected, for instance, in the withdrawal of the China Inland Mission from the ecumenical bodies. More importantly, Oldham and Warnshuis, soon after Mohonk, felt that while the IMC national bodies were now properly recognized as basis of the IMC, the functional relationships between the IMC and the national bodies had been left dangerously undefined.[29] A good deal of work, naturally, was being done by the appropriate national bodies (for example the CMSBI on German missions in British territories). Moreover, and as was to be hoped, the number of national missionary bodies was steadily increasing. In a memorandum to the CMSBI and the Foreign Missions Conference Oldham

[28] See Hogg for the whole story.
[29] *Ibid.*, p.218.

and Warnshuis stated that in the 1922–23 period the IMC amounted "practically to nothing more than a conference held every two years."[30]

With such questions, naturally, came that of the role of the secretaries themselves. There were evidently two expectations, not mutually exclusive but differing in emphasis, of what Oldham and Arnshuis were meant to be doing: travelling and sharing information or carrying out executive responsibilities for specifically assigned problems. It was this latter which brought down to a personal level the congenital problem of the respective spheres of activity for the national and international bodies. What was it that the IMC *could* and *had* to do, and therewith its two secretaries, which the national bodies could not? Oldham argued that very specific problems requiring only a small part of an administrator's time should be left to national executives. To the IMC should be given the comprehensive study of some broad problem – and also the task of acting as antennae to the changing world scene and the new demands for mission. Thus might the Council become an instrument to help bring into being those new creations or movements "which lie hid in the purpose of God for the world as it is today".[31] Oldham's high estimate of the role of national bodies was to influence considerably his view of the role of *international* bodies, up to and beyond the formation of the World Council of Churches many years later.

It was at the meeting of the IMC committee in Atlantic City in 1925 that major attention to these matters was given, and a definite direction given to the future development of the IMC. What was remarkable was how the range of the IMC's interests and work had expanded in just five years: religious freedom, race relations, indigenous churches, Christian education, opium traffic and other social evils – all these were recognized as the concerns of *mission* (itself a significant stance) and moreover requiring *international cooperation* both in study and execution, and as such rendered the IMC indispensable (and were also dealt with as major topics in the *IRM*). It should therefore concentrate on the larger problems confronting the boards.

W.R. Hogg says of Oldham: "When [he] came to a job, he concentrated on it with a single mind and with all his energy. When he had exhausted all that he could give to a particular task, he moved on to the next thing. In giving his best, he centred on one thing at a time."[32] This is somewhat overstated, especially when contrasted with Mott "who carried on a broad range of activities simultaneously"; for while Mott certainly showed a masterly ability to advance on several fronts at once, Oldham, while more focused in his interests, was markedly capable of attacking several issues during the same week if not the same day. As will become only too clear, in the 1920s Oldham had a diverse and complex agenda which makes any straightforward narrative difficult. It will be

[30] *Ibid.* See also Oldham on significance of national bodies especially in India and China, in "New Spiritual Adventures in the Mission Field", *IRM*, vol. XI, no. 44, Oct. 1922, pp.526–50.

[31] Hogg, p.219, n.53.

[32] *Ibid.*, p.221.

convenient, therefore, and not wholly arbitrary, to use the Atlantic City meeting of 1925 as a point to mark off a certain phase in Oldham's post-1918 career, for after that date his agenda proliferated even more. Moreover, from about that year, having set up and set in motion the IMC and clarified its objectives and methods, a change of emphasis is discernible in Oldham. Hitherto, the IMC as such had been the object of his attention and concern. From the mid-1920s, the IMC becomes progressively less important to Oldham as an organization in itself. From now on, it is mainly significant to him as supplying the context within which he could think, write and organize on what he was discerning to be the next critical issues in the contemporary world requiring a response from the missionary church. At the same time, as will be seen, a crisis of confidence developed between Oldham and his longest-standing colleague John Mott, on the kind of leadership now required by the IMC.

The early 1920s for Joe Oldham had seen real accomplishments. A note of sadness in his and Mary's life, in addition to their childlessness, was the loss of the one who perhaps above all would have rejoiced in what his son was bringing about. Colonel George Oldham died in 1923. A few years later Joe wrote to a friend who had been likewise bereaved: "I lost my father some years ago and for many years, and even now, the wound was opened afresh whenever I had some experience which I knew he would have shared with keenest delight, had he been alive. These severances come with a call to walk with a renewed devotion in the paths which those taken from us faithfully trod."[33]

[33] JHO letter to "Jim" 27 Oct. 1932 [OA].

# PART III

# MISSION AND THE CORRIDORS OF COLONIAL POWER

CHAPTER 9

# *Mission, Empire, Race and Prayer 1919–25*

JOE OLDHAM had never yet been to Africa, but in 1916 in *The World and the Gospel* he had written: "The problem with which we are confronted in Africa is one of the great issues of history. Have we eyes to see its immense significance? Shall the African peoples be enabled to develop their latent powers, to cultivate their peculiar gifts, and so enrich the life of humanity by their distinctive contributions? Or shall they be depressed and degraded and made the tool of others, the instrument of their gain, the victim of their greed and lust?"[1] While his own early overseas background had been formed by India, for some years the needs and potential of Africa had been exciting him. He was an active member of the Anti-Slavery League, constantly in touch with its secretary John Harris. In 1913 Harris completed a far-reaching tour of Africa, returning with shocking reports on the exploitation of Africans especially in the Portuguese colonies (there had previously been widespread outcries about the harshness of Belgian rule in the Congo). Another important contact was Lionel Curtis of the Round Table.

## Kenya and enforced labour

That Africans, anywhere, should be the tool, instrument or victim of others' greed and lust would be shocking enough to Oldham. But just after the end of the 1914–18 war it became evident that this was happening in Kenya, a British colony. In October 1919 the government of Kenya passed an order in council authorizing forced labour by Africans on the private estates of Europeans. The memorandum issued by the governor was accompanied by a circular from the chief native commissioner, instructing district officers to put every pressure on Africans to get them to comply. Two or three district officers refused. The

[1] *The World and the Gospel*, London, United Council for Missionary Education, 1916, pp.137f.

Anglican bishops of Mombasa and Uganda, and Dr J.W. Arthur of the Church of Scotland Mission, criticized the circular strongly but, apparently resigned to the inevitability of compulsory labour, "urged that so long as it was clearly necessary it should be definitely legalized"[2] – with the added proviso that protection be given to women and children. For the bishop of Zanzibar, Frank Weston (scourge alike of theological liberalism and racial injustice) such temporizing was to condone evil, and he vehemently protested against any legal recognition of forced labour. He appealed to the archbishop of Canterbury, whose concern was immediately aroused.

Weston came to England in the spring of 1921 to campaign on the issue. Through the missionary connections, the matter inevitably came to the attention of the CMSBI and Oldham in particular. Weston came to see Oldham. He said: "For many years I have been fighting against those who seem to deny our Lord doctrinally, but if it comes to bishops of the Church of England denying Him in matters of conduct I am going to quit."[3] Oldham commented a few years after:

> He was very hot on the subject. I think he did his fellow bishops an injustice. I felt as strongly as he did that the line taken in the Bishops' memorandum was most unfortunate and open to grave misunderstanding ... What I think he failed to recognise was that the intentions of the authors of the Bishops' memorandum were good and that, while some of the expressions used were unfortunate, the issue of the memorandum was a courageous act intended to stop abuses ... [Weston] was, however, not inclined at first to recognise this and was desperately afraid of any compromise in what seemed to him a clear issue of right and wrong.[4]

In fact Oldham's own handling of the issue typifies the approach of the "wily saint". He knew that the churches would only be listened to and taken seriously by the politicians if they presented a united front on the issue. Weston's "flaming campaign" (as Oldham put it), if it took the form of a "frontal attack", was bound to fail since the prime minister (David Lloyd George) could easily point to the fact that while the bishop of Zanzibar took this view, the missionary leaders right on the scene took a different line, showing that there are always two sides to every question. Oldham, like Weston, thought that the line between forced labour for private gain and slavery was impossible to draw. As was his custom, however, he also armed himself as fully as possible with the facts of the case, and worked towards a position which, while it might not satisfy everyone's moral passion, might at least draw sufficient united support to achieve a practicable change in government policy. He succeeded at a week's notice in calling a small meeting at Edinburgh House bringing together the three bishops (Uganda, Mombasa and Zanzibar) and a few representatives from other

[2] G.K.A. Bell, *Randall Davidson: Archbishop of Canterbury*, vol. II, Oxford, Oxford Univ. Press, 1935, p.1230.

[3] JHO letter to H. Maynard Smith 24 April 1925. Smith wrote the biography of Weston, *Frank, Bishop of Zanzibar: Life of Frank Weston 1871–1924*, London, SPCK, 1926.

[4] JHO letter to H. Maynard Smith 24 April 1925.

missionary societies. "We managed at this meeting to secure agreement in principle that the best plan was to press for an enquiry."[5] A memorandum was also prepared, largely the work of Oldham himself, to be submitted to the secretary of state for the colonies, Lord Milner.

On 16–18 June 1920 the CMSBI held its annual conference, and Oldham laid the matter before the gathering together with the draft memorandum. The timing was critical as the matter was due to be debated in the House of Lords at the end of the month. Oldham secured the unanimous agreement of the conference – which meant in effect the leading representatives of nearly all the non-Roman Catholic missionary societies in the country. The substance of the memorandum ran:

> The proposals in the circular for obtaining the native labour required for non-native farms and private undertakings aroused considerable disquietude in the minds of members of the Conference. While compulsion is not explicitly mentioned, in the opinion of the Bishops of Mombasa and Uganda and for the reasons given in their public statements "practically compulsion could hardly take a stronger form".
>
> The Conference accepts Lord Cromer's view that there are circumstances in which compulsion may be necessary for "indisputably and recognized purposes of public utility", but it views with concern any extension of the system and holds with Lord Cromer that it should be introduced only "under all possible safeguards against the occurrence of abuses", and that every effort should be made to create conditions which will make it no longer necessary.
>
> The members of the Conference desire to express their unqualified opposition to compulsory labour for private profit, which they believe to be morally wrong and fundamentally at variance with Christian conceptions of life and duty.[6]

The statement noted "with satisfaction" that a government spokesperson in the House of Commons had deprecated the application of force to make people work for private employers, and requested assurances on how this would be made good. Anxiety was expressed at the statement by the Native Commissioner that efforts were also being made to obtain native labour from adjacent conquered (i.e. ex-German) territory, with the comment that this was not easy to reconcile with the intent of the League of Nations covenant on mandated territories. While admitting that many of the societies represented at the conference were not directly engaged in East Africa, the memorandum concluded: "But it is a vital interest of the work in which they are all engaged throughout the world that British rule over subject races should be exercised in accordance with Christian standards."[7]

Cast in the form of a letter, signed by Oldham with the agreement of all present at the conference, the memorandum was sent to Lord Milner, secretary of state for the colonies. Using his personal acquaintance with the editor, Oldham also managed to get it in first place in the correspondence columns of

[5] *Ibid.*
[6] Cited in Oldham, *The Missionary Situation after the War*, London, Edinburgh House, 1920, p.53.
[7] *Ibid.*, p.54.

*The Times* on 29 June, the day before the debate was scheduled for the House of Lords. As it happened, at Lord Milner's request (was he taken aback by the rising scale of protest?) the debate was postponed until 14 July. When the occasion came, Archbishop Davidson spoke second, and very effectively, having been in close touch on the issue with Oldham as well as with the African bishops.

A month later, Milner issued a dispatch to the governor of East Africa, stating that a policy of compulsory labour for private employment "would be absolutely opposed to the traditional policy of His Majesty's Government".[8] Unsatisfactory conditions, however, still attached to the permission for compulsory labour for public utilities. On 14 December, the archbishop led a delegation to Milner, comprising Oldham, Lord Salisbury, A.E. Garvie, the bishop of Winchester (Talbot), Donald Fraser and Kenneth Maclennan, and presented him with a further memorandum signed by leaders of the societies and a large number of political and public figures.[9] It appealed also for a Royal Commission. This request was not granted. But at least, on 5 September 1921, the new secretary of state, Winston Churchill, issued a dispatch stating that it was the government's declared policy to avoid recourse to compulsory labour for government purposes except when absolutely necessary for essential services – and also that the requisite powers could only be used with the previous sanction of the secretary of state.

Not only was a royal commission on forced labour on Kenya refused;[10] Winston Churchill's speech on "Africans in East Africa" given at a "Kenya Colony and Uganda" dinner on 27 January 1922, dismayed Oldham. Churchill expressed strong sympathy with settler interests and stated: "The democratic principles of Europe are by no means suited to the development of Asiatic and African people." He promised to honour the pledge to maintain the highlands purely white, to regulate strictly the immigration of Indians, and looked forward not only to "complete self-government" of the colony but to an eventual federation of Kenya, Uganda, Tanganyika and Zanzibar.[11] "If this really represents the policy of the imperial government," wrote Oldham to Marion Hunter from India on 2 February, "it will have to be fought, for it is impossible to maintain the Empire on such a basis." And fight it, as will shortly be seen, he did.

### India: nationalism and a National Missionary Council

To be concerned for the worldwide mission of the church involves setting goals and determining achievable strategies. But it also means responding to that

[8] Bell, p.1230.

[9] See R.L. Tignon, *The Colonial Transformation of Kenya*, Princeton, Princeton Univ. Press, 1976, pp.171–73, for Oldham's role.

[10] K. Bliss's account of the whole episode in "The Legacy of J.H. Oldham", *International Bulletin of Missionary Research*, Jan. 1984, pp.18–24, is exaggerated both in the role it ascribes to Oldham himself at the expense of other actors (no mention, for example, of Weston), and in the extent of actual long-term policy change.

[11] *The Times*, 28 Jan. 1922.

agenda which, like it or not, the world itself decides to set, often capriciously. This twofold nature of the missionary task is well illustrated by the way in which, immediately after the first world war, Oldham was confronted by the new challenge of the country of his birth and of his own first-hand missionary experience, India. It is also important to bear in mind that Oldham's work in these years was set in the context created by John R. Mott's world tours since the Edinburgh 1910 conference, which greatly stimulated the formation of national bodies for the furtherance of cooperative Christian witness and service. But these developments generated crucial questions and tensions: were such bodies primarily those of (Western-based) missions or of the indigenous churches? The questions were being posed in a world now stirring with nationalist aspirations in face of imperialist and colonialist domination. They had explosive potential.[12]

India, in the aftermath of the war in which so many of her men had fought for the British empire, in the wake of the Russian Revolution and in the light of President Wilson's famous Fourteen Points which had contributed to the Versailles peace, was stirring with new national aspirations. "If the greatest autocracy could crash overnight, why should the Indian autocracy endure? And if European peoples could determine their future, why not India? Indians considered themselves adult members of the world society; the Gokhale attitude of requests for concessions gave place to the Tilak line of demands and assertions of rights."[13] Moreover, constitutional reform was in the air, which would lead to the India Act of 1921 embodying the Montford reforms and granting self-government over greater areas of Indian life. But on 13 April 1919 occurred the massacre at Amritsar. A crowd was broken up by troops without warning, resulting (on official estimates) in 379 dead and 1,200 wounded. This, together with other disturbances around that time, plunged the sub-continent into a new wave of bitterness and distrust between British and Indian which was perhaps never finally dissipated until independence three decades later. Even in 1997, on the visit of Queen Elizabeth II to India, the recollection of the atrocity still aroused acute sensitivities.

Soon after Amritsar, Joe Oldham found on his desk a letter written on 6 May 1919 from his longest-standing and closest Indian friend S.K. (Ernest) Datta, now joint general secretary of the Indian YMCA. He had spent part of the war years in France working with the YMCA among the Indian troops. That had provided him with an uplifting, never-to-be-forgotten experience of brotherhood and comradeship across the ranks and races. Now had come complete disillusionment, and the letter is bitter from start to finish. The British, if they ever could, can never be trusted again, and moreover unless something radical happens the cause of Western Christian missions in India is finished. "The other day an old friend, a Hindu bookseller of Lahore said to

[12] As background to this section, see Oldham, "The Church and Missions in India", *IRM*, vol. IX, no. 34, April 1920; Oldham, "New Spiritual Adventures in the Mission Field" *IRM*, vol. XI, no. 44, Oct. 1922, pp.526–50; Oldham, "Five Conferences in India", *IRM*, vol. XII, no. 46, April 1923, pp.262–76.

[13] P. Spear, "India", in *New Cambridge Modern History*, vol. XII, Cambridge, Cambridge Univ. Press, 1968, p.300.

another friend, a missionary, 'Why should you waste your time trying to evangelize us? Christianity to us means the bayonet and the machine gun.'" The cause of Christianity in India depends less on flooding the country with missionaries than with changing English public opinion at home. More than "concern" is needed at this point. "Will you not write to me and tell me your thoughts? . . . Still in spite of this disillusion, to you I can say, I continue to believe in the final triumph of the right. This is my comfort and solace during these days. Can you not help some of us to strengthen our faith more wholeheartedly in your people?"

Oldham was sufficiently moved by Datta's appeal, and what it represented, as to have it copied and circulated to a number of associates.[14] In replying he was, as would be expected, deeply sympathetic to Datta's case – almost to the point of agreeing that no more missionaries should be sent to India, or at least that "only a certain kind of missionary can be of any use to India at the present time".[15] But whereas Datta had declared that in the present situation individuals can only be seen as representatives of their racial communities, Oldham argued that in Christian perspective "in the end of the day race is an accident and . . . God and the individual soul are the eternal things". Had not Rabindranath Tagore warned against generalizations in racial relationships, and had not Gandhi recently stated that "Europeans too are our brothers"? And would it really help for British and Indian ties to be completely severed? But Oldham ends positively: there might well be value in Datta coming to Britain again to help interpret the Indian situation to public opinion.

The impassioned correspondence with Datta continued for many months, as did a similar exchange with K.T. Paul, another of the YMCA general secretaries in Calcutta who enthusiastically embraced Gandhi's policy of total non-cooperation. Like Datta, Paul felt that "the Battlefield is Britain, not elsewhere",[16] and wished to come to England to speak with key church leaders. That Oldham spent so much time and care in reading and replying at length to such letters shows how deeply he was concerned that both himself, and the wider church constituency, should really hear and understand what was being said from within this new wave of Indian nationalism: and not least from those Indian Christians who were caught in an agony of tension between evidently diverging loyalties. Oldham was to be instrumental in seeing that both men were able to travel and receive a personal hearing on the international scene, and talked at great length with Paul who did manage to visit England in the late summer of 1919.

Meanwhile other notable Indians were visiting Britain. Oldham sought out C.Y. Chintamani who was in London in June 1919, and also Srinivasa Shastri, the leader of moderate, liberal Indian opinion. Oldham and Edwyn Bevan dined with Shastri at the Athenaeum, and Shastri was also invited to Oldham's

[14] JHO letter to Hartog 2 June 1919 [OA].
[15] JHO letter to Datta 10 June 1919 [OA].
[16] Paul letter to JHO 27 June 1919 [OA].

*K.T. Paul*

home at Chipstead. The following year brought the charismatic figure of Sadhu Sundar Singh to Britain. The mystic–social-activist–evangelist made a considerable impact, especially through sharing in the life of working-class communities in the north of England. He spent a night with the Oldhams at Chipstead, and a warm mutual regard quickly grew. Singh also wished to visit the United States, despite doubts on both sides of the Atlantic as to whether his reception there would compare with that in Britain. However, as Oldham wrote to R.P. Wilder on 9 April 1919, "There is no use pointing out difficulties. He is one of those difficult (or perhaps utterly Christian) people who believe that with God nothing is impossible." Oldham provided him with a number of introductions to prominent Christian leaders in New York and elsewhere on the east coast, and the Sadhu duly sailed. From Pennsylvania he wrote a letter on 6 June 1920 in which glowing gratitude for all Oldham's help mingles with disappointment at what he found in America, in contrast to Edinburgh House and Chipstead:

> Here some laymen are helping me for meetings. I am rather disappointed to see the indifference of the what you called great leaders. I don't ask money or any help from them, but I expected Christian fellowship which could have help [*sic*] in my spiritual life. But I see that they have no regard for any man. It appears that their religion is

not Christianity but organization. They seem to me artificial spiritual leaders, if I am not mistaken if Christ would have come today here from Palestine these leaders would have rejected Him as a coloured man. I shall always remember that blessed time with you the 23rd of March.

If it was important that such as Datta and Paul visited the West, they in turn felt it essential that Oldham should visit India.[17] They feared that even Oldham could not fully appreciate the rapid disillusionment of younger Christians in India, who were increasingly turning to public and national affairs, not the church, as channels for their enthusiasm and service. Oldham was not willing to proceed without a legitimate invitation, and this was provided by John McKenzie, principal of Wilson College, Bombay.[18] Datta arrived in England during the summer, and he and Oldham journeyed together to America for the International Missionary Council meeting at Lake Mohonk in the autumn. Datta stayed on in the new world for speaking engagements, considerably ruffling some Canadian feathers by his outspoken attack on aspects of imperial rule, while Oldham returned home to prepare for the Indian visit.

Once again he was accompanied by Mary Oldham and Betty Gibson, sailing early in November. For Joe and Mary it was their first return to the land to which they owed so much in parentage and upbringing, as well as their missionary experience cruelly cut short by illness twenty years ago. As they approached Bombay Oldham wrote to Marion Hunter on 17 November, describing how being shut in with a British crowd of travellers, including a number of missionaries, gave a curious sense of Britain's place in the world:

I have pictured to myself the successive shiploads of similar companies which, for the past half century, have travelled week by week by this same route, from Port Said, down the Canal to Suez, through the Red Sea, and then across the Indian Ocean to Bombay and Colombo, some of them to govern, others to protect the frontiers of the Empire, others to trade, others to propagate their faith, all in their own way fulfilling the mission of their race. I write this not in any imperialistic sense, and fully conscious that only when the books are opened can the final verdict be passed on whether the nation has worthily fulfilled its mission; but the drama is profoundly moving.

Oldham's routine on board was largely filled by his daily average of seven hours reading and writing. He and Betty Gibson were already reading up material for the book on race. Mary Oldham had typed out a memorandum in which Joe had tried to set out Gandhi's creed as he could understand it thus far, and he had worked out a list of questions on the racial situation in India.

The itinerary for this Indian visit, as originally worked out, was to begin with four days in Bombay, meeting with the Bombay district missionary council and conducting personal interviews, followed by the Telegu Missions conference at Bazwada. There would follow an extremely concentrated week in and around Madras, visiting the district missionary council, the women's Christian college,

[17] Carter letter to JHO 19 Feb. 1921 [OA].
[18] McKenzie letter to JHO 5 March 1921 [OA].

the Vellore teaching hospital and other institutions, with meetings to discuss matters ranging from German missions to religious education, not to mention many personal interviews. December would be spent in Calcutta, Cuttack and Ranchi, and after a holiday the group would meet with the National Missionary Council at Poona in mid-January. No advance arrangements had been made to follow Poona – which was as well, as events proved.

Whatever the general value of such a visit in terms of renewing first-hand acquaintance with the Indian scene and the current missionary situation, there had been from the very beginning in Oldham's mind one clear target: the meeting of the National Missionary Council in Poona. This Council, like a number of such national bodies in Asia, was a product of John Mott's post-Edinburgh Asian tour in 1912. Oldham considered that a decade later, another kind of structure was needed if the Christian mission in India was truly to become an operation of the indigenous Christian leadership. As it was, the foreign mission boards remained the dominant controlling bodies, and too much of the direction of Indian mission enterprise remained in the hands of European staff. The IMC at Lake Mohonk had already passed resolutions calling for full responsibility in the various mission fields to pass to indigenous leadership. Above all, Oldham felt that while indeed the Christian movement was a minority in India, it still had immense potential, as yet unrealized, for serving the needs of Indian society especially in education. How could such resources be released?

Oldham probably had a scheme in mind before he even left England, but he kept his cards very close to his chest until he began to meet with both the Indian Christian leaders and the Bombay Representative Council of Missions, the Telegu Missions' Conference and the Madras Representative Council of Missions. He also discussed the matter at great length with Bishop Samuel Azariah, who as a young speaker had made such an impact at Edinburgh and was now an outstanding Indian Christian leader. Oldham's suggestion, as set out in a letter to Datta[19] was that the National Council needed a central secretariat, a close-knit team of about five people, who could give greater direction to the Indian missionary movement as a whole, and especially focus on particular needs such as training for rural education, and seeing that the genuine educators were properly used. The group would also act as, in effect, talent-spotters for "a very considerable number of Indian Christians of character and ability, and see first that they got the training in India or abroad that would fit them for leadership; and secondly, that they were put in positions of responsibility for which they were qualified". Such a central group should comprise both Indian and foreign persons. Their most important function "would be to minimize as rapidly as possible the disadvantages of the movement arising from its foreign character, and getting the main direction and control into Indian hands".[20]

[19] JHO letter to Datta 6 Dec. 1921 [OA].

[20] *Ibid.*; cf. Oldham, "New Spiritual Adventures in the Mission Field" (note 12 above), esp. p.530.

It was always characteristic of Oldham's sanctified pragmatism to ask not only what was desirable (in this case, the transition to indigenous leadership) but what were the practicable steps towards the desired end. The "what" was typically the subject of conference resolutions. The "how", Oldham always believed, obviously involved programming and organization, but even more, the *right people* to get things done and to motivate others in turn. The Indian missionary scene was fraught with sensitivities. The missions and their home boards were suspicious of any apparent threat to their sovereignty. The regional missionary councils in India itself were wary (especially in the Madras case) of any centralizing tendency. A number of Indian Christians were only too happy to remain under Western direction and be spared the burden of responsibility.

But there was also goodwill and acknowledgment of the desired goal, not least in the mission boards. The right core group could foster such aspirations, identify promising initiatives and nourish new confidence. There was obviously the risk, as Oldham admitted to Datta, that in the wrong hands such a central secretariat could turn the clock back to the days of Western hegemony. But the task was to ensure that the right hands were called in.

As far as the right people were concerned among Western personnel, though he mentioned several possible names to Datta, he did not mention one in particular: William Paton. Twelve years younger, Paton was already well known to Oldham. He was of Presbyterian stock, educated at Oxford and Westminster College, Cambridge, and from 1911 to 1921 had served as a secretary of the SCM and then, after a year in India with the YMCA, as secretary of the Student Volunteer Missionary Association. In 1921 he returned to India as general secretary of the YMCA. Powerful in physique and of seemingly boundless energy, within a very short time he was travelling the length and breadth of India and making his mark on the Christian scene there. He was exactly the kind of leader Oldham envisaged for the new task.[21] The problem was, of course, that the YMCA would need an immense amount of persuasion to release someone of such gifts who had only joined them so recently.

In taking his soundings prior to the Poona meeting, Oldham received reactions varying from approval to the cautious, with no overt, outright opposition. Naturally in Calcutta he talked about the scheme at length with Paton himself, who wrote on 20 December to Tissington Tatlow:

> . . . We have had Joe staying with us which was a great pleasure and his wife and Miss Gibson too. Joe looks terribly over-worked, but he is creating a very good impression. I can't outline his great scheme here but I think his proposals are on the only line which can save the missionary movement from being quite outside the stream of Indian life. For there is no manner of doubt that with all the hate and ill-will in India just now, and heaven knows there is enough of it, there is a wonderful readiness to

[21] On William Paton, see Eleanor M. Jackson's comprehensive study *Red Tape and the Gospel: A Study of the Significance of the Ecumenical Missionary Struggle of William Paton (1886–1943)*, Birmingham, Phlogiston Press and Selly Oak Colleges, 1980.

> listen to the Christian message when it is made clear that it has nothing to do with the racial-superiority–Western-superiority stunt ... the fact is "we are the Indian problem".

At this stage Paton did not mention to Tatlow that Oldham was already inviting him to take a leading part in the new secretariat if it transpired.

The National Missionary Council met at Poona 11–17 January. Oldham considered it touch-and-go whether his proposals would be accepted and in fact some quite spirited opposition emerged, particularly from some representing the Madras region. Oldham, however, was given opportunity to make two presentations. He did not try to force or cajole, but set the situation in the broadest possible context of the IMC (which he explained at some length) and on the steadily proven value of cooperation in many countries – not least in Britain, citing the case of the united protest against Kenyan forced labour. The opposition melted away – or least fell silent. The proposals were accepted for a new body to be formed: the National Christian Council of India. Half of its governing body would be Indian. Subject to finances, a staff of five officers would be appointed to carry out the kind of tasks envisaged by Oldham. Oldham wrote to Mott[22] while the meetings were still in progress and to his London colleagues immediately afterwards,[23] and Paton likewise to Tatlow.[24] There was relief rather than jubilation. The new constitution would need ratification in a year's time. Moreover, the devil as always was in the detail, above all the detail of names to serve as officers. The Council after a short discussion settled on Rai Banadur, A.C. Mukerji and William Paton to start with. A longer discussion ensued on whether S.K. Datta or K.T. Paul should also be appointed. Eventually the lot fell on Datta. There was good reason for this in that if the YMCA was to surrender Paton, it would be much harder for them to give up Paul as well. In another sense, however, the vote for Datta was a telling message from the Indians. Much of the money promised for the scheme thus far was from Canada. Oldham had told the gathering how unpopular Datta had made himself in that country by his outspokenness the year before, and the leading Canadian missionary present said that, to quote Paton, "if Datta were appointed it might dish the scheme as far as Canadian support was concerned".[25] In face of this possibility, the vote for Datta was nevertheless unanimous, demonstrating enough belief in the scheme not to wish it to be wholly dependent on funding from one country. In the event, it was in fact to be Paul, not Datta, who joined the new team.[26] For his part, Paton was to go through an agony of self-questioning before accepting appointment as secretary of what, in due course, became the National Christian Council of India, to which he gave outstanding leadership for the next five years.

[22] JHO letter to Mott 13 Jan. 1922 [OA].
[23] JHO letter to colleagues 19 Jan. 1922 [OA].
[24] Paton letter to Tatlow 18 Jan. 1922 [OA].
[25] *Ibid.*
[26] JHO letter to Datta 25 March 1922 [OA].

In addition to all this ecumenical engineering, Oldham used his time in India to the full to study the racial and political scene. In particular he developed a much greater understanding of Gandhi, whom he now saw as essentially a religious and only incidentally a political person. He corresponded a number of times with Sir Alexander Whyte of the legislative council in Delhi, who typified the more enlightened government attitude, sympathetic to Indian aspirations but exasperated at what seemed to be capricious tactics by Gandhi. He conceded Oldham's point that the problem of relationships between Britain and India was in large measure psychological: but that, he felt, did not by itself make Gandhi's mind any easier to follow.[27]

## Around the world

It was as well that there had been no firm plans for work after Poona, for at the very start of the meeting came a cable from Oldham's London missionary colleagues urging him to attend the national conference of the China Continuation Committee in Shanghai, 2–11 May 1921. The very same day there arrived a letter from E.C. Lobenstine, secretary of the China Continuation Committee itself, urging his presence. At Lake Mohonk it had been decided that Oldham should not attend, and he had consequently dismissed the idea from his mind – just as he had accepted Mott's judgment in 1913 that he should not accompany Mott to China then. But now matters were being viewed differently. If there was to be birth of a national Christian council, it was likely to be amid some controversy. That two such communications should have come so unexpectedly and simultaneously had almost the force of a divine summons. There was also a practical side to a recognition of providence: in view of the Indian scheme and the delicacy of its Canadian situation, a visit to Canada would also have been required in any case within the next few months. At very little, if any, extra expense, it would make sense for the Oldham entourage to proceed to Shanghai, thence across the Pacific to Vancouver and then continue home eastwards. Oldham penned all this in haste to Mott on 13 January 1922.

The last weeks in India brought debilitating bouts of stomach upsets to Joe Oldham. The party journeyed southwards and looked at Christian education work in South India. With Joe weak and utterly exhausted through sickness and travel, they at last reached Ceylon and the delight of a brief respite in the beautiful surroundings of Trinity College, Kandy, where Mary's brother Alek Fraser, as ever bubbling with humour, was coming towards the end of a notable spell as head. On 27 March they boarded the P. & O. ship *Plassey* and, after all the ardours of the past weeks, felt no compunction in transferring for once to first-class.[28]

[27] Cf. JHO–Whyte correspondence of 1922 [OA].
[28] JHO letter to Hunter 29 April 1922 [OA].

Oldham arrived in Shanghai with enough time to spare before the meetings to enable him to appraise the situation. A major issue was the attitude of the China Inland Mission (CIM), the largest and most decidedly evangelical of the Protestant missionary agencies, to the proposed national council. The CIM would only join if there was an acceptable doctrinal or credal basis to the organization. Oldham was able fully to brief Mott who arrived just before the meetings and had a lengthy interview with D.E. Hoste, head of the CIM.[29] The result was that, although the CIM did not join the national council, enough of the conservative apprehensions were dealt with to ensure that neither did it oppose the new body. The conference itself was large by any standards – over 1000 delegates, more than half Chinese. The National Christian Council was set up on the same basis as the IMC and was affiliated to the international body.

Oldham's brief China experience, limited largely to this single event, seems to have left relatively little impact on him, certainly as compared with either India or Africa. The Oldham party sailed to Vancouver with Mott. They drew their breath at the grandeur of the Rockies viewed from the Canadian Pacific observation car. Oldham made his Canadian contacts as required. What had begun as a visit to India, adventurous enough in itself, had turned into a circumnavigation of the Northern hemisphere, and the party reached Liverpool in the last week in June 1922.

## India again 1922–23

It was obvious that for the sake of consolidating and implementing the Poona decisions Oldham would have to return to India the following winter and meet again with the fledgling National Council. This became even more necessary since, despite the firm recommendations at Poona, vociferous opposition was still voiced in some quarters, notably from some of the leadership of the American Methodist missions and from the Madras area. No less worrying was the fact that several of the mission boards back in England were complaining about what had appeared to them, from a distance, to be Oldham's high-handed pushing through of the proposals, not to mention their financial implications.[30] They were capable of persuasion, and proved to be so. But there were many other details to be thrashed out, down to the matters of the salaries for Bill Paton and K.T. Paul as secretaries.

Once again, then, Joe and Mary Oldham and Betty Gibson were in India by November 1922. Almost immediately Oldham met with the executive of the National Council for immediate preparations for the main meeting at Ranchi in the new year, and for working out the final proposals. The American

[29] Hogg, pp.607–09.

[30] See Jackson, pp.103–06. It is clear that Oldham incurred great suspicion in missions board circles in Britain and in missions administrations in India. Had he not been able to secure Canadian funding for such as Datta's proposed post, he might well not have been able to sell the scheme.

Methodist Bishop Robinson had to be met and mollified over his complaints about British predominance on the Council. More to Oldham's taste, just before Christmas he addressed the convocation and graduation ceremony of Serampore College, India's oldest theological institution, and took part in a conference on higher theological education there. To share in such events at the site created by the Baptist pioneers Carey, Marshman and Ward over a century earlier stirred him profoundly: "They were certainly giants in those days. We of a later generation seem pygmies beside them."[31]

So to the National Council meeting at Ranchi, mid-January 1923. The scheme was given final approval. Not surprisingly, once again it was the detail which caused the most fraught discussion, especially the allocation of the financial support as between mission boards in Britain and North America on the one hand, and the Indian churches themselves. And the proposals to pay Paton and Paul what seemed like relatively high salaries needed explanation and defence. Overall the problem was how to keep the budget as low as possible while still being able to resource what promised to be one of the most vital parts of the new Council's work, specialist support for rural education, together with a woman appointee among the officers.

## East Africa and African "paramountcy"

Oldham's most substantial work for the organization of Christian leadership in India, a continuing role as wise counsellor apart, was now accomplished. But it was by a strange twist of fate, or providence, that on this same visit he became plunged into a new dimension of India's saga, and one which in turn led him back to Africa where the real drama was being played out. India in 1923 was seething with protests, especially among the young, about the situation of their compatriots in East Africa. They were demanding that pressure be put on the Colonial Office to allow Indians equal rights with whites there. There were demonstrations. Many missionaries supported the Indian cause: the India Office, always nervous of trouble, did indeed put pressure on the Colonial Office: but white settlers dreaded a flood of Indian immigrants and were up in arms. Indians already had a monopoly of trade within Kenya. A proposal was made for a new franchise giving the Indians a much more favourable representation on the executive council and this caused a considerable stir (for different reasons) among both settlers and Indians in Kenya. It was not altogether fanciful to think that Indians might take over the country. On the other hand the white settlers had been promised "responsible government": which could only mean, in their view, elected government firmly in their own hands, or a white-only enclave. If the latter, why should not Indians have one too? Oldham tried to put to his Indian friends another point of view but it was clear that violence would increase unless a settlement was made. The one man

[31] Letter JHO to Hunter 20 Dec. 1922 [OA].

they would trust was C.F. Andrews, the friend of Gandhi and a great fighter on behalf of Indians lured abroad as indentured labour to South Africa and Fiji. Gandhi had been referred to as "a naked fakir" but in the eyes of the India Office and the Colonial Office Andrews was worse: he was white, English and a clergyman of the Church of England. Oldham convinced them that it was Andrews as mediator or mounting violent protest in India. In all this, the Indian government was championing the Indian cause against the Colonial Office.

Back home in England in the spring of 1923, Oldham plunged himself into the background and facts of the case. Already while in India he had got Marion Hunter to elicit the view of Norman Leys, an authority and author on the Kenya case.[32] He spent a good deal of time in contact with Lambeth Palace, the archbishop having been alerted to the seriousness of the situation. Davidson was also in conversation with Andrews and a number of people with church and government experience both in India and Kenya, together with Srinivasa Shastri, leader of an Indian delegation.[33] Oldham also saw C.F. Andrews on a number of occasions and entertained him at Chipstead for a weekend. He made personal contacts in the Colonial Office, as he had done on the issue of forced labour. Moreover he began an intensive correspondence, and a series of conversations, with Sir Frederick Lugard, perhaps the most celebrated British governor in Africa and exponent of the "dual mandate" concept of colonial government. He introduced Lugard to Andrews, commenting:

> If Shastri were to consent to a settlement it would not follow that Indian opinion would endorse it: if Andrews were to say that it was just and fair there is a big probability that he would carry India with him . . . Unfortunately the fact is not realized by the authorities here.[34]

Oldham and Lugard found themselves in a good deal of agreement. Both saw that the imperial government must exercise responsibility for native affairs. In the case of Kenya this would mean recovery of certain powers that had been given to the settlers. Lugard and others felt that a *quid pro quo* would be necessary to satisfy the settlers, in the form of enlarged powers within an enclave. Oldham pointed out the difficulties this would present for a division of labour between a central and essential municipal government. Would the settlers accept this? Moreover:

> Is it possible to establish a self-governing community in the heart of tropical Africa composed of vigorous, energetic and aggressive Europeans without their insisting on gaining control over the surrounding territories, even in the last resort by recourse to violence?

Furthermore, Oldham pointed out the self-contradiction in the notion of "responsible government" as white self-government. A minority both

[32] Letter Leys to JHO 18 Feb. 1923 [OA].

[33] Bell, p.1231.

[34] JHO letter to Lugard 22 May 1923 [OA], and other correspondence.

surrounded by and fiscally dependent upon a majority native population could scarcely be called "self-governing". Surely, Oldham argued, the point to maintain is that which has always been claimed to represent the best in British colonial tradition: trusteeship. Settlers as such should have no more rights in *government* than any other community in the territory, and as evidence of his historical homework on this point Oldham cited the report of a select committee of the House of Commons on aboriginal tribes as far back as 1837: "The settlers in almost every colony have either disputes to adjust with the native tribes or claims to urge against them, the representative body is virtually a party and therefore ought not to be the judge in such controversies."[35] Lugard, a month later, commented: "I find the conviction growing upon me that the point on which to concentrate is adherence to our traditional colonial policy that native populations shall not be placed under the rule, direct or indirect, of a local oligarchy of alien nationality."[36] There was indeed convergence here. But Lugard was primarily forever assuming that *someone* would always have control over the natives. Oldham acknowledged that *at present*, native Africans were not ready for Western-style forms of government for themselves. But clearly he reserved his position on the distant future. And Oldham, for his part, was always more deeply aware of the strength of Indian opinion than was Lugard who was seeking to limit the likely offence to white settler opinion.

Oldham was closely involved in the drafting of a memorandum which Archbishop Davidson and he delivered to the colonial secretary, the Duke of Devonshire, on 29 May 1923. The memorandum suggested the following policy:

(1) H.M. Government to declare that it is their policy that the East African Crown Colonies and Protectorates, including Kenya, shall be administered under the direct authority of the Imperial Government acting as trustee for the native inhabitants and for civilisation as a whole, and that as between the different communities inhabiting these territories the interests of the native population are paramount.
(2) A royal commission be appointed to consider and report how this principle can best be applied to conditions in Kenya, with due regard to the rights and claims of each of the alien immigrant communities.
(3) No material change to be made to the disadvantage of any of the three communities until the commission has reported and H.M. Government has acted upon the report.[37]

Much correspondence and many interviews followed between the India Office, the Colonial Office, Lambeth Palace and Edinburgh House. Oldham himself discussed the memorandum with C.F. Andrews and other representatives of Indian opinion, and on 11 June wrote to Sir James Masterton Smith at the Colonial Office, assuring him that "it is possible to avert a break with

[35] *Ibid.*
[36] Lugard letter to JHO 1 June 1923 [OA].
[37] Bell, p.1232.

India at the present time" if a settlement could be reached on the lines presented to the secretary of state. The crucial first paragraph of recommendations as now made by Oldham ran:

> (1) An announcement that His Majesty's Government regard the East African colonies and protectorates, including Kenya, as essentially native territories and that it is their policy to administer Kenya under the direct authority of the Crown acting as trustee for the native population and for humanity as a whole, and that as between the different communities the interests of the natives are paramount.[38]

Constitutional modifications should be implemented as necessary; restrictions on immigration to be lifted – or to be applied equally to Europeans; India, while not relinquishing her claims, to refrain from the present from pressing the claim for land in the highlands; and the principle of no segregation on purely racial lines, already accepted by the Colonial Office and Indian government, to be maintained. Oldham believed such a settlement would be in the long-term interests of the settlers themselves.

It became clear that there would be no royal commission – if for no other reason than that it would be virtually impossible to find any membership of it which would be trusted by all parties. On 23 July 1923, however, the colonial secretary did issue a white paper which stated that "Primarily, Kenya is an African territory and . . . the interests of the African natives must be paramount, and that if, and when, those interests and the interests of the immigrant races should conflict, the former should prevail." The term *paramountcy*, in particular, which the memorandum of 29 May had suggested, was due to Oldham.

The Indians got something far less than they wanted. C.F. Andrews considered the white paper a sell-out – what did it matter to assure black Africans of their "paramountcy" at the expense of Indians when in practice it was white settlers who would remain on top? But *paramountcy* at least entered the vocabulary of government officials, providing a yardstick for policy which was not inherently in favour of the settlers. But of course it was an empty phrase unless backed by deeds. The important thing was that the settlement was eventually ratified by parliament and could therefore be used as a touchstone of British policy. It was not a great leap forward for justice, but it was a manifest obstacle to likely *in*justice, in seeking to safeguard the interests of Africans, the most vulnerable sector, in the face of sheer exploitation.

## Christianity and the Race Problem

Oldham had already, during the Great War, recognized race to be one of the key issues of the day, and attempts at racial domination to be one of the symptoms, along with the war itself, of the malaise underlying the "Christian"

[38] JHO letter to J.M. Smith 11 May 1923 [OA].

West. His three months in the United States early in 1921 brought him his first direct encounters with the black communities of America and, as it seemed to him, the exciting developments in black educational institutions. Moreover, that visit provided his first meetings with educated Africans.

At the Lake Mohonk meeting of 1921, the new IMC requested that Oldham devote attention to the issue of race, and back home the United Council for Missionary Education invited him to write a book on the subject (as it had done with *The World and the Gospel*). Not only would Oldham have needed little encouragement to embark on this project, but it is highly likely that he fed these bodies with prevenient suggestions of the importance of the subject and his personal interest in it. Be that as it may, *Christianity and the Race Problem* was published by SCM Press in 1924. Not only was it Oldham's main contribution to thought in this period, it was the most substantial single piece of writing (256 pages) of his whole life, and by itself would have firmly established his place as a pioneer in Christian social thinking.

The actual writing was undertaken under great pressure, and even the basic research was not begun until after the return from the visit to India and China in June 1922. In fact a good deal of the work, in terms of information gathering and preparation of the manuscript for the press, was carried out by the indefatigable Betty Gibson. Evidently on the homeward journey from China she and Oldham had planned ahead. She wrote to her family on 23 June, just before disembarking at Liverpool: "I am going to be very busy with the Race Book. I'll have to go at it very hard in order to make use of libraries etc. while I can get them. Of course if Joe does not go to India next winter there won't be such a stew, but if he goes, whether I go or not I'll have to get as far on before he goes." Even after the second Indian visit, on which Gibson had also gone, Oldham was still looking for help. In May 1923 he gratefully accepted an invitation from Edwyn Bevan to speak on "Christianity and Racial Awareness" at the meeting of the London Society for the Study of Religion. "If I am to write the book which I have promised," replied Oldham, "I think the group of people who I should meet at your dinner are just the kind of people who would give me a great deal of help and stimulus."[39] It may be assumed, then, that most of the actual writing-up was concentrated into the autumn and winter of 1923–24.

In a quite unprecedented way, the international context of the 1920s was raising race as an inescapably challenging issue for worldwide Christianity. The Great War had itself shaken the assumed self-confidence of Europe in the superiority of white civilization. India was stirring with aspirations towards self-government. One consequence of British rule in Africa acquiring more territory from the defeated Germans was that the spotlight was being turned upon African rights; and in South Africa the legal apparatus of segregation was already rolling, to lead a generation or so later to the full implementation of

[39] Letter JHO to Bevan 4 May 1923 [OA].

apartheid. In the Pacific, Japanese military and economic muscle, not to mention immigration into the western seaboard of the United States, was arousing American fears about the "yellow peril" (and at the Paris peace conference, the Japanese had been aggrieved that the president of the United States, of all people, refused to allow into the peace treaty a clause affirming the inherent equality of all people). Within the United States itself racial segregation and discrimination against black people remained the legacy of slavery, but more articulate voices were being heard from within the oppressed communities, and not least in the black churches.

There had as yet been little, if any, systematic Christian theological or ethical thinking on race. Plenty of ad hoc attention had been given to particular wrongs, and many a sermon was preached against "racial antagonism". But the climate of the post-war world meant that more than well-meaning sentiment was required to tackle the issues responsibly – or indeed to see what the issues actually were. In educated circles as well as in the more popular Western media, intellectual respectability was being given to beliefs in white superiority by such writers as Lothrop Stoddard and C.C. Josey. Propounding a "biological" view of human nature and attaching an exaggerated importance to certain ideas of heredity, they foresaw the future of human history as one of interracial conflict which the white or Nordic race could and must win. But, even if such views were to be rejected as pseudo-scientific ramblings, there remained the fraught political questions of dealing with actual situations where, like it or not, antagonism and conflict were real. In the complexities of the late afternoon of empire, how could biological, cultural, sociological and political factors, let alone the ethical, be teased apart?

*Christianity and the Race Problem* answered this situation in a masterly fashion and set a standard for all subsequent ecumenical writing on social ethics. It is broad in its sweep and yet, where necessary, detailed in its analysis. It is visionary in its hold on the Christian theological understanding of humans as created by God and of God's purpose in which human life finds its fulfilment; and at the same time it is rooted in the earthly facts of human existence as known to the best science of the day and as experienced in the life of actual communities. It does not harangue, but pursues its argument by patiently allowing conflicting opinions to have their full say, however unpalatable they may be, before making a considered (and not necessarily final) judgment. It is wide-ranging in its use of sources, around 100 authors – mainly in anthropology, genetics, psychology, and cultural studies and reports on specific situations – as well as drawing on Christian theologians past and present. A particularly important role is played in Oldham's mind at this time by the American philosopher and educationist W.E. Hocking, whose *Human Nature and Its Remaking* had first appeared in 1918 and whom Oldham had got to know on his recent American visits.[40]

"The ultimate political problem of the world is how the different races which inhabit it may live together in peace and harmony." Oldham certainly begins

[40] 2nd ed., New Haven, Yale Univ. Press, 1923.

with a broad sweep over the immediate post-war context: Western expansion has in a sense unified the world, politically, commercially and technologically. "For better or for worse the various families of mankind have been bound together in a common life, and have to learn how to adjust their relations in this unified world." But at the moment the moral and spiritual unity is lacking. It is not clear whether the Western peoples, responsible for bringing the world to this present situation, have the capacity to lead it to peace. Much of Europe itself, after the widespread collapse of monarchies in 1914–18, has found itself "without any principle of authority whatever" and with very little tradition of democratic experience to draw upon. Its peoples are thus "exposed to the risk of drifting without a compass, and become the prey of any adventurers who may be strong enough to impose their will"[41] – a prophecy which was to prove itself only too true in less than a decade.

Christian moralists are apt to deal with issues by, in effect, saying, "here are the problems, these are the Christian answers". Oldham is both far more circumspect and more penetrating, as shown by his exploration of what is "the Christian view" and *how* it relates "to the facts". He deeply sympathizes with Graham Wallas for his humane consideration of current social needs and the need for moral responses to them. Wallas, however, is dismissive of Christianity's claim to offer guidance on long-range ethical problems. Oldham's response is to accept much of the criticism about the failure of the church to offer such wisdom, but also to challenge the assumption that Christianity is primarily "a code of morality". It is, rather, a relationship with God and consists in seeing everything in relation to the eternal realm of God. And it is not primarily a command but good news. "It reveals what God is like. It tells us that he is love." From the Christian view of God as known in Jesus certain consequences for human relationships follow. There is first the call to seek God's kingdom of righteousness, and in the light of that "natural differences which exist among men become insignificant. Moral values are supreme." Further, God's love for humanity gives to each personality an inestimable worth, both in body and soul. Finally, inspired by the love of God, Christians are constrained to the service of their fellows, surmounting all barriers. Therefore it can be said: "What Christianity gives us . . . for our help and guidance in dealing with the problems that will come before us is certain fundamental beliefs regarding the meaning and purpose of life. It does not furnish any explicit direction in regard to the problems of race and nationality."[42] The New Testament furnishes no social programme, certainly not one for the complexities of modern industrial life. Yet, as Ernst Troeltsch puts it, it points to a final goal beyond the relativities of our earthly existence but one which "lifts men above the world without denying the world."[43] As much as anything it is a temper, an outlook which Christianity

[41] *Christianity and the Race Problem*, London, SCM, 1924, pp.5, 7.

[42] *Ibid.*, pp.18f., 21.

[43] *Ibid.*, p.22 (Ernst Troeltsch's massive *Social Teaching of the Christian Churches* was highly important to Oldham).

supplies – but it does so not in abstraction from the world but precisely in deep engagement with it, with all the facts and the realities of experience:

> Viewed from the purely religious standpoint, and in the light of eternity, race and nationality are of negligible importance; but from the temporal standpoint and in relation to the course of this world they are of immense significance. In the political sphere they are factors that cannot be neglected. A cosmopolitanism or internationalism which takes no account of them must come to grief on the rock of reality. Humanity exists only in the endless diversities of its component parts, each with its separate history, customs, institutions and civilization. The individual life must everywhere strike its roots into some particular soil and derive from some particular environment the nurture that it needs.

In all controversies, it is ascertainment of the *facts* that is the first step towards a solution – and often most of the steps too. But "knowledge of the facts is sought for the purpose of action". Mere scientific acquisition of knowledge is inadequate to our nature which is to feel and to will. "We are here not merely to know but to act", and this leads Oldham to one of his most memorable and oft-quoted utterances:

> Christianity is not primarily a philosophy but a crusade. As Christ was sent by the Father, so he sends His disciples to set up in the world the Kingdom of God. His coming was a declaration of war – a war to the death against the powers of darkness. He was manifested to destroy the works of the devil. Hence when Christians find in the world a state of things that is not in accord with the truth which they have learned from Christ, their concern is not that it should be explained but that it should be ended. In that temper we must approach everything in the relations between the races that cannot be reconciled with the Christian ideal.[44]

Neither "idealism" nor "realism" by itself is adequate to political affairs. "We cannot afford to lose sight either of our ideals or of the facts." With the dynamic supplied by the tension between these two poles, we are then taken stage by stage through the contemporary issues. At the end of the day, the causes of racial antagonism are due not to inherent differences of race but to other causes, of upbringing, political relationships (especially of power and dominance). Man is only partly a function of heredity. Environment and nurture are at least as important, and "race" is, zoologically speaking, a dubious term. There are many and deep inequalities in the human scene, but in the main these are explicable as due to inequalities of nurture and privilege, of education and experience, and not inherent qualities of race. There is an even greater truth of equality, as already acknowledged wherever equality before the law is acknowledged in society.

The only justification of empire, Oldham argues, lies in a commitment to enabling the development of the subject peoples towards full political maturity and self-governance, and that means a real commitment to education by the present governing powers. In *Christianity and the Race Problem* India receives a

[44] *Ibid.*, pp.23, 24, 26.

whole chapter to itself. Perhaps that is not surprising in view of the author's background and experience, but it was also a deliberate choice to look at the jewel in the crown of the British empire, where the issues of race were so intimately linked with the factors of power and domination. It was, Oldham later confessed, "the most difficult of all to write and I nearly gave up in despair".[45] British administrators arrive at what seem to be eminently moderate and fair conclusions, but which leave totally out of account what is most vital in the Indian consciousness. Oldham's sensitivity of understanding comes out well when he states:

> Indian opinion in the main ... does not desire the severing of the British connection, yet to Indians the question is always present how that connection can be maintained consistently with their self-respect ... To know from day to day that decisions regarding the affairs of one's country are made by alien rulers, to be conscious of social exclusiveness among the governing race, to incur social slights which seem to cast a stigma of inferiority, to run the risk of being exposed on occasion to insolence, insult and humiliation which rankle in the memory – such experiences alike in their larger and their more petty aspects are calculated to arouse the strongest and most intense feelings which the mind can entertain.[46]

The psychological problem on the British side, Oldham maintains, is that while the Government of India Act of 1919 commits Britain to the policy of the development of self-governing institutions, "a life-long habit of taking decisions is not one that those who govern India can easily change, however sincere may be their desire to give effect to the new policy".[47]

In all this, of course, Oldham was speaking out of the depth of his own – and perhaps his parents' – experience of India, of making friends with Indians and of letting them be friends to oneself; not to mention the mistakes he saw missionaries, no less than civil servants, often making. The book continues with examinations of immigration policy in the United States, East Africa and Australia, and of the issues of population control, intermarriage, and social and political equality. Particularly interesting, from the vantage point of the end of the century, is his warning that, however benevolently intended they may be, and however ostensibly fair, policies of segregation which afford subject races their own "self-government" over a limited range of affairs, beg the question of whether this is just another form of racial domination by the powerful – and the non-white communities are bound to see them as such. He has in mind South Africa, and one cannot help feeling how much blood and tears would have been saved if these words had been heeded:

> Communal representation can help towards a solution of political problems in which different races are involved only if there is no ground for suspecting that the plan is put forward as a means of maintaining a position of privilege and dominance and if it is recognized to be a stage in the evolution towards a genuine community.

[45] JHO letter to McKenzie 16 July 1924 [OA].
[46] *Christianity and the Race Problem*, p.115.
[47] *Ibid.*, p.119.

> It is a serious question, however, whether even as a stage in evolution it is wise to encourage the growth of political organization on racial lines. Disputes between races are apt to acquire a peculiar bitterness ... A potent cause of misunderstanding and conflict will be removed if associations and loyalties can be based on other interests than the physical bond of race or colour.[48]

Oldham's overall conclusions as to "the facts" are that while human differences are real, they are set within a fundamental human unity, in which diversity ministers to the fulfilment of a common social purpose. Racial antagonisms are primarily political, revolving around inequalities of power and economic resourcing, and ingrained cultural or historical prejudices, not ineradicable biological differences. It is Christian faith which both provides an unassailable ground for belief that this is indeed how things should be, and draws upon the love of God who invites us to cooperate with his loving purpose for the world. It is the Christian calling to see all these facts and problems and opportunities in the light of that living and creative purpose. There is need for a new spirit within the churches themselves which, for all their dismal failures, do have the potential for displaying within their own life the nature of the gospel, and for relaying this to the world in the form of joint, inter-racial enterprises and action on issues which affect all people, of whatever race. This becomes a charter for the *whole* church:

> wherever the separation [of races in the Church] is not a natural segregation but is imposed, a vital and essential truth of Christianity is compromised. It is not for those who are at distance to pass judgment on what should be done where racial problems are acute ... But ... the race problem is a world problem ... It is a matter in which the whole Church of Christ is concerned, the essential nature of the witness of the Church to the world is involved. The Church must stand for something in the world's eyes, or it will be swept aside as meaningless. It is committed to the principle that in Christ Jesus there is neither Jew nor Greek, bond nor free. On the Christian view the moral issues of sin, redemption, grace, service, brotherhood are so tremendous that natural differences lose their significance. The body of Christ is one. All partake of the one bread. Take away this unity in Christ and the heart falls out of Christianity.[49]

Half a century later, Protestant theologians engaged with apartheid would be talking of racism in terms of a *status confessionis*, but no one expresses the heart of the matter more clearly than Oldham does here. In practice the Roman Catholic Church, says Oldham, has been truer to the genius of Christianity than the Protestant bodies – and Islam too may boast of a more real brotherhood than Protestantism. All this is to stimulate a call to a new and deeper understanding of mission, and the closing sections of *Christianity and the Race Problem* repeat the call made in *The World and the Gospel* for mission to penetrate areas of life and thought as well as geographical areas on the earth's surface. The church must be at the centre of the tides of human affairs and, equally, sustained in prayer and worship by the vision of God.

[48] *Ibid.*, pp.105f.
[49] *Ibid.*, pp.262f.

*Christianity and the Race Problem* made a deep, wide and lasting impact, and not only in Britain where F.A. Cockin produced a set of study outlines based on the book for use in local groups. *The Times Literary Supplement* carried a two-column review. Dean Inge wrote two articles on the book for the front page of the *Morning Post.* Oldham was gratified that at the other end of the political spectrum the Glasgow Socialist *Forward* "wrote a three-column article on it entirely favourable and saying that if this was the kind of contribution that might be expected from the Church the labour movement would have to pay much more attention to it than in the past".[50] Norman Leys, the radical advocate of African political rights, paid Oldham a somewhat double-edged compliment: "I have read your book with great admiration and nearly complete agreement. Will you forgive me for saying that I had no idea you could write so good a book?"[51] In India, P.A. Popley, a YMCA district secretary for South India, got into a tangle in turn with the Calcutta *Guardian*, with Oldham, and eventually (so it seems) with himself over what he finally admitted were misconstructions which he had placed upon Oldham's treatment of India. Oldham stoically remarked that such was the price to be paid for trying to be "balanced".[52] This little episode was more than compensated for by another Indian reaction to two addresses drawing upon the book, which Oldham gave at an SCM conference in January 1925, on "India in the Twentieth Century" and "The Problem of Race".[53] The *Indian Social Reformer*, a Hindu weekly, was enthusiastic. The first address, wrote the reviewer, was in marked and refreshing contrast to the literature "produced by Ex-Governors and retired civilians who, having never come in contact with the masses and with no knowledge of the conditions of rural India, pose as experts on Indian affairs and exploit the credulity of the people of the West."[54] The second address was hailed as "a forceful sermon to white imperialists whose vision is blurred by exaggerated notions of their own superiority".

In ecumenical circles, where racism came to the top of the international ecumenical agenda in the late 1960s and 1970s, the book is still recognized as the pioneering systematic study in the field. On the more immediate level, Oldham had established for himself the method of relating the gospel to the contemporary world, by combining a deep theological and spiritual vision with a painstaking, even laborious, concern with "the facts".

### A Devotional Diary

Contrasts are among the most fascinating aspects of biography. The year immediately following the publication of his largest book, dealing with a

[50] JHO letter to Mott 21 July 1924 [OA].

[51] See J.W. Cell, *By Kenya Possessed: The Correspondence of Norman Leys and J.H. Oldham 1918–1926*, Chicago, University of Chicago Press, 1976, p.227.

[52] Popley letter to JHO 22 Oct. 1924 [OA].

[53] In *The World Task of the Christian Church*, London, SCM, 1925, pp.91–104.

[54] *Indian Social Reformer*, 27 June 1925 [OA].

burning contemporary social issue, Oldham brought out his smallest one, comprising a collection of meditations and prayers for private use. In fact *A Devotional Diary* proved to be his most widely circulated and popular work. Size apart, the contrast should not be overdrawn. "Ministry, service, fellowship", wrote Oldham in *Christianity and the Race Problem*, "depend for their inspiration and vitality upon worship."[55] Both corporate and private worship were central to Oldham's life, and mention has already been made of his simple but heartfelt pattern of devotions at home. It was in 1924 while visiting Selly Oak, Birmingham, that Oldham was given by the principal of Kingsmead College, John Hoyland, two copies of a little devotional book produced by his son Jack.[56] Oldham was intrigued by the inclusion in the book of spaces for recording the amount of time spent daily in quiet, as well as a short selection of texts for each day of the month as a guide to meditation.[57] He found the book helpful, and decided to produce one of his own on similar lines, in the form of an anthology of material which he personally had found inspirational and enlightening in prayer and meditation. Mary Oldham did much of the collation and referencing of material. At first Oldham intended a publication for purely private distribution to a number of friends and associates, at his own expense. Hugh Martin, however, at that time literature secretary of the SCM, became interested and thought there might be a market within the student constituency. Even so there were misgivings on the SCM side, especially over the "diary record" pages, and in the end Martin was persuaded to take on the book only because Oldham himself offered a subsidy of £25 and moreover placed an order for 200 copies.

So appeared in 1925 the first edition of *A Devotional Diary* – a tiny volume which would hardly be noticeable in an inside pocket or a handbag. It comprised one weekly and two monthly cycles of biblical texts, prose meditations or poems drawn from a wide variety of sources, and a prayer for the day. But most of the first half of the book consisted of the pages for recording one's daily allotment of time to this spiritual use. For Oldham it was the essential part of the diary: "an aid against self-deception".

The book had been put together somewhat hurriedly in view of Oldham's trip to America in the autumn of 1925, and there was not even time for proper proof-reading. It was no more than an experiment, and all Oldham could do was await the result. In fact it soon became apparent that *A Devotional Diary* struck a chord and met a need in a surprising number of people. Oldham quickly set about producing a larger and revised edition, using a wider variety of material and based on a four-monthly prayer-cycle. The daily structure of scripture, material for meditation and concluding prayer remained, as did pages for recording one's time-keeping (despite criticisms by some of "spiritual account keeping"), though these now were placed at the end of the book. This

[55] *Christianity and the Race Problem*, p.259.
[56] Cf. Letter JHO to Hoyland 8 Oct. 1925 [OA] and other correspondence.
[57] Introduction to *A Devotional Diary*, 1st ed., 1925.

was the version which became famous, going through sixteen printings and 51,000 copies by 1947.

*A Devotional Diary* broke new ground in a genre which was to become increasingly popular between the two world wars. Oldham's offering appealed to those who relished a combination of contemporary theological material (Baron von Hügel, B.H. Streeter and John Baillie for example) with well-established poets (Shakespeare, Wordsworth, Browning . . .), set in the framework of biblical text and prayer, and grouped under such broad themes for each day as "Life", "More Abundant Life", "The Crucifixion", "God of Nature", "Faith", "The Need for Labourers", etc. Oldham confessed to being able to offer his readers a somewhat more restricted choice of fare than would have been presented by someone with greater opportunities for wider reading than he had, in the busy life of the past three or four years. What does emerge from his anthology, however, are clear pointers to where his own spiritual nerve centre lay at this time. No one, for example, is more important in *A Devotional Diary* (scripture apart) than Friedrich von Hügel with his sense of religion as communion with a God who is near, indwelling, yet ultimate mystery: indicated, but not bound, by doctrines and institutions; whose grace is the source of all that is vital and creative in human life and experience. "Christianity is essentially, centrally, a heroism," von Hügel declares on the second day of the first month under the theme "More Abundant Life". That same page contains an anonymous quotation, possibly a paraphrase by Oldham of what he had heard or read elsewhere which, original to Oldham or not, certainly sums up the heart of his own belief and attitude to life: "To live is to meet life eager and unafraid, to refuse none of its responsibilities and to go forth daily with a gay and adventurous heart to encounter its risks, to overcome its difficulties and to seize its opportunities with both hands."

For a great many people *A Devotional Diary* certainly opened new windows onto spiritual resources and discipline, and its range of sources itself provided an example of ecumenism. "What did I learn from Joe Oldham?", asked a prominent headmaster: "How to pray in a new way."[58]

[58] Quoted in K. Bliss, "The Legacy of J.H. Oldham", p.21.

CHAPTER 10

# "Friend of Africa" 1920–30

THERE is no clearer demonstration of Joe Oldham's holistic view of mission than his engagement with Africa throughout the 1920s. We have already examined his involvement in the Kenya forced labour issue of 1920, and his advocacy of the paramountcy of African interests in the 1923 debates on the constitution of Kenya as a crown colony. Much of his continuing interest in the continent was to remain focused on Kenya and elsewhere in central and east Africa, but he was acutely aware that the issues with which he was dealing pertained to the whole of Africa in the afternoon of empire. These years formed an extraordinarily intense period of Oldham's life. What took place, as described in this chapter, was in addition to all his other full-time commitments as secretary of the IMC. As well as taking him on two extensive and vitally important visits to the scene, his African activities meant that he became as familiar a figure to many colonial governors, Colonial Office officials, parliamentarians of all parties, experts on tropical medicine and agriculture, and educationalists from Britain and America, as he did to mission boards and church leaders. It was here, more closely than at any other point in his life, that he found himself personally applying what he had called for in 1916 in *The World and the Gospel*: far from withdrawing from the world, going into the heart of secular life "meeting its difficulties, battling with its evils, bearing witness to [God's] truth".

## Mission and education

It was through what he did in this decade that Joe Oldham earned one of the titles etched on his memorial in Geneva: "Friend of Africa". He, no doubt, would have preferred to hope that in some way he had helped Christian missions themselves to be thought of as friends, not intruders, in Africa, and as real participants in the making of a new history of humankind there. It is no accident that as Oldham's African involvement increased so also did his anxieties about the future of missionary cooperation, and the IMC itself. Tensions arose between Oldham and Mott, and with other colleagues in America, and they were due not only to his allocation of time and energy. From Oldham's side, they also involved diverging perceptions of the nature of mission on the international scene, and fears that the missionary movement was now drifting into a backwater of the contemporary world. Since a biography tries to deal with a life in its wholeness and with the interconnectedness of its subject's activities and experiences, it is important to note that what is narrated in this chapter, while focused on Oldham's African work in the 1920s, was to have a crucial bearing on wider concerns which he not only brought to bear upon the African scene but which in turn shaped his view of the IMC itself.

While a number of factors were responsible for turning Oldham towards Africa, he would not have become engaged in the way he did without his wider, and prior, passionate concern for education. Of course he had a natural disposition towards such an interest, having been so well-educated himself and so closely identified with the student movement in his own missionary activity, at home as well as abroad. It was an interest, moreover, now given intellectual stimulus for him by the writings of W.E. Hocking. In the United States he had been fired by what he saw in the black educational centres at Tuskegee and elsewhere and by meeting African students working for higher degrees.

In one sense the contemporary missionary movement needed no encouragement to take education seriously: far from it, the provision of schools and higher educational colleges had by the turn of the century become one of the most familiar and unquestioned features of Western missions throughout Africa and Asia. Through such institutions the missions would have a direct impact on the population, and through the training of character as well as imparting learning, education would itself be a decisive way of Christianizing the country. Education had come to occupy a central place in mission, and without the missionary contribution the story of development of the countries concerned would have been very different. During 1914–18, from his Edinburgh office Oldham himself had been closely concerned for the development of educational work in India, particularly for women and in villages, and this need had been a prime factor in motivating his desire for a more effective national Christian body to succeed the National Missionary Council.

However, precisely because he did take Christian education so seriously, Oldham was one of the first to raise critical questions about the apparent success of this part of the missionary enterprise and about its future. In November 1921 – soon after the first meeting of the IMC at Lake Mohonk – he published, together with papers by Sir Michael Sadler and Paul Monroe, a paper for the IMC on "The Crisis in Christian Education in the Mission Fields".[1] It is essentially a warning that while the missionary educational contribution in the past has been immensely important, current developments in many mission

[1] In *Papers on Education Problems in Mission Fields*, London, IMC, 1921.

field countries will soon call for drastic changes. The crisis consists in the fact that few of those responsible for mission schools and colleges seem to be aware that such changes are afoot, and there is a danger of complacency. The critical developments are, first, that governments are everywhere assuming greater responsibility for education; second, that as a result mission schools will have to be meeting much higher standards; and third, the emphasis of government education is more and more that of building a common national culture with a consequent danger of state-imposed conformity to the detriment of that space for freedom and variety which is vital for any Christian understanding of personality as created by God. Mission institutions would have to face all these challenges with the additional handicap of being seen as foreign to the scene.

Oldham rejected any idea of surrendering the educational branch of mission for the sake of evangelism. For one thing, it would be to say that education and character-building lie outside the kingdom of Christ who is the way, the truth and the life for all. For another, it would be to deprive the indigenous church of an adequate leadership in the future. But a definite *policy* is needed, and to ensure the maintenance and raising of standards it should be a policy of *concentration*: "What we do at all we must do well, even if we have to do less . . . [T]he fact remains that mission boards are carrying on a good many schools at the present time without any other real justification than that a school was once started in a certain place."[2] Mission means movement in depth as well as geographical breadth – an Oldhamite theme we meet repeatedly. He believed that qualified people on the mission field should be set free to serve as educational specialists and advisers.

Oldham, far from applying double-standards as between the home and mission fields, was just as concerned that depth was being compromised within the West itself. As we have seen, he was sceptical about the adequacy of much of the preparation available for missionary candidates in the United States and strongly advocated to John R. Mott a policy of concentration of resources in just one or two centres. He was also concerned, in Britain as well, to ensure calibre as well as numbers of missionary personnel.

As far as his own understanding of education was concerned, the greatest single influence on Oldham at this stage was the American W.E. Hocking, who for a decade Oldham confessed to regarding as his "guru". In *Human Nature and Its Remaking* Hocking had set out a philosophical basis for Christian education, in reaction to current "naturalistic" understandings of human nature and behaviour as governed solely by heredity and "instincts". Human beings, argued Hocking, have a part in their own making: "Human beings as we find them are accordingly artificial products . . . Nature has made us: social action and our own efforts must continually remake us. Any attempt to reject art for "nature" can only result in an artificial naturalness which is far less genuine and less pleasing than the natural work of art."[3] Education therefore involves a

[2] *Ibid.*, p.66.
[3] 2nd ed., New Haven, Yale Univ. Press, 1923, p.7.

highly conscious and selective exposure to what is thought most worthwhile in the cultural inheritance, while leaving space for a proper individuality to develop. Morality is a matter of growth. And for Hocking the Christian, it was exposure to and active participation in the love of God as source of all goodness, which lead to such moral growth. It was highly significant that it was on his visits to America in 1920–21 that Oldham encountered Hocking and his work, at the same time as he discovered the educational work among the black communities. Education as both the possibility and means of "development" became indissolubly fused in Oldham's mind as a crucial activity of *mission*. Thus was a vital perspective on the African scene, for both missions and government, forged for Oldham. He enthusiastically reviewed *Human Nature and Its Remaking* in the *IRM* – significantly under the title "A Philosophical Interpretation of the *Missionary Idea*" (emphasis mine).[4]

Oldham's 1921 paper on the crisis in Christian education clearly sees the challenges facing missionaries as educators. He had proposed one main way forward: *concentrate* to ensure and raise the standards. But, it might be asked, could or should Christian responsibility for education be expressed only through Christian schools? If government is to take a much greater role in the provision, might not churches, mission agencies and individual Christians seek to influence state education, both its policy and its practice? Might there not be partnership rather than competition? By the mid-1920s, as will be seen, Oldham had faced this question and was answering it.[5]

## Britain and East Africa in the 1920s

In 1920 what had been known as the British East Africa Protectorate became Kenya Colony. More than a change in name was involved, as shown by the differing reactions of white settlers, Africans and Indians. The settlers had already been assured of land rights in the highlands (denied to the Indians), had obtained the franchise in 1919, and had long been calling for this change in status of the territory which appeared to entrench their claims to dominance. Confirmation that it did so was provided in 1922 when the chief justice found that native rights in their reserves had disappeared, the Africans in effect being left as tenants at the will of the crown.

Kenya was the prime focus of debate on British imperial and colonial policy in Africa in the decade and a half following the 1914–18 war. Apart from the controversies over forced labour in 1920 and the rights of Indians in 1923, it seemed that nearly all the questions on which hung the justification (or otherwise) of empire were being raised in Kenya: or, at least, in Kenya and the immediately neighbouring territories. Britain had acquired the former German colony of Tanganyika (present-day Tanzania) under League of Nations mandate.

[4] *IRM*, vol. X, no. 37, Jan. 1921, pp.63–76.

[5] Cf. also Oldham, "Religious Education in the Mission Field", *IRM*, vol. XIII, no. 52, Oct. 1924, pp.500–17.

This meant that Britain now ruled a continuous, huge swathe of central and east Africa, running from Kenya and Uganda south through Tanganyika, Northern Rhodesia and Nyasaland to Southern Rhodesia and Bechuanaland – with the Dominion of South Africa to the south, and to the north the condominium of Sudan and (until 1922) the Protectorate of Egypt for good measure. While it might have seemed that this was the apotheosis of empire, such aggrandizement only raised even more acutely the questions of what the empire was for, how it was to be governed, and in whose interests.

These questions were stimulated a good deal by the concept of "trusteeship" which had been generated by the Paris peace conference. "The wellbeing and development of peoples not yet able to stand by themselves, form a sacred Trust of Civilisation," stated article 22 of the League of Nations. This appeared to inject a moral element into the concept of empire, though critics were apt to point out that it might equally have lent sanctimonious self-justification to the activities of the imperialists (who were themselves largely responsible for framing the post-war settlements). But at least there was a sense that those states now acquiring new territories from the defeated Germany and her allies, being mandated to do so by the international community as a whole, were to be held accountable (by what machinery it was not clear) for the just governance of those lands and to act for the advancement of their peoples. Within the British empire the most eloquent exponent of the moral obligations attaching to "trusteeship" was Sir Frederick Lugard, whose book *The Dual Mandate in British Tropical Africa*[6] appeared in 1922 and became the bible of enlightened (that is, by today's standards, paternalistic) government of Africa. Lugard was himself the empire's most famous African governor of the day, having served as high commissioner in Nigeria for six years from the turn of the century, and then after five years in Hong Kong returning to Nigeria as governor-general 1912–19. His book is a massive, not wholly coherent yet fascinating collation of history, personal reminiscence and anecdote, commentary and argument, practical advice for new recruits to colonial service and statements of broad principle. (It is in one sense one of the first manuals on management: "The Governor, by delegating work to others, would seem to lighten his own task, but in point of fact the more he delegates the more he will find to do in coordinating the progress of the whole.") By the *dual mandate*, Lugard meant that empire had a duty towards the advancement of both its own industrial society at home, and the peoples it ruled abroad. Imperial or colonial rule served to develop the economic resources of both peoples, and as such is conscious of a wider duty to the whole of humanity. Here Lugard acknowledged that this was no more than what Joseph Chamberlain had stated twenty-four years earlier in describing the custodians of the tropics as "trustees of civilisation for the commerce of the world". The resources of the tropical countries "are to be developed alike in the interests of the natives and of the world at large". Lugard, however, was careful to add that trusteeship (especially since the advent

[6] Edinburgh and London, William Blackwood, 1922.

of the League of Nations) included an obligation on the controlling power "not only to safeguard the material rights of the natives, but to promote their moral and educational progress". At the same time, "the era of complete independence is not as yet visible on the horizon of time". But neither should rule be by the direct rule of force. The natives can and should be the agents of developing their own resources, but under European guidance which need not involve the European *ownership* of their lands. "As in the sphere of political, so also in that of material progress – teach the native to manage his own affairs and better his own methods ... The development must be under British guidance, without encroaching on native rights, or reducing the African to a state of serfage."[7]

Lugard thus supplied a moral as well as a political and economic perception of what empire was about in Africa. It was the evidence that this was *not* what Kenya was in fact about which sparked so much controversy in the 1920s, as reports were heard of settler brutalities towards Africans and the whole forced labour issue exploded in 1920. In 1924 Norman Leys, a former medical officer working among the Masai, published *Kenya*, a highly critical account of the colony. Oldham had been in contact with Leys since 1918, and their correspondence during the 1920s is a rich source for Christian thinking on colonial Africa and the tensions between differing perspectives: Leys the ardent Christian Socialist, Oldham the high-minded but pragmatic missionary diplomat.[8] Another former civil servant, W. McGregor Ross, also produced his controversial *Kenya from Within* in 1927. Both books supplied plenty of ammunition for critics of colonial policy. At the same time, whatever the political complexion of the government in power at Westminster at any given moment, the white settlers were never given unconditional endorsement from London. For one thing, the India Office brought pressure to bear regarding the status of Indians in East Africa. The contrast with the permissive attitude towards the settlers in Southern Rhodesia, who were accorded virtual self-government in 1922, was significant.

East African affairs were in the hands of the Colonial Office. The frequent changes in government following the first world war naturally brought a succession of colonial secretaries. Under Lloyd George's 1919 coalition government, the colonial secretary was Lord Milner, to be succeeded by Winston Churchill in February 1921. Under Bonar Law's Conservative government of October 1922, the Duke of Devonshire came to the Colonial Office, remaining there in Stanley Baldwin's first Conservative administration until January 1924, when Ramsay MacDonald's first Labour government came to power and J.H. Thomas became colonial secretary. Eight months later Leopold S. Amery took over with Baldwin's second Conservative government, adding responsibility for the dominions to his post in June 1925. Amery

[7] *Ibid.*, pp.18, 97, 198, 506f.

[8] See J.W. Cell, *By Kenya Possessed: The Correspondence of Norman Leys and J. H. Oldham 1918–1926*, Chicago, Univ. of Chicago Press, 1976.

remained at the Colonial Office for the full further four years of the Baldwin government – the longest-serving incumbent in the period under review and, as will be seen, the one with whom Oldham developed the closest working relationship. Lord Passfield (Sidney Webb) became Colonial Secretary under MacDonald's second Labour government in June 1929. Such changes may have brought different angles to the view from Whitehall, but on the whole they were remarkably in the same direction. "For the quarter of a century between the end of the first world war and the end of the second, the feature of British colonial policy that stands out in retrospect is the tranquil assumption of the long-term character of colonial rule. It was an assumption accepted by many, perhaps most, of the radical critics of that policy who were often more concerned to purify, supervise, or even internationalize, such rule than to advocate its rapid replacement by independence."[9]

Also regardless of changes in ministerial leadership was the character of the Colonial Office itself. Its staff had purely administrative – that is, supervisory and controlling – functions. Except in extreme circumstances it had no executive financial powers, and therefore no means of granting or directing economic assistance to any of the colonies – and the significance of this for Oldham's initiatives will be seen presently. "The Crown Agents for the Colonies acted as commercial and financial agents for all the non-self-governing territories and were financed entirely by the payments those territories made for their services."[10]

Furthermore, apart from a legal adviser, there was no specialist personnel with expertise on medical, agricultural, technical or scientific matters in the Colonial Office. And while the department could call on the services of a wide range of centres of expertise in an advisory role, from the London School of Tropical Diseases to the Royal Botanic Gardens, it could hardly itself give the impression of initiating research and promoting the gathering of vital information. The walls of the offices in Whitehall proudly displayed the maps of the vast British possessions in Africa, but those who sat at the desks – and therefore those in parliament and in government whom they were to serve – could be remarkably devoid of information on what was actually happening to the people, the soil, the forests and the rivers under their care. Lord Milner, when he left the Colonial Office in 1921, bitterly remarked on that office being the Cinderella of all the great public departments when it came to funding. This, too, is vital background for the battles that Oldham was to fight through the 1920s.

It was to Kenya, where the potential riches seemed greatest and yet the tensions were also the most fraught, that attention was again and again directed.

[9] K. Robinson, *The Dilemmas of Trusteeship: Aspects of British Colonial Policy Between the Wars*, London, Oxford Univ. Press, 1965, p.7.

[10] *Ibid.*, p.30.

### African education and research: Oldham and Lugard

In order to appreciate fully Joe Oldham's involvement with African affairs at this period, four sets of players with whom he was dealing need to be identified – in addition to his church- or missions-related colleagues. First, there was the Colonial Office itself and in particular its under-secretary of state, a post held by W.G.A. Ormsby-Gore during Stanley Baldwin's long, second Conservative administration from November 1924 to June 1929. Second, there were the African colonial governors themselves, with a number of whom Oldham became a close associate by personal meeting both in London and while visiting Africa, and by lengthy correspondence. Particularly important to Oldham were Donald Cameron who went to Tanganyika in 1924, and Edward Grigg who replaced Robert Coryndon in Kenya in 1925. Third, there were the powerful American trust funds and corporations desirous of helping worthy humanitarian causes at the international level: in particular the Phelps-Stokes Fund administered by the educationalist Dr Jesse T. Jones, and the almost legendary Carnegie and Rockefeller Foundations. Fourth, there was the informal network of associates with a keen interest in African affairs: academics like Lionel Curtis (All Souls, Oxford, and Chatham House, founder of the Round Table) and Sir Michael Sadler (master of University College, Oxford), groups like the Ralegh Club, retired diplomats and so forth.

In this latter set, one figure was pre-eminent: Sir Frederick (later Lord) Lugard. Having retired from the governer-generalship of Nigeria in 1919 and with his treatise *The Dual Mandate* appearing in 1922, he was unrivalled as an authoritative figure speaking with the voice of a lifetime's experience in colonial government. As has been seen already, his vision of colonial management was relatively enlightened for that time, advocating as he did as much "indirect" rule as possible, allowing Africans to develop their own resources by their own means, under European guidance. If that appeared far too liberal for many, whether in the settler communities in the colonies or on the Conservative benches in parliament, no one could gainsay the first-hand experience out of which he wrote. Lugard was not an academic, and had entered the colonial service from a military career. At first sight he and Oldham might have seemed poles apart. Lugard had by middle life lost the orthodox Christian faith of his upbringing, though not the Christian ethic. *The Dual Mandate* treats missions in a sympathetic yet detached way as acceptable contributors to human welfare provided the missionaries take account of the realities of the country they are working in, and do not presume that suffering, privation and worse constitute an effective witness: "I recollect a case of a missionary too poor to take his dying wife out of the country. These things do not promote the cause of the gospel. They do harm."[11] He has sharp comments to make on

[11] Lugard, p.589.

the negative effects upon missionary work of "sectarian rivalries and differences in teaching"[12] – and here at least Oldham would heartily concur with him.

In fact Lugard and Oldham became not only collaborators but close friends. Perhaps being the son of a colonel in the Indian army gave Joe Oldham a sympathetic point of access to Lugard's own background. Quite when or how they actually first met is not clear, but by the time of the Kenyan franchise issue in 1923 they were in close and frequent contact. They lived not far apart in Surrey. But it was above all their common interest in *education* for Africans that drew them closely together. Lugard's biographer, Margery Perham, is eloquent on this friendship, and indeed on Oldham himself, and deserves quoting:

> It was one of the joys of Lugard's release from both the restraints of office and service overseas that he was now free to express his great capacity for friendship . . . And his partnership with Dr Oldham was perhaps the most complete and effective of these later years . . .
>
> Sincere, selfless, thoughtful, a small man and very gentle, but with steel behind the gentleness, [Oldham] and Lugard fitted perfectly in character and aims . . .
>
> From January to July of 1923 the two friends were intensely busy [on the Kenyan franchise issue] behind the scenes and the technique of their long partnership, with its division of functions, began to take shape. Lugard provided the dignity of his name and age; he was the practical administrator with immense knowledge of Africa and Africans . . . Oldham was above all the diplomat. More than any other man I have known he illustrated the meaning of that rather startling injunction of Christ, "Be ye wise as serpents and harmless as doves". A Christian of an ecumenical cast of mind, his political principles were based upon religious belief. He gave practical effect to these by working upon the people, *all* the people, who were in any way important in a given situation. His complete personal disinterestedness was a source of great strength . . . He and Lugard – and Oldham in his unobtrusive way was captain of the team – would continue the treatment with further talk in clubs – especially, of course, the Athenaeum – or at weekends at Little Parkhurst [where Lugard lived]. Colonial Secretaries and Parliamentary Under-Secretaries of State at the Colonial Office came at the top of their list, but Prime Ministers and others in the Cabinet also occur. And the high-minded conspirators were quick to deal with possible successors to office . . . Archbishop Davidson was a constant and powerful ally . . . Both chose to work quietly in the background; both recoiled from extremists or public clamant egotists. For the decade following 1923, but especially from 1929 to 1931, there were many periods when they were often corresponding or seeing each other in London or Abinger several times a week and were even in daily contact during a crisis.[13]

Lugard had religious doubts, but these were no hindrance to the Oldhams' warm regard for him. After his death in 1945 Mary Oldham wrote to his brother that she and Joe "have often thought and said to each other that in Lord Lugard, as in few others, we were conscious of the presence of Christ . . . To us his life was an inspiration."[14]

[12] *Ibid.*, p.588.
[13] M. Perham, *Lugard: The Years of Authority 1898–1945* (2nd part of life), London, Collins, 1960, p.658.
[14] *Ibid.*, p.710.

## The Phelps-Stokes Fund and the advisory committee

It is clear that Oldham, following his 1921 paper on the crisis in education on the mission field, was seeking some contact with the Colonial Office on the issue. He raised the question of education in conjunction with the package of issues relating to the rights of Africans, in his confidential "Memorandum on Native Affairs in East Africa" written in the spring of 1920. This episode which eventually culminated in the recognition of African "paramountcy" has already been dealt with in the previous chapter. The story in which Oldham played a central role from this point onwards has been chronicled in detail by F.J. Clatworthy, who describes Oldham as "a dynamic synthesiser, a genius at influential action, and one of Britain's most unrecognized public servants".[15]

A number of positive influences were already at work. In 1920, the Phelps-Stokes Fund, based in New York, at the urgent request of American mission societies had agreed to fund a commission of missionaries and educationists to survey the various situations of education in West Africa and South Africa. The commission was led by the director of the Phelps-Stokes Fund, Dr T. Jesse Jones (whom Oldham had first met in London in 1919) and included an African member, Dr J.E. Kwegyir Aggrey of the Gold Coast (present-day Ghana). Its primary remit was to examine what effects current European styles of education were having on African communities, and to ask how education could be more adequately related to the physical and cultural conditions of African life. The commission reported in 1922, and immediately excited the interest of colonial governments who had long been uneasy about both the feasibility and desirability of Western-type literary education for "primitive" societies. What was doubly significant about the Phelps-Stokes report was that it was in large measure an exercise in self-criticism by the missions themselves, who hitherto had largely held a monopoly on education in tropical Africa and to whom therefore most of the mistakes had to be attributed, and who were now looking constructively towards a more responsible future. It could not be ignored by governments, and nowhere was the interest greater than in the Colonial Office in London. In fact it was through Oldham, who remained in very close touch with Jesse Jones throughout this period, that some British colonies had been included in the remit of the commission and that the Scottish missions were represented on the commission by Rev. and Mrs Arthur Wilkie.[16] Meanwhile, as seen in the previous chapter, Oldham's concern for a coherent missions policy on education as shown during and after the Lake Mohonk IMC meeting of 1921, was growing.

Early in 1923, very soon after his return from the second India visit, Oldham sensed that the time was ripe for another approach to the Colonial Office. He

[15] F.J. Clatworthy, *The Formulation of British Colonial Education Policy, 1923–1948*, Michigan, Univ. of Michigan School of Education, 1971.

[16] *Ibid.*, p.14.

spent the evening of 8 March with Sir Michael Sadler, who was not encouraging, evidently fearing that Colonial Office officials might suspect that special privileges were being sought for mission schools. Oldham sought to reassure him by letter next day that this was far from the case. He was simply concerned to argue that such schools should serve the educational good of Africa, that schooling needed a religious basis and that (as shown in India) there were real benefits in allowing room for private initiative and experiment.[17] The question though was how to initiate government action. The imperial education conference was scheduled for the summer of 1925, but Oldham foresaw that with its being largely composed of officials, largely official views would prevail. He chose instead to approach the Colonial Office personally. Sadler acquiesced in this: "As always it was a memorable thing to meet you when in London. You say a lot without saying it. I have chewed the cud since."[18]

Oldham accordingly wrote to the under-secretary of state, Ormsby-Gore, on 13 March 1923, requesting an opportunity to discuss African education. Ormsby-Gore in turn immediately invited Oldham to meet him on 22 March and to submit suggestions for cooperation between missions and government. Oldham had imagined that any such system would require very careful discussion and planning over two to three years, and was somewhat taken aback by the under-secretary's eagerness. He would have preferred a second commission to have gone, this time to East Africa and again under missionary auspices, to survey the scene and allow the missions themselves to make considered recommendations. In fact already, in Tanganyika in 1921, the Church Missionary Society (CMS) had requested the governor to introduce grant-in-aid to mission schools in exchange for expanding their numbers and raising standards in order to cope with the phenomenal rise of African interest both in schooling and in Christianity.[19] Oldham's initial caution was born less out of suspicion of government intentions than out of fears that sudden windfalls of government subsidies and concessions would cocoon the missions into further complacency about the need to re-think aims and *improve* quality – the fears that underlay his 1921 paper on education on the mission field.[20]

What exactly was said between Oldham and Ormsby-Gore is not known for certain but the rapport must have been instant, for almost immediately Oldham was cabling and writing to Jesse Jones urging him to bring forward his planned visit to England in the summer: the three governors from British west Africa would be coming to London early in May, as would the governor of Kenya Colony. There would in effect be an opportunity for a conference with the Colonial Office and key governors on educational policy. For this, Oldham knew that a carefully prepared memorandum would be essential, and that it would have to be written by none other than himself. Other forms of preparation were also necessary, not least that of ensuring that the missionary

[17] *Ibid.*, p.18.
[18] *Ibid.*
[19] R. Oliver, *The Missionary Factor in East Africa*, London, Longman, 1952, p.266.
[20] See earlier, pp.172, 212–14.

societies themselves would recognize the significance of this door opening from the Colonial Office side.

Oldham reported Ormsby-Gore's interest to Garfield Williams, the education secretary of the CMS. He also corresponded and conversed intensively with Lugard (who was already advising the government in his own capacity), and in fact it was working together on this issue that brought Oldham and Lugard "swiftly from acquaintanceship to trust and affection".[21] No less crucial was his winning the interest and active support of Archbishop Davidson. A situation quite unforeseen two years before had arisen: government was suddenly taking education of Africans very seriously, and turning to the missions since, for better or worse, it was their schools which were already on the ground in the colonies. At the same time, the missions were beginning to subject themselves to severe questions about their adequacy for the task ahead. So instead of a two-year process of commissioning an enquiry, sending it to East Africa, receiving and digesting its report, came a hectic two-month period of preparation of a confidential memorandum by Oldham.

Oldham sent out to his colleagues the first draft of his memorandum "Educational Policy in Africa" on 12 April. The education committee of the CMSBI, in whose name Oldham was preparing the paper, met on 4 May. The previous day came a letter of opposition from G.T. Manley, the Church Missionary Society representative on the committee, who feared that the concept of "partnership" between missions and government must mean interference from the latter side.[22] Oldham immediately got on to Garfield Williams in order to convince Manley that this would not happen.

Oldham's memorandum was in six sections, with an appendix of five statements on the importance of religion in African education. Its starting-point was diplomatically well chosen: a statement by Ormsby-Gore himself during a parliamentary debate on empire trade on 10 April that year, that "the first duty is to give the native a chance to advance in the scale of civilization and in moral and material prosperity".[23] The rest of the paper set out with frank realism the case for cooperation between government and missions on schooling. In some of the British colonies and protectorates in Africa, the whole, and in most of the others at least nine-tenths, of African education was being given in mission schools. Moreover, since qualified staff could be attracted to mission schools for lower wages than in any government school, mission schools represented a vastly more economical provision, financially speaking, than government schools. Moreover, stated Oldham, there was overwhelming testimony that if education was not to be destructive of morality and social order it must have a religious basis.[24]

The CMSBI education committee endorsed the memorandum. Oldham had also sent a copy to Archbishop Davidson, requesting that if possible he

[21] Perham, p.659.
[22] Clatworthy, p.21.
[23] *Ibid.*, p.22.
[24] Oliver, p.268.

should see the Duke of Devonshire and also the president of the Board of Education. He lunched with the archbishop on 9 May, and Davidson agreed to his requests. No less important, Lugard arranged for Oldham to meet a number of the governors privately and informally in advance of the main meeting. Equally, Oldham saw that strategically it would *not* be good for certain individuals or groups, worthy in themselves, to be associated with the cause: John Harris of the Anti-Slavery Society, for example, of whose committee Oldham was himself a member.[25] On 25 May Oldham himself had another interview with Ormsby-Gore. Before the conference met, Oldham had been able to secure the personal agreement of nearly all those who were to take part.

The climax to the whole process came on 6 June, with the conference itself, chaired by Ormsby-Gore. The gathering was noteworthy: the archbishop of Canterbury, Oldham, Jesse Jones from New York on behalf of the Phelps-Stokes Fund, Garfield Williams of the CMS, Lugard and five governors – Nigeria, Gold Coast, Sierra Leone, Kenya and Nyasaland – and the colonial secretary of Tanganyika, together with Colonial Office officials. That it took place on Derby Day, thereafter always being referred to as the "Derby Day meeting", provided a note of amused self-congratulation to some members at least of the group, an issue like African education for once being placed higher than this peak on the social calendar.[26] The main outcome was a decision to form in London a Permanent Advisory Committee on Native Education in Tropical Africa, on which the under-secretary of state and the head of the Africa department at the Colonial Office would regularly meet in consultation with representatives of both Protestant and Roman Catholic missions, and with educational experts, to study and advise on the wider questions of policy. The respective colonies would also have advisory boards of education, to be set up by the returning governors and to include missionaries.

The first members appointed to the committee were: Ormsby-Gore (chairman); Oldham; Sir Herbert Reid (Colonial Office); Bishop Bidwell (Roman Catholic representative, nominated by Cardinal Bourne); the bishop of Liverpool (A.A. David, a former headmaster of Rugby School); Lugard; Sir Michael Sadler; and Sir James Currie. Oldham was immensely encouraged by this step, described by one commentator as "a turning point in the history of African education".[27] One may note, too, that it was one of the most genuinely ecumenical enterprises of the time, including as it did Roman Catholic representation – a further testimony to the significance for Christian unity of outward-looking, world-oriented mission.

There was one matter, however, not settled at the Derby Day meeting, that of the appointment of an executive secretary. Oldham and Lugard were

[25] JHO letter to Ormsby-Gore 10 May 1923 [OA].

[26] Cf. Oldham, "Educational Policy of the British Government in Africa", *IRM*, vol. XIV, no. 55, July 1923, p.423. The article summarizes the whole story of the formation of the advisory committee.

[27] Oliver, p.270.

determined that someone of highest calibre be found. They were not encouraged by the Colonial Office officials' recommendation of a salary of £500 per year. Two days later, however, on 8 June, the colonial secretary (the Duke of Devonshire) invited Oldham to attend another meeting at the Colonial Office. Clatworthy records:

> He sat through the whole morning session without saying a word. Finally the Colonial Secretary asked Oldham to say a few words on education in the colonies. As it was nearly one o'clock and the whole morning session had been spent discussing education Oldham thought there would not be any further point to his prolonging the meeting. The Colonial Secretary asked for just five minutes. Oldham talked for more than five minutes on the salary allocation for the Executive Secretary of the Advisory Committee, and in his opinion, it was the most important five minutes he could ever have given to African education.[28]

The upshot was that the proposed salary was tripled to £1,500, more in line with what Oldham, Lugard and Ormsby-Gore envisaged and hoped for. The eventual choice for executive secretary was Major Hanns Vischer, one of the most colourful of Oldham's new associates. Of Swiss background, an anglophile and deeply religious (St Francis of Assisi was his hero-saint), he had gone out under the CMS to Nigeria in 1901 but soon decided he could do more constructive work in government employment. Showing a remarkable gift for languages, for surveying and for study of African culture, he became a protégé of Lugard and pioneered a good deal of educational work in Nigeria.

The committee was to more than prove its worth in the next few years. It met monthly and spawned a number of sub-committees covering subjects as varied as educational grants-in-aid, religious teaching in government schools, biological education in East Africa (strongly advocated by Prof. Julian Huxley) and British education staff. In turn it gave rise to the Inter-University Council for Higher Education in the Colonies, and was itself expanded in 1929 with a more wide-ranging brief, as the Advisory Committee on Education in the Colonies. Margery Perham judged it "one of the most, if not *the* most, constructive official body which I had ever attended"[29] though perhaps it was never so creative as in those first five years of its life when it dealt solely with Africa and the urgent issues awaiting it there. What is more, the advisory committee set an important and much-followed example in Colonial Office methodology, that of securing expert technical advice through voluntary committees.

## "Essential things to be done"

The decision to set up the advisory committee in June 1923, followed next month by the Kenya white paper, greatly encouraged Oldham to feel that at last Africa was being viewed with real seriousness and decisive actions would be taken. Almost at once the advisory committee got to work with a proposal that

[28] Clatworthy, pp.35f.
[29] Perham, p.660.

there should be another Phelps-Stokes Fund Commission, this time to East Africa, and again to be led by Jesse Jones. At the end of July Oldham was writing to Donald Fraser in Scotland, soliciting his interest in joining the commission but then confessing an ulterior motive: "To tell you the honest truth ... what we covet even more than yourself is the help of Mrs Fraser. There ought to be a woman on the commission and we cannot think of anyone who would be half so good as your wife."[30]

The second Phelps-Stokes Commission went out to East Africa early in 1924. Oldham himself was not a member of the commission (he was, for one thing, in the last stages of completing *Christianity and the Race Problem*), but by correspondence he kept in regular contact with Vischer who participated as secretary of the advisory committee, urging him to send preliminary reports on Uganda and Kenya as soon as possible. Vischer also needed to be kept informed of developments at home. Ramsay MacDonald's first Labour government was now in power, with J.H. Thomas as secretary of state at the Colonial Office. In March Oldham discovered that Thomas was considering an initiative for the application of the principles of the 1923 White Paper on trusteeship in Kenya. Having contacted a number of MPs, and hurriedly redrafting a paper drawn up by John Harris setting out major points for consideration, Oldham was disconcerted to learn that this paper had gone to the secretary of state as a memorandum "which is not what would have happened if I had been in charge of the business"[31] and backed up by a weighty deputation including Ormsby-Gore (now of course on the opposition benches) and Harris. Oldham's chief concern was that any new committee should bear in mind the existence of the advisory committee – since no treatment of trusteeship could afford to ignore education and, equally, there was a danger of crossed-wires and overlapping, even if (as seemed possible) someone like himself might be asked to serve on the new committee.

The Phelps-Stokes Commission, as before, reported in a thorough and workmanlike way. The facts were grotesque: in Kenya, Uganda and Tanganyika the colonial governments were spending, respectively 4 per cent, 2 per cent and 1 per cent of their revenue on education. "Uganda, though subsidising mission schools to the extent of £10,000 a year, had no Education Department at all. In Tanganyika, the Director of Education was the only man in a staff of five who was not actively engaged in teaching; and no grants-in-aid had been paid to missions since the establishment of the British administration."[32] Yet the mission school systems were desperate for expert advice, a professional inspectorate and resources to train African teachers more adequately. On the plus side was the fact that all three governments were already planning reforms. Oldham reported on the commission's work in *IRM*.[33]

[30] JHO letter to D. Fraser 26 July 1923 [OA].
[31] JHO letter to Vischer 10 April 1924 [OA].
[32] Oliver, p.270.
[33] Oldham, "The Christian Opportunity in Africa: Some Reflections on the Report of the Phelps-Stokes Commission", *IRM*, vol. XIV, no. 54, April 1925, pp.173–87.

This report acted as a further spur to the Labour government's concern. The result of J.H. Thomas's initiative, quite possibly influenced by the intervention of Oldham and his colleagues ("It a little looks from this narrative as if I had been a principal agent in getting the committee appointed. This, of course, is not the case. All I did was to help to steer the movement off certain rocks"),[34] was the setting up of an East Africa Commission under the chairmanship of Ormsby-Gore – a wise choice since his experience at the Colonial Office had made him probably the most knowledgeable parliamentarian in the field. The commission visited East Africa in July 1924. Meanwhile the focus on Africa continued within the missionary circle itself, with a conference on African Missions at High Leigh in September. Its main purpose was to consider the Phelps-Stokes Commission report, and Oldham reckoned it one of the best missions gatherings he had ever attended.[35]

Oldham was now, as a matter of course, inhabiting corridors of power and collaborating with politicians and their advisers to a degree well outside the usual ken of church-related officials. There is no doubt that he relished this, especially as in November 1924 the return of a Conservative government brought Ormsby-Gore back to the Colonial Office, where he would remain for the full term of the new parliament. Oldham wrote to Mott on 18 November:

> The Secretary of State for the Colonies is Amery. The Under-Secretary is Ormsby-Gore. They are likely to hold office for five years. Ormsby-Gore is a personal friend. He is sympathetic to all we wish for and will gladly accept anything really sound that we can put before him. Amery has brains, imagination and drive. He will certainly do things while he is in office, and I think that he can be got to do the right things. I do not yet know him personally, but I have several influential channels of communication open to me, and have already made a beginning in developing them. The contribution Dr Jones [of the Phelps-Stokes Fund] has made, and will make still more effectively in his new Report, is of enormous importance. Round his central ideas we can rally a large body of both missionary and official support. His policy was endorsed by the hundred missionary representatives at High Leigh. We are daily gathering adherents for it in the most influential circles. Amery and Ormsby-Gore have the power to translate it into action.

The context and overall purpose of this letter to Mott will be dealt with later. It is enough to note at this point the clarity of Oldham's strategy: identify points of common interest and possible cooperation between governments and mission, draw in the bodies with influence (and money) to find facts and develop ideas, enthuse both missionaries and officials with commitment, and develop the personal relationships of mutual trust and respect which can make things work.

The year 1925 saw even greater intensification of this Africa-related activity. First, early in the year the advisory committee put out its first and perhaps most important document, its white paper *Educational Policy in British Tropical*

[34] Clatworthy, p.18.

[35] JHO letter to Mott 15 Sept. 1924 [OA].

*Africa*, setting out the principles which were to prove the basis of policy for years to come. The drafting was largely Lugard's, with some suggestions by Oldham and Sadler. It was in effect an amplification of Oldham's original memorandum, and calling for partnership between government and missions on education. It laid down the need for missions schools to come under government supervision and to work alongside government schools. Religious and moral instruction was to be given highest importance. Lugard's "indirect" principle of colonial management was to be followed here in education, which "should be adapted to the mentality, aptitudes, occupations and traditions of the various peoples, conserving as far as possible all sound and healthy elements in the fabric of their social life".[36] The paper was sent out to all African governors, who were generally grateful that at last a coherent and practicable policy had arrived. It was twice reprinted in the 1930s for more general use.

Next, the parliamentary commission on East Africa under Ormsby-Gore produced its report. Ormsby-Gore sent Oldham in confidence a copy of the draft on 23 April. In general, the commission found in favour of the approach of the governor, Sir Robert Coryndon: setting up local native councils, and the dual policy on development. Oldham expressed unqualified admiration for the report and its sense of perspective.[37] He did however raise a question on its proposal for a loan to develop transport facilities in the region. He wrote to Ormsby-Gore:

> Your loan is not in reality a transport loan; it is a loan for the purposes of economic development, i.e. transport is only for the sake of an objective and whether you reach the objective depends on other factors.
>
> If there is to be successful development in East Africa there is something more important than transport. It is mind in the creative sense – statesmanship, policy, mastery of the facts. There are certain vital and I think essential things to be done in this region and as far as I can see they will not be done and economic development will suffer in consequence unless you and Amery have the means at your disposal to get them done.[38]

What these "essential things" were will soon be made clear. Meanwhile the report was meeting with a mixed reception in East Africa itself. The Kenyan settlers were unhappy with the application of a dual policy if it meant that Africans, being encouraged to become more adequately self-supporting, were to be less available to Europeans as a labour supply. On the other hand Donald Cameron, the new governor of Tanganyika, wrote to Oldham highly critical of the "sweeping statements" in the report based on dubious evidence. He told Oldham: "Economic development has been forced and little else has been thought of. The native has been de-tribalised and Europeanized and no thought at all has been given to the place that he is to fill in the political future of the

[36] Perham, p.661.
[37] JHO letter to Ormsby-Gore 1 May 1925 [OA].
[38] JHO letter to Ormsby-Gore 13 April 1925 ]OA].

country: we shall if we continue the practice of the past create another India or Egypt."[39]

What were the "essential things to be done"? In short, the facts of the situation had to be grasped by systematic research as the only possible basis for sound policy. It was partly in order to illustrate this that on 24 April 1925, the same day as he received Ormsby-Gore's draft of the East Africa Commission's report, Oldham in turn sent Ormsby-Gore a copy of a report he had recently come across while in Belgium, on the labour situation in the Belgian Congo, *Rapport de la Commission pour l'étude du problème de la main d'oeuvre au Congo-Belge* (1925). Oldham had been impressed by the detailed survey work behind this document, which asked two main questions: How much demand is being made upon African labour by European enterprises? What effect is this having on African tribal life? Its conclusion was that the recruitment of labour must be effectively controlled by government and that machinery must be set up for this purpose. Decision must be made on what labour may be called upon without damage to African communal life, and a balance must be sought between the needs of employment and African welfare. The situation was particularly serious in view of what appeared to be a declining population level in the Congo. Oldham also got in touch with the editor of *The Times*, Sir Stanley Reed, whom he had got to know en route to India in 1921, and wrote an article summarizing the report. This appeared under the by-line "From a Correspondent" in *The Times* of 12 May 1925 as the first item under imperial and foreign news, "Progress in the Belgian Congo – the Labour Problem".

Nor was this all. On 20 May came the debate in the House of Lords on Kenya and the report of the East Africa Commission. The archbishop of Canterbury had been thoroughly briefed by Oldham, and spoke second.[40] Stressing the "tremendous responsibility" for the natives, his speech was a plea for the long-term view. How would our actions now be viewed in thirty or forty years' time? The days of forming colonies were surely past: *trusteeship* was the watchword in the age of the League of Nations. He then drew attention to the recent *Times* piece on the Belgian report, and called for information on the relative amounts of public grants being spent on settlers and on Africans. The speech was Davidson at his best – or one might say, Oldham incognito but in public. Two days later *The Times* took up the issue again in its leader, welcoming Ormsby-Gore's report and commending the archbishop's "admirable" speech. Above all, it welcomed Lord Balfour's announcement of an imperial committee to study all such facts in East Africa thoroughly and scientifically.

In his letter to Ormsby-Gore of 13 May, Oldham had expressed disquiet about the use of a proposed loan to Kenya solely to develop a railway system. That, argued Oldham, would not meet the more fundamental need of Kenya. The colonial secretary should be allowed a degree of freedom to devote

[39] Cameron letter to JHO 1 June 1925 [OA].
[40] *The Times*, 21 May 1925.

a small proportion of the loan to other purposes. Much of the remainder of his letter is very revealing of how his mind was working – not to mention the fact in the first sentence it is very much the son of Colonel Oldham who is speaking:

> Everyone recognizes that building a railway involves preliminary engineering survey. It is necessary to get expert advice before investing capital. It is coming to be recognized also in modern large-scale business that it is necessary to spend money on a staff of experts on research, on good health conditions for the workers and even on studying their psychology . . .
>
> I do not believe it is possible to maintain that what actually exists in Kenya corresponds to the policy laid down in the White Paper of 1923, and in other declarations of policy. I am not attacking anyone because I am more and more inclined to believe that such evils as exist are due less to evil intention than to the fact that we have not got enough control over economic forces. I am of opinion that if proper provision can be made to ascertain economic facts and relate policy to them the things that are wrong will gradually be set right. But if this is not done I cannot help fearing that things will get worse because facts are being ignored and in that case there is no alternative for Christian public opinion which is seriously exercised about conditions in Kenya, except to carry on an agitation against what appears to be injustice to the natives but which in my belief is the result of helplessness in the face of economic factors that are imperfectly understood and brought under control. My belief is that the best way of getting a firm grip on the moral problem lies in getting a firm grip of the economic problem.

The need for thorough, scientific investigation into conditions in East Africa was Oldham's besetting theme throughout 1924–26. He tirelessly – some would have thought obsessively – pursued it in the advisory committee on education, in conversation and correspondence with Ormsby-Gore, and in a voluminous correspondence with a number of the colonial governors, especially Edward Grigg (with whom he spent much time just before his departure to Kenya in late 1925) and Donald Cameron of Tanganyika. Cameron was not easily convinced that sound policy need always wait for science.[41] Grigg was more interested. The crucial question was the funding for such research. Oldham on his visits to the United States, and in correspondence, had long and close dealings with representatives of the Carnegie and Rockefeller foundations, not to mention lengthy lunches whenever they were in London. There was sympathy on the American side, but also a natural wariness if the projects were to be seen to be too narrowly British rather than of universal human concern. Equally, the Colonial Office was anxious to avoid the impression of being beholden to American charity in order to carry out its own work. Oldham and Ormsby-Gore even lunched with Lord Balfour, Lord President of the Council, in December 1925 to try and win his support.[42]

[41] Cameron letter to JHO 26 June 1925 [OA].
[42] There is multitudinous correspondence, complete or in extracts, in OA.

## The International Institute of African Languages and Cultures

It was often a frustrating endeavour for Oldham. Two developments, however, in part answered his hopes. The first was the foundation in 1924 of the International Institute of African Languages and Cultures. Some attribute its genesis primarily to Oldham in conjunction with his German colleague Hans Westermann, some to Hanns Vischer. In fact Oldham and Vischer shared an equal concern for scientific research into the impact of European influence on African society and both were essential to the Institute's formation. Much of the planning in fact took place at the missionary conference at High Leigh in September 1924, which discussed the implications of the Phelps-Stokes Commission's report on East Africa. The priority was to lie in linguistic studies, including the immense and detailed work of recording and orthography, together with research into African social structure undergoing rapid change. The Institute was to be genuinely international, "a centre for world-wide contact between scholars and for the promotion of research and publication".[43] Some Rockefeller money was obtained to fund it. Lugard was chairman, Vischer secretary-general and, from early 1931 when financial stringency set in, Oldham became administrative director with the Institute contributing a quarter of his salary to the IMC, an arrangement which lasted until 1938. It launched the important journal *Africa* and organized seminars for promising young anthropologists led by the anthropologist Bronislaw Malinowski. Missionaries, advisedly handpicked by Oldham, often shared in these seminars. Interdisciplinary learning was a *sine qua non* to Oldham by now. Margery Perham sketches vividly the scene when larger international gatherings of scholars met: "Lugard, a little shy, a little aloof, combining courtesy with dignity and quite unconscious of the great reputation that gave him the primacy; Oldham, far-sighted, sharing, perhaps, with some eminent continental in a quiet corner his understanding of the depth of Africa's problems: Vischer, handsome, witty, cosmopolitan, circulating confidently in three languages amongst the mixed company and making everyone feel happier and more intelligent as they sparkled in the glow of his humanity."[44]

The second was that decision, announced by Lord Balfour during the House of Lords debate on Kenya in May 1925, to institute the committee of civil research in May 1925. The original scope envisaged for its work by Balfour was never in fact realized due to financial stringencies, but it did over the next few years carry out important work for East Africa on topics such as soil chemistry, African diet and sleeping sickness.

All this time, Oldham's contacts on African affairs continued to widen. During and after 1925 he was involved in extensive correspondence with, and about, Raymond Buell, the young American scholar and writer on political

[43] Perham, p.699.
[44] *Ibid.*, p.700.

and international affairs who was shortly to visit Africa to study a number of colonial countries. Oldham made a number of contacts for him during his visit to London, and was later to comment on aspects of his work. A particularly vital opportunity for live contact with the African educational scene, though not in fact with East Africa, came in 1924 when Alek Fraser moved from Trinity College, Kandy, to take charge of the newly founded Achimota college in the Gold Coast. This was expressly designed to explore new paths of education in Africa, and received government funding for this purpose, together with the services of J.E. Kwegyir Aggrey, himself from the Gold Coast and one of Africa's own pioneering educationalists and who had served on the Phelps-Stokes commissions. Achimota, declared Fraser, was to be about education *with* Africans, not *for* them. His letters fizzed with excitement at the possibilities, and with criticisms of others' short-sightedness. When his missives found their way to the advisory committee Oldham sometimes found their reception an embarrassing experience. He wrote to Fraser with counsel on how to get his ideas into practical reality, saying: "I think that at the moment you rather enjoy the reputation at the Colonial Office of a somewhat hair-brained sort of person who, lacking the standardising and concentrating influence of a long career in official harness, is apt to throw out all kinds of ... wild ideas."[45] Some of his letters were "apt to be misunderstood in that staid and respectable company".

By the end of 1925, then, Oldham was becoming known as quite an authority on Africa. But he had still never yet been there himself.

## Oldham's first African visit 1926

One evening in late August 1925 Oldham, Ormsby-Gore and Edward Grigg – shortly to be governor of Kenya – dined together in London and discussed further the possibilities of setting up properly funded research in Kenya. Afterwards Ormsby-Gore and Oldham were walking part of the way home together when the former suddenly said, "I wish you could go out to East Africa. If you were free this winter I think you might be able to do some good by a visit."[46] Oldham wrote to Grigg to sound his views on whether, as the governor-to-be, he felt such a visit might be useful especially in terms of the project they had in mind. Grigg's view would of course be only one, but a crucial one, of the opinions Oldham would have to sound out before deciding. His London and New York colleagues in the IMC, for a start, would have to be consulted about a visit which would taken him away from his desk for several weeks if not months, though it is hard to believe that the idea of visiting Africa had never occurred or appealed to Oldham before. Grigg's reply was hesitant: "... I am dealing here with a community and a country which I do not yet know and cannot easily estimate. The reasons for your coming are strong – contact with the problem on the spot, with local opinion, with everything one

[45] JHO letter to A. Fraser 5 Jan. 1927 [OA].
[46] Cf. JHO letter to Grigg 1 Sept. 1925 [OA].

means by atmosphere – and I personally should welcome it. But against this I feel bound to place the consideration that the white community is already on edge and that more harm than good *may* be done at the moment by the attention of visitors whom they would regard as theorists without practical responsibility . . . [T]he hardest question at the moment is not what to do but how to get it done. I am much confirmed in this by Cameron's agreement."[47]

Oldham acquiesced perfectly in this hesitation and the need to wait further for a final judgment. He did, however, have at least one other string to his bow in the form of his IMC and CMSBI responsibilities. For September 1926 there was being planned the very important international conference on African missions, to be held at Le Zoute in Belgium. How could the secretary of the IMC be so involved in it without a first-hand acquaintance with missions on the ground in Africa? The CMSBI early in October recorded its wish that Oldham should visit. Oldham wrote on 6 October to Grigg, by now in Kenya, with this news but stating that he had not intended to get involved in the issues discussed before Grigg left England: he was only informing him of the plan in case he heard about it from the Church of Scotland Mission representative in East Africa, J.W. Arthur. Grigg however read between the lines correctly and dispatched a cable to Oldham on 26 October: "Strongly advise your visiting Kenya earliest will gladly give all facilities here Grigg."

By late November Joe Oldham's plans were taking shape. He and Mary would sail for Cape Town on 8 January, spend four or five weeks in South Africa, and aim to reach Mombasa, from where they would sail home, by the end of March. From Cape Town onwards they would be accompanied by Charles T. Loram, formerly chief inspector of native education in Natal, and for part of the time would also have as travelling companion a Miss Whitelaw, a well-known Australian-born British educationalist. While Oldham would obviously give major attention to East Africa, he cherished the hope of including the Congo on the way.

On arrival in Cape Town Oldham found that C.F. Andrews was also there on behalf of the National Christian Council of India, and speaking to the clergy of the area on the Asiatic bill then going through the South African parliament. S.K. Datta had also come but had been refused permission to land. Oldham commented on the bill:

> Probably none of the promoters . . . have the slightest inkling of its effects on public opinion, not only in India, but in the Moslem world generally, and even on opinion in China and Japan . . . I should not be surprised if thoughtful minds throughout the whole of Asia were drawing inferences, right or wrong, from the American-Japanese Exclusion Act and the present legislation in South Africa.[48]

It was indeed a critical time in which to be in South Africa. The colour-bar bill was also going through parliament. Oldham met and talked with representatives of a wide variety of white opinion in Cape Town: newspaper editors,

[47] Grigg letter to JHO 7 Sept. 1925 [OA].
[48] JHO letter to anon. 31 Jan. 1926 [OA].

civil servants, politicians, academics, native administrators and the like. He was entertained by the governor-general at Government House where he also had long conversation with General Jan Smuts: a fascinating experience yet by the end deeply disappointing since Smuts seemed to have no genuine interest in the African communities: "for him the problems of South Africa were essentially those of the development of White civilization, in the working out of which the Native could, for practical purposes, largely be left out of account".[49] Among others, he met the governor of Southern Rhodesia, Sir John Chancellor, who happened to be passing through Cape Town at the time, and spoke at the University Club and the Rotary Club. He had a morning's conference with a group of missionaries; visited the archbishop's residence, Bishopscourt, revelling as every visitor there does in the natural beauty of the place, and spent a day at Stellenbosch University. He met with ministers of the Dutch Reformed Church. His contacts seem to have been almost wholly with representatives of the white communities, but there was one evening spent with the Native Welfare Society, a joint body composed of both blacks and whites. Altogether he found it a sombre experience, with a white population largely ignorant of and indifferent to the situations of the African population and the trend of current legislation. "It has been an extraordinarily interesting week," Oldham wrote home. "I shall not be altogether sorry, however, to have two days in the train in which to rest and think things over, and to escape to the presumably less exciting atmosphere of Lovedale and the Transkei."[50]

Unfortunately there is practically no surviving record of the remainder of Oldham's South African visit – except it is known that he was ill in Pretoria and that he gave an address in Natal. He also visited Lourenço Marques in Mozambique on account of difficulties which the Protestant missions there were having with the Portuguese authorities. The Oldhams sailed from Delagoa Bay for Dar es Salaam on 3 March. It had become apparent that to try to include the Congo in the itinerary would be quite impossible, and even visiting the Rhodesias and Nyasaland had to be abandoned as impracticable.

At Dar es Salaam they were warmly greeted by Donald Cameron and his wife and entertained at Government House, and their arrival could not have been more timely. A meeting of the new advisory committee on native education in Tanganyika Territory was due to begin an hour after their ship dropped anchor in the harbour. Oldham was taken to the meeting straight from the boat, and attended it for the next four days. This provided a thrilling experience in every way, for by it Oldham was able to see at first hand further concrete results, in Africa itself, of the efforts made in 1923 to secure cooperation on education between governments and missions. Under Cameron's governorship, within a matter of months a previously suspicious, if not hostile, relation between government and the missions had been transformed and "the heartiest

[49] *Ibid.*
[50] *Ibid.*

cooperation prevailed".[51] In addition to the national committee, which included both native and non-official European representatives as well as government officers and missions representatives, there were provincial committees on similar lines. The particular meeting in Dar es Salaam was dealing with new education ordinances and regulations. "Nothing could have been better than the spirit of cooperation displayed on all sides . . . The outlook is full of promise, and if things develop on the lines on which they have been started Tanganyika ought not to be far behind the Gold Coast in giving a lead in education to the African colonies . . ."[52] Expenditure on education was increasing at a meteoric rate – from £4,000 five years previously to £60,000 in the current year, quite apart from subsidies to the missions.

Oldham was also impressed with the quality of the government health programme in Tanganyika. His admiration for Cameron as a governor knew no bounds. The proposed railway linking Tanganyika with Nyasaland and the two Rhodesias would bring in more white settlers but Cameron, Oldham felt, was determined to stand by Africans' land rights. The disappointment of the Tanganyika leg of the trip was the impracticability – within the limits of the Oldhams' travel budget – of getting into the interior of the country, still less travelling up into Kenya via the Moshi area. Hence little was seen at first hand of missions work, and they had to go to Mombasa by sea.

In Kenya the host was the governor, Edward Grigg, whom Oldham had got to know so well in London the previous year. Again, a wide variety of contacts was made in the country. Oldham made a point of not ignoring the white settlers and met at least once with Lord Delamere, leader of the settler community. He got on particularly well with Major Eric Dutton, private secretary to the governor. But his particular interest was, as usual, in education, and above all in the development of the "Jeanes School" at Kabete. This imaginative venture, soon to be copied in neighbouring countries, aimed at training teachers of both sexes for work in rural areas, and also to provide courses for people in particular positions of responsibility (such as tribal chiefs and local authority councillors). Oldham's specific aim on this visit was to persuade Grigg that the Carnegie grant given for such work in Kenya should be spent not (as the advisory committee in London had short-sightedly recommended) on buildings, but on increasing and diversifying the staffing to include such as an agriculturalist, a woman teacher of domestic science and a specialist in health and sanitation. This required some deft footwork in dealing with the government staff in Nairobi, some of whom seemed dourly unimaginative. The director of the school was himself well-intentioned and conscientious but, whether by design or default, obstructive of any development along the lines envisaged. The chance of a breakthrough came when he went on home leave (never in fact to return). Oldham and Loram immediately went to work on Grigg himself, who had previously been sympathetic but pre-

[51] JHO letter to anon. 15 Feb. 1926 [OA].
[52] *Ibid.*

occupied with other matters – and indeed had himself found the director a source of frustration. Grigg expressed a wish to visit the school. "We left at three o'clock, and the Governor, as the motor car was starting, gave instructions to his A.D.C. to make arrangements for a game of golf at five o'clock. At half past four his interest in the Jeanes School was so keen that he sent the car back to Nairobi to cancel the game of golf, and remained at the school till after six. He was there altogether for over three hours." [53]

## Follow-up and the Le Zoute conference

The Oldhams sailed from Mombasa in the second week in May, reaching London by the end of the month. Oldham lost no time in communicating to as wide a public as possible what he had gleaned about the situation in East Africa, and in Kenya above all. He supplied two articles for *The Times* which appeared over his name under the heading "Kenya and Its Problems: A Recent Visit" on 9 and 10 June respectively. The first dealt mainly with native health and education. Kenya, stated Oldham, needed greater recognition of its problems. The settlers were not wholly irresponsible, and in fact in some instances were contributing to native education. The exemplary significance of the Jeanes School was stressed. The second article covered the dual policy and the importance of research. Land and taxation were crucial immediate issues, but no less significant were certain longer-term considerations:

> A serious adoption of the dual policy implies that the native point of view as well as that of the white minority must have a share in determining the course of evolution in East Africa. How the native point of view is to find political expression is a difficult question. Few would favour inclusion in a register of white voters. But the implications of the dual policy should be forcibly recognized.

By the standards of the time, Oldham's assumption that the Africans were entitled to, or even capable of, a "point of view" must have sounded almost revolutionary. A "disinterested outside power" should take responsibility for ensuring even-handed justice – a notion of imperial responsibility which Oldham was to develop over the next few years. *The Times* leader on the second day warmly commended the two articles.

Throughout the rest of the year, Oldham kept up a vigorous correspondence with a number of his contacts in Africa, especially Eric Dutton and James Dougall, deputy director of the Jeanes School at Kabete. Strenuous efforts continued to secure a grant from America for research in Kenya, a project which had Edward Grigg's enthusiastic backing and even, so Oldham learned, had won support from Lord Delamere. Allied to the project was a proposal to appoint a director to supervise and coordinate the research through a research committee, and Oldham knew enough to be aware that he himself was being considered (with Grigg's strong advocacy) for this post.[54] This would have

[53] JHO letter to T.J. Jones 14 May 1926 [OA].

[54] Cf. letters E. Diss to JHO 14 June 1926 and JHO to T.J. Jones 7 July 1926 [OA].

involved him spending considerable periods of time in East Africa and would therefore raise major questions about his future role within the IMC. The proposal, however, was remitted in the autumn to a sub-committee of the committee on civil research where the mood was hostile.[55] The government was coping with the prolonged and bitter coal strike, there had just been an imperial conference and thus preoccupation had centred on other matters.

On the missions front, the major event was the international conference on the Christian mission in Africa, held at Le Zoute in Belgium in September 1926. Preparations for this had been considerable, not least the material made available beforehand – the July 1926 issue of *IRM* had been a double-sized number devoted entirely to Africa.[56] Every important Protestant and Anglican missionary society from Europe and North America was represented.[57] Black leaders from both Africa and North America were present. So also was Frederick Lugard. The four main subjects were evangelism, education, the church, and race relations. "The whole work of the Conference", Oldham reflected afterwards, "was done under a sense that a human drama of absorbing interest and deep significance was being enacted with the African continent as its stage. Within the lifetime and memory of many of those present the opening up of its vast interior had taken place . . . Now for the first time these peoples are being swept into the main stream of human history, and what their development is to be under the impact of the new forces has become one of the major questions of the twentieth century." Education received thorough attention and affirmation. Less conclusive was the sectional discussion on evangelism, and Oldham himself was disappointed that "a more ringing and challenging note" was not sounded. Expounding his by now familiar theme of mission as extending the gospel not just geographically but also thematically into the life of peoples and societies, Oldham himself issued a striking challenge towards the close of the conference:

> Our attention has been directed in this Conference to the powerful new forces that are reshaping the life of African peoples. We are not discharging our missionary obligations if, while present physically in Africa, we ignore these new forces and remain apart from them. They are a vital part of the world in which our Christian witness has to be borne. To be truly missionary we must be in among them, in living relation with them, bringing to bear on them the leavening influence of the Christian revelation. Not to rest content with being in Africa and preaching on African soil, but to get as near as we can to the throbbing heart and centre of the movement of African life is the further call that comes to us, as our understanding of the missionary task expands and deepens.

Resolutions on education, health, native welfare, land and labour were passed. The resolutions on education recognized what Oldham and others had

[55] JHO letter to E. Dutton 24 Nov. 1926 [OA].

[56] Oldham himself contributed a technical article on "Population and Health in Africa" (pp.402–17).

[57] See Oldham's own report on Le Zoute, "The Christian Mission in Africa as seen at the International Conference at Le Zoute", *IRM*, vol. XVI, no. 61, Jan. 1927, pp.24–35.

long been advocating: a new partnership with government, a concentration on village life, an awareness of the conditions of African community life, and the need for missions schools to use governmental aid to reach the same standard of efficiency as found in government schools. "On many important issues the missions have a clearly defined policy in which they can unite. It remains only to act . . ."[58] So Oldham felt after Le Zoute, and at the end of 1926. If there is also in his words a hint of some impatience with the unabated love of conferences, we shall find it fully confirmed as the 1920s progress.

## The Hilton Young Commission 1928

The tensions over British policy in East Africa came to a head during 1927–31. In Kenya the white settlers continued to press for what amounted to self-government, and there was also a strong move towards "closer union" of the British East African territories as a whole. In Kenya, Edward Grigg as governor was known to be strongly sympathetic to the white settler cause, partly on the realistic political ground that the settlers, if determined enough, could probably at the end of the day take by force what they wanted and call any bluff from Westminster. By contrast, in Tanganyika the liberal Donald Cameron, Frederick Lugard's protégé and practitioner of his "indirect" policy of colonial rule, was vigorously and increasingly vocal in his opposition to all such moves.

On his appointment to Kenya in 1925, Grigg had been encouraged by the colonial secretary Leopold Amery to consider means of securing native lands. Grigg set out his ideas in a memorandum of March 1927, which recommended the permanent establishment of native reserves. In addition Grigg, supported by Amery, believed that the settlers themselves should constitute the trustees for the African territories and their administration. At the same time, Frederick Lugard was putting forward the idea of separate territories but with quite separate administrations for the African and white communities, with a joint council for common concerns. Lugard was not as sanguine as most Conservative opinion at Westminster, that if *given* responsibility the settlers would actually *become* responsible. His doubts were shared by Oldham who in turn, however, was dubious about Lugard's ideas on separate administration. Oldham, as will be seen, continued to maintain his line laid down in 1923, on the principle of the paramountcy of African interests combined with a strong imperial grip on government.

In the summer of 1927 the East African governors were called to London for consultation. Grigg made clear that he wanted to go a long way towards meeting his Kenyan settlers' demands for "closer union" on their own terms (he may possibly have been encouraged by Amery to harbour ambitions of becoming governor-general of an East African federation). Cameron was adamantly opposed (if Grigg had his ambitions, one should equally suppose that Cameron, for his part, in addition to his liberal convictions, would have a determination

[58] *Ibid.*, pp.27, 28, 30, 35.

to resist anything which might subsume his responsibilities under those of Grigg). Delamere and the settlers were hostile to Lugard's ideas for division of Kenya which would completely "devitalize" them as a colony. The deadlock at this level was reflected in heightening controversy over the issues in British public opinion (insofar as that opinion was taking notice of matters outside the troubled political and economic scene at home). It was also being matched by fierce dissension in Stanley Baldwin's cabinet. It was potentially deeply embarrassing for an imperial government to have two neighbouring colonies, Tanganyika and Kenya, pitted against each other, especially as Germany was campaigning for the retrocession of her former territories. It was in this context, particularly the confrontation between Cameron and Grigg,[59] that Amery decided on the familiar political means of buying, if not a solution, then at least time, in the shape of a royal commission. Time was what the more liberal side of opinion was also wanting, in order to build up opposition and prevent any hasty moves towards closer union or satisfaction of the more short-sighted settler interests.

It was in the last week in June that Oldham first heard from David Ormsby-Gore that he might be approached with a view to joining such a commission, and cabled Mott:

> MOST STRICTLY SECRET AND PERSONAL GOVERNMENT MAY INVITE ME FORM ONE OF THREE MEMBERS COMMISSION TO VISIT EAST AFRICA REPORT FUTURE POLITICAL ORGANISATION OF FIVE TERRITORIES POSITION OF NATIVES RESEARCH ETC. STOP REPORT MAY DEEPLY INFLUENCE FUTURE RELATIONS WHITE AND BLACK IN AFRICA STOP PROPOSAL ENTIRELY IN LINE WITH RATTVIK RESOLUTION THOUGH PROBABLY NOT INVOLVING ANY CONTINUING OBLIGATIONS STOP PAST CONNECTIONS AND GOVERNMENT CONCURRENCE IN VIEWS I HAVE BEEN ADVOCATING MAKE REFUSAL DIFFICULT . . .

The visit to East Africa would occupy the first four months of 1928, and would thus debar Oldham from being present at the Jerusalem missionary conference. Back from Mott came a cable in support of accepting any invitation which might be formally made to join the commission. There would at least be a chance for the two to meet and discuss matters further in Switzerland during August. Apart from Mott, the only persons in whom Oldham confided on the invitation before it became formal and public, were William Paton and Archbishop Davidson.[60] One senses that Oldham knew that his own defining moment, the *kairos* of his whole career thus far as well as a critical moment for Africa, was dawning with this invitation.

The commission, officially called the Royal Commission on Closer Union in East Africa, was to be chaired by Sir Edward Hilton Young (later Lord Kennet), a Liberal member of parliament who had earlier chaired the 1926 royal commission on Indian currency and finance. In addition to Oldham, the others were Sir George Schuster (a person with experience of the Sudan) and

[59] Perham, *Lugard*, pp.680f.
[60] JHO letter to Mott 30 June 1927 [OA].

Sir Reginald Mant of India. The significance of Oldham's inclusion has been viewed variously by different historians. George Bennett describes his appointment as very welcome to the settlers and to Grigg because of his previously sympathetic appreciation of their position,[61] with the implication that he was at that stage relatively innocent of East African affairs at first hand. Perham however attributes a good deal of Grigg's acute *anxiety* at the commission's coming to Kenya to Oldham's presence and the fact that "his now considerable knowledge of the issue together with his subtlety and persistence of mind promised to make him a dominant element".[62] At the very least the inclusion of Oldham signified a recognition of the missionary interest and experience of the region. For his part, Leopold Amery certainly hoped that the commission when reporting would pave the way for federation in East Africa.

As well as several assistants and secretaries, the party was to include as unofficial companions Mary Oldham and Lady Mant. The Oldhams left England just before Christmas 1927, crossing the Channel and then proceeding by train to Venice where they met up with Hilton Young and the Mants, flying thence to Cairo. In Cairo there was a glad reunion with the Oldhams' old Oxford friend Temple Gairdner who, despite feeling ill, guided them around the wonders of the Pyramids (it was to prove no passing fever: Gairdner was dead within weeks). Schuster joined them on the Nile steamer (named appropriately, perhaps, the SS *Lugard*). Throughout the tour Mary Oldham wrote copious letters back home to Betty Gibson, and these comprise a superb diary on the unofficial aspects of the tour in vivid and entertaining detail: the splendours of the Nile; dust and heat on train and car journeys; the excitement of watching big game; colourful African life and customs; the unpredictable conditions aboard the coastal steamers; the quirks of colonial governors, their wives and servants; the fun and (mostly minor) irritations that developed within the group as a whole. It is superb travelogue. Joe Oldham's health, for the most part, stood up to the rigours surprisingly well. It was Mary who suffered more from minor fevers, and Joe who cheered her up with aptly-chosen limericks.

For its actual work, the commission first visited Uganda, and then Kenya. The group arrived in Nairobi just when the elected (or "unofficial") members of the legislative council were strongly supporting the passage of the native lands trust bill through the legislative council. Canon Leakey, representing native interests on the council, expressed severe reservations about whether white settlers would really be trustworthy trustees of African interests (an Indian, A.H. Malik, likened it to setting a cat to watch over the interests of a mouse).[63] Several senior Commissioners had also broken their usual rule of silence and spoken out against the measure. The Hilton Young Commission

[61] G. Bennett, "British Settlers North of the Zambesi, 1920 to 1960", in L.H. Gann and P. Duignon, eds, *Colonialism in Africa 1870–1960. Vol. 2: The History and Problems of Colonialism 1914–1960*, Cambridge, Cambridge Univ. Press, 1970, p.66; and "Paramountcy to Partnership: J.H. Oldham and Africa", *Africa*, vol. XXX, no. 4, Oct. 1960, pp.356–61.

[62] Perham, p.681.

[63] Bennett, "British Settlers", p.65.

persuaded the council – against the wishes of Grigg and the settlers' representatives – to defer any further progress of the bill until its own report had been made and considered by the Colonial Office.

The commission heard the whole spectrum of views in Kenya. Archdeacon Owen of Kavirondo, one of the sternest critics of the settlers, was so handled by the chairman "that his intervention made little impression".[64] Other more moderate but percipient missionaries such as Leakey were more successful. The commission went on to Tanganyika, Nyasaland and Rhodesia. Perhaps the most influential views upon Oldham were those of the Scottish and Anglican missionaries of Nyasaland, with their more general criticism of the settlers' mentality as inimical to Africans' development. It was in Livingstone, Nyasaland, that the party felt they had reached rock-bottom as far as official hospitality was concerned. At dinner one evening, the subject of genetics came up and Joe Oldham got into an argument with the governor who "knows everything, and knows that he knows it; so there is no more to be said".[65]

### Aftermath of Hilton Young: the home campaign

The commission returned to England in early May 1928. Oldham had found himself drawn progressively closest in viewpoint to Schuster as the tour progressed. Together with Sir Reginald Mant they produced the majority report of the commission. This was issued on 17 January 1929: *Report of the Commission on Closer Union of the Dependencies in Eastern and Central Africa* (1929, Cmd. 3234). It was a long and informative document, with African interests given prominence. It advocated, as Oldham had so persistently argued since 1923, the maintenance of imperial trusteeship and the refusal to the settlers in Kenya of an unofficial majority. Hilton Young himself expressed some minority opinions. Nor did the commission accept Lugard's "administrative separation". They did recommend a moderate, flexible form of closer union "in which an authoritative governor-general would make imperial control, especially of native policy, a local and intimate reality".[66]

The Hilton Young report was scarcely off the press before it was under fire from pro-settler opinion. Grigg was in England at the time, and to him it was "disastrous". Lord Delamere cabled a furious denunciation from Kenya. Oldham had enough political nous to be prepared in advance for such reaction. He, Lugard and others quickly got to work. Oldham himself dealt with much of the press, English and Scottish. For the church constituency he wrote a pamphlet *What Is at Stake in East Africa*.[67] Baldwin's second Conservative administration was entering its last months of life, and Oldham made contact

[64] *Ibid.*, p.66.
[65] M. Oldham letter to Gibson 9 April 1928 [OA].
[66] Perham, p.682.
[67] Issued anonymously but definitely by Oldham: *What Is at Stake in East Africa*, London, Edinburgh House, 1929.

with the newly hopeful Labour party through De Lisle Burns, and also with the prime minister through Tom Jones. Lugard – by now a peer – put down a motion for debate in the House of Lords and prepared to make his maiden speech. Cameron arrived from Tanganyika to fight for the cause. Grigg fought back. The emotional temperature soared.

The outcome of the report was far from certain. The mobilization of parliamentary and public opinion was crucial, but for Oldham, as for the other commissioners, there were limits and proprieties to be observed in public activity. However, he was used to working behind the scenes, and in facilitating actions by his allies who could and did have a more public persona. Chief among these were Lugard and Archbishop Davidson.[68] A letter from Lugard in *The Times* would carry considerable weight. But it was at this precise moment, on 25 January 1929, that Frederick Lugard was plunged into grief and anguish with the death of his wife Flora. Oldham himself was caught in an agony of indecision between respect for Lugard the private mourner and increasing desperation over the future of Kenya. Eventually he took the plunge, and years later recalled:

> I could see no means of preventing it [Government action on Kenya] except an intervention by Lord Lugard . . . I travelled to Little Parkhurst . . . When we settled down in the study for a talk after dinner I explained to Lord Lugard the situation as I saw it, and said that I saw no way of arresting action which we both believed to be mistaken, except a letter by him to *The Times.* He visibly shrank from this suggestion, and said that it was contrary to his deepest feelings to come before the public in any way at such a time. I at once accepted this, and we talked for an hour about other matters. He then rose from his chair and went over to his desk, and began writing. I sat in silence while he did so. He came back and handed me a sheet of paper with the words: "You can send that to *The Times* tomorrow."[69]

Oldham next day took it along to Lambeth Palace. Randall Davidson agreed that it was precisely what was wanted, and off it went to *The Times*, appearing the following day, 7 February. It was essentially a plea for delay, in recognition of the gravity of the issue and the threatened break in customary crown colony procedure, and also the imminence of a general election. But it was imbued throughout with the long-term view: "Nor is it less desirable that the settlers in Kenya, for whose achievements and desire to come to a just and right decision I yield to none in appreciation, should have ample time to consider, and perhaps to revise, their first impressions. For it is my sincere belief that further consideration may lead them to doubt whether conclusions which seem desirable for the solution of present-day problems are in the real interests of their children's children."

Oldham was deeply moved by the confluence of private pain and public responsibility which he had witnessed in Lugard, and its issue in service to the wider good. "I cannot tell you", Oldham wrote to Lugard the day after his visit

[68] Cf. Perham, p.682.
[69] *Ibid.*, p.673.

to Little Parkhurst, "what last night meant to me."[70] His later reminiscences of Lugard at his desk that night continued:

> I do not think that I have ever had a stronger sense than during that half hour of what is sometimes called the "numinous" or witnessed a greater manifestation of supernatural heroism and devotion to duty. It is impossible to convey the impression in a letter. One has to know what Lord and Lady Lugard were to one another, and the way in which his life was torn in two by her death, to understand the courage and iron resolve which enabled him to do what he did.[71]

Efforts continued. Lugard and Oldham decided that the best way of securing full consideration of the whole issue would be by a joint select committee of both houses of parliament. More frantic activity, and on 25 February a letter appeared in *The Times* making this demand, signed by Lugard and six other peers. Then came the House of Lords debate on 13 March. Lugard had prepared his speech in close collaboration with Oldham. He reiterated his earlier interests in dual policy, indirect administration of native affairs, and the crucial importance of education. Overall he argued for a joint select committee of both houses, as had dealt with Indian affairs.[72] Oldham, watching from the Strangers' Gallery, was deeply gratified and impressed.[73] "The outstanding feature of the Debate was the extraordinary expression of confidence in him from every quarter of the House." Archbishop Davidson, for all the weight of his advancing years, also "did very well, better than expected". Oldham spoke at Chatham House on 19 March to a large audience but, in his view, "the best people" did not speak and the discussion was ill-informed.

The danger of precipitate action by the colonial secretary remained – as did the possibility of unilateral action in Kenya itself. Oldham told Cameron of his strong suspicion "that Kenya is determined to go its own way and that Grigg will take the same line". Amery, it later transpired, was indeed hoping to bypass the report and was angered at the cabinet's hesitancy and division on the issue. A cabinet committee was appointed. The in-fighting waged by Cameron and Grigg at the Colonial Office continued.

Amery was in a dilemma. The majority report of the Hilton Young Commission went against his political grain. But the public opposition to his views could not be gainsaid. Party political confrontation was sharpening, aroused as it was since the general strike of 1926 and now being further excited with the approach of a general election. Three weeks after the debate, Amery took refuge in yet another commission, this time a one-person affair in the shape of Sir Samuel Wilson, the permanent head of the Colonial Office. Wilson was in fact already decidedly (if privately) in sympathy with the views of Amery and Grigg. Oldham knew this, and also knew before most people of the plan to send Wilson out, and told Cameron, "In many ways you hold the key."[74]

[70] Perham, p.683.
[71] *Ibid.*, p.673.
[72] *Ibid.*, p.684.
[73] Letter JHO to Cameron 20 March 1929 and cited in Perham, p.685.
[74] *Ibid.*

Wilson duly went out to East Africa and returned in July with a report, not surprisingly, much more favourable to the settlers than the Hilton Young report had been, suggesting an unofficial majority in the legislative council and a reduced role for the high commissioner. Donald Cameron, however, had rejected it conclusively and his views were contained in an appendix. Meanwhile, on his return Wilson found that he now had new political masters at home. The Conservatives were out, Ramsay MacDonald's second Labour government was in, and there was a new Colonial and Dominions Secretary, Lord Passfield (Sidney Webb, the "bearded Fabian"). Lugard, Oldham and their circle turned to the new ministers "like flowers to the sun" (Margery Perham), but their chief aim, in view of the precarious position of the new government (it had no overall majority) was an all-party decision through a select committee. Lugard worked on Passfield (who, Oldham noted with amusement, would deal only with peers), entertaining him to dinner and midnight conversation at Little Parkhurst. Oldham and Lugard together saw Ramsay MacDonald's son Malcolm before he left for the United States, obtaining from him promise that there would be a select committee, and took tea with J.H. Thomas, the lord privy seal. David Ormsby-Gore's successor as under-secretary at the Colonial Office was Drummond Shiels who proved very amenable. Philip Kerr and Geoffrey Dawson of *The Times* were helpful. Close contact was maintained with the archbishop of Canterbury, and while Oldham worked on Oxford opinion, Lugard was in touch with commercial interests through his friend Sir Humphrey Leggat, chairman of the Joint East African Board.[75]

All concerned had to wait nearly a year for Passfield to declare his policy in June 1930, and it came with devastating clarity in the form of two white papers. They decisively rejected the Grigg-Amery-Wilson line. Passfield had kept his cards so close to his chest that not even the East African governors themselves were consulted beforehand, but received his memoranda as sealed packages to remain unopened until the actual publication date. Kenyan settlers called them the "black papers", and a chorus of white hostility rang throughout British colonial Africa. Moreover, Passfield accepted the plan of Oldham and Lugard for a joint select committee to consider the constitutional proposals. Passfield declared, when the matter was debated in parliament on 3 July, that East African policy required a sanction beyond that of any party government.

The joint select committee was duly appointed, and first met on 4 December 1930. As well as Passfield and Shiels it included the previous ministerial occupants of the Colonial Office, Amery and Ormsby-Gore. Edward Grigg by now felt totally alienated from what appeared to be a liberal and socialist ménage in charge of colonial policy. Neville Chamberlain urged Grigg to advise the settlers "not to think that the case had been lost 'because the old nanny-goat [Passfield] has issued these two white papers'".[76]

[75] Perham, p.687.
[76] *Ibid.*, p.688.

The work of the committee was long and arduous. Lugard was conscientious, attending nearly all the sessions and keeping in close touch with Oldham on every move. A notable contribution to the testimony it received in person was made by a number of Africans. Almost for the first time in Westminster, black Africa was speaking for itself and having to be listened to. Little Parkhurst became the off-stage centre for reflecting on the dramatic struggle. Oldham was a constant visitor there, side by side with governors such as Donald Cameron and Grigg's successor Joseph Byrne, settler representatives, intellectuals such as Julian Huxley and all manner of parliamentarians and Colonial Office staff. Lugard helped with much of the drafting of the report, which was carried out against the background of continuing political turbulence at home culminating in the formation of MacDonald's first "national" government at the end of August 1931, to be followed by the bitterly-fought general election which gave the national government victory in November. East Africa by now took a fairly low place on the public agenda, and indeed when the committee's report was issued on 6 October it seemed at first something of an anti-climax after so much effort. Perhaps nothing more should have been expected from a joint committee of both houses, and reflecting all major party opinion. But if the recommendations were compromises, at least they were clear. Closer union was rejected, and for the time being remained buried as an option. The Kenya council should remain *advisory* and the only change recommended was for a larger representation of African interests. Thus, even if closer union had been recommended, the Kenyan settlers would not have been able to realize their ulterior ambition of dominating the union that would have resulted. African paramountcy was reiterated, though perhaps in terms slightly less intimidating to the settlers. Lugard's doctrine of administrative separation was fully expounded, and while this was not adopted the way was left open for the development of native councils and a higher role for the chief native commissioner. Further, special commissions were to investigate the perennially controversial matters of native lands, and the distribution of revenue between Europeans and Africans.

Few victories are complete in the political arena, but Oldham, with Lugard, had seen most of the salient ground safeguarded. Closer union was out. On the basis of an all-party authority, African paramountcy and the need to build up a positive African participation in Kenyan affairs were affirmed. Settler opinion would remain unremittingly opposed to such policies, but the nearness to success which it achieved in the Amery-Grigg period was never to be repeated. Perham's judgment on who could take chief credit for this is striking:

> It remains to assess the reasons why the Amery-Grigg policy, which had so much Conservative support, failed. It was due to a combination of political events and personal efforts. Chief amongst the events were the advent of Labour to power with the appointment of Passfield as Colonial Secretary. His tenure was brief and he had his shortcomings. But . . . he approached the question not as a mere Labour doctrinaire, but as a trained administrator who had to see both sides of any issue, in

this case the native as well as the settler side. But perhaps no individual played a greater part from 1923 onwards than Oldham and we have seen that in the crucial years 1929–31 Lugard and he acted as one.[77]

No one would endorse that judgment more readily, though with considerable annoyance, than Samuel Wilson who from Whitehall had seen the Oldham–Lugard opposition building up and working so effectively. When he was sent out to Kenya in the summer of 1929 he lamented that Oldham and his allies had done their job so well that he himself was now "regarded by these damned doctrinaires as the permanent official sent out by Amery and chloroformed by the settlers".[78] In November 1929 he had complained in a letter to Grigg of Oldham and Lugard continuing "an intensive campaign in the press trying to mislead the British public"; and Amery likewise referred to the "mischievous lobbying" by Oldham and Lugard.

This was the high-water mark of Oldham's activist engagement with colonial policy in Africa – though not the end. "He was destined to leave a deep if, in part, a secret mark upon Africa",[79] and the story outlined here is where that mark was etched most decisively.

### Further reflections on Africa

By the end of the 1920s few people in Britain could speak on Africa with such authority as Joe Oldham. Following the setting up of the joint select committee in 1931, he was never again so heavily engaged in political footwork. But neither could his views ever be discounted. His two visits, his detailed mastery of so much information, his extraordinary array of contacts both in Africa and outside, and above all his clear principled stand on the interests of black Africans combined with a bent for practicable solutions, for a while gave him a unique stature alike in missionary, political and academic circles. He continued as administrative director of the International Institute of African Languages and Cultures until 1938.

Oldham always combined deftness in the hand-to-hand struggles with vision of the overall strategy and final goal. The manoeuvring with politicians never became just an enjoyable game, an end in itself. It was Africa he was interested in, not enjoying a reputation in the corridors of power as a remarkably skilled operator. That is shown by his ability at the end of the 1920s still to relate closely to the scene in East Africa, and to reflect on the major issues confronting the continent in the future. In 1929, a major controversy broke out in Kenya over the decision by the Scottish Mission churches to ban the Kikuyu practice of female circumcision. The issue became politicized when the Kikuyu Central Association, a new political movement, saw this as an attempt to denationalize

[77] *Ibid.*, pp.690f.
[78] *Ibid.*, p.691.
[79] *Ibid.*, p.658.

Kenyans and campaigned against the ban. Oldham counselled J.W. Arthur, head of the Scottish Mission in Kenya, to tread warily and not repeat the mistake made by some Western missions in India of allowing Christianity to become set in sheer opposition to nationalism.[80]

In retrospect, a major question hangs over Oldham's perspective on Africa in the context of the hey-day of colonialism. Adrian Hastings for example pays tribute to Oldham's extraordinary range of initiatives with both missionary bodies and government, and identifies him as the single most determinative influence on Western missionary policy in Africa in the 1920s and 1930s. Hastings concludes, however, "His benevolence was limitless, but its tone was profoundly paternalistic."[81] In seeking to ally missions and enlightened colonial policies Oldham was discounting the radical potential of African nationalism, which would in due course create a fateful dilemma for African Christianity. To this it should be said that "paternalism" undefined is not the most illuminating term. There are varieties and degrees of "paternalism". Oldham's emphasis was upon education as the prime need of Africa. It was indeed education in a European form which was his assumed perspective, but this was because he was also assuming "development" for eventual self-government as the ultimate end in view. Oldham in the 1920s may indeed have not given radical African nationalism its due attention, but can it be denied that those Africans who did eventually lead their peoples to independence from colonialism owed a debt to such education? Oldham did assume much of the colonial framework: not however as an ideology but as the means of actually improving matters within the foreseeable future.

Norman Leys, for his part, even before the Hilton Young Commission, had certainly grown increasingly impatient with Oldham's approach. At first, noting the success of Oldham's campaign against Kenyan forced labour, he had given Oldham the benefit of the doubt. But at the end of the day he was angry and disappointed:

> I hope you will forgive me for thinking that your occupation and habits dispose you to give too great importance to people in high position. You know them well, certainly meeting them in many countries. It is tempting to think that a thing is done when the hand of such a man is rightly guided. In the modern world it is not so. We are helpless unless the lever moves a powerful engine. That engine is public opinion.[82]

Oldham in turn lost patience with Leys, if politely:

> I give it up.
>
> This does not lessen my regard and admiration for you and for what you are doing or my desire to help, according to my lights, to further the ends you are seeking.[83]

[80] Bennett, "British Settlers North of the Zambesi", p.67.
[81] A. Hastings, *The Church in Africa 1450–1950*, Oxford, Oxford Univ. Press, 1994, p.552.
[82] Cell, p.242.
[83] *Ibid.*

A final judgment on Oldham in this respect should not ignore his position relative to other players in his context. Two very different books from the end of the decade reflect Oldham's most mature thinking on Africa in the changing world scene.

In November 1929 General Jan Smuts, former champion of the Boers, now the supreme empire loyalist and doyen of white benevolent paternalism in South Africa, gave the three Rhodes Memorial Lectures in the Sheldonian Theatre, Oxford.[84] They were broadcast by the BBC: years later Kathleen Bliss could "still hear that mellifluous voice coming through the crackling of the old crystal set".[85] Smuts presented an odd combination of argument for the value of white settlement in Africa and for the principles of the League of Nations. He quoted from Lugard and the Hilton Young report but hardly to such ends as the writers would have shared. The best prescription for native advancement was white settlement: "Without a large European population as a continuous support and as an ever-present example and stimulus for the natives, I fear that civilization will not go far and will not endure for long. From the native point of view, therefore, just as much as from the white or European point of view, nay, even more from the native point of view, the policy of African settlement is absolutely necessary." "The building up of a strong white community to hold and develop the healthy high lands which stretch from Rhodesia to Kenya would be a magnificent response to this call. Now that Great Britain holds these territories from north to south in one unbroken chain, she has an opportunity, greater even than Rhodes dreamt of, to carry out her historic mission and establish in the heart of the African continent and as a bulwark of its future civilization another great European community." The need was to develop civilization in Africa without injustice to the African, for "there is much that is good in the African and which ought to be preserved and developed". The African has remained a charming child-type – "No other race is so easily satisfied, so good-tempered, so care-free."[86] The best way of civilizing the African was by white settlement, and the best education for Africans was to be found in employment under whites. Segregation, but with the black males imbibing white values from the employers, was the best way forward. In all this, South Africa was showing the way for the rest of the continent.

Oldham heard the lectures and was incensed. He had met Smuts in Cape Town in 1926 and, even more than on that occasion, was again struck by how this high-minded idealism rested on sheer ignorance of, or lack of any real interest in, the reality of life for Africans. Moreover, Smuts was giving what a lot of already ill-informed people in Britain were wanting to hear about the decency of empire. Without waiting for the lectures to be published – the debate about East Africa was still raging and Passfield's white papers still being awaited – Oldham put pen to paper and produced his short but hard-hitting

[84] J.C. Smuts, *Africa and Some World Problems*, Oxford, Clarendon, 1930.
[85] K. Bliss, "The Legacy of J.H. Oldham", *International Bulletin of Missionary Research*, Jan. 1984, p.22.
[86] Smuts, p.49.

*White and Black in Africa*[87] which appeared in 1930. Significantly, he dedicated it to the memory of the late Kwegir Aggrey, who had represented the voice of educated black Africa and taken part in the Phelps-Stokes commissions.

*White and Black in Africa* takes Smuts apart thoroughly, if politely. Oldham and Smuts are at one in recognizing that Africa, pregnant with so many possibilities, represents one of the greatest and most exciting challenges to the modern world. He dismisses Smuts' claims, however, that South Africa shows the way ahead – and on purely factual grounds. Smuts had grandiosely claimed that wherever there is white settlement, black welfare increases. Oldham demands medical evidence in support of this and finds none, and in fact cites statistics of diseases pointing in the opposite direction. The facts of the South African situation just do not match Smuts' rose-tinted view of black betterment under white employment. What of the vast masses of blacks in the huge squatter camps? What are their chances of contact with whites? What prospects do the mine-workers have for better conditions or more skilled jobs? There is simply no economic advancement in view for the Africans: "The situation, as they view it, is one of despair. Except for the more fortunate few, there is only the barest subsistence to be obtained from the land."

On his wider African dreams, Smuts is revealed by Oldham to be embarrassingly ignorant on basic facts about the continent. There simply is no "belt of healthy high lands", congenial to European susceptibilities, stretching "from Rhodesia to Kenya"; rather, a mixture of terrains of very varying altitudes, soil conditions and diseases. But Oldham's most fundamental disagreement with Smuts is on African development. Smuts takes a rigidly stereotyped view of "the native", to be perpetually preserved in child-like dependency upon the white, while apparently totally unaware that the most disintegrating influence on present-day African society is exploitative Western colonialism. Oldham believes in the educability of Africans and in their own capacities for development. "The fundamental business of government in Africa is education. The responsibility of trusteeship means more than the protection of the native peoples from injustice. It calls for active exertion to help the African to make the best of himself."[88]

Nevertheless, towards the end of the book Oldham seeks to identify common ground with Smuts, who is laudatory about the League of Nations and its aims. Oldham, intrigued as to why Smuts can be so enlightened when thinking about responsible government at the world level yet so blinkered when it comes to Africa, believes that the principle of limitation of sovereignty of nations in face of international obligations might be applied to Africa. There is a need for the political expert who in the name of international justice can arbitrate between competing or conflicting interests. The principle is already at work in the increasing use of scientific expertise by the Colonial Office. A distinction

[87] Oldham, *White and Black in Africa: A Critical Examination of the Rhodes Lectures of General Smuts*, London, Longman, Green & Co., 1930.

[88] *Ibid.*, pp.17, 22, 41.

could be drawn between those issues which could be decided by a local legislative council and those requiring the decision of the colonial secretary, for example. Oldham, in other words, was reiterating his view of the strong arm of imperial government having the final say in matters where the paramount interests of Africans were at stake. This would not be arbitrary rule, but government informed by scientific wisdom and accountable to the international community's agreed standards of justice.

George Bennett comments on a certain irony in Oldham's response to Smuts. In 1931 the African Institute which Oldham had been instrumental in founding inaugurated its ambitious *Africa Survey*. Oldham arranged the introductory luncheon which brought together a senior representative of the Carnegie corporation and leading members of the Royal Institute of International Affairs. But, according to Bennett, it was Smuts' lectures which had been the most important public stimulus to the idea of the survey.[89]

The second book was not in reaction to such external provocation. *The Remaking of Man in Africa*[90] was the fruition of that whole decade of thinking about education in Africa which had taken root in Oldham from the end of the first world war, and its aim was to set out a strategy for a new missionary era. It was written jointly with Betty Gibson. Oldham and Gibson wrote drafts of their respective chapters, commented on and criticized each other's efforts and then rewrote accordingly. The result is a fairly seamless robe, itself a model of collaboration. Most of the themes were familiar by now to Oldham readers: the need for cooperation with governments, yet also to maintain a distinctively Christian basis of education; Christian education as the development of the whole person, and best mediated by the Christian life and experience of Christian community and worship; the requirement for education to be related to the experience of African life in society; teacher training; education of women and girls; the need to maintain, despite the tension, both the evangelistic and God-oriented activities of mission on the one hand, with humanitarian concern for education and the welfare of the whole person on the other.

Nevertheless certain notes are present which would not have been heard ten years earlier, except perhaps in a different key. "What a missionary can do for Africa by preparing Africans for positions of trust and responsibility and laying responsibility on their shoulders is immensely greater than anything that he can accomplish by himself." Moreover, the true relationship "is a comradeship in which Africans and those from the West seek together a growing understanding of life in the light of the Gospel".[91] Education is essentially "a comradeship in learning".

In fact it is striking that while the title of the book carries an obvious reference to W.E. Hocking, who had been so influential on Oldham's understanding of

[89] Bennett, "Paramountcy to Partnership", p.360.
[90] J.H. Oldham and B.D. Gibson, *The Remaking of Man in Africa*, London, Oxford Univ. Press and Humphrey Milford, 1931.
[91] *Ibid.*, pp.146f.

education, there is relatively little mention of Hocking in this work. The picture of the individual as the plastic object of influence is not totally displaced, but a different perspective is apparent, namely, that of the nature of community and of relationships between persons. There is also infiltrating a sense, too, that the relationship to the divine can be both problematic and surprising. The knowledge of God is a personal knowledge, a relationship with God as a Person who can never be comprehended in the depth of his being in quite the same way as we know human persons:

> God is not an object among other objects, and to think of him in this way is to involve ourselves in hopeless difficulties. God, as Professor Karl Barth has reminded us, is always Subject. We can know him only when he speaks to us and we are constrained to obey. The God of the Christian revelation meets us with the claim that we should surrender to him our heart. He asks for obedience, trust, love and uttermost devotion.[92]

This is the first published reference by Oldham to Karl Barth. Oldham was registering the new theological wind blowing from the continent, and also the emphasis on the "personal" in theologians nearer home such as H.H. Farmer in his *The Experience of God*. It was significant that he was picking up these new impulses ushered in by the "theology of crisis". That theology was to be at the centre of the struggles in Europe for the next decade, and it was once again to Europe, so soon to be in travail again, that Oldham's attention would now be turning.

[92] *Ibid.*, p.43.

CHAPTER 11

# *New Tensions: Oldham, Mott and the IMC*

FROM the previous chapter the impression might easily be gained that from the early 1920s onwards Oldham's Africa-related activities constituted a full-time occupation. They did. But Oldham led a more than full-time life. He was fully engaged as secretary of the International Missionary Council and editor of the *IRM*. He remained in close touch with all the major missionary agencies and the student movement, from the time when he had addressed the SCM Quadrennial conference in Glasgow in 1921. In the audience, and deeply impressed, was a young Dutchman called W.A. Visser 't Hooft who many years later still recalled Oldham's address as a milestone in his life.[1]

However, tensions did emerge between his increasing orientation towards Africa and his official responsibilities towards the IMC. They were partly, but not wholly, due to the competing demands on his time and energy and to differing expectations of his role especially as seen from North America. They arose also from gradually diverging perceptions on where the priorities for the missionary enterprise now lay and on the methods whereby international cooperation could best be pursued. There also developed, at certain points, serious frustrations on Joe Oldham's part with the kind of leadership role now being exercised by John Mott. All this may come as something of a surprise to students of ecumenical history who have been raised on a reading of the story from Edinburgh 1910 to the founding of the WCC as a smooth pilgrimage with an untrammelled Oldham–Mott friendship at its core.

## A holistic mission

The point to begin this aspect of the story is with the understanding of mission already held by Oldham around the time of the new beginning marked by the

[1] W.A. Visser 't Hooft, *Memoirs*, Geneva, WCC, 2nd ed. 1987, p.10.

formation of the IMC. While in New York in the winter of 1919–20, Joe Oldham was asked by E.A. Aiken for a summary statement on the goal of Christian missions, in preparation for a Student Volunteer conference. On his return to England, Oldham supplied him with the following statement[2] which merits quotation in full as a cogent expression of where his mind stood immediately following the first world war:

> THE AIM OF CHRISTIAN MISSIONS
>
> The aim of Christian missions is to make known to the whole of mankind the gracious and saving acts of God in history, which have their centre and crown in the person and work of Jesus Christ, and which make known His character and His purpose for the world.
>
> Since these acts of God are interpreted in human experience and their purpose is the redemption and richer fulfilment of human life the Christian witness is one not only of word but of life. The missionary task thus includes medical missions and other forms of philanthropy as a manifestation of Christian love; efforts through industrial and agricultural training to improve the economic life of the people where poverty is an obstacle to moral and spiritual growth; and Christian education generally as a means of forming character in accordance with the Christian view of the meaning and goal of life.
>
> A fundamental element in the aim of Christian missions is the establishment of a Christian society. This is essential, first, because the Christian ideal is social, as is shown by the central place of the Kingdom of God in Christ's teaching; and, secondly, because the missionary task can never be accomplished by foreigners. The primary object of foreign missionary effort is therefore to establish and to help to train for effective leadership an indigenous Christian Church.
>
> In so far as the aims of Christian missions need to be modified it would seem to me to be in the direction of a clearer recognition of the demands made by the complexity of modern life. Since the industrial revolution the relations of the individual are no longer as in the preceding ages mainly with individuals, but also with large organisations and with highly developed social groups. Under these conditions the attempt to win individuals necessarily involves the attempt to establish the rule of Christ over the whole life. Moreover, in view of the political and economic relations of the professedly Christian nations with non-Christian peoples it is necessary for Christian missions, if they are to bear true witness to Christ, clearly and publicly to dissociate themselves from selfish and materialistic influences in these contacts and to stand unequivocally for justice and brotherhood in international and inter-racial relations.

Whatever use the student conference in America made of it, this statement certainly serves as a manifesto for Joe Oldham's holistic understanding of mission, which undergirded all he attempted for the next ten years. His work for Africa is a direct expression of the thought of the final paragraph.

On the practical level, the restructuring of the secretariat of the IMC did recognize and allow for the heavy demands that came to be placed on Oldham. A.L. Warnshuis worked in the London office until 1924 when he moved to

[2] JHO letter to Aiken 17 Feb. 1920, with statement "The Aim of Christian Missions" attached [OA].

*William Paton*

New York to form an additional administrative base for the IMC there. The most significant development, however, came at the meeting of the IMC council in July 1926 at Rättvik, Sweden – that is, between Oldham's first African visit and the Le Zoute conference on mission in Africa. Here the decision was taken to invite William Paton to leave India and join Oldham as associate secretary of the IMC. The clearly stated need was to relieve Oldham of his present executive duties and to free him for the special lines of work that were making increasing demands on his time and strength.[3] Georgina Gollock was soon to retire and this alone made additional help necessary. It was not, however, simply a matter of providing more help for Oldham personally. It was a recognition that the IMC was itself developing and widening its scope, particularly in partnership with the increasing number of national councils and with the indigenous churches. There was also the Jerusalem conference to take place in 1928. Paton, who was himself present at Rättvik, agreed to accept after consultation with his colleagues back in India, and joined the London staff in early 1927.[4] In 1928 he took over the editorship of the *IRM*.

Oldham's relationship with Warnshuis eventually proved not so happy despite the early promise. Warnshuis showed himself an able enough administrator,

[3] IMC officers letter to Metropolitan of Calcutta 24 July 1926 [OA].

[4] See E. Jackson, *Red Tape and the Gospel*, Birmingham, Phlogiston Press and Selly Oak Colleges, 1980, p.112.

and an agreeable colleague. But, especially after Warnshuis's move to New York, Oldham was disappointed at what he saw as a lack of imagination and capacity for initiative, particularly in devising means of overcoming the conservative attitudes towards cooperation of some of the American mission boards.[5] Warnshuis, in turn, conveyed to Oldham a view which others in the United States probably shared, namely, that in his African activities Oldham was devoting too much time to sorting out specifically British colonial problems at the expense of the truly international missionary responsibilities which properly lay on his desk. Oldham strenuously denied this: "For a few months it is predominantly British, but only as a starting point for international cooperation on a large scale. Nothing that I have done has given me closer connections with the best elements in American life."[6] Oldham could cite not only the personal support of a number of American colleagues but also the generosity of the Phelps-Stokes Fund and Carnegie Corporation.

Further disagreement with Warnshuis arose in 1925 when the latter alleged that Oldham was stepping out of bounds in approaching American philanthropic trust funds directly and not via the American boards. Again, Oldham denied this was impermissible. The funds themselves were eager for international cooperation, and the work was ultimately on behalf of the IMC interest as a whole.[7]

## John Mott: what leadership?

It is, however, his correspondence with Mott that is most revealing of a degree of unease with the international missions scene, for all the advances represented by the IMC. In part, it was this very friendship, a long-standing relationship of trust, that enabled Oldham to share his anxieties about the movement with Mott. But in part, also, these anxieties arose around Mott himself. C. Howard Hopkins mentions this phase of their relationship only in passing, saying that "as Oldham unburdened himself the friendship between the two men deepened".[8] What happened was rather more complex than that.

As early as March 1921, Oldham was sharing his concern with Mott at what seemed to him to be the relatively low calibre of missionary recruits now coming through the Student Volunteer Movement in America, and also at the need to raise the quality of missionary preparation by concentrating teaching resources.[9] How far these concerns registered with Mott is not clear. Mott's real priorities still lay with the YMCA, and while he willingly undertook the chairmanship of the IMC, he gave the impression that it was one – albeit very important – among a number of his concerns. For Oldham and other members of the

[5] JHO letter 18 Nov. 1924 [OA].
[6] *Ibid.*
[7] JHO letter 2 July 1925 to Mott [OA].
[8] C.H. Hopkins, *John R. Mott 1865–1955: A Biography*, Geneva, WCC, and Grand Rapids, Eerdmans, 1979, p.638.
[9] JHO letters 15 March and 30 March 1921 to Mott [OA].

committee, however, the formation of the IMC, if it marked a real advance and a fulfilment of the Edinburgh dream, was surely *the* cause demanding heart and soul and strength for the new age. There was no other world figure who could match Mott for leadership – if he was prepared to give it. The IMC committee at Atlantic City in 1925 specifically asked Mott to devote more time to the IMC, and this undertaking he readily gave. Mott was now sixty. Years were inevitably marking even one as dynamic as he, and tastes were changing. Even within YMCA circles in America he was no longer regarded as the force he once was. But the evidence is that Oldham was on occasions more than a little puzzled that Mott seemed content to plough the seas and tour the conference platforms of the world in the old style, and still largely for the YMCA, when the hour both invited and enabled the new opportunities to be grasped and the new structures to be put to maximum use. On 9 October 1924, in preparation for the Atlantic City meeting of the IMC committee, Oldham sent Mott a statement, which he and Warnshuis had drawn up, on the need for quality recruitment and preparation of missionaries. He said in his covering letter:

> You will notice in the summary of questions at the end that we suggest that the Committee should freshly face the question whether missions are not at the present time drifting into a backwater outside the main currents that are shaping the life of the world. The tremendous task to which we are called, if we believe in the missionary undertaking, is to restore missionary effort to a central place in the life of the world.

This was being written by one who, with his African concerns, certainly felt immersed in "the main currents that are shaping the life of the world". Later that same month he wrote to Mott again, having just had Warnshuis spend a weekend with him. The conviction was growing within himself, said Oldham, that the missionary movement must experience a re-birth: "The Church must hear and respond to a call to larger things in some such way as it awakened to the needs of the unevangelized world more than a century ago. Nothing less than a re-birth is adequate to the present situation."[10]

Just three weeks later, on 18 November, he wrote yet again to Mott, at much greater length and, significantly, not from Edinburgh House but from his home at Chipstead. It was in fact a covering letter for the final version of the paper to be considered by the IMC committee at Atlantic City but Oldham took the opportunity of speaking frankly again of his hopes and fears for the future of the missionary movement. "In the missionary task to which you and I have both dedicated our lives we are facing a real crisis. It is clear that what exists at present is not adequate to the demands of the hour. Some new thing must be born as the foreign missionary movement was born more than a hundred years ago." Oldham drew on his own recent experiences of working with the Colonial Office in relation to Africa, stressing that this was not a narrow British concern but had vast potential for the international missionary community. Similar

[10] JHO letter 28 Oct. 1924 to Mott [OA].

opportunities would open up with France and Belgium, but these opportunities could only be exploited if there was a really effective means of international cooperation, and if the mission boards would realize that it was in the issues of education, rights of native peoples and so forth that the real access into the living heart of contemporary life would come. And it was the American boards who seemed most apathetic and negative in relation to these developments. The Atlantic City meeting would be crucial. The implied responsibility of Mott himself for the future could not be missed in Oldham's final paragraph:

> I have written to you thus fully and frankly because we shall have no opportunity of personal conversation. It means a great deal to me that we can face this issue together. International missionary co-operation has meant a great deal to both of us in past years. It was you who called me to my present task. I accepted the responsibility of the Continuation Committee after the Edinburgh Conference very much against my inclination, principally because the formation of the Committee seemed to me to provide you with a platform from which you could render immense services to the missionary cause. It may be that God has for us in the future still better things and a richer fellowship.

The Atlantic City meeting, as seen earlier, did take important measures, and Mott gave an important undertaking on the dedication of his time to the IMC. It also took the decision to hold a full-scale international missionary conference, the first since Edinburgh 1910, in 1927 or 1928, in Jerusalem. This had not been in Oldham's own mind, and from the start he had reservations about the idea. He confided to Mott his doubts about the value of such congresses, in view of the energy and expense they consumed with very little discernible result. "People get used to meetings of this kind and the hardened crowd of rather elderly people who are apt to form our constituency may easily go away from such a gathering very little changed."[11] What should be asked at the outset, said Oldham, is "what we hope may come out of such a meeting in the way of genuinely new insight, new life and new service". Having answered these questions it ought then to be asked critically whether they could be realized through such a gathering, or more effectively by other means. If a meeting still seems the most likely option, then it needs to be asked by what method the conference is going to produce the results. Present methods unthinkingly followed in conferences are proving failures, and much more thought needs to be given to them.

Shortly after his letter to Mott Oldham repeated to Ned Carter in New York his increasing concern with the conference mentality, so beloved of the missionary and church constituency. Most of the subjects dealt with at typical conferences, he suggested, were too large to be treated effectively within a few days. "The point that has for long been perplexing me is what particular and extremely limited objective, which alone is possible in the work of a few days, can most profitably be taken as the end to be achieved."[12] Getting conference

[11] JHO letter 1 April 1925 to Mott [OA].
[12] JHO letter 22 April 1925 to Carter [OA].

organizers and planners to think hard about what they really wanted out of such events, and what was realistic to expect, was to become a habit with Oldham right down to the first assembly of the WCC in 1948.

Oldham's scepticism about conferences was the other side of the coin of his conviction that, already, more was being achieved by committed action, based on principles already agreed, than by further large-scale deliberations. This is well borne out by another letter to Mott, dated 28 May 1925, in which yet again there is a plea for more overt involvement in IMC leadership. The letter merits citing almost in full:

> I have during my voyages, as you have no doubt done on yours, given much serious thought to the future of the International Missionary Council . . . The issues are so far-reaching and complex that an incomplete statement might confuse rather than illuminate . . .
>
> I should be deeply grateful if you could give me, even in the briefest possible form, some inkling of how your mind is moving in this matter. This would help me in thinking things out in preparation for our meeting. So much seems to me to depend on your decision that until I have some hint as to your present outlook my power to think to any purpose is largely paralysed.
>
> My personal approach to the future is largely coloured by the African situation, though I recognise clearly that this is only one element in the whole problem. I have become more and more deeply involved in the African problem. It has not been of my conscious seeking. I have felt that I have been led into it. I am now on terms of personal friendship with the governors of most of the British colonies in Africa and with the authorities at the Colonial Office. I have good connections with South Africa and with Belgium. Also, through Jesse Jones and others, there are American connections which might, in the Providence of God, make it possible to bring American influence to bear helpfully on the situation. The fact that one has the confidence of a good many of those who are directing affairs throughout the Continent makes it possible to render assistance in adjusting the relations between missions and governments in the present transitional, critical stage of development, and also furnishes an opportunity of making some contribution to the improvement of racial relations between white and black, which is one of the fundamental problems of the world to-day. I know very well that this confidence which exists at the moment is something that may easily be lost. But so long as it exists it is an asset and provides an opportunity to be seized.
>
> It is quite clear to me that if the opportunities which present themselves at the moment in Africa are to be improved and developed, they will need my more or less undivided attention for the next year or two. Africa is not the only opportunity that I see in the international sphere . . .
>
> It is clear, however, that Africa is not in itself a programme for the International Missionary Council . . . I do not see how I can at the same time both do what needs to be done in African questions and give the necessary attention to the home base of international co-operation and, in particular, do justice to the American end of things. I do not know how far, not being an American, I can succeed in retaining and developing the interest of American boards in the work of the Council . . . It is here that, apart from all other important considerations, your decision to me seems so vital. While you and I may differ in our mental approach to some problems, and

> while our methods of work may not always be the same, I believe that we are in fundamental agreement as to the kinds of things we want to see done; and you can carry American support.
>
> You will see, therefore, how vitally your decision affects my own position. If for any reason you should feel that your call is in some other direction, I am left with a problem for which at present I can see no solution.

There appears to have been no reply to this from Mott by letter, but Oldham met Mott while in New York in November 1925. Their conversation led Oldham to believe that while Mott would not be able to give a decision until the next IMC committee meeting in Rättvik the following July, he would, if asked, be prepared to devote the *whole* of his time to the IMC and drop his YMCA and WSCF work. In December Oldham reported this to the continental members of the IMC committee meeting in Utrecht, and conveyed their positive reaction to Mott.[13] At that meeting it was also strongly suggested, as it had been by a number of the Americans, that a major theme of the proposed 1927–28 meeting should be a new agreement on the aim of missions.

Oldham was in one sense relieved by Mott's willingness to consider full-time devotion to the IMC. At another level he was rather worried. What *kind* of leadership would he provide? On 5 January 1926, shortly before leaving for South Africa, and intending to reach Mott before he set sail on his Pacific Basin tour, Oldham wrote Mott a remarkable letter: remarkable for its length (23 pages); remarkable for the use of the familiar opening address "My dear John" in preference to the usual "My dear Mott" (the letter was also marked "private"); but remarkable above all for its frankness. Only a relationship of trust built up over many years and through so many vicissitudes could have enabled Joe Oldham to speak as he did here. Equally, only a passionate concern for the future of the cooperative international missionary movement could have nerved him to do it. Oldham repeats his insistence that the future of the IMC depends on Mott's decision, to the point where he queries whether, if Mott refuses, "we have at present a proposition that is worth going on with", since it is a matter of deciding on and concentrating on the best use of limited resources to do a few things really well. That will demand courageous leadership. Then comes the core of Oldham's appeal:

> I said to you when we talked in New York that I was much more concerned about what took place on the water while you are on your present tour than on what takes place on land. I do feel very strongly, as I said to you and as others said at Atlantic City, that if you are to take up this work it involves a quite fresh start. Our great need is that something new should be born, as the [World Student Christian] Federation was born at Vadstena thirty years ago. This means that you must have a fresh vision of something to be done and of the means by which it may be achieved. I think many, if not all, of your best friends feel that under the terrific pressure of practical demands in recent years you are, to some extent, following up beaten tracks and running on fixed rails rather than breaking along new trails. It is the latter which is required for the largest kind of leadership.

[13] JHO letter 16 Dec. 1925 to Mott [OA].

Oldham goes on to cite the other colleagues who, he claims, share his view, from Archbishop Davidson to Ruth Rouse. It is one thing for Mott to wish to bring into his new role what he has learnt in his other tasks – but he cannot continue with those other responsibilities, not even any executive office in his beloved YMCA. It must be a clean break. Above all, Mott's time-honoured way of holding and leading and addressing conferences must be rigorously reconsidered. Conferences must be subsidiary to clearly seen objectives, many of which can be reached more effectively by other means. Oldham refers to what he has seen and experienced, for example, of the use made of expertise by the American philanthropic trusts who have been aiding the work on Africa, not to mention the professionalism and scientific discipline of the new groups and advisory committees being set up in cooperation with the Colonial Office in London – "... in order that time and effort may not be wasted, I think we want to be continually submitting the results of our thinking about method to the criticism of first-rate minds, wherever we can obtain this help". "Where the creative mind is lacking, I am extremely sceptical about the value of conferences. Admittedly they do some good, but I question whether they do the greatest good." Hence he is doubtful about the proposed Jerusalem conference. The subjects must be much more tightly defined and focused: aims of missions today; race; education; missionary preparation, etc.

Is this the organizing secretary of Edinburgh 1910 speaking? It is indeed:

> We have got to go far beyond the Edinburgh Conference. It was generally recognised, I think, that the best of the eight reports at Edinburgh was the report of Cairns' Commission on the Christian Message. Notwithstanding this, I doubt whether it can be looked on as a really creative piece of work. I am sure that there have been volumes by individual writers that have had a more creative influence on missionary thinking even than this report. I should not think it worth while to put two or three years into work which issued in nothing more valuable than a report such as we got at the Edinburgh Conference.

Much of the rest of the letter is an exposition of the need to think realistically about what one or a few worthwhile things would be attainable by 1927. For all its outspokenness, it closes, as with all their letters, with heartfelt assurances of daily remembrance and prayer. What effect the letter had on Mott, assuming it did reach him before he set sail for the east, or it was forwarded to him, is not clear. No reply has been discovered, and in fact it does not appear in the Mott collection at Yale.

At Rättvik in 1926, the service of William Paton was obtained for the IMC. The value of Oldham's widening work was affirmed. And Mott did undertake to make planning for the Jerusalem conference (now scheduled for 1928) his major work. From this time his commitment to the IMC did increase. In 1928 he left the secretaryship of the American YMCA and the WSCF – though he took on the chairmanship of the World's Alliance of YMCAs in 1926.

After Rättvik, Oldham's relationship with Mott certainly eased again. It was with a genuine concern for the future of the IMC that early in 1927 Oldham wrote to Mott offering to resign his secretaryship if it would enable William

Paton's post to be more definitely financially secured. In itself this was a sign of his confidence in Paton rather than disenchantment with the IMC, but it is significant that Oldham was able to say, "I have no doubt that if my services are no longer needed by the Council some other opportunity of serving the cause of Christ will present itself." Oldham was sincere in his belief that what he would really like would be to continue with Paton, with a special brief on religious education, Africa, and consultancy on the overall policy of the Council. This in effect is what did happen.

Oldham's continuing problem now was less with Mott than with the Jerusalem conference coming into view in 1928. He continued to harbour doubts about the value of conferences in general, and the likely productivity of this one in particular. He did, however, share in a planning meeting at Mott's house in 1927. He had some influence on the agenda, and with Luther A. Weigle wrote one of the preparatory papers, *Religious Education.*[14] He insisted to Mott that African delegates be secured to attend.[15] He tried to enlist B.H. Streeter, the liberal Anglican theologian of Oxford, whose writings he was coming to admire, for Jerusalem. And he was in subsequent years to take up in his own way one of the chief themes of the conference, namely, secularism as an increasingly worldwide phenomenon. But clearly his heart was not in it – except to feel strongly critical of the lines of preparation emerging on the themes of the indigenous church, religious education, missions and industrial relations and race relations.[16] It was fundamentally, in his view, imprecise in its conception and too diffuse in its methodology.

## Oldham and the Jerusalem conference: an open question

In view of all this, it must be asked how far, when in August 1927 the invitation came to Oldham to join the Hilton Young commission, Oldham was motivated to accept by the fact that going to East Africa for the first four months of 1928 would mean he could *not* go to Jerusalem. It would at least distance him from an occasion for which he was duty bound to take some responsibility but of which he did not really approve. Probably this is an unanswerable question, even by Oldham himself. The fact remains that when it came to it, the secretary of the IMC, no less, asked to be relieved from attending what was the highest-profile event of the IMC thus far, and what would in many eyes be the most significant since Edinburgh 1910. Whatever his precise *motives* in choosing to go to Africa on a governmental commission rather than to Jerusalem for a missionary conference, Oldham was declaring his real values and interests. To him, these were now the real missionary interests: and here he was being true to his 1920 statement on the aims of missions. He was, very concretely, standing "unequivocally for justice and brotherhood in international and inter-racial

[14] J.H. Oldham and L.A. Weigle, *Religious Education,* Jerusalem Meeting of the IMC, New York and London, 1927.

[15] JHO letter 6 Oct. 1926 to Mott [OA].

[16] JHO letter 20 Dec. 1926 to Mott [OA].

relations", and believed he was doing so in a way which would in due course serve the wider missionary movement.

At this point arises the question of the part which the Jerusalem conference itself played in the development of Oldham's thought. While in Africa with the Hilton Young commission Oldham wrote to both William Paton and John Mott wishing the conference every success.[17] There is no reason to doubt that he meant what he said, his previous strong misgivings notwithstanding. There is also, however, a received opinion among ecumenical chroniclers that the Jerusalem conference made a profound impact on Oldham, marking even a "turning point" in his thinking on mission, especially through the paper by Rufus M. Jones on "Secular Civilization and the Christian Task". A main source of this interpretation is W.R. Hogg[18] who interviewed Oldham in 1948, and who is followed by Hans-Ruedi Weber,[19] W.L. Martin[20] and W.A. Visser 't Hooft.[21] Hogg writes:

> Jones' study convinced Oldham on his first reading that Christianity's real opponent in the East was not one of the ancient religions but *secularism.* Consequently he bent every effort to make it a paramount consideration at Jerusalem. His constant attention to the issue after 1928 was in large part instrumental in leading him into the program of Life and Work and the Oxford Conference.[22]

There is a danger of overstatement here. What is undeniable is that Oldham played a part in prompting Jones to write on this subject. In the spring of 1927 Oldham met with Mott in London to discuss the Jerusalem conference. Martin, following Hogg, states: "They decided that the International Missionary Council should consider the challenge to Christianity of another 'religion' beside the traditional faiths of Buddhism, Islam, Confucianism, and Hinduism. They gave this new 'religion' the title of 'rationalism' or 'materialism'. Mott suggested that they ask Rufus Jones, an American Quaker, to describe this 'religion' for the Jerusalem gathering."[23] But this in itself is revealing of the fact that Oldham was *already* keenly aware of the issue. Jones's paper was produced well before the conference, and Oldham read it in manuscript.

So much is certain, as is the impressive quality of Jones's paper which identified "secular" to mean "a way of life and an interpretation of life that include only the natural order of things and that do not find God, or a realm of spiritual

[17] JHO letters to Mott 1 March 1928 [OA] and Paton 3 March 1928 [OA].

[18] W.R. Hogg, *Ecumenical Foundations. A History of the International Missionary Council and its Nineteenth Century Background,* New York, Harper, 1952, p.241.

[19] H.-R. Weber, *Asia and the Ecumenical Movement 1895–1961,* London, SCM, 1966, p.158, n.1.

[20] W.L. Martin, "Joseph Houldsworth Oldham: His Thought and its Development", Ph.D. thesis, St Andrews Univ., 1967, pp.197–301. Martin however comments also on Weber's lack of attention to the range of Oldham's socio-political concerns after the first world war.

[21] W.A. Visser 't Hooft, *The Genesis and Formation of the World Council of Churches,* Geneva, WCC, 1982, p.32.

[22] Hogg, p.241.

[23] Cf. Martin, p.197.

reality, essential for life or thought".[24] Jones surveys in masterly fashion the shrinking hold of the churches in the West, the rise of humanism since the Renaissance and the near-complete dominance of science as the accepted explanation of reality for educated people in both East and West. He calls for a new Christian encounter with "naturalism" and "secularism" in both their strengths and weaknesses, and a "mobilization of spiritual forces" to demonstrate their inadequacy and to counteract them. That Oldham welcomed the paper is confirmed by his article of January 1928 looking forward to Jerusalem, "The Future of Christian Missions"[25] where he takes up Jones's term "secular civilization" as the context for the contemporary missionary movement and the focus for its new emphasis.

However, whether this amounted to a life-changing discovery for Oldham and was his prime mover towards Life and Work at the expense of the IMC is another matter. The main piece of evidence on which the received opinion rests is a letter written by Oldham to Mott in late 1934, explaining his decision taken in August that year at the Life and Work conference at Fanö, to devote his energies towards the Oxford conference. More will be said about this letter in the next chapter, but the significant passage in relation to the Jerusalem conference runs: "Though I was not present at Jerusalem that meeting had a more profound influence on my thinking and attitude than any other similar experience of my life. The contribution of Rufus Jones opened my eyes to the realities of the world in which we are living."[26]

Oldham was in effect arguing that it was precisely for the sake of furthering the missionary agenda on "secularism" that he was now working for Life and Work. It is just here, however, that caution must be exercised. Without necessarily, out of fear of hagiography, going to the extreme of scepticism in suspecting a subject's motives, the historian should beware of taking self-explanations at their face-value. This letter, dated more than six years after Jerusalem, was written to meet a particular situation of great tension in which Oldham was having by all means possible to justify to Mott his unexpected and unwelcome decision. To cite the Jerusalem conference at least offered a premise with which Mott could hardly disagree.

At least as pertinent to the case is what Oldham wrote *immediately* after Jerusalem. In his review of the published conference reports[27] he commends the volume on the Christian message, which includes Jones's article, as containing much that is vital and fresh. But in a total of three pages there is direct allusion to Jones's paper in only one sentence: "The volume . . . deals not only with the religions of non-Christian countries, but also with the secular view of life which among the educated classes everywhere is the most serious

[24] R.F. Jones, "Secular Civilization and the Christian Task", in *The Christian Life and Message in Relation to non-Christian Systems: Report of the Jerusalem meeting of the International Missionary Council, March 24th–April 8th 1928*, vol. I, London, Oxford Univ. Press, 1928, pp.284–338.

[25] Oldham, "The Future of Christian Missions", *The World Tomorrow*, vol. XI, Jan. 1928, pp.26–28.

[26] JHO letter to Mott 14 Nov. 1934 [OA]. Cited in Hogg pp.421f. and Martin p.200.

[27] Oldham, "The Jerusalem Meeting Report", *IRM*, vol. XVIII, Jan. 1929, pp.142–45.

rival of Christianity." Far more space is given to other themes in the material: the signs of greater international missionary cooperation, the "vast new provinces of human interest and activity to be conquered for Christ" as well as geographical areas, and, above all, the role of education in missions. If indeed Oldham, thanks to Jones's essay, had just undergone an eye-opening experience, one would expect considerably more excitement than is shown here.

It is true that after 1928 Oldham speaks frequently about "secular civilization". But this is a matter of language rather than of content. He did not need his eyes opening, by Rufus Jones or anyone else, to the "realities" which had already been apparent to him from the time of the first world war, if not earlier. If Jerusalem was an influence upon him, it was but one of several pressures leading him away from the IMC sphere and at most it acted to increase the momentum rather than change the trajectory of his movement. Moreover, while he adopted some of Jones's language, there was a significantly different line of attack. In his concluding paragraph Jones says that "we go as those who find in other religions which secularism attacks, as it attacks Christianity, witnesses of man's need of God and allies in our quest of perfection. Gladly recognizing the good they contain, we bring to them the best that our religion has brought to us, so that they may test it for themselves."[28] Increasingly, this was the kind of argument which Oldham was *not* to use as he moved into the 1930s and drew upon the neo-orthodoxy of Karl Barth and Emil Brunner. And for him, secularism was not so much a threat to Christianity seen as a "religion", but a call for Christianity itself to enter ever more deeply into the "secular" sphere and to risk itself in manifesting God's purpose *within* the world.

## Adventure?

The overall fact is that by the end of the 1920s, for Oldham the sense of *adventure*, which was always crucial to him and was indeed central to his spirituality, had gone out of the established missions and their conventional patterns of work. Adventure was now to be found at least as readily in the groups working for justice in race relations, in South Africa and East Africa and in India. He found it in the excitement of shared discovery as he worked with such as Lugard and Huxley, Ormsby-Gore and Cameron, on the needs of Africans and their education, and campaigned behind the scenes for British public opinion and governmental action. Here was life, risk, adventure, for the sake of others and the future.

By contrast the missions, all too often, seemed tame and concerned more for their own institutional life and spheres of influence. Their position became more difficult with the great depression at the end of the decade. In 1930, Oldham gave an address to the Church Missionary Society congress in London, on "The CMS and the Adventure of Today".[29] Here in effect he issued the

[28] Jones, p.338.
[29] Oldham, *The CMS and the Adventure of Today*, London, CMS, 1930.

same challenge to the CMS as he addressed to Mott four years earlier: the world has changed, a clean break is needed in the missionary movement. It must step into the realities of the life of Africans, for example, if the gospel is to be real to people. Missions must devote at least as much serious thought as governments are doing, in the field of education for instance. Above all, in any part of the world, the mission must engage with the social perplexities that beset people today. It is a mission for laypeople to act out in their daily lives. It is a mission centred on the needs of the world, not the church. It is a mission requiring the best thought of the finest theologians and scholars. What does it mean to be a Christian today? It is tempting to retreat to the old ways, says Oldham, and at heart the old answer may be the right one but it has to be rediscovered afresh as the word of God in this present hour: "Humanity has struck its tents and is on the march. It will not pay heed to those who ask it to retrace its steps. It will listen only to those whose faces are to the future and who speak out of a living contact with present realities."[30]

At the close of *The Remaking of Man in Africa* Oldham and Betty Gibson spoke of the need, even in the midst of difficulties, financial stringency and perplexity, for the missionary enterprise to be zestful and visionary. "A few people who see a true and worthy goal and set out resolutely to reach it will find new allies and support in unexpected quarters. Above all, here and now, whatever our difficulties may be, there is a road that leads from them straight to God. At any moment the eternal may break in on us, calling us to new tasks to be undertaken in God's strength, and giving us a power not of ourselves to accept and fulfil them."[31] It is this note of venturing and being prepared to meet the unexpectedly gracious breakthrough of God, which Oldham repeats in his CMS address. He concludes:

> What I have attempted to say to you may be summed up in one word: Listen. Let our attitude ... be that of listening for God's voice. Let us be ready for change, let us be willing to give up preconceived ideas, to surrender old methods, to strike out new paths.
>
> To those who listen God's whisper will come, and for those who can dare and suffer countless adventures are waiting in the days to come.

It was noted earlier how *The Remaking of Man in Africa* also registered the newer theology of crisis and the word of God, and the personalism of such as H.H. Farmer. As the 1930s opened, the world was indeed becoming a less certain place. Economic disaster and near-chaos threatened to engulf whole societies. Totalitarianisms arose in Europe, and nationalisms stirred in Africa such as in the Kikuyu movement. The world seemed to be a less certain, a more irrational and unpredictable, place. Theology needed to be less idealistic: more realistic in earthly terms and more expectant of heavenly judgment and grace. Oldham was registering all these seismic changes. And if Mott was not fully prepared for new paths, he himself certainly was.

[30] *Ibid.*, p.8.

[31] *The Remaking of Man in Africa*, London, Oxford Univ. Press and Humphrey Milford, 1931, p.148.

PART IV

# CHURCH, COMMUNITY AND STATE

CHAPTER 12

# *Oldham in Transition – to Life and Work*

THE period from 1928 to 1934 was one of the most pivotal in the story of the ecumenical movement, of the European churches (particularly German) and of theology. It was also a period of further decisive change for Joe Oldham, involved as he was in these developments, not only being influenced by them but also helping to shape some of them significantly. To gain some measure of the scale of change for Oldham, both a backward and a forward glance from the year 1928 are instructive. That year, we have seen, was the year of the international missionary conference in Jerusalem, an event for which Oldham took some responsibility in shaping but about which he was distinctly diffident and from which he was in fact absent due to his participation in the Hilton Young commission in Africa. We have noted also his growing concern at the course which the international missionary movement was taking, and his sense of a new "adventure" to be sought.

### A slow conversion?

Back in 1921 Oldham, then at the helm of the recently launched International Missionary Council, had been asked by Tissington Tatlow for his opinion on the proposals of Nathan Söderblom, Bishop of Stockholm, for a universal Christian conference on Life and Work being proposed for 1924.[1] Oldham was dismissive "that those of us who have jobs that are worth doing have not time to be drawn in to an attempt to pull on to sound lines a movement which could at best accomplish anything of central importance and which in present circumstances would demand an immensely greater amount of time to salvage than the effort would be worth".[2]

[1] The conference in fact took place in 1925.
[2] JHO letter to Tatlow 24 May 1921 [OA].

*J.H. Oldham* ca. *1932*

History quickly proved Oldham wrong. Much did come out of the Life and Work conference.[3] And the forward glance reveals Oldham thirteen years later in the summer of 1934 taking a decisive leading role in the movement generated at Stockholm and becoming the single most important shaper of the next Life and Work conference, that of Oxford 1937.

Did this simply represent a change of mind on Oldham's part, or even an attempt to jump onto a bandwagon that was now proving to be rolling irresistibly? Or was it Life and Work that changed in the course of a decade? The answer is more complex, and more interesting, than either of these judgments. As we have seen, at the end of the 1914–18 war Oldham's conception of Christian mission was remarkably inclusive. The agenda of the IMC was correspondingly broad: it had to engage with whatever issue in society and international relations required the challenge of the gospel, from education to race relations, from economics to the rights of Africans under colonial rule. Equally, as we have seen, by the late 1920s Oldham was becoming frustrated and impatient with what he saw as a growing introversion of the traditional missionary agencies. A new, adventurous leap into the *world* and its emergent currents of fears and hopes and possibilities was required.

[3] See N. Ehrenström, in Rouse and Neill, eds, *A History of the Ecumenical Movement 1517–1948*, London, SPCK, 1967, ch. 12.

There are on the one hand those who serve organizations efficiently and loyally to the end. They are not necessarily unaware of the wider world, and indeed may well concede the need for development and adaptation to a changing context. But their horizons are primarily those of the institution, seen from the inside. On the other hand there are those whose main passion is for the issues, and how they are to be engaged with. They will look for organizations as tools for that engagement, and will be prepared both to take up and to drop these implements according to their usefulness or otherwise. Oldham was of this latter kind. But he had an additional, and rare, facility: to *create* the tool, or at any rate to shape and sharpen what he perceived to have the potential to be effective. And he had the even rarer capacity, when necessary, to be critical of and even to drop what he himself had helped to create.

Seen in this light, there is a consistency in Oldham's developing relationship with Life and Work. By the early 1930s the movement was showing signs of developing a methodology more in line with his own approach which was to focus on particular issues and to research them adequately. As such it began to draw his interest, at the same time as the IMC was losing its appeal. Life and Work had the potential, more than anything else in view at that time, for being shaped into a tool for tackling the issues of society, and at an international level, with which he was concerned. In 1934, at the Fanö meeting, he grasped it decisively.

The change in emphasis did not mean that he dropped all his missionary interest and commitment. In January 1933, for instance, he gave in Scotland the Alexander Duff lectures on missions. Due to the pressures of other work, Oldham had to ask repeatedly for postponement of the lectures, and he was never able to fulfil his contract to produce them in a form for publication. But an important stimulus in their preparation came with a visit in September 1931 from W.E. Hocking, Oldham's American mentor for over a decade, who was leading the "Laymen's Commission of Enquiry" into the work of the American missionary agencies in Asia. This enquiry had originated from the response of a group of Baptist laypeople to Mott's account of his recent Asian tour, which had highlighted the increasingly critical situation of missions due to falling income and uncertainty about their role. The commission, comprising educationalists, business people and others from several Protestant denominations, devoted considerable attention to the work of missions in Asia. They sent out questionnaires and a party of "fact-finders" in advance of their own visits. Aided by a generous Rockefeller grant, they both thought and acted quite independently of the missions boards themselves. This at least was a sign of life in the movement which, as Oldham repeated to Mott,[4] was at a critical moment in its life, demanding new and radical thinking.

When the report, *Rethinking Missions*, appeared in the autumn of 1932 it aroused considerable controversy in North America and sent ripples abroad as well. Oldham was present at its presentation to the American societies and so

[4] JHO letter to Mott 30 Sept. 1931 [OA].

was well placed for a first-hand assessment both of the report itself and the reactions to it. The report, written from a decidedly liberal theological standpoint, was highly critical both of the underlying philosophy and the practical outworking of contemporary missions.[5] In seeking to present and embody the spirit of Christ, the goal of missions should be to seek common grounds with other peoples and their faiths, whereas in practice missions were promoting narrowly conceived and sectarian versions of Christianity. Oldham's own responses to the report, as shown in his correspondence with Hocking, William Paton and others, are paradoxical. On the one hand, he clearly does not share the liberal presuppositions of the authors nor does he consider many of their recommendations to be either new or practicable. On the other hand he considers it to be of critical importance precisely because it *has* dared to raise the fundamental theological issue, which must be faced and continued in debate, for missions. Moreover, a searching study of missions from outside could only do the movement good[6] and it would be tragic if the only reaction were to be defensive. "It may be that God is speaking to us through it."

## Oldham and the changing theological climate

Where Oldham is at his most critical of the American report, underlines the theological direction he was now travelling:

> The central issue in regard to Christianity is not fully faced. It is questionable whether the Commission are right in assuming that there is a common basis of agreement between Christians and the followers of other religions, and further common ground between Christians who differ from one another in their understanding of Christianity, and that to these beliefs held in common further beliefs may be added. If there is a divine revelation, as Christianity claims, when a man hears God's Word spoken in Christ and responds to it, everything is transformed and the old meanings are seen in a wholly new light . . .
>
> Christianity, as it has been understood in the past has had to do not with man's quest for God, but with God's gift to man. It has been bound up with the belief that God has acted in history. He has spoken to men. It is not our search but God's gift and commission on which everything hinges. It is not a question of our sharing with others "the deeper spiritual values of our lives", which for most of us are not very much to share but of bearing witness to a grace and truth outside of ourselves. The presentation in the report is concerned largely with religion as a way from man to God. The theme of the New Testament is the coming of God to man. The Christian mission in the sense in which it has hitherto been understood stands or falls with the question whether it is the bearer of a Word from God.[7]

Clearly, this is the voice of one who has begun to listen to Karl Barth, and the neo-orthodox movement for a return to a biblically based theology of revelation, instead of the liberal emphasis on human religious aspirations and

[5] See E. Jackson, *Red Tape and the Gospel*, Birmingham, Phlogisten Press and Selly Oak Colleges, 1980, pp.114–21.

[6] JHO letter to Paton 9 Nov. 1932 with attached paper "Rethinking Missions" [OA].

[7] Oldham, "Rethinking Missions".

*Karl Barth*

ethical insights. It should be noted, however, that Oldham from the time of his student conversion under D.L. Moody had *always* been an "evangelical" in the sense of holding to a specific, transformative gospel of the God who has acted in grace through Jesus Christ.

Oldham now had a new interest in continental theology. In April 1926 he had shared in a conference organized by George Bell (then Dean of Canterbury) at Canterbury on "The Kingdom of God". From Germany Gerhard Kittel, K.L. Schmidt, W. Stählin and H. Frick participated. The British contingent comprised Bell, E.G. Selwyn, A.E.J. Rawlinson, J.K. Mozley, Edwyn Hoskyns, C.H. Dodd and Oldham. Oldham took part in the return visit to Eisenach in August 1928.[8] From now on, it was to the European continent that Oldham was progressively drawn in his search for theological renewal, and this search was closely bound up with the programme of the IMC for a theological investigation into an adequate presentation of the Christian message for the contemporary world. The idea was to form groups of leading Christian thinkers on the continent, in Britain and North America. In January 1930 Oldham travelled to Germany and Switzerland to make preliminary enquiries, visiting Berlin, Marburg, Tübingen, Basel and Zurich. The highlight was evidently a three-hour conversation with Emil Brunner in Zurich. This and other

[8] See R.C.D. Jasper, *George Bell. Bishop of Chichester*, London, Oxford Univ. Press, 1967, pp.66f. Also correspondence in OA.

interviews convinced him that "the 'dialectical' theology is of first-class importance . . . it seems to me to be the most important thing in religious life at the present time".[9] In June of that year he helped to host Karl Barth's first visit to England. Barth stayed with the Oldhams at Chipstead for a weekend, and Oldham arranged a small dinner party for him to meet with English theologians. "We had a most interesting evening but it became apparent at the end of a long discussion that on one important point the apparent differences of opinion were due to the fact that terms were being used in different senses."[10] "You are all Pelagians!" Barth felt moved to exclaim at one point.[11] Moving on to Scotland and its Reformed atmosphere he evidently found himself a little more at ease.

Four months later, in October 1930, there took place in Basel, and at Oldham's invitation, the first meeting of continental theologians on the "Message". Emil Brunner and Karl Heim (famous for his attempt to relate scientific knowledge with Christian revelation) were present. Parallel to this "Brunner group" as it became known, Oldham had similar ambitions for America, and for a world group to meet the following year or soon after. The early summer of 1931 saw Oldham on the continent again, in Paris and in Frankfurt where he met Paul Tillich "who seems to me an important man. He and Frick may get together an extremely important group this summer and if so I shall try to attend it."[12] The Brunner group met again in Marburg in October.

Oldham's thirst for theological thought, old and new, from the continent remained unassuaged. In May 1932 we find him ordering copies of works by Dilthey and Franken, and – intriguingly in view of the author then being almost completely unknown – the young Dietrich Bonhoeffer's *Akt und Sein.*[13] Of the contemporary theologians, however, it was to Emil Brunner that he was most drawn. Brunner was no less concerned than Barth for a theology based on revelation through the divine Word but also insisted that theology must include an "anthropology" of the human capacities for receiving that word and for ethical response to it. Central to Brunner's thought was his emphasis on faith as *personal encounter* between the one who hears the Word and the God who speaks and draws near in grace, as distinct from a credal acceptance of abstract propositions of belief. Christianity thus sets forth "truth as encounter". Brunner's major impact thus far had come through *The Mediator* and *The Divine Imperative,*[14] and in Brunner Oldham saw the possibilities for establishing a new and urgently needed dialogue between evangelical theology and the contemporary human sciences – vital if the churches were to address seriously the current world context.

[9] JHO letter to Mott 18 Jan. 1930 [OA].

[10] JHO letter to Mott 19 June 1930 [OA].

[11] E. Busch, *Karl Barth. His Life from Letters and Autobiographical Texts,* London, SCM, 1975, p.204.

[12] JHO letter to Mott 4 June 1931 [OA].

[13] Letter B. Gibson to Reimer booksellers 25 May 1932 [OA].

[14] *Der Mittler,* Tübingen, J.C.B. Mohr, 1927; English tr. *The Mediator,* London, Lutterworth, 1946. *Das Gebot und die Ordnungen,* Tübingen, J.C.B. Mohr, 1937; English tr. *The Divine Imperative. A Study in Christian Ethics,* London, Lutterworth 1937.

*Emil Brunner*

Oldham's interest in an "anthropology" was resourced not only by such "theology of encounter" *per se*, but by the contemporary personalist philosophies running closely parallel to and indeed feeding it. He had made early acquaintance with Martin Buber's *Ich und Du* which was not to appear in English until 1937, and we have already noted the influence of the "I–Thou" thinking, and the emphasis on the centrality of interhuman relations, in Oldham's writing on missions and education in the late 1920s. But *the* thinker in this vein who excited him during the 1930s was Eberhard Grisebach, German-born and professor of philosophy and pedagogics at Zurich from 1931, and relatively unknown then (and now) in the English-speaking world. For Grisebach, the foremost task of philosophy was not to reach a theoretical knowledge of "reality", but to educate for actual living. In his *Gegenwart* (1928) he had trenchantly rejected the idealistic tradition which presupposed that truth could be reached by a kind of self-reflective inwardness on the part of an individual. "Reality" – certainly in the sense of an assured ethical knowledge – is not found *within* us, but becomes *present to* us in the encounter with others, and only in facing and being faced by the other person to the point of contradiction do we come to recognize it. Human nature is only understood in the interhuman realm of concrete encounters, demands and opportunities. Oldham included a brief exposition of Grisebach in his address "The Dilemma of Western Civilisation" at the European SCM conference in Germany in 1932.[15]

[15] Oldham, "The Dilemma of Western Civilization", *Student World*, XXV, 3, 1932.

(At the same meeting was Nicolai Berdayev. Oldham was struck by how some passages in their papers were almost identical.)[16]

It is tempting to say that in Grisebach Oldham had found a continental equivalent to W.E. Hocking, a philosopher concerned with ethical education and personal formation. But the two mentors obviously represented very different philosophical approaches. Could there be loyalty to both? In fact this question is part of a wider and increasingly fraught issue that faced Oldham as the 1930s wore on, and which was to result in a severe test in ecumenical relationships: the increasing disparity, for a time, between European and North American theology and religious thinking. It quickly became evident in the attempts to coordinate the IMC project of theological groups working on the Christian message. The Americans, still riding on the liberal tide, were suspicious of the new "Barthianism" on the continent.[17] In fact it was Brunner's *Ethik*, rather than any work of Barth, which was providing the material for the continental groups,[18] and in Britain itself Oldham was taking a fairly pragmatic line on the starting point for discussion, whether "What is Christianity?" or "Religion and Communism", so long as it got people talking about faith and the modern world. Nevertheless Oldham had to spend some time reassuring Hocking that to follow Barth did not necessarily make one a narrow-minded and exclusivist dogmatician: "I do not think the Barthians or at least Brunner really want to excommunicate those who disagree with them. They are only insisting very vigorously on aspects of truth which they feel have been ignored."[19] In fact the interest of the British group did prove to centre on "Christianity and Communism".

But the Americans grew increasingly restive, feeling that Oldham was assuming that the agenda and approach of the European groups should be applied worldwide. Early in 1933 Henry P. van Dusen of Union Seminary, New York, warned W.A. Visser 't Hooft who was shortly to come to New York to visit America and address several meetings, not to make what he regarded as Oldham's mistake on his most recent visit: ". . . On his last visit the references to Grisebach, Tillich and Heim, not to speak of Barth and Brunner, were so numerous that it tended to give his discussions a temper almost wholly unrelated to American problems and thought."[20]

It is ironic to reflect that in the post-1945 world, for a time at least, a favourite theological quip was that when Europe catches a cold, America gets pneumonia. In the 1930s the virus travelled more slowly.

[16] JHO letter to Mott 19 May 1932 [OA].

[17] See for example the resistance to Dietrich Bonhoeffer's efforts at communicating the thinking of Barth at Union Seminary, New York, during 1930–31: E. Bethge, *Dietrich Bonhoeffer*, London, Collins, 1970, pp.116–19.

[18] JHO letter to W. Hocking 18 Aug. 1934 [OA].

[19] JHO letter to Hocking 28 Feb. 1933 [OA].

[20] Van Dusen letter to Visser 't Hooft 10 March 1933 [OA].

## Ecumenical developments

At this point it is necessary to trace in outline those developments in ecumenical life and structures, especially in Life and Work, leading to the decisive point of the Fanö conference of 1934.

The 1925 Stockholm Life and Work conference had set up a continuation committee, reconstituted in 1930 as a permanent body, the Universal Christian Council for Life and Work, of which George Bell (from 1929 bishop of Chichester) became chairman. The principle objective of the Council was "to perpetuate and strengthen the fellowship between the churches in the application of Christian ethics in the social problems of modern life".[21] In fact following Stockholm Life and Work immediately became "a laboratory of fertile ideas and projects",[22] establishing a number of commissions on international and economic issues, and in 1927 creating an International Christian Social Institute, based in Geneva, to study social and industrial issues in the light of Christian ethics. This was still in its infancy when the worldwide economic disaster of 1929 threatened the very existence of all such international projects. Despite the difficulties, the Institute's programme of study and education developed and in 1929 it appointed its first secretary for research, Hans Schönfeld, a trained economist and pastor from Germany and an adept at creating efficient groups of co-workers in research. Further staffing was obtained, and in 1931 the Institute was reorganized with Schönfeld director of its research department.

In 1928 Life and Work itself set up its headquarters in Geneva. That same year, following the Jerusalem conference, the IMC also established in Geneva its own department of social and economic research. Clearly there was a measure of convergence between these two streams of the ecumenical movement. Geneva, already the site of such international organizations as the League of Nations and the International Labour Organization (with both of which Life and Work maintained close liaison), was both encouraging and requiring the close proximity of international Christian bodies as the need for increased collaboration was increasingly recognized. In particular, Geneva was the location of the staff headquarters of the World Student Christian Federation (WSCF), the umbrella organization of the worldwide Student Christian Movement bodies, YMCAs and YWCAs which had been fostered by J.R. Mott on his worldwide travels and which, as has been seen in earlier chapters had been the seed-bed of much of the international movement for Christian unity. In 1924 W.A. Visser 't Hooft had come to Geneva from Holland to work for the YMCA, and in 1928 was appointed to work half-time for the WSCF secretariat. Clearly a rising star in the ecumenical sky, theologically he was a powerful advocate of Karl Barth.

[21] Ehrenström, p.553.
[22] *Ibid.*, p.555.

Life and Work, through its research programmes, commissions, conferences and publications, was developing quite impressively. The death of its founding genius, Nathan Söderblom, in 1931 marked the passing of its apostolic age but not of its momentum. The holding of a second world conference had been in the minds of the Universal Council for some time and was originally envisaged for 1935, an exact decade after Stockholm. In 1932 however the decision was taken to postpone it until 1937 in view of the pressing economic difficulties. At the same time the urgency of addressing major world issues was growing, signalled by the failure that year of the disarmament conference in Geneva, and the following year by the advent of Adolf Hitler to power in Germany and the onset of the church struggle there. In April 1934 Life and Work, in obvious reference to the crises in Germany and elsewhere in Europe, held a conference in Paris on "The Church and the State of Today". However, the danger of a preoccupation with Europe at the expense of the wider world was also being recognized. The original intention of the Universal Council had been to include in its structure a section on the "younger churches". This was never realized, but in 1934 it was decided that the national Christian councils in Africa and Asia should be recognized as fulfilling this function: a further instance of convergence with the IMC interest.

It was at the biennial conference of the Universal Council at Fanö, Denmark, in August 1934, that the most critical decisions in its history so far had to be made by Life and Work: in particular, on its stance in relation to the German church situation, and on the nature, theme and methodology of the proposed world conference. And it was here that Oldham, finally and decisively, seized hold of Life and Work to shape as his next tool for the job he wanted to be done.

## Grasping the tool

The 1928 Jerusalem conference had identified "secularism" as a growing, worldwide malaise. Oldham went along with this, but not in the manner of the conference itself, certainly not as far as the remedy was concerned. Whereas Jerusalem spoke of the need for a cooperation between all religions in confronting secularism, Oldham was by now – thanks to the new theological orientation from Barth and others – suspicious of "religion" as a general, undefined phenomenon. What was needed from Christianity was a new realization of its own specificity as a witness to God's self-revelation, *and* a new immersion, adventurous and pioneering, into the dilemmas and possibilities of the contemporary world. This, as we have seen, was the note in his own addresses to the Church Missionary Society and the IMC in this period.

It was a note Oldham sounded clearly in his first effective engagement with the leaders of the Geneva-based international Christian organizations in 1929. Over forty years later, Visser 't Hooft recalled the impact Oldham made on this occasion, which was the first time the two met personally. "Oldham spoke of a new adventure. He wanted to lead Christians out of the world of illusions in which they were still living. They had to understand once and for all that the world was not becoming more and more Christian. But it was not by defence, but by facing boldly and creatively the challenge of secular civilization that the church would come to fulfil its mission."[23] Hendrik Kraemer, another Dutchman destined for pioneering ecumenical leadership, spoke no less powerfully at the meeting.

This encounter with Visser 't Hooft was the start of another friendship which was to be crucial for the ecumenical movement. Much in the same way as Oldham in his younger days had experienced with Mott, so in turn Visser 't Hooft now found himself drawn into collaboration, fascinatingly educative, with an older visionary. Visser 't Hooft describes Oldham's way of getting together creative minds – especially lay minds – from all backgrounds and viewpoints to examine the real issues of the day: "He brought me into one of these curiously mixed groups. His role in the meetings was Socratic: he would simply put questions and so stimulate the discussion." Visser 't Hooft also vividly sketches his own version of a picture which still does the rounds of conversation about Oldham: his famous têtes-à-têtes in the Athenaeum, that most patrician of London clubs which Oldham joined in 1928:

> It was said at the time that for Oldham the road to the Kingdom of God went through the dining room of the Athenaeum ... For it was in that solemn setting that men of the most diverse backgrounds were put under the terrific pressure of Oldham's single-mindedness and almost forced to co-operate in his undertaking. Most of us, however, were grateful to be enlisted in his team and followed the leader gladly, even though on leaving the Athenaeum we realized that we had again to promise to attend another preparatory meeting or write another memorandum. And there was this further compensation that, thanks to Oldham, one had an opportunity to meet people from all walks of life whom one would never have met otherwise.[24]

Prominent among Visser 't Hooft's own contemporaries and collaborators was Francis P. Miller, a Virginian who succeeded John Mott as chairman of the WSCF in 1928 and a passionate advocate of the international role of Christianity. It was largely Miller who instigated the programme of study throughout the student world, closely parallel to that being led by Oldham for the IMC, on the basic message of the Federation. The WSCF programme organizers found in Oldham a challenging ally. Miller and Oldham came to have a warm regard for each other, not least because Oldham regarded the younger man as an intellectual equal and they carried on a vigorous correspondence for a time on all manner of subjects, from ecumenical strategy to the I–Thou philosophy of Martin Buber. Here at least was an American who, even if he disagreed with some current European theological trends, at least knew and understood what he was disagreeing with. Miller was later to play a leading part in the decision-making bodies of the World Council of Churches.

[23] W.A. Visser 't Hooft, *Memoirs*, Geneva, WCC, 1973, p.39.
[24] *Ibid.*, pp.41f.

*W.A. Visser 't Hooft*

Oldham, having suspected considerable potential in Visser 't Hooft, soon felt his judgment confirmed. "The more I see of him," he wrote to Francis Miller, "the more I feel that you have in him a very exceptional personality. He has an understanding of the religious situation almost unique in both its range and its depth. He also has unequalled gifts of interpretation and sees as clearly as anyone that I know that the primary task of the Church is evangelisation. He can in the present situation do what no one else can do."[25]

In the summer of 1930 Visser 't Hooft and Miller convened a meeting of about twenty-five people, including Oldham, at Zuylen in Holland to discover what could be said together about the message of the WSCF. Visser 't Hooft was chairman. Oldham repeated his earlier challenge: "What is so deeply disconcerting about our situation . . . is not secularism or the modern world in general, but the fact that the church, which pretends to have the word of God, has no word which comes to the modern world with real power."[26] In fact the meeting came to no firm consensus since, as Visser 't Hooft recalls, "the differences in spiritual and cultural background between the Continent and the USA, between Britain and China, and so forth, were too great". Oldham himself, rather than being discouraged, was impressed with the energy and vision of this new generation of leadership in the WSCF. At his invitation,

[25] JHO letter to Miller 8 June 1934 [OA].
[26] Visser 't Hooft, p.40.

Visser 't Hooft attended the meeting of the "Brunner group" in Basel in October that year. Likewise Oldham was anxious to get Miller involved in the American group, as he told Mott: "The more I go into this matter the more I feel that it is very important that we keep close touch with the Federation which is keenly interested in the same question. Both Miller and Visser 't Hooft are exceedingly keen on what we are doing and I think it would be a good thing if Francis could be linked up with the American group."[27]

This interplay of Oldham with the new student world was further highlighted two years later, when in May 1932 Oldham addressed the European Student Christian Movement leaders' conference at Bad Boll in Germany on "The Dilemma of Western Civilization". Here with striking effect he calls on a galaxy of contemporaries from the scientist J.B.S. Haldane to Aldous Huxley, from C.G. Jung to Bertrand Russell and Ortega y Gasset, to illustrate the impending crisis facing a civilization whose basic belief is progress founded upon science and the love of power. The final legacy of the Renaissance, whereby humankind thought to emancipate itself totally from spiritual control, is a materialistic individualism. He invokes Grisebach to point to an alternative way, the way of relationships with others, as the way to reality: "The call to us is not to withdraw into ourselves, but to accept life as it comes to us in the accidental, unforeseen, unexpected and searching demands made upon us by our fellow-men and to find in an unlimited response to these demands the true meaning of our existence."[28] Here too, more than anywhere else, Oldham makes clear that he has joined forces with Karl Barth in rejecting the Jerusalem 1928 espousal of "religion" in general against "secularism" in general. Referring approvingly to some remarks of Barth on communism and nationalism, he states: "When men abandon their belief in God, they turn to the worship of false gods." Visser 't Hooft was on the same track. Oldham laid down the same emphasis in his address to the SCM Quadrennial Conference in Edinburgh in 1933.[29] It was a powerful exposition, yet again, of the Grisebach view of human life as encounter and response. One person in the audience, Lesslie Newbigin, was to remember Oldham's words to the end of his days.[30]

Thus a new alliance was in formation, bonded by common concerns, shared theological approaches and personal friendships. Then came the critical year 1933 with the Nazi revolution in Germany and the onset of the church struggle. This threw into sharpest possible focus the question of the Christian vision of society in relation to totalitarian ideologies, and the relation of church and state. At the same time, a number of leaders of the various strands of the ecumenical movement began to take up the issue of a more carefully co-ordinated common strategy. It was William Adams Brown, veteran leader of

[27] JHO letter to Mott 10 Oct. 1930 [OA].
[28] "The Dilemma of Western Civilization", p.194.
[29] Oldham, "Faith in God and Faith in Man: Or, the Dimensions of Human Life", in *The Christian Faith Today*, London, SCM, 1933, pp.54–75.
[30] L. Newbigin interview with author March 1991.

Life and Work in the United States, who while visiting Europe in 1933 suggested to William Temple, Archbishop of York, that a meeting of the responsible leaders be held. Accordingly, Temple hosted a gathering of ten people at Bishopthorpe.[31] Oldham, with William Paton, attended on behalf of the IMC. Visser 't Hooft represented the WSCF. Faith and Order, Life and Work, the World Alliance for Promoting International Friendship through the Churches and the YMCA were also represented. It was a completely informal group with no official standing, but can be regarded as the starting point of that search for a common ecumenical instrument, which was to lead to the formation of the World Council of Churches.

Oldham was fully supportive of the need for closer cooperation of the IMC and the other groupings, but warned against the "consultative group" becoming anything more than just that.[32] In any case he was at this stage less interested in any grand ecumenical design than in finding a means for the churches to address the crisis in Western society. The real turning-point for him came with the conference in Paris in April 1934 organized by Life and Work on "The Church and the State of Today". Oldham attended, along with Visser 't Hooft. Such celebrities as Max Huber, Emil Brunner and Nicolas Berdyaev were among the participants. By now, as we have noted, Life and Work had developed an increasingly effective research department led by Hans Schönfield, now assisted by Nils Ehrenström of Sweden. Oldham was impressed both by the conference itself, and by the potential of Life and Work for furthering the cause he now saw as crucial: the Christian exploration of human life in society at a time when the false worship of power and domination was rampant. In fact even before the conference he was fully involved in the subject, and had accepted the chairmanship of a commission to prepare a small British conference on the subject at High Leigh in June. He also suggested to the BBC a series of broadcast talks on the subject of religion and the state.[33]

Preparations were now advancing for Life and Work's biennial conference on the island of Fanö, Denmark, in August. It would clearly be a critical meeting in which major strategic decisions would be taken in the light of the Paris conference and in relation to the world conference now being planned for 1937. George Bell, Bishop of Chichester and chairman of the Universal Council, invited Oldham to attend. In writing to H.L. Henriod, Life and Work's secretary in Geneva, Oldham cites as the rationale for his (or Bill Paton's) attendance the fact that "questions may very easily arise at the meeting of the Ad Interim Committee of the IMC at Salisbury in July which will make conference between us and the Universal Council of Life and Work desirable". Diary and holiday considerations would make attendance difficult, but on the whole it would be easier for Oldham himself rather than Paton to get to Fanö. "I am therefore reserving the dates in case it may be necessary for me to

[31] W.A. Visser 't Hooft in Rouse and Neill, p.699.
[32] JHO letter to Mott 8 May 1934 [OA].
[33] JHO letter to Siepmann 6 April 1934 [OA].

attend."[34] In view of what actually happened between Oldham and Life and Work at Fanö it is hard to believe that he could have been so hesitant about attending even at this relatively late stage. Was this diffidence a cover to offset any suggestion of ambitions? At any rate Oldham affects some ignorance about Life and Work and requests an updated copy of the constitution of the Council (but could he not have obtained it at least as readily from Bell?). Oldham's actions in the months leading up to Fanö certainly appear to be consistent with someone being drawn barely consciously, if not unwillingly, into close association with the movement. They are equally capable of interpretation as a clever camouflaging of his actual interests: too high a profile might well have aroused opposition in advance, not least from America, from both his friends such as Mott who would not wish him to desert the IMC fold, and those suspicious of his theological enthusiasms.

Oldham's thinking on ecumenical strategy in the early summer of 1934 is best illustrated in a letter to Francis Miller, dated 8 June:

> As you know the five so-called "ecumenical" movements have been drawing closer to one another and we have had during the last year two or three meetings of a small informal "consultative" group. I have also been drawn into rather close touch with the Life and Work Movement and attended the International Study Conference in Paris. The interesting thing is that all the five movements are finding themselves driven back on ultimate problems which are in their essence theological. We are all in the last resort concerned with one and the same problem though each movement approaches it and must continue to approach it from its own distinctive angle. This being so, it becomes increasingly clear that the real problem is how through consultation we can make the best use of the very limited resources at our disposal. By this I mean that the really first class minds which are thinking in a Christian way and at the same time in a way that is relevant to the actual situation are few in number. If all the movements make unrelated claims on them it is a danger that their energies may be dissipated and that they may not make their largest possible contribution which it is the concern of all the movements alike that they should make. Further, we have very few people who have both the gifts and training and also the time to co-ordinate the work of thinking and it is the common concern of all of us that the few people we have should be free to make this indispensable contribution and relieved from other responsibilities in order to make it. What matters in my view is the tasks and so long as they are done it is a matter of almost complete indifference to me whether they are done by the IMC or Life and Work or the Federation . . .
>
> I have had talks recently with Eric Fenn and Edwin Barker and Visser 't Hooft as well as with the Life and Work people and with Canon Hodgson, the secretary of Faith and Order. I think we are all pretty much agreed. To illustrate what I mean, I think that Life and Work are taking hold very effectively of the Church and Nation problem. That being so I think the Federation might be content to soft pedal on this subject and throw its energies into what Life and Work is doing. I incline to think that Visser 't Hooft and Eric Fenn more or less agree on this point . . .

[34] JHO letter to Henriod 11 May 1934 [OA].

> The other point is the personnel to co-ordinate this thinking. I wrote a letter a few days ago to the Bishop of Chichester to urge that Schönfeld and Ehrenström should not be overladen with administrative jobs but should be freed to do the kind of thing for which they are particularly qualified, to bring thinkers together on the vitally important questions of Church and Nation. The deeper I get into these questions the clearer it is that everything is bound up with everything else, and the subject of Church and Nation is not only important in itself but also because it is as good an approach as any other to the central questions such as What is man? What is God? What is the Church?

Oldham was concerned that Visser 't Hooft, in particular, should be freed from purely administrative work in order to contribute his unequalled gifts to the supremely important task, "the attempt to obtain a deeper understanding of the meaning and message of Christianity in relation to modern thought and the existing social order".

In the last week of June Oldham finally booked a hotel room at Fanö for himself and Mary. The conference met 22–28 August. Fanö, a small island off the Danish coast, provided a seaside-resort atmosphere and Oldham afterwards claimed to Mott that he and Mary had expected "that the conference would be to some extent a holiday".[35] But it proved sharply otherwise, being a major turning point for Life and Work, the World Alliance for Promoting International Friendship through the Churches which met jointly with the Council, and for Oldham himself. Fanö's importance in ecumenical history is that here "the Council solemnly resolved to throw its weight on the side of the Confessing Church in Germany against the so-called 'German Christians' and by implication against the Nazi regime".[36] The full story of this drama can be read elsewhere.[37] The conference has also been highlighted as a critical episode in the story of Dietrich Bonhoeffer who attended Fanö as a youth secretary of the World Alliance, and who not only was involved in the struggle of the Confessing Church delegation but also made one of his most famous declarations on the peace question.[38]

The main agenda at Fanö, however, was a broader consideration of the issues which had become so critical in Germany. Based on the findings of the Paris conference in April, the plenary sessions dealt with church and state, and the church and the world of nations. A meeting of the ecumenical youth commission met simultaneously and on the same theme. The strategic decision was made to focus the world conference, now definitely scheduled for Oxford 1937, on the theme of "Church, Community and State".[39] To prepare for this a strengthened advisory commission was appointed, to include Oldham, John Baillie, V.A. Demant, Leonard Hodgson, Wilhelm Menn, Henry P. van Dusen, and Visser 't Hooft.

[35] JHO letter to Mott 21 Sept. 1934 [OA].

[36] Ehrenström, p.583.

[37] See e.g. K. Scholder, *The Churches in the Third Reich*, vols I and II, London, SCM, 1987 and 1988.

[38] See Bethge, pp.298–315.

[39] The original ordering in the title was "Church, State and Community". The change was made very soon after Fanö, probably by Oldham himself, and was of some significance.

*The Fanö Conference 1934. Oldham is on the back row, 2nd left from the open door. Front row, from left: 8th Bishop Theodor Heckel; 10th Bishop George Bell*

Oldham was appointed chairman of the research commission. He explained to Mott by letter on 21 September:

> I was made chairman of the Committee on Programme for the 1937 conference and also had to take an active part in the other important committee dealing with the German Church situation …
>
> The Council decided to hold a world conference (probably of limited size) in 1937. My committee was not concerned with the question whether the conference should be held or not but only with the question whether, if there was to be one, what its programme should be. The subject that has been decided upon is the Church, the State and the Community. This is only one way of formulating the central problem which confronts Christianity in all parts of the world of its relation to the thought and life of our time.

Oldham sets out the universal significance of these issues and argues that the programme could make an important contribution to the concerns of the IMC, particularly as Life and Work has the services of such able people as Schönfeld and Ehrenström. He continues: "I yielded under very great pressure to allow myself to become chairman of the Research Commission of Life and Work. It will not mean an excessive amount of work …"

To "yield under very great pressure" was a device not unknown to Mott himself in pursuing influential positions, and he may well have suspected Oldham to have been employing it here. In fact within a few weeks it became apparent that this new work *would* be a time-consuming challenge, and it is hard to believe that with all his experience Oldham had really expected it otherwise. At any rate Mott was not pleased with Oldham's decision, nor was Warnshuis, and cautioned not to allow this new responsibility to encroach greatly on his time. Mott and Warnshuis, to say the least, had a point. The secretary of the IMC had, without any warning or consultation with his colleagues, embarked on a major enterprise with another ecumenical organization, an organization moreover which Mott rated low in significance at that time.

Oldham sought further to justify his decision in a long letter to Mott in mid-November, and which has already been cited in the previous chapter for the claim made in it by Oldham of the "profound influence" of the Jerusalem conference upon him.[40] The basic point, Oldham argues, is that the theme of the 1937 conference deals with the fundamentals of the message and nature of the church and these questions, far from being a divergence from the missionary task, underlie it. As for the status of Life and Work:

> We should be thinking and speaking of quite different things if you supposed that I see any large possibilities in the Universal Christian Council for Life and Work as it is at present. What has moved me is that it seems providentially to offer an opportunity of mobilising the best Christian thought of the world, both theological and lay, to meet the situation more effectively than has ever been attempted thus far.

[40] JHO letter to Mott 14 Nov. 1934 [OA].

Such is the hope for the 1937 conference, and Oldham lists the impressive names of bishops, theologians and leading lay people already committed on both sides of the Atlantic. Further, in Schönfeld and Ehrenström, Life and Work, in contrast to all other ecumenical movements has two full-time workers specially gifted for and devoted to this task. Oldham himself had the contacts to make their work even more fruitful. And far from being a diversion from the IMC agenda, Oldham saw the theme as a direct fulfilment of the Jerusalem 1928 recognition of secularism as a key issue. "The difference is that whereas I have been brought to despair in regard to doing anything about it because the resources in time were quite insufficient, new possibilities have presented themselves through the resources at the disposal of the Universal Christian Council. This transforms the situation." The programme would, moreover, directly benefit the missionary cause in equipping missionaries more adequately for the issues that were then worldwide in scope. Oldham acknowledged that the IMC committee might take a different view, and was prepared to wait till the following year for their judgment. Meanwhile, he would consider himself still as an officer of the IMC, but devoting part of his time to Life and Work. In fact the material being prepared for 1937 would also be highly useful for the IMC's next world conference being planned for 1938.

Oldham thus presented his decision at Fanö as the result of an unsought and sudden revelation of a new possibility for fulfilling what he had long been looking for, and trying to work for, in the IMC. Whether it was quite so sudden, or whether he had craftily manoeuvred himself into a situation where he was the obvious candidate, must remain an open question. In addition to the signs of his growing enthusiasm for Life and Work which we have noted prior to Fanö, one would like to know, for example, of the kind of conversations that are likely to have taken place between himself and Bell in the Athenaeum in the early summer of 1934. Visser 't Hooft certainly implies that it was the Paris conference which had been crucial in forming Oldham's mind.[41] But whatever tensions arose between Oldham and Mott immediately after Fanö, one denouement of this story is that when the world conference did convene at Oxford in 1937 it was under the chairmanship of – John Mott.

## Life as a whole

Oldham at Fanö had reached the age of 60, and was now on the verge of his last, and many would say greatest, term of official service for the churches and the ecumenical movement. This chapter has concentrated on his theological and ecumenical activities since the late 1920s. There was much more to his life, however. His involvement in African affairs, and the aftermath of the Hilton Young commission, heavily occupied him well past 1930, and in 1931 he accepted the arrangement whereby a quarter of his time was to be given to the Institute of African Languages and Cultures. He remained available to student meetings,

[41] Visser 't Hooft, p.41.

especially in Scotland. He joined the central council for adult broadcast education in 1931, and the following year served on an advisory group of the BBC to look at its Sunday broadcasting policy. The group included T.S. Eliot and Walter Moberly who were later to be key members of the "Moot", together with A.D. Lindsay and Nathaniel Micklem. Other advisory work for the BBC followed. Academic recognition came too, with an honorary DD from Edinburgh University in 1929.

His election to the Athenaeum had come in 1928 and, as we have noted from Visser 't Hooft's description, it was in the relaxed and upholstered ambience of the club that many of his personal meetings now took place. Often those lunchtime encounters originated with Oldham's reading of a book and, if it sufficiently interested him, desire to meet the author. But the Athenaeum still represented the world of work, and real relaxation required a discipline – and doctor's orders – to find its way into his diary. The Oldhams' favourite holiday activity was walking, or merely staying at home and gardening at Chipstead. There was also cricket to follow. Karl Barth, during his visit in June 1930, was bemused when in the midst of a weighty theological discussion Oldham suddenly begged leave to slip out into the street and buy a newspaper "to see how the Test Match was getting on". Barth claimed that this was one of the great moments of revelation to him of "the British way of life".[42] The dates 10–14 August 1933 in Oldham's diary are crossed out with "Oval" written through them (the West Indies were the touring side). Mary Oldham, as well as keeping a home both comforting for themselves and bountifully hospitable to visitors (conversation over sherry before dinner was the highlight of each day for many), carefully monitored the diet although Joe never seems to have quite espoused her vegetarianism. At times their experiments in this direction verged on the eccentric. In the summer of 1931 they spent three weeks at a "nature cure resort" at Tring eating nothing but oranges for practically the whole time. "It has done me an immense amount of good and I feel better than I have done for many years," Joe told his brother Jack.[43] There is no evidence, it has to be said, that the experience was ever repeated.

It was in these years also, however, that the affliction which was to mark the rest of his life began: an increasing and eventually almost total deafness. There is some evidence that it was a hereditary condition. Be that as it may, from about 1930 he began to experiment with hearing aids, most of which were not only cumbersome and liable to fall to pieces but dismally failed to live up to the claims made by their manufacturers. Eventually he did find one piece of apparatus which enabled him to hear what was being said – provided the speaker was a few inches away and spoke right into the ear-trumpet. Legend has it that in the Athenaeum Oldham favoured a particular couch (still there) at the top of the stairs leading to the library, where such "conversations" would be less

[42] Source of anecdote: Muriel Duncan (St Andrews, Scotland) letter to K. Bliss 18 July 1969 [OA]. Barth was equally surprised and amused by a like concern for the cricket score shown by Prof. Milligan of Glasgow in the midst of a learned discussion of ancient papyri.

[43] Letter JHO to Jack Oldham 17 Sept. 1931.

intrusive on others. But, as the late David Paton once related to the writer, it could still be embarrassing to have virtually to shout one's opinions on the archbishop of Canterbury in such an atmosphere. Alan Booth used to tell how once, on that famous couch, Oldham asked him whether he had read a certain article in *The Times*. "I don't read *The Times*", replied Booth. "I beg your pardon?" asked Oldham. "I don't read *The Times*," said Booth more loudly. Deafness combined with cultural incomprehension on Oldham's part resulted in an eventual fortissimo of "I DON'T READ *THE TIMES*!" resounding through an astonished Athenaeum library. People came to view the apparatus, which accompanied Oldham everywhere, with almost as much amused affection as the user himself. But it was an appalling affliction for one whose whole method of working was based on meeting others. That he achieved so much while thus handicapped is extraordinary.

Monica Wilson, who had a research fellowship with the African Institute during the 1930s, supplies a telling vignette of the Oldham style around this time. Speaking of both Chipstead and the Institute she says:

> I remember particularly Mrs Oldham's grace and warmth and her ability to make one feel welcome and at home. Joe himself was a little remote, partly because of his deafness.
>
> . . . [T]he impression I have of Oldham was of someone who did the strategic planning, who secured financial support, and who got the best people in any field to help him and carry out the plans, while he disappeared into the background. He was already very deaf, but had great charisma. Godfrey [her husband] and I were already using his "Devotional Diary" at this time, and there were affectionate jokes about his idea of "five minutes constructive thought while shaving".[44]

[44] M. Wilson letter to K. Bliss 16 Oct. 1970 [OA].

CHAPTER 13

# *Oldham and Nazi Germany 1933–37*

THE dramatic story of the German churches' response to the Nazi revolution is well chronicled,[1] in both its heroic and less glorious aspects. A vital part of the story is that of the involvement of the churches outside Germany, and the international ecumenical movement, and not least in Britain.[2] The stalwart support of George Bell – acting not only as a senior bishop of the Church of England but also as chairman of the Universal Christian Council for Life and Work – for the beleaguered Evangelicals, and his friendship with Dietrich Bonhoeffer in particular, form an inspiring chapter in 20th-century church history. Bell, however, was not alone in his stand. Not only was there widespread popular support in Britain for the witness of the Confessing Church[3] as representing about the only public, visible and corporate form of resistance to the total claims of the Nazi state, but Bell had a number of close collaborators much less in the public eye. Among them was Joe Oldham. From the Fanö conference of August 1934 onwards Bell and Oldham were of course officially linked in the programme of Life and Work, but their collaboration on Germany began well before that event. Moreover, Oldham at his IMC desk had his own specific reasons for quickly becoming involved in the German church scene.

[1] See J.S. Conway, *The Nazi Persecution of the Churches*, London, Weidenfeld & Nicolson, 1968; K. Scholder, *The Churches in the Third Reich*, vol. I, London, SCM, 1987, and vol. II, London, SCM, 1988; A. Boyens, *Kirchenkampf und Oekumene 1933–1939. Darstellung und Dokumentation*, Munich, Chr. Kaiser, 1969, esp. pp.20–22, 72–74, 87–89, 133–135, 156f.

[2] The most definitive overall study to date of this aspect is the unpublished Oxford D.Phil. thesis of Daphne Hampson, "The British Responses to the German Church Struggle 1933–1939", 1973. See also e.g. K. Robbins, "Free Churchmen and the Twenty Years' Crisis", *Baptist Quarterly*, XXVII, no. 8, 1977–78, pp.346ff.; A. Hastings, *A History of English Christianity 1920–1985*, London, Collins, 1986, ch. 22.

[3] In 1930s English parlance *Die Bekennende Kirche* was often rendered as "the Confessional Church". "Confessing" rather than "Confessional" has now become widely accepted and used as more accurate. In my own text I therefore use "Confessing", while retaining "Confessional" in quotations from the time.

As a leading ecumenical and international figure, already with much experience and many contacts in Germany, Oldham could not fail to appreciate what was happening soon after Hitler came to power at the end of January 1933: the strident demands of the so-called "German Christians" and their programme for a truly "Germanic" faith in conformity with the Nazi ideology of blood, race and soil; the attempt to introduce the *Führerprinzip* into the government of the church with the appointment of "Reich Bishop" Ludwig Müller and the imposition of state-appointed "commissars" in charge of regional and departmental church affairs; and the demands for "aryanization" of the church, that is, the exclusion of pastors of Jewish descent. Equally keenly, he noted the resistance to all this in the stand of Martin Niemöller and the emergence of the Pastors' Emergency League in the early autumn of 1933, followed by the free synod of Barmen at the end of May 1934 which set forth the famous Barmen Declaration, the charter of the Confessing Church. The fact that Karl Barth was so clearly instrumental in the theological resistance of Barmen and the Confessing Church merely underlined for Oldham where his sympathies should lie. In his paper "The Christian World Community" given in 1935, Oldham rhetorically asks what more momentous question can there be for a person than "whether there is a living Word which he may hear, which he may trust, which he can and must obey?"[4] The echoes from the first thesis of the Barmen Declaration are unmistakable. But Oldham knew, too, that it was not only Barth who was involved. There soon arrived on his desk a copy of the statement drawn up by the theologians of Marburg University, where Rudolf Bultmann was preeminent, rejecting the concept of an "aryan" church as inimical to the church of the Reformation.

## The German missions again – and the Confessing Church

It was specifically as secretary of the International Missionary Council that Oldham himself first became directly involved in the German conflict. The fate of German missions under the Nazi regime has hitherto received relatively little attention in accounts of the church struggle,[5] but for Oldham it was a major preoccupation for over twelve months from the autumn of 1933. In September of that year he received from D. Stange of Kassel, an emissary of Ludwig Müller, a reassuring letter containing a statement signed by the Reich bishop which affirmed the unity in Christ of the German church with churches throughout the world, and encouraging Oldham to visit Germany, preferably during the forthcoming 450th anniversary of Martin Luther's birth which, he promised, would create a deep impression upon him.[6] This however was followed quickly by a letter of 20 September from Alphons Koechlin of the Basel Mission, also encouraging Oldham to visit Germany but for rather

[4] Oldham, "The Christian World Community", *Student World*, vol. XXVIII, no. 4, 1935, p.376.
[5] Though see Boyens, pp.20–22, 72–74.
[6] Stange letter to JHO 10 Sept. 1933 [OA].

different reasons. The leaders of the German missions were becoming increasingly dismayed by the attempts of the "German Christians" to restructure and control their organizations. Overseas, the missions were to retain independence but "On the home base the church is getting a far greater power of control in all financial and administrative matters." The larger societies were being forced into a dependency on the regional *Land* churches, which were themselves now being treated as subdivisions of an increasingly centralized Reich church. Smaller missions were having to merge and a number of very small ones "are kindly invited to disappear". No one could doubt the need for more coordination but on the other hand "many proposed and in principle already agreed things mean a dangerous break in the history of German missionary societies and of course the possibility of being governed by an all too powerful and all too strongly nationalized Church is very evident". Nevertheless, said Koechlin, Karl Barth and others were encouraging a powerful resistance, and above all the work of God needed to be patiently looked for in this revolutionary period.

Martin Schlunk, *Missionswisschenschaftler* of Tübingen, was anxious for Oldham to intervene by letter to the German church authorities. Oldham consulted with Paton and Mott who felt that a visit to Germany would be more to the point. Oldham himself did not go at this stage, but in late October 1933 someone else did – Ruth Rouse, known to Oldham from SCM days and now educational secretary for the Church of England. She visited Siegfrid Knak, director of the Berlin Mission, and others, and on her return presented a very full, confidential report to the Conference of Missionary Societies in Britain and Ireland.[7] It made alarming reading. A "commissar" had been appointed to deal with missions, and Knak and one or two others had met with some members of the "German Christians" to try to draw up proposals acceptable to all sides. However, at a conference attended by about seventy members of nearly all the missions there had been uproar at the proposals, which included heavy-handed measures for control by the Reich bishop. Instead the meeting – which included only two "German Christians" and was heavily critical of that movement – drew up plans for a new structure to replace the German Missionary Federation (*Bund*), comprising representatives of all the German societies. The demand of the German Christians for a 75 per cent majority of seats on any such body was rejected, as was any "aryan" paragraph.

There was little chance of such plans being acceptable to the authorities. Equally worrying, however, according to Rouse, was the rising prejudice against financial help for causes beyond Germany. In some places collections for foreign missions had even been forbidden in favour of the "winter help" collections for the destitute within Germany. Knak had concluded with three suggestions on how friends in Britain could help the situation: continue "in all tactful ways" to make foreign opinion of German affairs in church and state known; offer

[7] "Report on Missionary Situation in Germany by Miss Ruth Rouse. Strictly Private and Confidential: Conference of Missionary Societies in Britain and Ireland" [OA].

financial help if the "winter help" seriously reduces missions income; and continue the facilities for German missionaries in India to learn English.

The seriousness of the German church scene was underlined for Oldham in February 1934 in a series of communications from Hans Schönfeld in Geneva who spoke of the "terrible church situation" there and commended some reading to him on the subject.[8] Financial help not just for the missions but for many pastors was becoming a priority which the churches abroad should address. Schönfeld, however, was not an unqualified admirer of Karl Barth. In answer to an enquiry from Oldham, he felt that Barth, being Swiss, did not fully understand the specific peculiarities of the German context.[9] Schönfeld's guardedness regarding Barth was repeated in letters later that year, and he once appealed to Oldham, whom he knew to have access to Barth, to try to enlist help from colleagues who might get him to tone down the asperity of his debate with Emil Brunner on "natural theology".[10] By mid-April 1934 – just after the Paris Life and Work conference – Oldham felt sufficiently involved and in command of the basic facts to send to George Bell the draft of an Ascensiontide letter for the chairman of Life and Work to send to the churches on the grave issues at stake in the German church situation, and therefore on the importance of both the forthcoming meeting of the Universal Council at Fanö and the report of the Paris conference which would shortly appear.[11] Oldham clearly felt that the German church situation was a crisis of the first order, in view of the intention of the totalitarian state to impose uniformity come what may.[12] It was at Fanö, in August, that Oldham was thrust directly into the church struggle as the Confessing Church fought for ecumenical recognition as the true representative of the church of Christ in Germany. As well as being put on the commission for the 1937 conference, Oldham was brought into the committee dealing with the German church issue and took an active part in the discussions. He later reported to Henry Leiper in New York that at Fanö the international Christian body was faced with its most difficult and delicate problem for a generation.[13]

But it was the plight of the German missions which returned insistently to the fore, and at Fanö Oldham heard at first hand of the extent of the crisis: owing to the difficulties of exchange the German societies were no longer able to remit funds abroad. Soon after his return from Fanö he relayed this news to Mott, and, after consulting with Bill Paton, decided he must visit Germany without delay. "We may be on the verge of complete collapse of German missions throughout the world. It is impossible for the missionary leaders in Germany in present circumstances to communicate about these

[8] Schönfeld letters to JHO 10, 19 and 22 Feb. 1934 [OA].

[9] Schönfeld letter 22 Feb. 1934.

[10] Schönfeld letter to JHO 12 Dec. 1934 [OA].

[11] JHO letter to Henriod 17 April 1934 [OA]. This provides further evidence of Oldham's strong interest in Fanö four months before the event.

[12] Cf. Hampson, p.88.

[13] *Ibid.*, p.69.

*Hans Schönfeld*

matters by post".[14] Hans Schönfeld was in any case wishing to meet Oldham in Cologne.

Oldham therefore made his first visit to Nazi Germany in the last week of September 1934 and met with Knak who was now acting as plenipotentiary on behalf of all the German missionary societies. Knak confirmed the grim picture and on his return Oldham wrote to Mott on 21 September: "There is almost as great a danger of a complete collapse of the missionary work as there was during the war, and some energetic action is called for." Oldham must have reflected on the irony that during and immediately after 1914–18 his efforts to secure the survival of German missions from British imperial depredations had met with misunderstanding and hostility from his German colleagues, and now the present leaders of those same missions were appealing to him for help in face of the policies of their own German state. Equally, these pleas showed that his efforts nearly twenty years earlier were now appreciated as having been sound, sincere and effective. But no less than the plight of the missions, this visit shook Oldham into an even deeper awareness of the church crisis as a whole and drew him into a still closer relationship with George Bell with whom he conferred at length in London early in October, and then at Chichester 10–12 October.[15] While on the train returning to London on 12 October, Oldham

[14] JHO letter to Mott 21 Sept. 1934 [OA].
[15] Cf. Hampson, pp.87–95.

read even more alarming reports in *The Times*: "Commissar" Jäger and Gestapo officers had raided the Bavarian church headquarters, announcing the compulsory retirement of Bishops Wurm and Meiser but also thereby provoking a spirited protest from thousands of Bavarian Protestants. The attempt to impose a Germanic faith by sheer force was all too real, and battle was being joined in earnest. Oldham and Bell decided that urgent action was required, and Oldham cabled Samuel McCrea Cavert, secretary of the National Council of Churches in the USA:

> GRAVITY OF GERMAN CHURCH SITUATION INCREASING. EVENTUALITY MAY ARISE WHEN ONLY MEANS OF AVERTING DISASTER WILL BE TO INFORM GERMAN GOVERNMENT PRIVATELY THROUGH EMBASSIES IN DIFFERENT COUNTRIES THAT IF ATTEMPT MADE TO DESTROY CONFESSIONAL SYNOD REPRESENTING EVANGELICAL CHRISTIANITY CHURCHES WILL BE COMPELLED TO TAKE MOST EFFECTIVE MEASURES TO SUBMIT FACTS TO THEIR CONSTITUENCIES. RESULT WILL BE THAT CIRCLES NATURALLY MOST FRIENDLY TO GERMAN PEOPLE WILL BE ROUSED TO INDIGNATION. TIME A VITAL ELEMENT. AVOID ALL PUBLICITY AND DELAY ACTION UNTIL RECEIPT OF LETTER OR FURTHER CABLEGRAM BUT TAKE VERY CONFIDENTIAL STEPS TO PREPARE FOR PROMPT VIGOROUS ACTION IF REQUIRED. SIMULTANEOUS ACTION IN ALL COUNTRIES DESIRABLE. BISHOP OF CHICHESTER CONSULTING COLLEAGUES PERSONALLY APPROVES THIS CABLEGRAM.[16]

Oldham followed this up by letter to Cavert who responded positively. Bell and Oldham maintained close contact with the archbishop of Canterbury and the leadership of the Free Churches. Oldham explained to Mott: "The fact that I happened to be in London and have had long international connections has enabled me to be of some service in collaborating with [Bell] . . . I do not think we can exaggerate the seriousness of what is taking place at the present time in Germany, and it has a profound significance not for Germany alone but for the whole of Christendom."[17] Another cable and letter went to Cavert. Oldham was convinced that the time had come for drastic action: churches throughout the world should be prepared, simultaneously and at the right moment, to make known to the German embassies in their countries that any attempt to destroy the Confessing Church would provoke unprecedented indignation against the German government.[18] At the same time he feared that too hasty and uncoordinated action, and especially any advance publicity of the plan, would disastrously suit the interests of Nazi propaganda, and he was alarmed that Cavert was already making some rash public statements.[19] It is significant that while it was George Bell who was becoming known as the public protagonist for the persecuted Confessing Church, of the two it was Oldham who, while acting more covertly, seems to have been far more aware that the Nazi leadership were gangsters by nature rather than "reasonable men".[20]

[16] [OA]
[17] JHO letter to Mott 16 Oct. 1934 [OA].
[18] Cf. also Hampson, p.92.
[19] *Ibid.*, p.96.
[20] *Ibid.*, p.93.

*Bishop George Bell*

The possibility of some kind of intervention by their own government was naturally also in the minds of Oldham and Bell. At the same time Oldham was concerned lest any overt diplomatic action by the British government, if it was known to have been prompted from church circles, would play into the hands of the Reich authorities who were only too keen to show that the church opposition in Germany was a front for political games aided from abroad. In the late autumn and winter of 1934, Oldham and Bell induced Archbishop Lang to write both to the foreign secretary, Sir John Simon, and to the British ambassador in Berlin, stating their basic concerns.[21]

Meanwhile, the missions again. On 12 November Oldham and officials of British missionary societies met in London with a deputation of four representatives of the German missions, led by Knak. The full extent of the financial crisis was set out: the Reichsbank was permitting only the most meagre amount of remittances to be sent abroad, hardly enough to cover the cost of missionaries' salaries let alone all the other aspects of missionary work. It could be said that what the German societies were facing was simply an extreme version of what all Western mission boards were having to cope with, namely, severe financial retrenchment following the international economic crash of

[21] *Ibid.*, p.111.

1929. But it *was* extreme, to the point of imminent catastrophe. Many of the German missions were already running at a drastically reduced level of personnel compared to the pre-1914 days. In the longer term, there would have to be massive restructuring of the German work. But that was not even worth contemplating if the immediate crisis could not be weathered. The meeting therefore proposed raising an emergency fund to aid the German missions, paid for partly by the British societies out of their ordinary funds and partly by seeking voluntary gifts and donations from the church constituency at large. Out of this fund, remittances would be sent directly to the German mission fields. Such donations would however (and the Germans themselves wished this) be regarded only as loans. Within Germany, the societies would pay into a German bank an equivalent amount to be held until conditions permitted repayment to Britain. Meanwhile the Germans would identify which fields and areas of work should receive priority. The possibility of non-German societies taking over some of the German work was not considered desirable (doubtless the bitter feelings of 1914–18 were recalled) but neither was it practicable since nearly all the non-German societies felt that their own work had been virtually cut back to the bone already.

This plan was largely of Oldham's (and William Paton's) devising. Oldham was not sanguine about the outcome. At best, the disaster could only be minimized, not avoided. But immediately after the meeting he wrote Mott on 13 November a full account of the discussions and proposals in the hope that a similar scheme might be set up in America. Six weeks later Oldham was able to report to Mott that a number of the British societies – the SPG in particular – were prepared to help. The overall results were modest and could only offer the briefest respite: "The German societies have to face the fact of catastrophe . . ." But at least, others were facing it with them. Largely under William Paton's direction, the scheme did go ahead and played a vital role in maintaining missionary cooperation, not least in India, even after the outbreak of war.[22]

## Heroes, heroines and officials

During 1934–35 Oldham, in addition to his close contacts with George Bell, became acquainted with a number of visitors and emigrés from Nazi Germany, and with British people who were active on the scene and had first-hand information. Among the Germans was Dietrich Bonhoeffer who in October 1933 arrived as pastor of the two German congregations in London. Bonhoeffer, we have seen earlier, had already come to Oldham's notice as a significant academic theologian but there is no evidence that they had met personally before Bonhoeffer came to London. Nor is it clear how the contact was made; as likely as not, it was through George Bell. Bonhoeffer had already shown his mettle in the early phase of the church struggle as an ally of Karl Barth and a trenchant critic of the "orders of creation" theology beloved of the "German

[22] See E. Jackson, *Red Tape and the Gospel*, p.194.

Christians" and others. He had also, since 1931, been a youth secretary of the World Alliance for Promoting International Friendship through the Churches. While in London he closely followed events in his homeland, frequently returning to Berlin, and ensured that the German congregations in Britain took the side of the Confessing Church. He remained active in the ecumenical peace movement, and was notably present at the Fanö conference in 1934. It was above all the close friendship which developed between himself and George Bell which ensured that his accurate and detailed information on the church struggle, and the wider scene in Nazi Germany, received an understanding ear in Britain.

Oldham met with Bonhoeffer in London a number of times, was impressed and in turn commended him to others. On 18 December 1934 he wrote to Eleonora Iredale, an Anglican member of the council of Life and Work who will figure conspicuously later in the Oldham story:

> Last night I had Bonhoeffer, who is in charge of the German Church here, to dinner. He is one of the best of the younger Germans. He is carrying a heavy burden of anxiety in regard to the German refugees. There are about three thousand in this country, nearly all belonging to the middle classes – lawyers, doctors, artists, journalists, etc. About half are Jews and are fairly well looked after by the Jewish community. The other half are in a bad way, and Bonhoeffer is in touch with a number of cases of actual destitution. Their anxiety is increased in some instances by not knowing whether their permit will be renewed after every six months. Is there any kind of action you can think of that might be taken to help these unfortunate people?

Early in 1935 Oldham was contacted by Dorothy Buxton. Together with her husband Charles Roden Buxton, a Liberal (and later a Labour) politician, she had a long and unusually intimate knowledge of German affairs, and from 1933 was campaigning vigorously to bring home to influential opinion in Britain the real nature of the Nazi regime and its brutality.[23] She was now anxious to visit Germany again in order to find out the attitude of German church leaders.[24] Oldham confessed to having much less to do with such leaders as compared with the missionary officials, but recommended her to contact Bonhoeffer and gave her his address in Sydenham: "he knows most of the leaders and has been acting as an intermediary between them and the Bishop of Chichester . . . He would be sympathetic on the subject of the concentration camps." Oldham however went on with a caution which provides an interesting comment both on that stage of the church struggle and on his own perception of the need to weigh the balance between protest and diplomacy:

> There is, however, a further real difficulty. Those who might be sympathetic on the subject are connected with the Confessional Movement. The position of the Confessional Church in its relations with the state is, at the present moment, so

[23] See K. Robbins, "Church and Politics: Dorothy Buxton and the German Church Struggle", in D. Baker, ed., *Church, Society and Politics*, Oxford, Blackwell, 1975, pp.419–33.

[24] D. Buxton letter to JHO 20 Jan. 1935 [OA].

*Dietrich Bonhoeffer*

> critical that I think that its leaders would feel a difficulty just now about being involved in the question of the concentration camps. Deeply interested as I am in this matter I think they may be right in their hesitation. Circumstances often allow us to do only one thing at a time and the Confessional Church has at the moment such a difficult problem to solve that it is doubtful whether in these critical weeks it should be complicated by the introduction of the other question, in spite of the fact that it is one in regard to which the Christian Church ought in normal times to take vigorous action.[25]

Buxton was later able to report that in Germany she had found Roman Catholic churchmen more aware and concerned about the issue than Protestants – with the exception of Präses Karl Koch of the Westphalian Church.[26]

Dietrich Bonhoeffer returned to Germany in April 1935 in order to take charge of the illegal seminary of the Confessing Church near Zingst on the Baltic coast. Before leaving London he wrote Oldham a warm letter of thanks for the support he had received from him – and expressing appreciation also for the fact that his cousin Charlotte von Leubuscher was working in one of the committees which Oldham had set up in preparation for the 1937 Oxford conference.[27]

[25] JHO letter to Buxton 1 Feb. 1935 [OA].

[26] Letter K. Hahn to JHO 6 March 1935 [OA].

[27] Bonhoeffer letter to JHO 12 March 1935 [OA]. Text now published in *Dietrich Bonhoeffer: London 1933–1935*, Dietrich Bonhoeffer Werke Band 13, Gutersloh, Chr. Kaiser, 1994, pp.284f.

Meanwhile Oldham was preparing for his own second visit to Nazi Germany, and in addition to Bell he was also in touch with the archbishop of York, William Temple. He was hoping to see not only August Marahrens, bishop of Hanover and other Confessing Church leaders,[28] but representatives of the Reich church government, including Bishop Theodor Heckel, head of the church office for external affairs. Oldham, doubtless through his contacts with Bell and Bonhoeffer, was already well informed on the role, ambiguous to say the least, which Heckel was playing as an intermediary between the German churches and the ecumenical movement. On 14 December 1934 he had communicated his doubts to Hans Schönfeld who had enquired about the possibility of Heckel being given a place on the committee preparing for the Oxford conference:

> I very much distrust Heckel and this is part of the difficulty. For this reason it would seem to me essential, if he is made a member of the Committee, that he should be balanced as proposed in your memorandum by others. I think we should be quite prepared to stretch a point and in present circumstances to give the German Church an enlarged representation, *if this is the best way of dealing with the German problem.*
>
> I am doubtful whether it is necessary to supplement Heckel with one of his collaborators who is a jurist. (emphasis mine)

Distrustful yet prepared to stretch a point: Oldham's viewpoint was characteristic of those ecumenicals who strongly identified with the Confessing Church yet did not feel it wise or practicable to cut off all relations with the "official" Reich church authorities. In fact the problem had germinated at Fanö. While that conference had indeed "solemnly resolved to throw its weight on the side of the Confessing Church",[29] Heckel had managed to get inserted into the resolution a small clause stating that the Council wished to remain in "friendly contact" with all groups in the German Evangelical Church. Few if any saw much significance in this at the time. But it was enough "to allow the Reich Church to put its foot inside the door"[30] – and keep it there. Hence Oldham could see no objection to committee documents being communicated to Heckel before publication, since he felt that the Committee itself should not be issuing public declarations which should be the task of leaders of the churches themselves. His further comment to Schönfeld is a blend of principle and realism:

> There is of course no reason in principle why the study work should not be related to Heckel's office in the same way as to the national inter-church organisations in Great Britain and America. On the other hand what Heckel fails to recognize is that at the present time circumstances are quite different. Geneva can deal with London and New York because the offices there are known to have the confidence of all the various sections of the Churches, but it is precisely uncertainty about this being true of Heckel's office that creates the difficulty in the German situation.[31]

[28] But see E. Bethge, *Dietrich Bonhoeffer*, p.325, on the ambiguity of Marahrens' position.
[29] N. Ehrenström, in Rouse and Neil, eds, *A History of the Ecumenical Movement 1517–1948*, p.583.
[30] Bethge, p.300.
[31] JHO letter to Schönfeld 14 Dec. 1934 [OA].

To the most radical members of the Confessing Church like Bonhoeffer, of course, Oldham's perception would not do complete justice to the situation. In their eyes, to speak in terms of "interchurch" or "various sections of the churches" in Germany was misleading. The Confessing Church claim was not that it was *a* church alongside others, or a section of the church, but the one true Evangelical Church in Germany.

It was with this background that Oldham travelled to Germany in May 1935. His primary object was to meet in Hanover with leaders of the Confessing Church on preparations for the Oxford conference. First however he went to Berlin to meet with Heckel who also called together General Superintendent Otto Dibelius, Karl Heim and H.D. Wendland. There he learnt of negotiations between the Confessing leadership and the government, and Heckel assured him that a settlement would probably be reached within a week.[32] A different picture was given to Oldham by *The Times* correspondent in Berlin, Ebbut, who came to see him on 12 May and told him that the negotiations had completely broken down due to an intervention by Hitler, that the Nazi party would soon be imposing a national church by force and that any future church opposition, Catholic or Protestant, would be treated with increasing severity. The church situation in Germany, Ebbut felt, was worse than it had been for months and he expressed surprise that there had not been more public expression of opinion in England.

Oldham went on to Hanover for the meeting with the Confessing leaders 13–14 May. There the sense of emergency was even greater: three pastors from the Rhineland had been interned in Dachau for over a month and the Confessing Church had prescribed weekly services of intercession on their behalf, and a few days previously the Confessing Church council's office in Berlin-Dahlem had been searched by the Gestapo. Oldham felt "a sense of impending tragedy" over the meeting. Bonhoeffer was summoned by telegram to Hanover and delivered a typically forthright warning that the ecumenical representatives abroad must no longer expect Heckel's office and the Confessing Church to work jointly for the Oxford conference, and that the Confessing Church must insist on a less equivocal attitude to its claims on the part of the research department in Geneva. "He went on to say that preparations for Oxford could only emanate from a theology supported by a real church; Geneva, however, was evading a decision as to which was the real Church in Germany."[33] Nevertheless the meeting unanimously resolved to cooperate in every possible way in the Oxford preparations and appointed a committee to supervise the programme.[34] On returning to England Oldham went on to an executive meeting of Life and Work in York where he shared with Bell the results of his visit. It was not only to Bell, however, that Oldham relayed his concern. In London he lunched with Barrington-Ward, editor of *The Times*,

[32] JHO letter to H. Henson 23 May 1935 [OA].
[33] Bethge, p.391.
[34] JHO letter to W.E. Hocking 21 May 1935 [OA].

and then wrote to Hensley Henson, bishop of Durham, now in his seventies but still capable of the most fiery utterances when roused in the cause of truth and righteousness. Would Henson join with others in initiating correspondence in *The Times*? Oldham set out the background from his visit to Germany and went on:

> I shall be having a talk with the Archbishop of Canterbury about the possibility in certain eventualities of concerted action by the Churches outside Germany. If the necessity arises of such concerted action and it seems desirable to take it, we have the machinery for bringing it about . . .
>
> Whether any action of this nature is called for, or not, however, it would seem desirable that there should be some public expression of the concern and indignation that are felt about the present tendencies to substitute a new paganism for Christianity in Germany and the imprisonment of ministers of the Gospel in concentration camps which Mr Baldwin said, in a recent speech, he had not expected to live to see in countries which we had believed to be civilized. I learned from Ebbut that they have knowledge which they cannot use or make public of brutalities of the worst kind which have been inflicted on some of the pastors . . .
>
> Hitler in his speech on Tuesday insisted that the attitude of national-socialism to religion, in contrast with that of communism, was friendly. A government, however, which sends pastors to concentration camps, forbids the use of public halls to Christian bodies while putting them freely at the disposal of the German Faith movement, and suppresses Church newspapers so that the leaders of the Church have to communicate with their congregations more or less surreptitiously by typewritten circular which may at any time be seized, cannot be regarded as unduly cordial in its attitude to Christianity.[35]

A few days later, the archbishop of Canterbury, Cosmo Gordon Lang, had an interview with the German ambassador, Ribbentrop. There was correspondence in *The Times*. On 5 June news came that the three Rhineland pastors had been released from Dachau. Oldham took some pleasure in thinking that such interventions as he and others had prompted might have had some effect but he knew it was a limited advance. On 6 June he wrote to A.C. Don, the archbishop's chaplain:

> The release of pastors means a great deal and the removal of restrictions on the freedom of the Church will mean more. Whatever may be achieved, however, I do not think we can regard it as more than a small tactical success in what must inevitably be a long struggle. The conflict with new pagan forces of Germany will go on and if I have one regret in regard to the correspondence which has been appearing in *The Times* it is that the letters tend to assume that Germany is pagan while England is Christian. Happily there is nothing here comparable to the attempt to impose a new pagan religion on the whole community by force by the State, but there are many ideas in the ascendant which are quite irreconcilable with the Christian understanding of life.

[35] JHO letter to H. Henson 23 March 1935 [OA].

## Prophecy and diplomacy

Oldham's actions, if discreet, stand well within the finest attempts at solidarity with the Confessing Church under persecution. It also has to be said that he was typical of those Western ecumenicals who did not always appreciate that to the theological leaders of the Confessing Church, even more important than what was happening to pastors and to the "freedom of the church" was what was happening to the confession of the gospel as declared at Barmen.[36] It was solidarity with *that* cause, and its implications for an exclusive recognition of the Confessing Church by the ecumenical movement, which was uppermost in the minds of such as Bonhoeffer and Karl Barth. Inevitably, for all their admiration and gratitude to him Oldham was linked in their minds with the somewhat equivocal stance of the research department of Life and Work in Geneva. Daphne Hampson is right in pointing out that in relation to the German church struggle, Life and Work on the one hand, and Faith and Order on the other, were much closer than some popular opinion in ecumenical circles has suggested;[37] and Oldham's stance in practice differed little from that of Leonard Hodgson, the secretary of Faith and Order, with whom Bonhoeffer had a heated argument in 1939.[38] Both movements were in fact careful to avoid being drawn into adjudication in an "internal church dispute" in Germany. Nevertheless, Life and Work was always to be *felt* by the Confessing Church leaders, and Bonhoeffer in particular, to be more in solidarity with them than was the case with Faith and Order. In any case Faith and Order's image was not helped by the fact that one of its most prominent English leaders, the bishop of Gloucester A.C. Headlam, long maintained a position of outright support for the Reich church, and even for some of the "German Christians", with a derisive stance towards the Confessing Church and Martin Niemöller (even after his imprisonment) in particular. And whereas Faith and Order always gave the impression that impartiality *per se* was the order of the day, Oldham and Bell during 1933–35 made clear that their fundamental sympathies were with the Confessing Church, and that as a matter of *strategy* it was as well to maintain contact with Heckel's office. Better an officially approved German presence in ecumenical gatherings which included a Confessing Church delegation than no German presence at all, and this might be better ensured by keeping Heckel on board. This of course even in terms of strategy was fraught with risks, and there is some evidence that in the preparations for Oxford Oldham, even more than he realized, was at least close to being manipulated by Heckel and German diplomatic staff in London.[39] Certainly, by the time of the meeting of the administrative committee of Life and Work in Paris in June 1936, Oldham was defending the idea of a single and inclusive German

[36] Cf. Bethge, chs 8 and 9.
[37] Hampson, pp.168–70.
[38] Bethge, pp.545–48.
[39] Hampson, p.182.

delegation at the Oxford conference in the belief that the German church situation had changed significantly, with the threat of an imposed uniform Reich church apparently receding and, depressingly, the Confessing Church in increasing disarray.[40] And well after the Oxford Conference, in June 1939, Oldham was reiterating to Visser 't Hooft (who was apparently in agreement) that Heckel, in view of his official church position, could hardly be denied a position on the provisional committee of the World Council of Churches, then in formation:

> I believe that we ought to go to all possible lengths to maintain any touch that we can have with the German Evangelical Church, even to the extent of making some temporary sacrifices of principle for the sake of keeping contact with them till things change for the better.
>
> On the other hand we must be to the fullest extent on our guard against allowing the ecumenical movement to be *used* in the interests of internal Church politics in Germany.
>
> I very much distrust Heckel and this is part of the difficulty.[41]

From 1936 on, Oldham's involvement with the church struggle was inseparable from his role in Life and Work circles and the preparations for the Oxford conference. The Life and Work council meeting at Chamby, Switzerland, in August 1936 (again attended by both Oldham and Bonhoeffer) was riven with debate on the German church situation, and Oldham was among those who moved that there should be discussion of the Jewish question. The preparations for Oxford 1937 had now become the all-consuming preoccupation – but the Oxford conference was itself to become part of the struggle, as will be seen.

## Getting the right information to the centre?

The subject of Oldham and Nazi Germany cannot be left without mention of his involvement in two related episodes which in retrospect may seem somewhat bizarre, if well intentioned. Understanding the background to these events in Oldham's mind is perhaps helped by a paragraph in a letter to Hans Schönfeld of 14 December 1934, where he had raised the question of how to get to the attention of the Nazi government the likely effect on worldwide opinion of an attempt to suppress the Confessing Church:

> I have realised for some time the peculiar situation of the present government in Germany. Up to the present there has been no European government which, if enough trouble were taken, it was not possible to reach through some channel or other. In the case of the present German government these means of communication are lacking. Having realised that this was the crux of the difficulty I was all the more interested to see a week or two ago that either Mr Baldwin or Sir John Simon – I

[40] *Ibid.*, pp.184f.

[41] Letter JHO to Visser 't Hooft 27 June 1939. Cited in Hampson, p.347.

forget which – in a recent speech called attention to the same difficulty which is obviously experienced by foreign governments also. He pointed out that with previous German governments there were far closer and more intimate personal links between diplomatists than with the present regime. This problem of getting the right information to the centre in the most effective way is one which must be explored from every possible angle.

In the spring of that year, Oldham had been contacted by Kurt Hahn, a German Jewish emigré and the founder-headmaster of Gordonstoun School in Scotland, who was trying to organize a group of leading figures in Britain to sign and deliver directly to Hitler a letter expressing concern at the reports of the concentration camps and other abuses of freedom in Germany. The rationale was that an appeal by influential figures who considered themselves friends of the country might bring home to the Reich chancellor the way in which the name of Germany was being besmirched abroad. William Temple and George Bell among the bishops were known to be sympathetic. Others included G.M. Trevelyan, J.M. Keynes and A.D. Lindsay from the academic world, and other luminaries such as Sybil Thorndike, Lord Buckmaster and Sir Michael Sadler. Oldham was drawn in, not as a potential signatory but as a facilitator of contacts. The result was a seemingly endless round of meetings during May 1934 in the Athenaeum and elsewhere in London, and a plethora of correspondence between Oldham, Hahn, Temple and Bell.[42] Should a copy of the proposed letter also go to President Hindenburg? Who should actually deliver it? What protocol should be observed in the Reich chancellery? What about the final wording? The letter was finally taken to Berlin in mid-May by Vernon Bartlett, editor of the *News Chronicle* but, for reasons which are obscure, was never actually delivered.

In December 1934, again instigated by Hahn, and joined by what seems to have been an independent initiative from Lady Barbara Wilson, plans were mooted for an actual delegation to try to see Hitler. Again there was much discussion and correspondence. Again Oldham played the role of ringmaster. Initially George Bell was especially supportive, and was prepared himself at least to go if not actually lead the delegation. Contacts were also made with German diplomatic channels. Following lunch with a German embassy official, Bon, on New Year's Eve Oldham reported to Bell that meetings with Rudolf Hess and Alfred Rosenberg (with whom Bell already had contact) were being planned: "... Frick and Rosenberg constitute a central group who would like to bring an element of moderation into the anti-Jewish campaign. There is an intense struggle going on between Schacht and Goering on the one hand, who are definitely opposed for economic reasons to the anti-Jewish campaign, and Goebbels and Streicher on the other ... Rosenberg appears to have given a definite assurance that if a group of representative Englishmen came to Germany they would have an interview with Hitler. His lieutenant, Bomer, is willing to come to London any time after the middle of January and escort the

[42] Correspondence in OA.

party."[43] The plan fizzled out by the beginning of February 1935. Bell in particular evidently had increasing doubts, events in Germany making him ever more pessimistic.

With the benefit of hindsight such efforts may be judged futile or naive. They presupposed that the Nazi regime would be amenable to reason, when the very ideology on which it was based was a cult of the irrational at its most demonic. Even Oldham who had fewer illusions than most about the nature of the regime, still had to appreciate that more fully. But that realization could only come through further experience, and if it is a fault to be highminded and unrealistic, it is far worse to be highminded yet indolent.

[43] JHO letter to Bell 31 Dec. 1935 [OA].

CHAPTER 14

# *Oxford 1937*

THE world conference on "Church, Community and State" which met in Oxford in July 1937 is easily described as one of the great ecumenical landmarks of the 20th century. It brought together over 400 delegates from 120 churches in forty countries to study, debate and formulate lines of thought and action for the churches in relation to contemporary society. It met at a time of deepening political crisis in Europe and the Far East. In Nazi Germany Hitler had just put Martin Niemöller in prison, and had banned any delegates from the German Evangelical Church from attending Oxford – which paradoxically made their witness even more powerfully present. China and its Christians were at the start of their terrible experience of the Japanese onslaught. In Russia the Stalinist totalitarian programme was bulldozing its way across everyone and everything, including religion, which represented an alternative view of society. The Western nations seemed powerless in the face of these new titanisms, and many people were querying how deep were the moral foundations of the democracies which they claimed to value. The hopes for international order which had been so high after 1918, and were still so strong at the 1925 Stockholm conference, had already long faded, with the League of Nations seen as little more than a talking-shop. Oxford 1937 represented an attempt to bring the churches together to face these brute realities and to identify the directions of response. It generated a slogan, "Let the church be the church!". Although this phrase did not actually appear in any of the final documents, it does capture much of the essence of what happened in preparation for Oxford, at the gathering itself and its aftermath. The church had a specific witness and challenge to make to the world, to its false gods and the idols being erected in their honour. In the face of all that was dividing and fragmenting the world, the churches were given a realization that they were to embody a new community among themselves, and promote the cause of community in the world at every level. It was in the creation of a sense of universal fellowship in Christ, which was not to be disrupted for racial or nationalistic ends, and was to be furthered in the pursuit of a common mission in the world, that Oxford was significant. That significance was fully revealed with the eruption of a new world conflict two years later. At many levels the churches remained together in that conflict and, moreover, were afterwards able to unite in the tasks of reconciliation and reconstruction in a way that would not have been possible but for the 1937 experience. It is arguably the case that in its preparation and execution Oxford 1937 – at least as far as thinking about church and society is concerned – generated a culture of shared language, values and methods which remained normative for the ecumenical movement until about the fourth assembly of the World Council of Churches at Uppsala in 1968, over thirty years later.

It is also easily, and correctly, said that Oxford 1937 owed more to J.H. Oldham – "the chief architect and outstanding exponent of the Oxford project"[1] – than to anyone else. It was indeed in a special way his event, and because of this to describe it as an ecumenical study conference on a world scale is especially apt. Comparisons with Edinburgh 1910 are instructive. The leading crew at Oxford were the same as at Edinburgh: Mott as chairman, Oldham as (effectively) organizing secretary. But whereas at Edinburgh Mott had been the decisive shaper overall, at Oxford he was brought in only in the final stages of preparation and had to be instructed by Oldham in some detail as to how he should conduct proceedings. There were others at Oxford who had been present at Edinburgh. William Temple was chairman of the committee which drafted the conference message. He had been a young steward at Edinburgh, as had John Baillie and Walter Moberly, two of the main contributors at Oxford. The pattern recurs continually in the ecumenical movement.

Oxford 1937, however, could too easily be described as simply another witness to Oldham's outstanding skills as both a thinker and organizer on a world scale. That picture would be valid only if it made visible all that took place behind the scenes in the preparations. Many of those who came to Oxford in July 1937 and were inspired by the plenary presentations, the group discussions and the daily sessions of worship in the Church of St Mary the Virgin, could have had little idea of the severe stresses and strains which developed in the three preceding years, of the uncertainties which mounted virtually until the eve of the gathering, and indeed of the near-chaos which at times threatened everything. That is likely to be even more the case with those of us who only have the published reports to go by. Indeed, despair sometimes nearly overtook the organizers during the conference itself. Eric Fenn, Oldham's assistant at Oxford, still vividly recalls how one day in the midst of proceedings he was met in the High Street by Hendrik Kraemer who wanted to know why he was looking so glum. Fenn told him how badly he thought things were going – the meandering sectional meetings, the poor drafting of reports and so forth. "Never mind," said Kraemer putting a friendly arm round the young man's shoulder,

[1] N. Ehrenström, in Rouse and Neill, eds, *A History of the Ecumenical Movement 1517–1948*, p.584.

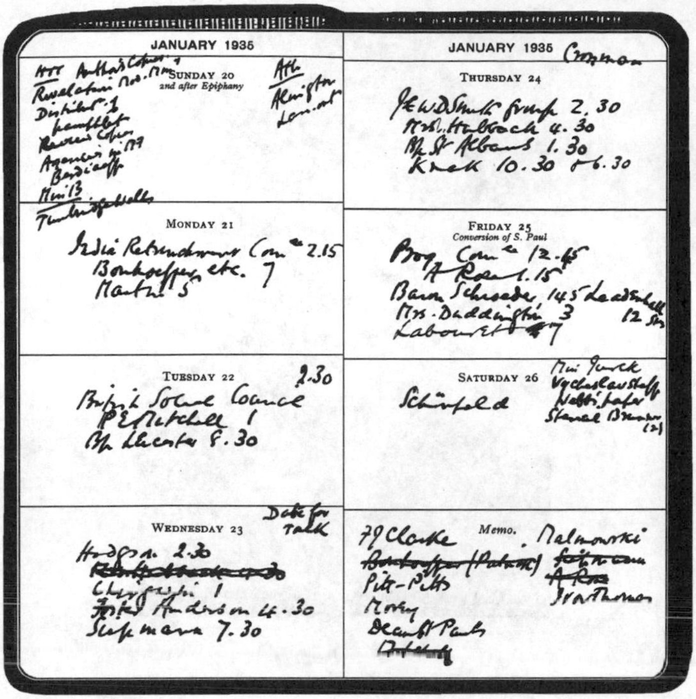

*A week in Oldham's diary, January 1935*

"it's always like this. 99% of these ecumenical gatherings is rubbish. What we have to look for is the other 1%."[2]

This section therefore aims to paint a fuller picture, in terms of what the preparations for Oxford 1937 meant for Oldham himself.

## The beginnings: Fanö 1934 and after

Joe Oldham, we have seen, was elected chairman of Life and Work's advisory commission on research at the meeting of the Universal Council at Fanö in August 1934, specifically with a view to preparations for the world conference. The decision to focus the world conference on "Church, Community and State" was taken by the Universal Council itself at Fanö. The "Explanation to the Churches" issued by the Council, as recorded in the minutes, shows every sign of Oldham's hand in the drafting:

> The great extension of the function of the State everywhere in recent times and the emergence in some countries of the authoritarian or totalitarian State raise in a new and often an acute form the age-long question of the relation between the Church and the State. The gravity of the modern problem lies in the fact that the increasing

[2] E. Fenn, interview with author – 25 October 1990.

*Eric Fenn*

> organization of the life of the community, which is made possible by modern science and technique and which is required for the control and direction of economic forces, coincides with a growing secularisation of the thought and life of mankind . . . No question, therefore, more urgently demands the grave and earnest consideration of Christian people than the relation between the Church, the State and the Community, since on these practical issues is focused the great and critical debate between the Christian faith and the secular tendencies of our time. In this struggle the very existence of the Christian Church is at stake.[3]

Whether Oldham had sought the key role, or whether it had suddenly found him, remain open questions but he certainly seized it decisively. He treated the preparations for Oxford as the heaven-sent opportunity to put into practice what he had long wished to see: a programme of study by the churches internationally, which would grapple with the meaning of Christian faith for contemporary society. In Life and Work he had found the tool – or what could be shaped into the tool – he had been looking for. The project both swallowed up and took further the International Missionary Council programme of study on the Christian message, and although he retained his desk at the International Missionary Council the preparations for Oxford became to all intents his full-time occupation for the next three years.

Of course he could not and did not wish to work alone. The advisory commission included notable names: John Baillie from Scotland, Emil Brunner

[3] Ehrenström, p.584.

from Switzerland, V.A. Demant and Leonard Hodgson (also secretary of Faith and Order) from England, Wilhelm Menn from Germany, Henry P. van Dusen from the USA and W.A. Visser 't Hooft from Geneva. Then there were the full-time staff at the Research Institute in Geneva, Hans Schönfeld and Nils Ehrenström. At Oldham's London office in Edinburgh House, Hugh Lister and Olive Wyon were brought in to help with administration. They were joined in 1936 by Eric Fenn, a young Presbyterian minister and a former general secretary of the SCM, to assist with preparations for the conference itself, and who acted as minutes secretary for the various preparatory meetings. Fenn was in fact Oldham's second choice. He also made strenuous efforts to recruit another SCM secretary (also a Presbyterian!), Lesslie Newbigin, even to the extent of pursuing Newbigin and his bride Helen to their honeymoon hotel in the Lake District.[4] But in vain: the Newbigins were determined to go to India. Wyon, Lister and Fenn were all highly gifted young people destined to have notable, if very different, careers after the Oxford conference.[5]

The executive committee of Life and Work met annually. Overseeing everything was of course the Universal Council itself, but this met only biennially. It was at Chamby in August 1936 that the Council met for the only time between Fanö and Oxford.

In the meantime Oldham had considerable freedom of action. The "meantime", however, was perilously short – less than three years for the most ambitious international programme of ecumenical study ever envisaged hitherto. One of Oldham's first steps was to write an introductory booklet, *Church, Community, and State: A World Issue.*[6]

The booklet, over 40 pages long, is effectively Oldham's manifesto for the Oxford conference and, moreover, for the programme of study leading up to and (he hoped) beyond it. It opens with a statement of what was now to be a central and continually reiterated theme of Oldham for the next decade, that is, until the end of the second world war: the issues facing human existence from the growth of the modern state. The assumption of responsibility by the state for so many areas of life, from railways to education, from health to agriculture, from housing to pensions, is not in itself to be resisted and has brought many benefits: "Organisation may be the means to a larger freedom." But there are grave dangers, seen in the extremities of the totalitarian states of Russia, Italy and Germany and in similar tendencies elsewhere. "The new absolutism of the state is a warning signal of dangers which confront the Church

[4] L. Newbigin, interview with author. At about the same time Oldham was in similar pursuit of Alan Richardson, then vicar of Cambo in Northumberland (A. Richardson letter to K. Bliss 14 Feb. 1969 [OA]).

[5] Olive Wyon had made a name both as a translator of continental theology and as a writer in her own right. Hugh Lister's career was tragically short: after an outstanding parish ministry in Hackney, east London, he joined the army and was killed in France in 1944. Eric Fenn, as well as continuing to collaborate with Oldham for a number of years, went on to distinguished work with the BBC Religious Broadcasting, and became a moderator of the Presbyterian Church in England.

[6] *Church, Community and State: A World Issue*, New York and London, Harper Bros, 1935; with a preface by William Adams Brown and introduction by George Bell.

everywhere. The issues are world issues and the common concern of the whole Christian Church." A totalitarian state is one which "lays claim to man in the totality of his being" and declares its own authority to be the source of all authority, refusing to recognize the independence in their own spheres of religion, culture, education and the family. Such a state declares itself to be not just a state but a church. "Underlying the claims of the totalitarian state are certain ultimate beliefs regarding the nature and destiny of man. In so far as these are incompatible with the Christian understanding of the meaning and purpose of man's existence, the Church must inevitably be involved in a life and death struggle for its existence." Soviet communism and Italian fascism represent such claims, as does H.G. Wells's vision of a "world state".

It is that form of the secular cast of mind which Oldham believes to be the universal menace. Centralization as such may bring benefits in certain situations. It is in the imposition on a community of a philosophy of life and pattern of living contrary to the Christian understanding that the chief danger lies. This can apply also to democratic societies, and the danger may be all the greater for occurring in less obvious ways: "It is when Christian people are unaware that their faith is being undermined that the greater harm may be done. The deeper meaning of totalitarian claims will be missed if they fail to open our eyes to a state of things which is found in every country." The drift and pressure of modern conditions is towards conformity, and Oldham describes educational trends in illustration of this. The question for the church is whether the common life and culture in which modern people are increasingly bound together will be inspired by Christian or pagan conceptions of the meaning and purpose of life.

Typically, however, Oldham does not propose reacting to danger only by a sense of alarm, but out of Christian hope. The last word is spoken by God in Christ. We are not responsible for the whole course of the world, which is in God's sure hands, but are to fulfil each day within our creaturely dependence the task assigned to us, trusting the outcome to God and thus girded by a confidence and a peace which passes human understanding. There is hope also lying in the opportunity of a new awakening of the church. Hope impels to action, and it is on this basis that the programme for the proposed world conference is set out.

A basic question is the nature and authority of the state, and the Christian relationship to it. Underlying this in turn are the questions of the nature of Christian ethics in relation to individual and collective action, as dealt with by Reinhold Niebuhr.[7] There are fundamental questions of theology to be explored, for instance how ethical imperatives are related to the necessities of a natural order and the laws of political and economic life. Here Emil Brunner is cited as the contemporary authority (*Das Gebot und die Ordnungen*). Following on from this are the questions of the kingdom of God in relation to history, and of human nature itself. Has the church a living word for these times, a

[7] Niebuhr's *Moral Man and Immoral Society* and *End of an Era* are cited.

word which addresses the current ideologies and social thinking? Above all, to the whole question of the life of human beings in relationship with others? "Only as the Christian Gospel is brought into a close relation to the realities and actual problems of the world to-day can we expect mankind to recognize in it a living word of judgement and redemption." But equally typical of Oldham is his final insistence that this is to be no abstract intellectual exercise. The conference will achieve its purpose only if it reaches beyond intellectuality "and becomes the expression of a Church which is a community of persons, in whose hearts is kindled the flame of evangelism, who find the fulfilment of life in the acceptance of responsibility towards their fellow men, in mutual respect and service and love, and who draw inspiration and strength for such a life from hourly dependence in trust and obedience on One Who has revealed Himself to us as our Father and has called us to live as His sons".

Oldham's introductory booklet has been summarized at some length because nothing gives a clearer indication of his mind and purpose at the start of the Oxford 1937 project. Moreover, there can be seen in his exposition the sources of some of the tensions and disagreements which the programme was to encounter. It is not hard to detect some major ambiguities. For example, is Oldham mainly concerned about the centralized state as such, or about the danger that the uniform ideology it may impose will be inimical to Christianity? Further, does he seriously believe that the issue can be so starkly stated, as lying between "Christian" and "pagan" conceptions? What the Oxford process was to reveal, was that a single, agreed "Christian" understanding was tediously elusive.

## A worldwide study programme

Edinburgh House might be the strategic centre, but could not be the only point for stimulating and coordinating action on an international scale. Regional, if not national, advisory groups or committees would also be required. In Britain an advisory council of about thirty leading church figures and academics from nearly all the main Christian traditions (except Roman Catholic) was set up under the chairmanship of Sir Walter Moberly. For the United States, a group functioned both as the American section of the Universal Council and as the department of relations with churches abroad of the Federal Council of the Churches of Christ. Henry S. Leiper, secretary of the Federal Council, directed an extensive programme of education based on the Oxford project, assisted by a special advisory council of which the secretaries were H.P. van Dusen and John C. Bennett. William Adams Brown, veteran ecumenical theologian and chairman of the administrative committee of Life and Work, was also involved. There was a continental committee, and as has been seen the German Confessing Church formed its own committee. To keep in touch with all such groups naturally meant a mountain of correspondence and a good deal of travelling for Oldham.

It was decided early on that the programme would cover nine main areas to be researched. The first group comprised three subjects implied in the conference title: the church and its function in society; church and community; church and state. Next came three related areas: church, community and state in relation to education; church, community and state in relation to the economic order; the universal church and the world of nations. Finally there was to be an examination of theological foundations: the Christian understanding of man; the kingdom of God and history; the Christian faith and the common life. This scheme represented both a continuation of earlier Life and Work studies, and also a focusing on a narrower range of issues than some would have liked. Earlier work had treated extensively of labour and employment questions and social welfare, for example, but Oldham insisted as always that hard choices had to be made on priorities especially where the churches' overall resources for this kind of work were so scarce. Moreover, at this critical point in history, these were the most critical and fundamental questions.

Some also asked whether with the prominence given to "Church" in the programme, Life and Work was losing its earlier prophetic social stance and in danger of becoming as ecclesiasticized as Faith and Order. For Oldham the case of Nazi Germany, and not just that one, was highlighting the fact that the questions of nature and role of the church and the nature and purpose of human society, while not the same, were inseparable in the contemporary world. He powerfully set out this view in an address to a student conference on "The Christian World Community":[8] the vital necessity, for the world's sake, of there being in the world a community which hears a saving word from beyond itself, a community which worships a God beyond itself, a community of people who live with and for one another in acceptance, forgiveness and service, a community which lives not for its own sake but for the world's sake, and a community which exists universally throughout the world. And he had quickly made up his mind that his own contribution to the programme would be precisely in the first section, the church and its function in society. Equally significant in this regard was Oldham's background booklet for the International Missionary conference to take place in 1938 at Tambaram, on *The Question of the Church in the World of Today.*[9] It follows much the same line as the preceding address: a sign of how Oldham was seeing the same fundamental questions as underlying challenges to all branches of the ecumenical movement. It was to be his last publication for the IMC.

Oldham's plan was for an international network of groups to work on assigned subjects. For each subject a small team of writers – theologians and lay experts – would be recruited to produce the preparatory papers. Each paper once produced in draft would be commented on by a circle of thirty or forty people representing a variety of theological and confessional standpoints and professional expertise, and revised accordingly – if necessary several times over. It was indeed the most extensive and intensive ecumenical study programme

[8] Oldham, "The Christian World Community", *Student World,* vol. XXVIII, no.4, 1035, pp.374–89.

[9] Oldham, *The Question of the Church in the World of Today*, London, Edinburgh House for IMC, 1936.

ever devised hitherto. The first task was to enlist the writers, and this Oldham did with his usual energy and persuasiveness – either directly when he already knew the persons or had received strong recommendations on their behalf, or using his collaborators on the various groups to act as recruiting agents. The list of contributors reads like a Who's Who of the theological world of the time, with eminences like Emil Brunner, Reinhold Niebuhr, C.H. Dodd, H.G. Wood, H.D. Wendland, Martin Dibelius, H.H. Farmer, Marc Boegner, Max Huber, C.E. Raven, William Temple, Paul Tillich, Edwyn Bevan and Stefan Zankov. Some were still rising stars, like John Bennett from the United States, and Austin Farrer of Oxford. What should be noted is that none of these had been recruited as "ecumenical theologians" (an anachronistic term, symptomatic of our present day). They were theologians drawn into the ecumenical enterprise because they were regarded as having something important to say. But not all were professional theologians either. John Foster Dulles, for example, to be a major if controversial voice in American post-war foreign policy, was a contributor to the section on the universal church and the world of nations. Of course many more writers were initially involved than those whose work finally saw the light of day – in all some 250 papers were produced. The commentators and critics came from even wider circles of interest: scientists, political and social thinkers, industrialists, literati and educationists as well as theologians had their say.

## The Atlantic: a stormy passage

To produce a coherent outcome from such a diversity of perspectives and contexts was expecting a very great deal, certainly in the space of barely three years. Oldham was not too daunted. For one thing, he was not expecting overall agreement from the contributors and he welcomed the sharpness of contrary opinions. What he did hope for was some overall perspective within which to set different approaches to the fundamental issue of how the church understands itself in relation to the gospel given to it, and in relation to the human condition of the time. For another thing, he was not too concerned about the time factor, and did not wish to create unreal expectations about what could be achieved within a space of two weeks in July 1937. Everything did not stand or fall by what would happen in Oxford. Again and again, almost *ad nauseam*, to preparatory meetings and conferences and in correspondence, he stated that what was afoot in the programme was a process demanding not three but twenty or thirty years' hard work by the churches, the issues being so fundamental and the implications so far-reaching. It has been seen in an earlier chapter that by the 1920s he had become dubious about the value of large conferences. With Oxford, it was certainly the study programme rather than the gathering itself which most excited him. In practical terms, however, he welcomed the necessary deadline and worked with all his energies to meet it.

Overall perspectives might be uppermost in Oldham's mind, but he could not ignore the tensions that arose between one context and another. The

German situation, we have already seen, became a major issue especially as far as representation was concerned. That, however, was more a matter for the administrative committee of Life and Work rather than the advisory commission on research. The severest problems Oldham had to face directly had to do with the authorship, content and methods of producing the preparatory material, and here serious disagreements came with the team in the USA. Perhaps, as Oldham twice sailed to and fro across the Atlantic during these three years, he reflected on the transatlantic tensions that had nearly shipwrecked the Edinburgh conference prior to 1910. Once again, an unusual combination of tact and firmness was called for.

Part of the reason for these tensions undoubtedly lay in the sheer physical distance between New York and London. More important was the psychological distance which, the Americans felt, separated them from where the vital decisions were being made. The theme of the conference, after all, had been greatly if not mainly determined by the crises in Europe and by the felt need of the European churches to respond to them. Further, a conference highly motivated by European concerns was taking place in Europe itself, and those chiefly responsible for the actual arrangements were in London and Geneva. Oldham, as the main organizer of the whole programme, was on his home ground. The enthusiasm for the conference in America was real, but in the offices of the Federal Council in New York it was hard at times not to feel that it was a European conference in which they were being graciously invited to join.

All went well for over a year following Fanö. Late in 1935 the advisory commission on research meeting in Holland endorsed entirely the plans thus far for Oxford. But rumblings of discontent soon came from the American group. Oldham's advisory commission had made a large number of reallocations of writers to particular subjects, and Henry van Dusen wrote in some alarm about these "drastic" changes which left him "with a very deep feeling of uncertainty as to what is projected for the next year and a half, and as to precisely how we in this country can most helpfully participate".[10] Most upsetting was the proposal to shift Paul Tillich, of all people, from the section on "Man" to that on "The Kingdom of God". Tillich, who had had to leave Germany after the Nazi advent to power, was now teaching at van Dusen's own Union Seminary, and with his formidable intellect was a prize adornment on the American scene. Van Dusen clearly feared an unpleasant scene with him. "Is he not likely to query why, when he has been urged to go so far in dealing with this particular subject, he should suddenly be shifted to another and Berdyaev substituted in his place?" Oldham replied at length, explaining the feelings of the Holland meeting. He admitted the delicate nature of asking changes of prominent writers.[11] He had had to write several letters which might well lead to some strain in relationships. But all writing had been invited on

[10] van Dusen letter to JHO 21 Jan. 1936 [OA].
[11] JHO letter to van Dusen 4 Feb. 1936 [OA].

*Henry P. van Dusen*

the clear understanding there was no commitment to publication. The "paramount" interest (did Oldham recall Kenya as he wrote?) had to be that of the conference itself, and a paper would be judged on whether it would be intelligible to the wider ecumenical constituency, and would not "create misunderstanding or provoke criticism in some section of the international community". Many contributors, including some of the ablest, Arnold Toynbee and Edwyn Bevan for example, had been willing to have their papers scrapped on this basis. As for Tillich, the line-up that had emerged for "Man" had included Brunner and Heim as well as Tillich and several others making for a rather imbalanced team. Neither Brunner nor Heim could be dropped "as it would be very difficult to find substitutes". But Berdyaev could certainly write on Tillich's subject and would make the group more representative. In any case, Tillich's paper at present was in the form of notes and, as one of the group put it, to make it suitable for publication he would have "to begin where he left off". This explanation, the hope that he would be able to use his work elsewhere, together with a £10 fee and expenses, Oldham thought should keep him amenable. As it happened, Tillich did write one of the final papers for the section "The Kingdom of God and History".

Of longer term concern to the Americans was Oldham's predilection, as they saw it, for Emil Brunner. Before taking on the work for Oxford, Oldham had already run into trouble in the USA for his enthusiasm for continental thinkers of this stamp. Van Dusen felt that many Americans would at important

*Henry Smith Leiper*

points find the "secular" views of "man" which Brunner was rejecting closer to the true Christian view than Brunner's, which should be supplemented by alternatives. Oldham defended Brunner, whose work would surely be rendered acceptable by extensive footnotes or slight modification. Brunner, Charles Raven had assured him, was saying essentially what a liberal like himself would want to affirm as the distinctive thing in the Christian understanding of human nature, "i.e., that man has his being, that is to say, his existence as man or person, in relationship or . . . in responsible self-hood. I believe that we have here an idea of quite inexhaustible significance, and that if the volume can bring this home to the general consciousness of Christian people, a great deal will have been achieved."[12] There is no question, Oldham assured van Dusen, but that the wide differences in the implications of this central assertion should be stated.

But van Dusen returned to the attack. One of the American group, R.L. Calhoun, had been at the meeting in Holland and brought back a report of the tenor of the discussion. The American committee's unanimous view was:

> that it would be a fatal mistake to endorse the presentation of the Christian view of Man to Brunner alone. Calhoun brought back the impression that, within your group, Brunner is being increasingly considered as a central figure, recognising the Barthian

[12] JHO letter, *op. cit.*

with the "British" point of view. It cannot be too strongly emphasized that the whole Barth-Brunner theology has thus far made almost no impression in America; to anyone in this country whatever Brunner writes is regarded as peripheral to the central Christian position . . . "The standpoint is not sufficiently representative and ecumenical". Of course you have a high measure of confidence that Brunner will see the light and radically modify his previous presentations. We hope you are right, but must in all candour state that nothing which he has previously done seems to us to give encouragement to this hope. I think it is not putting it too strongly to say that any volume coming to America in which Brunner was entrusted with the exposition of the "Christian conception" would be immediately discounted in a fashion which it would be very difficult to overcome.[13]

Oldham presently had to concede that there were strong criticisms of Brunner's paper also in England[14] – even, now, from Charles Raven. The aim must be to present fully both agreement and disagreement in the volume but also to relate them to each other. "Merely to piece together several different contributions will give us a very poor book." In the end Calhoun was one of the other contributors. But into the summer he and van Dusen were still debating whether to demand Brunner's exclusion. Calhoun shared with van Dusen a belief that this might even be welcomed by some in England: "My confidence in Oldham's resourcefulness is high, but I think many of his compatriots disapprove of his partiality to Brunner . . ."[15] Calhoun felt the matter to be an acute test "of our readiness for ecumenicity, and the very first volume may convict us of sin rather than encourage us to hope for speedy salvation". But to jettison Brunner now would be a woeful confession of failure, since Brunner had a good deal in common with both Barthians and liberals. "Yet how to make a genuinely catholic understanding emerge from the present confusion of tongues I do not see".

An important difference between the American and British or European contexts was revealed on another level, when van Dusen warned Oldham of the dangers of his repeated emphasis on the long-term aims of the programme at the expense of the conference itself. The American group, said van Dusen, felt that this was hardly likely to quicken interest in the total undertaking or to make the Oxford conference appear of any particular importance.[16] It was certainly fatal from the money-raising point of view. Moreover, in what was (presumably unintentionally) a rather self-revealing comment about the nature of his group, van Dusen stated that many of those most deeply interested had no hope of living out the twenty-five- or thirty-five-year period. He conceded that a cultural difference between Britain and America was probably also involved. Oldham's first reply was irenic: there was no fundamental conflict between thinking long-term and acting more immediately.[17] But a few days

[13] van Dusen letter to JHO 13 Feb. 1936 [OA].
[14] JHO letter to van Dusen 3 March 1936 [OA].
[15] Calhoun letter to van Dusen 7 July 1936 [OA].
[16] van Dusen letter to JHO 17 March 1936 [OA].
[17] JHO letter to van Dusen 1 April 1936 [OA].

later, having just conducted a retreat for SCM staff in Britain, he was more assertive on the need for fundamental thinking – "the open conspiracy" – long beyond the conference.[18] Moreover he was not greatly concerned about the attitude of people "who like myself will not in all probability be participating actively in the programme twenty years hence. My deep concern is that the younger generation should be committed to a task to which they can give their entire lives". With the SCM group, he said, he had felt more at home than in most gatherings of seniors.

The Americans were also worried about some of the practicalities of the conference and the programme. For instance, in medieval Oxford would there be a hall large enough to accommodate not only the 400 or so official participants but also the many other visitors? Oldham assured them that the Sheldonian Theatre and town hall would amply suffice.[19] Oldham in turn was more worried that enough of the "right sort" of Americans could be got across the Atlantic both for the Universal Council meeting at Chamby, Switzerland, in August 1936, and a preparatory meeting for Oxford to take place at York.

## Final plans: Chamby 1936

The Universal Council for Life and Work met at Chamby 21–25 August 1936. The final plans for Oxford formed the biggest item on the agenda and occupied more sessions than any other topic, as well as being dealt with at length by H.L. Henriod and Hans Schönfeld in their respective reports as secretary and director of research. Schönfeld, reporting in detail on the extraordinary development of the study programme, identified as of "decisive importance" the "wise leadership" of Oldham,[20] together with the collaboration of a number of others, notably van Dusen in America. Schönfeld also reported on progress with the nine preparatory volumes – and on the major disagreements which had often followed exchanges between Continental, British and American collaborators. None the less "the research meetings had often . . . left the deepest impression that common Christian thinking had been achieved". A question was raised as to "how far the Council was committed to the treatment of the subjects as outlined in the memorandum". Oldham himself intervened to say that "all the material in question should be regarded as a quarry from which to draw in the preparatory work, and that the significance of the volumes consisted in the fact that they embodied a large amount of ecumenical thinking with a view to clarifying, in a manner that could not be done in the busy ten days of the conference, the differences of view existing among Christians. The volumes represented . . . a study process of interchange of thought among the best minds in all countries."

[18] JHO letter to van Dusen 8 April 1936 [OA].
[19] JHO letter to van Dusen 1 April 1936 [OA].
[20] Universal Christian Council for Life and Work: Minutes of the Council Meeting, Chamby sur Montreux, August 21–25, 1936, Geneva, WCC, p.17. Following quotes from pp.38, 40f., 54.

Oldham himself presented the actual conference programme. Any American misgivings notwithstanding, he began by again insisting on the need to focus attention "not on the Oxford conference primarily, but on the tremendous human realities with which it was concerned, and on the actual existing conditions in the modern world". Every word in his report was a prayer "that God might use these insignificant efforts to be in His hands the means of bringing some help and redemption to suffering humanity". Yet the entire significance of the conference would depend "on how far it resulted in action", within the purposes of God.

A long and lively discussion on the programme followed, and the minutes record that:

> A wish was expressed for a simpler statement of the principles and purpose of the conference, for presentation to the laymen whose participation it was hoped to secure. It was suggested that there was a danger of absorption in technical questions of a social and economic nature, and of thus obscuring at the conference the aim of the realisation of united Christian thinking; and that more emphasis needed to be laid on the spiritual side of the meeting. Several speakers presented their impression that the Oxford Conference would be in danger of giving academic treatment to problems which were to them, in their respective countries, already burning realities, and a contrast was drawn between the world situation existing at the time of the Stockholm Conference, and the international background on which the Oxford Conference was being prepared, at a time when even the existence of certain churches was in question.

A suggestion was made to link the sensitive subject of "The Church and War" with that of "The Universal Church and the World of Nations". Some speakers thought the whole approach too theoretical and required an educational effort to bring home to the constituency "the actual existential character of the problems in question". In his final response, Oldham was clearly somewhat depressed by the demand for instant communicability of thinking which was still wrestling with weighty issues barely understood as yet by the best minds themselves. He again made his distinction between the total task of the churches, and the contribution which the conference itself could make:

> Demands had been made upon [the conference] in the discussion which it could not possibly meet. It could only survey the situation and make for more adequate treatment of the problems in the days to come. It was also necessary to distinguish between the task of continuing to seek for a more adequate answer, and the educative task of communicating to the outside public such answer as had already been secured. We had to give what we had got. It was possible to interfere with the process of thinking out the answers to the problems, by asking too insistently that they should be popularly interpreted in their intermediate stages to the ordinary layman.

One of the great difficulties in handling these vast problems, said Oldham, lay in discovering an adequate technique – and such a technique was now in process of development through the interchange of thought that had been taking place in the study programme. He was clearly anxious that the Council, an unwieldy body of some eighty people of varying ability, was in imminent danger of undoing the hard work of the study programme. However, careful politician that he was, he had two proposals up his sleeve which would assure the Council members that they still had ownership of the whole project, and at the same time would ensure the continuation of the project. He proposed that the administrative committee be asked to set up commissions on each of the subjects which it was decided to include at the conference; and further, for immediate action, that this council meeting should appoint a committee to report on the programme later in the meeting. Skilful footwork had evidently already been done in the corridors, for the chairman was able to announce the eight names suggested for this group, to include Oldham and to be chaired by Walter Moberly. The Council agreed.

This *ad hoc* group met, and reported two days later. The discussion was again intensive, and some proposals were referred back. The outcome was agreement for five sections: the church and the community; the church and the state; church, community and state in relation to social order; church, community and state in relation to education; the universal church and the world of nations. It was still left open for further decision whether the last-named section should include the topic of Christianity and war, or whether this subject should comprise a section on its own (eventually it was subsumed under the former). The administrative committee was entrusted with the task of appointing chairmen, and ensuring the provision of memoranda as a basis for discussion. Further aspects of the programme – timetable, worship, translations, the possibility of issuing public statements and other matters, were also dealt with.

On the final day of the Council, as well as practical details of accommodation, etc., the crucial question of the allocation of places was dealt with. Oldham stressed the vital importance of adequate representation of experienced laypeople. "If the outside world was to take notice of the conference, it must have a large proportion of laymen participating in it, and in fact the Life and Work movement must itself become fundamentally a lay movement." His proposals included increasing the membership of the conference by twenty-five, to provide for representatives of "other ecumenical movements" including the WSCF, YMCA and YWCA; and that in making nominations for the one hundred co-opted members the administrative committee take in view the desirability of including representatives of universities, public life, industry and commerce, the working classes, women and the younger generation. The proposals were unanimously adopted.

Oldham left Chamby fairly well satisfied. But following the meeting, it also emerged that for one of the Americans the main problem was considered to be Oldham himself. The ageing William Adams Brown, chairman of the administrative committee, asked to sit in on a meeting of the research commission and monopolized much of the time by cantankerously raising questions about how decisions had been made on the programme. He then demanded a two-hour private meeting with Oldham, accusing him of high-handedness and going over his (Brown's) head. Oldham replied quietly but firmly that such a

*Preparatory group for Oxford 1937 Conference, Bishopthorpe, York. Front row from left: 3rd J.H. Oldham, 4th Archbishop William Temple, 5th W.A. Visser 't Hooft, 6th Reinhold Niebuhr.*

programme could only be undertaken if someone took a leading responsibility. The respective accounts of this encounter by Brown and Oldham in letters to van Dusen, as might be expected, do not entirely tally. "It has not been altogether easy", states Brown, "to deal with Oldham who, with the best will in the world, has been tempted to carry matters with a somewhat high hand, and to resent any attempt to change plans which he has himself adopted. What has made it more difficult is that he fills his schedule so full that there is no time or opportunity for discussion of the fundamental issues which underlie all questions of detail."[21] "At Chamby", van Dusen learned in turn from Oldham, "Adams Brown was exceptionally difficult throughout the meeting and succeeded in irritating almost everyone."[22] Others present seem to have sympathized with Oldham, Henry Leiper and other Americans included, having found Brown's behaviour embarrassing to say the least. Oldham put it down, as well as to advancing years (he made comparisons with Lord Lugard), to resentment by Brown that the research programme in America had been in the hands of van Dusen and Bennett rather than himself. Some reconciliation was effected by further letters.

After Chamby Oldham made plans for a three-week visit to the USA by himself and Mary, which took place in November. This enabled him to meet

[21] Adams Brown letter to van Dusen 31 Sept. 1936 [OA].
[22] JHO letter to van Dusen 2 Sept. 1936 [OA].

with nearly all the American writers and speakers for Oxford and to attend a number of preparatory meetings for delegates and other interested people. He was impressed by the seriousness of the American preparations. A number of the problems felt from the American side had to be dealt with. But as the new year dawned, and with the conference now only six months or so away, new anxieties came to the fore – and some of the old ones continued. It was by now evident that, with the exception of the first one, the group reports (reduced in number from nine to seven at Chamby) would not be ready in time for the conference and would be published later. What would be supplied to the conference would be memoranda prepared by the sectional chairmen, based on the report material thus far available.

Early in March 1937 Oldham was laid low by influenza for several precious days. Chaos seemed to be threatening. Many of the reports, and even the memoranda, were still revealing massive divergences of approach. Moreover van Dusen was troubled by the fact that in some cases there were just as great divergences between himself and Oldham on their value. "Your distress can hardly be greater than my own", Oldham told him. "None the less I comfort myself with the thought that these are growing pains and we may get through to something useful in the end. I have never been under any illusions as to the difficulty of the job we are attempting and therefore do not allow myself to be unduly discouraged by the discovery that it really is difficult."[23] To Oldham the fundamental task was simply made more clear: to find where there is agreement on the church's task and therefore the next fruitful steps to take.

Even in mid-April, many matters on the programme of speakers were still unsettled. Should Brunner speak? Would Reinhold Niebuhr in fact be coming? Could more Americans be fitted in to the list of speakers? It was clear from van Dusen that the fundamental American anxiety had not been allayed. Oldham confessed to H.L. Henriod:

> The most serious problem we have to deal with at Conference seems to be America. They have the feeling that the whole Conference is a European set up . . . There is much truth in this since the Executive has been on this side. I can hardly exaggerate the extent to which the Americans feel that the whole of the thinking in the preparatory work has been given a European cast. We have had matters so much our own way on this side of the Atlantic that I cannot help thinking that it would be good policy to tip the balance in the other direction.[24]

At about the same time, van Dusen wrote to Oldham saying that for all the strain and tension of the past few weeks there could be no doubting the admiration felt for him in America.[25] Until almost the eve of the conference itself, however, van Dusen was expressing his disappointment with the quality of much of the reports. Oldham still maintained that they were material to work on, and that the labours of three years should not be jettisoned. The

[23] JHO letter to van Dusen 1 April 1937 [OA].
[24] JHO letter to Henriod 13 April 1937 [OA].
[25] van Dusen letter to JHO 10 April 1937 [OA].

chairmen of the sections ought to be entrusted with the decisions on how to proceed. But as always with such events, there comes a point where the occasion takes over from all the preparation, with all its strengths and weaknesses, for good or ill.

### Oldham's contribution: the church and its function in society

Almost the one thing on which all were agreed, in America and elsewhere, was that Oldham's own report was first-class. He completed it early in 1937, after it was circulated and subjected to comment and criticism as all the other reports. *The Church and Its Function in Society*[26] is in fact a composite volume. Oldham wrote a short, introductory Part I setting the scene for the Oxford conference. W.A. Visser 't Hooft wrote Part II, a largely descriptive survey of the historical and doctrinal distinctive of the various churches but concluding with a discussion of the meaning of the church as an ecumenical society. The major section, Part III on the function of the church in society, is Oldham's, although in the preface he generously pays tribute to Nils Ehrenström who assisted in the final stages. The book, technically the report of Section I, constituted the only material published prior to the conference itself. It was of such quality as to ensure that whatever the problems caused by the lateness of the other reports and the unevenness in the memoranda being supplied to delegates, the conference had a solid introductory basis to work on. Without too much exaggeration, it can be said to have gone a long way to saving the whole enterprise.

Oldham's essay is in the first place a summary, typically succinct and coherent, of the holistic understanding of the church and its mission which had marked his thinking since the first world war. Here again are made both the distinctions and the inter-relations, between the church as an institution and as a community of faith, between the givenness of the gospel of grace and the ethics which are a response to that grace, between the church receptive and the church active, between the church as a community of worship and the church as active in love, evangelization, mercy and witness. But the greatest value of the writing for the theme of the conference lies in the later sections dealing with the nature of secular society and the role of the Christian and the church within it. Rarely has the basic issue for faith of the necessity of corporate life in the world been stated so clearly:

> This fact of association with others in carrying out the purposes by which the community maintains, expands, and enriches its own life gives rise to one of the main problems of which account has to be taken in considering action in the corporate life. Where there is purpose there may be divergence of purpose. The purpose of the Christian is to carry out in all relations the will of God. But in every group of which he is a member, whether it be the nation or State, or a voluntary association, such as

[26] W.A. Visser 't Hooft and J.H. Oldham, *The Church and Its Function in Society*, London, Allen & Unwin, 1937.

> a trades union or employers' federation or an educational institution, he may be, and generally is, associated with those who do not share this Christian purpose. This group has a common purpose which is not identical with the Christian's purpose, but the realization of which, notwithstanding the imperfections of the process, is necessary for human existence or welfare. Where this conflict of purpose arises, the Christian is confronted with the choice of withdrawing from an association, the purpose of which he feels to be incompatible with his Christian calling (which is possible in the case of a voluntary association but not as a rule in the case of a nation or the State), or of remaining a member of the association and seeking by protest, or by the quality of his action, to bring the common purpose into fuller accord with what he believes to be the will of God. For the solution of conflicts between contradictory purposes there can be no easy, general or universally valid solutions. Such conflicts are the stuff of life. They arise in an endless multiplicity of new and unrepeatable situations. There is no escape for the individual from the responsibility of decision. In these responsible choices life finds its meaning. The only thing men take with them when the end comes is the character formed by their decisions.[27]

There is much realism in the essay, on the nature of institutional life and "the laws of things" which have to be recognized, yet also an insistence on the necessity and possibility of ethical guidance in secular affairs – an emphasis which Oldham noted had, ironically, been welcomed more enthusiastically by laypersons than by the professional theologians who had looked at his earlier drafts. And it is the emphasis on the role of the laity for expressing the gospel and Christian ethics within the world which is one of the highpoints in the essay:

> In relation to the issues which will come before the Oxford Conference nothing could be plainer than that if the Christian faith is in the present and future to bring about changes . . . in the thought, habits and practices of society, it can only do this through the living, working faith of multitudes of lay men and women conducting the ordinary affairs of life. The only way in which it can affect business or politics is by shaping the convictions and determining the actions of those engaged in business and politics. It remains inoperative and unproductive, except in so far as it becomes a principle of action in the lives of those who are actually carrying on the work of the world and ordering its course in one direction or another.[28]

Oldham however went further than this.[29] The concept of lay ministries had to be developed, and appropriate structures developed for them in the shape of cells or associations of those sharing the same contexts and responsibilities in secular life. Such insights were to prove seminal during and after the second world war for thinking and experiment in many countries on "the ministry of the laity". Equally, it should be noted, Oldham has important things to say on the proper function of the ordained ministry.

It is also in this essay that Oldham first suggests – surprisingly briefly in view of the large-scale use that subsequently came to be made of it by others – the

[27] *Ibid.*, pp.178f.
[28] *Ibid.*, p.117.
[29] *Ibid.*, pp.192–95, "The Witness and Action of the Christian Laity".

form of ethical statement that has come to be particularly associated with his name: "middle axioms". It is important to note the particular context in which Oldham produces this concept, since it is apt to be treated as a free-standing principle divorced from the total setting of the church, the gospel, the believer and society. The gospel is not a code of morals or a new law, says Oldham, but the mind that has responded to Christ must express itself in new forms of behaviour. To speak broadly about the law or love or social justice does not go far in helping to know what must be done in particular cases. That is an individual moral responsibility. Oldham continues:

> It is not the function of the clergy to tell the laity how to act in public affairs, but to confront them with the Christian demand and to encourage them to discover its application for themselves. Hence between purely general statements of the ethical demands of the Gospel and the decisions that have to be made in concrete situations there is need for what may be described as middle axioms. It is these that give relevance and point to the Christian ethic. They are an attempt to define the directions in which, in a particular state of society, Christian faith must express itself. They are not binding for all time, but are provisional definitions of the type of behaviour required of Christians at a given period and in given circumstances.[30]

Oldham goes on to illustrate by citing R.H. Tawney on wealth and materialism, and the principle of equality as it applies in the care and education of the young. There is much else in the section which still reads well for today. not least Oldham's double insistence that the church must speak out on social wrongs, and that ecclesiastical assemblies must beware of so speaking before a full study of the facts in each case.

Where today's reader may have doubts is in the discussion on whether certain political systems and allegiances can in themselves be deemed heretical. "If a Church declares a certain cause to be the work of Satan, it would seem to follow that it must exclude from its membership those who identify themselves with it."[31] The debate among a number of German theologians is cited. "It is doubtful", Oldham concludes, "whether the Church can, or ought to, pronounce judgment on Communism, or Capitalism, or Fascism as such, since each of these comprises a bewildering variety of aims and activities, and the judgment becomes significant only when it is stated much more precisely what features in it are approved or condemned."[32] Post-Auschwitz, post-Stalin, and (just) post-apartheid, we may well feel that certain systems have for themselves stated all too precisely just what they stand for. In that case, we should recognize that Oldham was not equivocating, but merely stating a condition that has in fact been fulfilled. In 1937 not all was seen which could only be seen in its fullest horrors a few years later.[33] It is important above all to recognize that

[30] *Ibid.*, p.209.
[31] *Ibid.*, p.227.
[32] *Ibid.*, p.228.
[33] The concept of *status confessionis*, which the Confessing Church in Nazi Germany applied to the issue of the "aryan clause", is today being discussed much more widely in relation to ethical issues in the socio-political sphere.

Oldham, far from believing that his essay or the Oxford conference itself represented a final vantage point for Christian ethics, still less a point on which all could agree at present, saw these efforts as but an early stage on the way towards unity in Christian thought. In his penultimate paragraph he is still pleading for the best minds and the deepest Christian insights, hammered out under the criticism of many different minds, and fed by the different streams of Christian experience and tradition, to work towards a comprehensiveness, balance and depth of insight, which would be a real expression of Christian unity. "That would seem to be the great adventure to which the Church in this time may be called."[34]

## The conference

Reinhold Niebuhr did come to Oxford. So did the 425 official delegates – 300 of them appointees of the churches, and 125 invited by the Universal Council – and nearly all the other main speakers hoped for, from Emil Brunner to T.S. Eliot, from Pierre Maury to T.Z. Koo of China (though the representation from the "younger churches" was still woefully small). A small conference of the officers, chairmen and secretaries of sections, took place shortly beforehand. John Mott, for once in his life, was privately insecure and, according to one close observer, Eric Fenn, miserable throughout the conference, even if his influence is held, in the opinion of another, to have been "tremendous".[35] It was an alien scene to that over which he had assumed command for a lifetime, of captive audiences waiting for the orders of the day to go out and proclaim the simple Christian message. Here, the question was what is the Christian message in the world of dictatorships and crumbling democracies? He and Oldham had breakfast together every morning, and Oldham briefed him on how to handle the day's proceedings.

The opening plenary took place in the Sheldonian Theatre, the archbishop of Canterbury giving his presidential address. Most of the others were held in the town hall. At the first main meeting, A. Runestam surveyed the story of Life and Work from Stockholm to Oxford, Oldham spoke on "The Meaning and Possibilities of the Oxford Conference", Schönfeld on the work of preparation and, significantly, van Dusen on "The American Approach to the Conference". When it came to the sectional meetings the memoranda, subject of so much debate between Oldham and van Dusen, were largely discarded, and the groups produced their own drafts, redrafts and final reports in that hectic process typical of such gatherings. There was no time for the reports to be fully discussed and adopted in plenary, but they were accepted as worthy of commendation for study by the churches. There can be no doubting the intensity and seriousness of the whole process, and the thoroughness of the work. Oldham was probably right in saying that the new documents "could

[34] Visser 't Hooft and Oldham, p.254.
[35] Hopkins, John R. Mott, p.687.

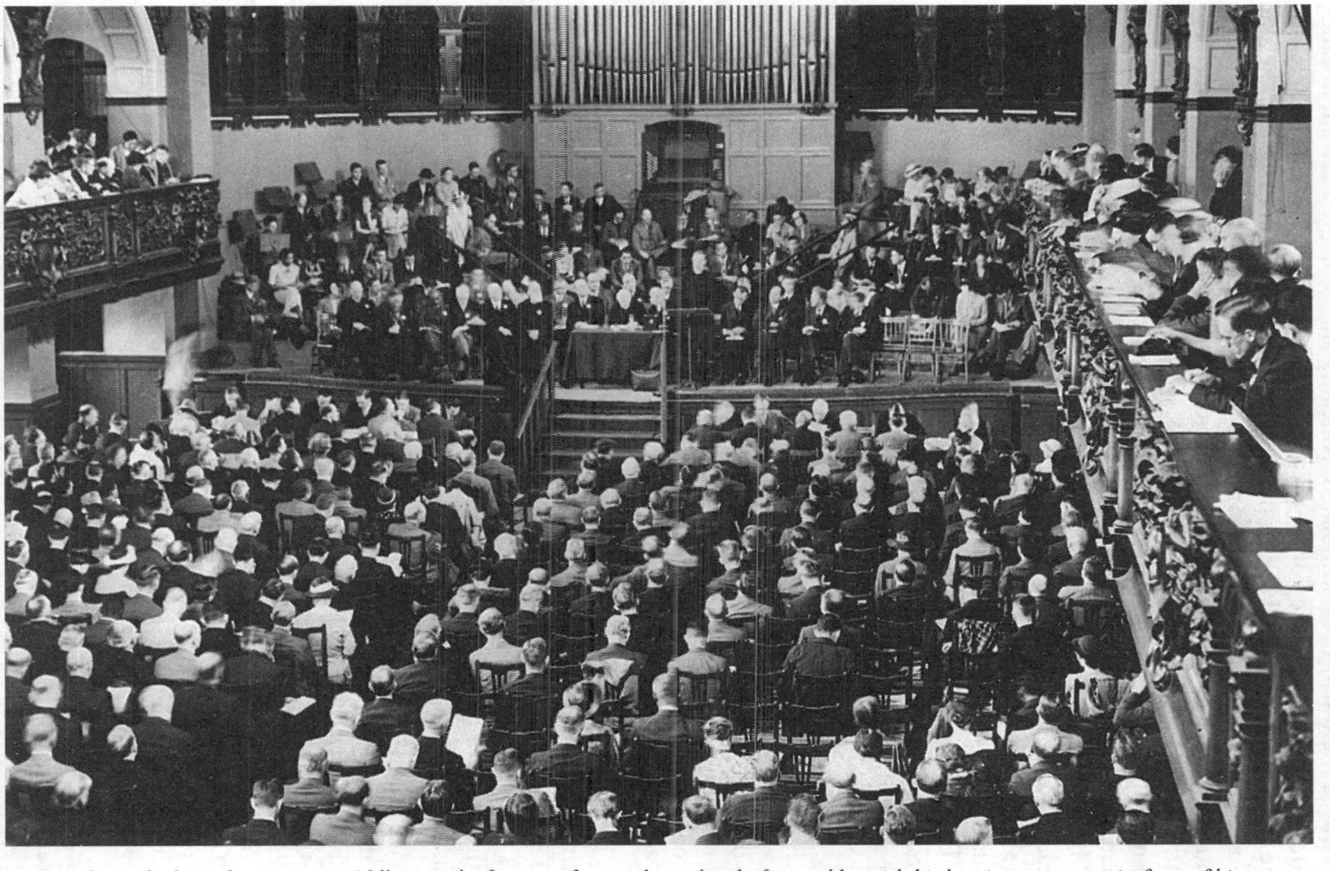

*The Oxford Conference, 1937. Oldham is the figure 1st from right at the platform table, with his hearing-apparatus in front of him.*

hardly have assumed the form they did ... unless the minds of those who produced them had been stimulated, educated and brought a certain distance along the road by the study of the preparatory material".[36] He, at least, felt that the study programme had been vindicated. Nor was it, Oldham stated, the aim of the conference "to issue authoritative pronouncements on large, difficult and controversial subjects".[37] Rather, what was offered was "as comprehensive and balanced a statement as was possible, in the time and with the resources at its disposal, of the present mind of the Church". What had resulted was material for further reflection. "The next step is to take these conclusions arrived at by prolonged common labour, to examine them critically in the light of practical experience, and so advance step by step to a deeper understanding of the mission and responsibilities of the Church in relation to the life of men today."

For many participants, the daily worship sessions, including silent prayer, arranged in St Mary's by F.A. Cockin (later bishop of Bristol) were as important a part of the experience as any other aspect of the two weeks. Oldham himself wrote:

> It is hardly possible to convey to those who were not present what the daily united worship in a company drawn from many countries, peoples, and races, meant to those who took part in it. In the periods of silence there was often an overpowering sense that things were happening in the spiritual world, and that in the coming years one might expect to see in the breaking out of new life in countless directions an answer to the prayers that were being offered together to God.[38]

The conference message was drawn up by a committee chaired by William Temple, and was largely his own work. It includes the famous statement "We do not call the world to be like ourselves, for we are already too like the world ... The call to ourselves and to the world is to Christ"[39] and ends with an affirmation of faith which, two years later as the world slid into war yet again, was even more apposite:

> We have tried during these days at Oxford to look without illusion at the chaos and disintegration of the world, the injustices of the social order and the menace and horror of war. The world is anxious and bewildered and full of pain and fear. We are troubled yet we do not fear. Our hope is anchored in the living God. In Christ, and in the union of man with God and of man with man, which He creates, life even in face of all these evils has a meaning. In His Name we set our hands, as the servants of God and in Him of one another, to the task of proclaiming God's message of redemption, of living as His children, and of combating injustice, cruelty, and hate. The Church can be of good cheer; it hears its Lord saying, "I have overcome the world".[40]

[36] Oldham, *The Churches Survey Their Task*: *The Report of the Conference at Oxford, July 1937, on Church, Community and State*, London, Allen & Unwin, 1937, p.23.

[37] *Ibid.*, p.25.

[38] *Ibid.*, pp.18f.

[39] *Ibid.*, p.57.

[40] *Ibid.*, p.63.

No one could have breathed a more fervent "Amen" to this than Joe Oldham himself. In the weeks immediately following Oxford he had to see to the compilation of the full reports of the conference. He and Fenn completed this by mid-August and the volume appeared in the autumn as *The Churches Survey Their Task*. Some sections have obviously dated. Other parts remain classic statements of perennial issues for Christian mission and ethics: the interrelationship of love and justice, of the commitment to peace and the legitimacy of the use of force in international order, and the tensions between national loyalty and membership of the universal fellowship of the church, to name but some. The autumn also saw at last the publication of the remaining six preparatory reports. These have never had their full due of recognition, partly because the main stock of copies was destroyed in the bombing of London. But with *The Church and Its Function in Society* and *The Churches Survey Their Task*, Oxford 1937 bequeathed a rich and continuing legacy for ecumenical thought. And Britain's most ancient university recognized the unique contribution of one of its sons by awarding J.H. Oldham an honorary DD.

The Oxford conference was followed almost immediately by the second world conference on Faith and Order in Edinburgh. Between the two meetings, and for participants in both, Archbishop Lang held a service in St Paul's Cathedral. The linking of the two conferences was significant. Oxford had not been solely occupied with the stated theme of the conference. Developments were already afoot on issues vital for the whole ecumenical movement and its future organization, and in these, as we shall now see, Oldham was also intimately involved.

CHAPTER 15

# *Towards a World Council of Churches 1933–39*

In historical retrospect, a sense of logical inevitability attaches to the formation of institutions which have now been in existence for half a century or more, during which time they have come to be taken for granted as central expressions of vital interests. Yet, if we date the start of the modern ecumenical movement from Edinburgh 1910, twenty-eight years were to elapse before the decisive and conclusive steps were taken in the formation of the World Council of Churches in 1938. True, immediately after the 1914–18 war the concept of a "League of Churches" was canvassed in a number of quarters, and in 1920 the Ecumenical Patriarchate put out a proposal for a *koinonia* of churches.[1] But it was only from about 1933 that the idea of a single inclusive ecumenical body began to be discussed seriously, let alone to take shape. And when concrete proposals were eventually set out in 1937, it was by no means inevitable that they would find universal acceptance among those churches and organizations which had hitherto been active in the ecumenical movement. Or perhaps one should say "ecumenical movements", for the International Missionary Council, the Universal Christian Council on Life and Work, Faith and Order, the WSCF and YMCA, etc. were all independent expressions of efforts at greater Christian unity. By the late 1920s each had developed its own sense of identity and purpose, its own method and style of activity.

On the other hand these bodies were by no means unrelated to one another. A good number of their leading personnel were involved in more than one of the organizations, and knew each other well. William Temple, for example, was not only president of the Continuation Committee of the 1927 Faith and Order conference, but had been active at the 1928 world missionary conference

[1] See W.A. Visser 't Hooft in Rouse and Neill, eds, *A History of the Ecumenical Movement 1517–1948*, p.697.

in Jerusalem and drafter of its message. People like Deissmann of Germany and Hamilcar of Greece were on the committees of both Life and Work and Faith and Order. John Mott had his feet squarely in both the IMC and the WSCF. Moreover, it became apparent that while the respective agendas of the various organizations might have distinctive priorities, at certain points they also manifested converging and even overlapping interests. Life and Work, for example, had been deeply concerned for interchurch dialogue as such and not just social-ethical issues; and we have seen how under Oldham's leadership the IMC had from the start embraced a concept of mission inclusive of the socio-political sphere.

By the early 1930s, the very growth of these bodies and the increasing demands they were making on their constituents meant that voices began to be raised on the need for greater coordination of effort and pooling of resources. Significantly, the concern was felt particularly in the student ecumenical bodies which represented a constituency concerned for the whole agenda of united Christian action, not one or another aspect of it. Why this confusing situation, it was asked, of having to relate to several such bodies? In 1932 George Bell, on behalf of Life and Work, enquired of a large number of church leaders on the desirability of holding the next world conferences on Life and Work and on Faith and Order at the same place and about the same time. There was overwhelming support for this plan, which effectively was realized at Oxford and Edinburgh in 1937.

## Oldham's role

J.H. Oldham himself, in his proposals at the international missionary conference in Crans, June 1920, for the formation of an International Missionary Council, had envisaged that the council "would probably have before long to give way to something that may represent the beginnings of a world league of Churches".[2] It is highly likely that Oldham had been influenced by the Round Table Group in England, led by Lionel Curtis, several members of which had been instrumental in the formation of the League of Nations.[3] There is no evidence, however, that in the following decade Oldham gave such grand schemes much further thought. His main energies had gone into making the IMC agenda as inclusive as possible, and into tackling the problems of Asia and (especially) Africa. But as we have seen, from the period immediately following the 1928 Jerusalem conference he was growing increasingly restive over the need for a more adventurous engagement with a growing secularist world, and casting around for a suitable instrument. He eventually found it in Life and Work. But his route towards this organization lay through the student

[2] *Ibid.*

[3] *Ibid.* In researching for his article Visser 't Hooft consulted Oldham by letter. Oldham's reply of 20 Sept. 1952 [OA] underlines the influence Curtis had on his views, especially on matters of constitutional principle and the need of a secretariat in international relations. Oldham also states that there was little connection between his own suggestions and the proposals of the Ecumenical Patriarch.

bodies. The significance for Oldham of his renewed contacts with the student scene from about 1930, especially the Geneva-based WSCF and YMCA and the new, young leadership being provided by the likes of W.A. Visser 't Hooft and Francis Miller, cannot be stressed too highly. It was here that he discovered a new openness to the contemporary world and, above all, future ecumenical leaders in whose character, gifts and vision he could place confidence.

It was on the initiative of William Adams Brown of the USA, then chairman of the administrative committee of Life and Work, that the first meeting took place which was to mark the first step towards a linking together of the various ecumenical bodies. As early as 1928 he had gone on record stating that Faith and Order and Life and Work could not be permanently kept apart.[4] In 1933 Brown spent much time in Europe and made ecumenical coordination one of his chief concerns.[5] He proposed to William Temple that the responsible leaders of the main organizations should meet together to see what could be done to achieve this. Temple not only agreed but hosted the meeting at Bishopthorpe Palace, York, in May 1933. Ten people attended: Oldham and Bill Paton for the IMC; Temple and H.N. Bate for Faith and Order; Brown and Samuel McCrea Cavert for Life and Work; Valdemar Ammundsen and H.L. Henriod for the World Alliance for International Friendship through the Churches; and Visser 't Hooft and Charles Guillion for the YMCA and WSCF. It was an entirely unofficial and informal gathering of people who for the most part already knew and respected each other. It did not produce any immediate results or even, apparently, shape any further proposals. But as Visser 't Hooft recalls: "The completely informal, non-prelatical atmosphere which the Archbishop and Mrs Temple created, the good stories that were told, always accompanied by that high-pitched laughter of Temple himself, led to the result that, without as yet committing ourselves to any specific plan, we became a group of people united by the common purpose of giving the ecumenical movement a more truly ecumenical shape."[6]

We have no record of whatever part Oldham played in this meeting. It is evident, however, that he regarded the issues as important enough to warrant continuing the discussion. About a month later, on 19 June, he wrote to Francis Miller: "You have probably heard from Visser 't Hooft of an interesting informal meeting at York of representatives of the five ecumenical organisations. I subsequently had Adams Brown and [Leonard] Hodgson, who has taken on the secretaryship of Faith and Order, down to stay with me and I am to spend half a day with Adams Brown at the end of this week." Apart from this, we have few indications of Oldham's thinking before the next meeting of the "Consultative Group", as it came to be called, in Paris in August 1934. By now, as we have seen, Oldham was increasingly interested in Life and Work – and was on the point of engaging with it at the expense of the IMC. He was also

[4] Visser 't Hooft, in Rouse and Neill, *History*, p.699.
[5] *Ibid.*
[6] W.A. Visser 't Hooft, *Memoirs*, London, SCM, 1973, p.77.

realizing that relating to the wider ecumenical scene as a whole was going to prove a particular challenge for the IMC itself. Early in May 1934 he and Bill Paton discussed these issues at some length, and Oldham wrote to Mott warning that "It becomes more and more plain that . . . the question of our relations with the other ecumenical movements cannot be evaded. It will come up in a quite definite form in connection with the proposed conference of Faith and Order and of Life and Work in 1937 and in particular with the latter since they will have to decide at the meeting in Denmark in August how they will organise their fifth section which relates to the mission field." Oldham was anxious to draw Mott into conversation with Temple and George Bell, and also with Leonard Hodgson, Visser 't Hooft and other members of the Consultative Group, when Mott would be in Britain later in the summer. At the same time, Oldham in typical fashion believed the Consultative Group should retain its unofficial status and informal style:

> In regard to the Consultative Group I have always held (in opposition to Adams Brown) that it is undesirable to give the Consultative Group either a definite constitution or a fixed membership or regular meetings. I think it will be most useful if it is nothing more than the occasional getting together of persons related to the various ecumenical movements as occasion requires. It does not matter therefore whether we call the little group that would meet when you are here a meeting of the Consultative Group or not.[7]

That Oldham, at this stage, was still thinking in terms of sensible co-ordination and agreed allocation of tasks among the ecumenical bodies, rather than the creation of a new organizational structure, is underlined by his remarks to Francis Miller a month later, in June; "it becomes increasingly clear that the real problem is how through consultation we can make the best use of the very limited resources at our disposal."[8] *Which* group should carry out which task was in itself of no consequence provided the most appropriate persons were doing it. Thus for example the Life and Work people were tackling church and nation issues – the WSCF should leave it to them.

Oldham attended the meeting of the Consultative Group in Paris in early August 1934, that is, shortly before the Fanö meeting of Life and Work which was to be so decisive both for that movement and for Oldham himself. Again, little is known of this Paris meeting but it appears that Adams Brown produced a detailed memorandum on the various ways in which the five main bodies might collaborate, and that Oldham introduced a discussion setting the whole question in the context of the total task of the church in the modern world.[9]

Thereafter, the next important step took place in late 1935, when the American sections of Life and Work and Faith and Order arranged for an informal consultation in Princeton, at the home of J. Ross Stevenson. William

[7] JHO letter to Mott 8 May 1934 [OA].
[8] JHO letter to Miller 8 June 1934 [OA].
[9] Visser 't Hooft, in Rouse and Neill, *History*, p.699.

Temple was visiting the USA, as were Oldham and Bill Paton. Thus the IMC was also represented, as were the World Alliance and the WSCF. This time, Temple took the lead in suggesting that the time had come for an "interdenominational, international council representing all the churches, with committees to carry on various projects now forming the objectives of the distinct world movements".[10] The meeting needed no further urging on this objective, but spelled out in more detail the need for greater coordination: the need to present the ecumenical task to the churches as a single common task; the need for a body through which the churches could speak together to the world; the more effective relating of the "younger churches" to the ecumenical movement; and, of increasing urgency in that historical context of resurgent nationalisms, the call for united witness in a world where nationalism was savaging the ideal of universal Christendom. The meeting recommended that the Consultative Group be given regular status, and that the bodies represented on it should take appropriate action to make the existing cooperation more effective. New opportunities – or at least expectations – were thus created at Princeton.

"The man who translated those opportunities into specific and concrete proposals was Dr J.H. Oldham," writes W.A. Visser 't Hooft in the official history of the ecumenical movement. Yet again, unfortunately, it has to be confessed that very little hard information has survived on what precisely Oldham thought and did between the Princeton consultation and the meeting of the council of Life and Work at Chamby in August 1936. But Oldham produced for Chamby a memorandum on the need to seize both the challenge of the urgent historic situation, and the opportunity created by the forthcoming Oxford and Edinburgh conferences:

> The holding of the ecumenical conferences in 1937 provides an opportunity which will not recur for many years, of having the whole question of the future of the ecumenical movement examined afresh . . . In the historical crisis in which the Church finds itself there is need of facing these questions with the greatest deliberation and of bringing to bear on them the best statesmanship that the Church can command. The best means of doing this would seem to be the appointment in consultation with the other ecumenical movements of a committee which would meet prior to the conferences at Oxford and Edinburgh and present a report to the conferences.[11]

Not, notice, a plan for a new structure: rather, a *method* for arriving at it. It was typical of Oldham's strategy, to hold to a long-term view but to declare only the next step along the way. The proposal actually put to the Chamby meeting, as presented by George Bell, was for a commission of 30 persons "to review the work of oecumenical cooperation since the Stockholm and Lausanne Conferences, and to make recommendations to the Oxford and Edinburgh Conferences regarding the future policy, organisation and work of the

[10] *Ibid.*, p.701.
[11] *Ibid.*, pp.701f.

oecumenical movement".[12] The commission would be nominated by the Consultative Group, and as well as comprising occupants of ecclesiastical responsibility in the churches, would include representatives of the point of view of laymen, women and youth, together with the officers of ecumenical movements. The Council unanimously approved the proposal. The committee of Faith and Order likewise agreed in September, and the committees of the World Alliance and the IMC followed suit. Implementation of the next stage fell to the Consultative Group which met in London in October 1936. The proposed committee to meet in 1937 would now comprise thirty-five people, and in fact was henceforth known as the "Committee of Thirty-Five". The Consultative Group drew up the list of thirty-five names. They included obvious choices among the seasoned ecumenical leaders and campaigners: Oldham himself, John Mott, George Bell, S.M. Cavert, William Temple, Marc Boegner, H.L. Henriod, Leonard Hodgson, Walter Moberly, Bill Paton, Hans Schönfeld and W.A. Visser 't Hooft. But also included were relative newcomers to the scene such as the Baptist M.E. Aubrey representing the British Free Churches and a young Dutch woman, C.M. van Asch van Wijck, for the YWCA.[13] The Committee of Thirty-Five would meet in July 1937, immediately prior to the Oxford conference.

The first six months of 1937, it has been seen, were already filled with well-nigh crushing responsibilities and anxieties for Oldham in the preparations for Oxford. The planning for ecumenical organization post-Oxford and post-Edinburgh was, as far as Oldham was concerned, a sub-plot within the main preparations for Oxford. But he knew that once the Committee of Thirty-Five had met that theme would take on a momentum of its own, and very quickly. Mental space needed to be found within all the pressing cares of church, community and state in preparation for that vital meeting of the Thirty-Five. In fact until late in the day he kept his cards very close to his chest, thinking only in the broadest terms of what the future organization might comprise: a means of bringing Life and Work and Faith and Order together, with appropriate links also for the other "movements"; offices in Geneva, London and New York; and with a continuing emphasis upon "research". On one matter, however, Oldham was precise and emphatic: what counted above all was the person who would be in overall executive charge. And, in private at least, he had no doubts who that person should be – Wim Visser 't Hooft. Indeed, Oldham is on record as saying that *only* if Visser 't Hooft was to be secretary of the new body did he consider it worth bothering with.

As the leading figures began arriving in Britain for the Oxford conference, Oldham talked with them severally at Chipstead or in London. An extraordinarily sharp picture of Oldham's thinking, and of certain of the anxieties he was provoking in others, is given in a letter from Henry van Dusen to John Mott of 3 July. Van Dusen (not a member of the Thirty-Five) had with

[12] Life and Work Council Minutes, Chamby 1936, p.55.
[13] For the full list, see report of the Oxford conference, *The Churches Survey Their Task*, pp.278f.

John Bennett been staying at Chipstead and discussed both Oxford and what might lie beyond:

Oldham's ideas of what should eventuate from the Committee of Thirty-Five, and which he will be sharing with you when you meet, seem to be on the whole thoroughly sound and just about what we have all been coming to. He appears to envision a new World Christian Counsel [*sic., passim*] into which would be funded the present activities of both Life and Work and Faith and Order, and also all that has been begun in connection with Oxford. There are two points at which I am not so sure of the wisdom of his views:

a. As to the structure and center of reference of the new Counsel. He seems to think of it as primarily concerned with the type of study and conference which he has initiated for Oxford. This is inevitable in view of his conviction of the preeminent importance of the undertaking he has been guiding. I am not confident that its *preeminent* worth has been demonstrated. We cannot be sure of that until after Oxford, perhaps until some years hence. It would be a major tragedy if the Committee of Thirty-Five were unduly swayed by Oldham's deep and sincere conviction that this way lies the one promising and greatly significant effort in Christian unity. Positively, I would think the new Counsel, if formed, should represent far more a genuine merger of the two existing movements with Oldham's plans for "research" holding an important but distinctly secondary place in the total enterprise. Moreover, although my own natural interests turn almost wholly to Life and Work matters, I am convinced that Oldham greatly underrates the significance of the Faith and Order movement and its present very real achievements.

b. As to the leadership of the new Council. Here, also, Oldham's general plan seems thoroughly sound offices in Geneva, London and New York, with a small staff at each center (eventually there should surely be a center in the Far East). And his ideas on personnel – himself and Fenn in London; Leiper and Bennett (for as much time as he can give) in New York; Schönfeld and Ehrenström in Geneva – are admirable. My only query here concerns the major executive leadership. Naturally, Oldham tends to think of someone whose main interest is in the one thing which seems to Oldham important. His best present suggestion is 't Hooft. Quite probably, 't Hooft is the best possible person who might be available, although many of the considerations which have somewhat limited his effectiveness in the WSCF would apply equally here. The important point is that there be a clear idea of the *kind* of person needed. It would seem to me that what is desired as General Secretary is a man of very real administrative gifts with a deep feeling for "the care of the churches" and a competent and unqualified sympathy with the importance of Oldham's plans for further study and conference. Cavert or Paton would represent the ideal; and, while it may not be possible to find such a man, it is important that the ideal be held in view.

Oldham was evidently hoping to continue as chairman of whatever committee on research would be set up by the new Council. Van Dusen found this prospect congenial – but warned against allowing Oldham to become chairman either of the Council or its administrative committee, and equally against someone "too readily subservient to Oldham's views" occupying these positions. This, said van Dusen, was written "in great frankness not at all through lack of appreciation of Oldham's matchless gifts and his invaluable contributions, but through recognition of certain limitations which have become increasingly apparent in the preparations for Oxford". What those limitations were, in van Dusen's and other American eyes, have been noted earlier: an overly Eurocentric outlook in theology and a somewhat narrow emphasis upon "study".

## The Westfield College meeting

The Committee of Thirty-Five met at Westfield College, London, 8–10 July 1937. In some ways the gathering was a kind of enlarged version of the Consultative Group, and certainly a degree of informality prevailed. Temple was in the chair. No specific plan was presented to the meeting on paper, and no formal minutes were taken.[14] There had evidently been sufficient conversation beforehand among the main architects – Oldham, Temple, Adams Brown and Cavert – to enable agreement on essentials to be reached quickly and, given a strong lead from Temple in particular, for a unanimously agreed report to be drawn up for presentation to the Oxford and Edinburgh conferences. The report was brief, the actual recommendations running to less than 900 words. Under the heading "A World Council of Churches" (the title was owed to Cavert), the first paragraph stated simply but with infinite care:

> That the Conference regards it as desirable that, with a view to facilitating the more effective action of the Christian Church in the modern world, the movements known as "Life and Work" and "Faith and Order" should be more closely related in a body representative of the Churches and caring for the interests of each Movement.

The new organization would have no power to legislate for the churches or commit them to action without their consent, but it must deserve and win the respect of the churches so that the most influential people in the life of the churches may be willing to give time and thought to its work. The next two paragraphs are Oldham through and through:

> Further, the witness which the Church in the modern world is called to give is such that in certain spheres the predominant voice in the utterance of it must be that of lay people holding posts of responsibility and influence in the secular world.
>
> For both these reasons, a first-class Intelligence Staff is indispensable in order that material for discussion and action may be adequately prepared.[15]

The responsibilities of the new body would include carrying on the work of the two world conferences; facilitating corporate action by the churches; promoting cooperation in study and the growth in ecumenical consciousness in the churches; an ecumenical journal; communication with the other various ecumenical bodies and worldwide denominational federations; and to call world

[14] See Visser 't Hooft, *Memoirs*, p.78 for a full account.
[15] *The Churches Survey Their Task*, p.279.

conferences on specific subjects as occasion required. There would be a general assembly of representatives of the churches meeting every five years, and a central council of approximately sixty members which would be the committee of the general assembly, meeting annually, its membership being constituted mainly on a regional basis and one-third to be laymen or laywomen as far as possible. This feature was advanced by Oldham and provoked the longest discussion in the whole plan, but eventually carried.[16] There would be a commission for the further study of Faith and Order subjects to be appointed at Edinburgh, and a commission similarly for Life and Work study "to be appointed by the Central Council with a view to facilitating common Christian action". Finally, the report recommended that Oxford and Edinburgh each appoint seven members to a constituent committee to complete the details and bring the scheme into existence.

Thus was drafted the ground-plan of what eventually became the World Council of Churches. The main features remained in the constitution adopted at Amsterdam in 1948, and still operate half a century later: a body representative of the churches but with no power to legislate for them or to carry authority over them, with a general assembly and a central council (committee). It was the regional, at the expense of the confessional, emphasis in representation on the central council which was to prove the most contentious feature of the Westfield proposals. It should be noted, too, that the Westfield meeting saw the crucial matter as being the linking of Faith and Order with Life and Work, the two bodies constituted by mandated representatives of the churches themselves. The relationship of the new body to the IMC, WSCF, etc. was regarded as important but a matter for further discussion.

If Temple was the overall architect of this plan, it was Oldham who was the design engineer for many of its most crucial features, and not only in the emphasis on the role of the laity. With Marc Boegner, he had insisted that the new council must be rooted in the life of the churches: "We want the national churches to think of their problems as part of an ecumenical body."[17] But for Oldham, the constitution to be set down on paper was only one aspect. Right at the beginning of the meeting he drew Visser 't Hooft aside and asked whether he would be willing to become the executive officer of a new ecumenical body if it was to be created. "To such a very vague question I could only give a very vague answer." Almost at the close of the meeting, Visser 't Hooft was asked to leave the room while the question of staffing was discussed. "After a while Archbishop Temple informed me that 'the 35' had unanimously expressed the conviction that I should be the principal staff member of the new Council. He said that by gifts and experience I was clearly the man to take this place."[18] Oldham's view, conveyed by quiet lobbying as much as by address to the Thirty-Five as a whole, had prevailed. Visser 't Hooft later likened this to being invited

[16] Visser 't Hooft, *Memoirs*, p.79.
[17] *Ibid.*, p.78.
[18] *Ibid.*

to live in a house for which there was as yet only a blueprint and even the prospective owners (the churches) had still to give an opinion as to whether they wanted it. Due both to circumstances and to caution about his own capacities, he was to remain uncertain for many months. But clearly a process was afoot opening up a daunting prospect of responsibilities for someone only 36 years old.

Just two days after Westfield, the Oxford conference opened. The report of the Thirty-Five was presented by William Temple to a plenary session on 19 July, with final voting three days later. The proposals had a notably smooth ride. The report was adopted. It was agreed to appoint a Constituent Committee, if the Edinburgh Conference likewise agreed. The business committee, at the request of the conference, nominated the seven names: Marc Boegner, William Adams Brown, George Bell, Archbishop Germanos, Bishop Marahrens, John Mott, and Oldham.

## Faith and Order: married yet staying single?

Everything now depended on the Faith and Order conference, meeting at Edinburgh 3–18 August. Oldham was not a participant at Edinburgh, visiting the conference only fleetingly to meet with the Oxford appointees to the Constituent Committee. For once, and somewhat disconcertingly from his point of view, events in the ecumenical process were quite outside his control or direct influence. Not only was Oldham not physically present at Edinburgh, these two weeks revealed an Achilles heel in his ecumenism: Faith and Order, alone of almost all the ecumenical movements, had remained a world outside his ken. True, he had always taken the church seriously, theologically and practically, and it was precisely his perception of the need for a new self-understanding of the church as a community in relation to society, that had undergirded his work for the Oxford conference. But for Oldham, issues of visible, structural unity and intercommunion were always marginal to the questions of cooperation and united witness in society. This is a legitimate emphasis and the tension between "Life and Work" and "Faith and Order" approaches continues in ecumenism down to the present. But to be without any real experience of or empathy with the concerns of Faith and Order suddenly became a critical disadvantage in the delicate process of bringing that movement together with Life and Work in a new, inclusive ecumenical body. It was at this point that, undoubtedly, the major credit must go to William Temple, not Oldham, for piloting the ecumenical ship safely. Essentially a Faith and Order figure yet deeply involved at Oxford and committed to the Life and Work agenda, only Temple had large enough stature in each movement to carry complete confidence from both constituencies.

By the end of the Oxford conference it was apparent that while Life and Work had uttered a virtually unanimous "Yes" to the Westfield recommendations, trouble would be met from other quarters. One such quarter was the Reich church of Germany. Bishop Heckel, for his own strategic reasons, was alarmed at the prospect of Faith and Order, where he saw greater prospect of ensuring ecumenical contacts for his Reich Church, now uniting with Life and Work where, its "friendly contact" with all German church groups notwithstanding, more overt sympathy was expressed for the Confessing Church. Temple and Oldham shared with each other their correspondence with Heckel.[19] Both agreed that for the present all that could be said was that the scheme would only be brought into existence by the will of the churches. More immediately and substantially to be faced was the disquiet from circles within Faith and Order itself, most notably from A.C. Headlam, bishop of Gloucester. Moreover, for good measure, Headlam was a vociferous supporter of the Reich church – and even of some of the "German Christians" – and highly critical of the Confessing Church leadership. Oldham met Headlam for a talk at the Athenaeum immediately after Oxford. Archbishop Lang had also told him that some of the American Episcopalians were similarly distrustful of a proposal which seemed to threaten the identity of the Faith and Order movement and the furtherance of its distinct concerns. Oldham arranged to meet one of the leading Episcopalians, Bishop Perry, for discussion. Oldham wrote to Temple:

> I think the answer to all these people . . . is that the intention of the new move is to bring into existence a more representative and weighty body than the Universal Christian Council and that if the new council can be made truly representative of the Churches we ought to trust their collective wisdom since there is nothing better that we have to trust. I tried to impress on the Bishop of Gloucester that the new council would be just as dependent in the last resort on the Churches themselves as Faith and Order is and also that precisely because of the dangers he scents of the Churches getting mixed up in politics we ought to have a body which can enlist the wisest minds at the disposal of the Church in the continuous study of these difficult questions. I made the same point to the Archbishop of Canterbury who heartily agreed that it was the real and convincing answer.[20]

Headlam went to Edinburgh with his fears unallayed by Oldham. There was lively discussion on the Westfield proposals. Most were strongly in favour, or at least were persuaded by Temple, Mott and Boegner that the new council would safeguard and advance Faith and Order's concerns. But the recommendations were agreed to only if certain conditions were fulfilled in the constitution of the new body. The matter of "political" interference was raised again by Headlam during discussion of the report on the section on the church's unity in life and worship. But few were disposed to take seriously the views of a prelate who evidently considered that Bishop Bell's letters to *The Times* in support of Martin Niemöller were "political" while his own welcoming of a visit from Joachim Hossenfelder, leader of the "German Christians", was not.

The reports of suspicion and caution at Edinburgh reached Oldham in London. He professed not to be unduly worried. Such an atmosphere easily

[19] Temple letter to JHO 24 July 1937, JHO letter to Temple 29 July 1937 [OA].
[20] JHO, letter to Temple 29 July 1937 [OA].

arose "especially when people are tired". Quiet work with individuals would be in order.

Oldham was alarmed, however, on being told that Faith and Order, regardless of progress towards the formation of the new World Council, intended to reappoint its own Continuation Committee and keep it in being for the foreseeable future whereas at Oxford Life and Work had taken the plunge to sink its own structure and identity entirely within the new body. Oldham wrote to Temple at Edinburgh suggesting that if there was to be a Faith and Order Continuation Committee, it might be reduced in size and function, comprising a small group of theologians. Faith and Order concerns generally would be catered for within the central council of the new body. He also enlisted Mott in pushing this idea, on the assumption that the veteran American would inevitably carry weight. Temple's reply from Edinburgh was one of the most vigorous rebuttals Oldham ever received from anyone:

> I have very seldom found myself in almost diametrical difference from you, and as that happens on this occasion I feel obliged to attribute the fact to your having had no close associations with the Faith and Order Movement. Its whole essence has been conversations of the widest possible scale: and if we were now to propose that its Continuation Committee should be confined to a small group of theologians, while a body also responsible for many other interests [the Central Council] became the focus of these conversations, I think that all the goodwill that we have now gathered here would be scattered in a moment, and the chances of cooperation ruined. I find this view shared by everyone I have consulted, who is intimately acquainted with the movement. There is also, whether fairly or not, a sense in many quarters that the movement is under threat of being "managed" by people whose association with it is mainly due to their concern for the new organisation rather than for its own business. If I were to reveal the fact that Mott, who has never been at one of these meetings before, himself prepared a list for the American representation on a reduced Continuation Committee I should evoke boisterous laughter and determined resistance. But I have managed, I think, to keep that secret from everyone except my wife![21]

Mott and Adams Brown, who were on the business committee at Edinburgh, eventually had to concede the Faith and Order anxieties: the new council might not be in existence for quite some time, and it could not be known how much time and effort the new assembly would devote to Faith and Order matters. To keep the Continuation Committee in being seemed a natural precaution. Faith and Order, Temple told Oldham, must be permitted to grow into the other "and not be transferred into it by abrupt administrative action". And, Temple concluded, "I think the fashioning of the new instrument is going to be a matter of very great delicacy, and I think that many of the Churches are going to take a great deal of persuasion."

Oldham's instant reply to Temple was emollient but equally frank:

[21] Temple letter to JHO 14 Aug. 1937 [OA].

> You are quite right in thinking that in putting forward one side of considerations I underestimated through lack of a sufficiently close touch the things that would weigh with the Faith and Order Movement. I am quite satisfied that there is a way out along the lines of your letter, even though progress may be smaller than it might have been. My anxiety was (and to some extent still is) that people at Edinburgh may lose sight of the urgency of the problems with which the Oxford Conference was concerned and fail to realise that the Oxford Conference, on the strength of a report from a committee so representative as the Committee of Thirty-Five, put all its eggs into the one basket and made no provision for an alternative scheme for carrying forward its work if this should fail.[22]

It was, said Oldham, "rather unfortunate" that the Life and Work interests at Edinburgh had been in the hands of Mott "who has no great understanding of the ecclesiastical mind", and of the ageing Adams Brown. Oldham felt he could himself do a better job if he could sit round a table with the likes of Headlam: "There would not be much difficulty in arriving at an understanding which would give them what they want, and at the same time secure what seems to me important." Oldham hurried to Edinburgh for one day and after conversation with Temple thought that he had changed the archbishop's mind. Eight months later he could still write with some bitterness of the episode:

> Speaking quite confidentially I have always regarded the action of the Edinburgh Conference as short-sighted and stupid. The ease with which a large body of intelligent people succumb, as they continually do, to the temptation to both have their cake and eat it constantly mystifies me. What the resolutions of the Edinburgh Conference say on any objective view of their meaning is that the Faith and Order Movement intends to be married and with equal determination to stay single. I did my best in the one day I was in Edinburgh to stop this folly and thought I had persuaded the Archbishop of York. But other people got hold of him and he failed to stand by his guns.[23]

## The Committee of Fourteen

At any rate, the Edinburgh conference appointed its seven members for the Constituent Committee, and this met for a preliminary consultation in London on 19 August, the day after the Edinburgh conference ended. Temple was in the chair. It opened with tension and anxiety on both Life and Work and Faith and Order sides – Oldham felt particularly the disadvantage faced by the former group in not having time to meet together beforehand and consider the implications of the tactics adopted at Edinburgh – and it lasted only three hours. However, the meeting came up with the concrete proposal for the next vital step: for invitations to be issued to the churches to send representatives to a provisional conference in Holland, 9–13 May 1938. This conference would draw up a constitution for the proposed World Council to be submitted to the

[22] JHO letter to Temple 16 Aug. 1937 [OA].
[23] JHO letter to Visser 't Hooft 26 April 1938 [OA].

churches, and also make provision for the maintenance of the work of both Life and Work and Faith and Order for the period prior to the first general assembly. Oldham fought very hard for this second provision, "pointing out that Faith and Order had provided for their future by appointing a continuation committee, while Oxford had made no such provision".[24] This decision would be implemented by a committee comprising Temple, Boegner, Adams Brown, Bell, Archbishop Germanos, Ross Stevenson, Mott and Oldham, with the assistance of Hans Schönfeld. Since only Oldham and Schönfeld would be in a position to devote their whole time to the work, Oldham felt gratified that the actual preparation would in fact be in their hands. This London meeting was another of those moments in his career when Oldham felt that through sustained effort and a sovereign providence, more than could have been hoped for had been achieved, and problems overcome in a miraculous way: "It was a strenuous and sustained fight to secure points that seemed to me vital – often of apparently minor character, but actually if decided wrongly likely to create insuperable difficulties for Life and Work. In the end we secured everything that seemed to me essential – and with the complete goodwill of the whole committee."

For the next few months, as well as the follow-up to Oxford, preparations for the meeting in Holland were a main preoccupation for Oldham. There were, however, those who challenged his assumption that this preoccupation should be mainly his, or shared with Schönfeld. The hurried meeting of the Committee of Fourteen in London on 19 August had left unclear just who had executive responsibility for preparing for the meeting in Holland. Cavert (Life and Work) and Hodgson (Faith and Order) had acted as minute secretaries. When Oldham began acting on the assumption that for obvious practical reasons the preparatory work would be up to himself and Schönfeld, H.L. Henriod, secretary for Life and Work, evidently felt threatened and marginalized. Henriod, who had not even been made a member of the Constituent Committee, and whose effectiveness as an executive was questioned by not a few ecumenical colleagues, wrote to William Adams Brown querying the role that Oldham was playing. Oldham received a copy of the letter, and immediately wrote a long letter to Adams Brown in explanation of the position as he saw it.[25] Hodgson and Cavert had acted as minute secretaries at the London meeting of the Constituent Committee – but with no implication that they had any further executive role, and in fact neither of them was in a position to take on any such responsibility. Oldham agreed that the "topsy-turvy" position needed to be cleared up immediately. Energetic action was needed for May 1938. Such church leaders as Oldham had talked to were wholly in favour of the work being done by such as himself and Fenn in London, Schönfeld and Ehrenström in Geneva. Henriod was in any case devoting more time to the World Alliance. Oldham declared himself to be without any personal ambition

[24] JHO letter to Visser 't Hooft 20 Aug. 1937 [OA].
[25] JHO letter to Brown 4 Oct. 1937 [OA].

in the longer term future of the new council – his only concern was for the May 1938 meeting. His view all along had been that the new council must be free to choose its own executive officers and staff.

William Temple tried to settle the matter as chairman of the Committee of Fourteen, with a letter to all members of the Committee, dated 12 October 1937, stating that Oldham, Cavert and Hodgson were joint secretaries, with the task of preparing for the May 1938 meeting to be shared between them "and Dr Oldham can call on the help of the Staff of the Universal Council, which would be at his disposal for this purpose". But his letter made no mention of Henriod, which William Adams Brown felt could create further difficulties.[26] Hodgson being secretary of Faith and Order, his opposite number in Life and Work was neither Cavert nor Oldham but Henriod. Would it not be better to state that Oldham would be working in conjunction with the secretaries of both movements? Cavert, for his own part, in any case wished only to be involved on the American side of preparations.[27] The matter was evidently not solved to everyone's satisfaction, but Oldham continued to work as the main executive in preparation for the May 1938 meeting – on the clear understanding that it was precisely for that meeting, and no further stages, that he was so acting. The official letter-heading for the "Proposed World Council of Churches" listed the Constituent Committee with Temple as Chairman and Cavert and Hodgson as "Secretaries", below which came a sub-heading "Committee of Arrangements for the Conference in Holland", listing no names except that of Oldham as "Chairman".

But if not ambitious for himself, Oldham still had definite convictions as to the person who should be chosen for the chief executive role in the new council. From the close of the Oxford conference he kept Visser 't Hooft fully informed of developments at Edinburgh, in the first meeting of the Constituent Committee and in his correspondence and discussion with ecumenical colleagues, and Visser 't Hooft in turn confided his concerns to Oldham. Soon after Oxford he was wanting clarification on the particular responsibility the council was wanting him to accept, especially as regards the relationship of general secretary to director of study and research.[28] Further, he wanted assurance that he really would be relating equally to Life and Work and Faith and Order – the attitude taken by Faith and Order at the Edinburgh conference worried him as it did Oldham.[29] And what staff would be available to him? Moreover, what really would be the basis of the council – a genuine council of churches or "merely a Federation of Religious Associations"?

Oldham, for his part, was largely concerned with assuring Visser 't Hooft that while a formal invitation would have to await a further stage in the setting up of the Council, there could be no doubting the conviction of people like

[26] Brown letter to Temple 19 Oct. 1937 [OA].
[27] Cavert letter to Temple 19 Oct. 1937 [OA].
[28] Visser 't Hooft letter to JHO 14 Aug. 1937 [OA].
[29] Visser 't Hooft letter to JHO 26 April 1938 [OA].

Temple that, at the very least, Visser 't Hooft's association with the research department would be widely welcomed.[30] To take such assurances as the whole of the story, however, was dangerous. Everyone knew that since the Westfield meeting Visser 't Hooft was a widely tipped favourite for the chief executive post in the new council. But not only was this as yet a quite informal proposition, it was not universally agreed either. Not least was the question of his relative youth. And even among those who had been present at Westfield there were now doubts as to the wisdom of taking that preliminary step. Adams Brown told Temple: "As you know, the action taken at Westfield with regard to Visser 't Hooft has created a situation of tension and embarrassment which I believe would be accentuated by ignoring Henriod further in the form of the appointment."[31] Moreover, during the winter of 1937–38, queries were raised in the United States about the suitability of Visser 't Hooft as overall leader of the new council in comparison with, for example, William Paton. Samuel McCrea Cavert and van Dusen conveyed these doubts to Oldham. Oldham felt that for Paton to go wholly to the World Council "would kill the IMC",[32] but was entirely supportive of Paton having some associated office with Visser 't Hooft – an arrangement he knew would be satisfactory to the latter, anxious as he was to have colleagues of the highest calibre. Early in January 1938 Oldham talked with Visser 't Hooft at a theological students' conference at Swanwick, and was alarmed to hear that rumours had reached him that even Mott had grave doubts about his being made an officer of the World Council, and thought he should continue in the WSCF.

Those familiar with politics, ecclesiastical no less than secular, will recognize the difficulty of discerning motives at this point. Was Oldham really concerned for the future of the IMC, or simply determined that Paton should not be a serious rival to Visser 't Hooft for the WCC post? And was Mott really doubtful about Visser 't Hooft's capacities for the WCC post, or more concerned for the future of the WSCF? Oldham certainly talked the matter over with Bill Paton, who apparently shared his view that Visser 't Hooft could not be thought of otherwise than as at the helm of the WCC and would gladly work with him. Meanwhile Oldham reiterated to van Dusen that he could throw himself into the effort to form a World Council only if it was going to do something substantial, that it could do this only if it had leaders of outstanding calibre, and that there was no one in sight to match Visser 't Hooft's gifts.[33] Suddenly he bursts into one of those theological sallies of enduring significance:

> I believe that efforts of voluntary cooperation between the Churches can succeed only if they have at their disposal an original and creative leadership. It has not pleased God Almighty to create such persons possessing at the same time an all-round balance. We have got to take them with their human limitations and onesidedness and seek

[30] JHO letter to Visser 't Hooft 20 Aug. 1937 [OA].
[31] Brown letter to Temple 19 Oct. 1937 [OA].
[32] JHO letter to van Dusen 7 Jan. 1938 [OA].
[33] *Ibid.*

to supplement them with others possessing complementary gifts. So far from rebelling against this limitation it seems to me to belong to the conception of the Body of Christ that no individual is self-sufficient and that we are all dependent on the gifts and qualities which God has withheld from ourselves and given to others. I have from the beginning shared the anxieties which you and others felt in regard to the sole leadership of Visser 't Hooft. I have said to him quite frankly in almost every conversation that I have had with him that I did not think that we could float the World Council on his sole leadership. It is for this reason that the case seems to me of such overwhelming strength that Paton should be associated with it.

Oldham then schemed to get van Dusen to sound out Mott further on his "doubts", and he himself would also approach Mott without any mention of his contact with van Dusen. Van Dusen's reply[34] showed that the American scene was in one sense more reassuring, and in other senses decidedly less so, than had at first appeared. Mott's "doubts" about Visser 't Hooft, said van Dusen, were probably to be dated before the meetings and conferences of the previous summer, when Mott was still somewhat dubious about the idea of a World Council and mostly concerned with the future of the WSCF. Mott, like all the Americans, had no doubts whatsoever about Visser 't Hooft's indispensability to leadership in the World Council. But their perception of *which* post he should fill was rather different to Oldham's. "In all of the informal conversations before and during Oxford, it seemed to be unanimously understood that 't Hooft was quite indispensable in the leadership of the Council but that he was not the man for the post of Executive Secretary."[35] Visser 't Hooft, they were hoping, would head up the research department, leaving the executive secretaryship to someone else, preferably Paton.

The situation was virtually impossible to resolve in advance of the formation of the only body which could decide on the posts, and which could only take place at the forthcoming meeting in May 1938. Meanwhile much remained to be done, and quickly, in setting up that meeting. Major misunderstandings concerning the nature of the proposed Council kept rearing their heads. In October Oldham was complaining to Temple that even such as A.E. Garvie, one of the leading Congregational ecumenists, did not seem to have grasped that the main responsibility would be laid on the churches themselves.[36] Oldham laid much of the blame for the "widespread misunderstanding" on what had taken place at Edinburgh in the Faith and Order conference,[37] but he was comforted by the whole-hearted support the project continued to receive from the archbishop of Canterbury, Lang. A major challenge however lay in securing the interest and commitment of the Orthodox churches, and here Oldham was prepared to lean heavily on the advice of the Anglo-Catholics in the Church of England. He had two long conversations with Canon Douglas and Paul B. Anderson, as a result of which he drew up a memorandum

[34] van Dusen letter to JHO 28 Jan. 1938 [OA].
[35] *Ibid.*
[36] JHO letter to Temple 11 Oct. 1937 [OA].
[37] JHO letter to Mott 20 Oct. 1937 [OA].

containing a list of nine Orthodox names to whom the invitations to the provisional conference might be sent, and shared this with Temple and Mott.

Oldham also prepared for Temple the draft of the letter of invitation to the provisional conference, now set to take place in Utrecht 9–13 May 1938.[38] It went out over the names of Temple and Adams Brown as presidents of Faith and Order and Life and Work respectively, together with notes designed to counteract the various "misunderstandings" of the proposal. At the same time Oldham was concerned not to let the Oxford 1937 kind of study emphasis be lost and, as can be seen in correspondence with Henry van Dusen at this time, he was clearly starting to think afresh on how "research" might be conducted ecumenically in the future.[39] A whole series of problems had to be sorted out regarding American representation at the provisional conference: the relation between members of the "Fourteen" and the Council which the conference was to bring into being, the proportion of lay people, and so forth.

## The Utrecht conference, May 1938

May 1938 finally came, and the sixty or so participants gathered at Utrecht under William Temple's chairmanship. The constitutional structure agreed was largely that set out in the Westfield proposals, but those who advocated a confessional rather than simply regional basis for representation on the central committee reserved the right to raise the issue further. What provoked the most intense discussion was the stated theological basis of the Council. The basis finally agreed was: "The World Council of Churches is a fellowship of Churches which accept our Lord Jesus Christ as God and Saviour." A Provisional Committee was appointed to handle affairs before the first general assembly could meet (it was hoped in 1940 or 1941), comprising the Committee of Fourteen and others appointed by Life and Work and Faith and Order. This met first on 13 May, electing Temple as chairman and Mott, Boegner and Archbishop Germanos as vice-chairmen. As agreed at Oxford, the administrative committee of Life and Work had transferred all its responsibilities to this committee. Faith and Order maintained its Continuation Committee. At its meeting in Clarens, Switzerland, at the end of August, Temple still had to face a barrage of critical questions from Headlam and others before the scheme was finally accepted as conforming to the conditions laid down at Edinburgh.

Faith and Order's "marriage but remaining single" still rankled with Oldham. But Utrecht otherwise saw the almost complete fulfilment of all that he had striven towards for over two years. Above all, the question of the general secretaryship was settled as he wished. Visser 't Hooft was invited by the new Provisional Committee to become "General Secretary of the World Council of Churches in Process of Formation" with Bill Paton and Henry Leiper (USA) as associate general secretaries. Temple himself finally drove through any lingering

[38] JHO letter to Temple 23 Oct. 1937 [OA].

[39] JHO letter to van Dusen 18 Nov. 1937 [OA].

doubts on Visser 't Hooft's relative youthfulness. The appointment of Bill Paton, who would continue to work from Edinburgh House in London, was not only satisfactory in bringing into the Council his outstanding gifts.[40] It was also of major strategic importance, since Paton would continue to work part-time for the IMC and thus be instrumental in forging a link between the "younger churches" for which the IMC was a major instrument, and the new World Council. Oldham's canniness had borne fruit yet again.

Oldham was a member of the Provisional Committee, by virtue of being one of the "Fourteen". He was also, by his own choice, appointed as vice-chairman rather than chairman of the study commission appointed at Utrecht. He might be thought to have seen the ecumenical movement reach its awaited goal and therefore ready to bow himself out. But he was far from finished yet.

[40] On Paton's own low-key role in the formation of the WCC, see E. Jackson, *Red Tape and the Gospel*, ch. X.

CHAPTER 16

# "A fighting chance": The Council on the Christian Faith and the Common Life

As if the preparations for the Oxford conference, and its follow-up, together with the setting up of the World Council of Churches, were not enough occupation for a busy man, during the summer of 1937 Oldham was devoting a good deal of energy to yet another project. In Oldham's mind it was all of a piece with these other objects, and especially with the setting up of the World Council. It was the attempt to establish an ecumenical body in Britain, composed of church leaders and specialized, influential lay experts, to promote a new understanding of the relationship between Christian faith and society. What finally emerged from this effort in 1938 was the Council on the Christian Faith and the Common Life (CCFCL), an organization which together with the larger Commission of Churches for International Friendship and Social Responsibility was subsumed into the British Council of Churches on its formation in 1942. To some extent therefore, Oldham can be regarded as a pioneer on the path of specifically British, as well as worldwide, ecumenism. Pioneering this venture certainly was, but as will be seen its actual significance is not exactly clear.

## The World Council – in Britain

Oldham was already looking beyond the Oxford conference even before it had taken place, and was asking how the basal issues in society could be studied in depth, in the light of Christian faith, in the specifically British context. The Oxford conference showed what could be done on the worldwide scale. Or at least, it gave a vision and a challenge for this task: Oldham was not disposed to claim too much for the actual achievements of Oxford, just as he had from the beginning warned against setting too great hopes on what might be accomplished within twelve days of meetings. He was to be dismissive, for instance, of the value of the conference section report on education. By the spring of 1937 there had begun to form in his mind the idea of bringing together "the best minds" in Britain, particularly from the universities, and under the patronage of the leaders of all the main Christian denominations, to look at certain social issues theologically and in terms of public policy. Early in June he began to talk about the idea with Sir Walter Moberly and also Eleonora Iredale.[1] Moberly, chairman of the University Grants Committee, had long been a collaborator with Oldham within Life and Work, and Oldham regarded him as the most influential layperson on church affairs whose judgment would carry a weight second only to that of the archbishop of Canterbury. Iredale, a product of the SCM and a member of the council of Life and Work, was not only a voluble and forceful character with forthright views on social ills and their remedy; she also had a persuasive gift for finding and tapping sources of money for good causes, and had in fact done much in this way to save the Oxford conference from financial embarrassment. Oldham reckoned that £50,000 would be needed to fund what he had in mind, which would also serve largely to cover the British contribution "to any international plan" (that is, the World Council). Along with Iredale and Moberly, T.S. Eliot was drawn in as a firm supporter of the scheme, and eventually Oldham did secure some support from the leaders of the main British churches.

Oldham lunched and talked also with Dr Berry of the Congregational Union, until recently president of the Federal Council of the Free Churches, and with Dr Bond the Methodist leader. Both apparently were reassuring on finding moral and financial support from their churches. Still more crucial was the securing of the support of the archbishop of Canterbury, with whom Oldham also talked in that same month of June, and succeeded.

Most important of all, in Oldham's view, would be to find the right executive staff. Oldham made no attempt to conceal his own interest in playing a leading role, though not on his own. There are hints in his correspondence during 1937 that, while not projecting his services for the new World Council beyond the Utrecht meeting of 1938, he was in fact keeping his options open. He evidently did not want to be so committed and tied down to a British post that he could not, if pressed, serve also in the World Council. But Oldham was now 63 years old and it was obvious that younger blood must be looked for to provide leadership, or at least to share it, for his British scheme. As with the project to form a World Council where Oldham's enthusiasm was dependent on his perception of W.A. Visser 't Hooft as the only candidate worth considering for the general secretaryship, so his British dream also became inseparable from his conviction that one, and only one, person was adequate to the task.

[1] JHO letter to Mott 9 June 1937 [OA].

## The hunting of Hunter

In this case, the person who had caught Oldham's hawkish eye was Leslie Hunter, the Anglican archdeacon of Northumberland. Hunter was an SCM product, had been closely associated with William Temple in the COPEC conferences of the 1920s and, having a major concern with unemployment, had set up a bureau of social research on Tyneside. Through the summer and autumn of 1937, in personal meetings and frequent – sometimes lengthy – correspondence Hunter experienced as few others ever did the full force of Oldham's powers of dogged persuasion. The assault began in late June with a meeting in London, followed up by a letter to Hunter in Newcastle-on-Tyne. Oldham drew a rich picture full of the possibilities of the scheme and the range of its likely activities, and the exciting demands it would offer those involved:

> Only a fraction of the possible tasks can be taken effectively in hand; but even this fraction involves so many intimate contacts with a) church leaders – not only the two Archbishops and the secretaries of denominations but a much wider circle of the influential clergy; b) Christian youth organisations; c) those directing the social services throughout the country and leaders of education; d) leaders in public life, administration and industry; e) representatives of the labour movement – quite essential; and f) particular movements of various kinds. The enumeration is doubtless far from complete. Even a team of three or four people could maintain only a fraction of the desirable contacts.[2]

There was, said Oldham, ground for believing that there would be "solid support" from church leaders and others "for a bold move at the present time". But, he went on, "the only person round whom we can rally this potential support, so far as we [*sic*] can see after much careful thought and enquiry, is yourself. If you are unable to respond, the project, so far as I can see, must lapse." This appeal could be read like an honest *cri du coeur*. It could equally come across as moral blackmail, though doubtless Oldham was entirely sincere when he asked Hunter, as he did more than once during these weeks, to consider whether a call of God might be involved here. At any rate, Hunter's reply to this initial approach was cool.[3] He did not feel attracted by the kind of work described by Oldham, which was far removed from what he had envisaged for himself at his ordination and which could just as well be done by a layman. There would be need for generous financing of the project, on which Oldham had so far been somewhat vague. Nor could he easily see himself working very closely with Eleonora Iredale (whom most people, Oldham excepted, seem to have found brilliant but intimidating and impossibly opinionated). And Robert Mackie, secretary of the WSCF, having heard of the scheme, was distinctly unsupportive since Oldham had apparently eliminated Scotland from involvement in it. The real problem for Hunter, however, lay in what would be

[2] JHO letter to Hunter 27 June 1937 [OA].
[3] Hunter letter to JHO 3 July 1937 [OA].

the relationship between himself and Oldham in the project. He pointed out shrewdly:

> I should value your co-operation – especially in view of the necessity of a rapid start and don't doubt our ability to pull together. But although you might be ready to play second fiddle, the general public and the Church leaders would always think of you as the head – unless somehow or other you had a special commission. Moreover, I do not think you ought to feel yourself too tied down to one specific job.

This was, to say the least, hardly a positive reply but Oldham felt encouraged enough by Hunter's willingness to consider the proposal and was content for the present "to leave future steps in the hands of God"[4] and to have some more conversation with Hunter during one of the more leisured periods in the Oxford conference. This did happen, and after Oxford Hunter wrote to Oldham: "Nothing that happened at Oxford lessened my personal reluctance to undertake the work proposed, but everything that happened strengthened my sense of its importance, could it be undertaken. The considered opinion of your weighty group that I was the only available person, supported as it was by the Archbishop of Canterbury's counsel, leaves me unable to refuse."[5] He would accept the invitation when it was made, provided certain conditions were met, including not just the approval but the public support of church leaders, and a secure income and funding to secure first-rate staff of his own choosing. The main difficulty remained that of defining his and Oldham's areas of work and the relation between them. Again, he was perceptive and to the point:

> Your co-operation would be a real strength – especially at the outset. The only difference of function between you and me which the public could appreciate in view of your standing and which in my judgment would be workable, would be for you to become Oecumenical Secretary and to hold all the threads with the World Council – having charge of a more or less self-contained department with a staff of your own choosing. Any association between us which was less explicit would lead to confusion, however good a personal relationship we had. If, as you suggested, you were to be head of "Intelligence" the overlap would be complete for at the moment there is not much else to it than an Intelligence Bureau of the Churches. Moreover, could you actually lay aside your oecumenical and missionary responsibilities seeing that your knowledge and experience in both fields are unique?

This letter is an ironic compliment to Oldham's recognition of Hunter as a man of unusual gifts. Probably never before in his life had Oldham been so shrewdly assessed to his face. Hunter had put his finger right on the spot, that Oldham was now limited by success and reputation which would simply *not* permit him in a "co-operative" role especially with a younger person. There was also a very sharp exposure of where Oldham's priorities were really lying in the emphasis on "Intelligence".

[4] JHO letter to Hunter 5 July 1937 [OA].
[5] Hunter letter to JHO 6 Aug. 1937 [OA].

The conditions which Hunter had laid down were never finally met, and the uncertainties which he had identified as in need of clarification remained unresolved. (Visser 't Hooft might have had similar problems with the nascent World Council, but at least in that case there was an agreed process and timetable of decision-making.) The correspondence and the meetings, both in London and in Newcastle, dragged on into 1938. On 14 January 1938, meeting at Lambeth Palace, the group convened by Archbishop Lang to look at the proposals for the World Council decided to set up a small committee to explore further Oldham's scheme; moreover, the group issued a formal invitation to Leslie Hunter to be a member of the secretariat of the new British Council on the Christian Faith and the Common Life, along with Oldham. Temple wrote to him on 20 January with this news. But as far as Hunter was concerned, all the previous problems and doubts remained. Oldham himself did not help matters by repeating Temple's invitation with no greater clarity than before[6] on the division of labour expected between them. In some exasperation Hunter wrote to Temple on 1 February:

> To tell the truth I was more disposed to the venture before Joe got to work on me by prayer and propaganda than after! I felt that he made up his mind too absolutely that I was the required person – and then put the proposal in the form – "We are not clear what the job is but we want you because you are most likely to discover what it is – anyway we are not likely to go forward in the matter unless you sign on. It's your job or nobody's."
>
> That line of attack may flatter a man's vanity but it doesn't persuade such wisdom as he has or appeal to a sense of vocation. If there really is a job – and one worth giving up much in order to do – it ought to be so clearly envisaged that its promoters are ready to go forward with it – with the team they can secure when the time comes.

Hunter found a sympathetic ally in the one who perhaps had the most experience of working with Oldham as a near-equal, Bill Paton. Hunter had shown him Oldham's latest letter and shared his frustration. Paton's reply bit deep:

> I sympathise with you over Joe's letter, though I am so well used to him that it does not affect me quite so badly. The dear man always fancies that he is frightfully good as a worker in a team and he just isn't. But I doubt whether he really means more than that when the group, whatever it finally is, gets down to business they have got to look at the whole programme together and find out which can best do which.
>
> What has got to be made clear, and what Joe evades, is that there is a definite need for the sort of initiative and leadership that you can supply. It is quite preposterous to ask you to leave your present and your possible future job for a vague share in a programme with undefined persons. I am writing to Joe tonight. I shall tell him that this way of doing things is likely to rot the whole business up, and that as the World Council more or less goes with it, so far as British support goes, I do not intend to

[6] JHO letter to Hunter 20 Jan. 1938 [OA].

come in or to try to bring in the IMC unless it is cleared up. It is obviously time for the committee to get to work and to prevent Joe's changing moods from messing up the whole business.[7]

A.D. Lindsay, Master of Balliol College, Oxford, suggested that Hunter might combine the post with the chaplaincy of Balliol. That would ease the financial situation, but Oldham was insisting that only a full-time commitment would suffice. William Temple and George Bell in turn tried to mediate in a situation increasingly riven by "misunderstandings". A further meeting at Lambeth Palace took place on 17 March 1938.

As late as May 1938, following the Utrecht conference, Oldham was still writing optimistically to Leslie Hunter.[8] But Hunter never did join the Council on Christian Faith and the Common Life, which until the formation of the British Council of Churches in 1942 always remained a modest enterprise, with Oldham as sole secretary on a part-time basis. Hunter went on to become bishop of Sheffield. During 1939 Oldham did secure the services of another promising young priest and former SCM secretary, Oliver Tomkins, who also helped him in organizing early meetings of the "Moot". Tomkins had a tremendous admiration for Oldham and believed passionately in the need to participate in Oldham's "fantastic gamble" for the sake of a "new Christendom".[9] But again, lack of funds prevented any permanent and full-time employment of him.

## A flawed vision

There was in fact something deeply flawed in the whole scheme. It was not simply that, as Hunter and Paton both agreed, to try to recruit a leader before anything was clearly set up or job-descriptions had been worked out, was bizarre. The contradiction lay deeper. Oldham's vision was for a movement which would relate the churches to the challenges of contemporary society, and recruit "the best minds" for this task. Early on in his appeals to Leslie Hunter he had pointed out that "the danger of all efforts of the kind proposed is that they become clericalised".[10] But oddly, of all the instruments with which he was ever involved in forming, the CCFCL seems to have been set up with the most ecclesiastically top-heavy leadership. Why this sudden concern for approval by the prelacy? One of the most interesting passages in all of Oldham's correspondence with Leslie Hunter runs:

I am compelled . . . always to go back as far as one can to fundamentals. The heart of my philosophy in regard to this venture is, I think, expressed in the idea of "The Church *within* the Church". I believe that we have in the last resort to choose between three courses. We may work with the small body of elect souls. But in that case what

[7] Paton letter to Hunter 15 Feb. 1938 [OA].
[8] JHO letter to Hunter 18 May 1938 [OA].
[9] Information on Tomkins' diaries kindly supplied by his biographer, Prof. A. Hastings.
[10] JHO letter to Hunter 27 June 1937 [OA].

we do is confined within narrow circles; and it is hardly possible to achieve anything in the way of a national effort. Or, alternatively, we might work solely with the organised churches, taking them as they are. That would mean that none of the things you and I care about would get done. The third course is that we should try to work with the progressive and forward-looking group within the church, *under cover of and with the backing of the official church.* I am under no illusions that this may in fact prove to be impossible. But I believe (with some confirmation in experience) that there is a fighting chance along this line; and so long as it is true, I believe it is our duty to take it, since so much more can be accomplished in this way than in any other.[11] (emphasis mine)

The contradiction lay in Oldham's fearing "clericalisation" yet at the same time wishing for hierarchical approval and support. In the end, the CCFCL failed either to stimulate sufficiently the progressive "church within the church" or to win enough real backing (or cover), not to mention funding, from the official church leadership. And by 1939, as will be seen, another player was in the field in the shape of the Commission on International Friendship and Social Responsibility. Not that the CCFCL was of no significance whatever. As will be seen, it did play a role, though not the one which Oldham envisaged, in the emergence of a lasting ecumenical British body. But it has to be labelled one of Joe Oldham's brave failures, an adventure that finally got nowhere, and not just because of the mistaken pursuit of Leslie Hunter. Equally, it may be judged that a career of such productivity as Joe Oldham's can surely afford at least one such disappointing episode. He knew it was a "fighting chance", and fighting chances, by definition, have no guarantee of success.

By the time it became clear that the Council was not proving the great way forward, Oldham was practically at what would be retirement age for most people. Had his working life, or indeed his life itself, ended then he would have been seen as having had a brilliant career which, after the crowning achievements of Oxford 1937 and the setting up of the World Council, had hardly anything left to say. The extraordinary fact is that precisely now he did discover yet another track along which to venture, and which led him into another decade or more of immense creativity – some would say the period of his most creative contributions of all to Christian life and thought. For, in setting up the "Moot", starting *The Christian News-Letter* and subsequently the Christian Frontier Council, Oldham did all – and arguably far more than – he hoped might be achieved in the Council on Christian Faith and the Common Life. And all with less cover and backing of the "official church" than he had hoped for for that Council.

[11] JHO letter to Hunter 28 Sept. 1937 [OA].

# PART V

# CRISIS, WAR AND SOCIETY 1938–45

CHAPTER 17

# *The Moot*

ON 4 December 1936 Oldham wrote to Hans Schönfeld in Geneva: "I have arranged for an all-day meeting of the Moot (i.e. Miss Wyon, Fenn, Richardson, Miss Iredale, etc.) on Tuesday December 15th. We had a meeting yesterday and found that we could not overtake all the matters which have to be considered in regard to the Oxford Conference." This appears to be Oldham's earliest reference to a "Moot", and in this case it apparently signified a close-knit but ad hoc group of his colleagues most intimately involved in the planning for Oxford 1937. Schönfeld, Oldham hoped, would be able to attend the next meeting, along with his Geneva colleague Niels Ehrenström. Today, no doubt, such a group would be called a "think-tank", witnessing to the dominance of language by the pseudo-technological idiom. Typically, Oldham with his fondness for the personalist motif of "encounter", delved into Old English for the word meaning an assembly, or *meeting-point*.[1]

Apart from the fact that Fenn, Iredale and Oldham himself were to be members, what came to be established in 1938 as "The Moot" had little continuity with this pre-Oxford conference group. But it is clear that even as he was preparing for Oxford Oldham was looking beyond the conference to a variety of ways in which some of its main themes and concerns could be pursued in depth by "the best minds". It was to be small in size and exclusive in nature, yet in retrospect the Moot is justly viewed as one of Oldham's most creative ventures, largely due to the unusual calibre and extraordinarily contrasting personalities of those whom he drew together in it.

## A perception of crisis – and the need for response

Two particular points in the background to the Moot should be made. First, Oldham was undoubtedly responding to the note of crisis in Western societies

[1] Interview of K. Bliss with D. Forrester 11 Sept. 1989. Eric Fenn may have first suggested the term.

in face of the totalitarian menace. This had already been registered at Oxford. The point needs underlining because in the public eye Oldham's perception of crisis became linked with a celebrated letter from him published in *The Times* on 5 October 1938 immediately following the Munich episode. The letter in full reads:

> The lessons which are being drawn from the unforgettable experiences through which we have lived during the past few days do not for the most part go deep enough. The removal of an immediate danger does not mean that effective steps have yet been taken to stem forces that threaten the disintegration of modern society. The respite that has been given us may be no more than a postponement of the day of reckoning unless we are determined to root out the cancerous growths which have brought Western civilization to the verge of complete collapse. Whether truth and justice or caprice and violence are to prevail in human affairs is a question on which the fate of mankind depends. But to equate the conflict between these opposing forces with the conflict between democracies and dictatorships, real and profound as is the difference, is a dangerous simplification of the problem. To focus on evil in others is a way of escape from the painful struggle of eradicating it from our own hearts and lives and an evasion of our real responsibilities.
>
> The basal truth is that the spiritual foundations of Western civilization have been undermined. The systems which are in the ascendant on the Continent may be regarded from one point of view as convulsive attempts to arrest the process of disintegration. What clear alternative do we have in this country? The mind of England is confused and uncertain. Is it possible that in these circumstances a simple question, which some would answer in the affirmative as a matter of course, and many more regard as wholly beside the mark, might unexpectedly become a serious and live issue? May our salvation lie in an attempt to recover our Christian heritage, not in the sense of going back to the past but of discovering in the central affirmations and insights of the faith new spiritual energies to regenerate and vitalize our sick society? Does not the public repudiation of the whole Christian scheme of life in a large part of what was once known as Christendom force to the front the question whether the path of wisdom is not rather to attempt to work out a Christian doctrine of modern society and to order our national life in accordance with it?
>
> Those who would give a quick, easy, or confident answer to this question have failed to understand it. It cannot even be seriously considered without a profound awareness of the extent to which Christian ideas have lost their hold over, or faded from the consciousness of, large sections of the population; of the far-reaching changes that would be called for in the structure, institutions, and activities of existing society, which is in many of its features a complete denial of the Christian understanding of the meaning and end of man's existence; and of the stupendous and costly spiritual, moral and intellectual effort that any serious attempt to order the national life in accordance with the Christian understanding of life would demand. Realistically viewed the task is so far beyond the present capacity of our British Christianity that I write as a fool. But if the will were there, I believe that the first steps to be taken are fairly clear. The presupposition of all else, however, is the recognition that nothing short of a really heroic effort will avail to save mankind from its present evils and the destruction which must follow in their train.

But for Oldham, Munich was not the point of revelation of the underlying crisis, rather simply the occasion which illustrated beyond doubt what he had long seen. By the time of Munich the Moot had already met twice.

The second point is that while it is clear that Oldham was indeed anxious to collect "the best minds" to tackle the fundamental problems of society in the light of Christian faith, from the start his goal was not thinking for thinking's sake, but action. And by action, Oldham meant above all the actions of lay people in their responsibilities in the secular world. But unlike those theologians or church leaders (William Temple among them) who were content to urge in a general way the responsibilities of lay people for witness in society, Oldham was arguing for the appropriate *organization* of lay people, modest yet appropriate to their day-to-day situations. In the preparatory volume for Oxford he had written:

> Wherever there has been a revival of Christianity of an enduring kind it has generally found expression in the spontaneous activity of small groups meeting for mutual encouragement, fellowship, and common effort. The conception of "cells" is wholly congruous with the genius of Christianity. May not the formation of such cells of Christian witness and service be the distinctive Christian contribution to the social and political struggles of our time? To be effectively changed a social system must be changed from within and in all its parts.[2]

So Oldham envisaged "a multitude of centres of spontaneous activity" whereby Christians in neighbourhoods or professions combated evils in social and political life. The Moot was, in part, a particularization of this idea. Those whom he would invite would indeed be original, intellectually sharp thinkers, but among them would be people in highly influential roles in public life. As well as "cells" among the population at large, the idea of an *order* of people in key positions began to take shape in his mind; and the Moot could be the genesis of such an order. This in fact proved to be a vision which both stimulated and frustrated much of the discussion in the Moot.

## The first Moot

Twelve people, including Joe and Mary Oldham, met for the first meeting of the Moot from 1 to 4 April 1938 at High Leigh in Hertfordshire. It was indeed a highly eclectic group. Two were academic theologians, both Presbyterians and identified with the newer personalistic strain in theology: *John Baillie*, recently returned from New York to occupy the chair of divinity at New College, Edinburgh; and *H.H. Farmer* of Westminster College, Cambridge. Representing the philosophical world was *H.A. Hodges*, professor at Reading University, a devout Anglican, an admirer of Thomas Aquinas and an authority on the 19th-century German thinker Wilhelm Dilthey. *T.S. Eliot* was there,

[2] Oldham in Oldham and Visser 't Hooft, *The Church and Its Function in Society*, London, Allen & Unwin, 1937, p.198.

*John Baillie*

already long famous as the poet whose *The Waste Land* (1922) had for many brought poetry into the 20th century, and who had converted both from agnosticism to Anglo-Catholicism and from American citizenship into High Tory Englishness. At his desk as editor of the *Criterion* and as a publisher he was as much a literary critic as a poet in his own right, and furthermore was deeply interested not only in culture but in the nature and basis of society as such, as was to be seen in his *The Nature of a Christian Society* (1939). Oldham had known Eliot since the early 1930s, and their mutual acquaintance seems to have been brought about through George Bell.[3] At their first meeting Oldham had been delighted with Eliot's question "Who is John Mott?" for convincing him that he had at last got outside his customary religious world.

In mighty contrast to all these figures was *John Middleton Murry*. His self-description as "author and farmer" hardly did justice to his colourful career which had by turns taken him into journalism, art and literary criticism, the

[3] R.C.D. Jasper, *George Bell: Bishop of Chichester*, London, Oxford Univ. Press, 1967, p.125. Eliot recalled a train journey with Bell in 1930, when the bishop first mentioned Oldham's name to him.

political intelligence department during the 1914–18 war (he became chief censor in 1919) and prolific writing on social and ethical issues. By now an uncompromising Christian pacifist and communist, he led a decidedly unconventional life-style involving an experiment in communal living on a farm. He was twice-widowed, one of his wives being the writer Katharine Mansfield with whose works he confessed an abiding obsession.

Combining the academic and man of affairs, (Sir) *Walter Moberly* was perhaps the nearest anyone ever attained to Oldham's ideal of the theologically aware and responsible Christian layperson. Trained in philosophy, as a young Oxford don he had contributed two essays to the controversial volume of liberal theology *Foundations* in 1912. He fought in the 1914–18 war, receiving the DSO for gallantry, and afterwards returned to academic life, first as professor of philosophy at Birmingham, then successively principal of University College, Exeter, and vice-chancellor of Manchester University. Since 1935 he had been chairman of the University Grants Committee, the most powerful and politically influential position in higher education in Britain. His close association with Oldham was already long-standing: he was an active member of the Council of Life and Work, and at the Oxford conference had chaired the section on church and community.

The only woman apart from *Mary Oldham* was *Eleonora Iredale*, already encountered in the Oldham story, and with more than enough force of personality not to be intimidated by this prestigious male company. But Oldham was concerned that the group, if it was really to look at the questions affecting the whole of society, should not be confined to the by-now customary "ecumenical" clientele. Not only had he recruited *Christopher Dawson*, the young Roman Catholic historian and editor of the *Dublin Review*, and one of the ablest minds then engaged on social issues, but also *Adolf Löwe*, a Jewish refugee from Nazi Germany. Löwe had been professor of political philosophy at Frankfurt and a leading light in the movement of "religious socialists" in the 1920s. A number of his students were to be active in the intellectual circles of the German resistance to Hitler. Finally there was *Eric Fenn*, Oldham's assistant for the Oxford conference, to whom was assigned much of the secretarial work for the Moot.

As always when new groups gather, this first meeting was largely given to the members sharing their own perspectives and backgrounds.[4] Oldham had circulated a preparatory paper setting out his understanding of the "crisis" facing British society and the need for an "order" to counteract the slide into moral uncertainty and state absolutism. Members reacted variously. Moberly largely agreed with Oldham's diagnosis: an increasing divorce between the life of the church and the life of the community. For Baillie, the main rift was within the Christian mind itself, dating back to the Renaissance and the emergence of a secular humanism apparently inalienable to religious belief. Eliot wanted both

[4] 1st Moot Minutes. A full set of Moot Minutes and Moot Papers is in the Oldham Archive [OA] in New College, Edinburgh.

*Eleonora Iredale*

a longer historical perspective and a more precise definition of the problem. As a German and a Jew, Löwe confessed to unease at the decline of a sense of moral responsibility in British society, manifested in the acquiescence in the Nazi advance over Europe. Farmer's main concern was "the complete lack of understanding of Christian faith by increasing numbers of people". To be effective an "order" would have to be rooted in "the soil of the common life" – might not something have to be learned even from the Nazi party here? Dawson acutely asked whether an "order" as traditionally understood was appropriate to today since such movements had typically asked for total submission at the expense of individual freedom, and the church itself has become an adjunct to the community instead of a place where people find fullness of community. Middleton Murry (as he was to do repeatedly in the course of Moot meetings) confessed his "isolation as a thinker" and prescribed "a renaissance of the Christian imagination" which would challenge and revivify society for a true community. Hodges agreed with much of Baillie's diagnosis, and was looking for a new catholic "synthesis" for the 20th century, in which the distinctive discoveries of the Reformation would nevertheless be safeguarded.

The discussion developed into a long debate on whether a Christian regeneration of society could involve anything other than some form of "Christian totalitarianism". In it all, Oldham himself was almost wholly silent, except for the occasional request for further definition or clarification. Towards the close of the meeting, members shared information on their own current preoccupations and writing projects, and there was more discussion of the possibilities of an "order". Interestingly, Dawson raised the question of more Catholic participation in the group, the likelihood being that laypeople rather than clerics could be recruited.

## The second Moot

Thus was the Moot launched. It met next 23–26 September 1938 at Westfield College, London. Two papers were prepared in advance and circulated among members, who in turn submitted comments which were also distributed before the meeting. One was by Middleton Murry on "Towards a Christian Theory of Society", the other by Oldham on "Problems and Tasks of the Council on the Christian Faith and the Common Life". This was not the only preparation by Oldham: several more members were recruited. *Walter Oakeshott* was a notable teacher and about to become high master of St Paul's School. Author of *Commerce and Society* (1936) he had been a member of the Pilgrim Trust Unemployment Enquiry. *Gilbert Shaw* appeared. *Alec Vidler*, though he later claimed never to have understood quite why he was asked to join, strengthened the theological muscle of the group still further. Some years earlier, as an Anglo-Catholic and socially outspoken priest in Birmingham, Vidler had made a name for himself by repeated controversy with Bishop E.W. Barnes, notorious for his liberalism in theology but, according to Vidler at the time, decidedly intolerant of clergy wayward in matters of ritual. Vidler had subsequently been warden of the Oratory House in Cambridge, where he had researched extensively in social theology and Catholic Modernism, and at the time of the second Moot meeting was in process of taking up the post of warden of St Deiniol's Library, Hawarden, and the editorship of the influential journal *Theology*.[5]

*The* big recruit, however, and the most important (in his eyes at least) Oldham ever secured for the Moot, was yet again from outside the strictly Christian camp. *Karl Mannheim*, Jewish as was Adolf Löwe, had lost his chair in sociology at Frankfurt in April 1933 with the Nazi advent to power and found refuge in London as a lecturer at the London School of Economics. Already of international repute through such major works as *Ideology and Utopia*, his work on the sociology of knowledge was setting the agenda for a whole new generation of social scientists. Why such a critical mind from an (apparently) agnostic Jewish background should have so readily accepted the invitation to join the Moot has puzzled some Mannheim scholars.[6] Quite probably, as an immigrant intellectual he was attracted by the possibility it

[5] See Alec Vidler, *Scenes from a Clerical Life*, London, Collins, 1977, for his autobiography. Pages 116–19 describe his experience of the Moot. He also comments on it in his interview in Ved Mehta, *The New Theologian*, London, Pelican, 1965, pp.83f.

[6] See D. Kettler, V. Meja and N. Stehr, *Karl Mannheim*, London, Tavistock, 1984. The account of Oldham and the Moot as a context for Mannheim's thinking (pp.130–32, 138–44) is perfunctory and superficial compared with that by R. Kojecky in the case of T.S. Eliot (see note 34 below).

*Alec Vidler*

offered of deepening his understanding of his new context from the inside. But further, Mannheim, whatever his personal beliefs, took other people's beliefs seriously and was deeply interested in both the ethical dimension of society and its connection with things "spiritual". Oldham, for his part, clearly relished the healthy challenge such an "outsider" could bring to the mainly Christian group which in any case was there to reflect on *society.* As it happened, before long Mannheim was to be very much an insider to the Moot.

Two other names, more familiar in the Christian world, appeared on the attendance list: *William Paton*, Oldham's IMC colleague, and *Lesslie Newbigin*, whom Oldham had so much admired as a leader in the SCM, now home after a first spell of missionary service in India.

Middleton Murry's paper, which provided the meat for the first part of the meeting, was a fascinating argument, drawing upon Rousseau, Coleridge and Thomas Arnold, for the state to be a moral organization and for the "national church" to be inclusive of the whole of society and at one with the state. In the modern industrial age, Christian civilization could continue to exist only as an inclusively national and Christian society, led by the national church with the state as its organ. In response some Moot members – Baillie, Löwe and Eliot in particular – jumped on Murry's assumption of the nation as the boundary of society, especially as far as the church, which was universal in nature, was concerned. The discussion moved on to the question of secularization, and the place of mutual, personal relationships in modern society. Oldham asked whether a "Christian" society could only properly mean the spheres in which personal relationships could operate, and whether therefore the world of "remote relationship" was sub-Christian? And what was the relationship of law to personal relations? Mannheim agreed with Oldham's distinction but preferred a historical, rather than moral or theological, perspective: there was no *simple* distinction between the spheres. Institutional relationships (as in modern health care) had replaced simple neighbourly care, but "institutional life was no longer empty of personal significance, and primary relationships were dependent on social relations".[7]

From secularization to the relation between religion and science, from the question of the role of the church to the strength of its numbers in society, from specifically Christian belief to natural law, the discussion leapt forward like a bush fire. A short sample from Eric Fenn's virtually verbatim minutes conveys well the atmosphere:

> *J.M. Murry* pointed out that there were two different angles of approach (a) to the sociologist the Church was a social grouping desirable as a check on the natural workings of the community; (b) but by a preponderance of Christian men in the governing group was meant men who accepted the Christian faith. This immediately involved the Church in some sense. The Church was therefore eternal and must find expression in some form.
>
> *Alec Vidler* said that we could not be dependent for safeguards on men of Christian belief, but would need institutional safeguards of the distribution of power. Of these safeguards the Church was one.
>
> *J.M. Murry* agreed, but desired to go further and to conceive that the quality of the Christian men concerned would be such as to hold this even in opposition to their own power.
>
> *W. Paton* referred to the original question and asked whether we were agreeing about the all-embracing nature of modern society and that government must be all-embracing and centralised . . .
>
> *Gilbert Shaw* questioned the use of the terms "check" and "safeguard". The worshipping society was a leaven. Murry and Löwe seemed to postulate a Messianic redemptive order, whereas organised Christianity took over the colour of the world.
>
> *Alec Vidler* said that he did not wish to press the term "safeguard", but in the case of Germany could the Church not have been a more effective check if it had been stronger?
>
> *John Baillie* asked whether this meant checking totalitarianism or changing its quality.
>
> *Alec Vidler* said that what he had in mind was a much greater tension between Christianity and neo-paganism.
>
> *Adolf Löwe* asked why the Church had been so weak in the 150 years before Hitler. There had only been one religion in Germany in the 19th century, namely Marxism. The Church had been identified with class and privilege. He felt that there was a permanent risk in any final check in a planned society determined by Christianity. There would always be a temptation to misuse power . . .

[7] 2nd Moot Minutes, p.3.

*J.H. Oldham*, while accepting this view in general, urged that amongst the principles accepted by a Christian society must be one that allowed the maximum field for thought and freedom. It seemed to him that both Löwe and Murry accepted this view.

*Adolf Löwe* agreed, but believed that we should see saints burning again.

*John Baillie* asked if this meant that saints would be burning heretics.[8]

Next day the discussion moved on further into what was meant by a "Christian society" and how it might be brought about. Oldham reiterated his plea for a declaration by a sizeable body of people on the principles that society must adhere to in order to deserve the title "Christian". The church, dominated by clergy with a narrow interest in "religion", had ceased to *think*, and to think collectively about society. William Paton, somewhat disingenuously, said that he could not really see what the problem was since Britain still had a large measure of formal adherence to Christian norms, citing the recent coronation and the debate about divorce law. He was given short shrift by John Baillie. Paton's examples "showed rather a concordat between the State and the Cultus", whereas Murry was pleading for public policy directed by Christian principles. "The fact was a deep separation between politics and religion, and people were 'equally horrified at hearing Christianity doubted and seeing it practised'." Murry and Shaw in turn pleaded for a strong moral movement within the church which would give people something they wanted to convert into, and Oldham agreed with this. "It seemed to him that the greatest contribution in a given situation might be the posing of the right question to the public conscience." It would open up a sphere for evangelization, hitherto non-existent, by a devoted group.

In fact it was Karl Mannheim who introduced the most optimistic note into this discussion. The situation, he felt, was not as difficult as twenty years earlier. "Fascism had created a new opposition, both to the Christian and to the humanitarian mind. The two groups found themselves driven together and the free intelligentsia were rather nearer therefore to religious tradition. We required to revitalise the traditional elements and re-adapt them to new social needs."[9] Likewise the international crisis would inevitably raise either the question of what was being fought for, or what new aims should be set now that the danger is past. "In either case the Church would find itself in a much more living society and would be bound to return some answer."

The last day was taken up in a long and inconclusive discussion about possible action, including a response to the eventuality of war. Should action be left to individuals, or could the group as such be the nucleus of a wider movement? If so, how would it work? A small, concerted effort or a widespread campaign? Either way, should it speak in a specifically Christian way to provoke an awareness of sin and the Christian answer? Or would it suffice – as H.A. Hodges felt – to stimulate what was already a half-Christian consciousness in

[8] *Ibid.*, pp.8f.

[9] *Ibid.*, p.12.

much of the population? Some members were clearly depressed about the dead weight of apathy and indifference in the churches. Eleonora Iredale urged a recognition that many people with no contact with the church were already trying to live "the life of God" and would welcome a lead. Oldham himself refused to be tied down by hard opposites: much could be achieved "through a multitude of prophetic utterances". At any rate, the group readily agreed to meet again.

Not quite all, however, were invited again. Lesslie Newbigin had tried to intervene constructively at several points, but just prior to the meeting had had "a rather tough session" with Oldham at the Athenaeum.[10] On the morning following the discussion of Middleton Murry's paper "it was clear that Oldham did not want my viewpoint and it seemed best to keep silent and not interfere with the discussion". That was his one and only experience of the Moot. William Paton fared likewise.[11] By now the core membership and pattern of working of the Moot were already established. It was firmly Oldham's project. He issued the invitations, largely determined or sanctioned the agenda, decided on the papers to be circulated beforehand, and chaired each meeting. The minutes, taken by Eric Fenn almost verbatim and typed up by Mary Oldham, were duplicated and issued to each member. They, and most of the papers, were marked "Strictly Confidential to Members of the Moot". It was indeed a cell. Within it Oldham reigned supreme thanks, in a peculiar way, to his deafness. In order to hear what was being said, he had to come and sit close enough to each would-be speaker in turn so as to enable him or her to address his ear-trumpet directly. As well as imposing an unusual degree of order on proceedings, this probably encouraged a deliberateness of delivery, and perhaps of thought as well. The sight of Oldham shuffling his stool (or sometimes a cushion) around the room with his cumbersome hearing device provided many of the members of the Moot with their most endearing memories of him, the more so as, once in position, he was all attention. Marjorie Reeves, who attended one or two of the later meetings as a guest, and though so relatively young was encouraged to speak, recalls Oldham's elfish little face and keen blue eyes riveted in upward gaze on her as though she was saying the most important thing in the world.[12] It was all hard, if stimulating, work. The usual three-day periods spent together gave little concession to free time but, typically for Oldham,

[10] L. Newbigin, *Unfinished Agenda*, Edinburgh, St Andrew Press, 1993, p.46.

[11] E. Jackson, *Red Tape and the Gospel*, p.265, states that "Paton was deeply hurt to find himself excluded" from the Moot, but that if he had been allowed to participate he would "of his own accord have dropped out when he saw the abstract and totally theoretical nature of the subjects chosen for discussion". Jackson is evidently unaware that Paton did attend the second meeting.

[12] M. Reeves interview with author, 20 Dec. 1996. Daniel Jenkins in an interview with author 17 March 1998 confirmed this experience while also recalling that Oldham's concentrated attention on what one was saying could also be inhibiting in the sense of making one weigh one's words *too* carefully, when a process of "thinking aloud" might have been preferred. Ronald Preston has an even more intimidating recollection: "If he thought what you were saying not very interesting you could see him quietly switching [his hearing aid] off" (letter to author 20 March 1998).

there was time for prayer each day even though, in Alec Vidler's words, "some members were would-be rather than professing Christian believers".[13]

### The third Moot: readiness for war and planning for freedom

The Moot met for the third time on 6–9 January 1939 at Elfinsward, Haywards Heath. Attending again were Baillie, Eliot, Fenn, Hodges, Iredale, Löwe, Mannheim, Moberly, Murry, Shaw and Vidler, with a new recruit, the young Oliver Tomkins. First item on the agenda was a review by John Baillie of *True Humanism*, the recent work of Jacques Maritain, the French Catholic personalist social theologian.[14] Most of the next day was spent in discussion of Oldham's paper held over from the last meeting, "The Problems and Tasks of the Council on the Christian Faith and the Common Life". Running to ten pages, the paper gathers up much of Oldham's approach to Christian social thinking from his past twenty years. First he states the need to view everything in the proper theological context of God's self-revelation in Christ and of his kingdom, in contrast to current trends such as both Nazism and communism which are an illusory, man-centred "attempt to escape from the relativism of human wishes and aspirations and to find support in a reality which commands us".[15] While sympathetic to Middleton Murry's attempt to expound an all-embracing "Christian society", Oldham wishes to state more clearly the distinct nature of the church as community founded on transcendent values, while equally affirming that these values must as far as possible also be worked out in the all-too-human wider society. Thinking through the relation of faith to the common life must therefore be "bi-polar". A society which is not the church, but nevertheless could be designated as "Christian", would manifest a "secular morality vitalised and regenerated by the Christian understanding of life", the aims of which could be endorsed both by Christians and many who did not consciously share that faith. Among these aims would be:

(1) A social environment in which God's love for men is reflected at least fitfully in the actual conditions of their lives and does not appear to those conditions a hollow mockery.

(2) A society in which men can live as those who are responsible to God and consequently to one another, and who have, therefore, the opportunity of responsible choice.

(3) A society in which there is a growing realisation of our membership one of another.

(4) A society which has a respect for the claims and rights of all men, as created by God and the objects of His redeeming love, and has as its purpose the service and well-being of mankind.

[13] Vidler, *Scenes from a Clerical Life*, p.128.

[14] On this discussion, see K. Clements, "John Baillie and 'The Moot'", in D. Fergusson, ed., *Christ, Church and Society: Essays on John Baillie and Donald Baillie*, Edinburgh, T. & T. Clark, 1993, pp.212f.

[15] This and following quotations from 3rd Moot Minutes, pp.1, 3, 7, 9.

The council, Oldham suggested, should not itself try to formulate social policies but should raise the basic questions on how far these aims were, or were not, being fulfilled in present society, and should stimulate in-depth study of particular issues so that the representatives of the churches could speak with authority backed by sound knowledge. He looked forward to there being two or three more "Moots" being formed to help in this process.

The discussion centred largely on the strategy to be followed. Oldham in fact hoped that a pamphlet might be produced, under the auspices of the Council, on the basis of his paper, setting out the aims of the "Christian society" – it would be a Christian analogy to *Mein Kampf* and distributed to about 300 people, and then published only if most of them felt committed to its main positions. Those who backed it would be invited to form some kind of movement or order. Alec Vidler was doubtful: it would be encouraging people to "go underground" in a movement of investigation and experiment without any suggestion that anybody had a programme or solution. Also he had serious misgivings on the relation to the institutional churches – "They were part of the thing that was bankrupt." Others felt that many laity were wanting such a word: but John Baillie felt that while Oldham was right in substance, as yet it hardly amounted to a clarion call in the style of Luther or John Knox, which was what was needed to engage people. Eliot had questions about the addressees: the people who were meant to become part of the movement, or the public at large, or who? It was in fact Walter Moberly who put his finger on the nub of the issue. Oldham was wanting the document to go out under the auspices of the council, a body which was deliberately set up with official church backing, yet at the same time the paper's presupposition was that the church was incapable of meeting the present need and a radical movement of questioning was needed: "The question was whether it was possible to combine the official blessing and countenance of the Church with living freedom." Eliot agreed. Oliver Tomkins, already manifesting the shrewdness of his later ecumenical and episcopal career, agreeing that the paper lacked concreteness, felt "that the question, Who should back the statement, must be answered by the attempt to get the Council to do so, leaving the initiative to them whether they were prepared to go on or not". Beyond agreeing that some kind of "movement" was necessary, the discussion was inconclusive.

In the evening the group turned to Karl Mannheim's paper "Planning for Freedom".[16] Running to nineteen pages, the paper is of unusual interest on several grounds. In the first place, it was this piece of writing which, more than any other single contribution, decisively set the long-term agenda for the Moot. Mannheim shared with the other members the sense of alarm not only at the emergence of the totalitarian dictatorships, but also at the growth, inexorable and seemingly unexamined, of the impersonally planned societies in the democratic West. Unlike Oldham and most of the others, however, he did not see "planning" and "freedom" simply as antitheses, and was therefore not

[16] Mannheim, "Planning for Freedom" (Moot Papers).

reduced to a desperate rearguard action to defend "personal freedom" at all costs against the encroaching impersonal state. He took a much more matter-of-fact view of the growth of the industrial and technological society, and a calmly pragmatic approach to what needed to be done here and now: "we ought to consent to any innovation which increases the efficiency of social institutions but we ought at the same time to watch these steps with the greatest possible care, insofar as they are likely to endanger our freedom, democracy and social progress." What was required was that a group of conscientious and thoughtful people should first think out a long-range policy, a kind of "Summa" for a new social system, and then make an actual survey of the concrete changes presently taking place. Planning and freedom need not be simply opposed. One could plan *for* freedom, for example by deliberately refraining from "superfluous management" – a radically different policy from the "purposeless non-interference of a *laisser-faire* society". Such planning, for a start, would move in the direction of social justice.

Second, the paper is revealing for showing how close, from very early in the life of the Moot, Mannheim and Oldham were in their view of the need for some kind of "order" to permeate the decision-making positions in social and public life for the sake of bringing moral and spiritual values to bear on policy. And it is not clear who was the greater influence on the other. The order, Mannheim felt, was to "revitalize the social body and to spread the spirit". Standing midway between the huge organized bodies and the individual, its task "is not merely to get in touch with the people, find out what is going on in the nooks and corners of society and invent new methods of adjustment where the old ones have failed, but also to persuade organised bodies like the Churches and the Civil service to accept the new ideas and the practical purposes which are necessary in an age of democratic change". It would be a *combatant* order, the nervous system in the social organism.

Third, the paper demonstrates just how seriously Mannheim, though an outsider to Christian belief, did take the churches as social institutions and as potential instruments of social change. There is a whole page on the role of the church in expressing public sentiment, and even a paragraph on "prayer as one of the more significant forms of social integration" and the eucharist and ritual as a means of spiritualizing mass emotion "in a way which is directly opposed to the fomentation of mass hysteria in modern society".

The discussion in the Moot was also revealing, in that Mannheim seemed both to sharpen the diagnosis of the "machine age" and at the same time to underline the responsibilities and potential influence of the churches even more than some of the Christians in the group were prepared to do. Oldham asked him whether he was actually saying that "granted Mannheim's point that planning would be blind and disastrous unless criticism was brought to bear on it, any body of people existed who could provide this criticism other than the churches?"[17] Mannheim replied that he saw no hope in the universities, but

[17] 3rd Moot Minutes, p.17.

if the church had the courage to study things thoroughly this could stimulate the universities and so penetrate society. Alec Vidler felt that the machine age was irredeemable but there was no way out of it, and "we had to go on with a programme such as that outlined by Mannheim, even though it might fail". Middleton Murry did not like the plan outlined by Mannheim "but was forced to agree with it". The discussion was summarized thus:

> *J.H. Oldham* pointed out that a decision would have to be reached shortly, but he was anxious to take it within the fellowship of this group. It involved a venture into the unknown of a group which was prepared to say the Christian revelation was true and that they were prepared to follow out its implications. This demanded a testing of institutions, the initiation of a movement of thought and action, and the acceptance of the sacrifice involved. If, as he judged, Mannheim's programme was accepted by the group as a whole, this would become an integral part of the programme.[18]

The Sunday morning was occupied with H.A. Hodges' paper "Towards a Plan for a New *Summa*", a proposal to attempt a new Christian philosophy which would reintegrate Catholic and Protestant thought, the scientific viewpoint, and ethics, in a socially relevant way. The meeting concluded with a further debate on strategy, and the best use of Oldham's document. He was encouraged to revise it, send it to 200–300 people, and then get it printed privately and let it be available on demand, rather than attempt to issue it with the sanction of the Council on Christian Faith and the Common Life.

## The fourth Moot: a "Christian order"?

This effort in fact appears to have sunk without trace. Not a word was breathed about it at the fourth meeting of the Moot, held 14–17 April 1939 at Old Jordans Hostel, Beaconsfield. Instead, Oldham delivered an introductory statement on the nature and purpose of the Moot itself, in relation to the wider movement which it would help to stimulate. The Moot was concerned primarily with thought, and this task required a wider body of people than the present membership of the Moot. Should the Moot be enlarged, or continue as the central planning group? In answer to questions, Oldham said that the distinction in his mind between the Moot and the "Order" was that "the Order would include a body of people working for a new Christendom otherwise than in the realm of pure thought".[19] In fact while further discussion of Mannheim's and Hodges' papers formally set most of the agenda for this meeting, the discussion continually turned towards the question of what the Moot was for, and what the wider movement or Order should be and do. Mannheim again used his analogy of the nervous system in the organism. Alec Vidler wanted a new political movement in place of the discredited main parties. Gilbert Shaw said the Order should only point the way towards redemption,

[18] *Ibid.*
[19] 4th Moot Minutes, p.3.

that is, set out fundamental principles – "a kind of collectivised Jeremiah". Mannheim retorted this would be to allow fascism and admit defeat even before starting. Again it was Moberly who saw the issues clearly:

> *W.H. Moberly* said there were two questions involved. There was the need to get action taken, and that raised the question of what action and by whom? There was the different issue of the need to get together on the basis of a way of life in view of spiritual issues which were greater than that of totalitarianism. Clearly on either ground we needed a small body of deeply committed persons; but were we the possible people to undertake political tasks of this magnitude? It might be laid on us to do something in regard to the deeper spiritual issues, but we could hardly be the spearhead of a new political movement.[20]

Oldham claimed that there were already about forty or fifty people in agreement with the aims of the total project. What was required was some bond between them which would give meaning to their association. But what bond? What precise aims? Moberly pressed his point, but Oldham would say no more than that these were necessarily intangible at the moment. He was evidently thinking, still, that the Council on Christian Faith and the Common Life might provide the necessary staffing and resources for the project. If not, then the Order would provide a readily available pool of committed people to see the project through. T.S. Eliot suggested that successive stages of commitment might be envisaged as the project opened up. Oldham suggested that the Order should have an annual meeting, part of the time of which would be spent in groups. Its function would be to review the most urgent tasks, "and it was assumed that members would try to back any action that was appropriate". They would accept some kind of discipline of daily prayer throughout the year. Oldham also used the analogy of the Round Table on Africa, but as Moberly pointed out this had begun with a few like-minded people gathered round a concrete situation, and attached to Lord Milner in South Africa. This was very different from collecting about sixty people in the way suggested. Eric Fenn finally brought both clarity and realism in suggesting that what, in the end, was being suggested was that the Moot be enlarged and form *itself* into an Order. This brought much assent, and some time was spent discussing possible names: Koinonia; The Brotherhood of the Common Mind; The Christian Conspiracy.

None of these names was adopted, because the Order never transpired and the Moot remained as it was. The discussion periodically resurrected itself at subsequent meetings (in one form in particular in 1941, as seen below), but the fact was that the Moot, in its size and composition and style, was by now too fully satisfying to its present members for them seriously to contemplate radical change. Moreover, the "Order" remained a perversely nebulous idea in Oldham's mind. It was never, for instance, ever really asked just *how*, say, a member who was a civil servant in the Home Office might expect actually to change or

[20] *Ibid.*, p.17.

modify a governmental policy as a result of his commitment. It is striking that Oldham does not seem to have drawn on his own positive experience of influencing colonial policy in Africa ten years earlier. That had required a long-term, developing partnership and dialogue with the decision-makers, and about very specific issues. Compared with that phase of his work, this aspect of the Moot proceedings remained abstract and ethereal, never getting beyond an affirmation of the need for study, public declaration and an undefined commitment in some kind of association.

Moreover – and here Christopher Dawson and Walter Moberly had come very close to exposing them – were there not anti-democratic tendencies lurking in the talk of an "Order"? It was intended to safeguard the dimension of personal freedom and responsibility but, quite apart from the question of how far these are compatible with an "Order" (and some in the Moot were not averse to seeing what might be learnt from the fascist and communist party methods), the people whom Oldham envisaged as members of it seem largely to have been "key" figures in government, education and other public services. That is, those who already have power. He seems relatively uninterested in the people at large, that is, precisely those who were allegedly most threatened by the planned society. Here we come close to one of the paradoxes in the Oldham mind. He had a deep concern that power be not misused, whether in Whitehall or colonial Africa or in Nazi Germany. He was deeply concerned over issues ranging from race relations to unemployment. But at the end of the day he does seem to pay more attention to the powerful decision-maker than to those affected by the decision. Eric Fenn recalls how, in September 1938, Oldham told him that Prime Minister Chamberlain was going off to Munich. "What is he going to do there?" asked Fenn innocently. "He's going to make *peace*", said Oldham in hushed tones of awe.[21]

This fourth Moot meeting drew up an outline programme of study groups preparatory to conferences on the idea of university, education, the essence of Christianity, and politics and economics. It sounded as if the Oxford conference was indeed being extended. An enlarged meeting of the Moot itself would be held in September, with a number of additional names to be invited including William Temple, Leslie Hunter and A.D. Lindsay. Finally, contingency plans were agreed upon for the eventuality of war, including: contact to be maintained, a skeleton Moot to be convened as soon as possible, and briefing to be prepared to encourage church leaders "to take a definite line in accordance with the fifth report of the Oxford Conference" against hatred of enemies, on a generous attitude towards conscientious objectors, against retaliation and "the more brutal methods of war", and a concern from the outset with "the temper of the peace". Oldham suggested that one practical task that might be called for immediately was how the church could be prepared for the emergency of the next war and whether it could be prevented from being swept into the same attitude as in 1914. If it was possible to build up a body of thought within

[21] Fenn interview with author, 20 Oct. 1990.

the church, both pacifist and non-pacifist, to guide the leaders of the church in such an emergency it would be a great contribution to the witness of the Church.[22]

### The Moot goes to war

As it happened, there was no need for a "skeletal" Moot meeting on the outbreak of war. Britain declared war on Germany on 3 September and the enlarged meeting of the Moot had been fixed for less than three weeks hence, 23–24 September. On 6 September Oldham wrote to the Moot members:

> The immense danger in which we stand is that the fact that what the nation is fighting is something utterly inhuman and evil may make us forget that anti-Christ is not only incarnated in the Nazi leaders, but is an active and present force among ourselves and in our hearts. Only the strongest spiritual effort can save us from being assimilated to what we oppose. The war will evoke tides of passion which it will be hard to stem, but if everything that matters is not to be lost, we must make from the start the utmost effort of which we are capable to rally all the spiritual forces in the nation to combat the evil in ourselves and to strive for a just, real and lasting peace. The need for committing ourselves to God to be His instruments for the coming to birth of a reborn Christendom in His time and way has become more urgent than ever. Only in that direction is there any gleam of hope for mankind.

Oldham insisted that the Moot meet as planned. It did so at Annandale in north London, and in addition to the regular membership of the Oldhams, Baillie, Eliot, Farmer, Fenn, Hodges, Iredale, Löwe, Mannheim, Moberly, Middleton Murry, Shaw, Tomkins and Vidler, it was attended by a notable array of church leaders and thinkers: Archie Craig (secretary of the newly formed Commission on International Friendship and Social Responsibility), O.S. Franks, A.C. Goyder, W.D.L. Greer, Philip Mairet, R.A. Tawney, C.G. Vickers – and Reinhold Niebuhr who was in Britain on a lecturing visit. The first five hours were spent simply allowing members to state their feelings and questions now that war was a fact. Never was so much self-confessed confusion and uncertainty evident. Oldham himself had in fact given a radio broadcast soon after the declaration, stating the need for a fight "on two fronts": against the obvious enemy without, but equally on the need for a new basis of values for our own society. Most of the Moot were sympathetic to this, but felt in need of much greater clarity. Moberly for example wanted to know what sort of criticism could be made of the government without sounding doctrinaire. There was the danger of pharisaism arising from the knowledge that one is fighting wrong. John Baillie said that never in his life had he been so unable to bring his thoughts into focus. "In 1914 there was very little confusion and a desire to be in it. To-day he found students confused but glumly determined."[23]

[22] 4th Moot Minutes, p.15.
[23] 5th Moot Minutes p.2.

Middleton Murry found himself deeply alienated by the whole business. Germany and Russia had taken the initiative in answering the breakdown of society but the process had become diabolical in their hands. Christianity had become irrelevant and the best thing might be to keep quiet on the "Christian" element in it all. He had had an article for the *Times Literary Supplement* rejected for suggesting that Christian principles might concur only in defeat, and another article criticized for *not* saying that the German people must suffer everything necessary for the eradication of Hitlerism. Alec Vidler (who was himself to get into mild trouble with the publishers of *Theology* for an editorial warning against national self-righteousness)[24] recognized that national effort must depend on crude over-simplification but "could someone say in public while there is yet time that the issue is confused?"[25] Significantly, it was Mannheim and Löwe, who knew the enemy at first hand better than anyone else in the group, who called both for conviction on the necessity for fighting to win, and for clarity on the deeper issues being fought for. Reinhold Niebuhr, as would be expected, was trenchant:

> Our despair is partly due to our moralism, to the feeling that we are the good people but not good enough to overcome the bad ones, but the atonement means that there is no resolution of the moral conflict of good and evil in history. The Christian problem is what to do with a bad conscience. One way is to bring forth fruits meet for repentance and to let God's mercy look after your bad conscience.
>
> English moral sensitivity has created many good things but it did not know what to do with a bad conscience, ever since Versailles. Human history is always tragic and looking at the present situation from this perspective we see that we are sinful people, fighting sin, but we also have to stand for right. There is a danger of getting a moral squeamishness which makes us forget it is *evil* we are fighting.[26]

At any rate, it was with confusion and hesitation rather than, as Oldham had feared, "tides of passion" that the Moot members felt faced. The mood was notably different from that of August 1914. The constructive time at this Moot was a discussion of Oldham's plan for a newsletter, which will be dealt with in the next chapter. There was also yet again a discussion on an "Order", and the relation of the Moot, enlarged or otherwise, to this. Yet again, no conclusion was reached. Fenn summarized the outcome: "In general it was felt that the group was agreed that our war aims might be called a fighting for the potentialities of our freedom and that consequently the plans on which the Moot has become engaged remain more vital than ever."[27]

## The Moot established

What happened was that the Moot continued in much its present form for the duration of the war, and for a time beyond. Space does not permit more than a

[24] See Vidler, pp.114–16.
[25] 5th Moot Minutes, p.4.
[26] *Ibid.*, p.6
[27] *Ibid.*, p.12.

generalized account of its continuing life and discussions, but enough can be said to give a picture of a quite remarkable achievement.

From September 1939 to December 1944 the Moot met two or three times a year, and in fact in 1941 met four times. The pattern remained as before: a weekend in a large house, each meeting preceded by circulation of the full minutes of the previous meeting and usually also a weighty dose of papers for discussion, either prepared specially by one or more members, or culled from writings elsewhere. The venues varied. There seemed no shortage of suitably large and hospitable houses within reach of London. The Old Hostel at Jordans was popular, as was 13 Norham Gardens, off the Banbury Road in Oxford, but the most regular meeting-point later in the war was St Julians, the missionary retreat centre near Horsham in Sussex founded and run by Florence Allshorn. Though generously accommodating in size, beds and quietness, under wartime austerity the hosts could provide little more. Before long, the letters giving members travelling directions also came to include requests to bring their own precious rations of butter and sugar. The fact that the members, beset as was most of the population by more than enough to do in war-time, were prepared to make this regular commitment under such tedious conditions, is itself noteworthy. One thinks particularly, for example, of John Baillie and the tiresome journey to and from Edinburgh on overcrowded, blacked-out trains.

Two further significant recruits not hitherto listed, both of them distinguished educationists, should be mentioned. *Fred Clarke* (knighted in 1943) had taught in South Africa and Canada as well as Britain and was now professor of education and director of the Institute of Education at London University. *Sir Hector Hetherington* was principal and vice-chancellor of Glasgow University and had a string of committee responsibilities in the areas including unemployment insurance, hospitals, economic research and wages agreements. In these and others Oldham had therefore mustered not only academic acumen but a considerable range of experience in public policy formation.

The membership remained impressively constant and an attendance "register" will be found as an appendix to this book. If the attendance at the twenty meetings from April 1938 to December 1944 is examined, then a clear picture emerges. The innermost core comprised six persons: Oldham himself, Hodges, Mannheim, Vidler, Moberly and Fenn, each of whom attended sixteen or more meetings. Mary Oldham, Gilbert Shaw, Eleonora Iredale, T.S. Eliot and John Baillie each attended eleven or more times. Eleven people thus constituted the most solid, regular membership. Around this team were five people who attended less often (for good reasons) but were certainly considered by the others to belong: Middleton Murry and Fred Clarke (nine attendances each), Adolf Löwe (six), Hector Hetherington and Walter Oakeshott (five each). Finally comes a tail of people who attended three times or less. They include Christopher Dawson whose travels and other commitments made him a particularly sad loss to the group (though he remained an important correspondent with Oldham) and H.H. Farmer who had to resign soon after the outbreak of war due to sheer pressure of work. They also include the unfortunates like Lesslie Newbigin and William Paton whom Oldham did not invite again, and Oliver Tomkins who was drawn into other activities. Adolf Löwe was also a serious loss to the group after such a regular and committed beginning: he left for the United States in 1940. The kind of commitment shown to the Moot is perhaps best illustrated by John Baillie. He would certainly have been in the top bracket of attendances but for two enforced periods of absence, during 1940–41 when he was serving with the YMCA among the troops in France and visited the United States, and during 1943–44 while he was moderator of the general assembly of the Church of Scotland. The fact that after both these terms he got back to the Moot as soon as possible – and during them remained in correspondence – says it all.[28] Later in the life of the Moot, a number of younger figures appear, either as members or guests, including Kathleen Bliss, Daniel Jenkins and Donald Mackinnon. Oldham certainly did not lose his eye for spotting potential, as testified by the subsequent careers of these recruits. Another prize catch was the scientist and philosopher Michael Polanyi who made his first appearance in June 1944.

The subjects dealt with by the Moot continued to focus on social transformation and the necessary tension between planning and freedom. Sometimes the starting point was the social topic itself, sometimes an element in Christian belief which should inform the social philosophy. With Fred Clarke in attendance, education, religious education and the role of the modern university received a good deal of attention. Natural law and social ethics, a "Bill of Duties", the "Christian Imagination", "Freedom and Vocation", the metaphysical presuppositions of Christianity, the question of power, post-war reconstruction in Europe – these were but some of the successive agenda items. A lively theological debate sprang up when, at John Baillie's instigation, the group was made to consider the significance of contemporary Barthian thinking. After the twelfth meeting which discussed a paper by Hodges on "Christian Thinking Today" Baillie was more than ever concerned that the group, the majority of whom were of philosophical or liberal theological bent, needed to be put in touch with the neo-orthodoxy more typical of the generation of students he was teaching at Edinburgh. Oldham concurred with this, and so Thomas F. Torrance was asked to produce a paper in response. It was a Barthian broadside on Hodges' whole notion of making Christianity "intelligible" and "satisfying" to certain human impulses.[29] Hodges wrote an equally spirited reply.[30] Some Moot members felt this Barthian intrusion a waste of their time but it did stimulate Hodges to some creative and original writing in some further Moot papers on human "archetypes" operative in society and culture. On ethical issues, some of the most interesting discussions took

[28] See, in addition to Clements, "John Baillie and 'The Moot'", K. Clements, "Oldham and Baillie: A Creative Relationship", in A.R. Morton, ed., *God's Will in a Time of Crisis: A Colloquium Celebrating the 50th Anniversary of the Baillie Commission*, Edinburgh, Centre for Theology and Public Issues, New College, 1994, pp.45–59.

[29] T.F. Torrance, "Christian Thinking Today" (Moot Papers).

[30] H.A. Hodges, "Barthianism and Christian Thinking" (Moot Papers).

place in the sixteenth and seventeenth meetings. To the former (8–11 January 1943), Frank Pakenham (later Lord Longford) came as a guest, fresh from his work as assistant to Sir William Beveridge, and gave a presentation both on the Beveridge report and his paper "Grey Eminence and Political Morality" which had recently appeared in the *Political Quarterly*. At the latter (18–21 June 1943) Reinhold Niebuhr was present to weigh into Middleton Murry's "Christian society" as offering a form of monasticism rather than an ethic for the real world.

Hodges wrote copiously for the Moot, but the most prolific was Karl Mannheim. The subjects of his lengthy papers – never just "notes" but detailed, closely-argued essays – themselves convey just how seriously he was wishing to engage with the group and how much he expected from it: "Planning for Freedom"; "Towards a New Social Philosophy I: A Challenge to Christian Thinkers by a Sociologist"; "Towards a New Social Philosophy II: Christian Values and the Changing Environment"; "The Crisis in Valuation"; "A Syllabus on Power".

If Oldham played the role of skilled organizer and director of a rolling seminar, he had also to be a wise tactician of human relationships. Of all the people who might have seemed obvious choices to belong to the Moot but who were *not* invited, William Temple is most conspicuous (though he was at first suggested for the enlarged meeting of September 1939). Eric Fenn, closer than most to Oldham at the time, believes that this was Oldham's conscious choice, made on the grounds that by his sheer stature Temple would have dominated the group to the detriment of the kind of discussion being looked for.[31] As it was, although some close friendships grew up in the Moot there were also at times tensions and personal frictions. Middleton Murry, in particular, sat uneasily with some of the more urbane and academically philosophical members and eventually his patience wore out. At the fifteenth meeting (11–14 September 1942) he conspicuously refrained from taking any part in the long discussion of Hodges' two papers on "Archetypes". Immediately after the meeting, on 14 August, he wrote at length to Oldham to give "some rational account of my unsatisfactory behaviour at the Moot". He confessed to a confused anger about what the Moot is supposed to be:

> I do not think it is the proper business of the Moot to criticise in detail papers written by specialists along the lines of their specialism . . . I will take the example of Hodges' paper. What am I to conclude from it? That a new archetype is necessary for creative social change for the better? That a new archetype, though necessary, cannot be created by conscious intent? Both together? Neither? The point I wish to make is that the argument breaks off at the point of relevance. Why should we spend our time on the prolegomena?
>
> . . . I am not in the least criticising Hodges' paper – except as material for the Moot. If the Moot is a philosophical club, well and good. But I believed it was something different . . .

[31] Fenn interview.

Murry did not attend again. Oldham had the letter copied and (presumably with his permission) circulated to all the Moot members. Sometimes other Moot members could save a situation, and with humour, as when the young Donald Mackinnon exploded "The Oxford don is a *bloody* thing!", and in the nervous silence which ensued John Baillie's quiet tones were heard, "Mr Chairman, there must be another word."[32]

## Fruits of the Moot

What, at the end of the day, did the Moot actually produce apart from an enriching and intellectually stimulating experience for its members? In one respect the answer is, not much. Oldham's hopes that from this nucleus some kind of "Order" to re-direct and reinvigorate British society would emerge were never realized. The long, tortuous discussions on "strategy" finally got nowhere. On the one hand the Moot itself was too small, too intellectually preoccupied (rightly so in the eventual opinion of most of its members) to be action-oriented. On the other hand, the Council on the Christian Faith and the Common Life, which Oldham saw as the bridge between the thinking of the Moot and a more public form of collective action, was too weak in organization and resources to mobilize that wider action. Oldham did resurrect the idea early in 1941 when he conceived of a "Fraternity of the Spirit", an association of people committed "in the power of the Spirit" to the practice of fellowship and the pursuit of a society based on freedom before God and on inter-dependence. He wrote to the Moot members on 2 April 1941 with this idea, and it is intriguing to speculate what connection there was in his mind with the visionary but short-lived "Sword of the Spirit" movement initiated by leading Catholics with the strong support of Cardinal Hinsley (who apparently invented the name of the movement).[33] Christopher Dawson was among its leading spokesmen, it had strong support from prominent Anglicans including George Bell, and it was coming to its fateful climax at about the same time as Oldham was communicating his idea to the Moot. The question of a possible connection is even more interesting in that Christopher Dawson was due to attend the Moot eleventh meeting virtually the next day after Oldham wrote (4–7 April) but was prevented by illness.

In other respects, however, the Moot was highly productive. From the start Oldham had in fact argued that much of its fruit would be found in the day-to-day work of its members and their already existing individual pursuits and responsibilities. There is no doubt that this was the case for many of the members. Eliot, for example, was powerfully resourced and stimulated for his writing on culture and society, seen notably in his *Notes towards the Definition of Culture* (1948), as has been well documented by R. Kojecky.[34] Fred Clarke,

[32] *Ibid.*

[33] See A. Hastings, *A History of English Christianity 1920–1985*, London, Collins, 1986, pp.383ff.

[34] R. Kojecky, *T.S. Eliot's Social Criticism,* London, Faber & Faber, 1971, esp. Ch. IX, "A Christian Elite".

one of the most formative minds on education in the postwar years, was likewise stimulated and played a major role in the higher education group which produced the series *Educational Issues of Today.*[35] Walter Moberly also shared in that development. Some of the stimulus was longer term as well as immediate. Alec Vidler not only found his theological awareness both widened and sharpened still more, at just the time when he was beginning as editor of *Theology* and thus to engender through that journal a wider awareness of the critical context in which Christian thought was finding itself. Looking back in Cambridge nearly twenty years later, he described the Moot as "the best group I have ever been a member of, and the most high-powered",[36] and it was in conscious recollection of it that he convened the group of questioning Cambridge theologians who eventually produced the symposium *Soundings* in 1962. Hodges, too, used the Moot both to air his philosophical explorations and have them constructively criticized. He continued to write creatively on both philosophy and theology until well into his later years (he died in 1976). But, again, it was above all Mannheim who both gave to and gained from the Moot so much that bore fruit in his writing. His Moot papers were unashamedly the seedlings of what was to appear in his later (and posthumous) works such as *Man and Society in an Age of Reconstruction* – as well as deeply informing Fred Clarke's studies on education. "Planning for Freedom", a phrase first tossed around the Moot, became something of a slogan for a generation of social thinkers.

As for Oldham himself, it is almost impossible to disentangle his own thinking in the Moot from what which he expressed in his own wartime writing and broadcasting, an account of which is given in the next chapter on *The Christian News-Letter.* That particular venture is one which overlapped considerably with the Moot, the more so as several Moot members – Eliot, Vidler, Iredale and Moberly in particular – were Oldham's collaborators in it, not to mention contributors to its pages.

The Moot produced relatively little by way of collective writing, but certain pieces emerged by consensus and, thanks to Oldham's connections, had some wider significance. William Temple may have been kept at a safe distance from the Moot but Oldham kept in close touch with him by correspondence. His accession to Canterbury in 1942 meant that the Church of England – and one could say in a real sense the whole of organized Christianity in the land – now had as its leader one much in tune with the questions being explored in the Moot. He too felt a responsibility to continue the agenda of Oxford 1937, as seen in his wartime speaking and writing and above all in his immensely influential paperback *Christianity and Social Order* (1942). The seventeenth Moot meeting (18–21 June 1943) had before it a draft of Temple's "Beckley Lecture" and in turn the Moot resourced Temple at a number of points, most

[35] See William Taylor, "Education and the Moot", in R. Aldrich, ed., *History and Education: Essays in Honour of Peter Gordon*, London: Woburn, 1996.

[36] Mehta, p.83.

notably in a memorandum sent to him in autumn 1943 on "The Christian Witness in the Present Crisis", which as will be seen in the next chapter formed the basis of an important supplement appearing over Temple's name in *The Christian News-Letter*.

There was moreover one corporate church initiative, in itself of major significance, on which the Moot had a vital influence through one of its members. In 1940 the general assembly of the Church of Scotland appointed a "Commission on the Interpretation of God's Will in the Present Crisis". John Baillie was called upon to chair it. It worked for over four years, producing reports on the nature of the church, the presentation of the faith for today, and social order. Marriage and the family, education, social and industrial life and international reconstruction, were all covered. For Baillie, the Moot was of capital importance as a resource for this work, and this alone accounts for much of his commitment to the group. A full account of the mutual influences of the Moot and the "Baillie Commission" can be found elsewhere.[37]

There were other and still wider reaches of currents from the Moot. Oldham remained in touch throughout the war years with W.A. Visser 't Hooft at the embryonic World Council of Churches in Geneva. The WCC in fact became a point of contact between the churches outside Germany and the Christian resistance inside Nazi Germany. Several of the Moot papers were sent to Geneva, and there is circumstantial evidence that at least one found its way to the Kreisau circle of intellectual resisters led by Helmut von Moltke – which was itself a kind of Moot planning for a non-Nazi Germany and a new Europe. There was a connection on another level between the Moot and Kreisau: among Adolf Löwe's former students and followers in the "religious socialist" movement before the Nazi period were Horst von Einsiedeln and Carl Dietrich von Trota, by now key members of the Kreisau circle. The Moot was one nexus in a web of Christian social and theological enquiry transcending the lines drawn by war.[38]

## The death of Mannheim – and of the Moot

The Moot continued after the war. Its membership was changing. New and younger members were coming in. Then, in January 1947, Karl Mannheim died at the sadly early age of 53. The Moot members wrote through Oldham a letter of condolence to Karl Mannheim's widow, Julia. Perhaps it was only when they read her short but moving reply that they fully realized all that the Moot had meant to him, and what it might mean to each of them:

> It was the spot for him to be as he was without the slightest reservations because he knew that you all wanted and do not mind if he gives himself as he is. Only in his first youth has he had something similar to this – *silicet parva componere magnus.* That was the circle around George Lukacs in Hungary before he had to leave the

[37] See Clements, "Oldham and Baillie".
[38] See *ibid.* for more details.

country for his political belief and convictions some 27 years ago. Until the formation of the Moot he was longing for that safe and free place for the mind, soul and spirit and your circle has given that to him and I should like to bless everyone of you for having taken him in so completely. You all shared his ultimate aims and endeavours of what is important. I thank you also for your prayers for him and for me. I am a strong believer in gratitude and I know it will never fade out towards every one of you.[39]

The Moot members also contributed to a fund towards the initial expenses of publishing Mannheim's unpublished papers, and the cost of a visit by Julia Mannheim to the USA where further plans for the series of publications, under the editorial direction of Adolf Löwe, were made.

The Moot met for the last time in November 1947. Oldham told the group he had decided to call it a day as far as the Moot was concerned – or at any rate he himself was not prepared to go on leading it.[40] Perhaps he was already looking for a pretext. He was always averse to prolonging a project, however valued, for its own sake and the Moot would soon be ten years old. New problems were beginning to preoccupy him. But the explicit reason he gave for terminating the Moot was that with Mannheim's death it had lost its prime intellectual mover. Baillie, for one, was deeply disappointed but Oldham remained firm. Some members continued to gather for a time at Julia Mannheim's home in Hampstead, and as late as 1950 Alec Vidler sounded out the possibility of reviving it.[41] But the Moot was now definitely a thing of the past.

[39] J. Mannheim letter to Moot members 19 Jan. 1947 [OA].
[40] JHO letter to Moot members Nov. 1947 [OA].
[41] Vidler letter to JHO 11 May 1950 [OA].

CHAPTER 18

# *The Christian News-Letter*

UNLIKE August 1914, when conflict burst like an unexpected thunderstorm, the second world war had been awaited for months, if not years. For September 1939 Joe Oldham was certainly well prepared. The Oxford 1937 conference had in itself in some respects been a preparation for the scenario of war, in which the churches accepted the challenge of declaring themselves an international fellowship, come what may. In the British context the most urgent challenge to be addressed, in Oldham's view, was the self-understanding of British society. What was it, apart from sheer national survival, that was to be fought for? If "Hitlerism" was to be defeated, what was to be put in its place? What in British society was *worth* defending, and what was under judgment, meriting dissolution? This, as we have seen, was essentially the question he raised in his letter to *The Times* of October 1938.

## A plot is hatched

The fourth meeting of the Moot, 14–17 April 1939, in considering the steps to be taken in the event of war, agreed that "there would be an immediate need of literature dealing with the issues raised by the war for Christians, in the form of articles and pamphlets".[1] No more was said at this stage, but it is clear that during the remaining months of peace Oldham and his closest associates were busy putting in place a mechanism for enabling this provision. Oldham was already attracted by the example of Stephen King-Hall's *National News-Letter*[2] and had in mind a weekly bulletin to be produced under the patronage of the Council on the Christian Faith and the Common Life. It was Eleonora Iredale who immediately started seeing to the practicalities, and who not only started

[1] 4th Moot Minutes, p.22.

[2] Cf. Vidler, *Scenes from a Clerical Life*, p.120.

to raise some funds but had the foresight to purchase thirty tons of paper and so forestall any wartime austerity measures.[3] From the start Oldham envisaged it as a collaborative exercise exploiting his large network of contacts, not least the members of the Moot.

By the time Neville Chamberlain broadcast to the nation on 3 September that Britain was now at war with Germany, Oldham's plans were already clear. *The Christian News-Letter* would be produced, he hoped, weekly rather than fortnightly. The group responsible for it would not support a particular political solution but it would aim at political effect. It would seek to keep alive awareness of moral values and hold together those trying to overcome either fear for themselves or fear of deep changes. He hoped that the Council on the Christian Faith and the Common Life would give it approval and appoint its editors, but not control its policy. The editors would be assisted by an editorial board, basically the Moot and near-associates, plus a number of church officials. There was the distinct anxiety that if thought too outspoken, the News-Letter might be challenged or even suppressed, in which case it might then be floated as an independent journal helped by the advertisement which it gained. Its format would be a four-page quarto sheet carrying about 2,000 words. The articles would all result from group discussion and criticism, based on information and research carried out by the editorial staff. There would also be a two- or three-page supplement commenting on particular issues generated by correspondence from the readers.

Oldham worked very quickly indeed in the early days of September. He secured the support of the archbishops of Canterbury and York, and the Free Church leaders, to promote circulation of the News-Letter. Alec Vidler, now at Hawarden, was recruited as co-editor with Oldham, and agreed to spend two days a week in London. Oldham cheerfully pointed out that not only would Vidler's talents be well used, but it would be less than likely that *both* editors would be killed in air-raids and so continuity in the work could be reasonably assured. The editorial group was formed: T.S. Eliot, Philip Mairet and Lord Hambledon would meet weekly with Oldham and Vidler. Seven main areas were already sketched out for airing in the publication:

1 the religious interpretation of present events;
2 a survey of immediate issues raised;
3 drawing attention to the lessons of history;
4 practical problems such as evacuation and the 14–20 age-group;
5 the making real of the ecumenical church;
6 the defence of religious and democratic principles;
7 the formulation of war-aims.

Moreover, the Society for Promoting Christian Knowledge (SPCK) was agreeable to publishing a series of booklets expanding on the topics dealt with in the News-Letter, to be edited by Vidler.

[3] Information from M. Reeves.

Oldham brought his plans to the enlarged fifth meeting of the Moot on 23–24 September, making clear that only with the Moot's support would he proceed further. The group was enthusiastic but raised a number of questions, especially about the intended readership. Would it be sufficiently popular in style to reach the 10,000 subscribers Oldham was hoping for? Oldham said that he wanted the News-Letter to be of such quality that it would be thought by the Master of Balliol to be worth reading yet would equally appeal to schoolteachers and Workers' Education Association pupils.[4] Some cautioned against undue haste in launching the News-Letter on the ground that several issues would need planning in advance, and Adolf Löwe suggested that "if it were postponed until January that would give time for the public to become accustomed to the war when it really starts". Oldham was not disposed towards such discretion. There was, however, one particular recommendation to which Oldham submitted. He had been firm that the articles should be anonymous, written by different people though edited by one group. The Moot accepted this in principle but was unanimous that "some personal signature was essential, and that it must in fact appear to go out as a letter from Oldham".[5] For once, Oldham was persuaded to put self-effacement on one side, and this apparently small concession was in fact to add a vital touch to the News-Letter which contributed hugely to its success.

The advisory committee of forty-eight "collaborators" was also assembled. Essentially it was the Moot plus church leaders and officials such as William Temple, M.E. Aubrey (secretary of the Baptist Union), Cyril Garbett (bishop of Winchester), Leslie Hunter (now bishop of Sheffield) and the Methodist W.D.L. Greer; academics including R.H. Tawney, Arnold Toynbee and A.D. Lindsay; theologians such as C.H. Dodd, Nathaniel Micklem and V.A. Demant; and a variety of other creative figures like Dorothy Sayers, Kurt Hahn and Sir Alfred Zimmern. Reinhold Niebuhr also appeared on the list, and Oldham was anxious to keep in close touch with ecumenical partners abroad, particularly W.A. Visser 't Hooft in Geneva. Visser 't Hooft was himself hoping to have some kind of international network of theological thinking set up to inform the churches caught up in the conflict, and wrote to Oldham on this in the first weeks of the war. Oldham replied enthusiastically – "obviously it will be the greatest re-inforcement if we can link up with ecumenical thought" – and invited Visser 't Hooft to contribute to the News-Letter.

The first meeting of collaborators took place on 15 November at Lambeth Palace, with William Temple in the chair. "I should like to ask you all . . .", wrote Oldham in his letter of invitation, "to think of the News-Letter not as something to which you are invited, from outside, to contribute, but as a joint enterprise which we are trying collectively to create. What will give significance to the News-Letter and to the series of small books which are being planned in connection with it, is that there should be behind it a concerted and sustained

[4] 5th Moot Minutes, p.5.
[5] *Ibid.*, p.8.

effort of thought. We must settle down as soon as we can to see how far we can arrive at a common understanding of the situation and of what must be done to wrest good out of evil, and as our understanding deepens direct our efforts to the education of the public mind."[6]

## First shot

By the time of this meeting, four issues of *The Christian News-Letter* had already appeared. The first (no. 0) was published on 18 October and sent as what today would be called a "mail-shot" to a large number of targeted individuals. It began:

> Dear X,
>
> I know that I could hardly hit on a worse opening for a News-Letter than to begin by explaining that it is issued under the auspices of the Council of the Churches on the Christian Faith and the Common Life. The thought of organisation leaves most people cold, and to some at least whose interest we want to enlist any mention of the Churches is an unpromising beginning. But the purpose of the Council which was set up by the Churches in this country last year is one which I believe you will recognise to be necessary and important. Its task is to bridge the gulf which exists at present between organised religion and the general life of the community. A cell has been created which has links not only with the various activities of the Churches but also with many individuals and organisations outside them. Its existence makes possible much which there was no means of attempting before.

There followed an explanation of the thinking behind the News-Letter in much the same terms as Oldham had expressed to his Moot colleagues and other collaborators, and an invitation to subscribe at ten shillings and sixpence for a year (a moderate price for those days) and to enlist other readers. Over Oldham's signature it concluded: "If in a multitude of centres throughout the country there begins an active canvassing of ideas leading to imaginative, constructive, practical effort, a new society will be coming to birth even in the throes of war."

There was, too, a supplement even to this prototype number. Anonymous, "What is a 'Christian' News-Letter?" is quintessentially Oldham: God has acted in Jesus Christ bringing a new era in the life of mankind; this is the foundational faith for belief in the victory over the forces of evil; Christians share in the life of the world in all its confusion yet with a clear hope for a better life; they identify with all that is good in their nation yet their final loyalty is to eternal values, before which even their nation (in contrast to the Nazi religion of nationalism) is judged; there are even many Germans "who hate the evils we are resisting as much as we do"; the Christian church transcends the bounds of nationality; creative effort must be maintained precisely in face of the militarism which war breeds.

[6] JHO letter to News-Letter collaborators 9 Oct. 1939 [OA].

All very basic principles, perhaps, but it was being stated with a taut clarity and unmistakable passion: "Few thoughtful people suppose that even [*sic*] if we win the war we can revert to our accustomed life. The existing order of things is at an end. We must be ready for drastic transformation of ideas, values, relationships and social habit." The concluding paragraphs merit quoting in full:

> The only force capable of bringing to birth a new society embodying enough of the Christian values to entitle it to be described as a new Christendom is that of alert, adventurous, disciplined men and women, delivered from anxiety about their personal future or immediate effectiveness and from dread of radical social change, and dedicated to the service of a society founded on Christian truth and justice. This deliverance from self-centredness and inhibition comes from a complete surrender to the will of God.
>
> What holds us back more than anything else is fear – fear not only of death but of life.
>
> Christianity offers us freedom from fear through the assurance that God is working out his purposes in history even though they are hidden from our eyes, that the forces of truth and goodness are more real, and in the long run more powerful, than those of evil, and that our individual lives are in the keeping of a Power whom we can absolutely trust. Our hope is that the News-Letter may serve as a means of communication between those who are reaching out after this way of life.

This was the spirit in which *The Christian News-Letter* was launched. The first issue for subscribers appeared on 1 November, dealing with "Christian concern for the peace", "God as Creator" and "Christian realism". The following week it included comments on as diverse themes as the destruction of nature and the role of chaplains to the forces. The weekly routine, to be followed till the end of the war and beyond, was under way.

## A grateful readership

The response was immediate, and beyond even what Oldham himself had really dared to hope. In the two weeks following the preliminary issue 3,560 subscribers enrolled. A small room in offices in Balcombe Street had been hired, and Eleonora Iredale quickly had to recruit a body of volunteers, who included several "non-Aryan" Christian refugees from Germany, to help in the work of dispatching the copies. By the spring of 1940 there were over 10,000 subscriptions – and many copies were being read by far more than one person. The readership covered the whole of Great Britain. Moreover, discussion groups based on the News-Letter were already forming spontaneously within days of the first issue. And, exactly as hoped, a huge and lively correspondence from readers resulted, and from all sorts and conditions of men and women. Oldham reported to the Council on the Christian Faith and the Common Life in the spring of 1940:

> Among our subscribers are privates in the army, Anglican and Roman Catholic Archbishops, school teachers in elementary and secondary schools, lawyers, doctors, miners, business men, civil servants, nurses, housewives, every variety of person seems to be represented, and represented not only in their membership but also in the correspondence which we receive. This varies considerably. There are days when there are not more than 50 letters; there are others when there are nearly 200 in one day. We read every letter and answer all we can.[7]

All this took place despite rising costs of printing and postage in the first months of war, necessitating an increase in the subscription rates. In due course the supplement was limited to a fortnightly appearance. There were other discouragements. With the onset of the London blitz in 1940–41 the editorial office had for a time to move to Manchester College, Oxford.[8] The sheer effort in maintaining the weekly output was colossal. The number of subscribers remained at around 10,000 throughout the war, with a peak of 11,592 in March 1941.[9] By 1942 fifty-two local study groups were in existence.

What was the secret of the success of *The Christian News-Letter*? In large measure of course it was the content: topics of immediate practicality, long-term issues of social reconstruction and fundamental questions of faith were all offered. In the war-time context where the alternatives were so often pulpit banalities or political rhetoric, many people – inside or on the edges or right outside the churches – were hungry for this diet which combined realism with hope. Kenneth Grayston recalls how much it meant to a theological student early in the war, to find writing which *brought together* the newer "biblical theology" with the urgent public issues of the day and enabled one to see things whole.[10] But the right *form* had also been hit upon. Oldham was delighted when one day in 1940 an army private back from France marched into the Balcombe Street office and pointed out that he liked the News-Letter "because it was so brief and compact he could carry it in his pocket, and it gave him something to think about in long intervals".[11] Finally, the significance of the personal touch which the Moot had insisted upon should not be underestimated. It was a feature which mattered deeply in war-time Britain, as mass organization and mass communication, not to mention mass disruption, took an increasing hold on life. Radio, for example, became of great importance not simply because it provided information and entertainment as such, but because even in the most threatening circumstances it provided an assured access to the personal realm of household names for a whole population. People could feel in touch with real personalities, from the bizarre but loveable characters in the "ITMA" radio show, to the newsreader who (for security reasons) had to declare his name at the start of each bulletin. Each time *The*

[7] Oldham, "Report to Council" [OA], p.2.

[8] Vidler, p.122.

[9] "Report to Christian Frontier Council", Feb. 1942 [OA].

[10] K. Grayston interview with author 18 March 1998. Grayston was later involved in the work of the *CNL* and Christian Frontier Council.

[11] "Report to Council", p.2.

*Christian News-Letter* arrived over Oldham's own flowing signature people felt they really were receiving a personal *letter.* Some years ago, the writer heard a speaker recalling how "as Dr Oldham used to keep telling us during the war, 'life is meeting'". She was unconsciously testifying to the sense of personal address conveyed by *The Christian News-Letter.* And, perhaps more than he realised at first, through the News-Letter Oldham was in fact expressing that theology and anthropology of personal encounter which he had sought to promote in more literary form for several years.

Through the News-Letter, Christian debate entered the public forum, and at a popular but serious level, to a degree perhaps never equalled before or since in Britain. It was exchanged with a large number of secular papers and periodicals – often at their suggestion – ranging from the *Listener* and *Time and Tide* to *Picture Post.* Then in January 1940 came the first of *The Christian News-Letter* books, the series of small paperbacks (another feature which became vastly popular, of necessity, in war-time Britain) edited by Alec Vidler and designed to amplify certain of the issues raised in the News-Letter itself. This first was Oldham's own *The Resurrection of Christendom,*[12] based on the draft of a document he had prepared before the war for discussion in the Moot and to be submitted to the Council on the Christian Faith and the Common Life as a policy statement for the Council. It is basically a recapitulation of his thinking from Oxford 1937 onwards, on the necessity for a new engagement of Christian thought with the contemporary and changing world. The familiar themes appear: a belief in the purposes of God in history, the need for a new social philosophy based on human inter-relationships, the emphasis on the role of laypeople in society, and the need for the church to collaborate with other groups working for social justice and harmony. One new element appears, however: the call for a new reverence for nature: "The Christian mind will have an instinctive sympathy with efforts to re-establish a harmony between man and Nature and to resist the destruction and wastage of the resources of the earth."[13] It was a theme he was to repeat and enlarge upon in the war years.[14] If Oldham had been heeded more, perhaps the frequent charge of recent times, that Christian theology has not been ecologically friendly, would have had less substance.

Virtually anything that mattered to people in the life they were living now or the life they hoped for after the war, found room in *The Christian News-Letter* and its supplements: the aims of a just peace; unemployment; housing; life and attitudes in the armed forces; education; the scientific method; religious education; the role of clergy; marriage and family life in wartime; planning and freedom; social security and the Beveridge report; conscientious objection; evacuees; youth; religion in the country-side; the universities; and much else.

[12] Oldham, *The Resurrection of Christendom,* Christian News-Letter Books, no. 1, London, Sheldon, 1940.

[13] *Ibid.*, p.31.

[14] Cf. e.g. *Real Life is Meeting,* pp.15f.

The general approach was clear: topics were to be aired and issues were to be raised within a firmly Christian and ecumenical perspective, but never a doctrinaire one. People were encouraged to join a serious discussion, not to listen to moralizing lectures, and many readers responded with their own views. Hence the News-Letter was never quite predictable, which added to its appeal. It weighed in heavily against those in the national press who lusted for revenge against the Japanese.[15] On the other hand, while in the early years of the war there was extensive discussion of the ethics of the bombing of civilian targets, there was little echo of George Bell's 1944 protests against the mass bombing of German cities. Such comment as there was now confined itself to regret for the realities of war.

Important was the fact that often there was real *news*, otherwise very hard to come by, especially of the work of the churches in distant corners of the world, from Russia to China, from Africa to occupied Europe; not to mention activities nearer at hand such as the newly founded Iona community in Scotland.[16] Often there were notes on recommended reading. Nor were the more personal dimensions of faith and the spiritual life forgotten. Daniel Jenkins, for example, wrote on "Prayer"; Melville Chaning-Pearce, whose book *Midnight Hour* written under the pseudonym "Nicodemus" was a scarifying autobiography of spiritual struggle in wartime, wrote on "Mysticism and Meaning"; and the young Ronald Gregor Smith, then a parish minister in Selkirk, wrought out of his own existential struggles a Kierkegaardian piece, also titled "Midnight Hour".

Indeed, the authors of the supplements, for which the rule of anonymity was quickly dropped, as a whole comprised a remarkable array of the already-famous or soon-to-be-well-known among religious thinkers. They included, as well as those mentioned above, John Middleton Murry, H.H. Farmer, Barbara Ward, Dorothy Sayers, William Paton, Reinhold Niebuhr, T.S. Eliot, H.A. Hodges, V.A. Demant, William Temple, C.H. Dodd, John Baillie, John Marsh, Walter Moberly, Gerhard Leibholz (the brother-in-law of Dietrich Bonhoeffer and now a refugee teaching in Oxford), Kathleen Bliss, F.B. Welbourn, Marjorie Reeves, A.D. Lindsay, Kenneth Grubb, George Bell, Karl Mannheim, Alan Ecclestone, John Foster Dulles and Karl Jaspers. Special mention must be made of Karl Barth, a number of whose public letters on Christian responsibility and the war, addressed to the world at large or to Christians in particular countries such as France and the United States, were reproduced or extracted.[17] In some cases the rule of anonymity had to be reapplied to authorship of the supplements. "A Member of a Tribunal" wrote on "Conscientious Objectors" and "A European

[15] Cf. e.g. *CNL* 128, 8 April 1942.

[16] George Macleod's new Iona community venture was provoking controversy in Church of Scotland circles. *CNL* 4 in November 1939 gave publicity and support to Iona, causing sharp correspondence between Oldham and John White, a former moderator of the General Assembly of the Church of Scotland who felt that the official extension work of the Church had been denigrated. Cf. correspondence between Oldham, Macleod and White Nov.–Dec. 1939 [OA].

[17] Barth's supplements are 15, 66 and 222.

Neutral" on "Are There Two Germanies?". "A Church under Nazi Occupation" was supplied by W.A. Visser 't Hooft in 1942 on his native Holland, without his name attached for even more obvious reasons, and a similarly anonymous piece on "Present Conditions in the Evangelical Church in Germany" appeared in April 1941.

## Friends in Geneva, Germany – and beyond

*The Christian News-Letter* thus helped to keep international, ecumenical discussion alive, and in public, in keeping with the declarations of Oxford 1937. One day in Geneva in February 1941 Visser 't Hooft was tuning his radio to the British overseas service when he heard Oldham's familiar tones expounding his views on human relationships. He wrote soon after to express his delight, but also some frustration that the News-Letter was rarely reaching him:

> A certain number of magazines and newspapers are coming through, but the News-Letter is not among them. This is a very great pity, because the News-Letter gives a more intimate picture of British Christianity and tells us more about the thought of our best friends and colleagues. If we could get it we could pass on very much more of that thought to the many countries with which we remain in contact. I need not underline how important this is in view of the future.[18]

Visser 't Hooft clearly had in mind, among other things, his contacts with the German resistance. The matter was crucially important in these early months of 1941, since the News-Letter was full of discussion of Pope Pius XII's famous "five peace points" issued in December 1940 and taken up by the British church leaders. Oldham quickly rectified the matter of dispatching the News-Letter more efficiently to Geneva, and on 18 June Visser 't Hooft wrote again, in somewhat coded form:

> It is a very great joy to receive the News-Letter again quite regularly, though somewhat late. We use it to good advantage and show it to people from various countries who cannot receive it directly. Thus I had occasion to show your remarkable statement about the attitude to be taken to the country with which yours is at war, to a person from that country whom you met some years ago at Liverpool and Balliol [*sic*] and who is a very keen observer of the situation. He was deeply impressed by it and said that this would help him a very great deal in certain things on which he is working with his friends. The knowledge that there is a group such as the one of which you are the centre who take this kind of attitude gives him and others real hope concerning the future.

The German referred to was clearly Adam von Trott. Visser 't Hooft went on to emphasize the importance of people in Germany being given a hope that defeat would not mean being "put at the mercy of revengeful nations" and of it being made clear "that there is a chance for a constructive peace in which no

[18] Visser 't Hooft letter to JHO 4 Feb. 1941 [OA].

nation will be treated as being on a basis of inequality with other nations". His German friend had emphasized that there was no "war hysteria", rather a "grumbling lethargy" in his country.

The most direct British link with the German resistance via Geneva at this time was provided by William Paton, whose relationship with the Visser 't Hooft contacts such as von Trott and Bonhoeffer in Germany, and with the Peace Aims Group and others in London, has been extensively researched.[19] Oldham himself was not directly concerned with the resistance as was Paton. His collaborators, however, included not only Paton but such as A.D. Lindsay, Alfred Zimmern and George Bell who were also deeply involved on the British side, and he would have been well aware of much that was going on. It can be said that the News-Letter, as with certain of the Moot papers, played a reinforcing role in the encouragement of the German resistance to believe that they had allies within Britain.

It was not only with the continent that Oldham was concerned to link *The Christian News-Letter*. Henry van Dusen and John Bennett made efforts to have it circulated in the United States.[20] John Mott wrote appreciatively. Van Dusen, Foster Dulles and Reinhold Niebuhr contributed to the Supplements. The international scope of the News-Letter was well reflected in the contents themselves. Marjorie Reeves[21] has drawn attention to the remarkably outward-looking stance which it displayed throughout the war: "Food shortages in Britain get few mentions, but 'hunger in Europe' occurs again and again." Not only the diverse activities of the worldwide church in war, but issues like Indian independence, the role of the British commonwealth in a new world order, the place of Germany in a future Europe, and British responsibility in reconstructing that new Europe out of the desolation of war, were all highlighted. For many readers it was a new window on the whole world.

## Real life is meeting

As well as in nearly every case (after the editorial discussions) writing up the actual News-Letter, Oldham himself wrote twenty-three of the supplements up to the end of 1945, by far the largest individual contribution. His subjects ranged from the theological and general ("What is God Doing?", "Christianity and Politics", "Superman or Son of God") to quite concrete matters ("Youth, the War and the Future", "Christians and the Beveridge Report", "The Church in Europe"). His *pièce de résistance*, however, was an essay which fused his theology with the concrete: "All Real Life is Meeting" appeared as the supplement to no. 112 in December 1941. Oldham, as has been seen, had known and enthused over Martin Buber's *Ich und Du* long before Ronald Gregor Smith's English translation appeared as *I and Thou* in 1937, and he had deeply

[19] See E. Jackson, *Red Tape and the Gospel*, ch. XII.
[20] JHO letter to H. van Dusen 2 April 1940; van Dusen letter to JHO 6 April 1940 [OA].
[21] M. Reeves, "The Christian News-Letter: Britain and the World", in M. Reeves, ed., *Christian Thinking and Social Order*, London, Cassell, 1999.

absorbed Buber's perception of the interpersonal realm in the development of his own emphasis on the relational character of authentic human existence. "All real living is meeting" was Gregor Smith's rendering of Buber's key phrase *Alles wirkliches Leben ist Begegnung*. Oldham gladly adopted and adapted it – and made it famous even to many who could have no idea of its origin but thereafter associated it pre-eminently with Oldham himself. The supplement neatly expounds both Buber and the similar thought of John Macmurray, and his conclusion from both these "prophetic voices" crystallizes not only their thought but his own fusion of theology, spirituality and ethics:

> There is that in the universe which is waiting to meet us. Let us go forth to meet it. What will come from the meeting is not in our hands. If it were, there would be no meeting; we should still be in the prison-house of our own self-chosen purposes in which we control and order things.
>
> What comes out of this meeting is God's affair. In every real encounter with our fellow-men we meet the living Spirit, the Creator of life. God is not to be found by leaving the world. He is not to be found by staying in the world. But those who in their daily living respond with their whole being to the "Thou" by whom they find themselves being addressed are caught up into union with the true life of the world. "Inasmuch as ye did it unto one of these My brethren, even these least, ye did it unto *Me*."
>
> Those who meet – who answer in responsible decision to the word addressed to them by another – are already sharers in eternal life. They are already bound together in community. They are allied with the power of the eternal Spirit – a power that can destroy the domination of things, overturn the proudest monuments of ambition and acquisitiveness and restore man to his true life which is realised only in community.

Shortened to *Real Life Is Meeting*, the Buberian phrase supplied the title to the fourteenth *Christian News-Letter* book the following year. This comprised several of the Supplements to have appeared in the News-Letter during the previous twelve months: in addition to "All Real Life Is Meeting", it brought together Oldham's pieces on "Return to Reality", "Superman or Son of God?", "A Fresh Approach to Christian Education" and "Planning for Freedom", with H.A. Hodges' "Christianity in an Age of Science" and Philip Mairet's "The Gospel, Drama and Society". Both Hodges' and Mairet's contributions were cast in the form of letters responding to Oldham's pieces. In effect the book was a public Moot discussion.

Meanwhile, Alec Vidler was proving as resourceful and creative an editor of the series of News-Letter books as he was of *Theology*. They conveyed, for example, John Middleton Murry's passion in *Europe in Travail*, O.C. Quick's clarity in *Christianity and Justice* and Gordon Rupp's vigorous theological expression in *Is This a Christian Country?* Marjorie Reeves and John Drewett produced *What Is Christian Education?* and C.J. Strauss *Japan in the World Crisis*. Moreover, from Karl Barth Vidler elicited his *A Letter to Great Britain from Switzerland*. No fewer than fourteen volumes had appeared from the Sheldon Press by mid-1942.

### The Archbishop speaks

Mention should be made of one further supplement and its provenance. In April 1942 William Temple was enthroned as archbishop of Canterbury. Oldham's relationship with Temple dated from more than thirty years earlier, when Temple as a student was active in the SCM, and he had been among the young stewards at the Edinburgh conference. They had been collaborators during 1914–18 in the *Papers for War-time* group, during the 1930s in the Pilgrim Trust enquiry on unemployment, in the Oxford conference and of course in the process of formation of the World Council of Churches and, most recently, in the launching of the News-Letter itself. (Oldham, it should be said, was not involved in the 1941 Malvern conference, chaired by Temple, although T.S. Eliot, Middleton Murry and H.A. Hodges from the Moot were.) They were on Christian name terms – in fact Temple was one of the very, very few people, outside of his family, with whom Oldham at that time used familiar address in his letters. For Oldham "Temple had an affectionate admiration",[22] and there is no doubt that the feeling was mutual, notwithstanding Oldham's innate suspicion of bishops as a species. Over much ground their minds were very close, especially on the need to create a new social order and for Christianity to be involved in this. There were also significant differences of emphasis between them. In ecumenical affairs Temple, it has been seen, felt that Oldham did not really understand how and why Faith and Order differed from Life and Work. Further, Temple's approach to Christian social engagement, as seen in his highly influential paperback *Christianity and Social Order*,[23] was to declare that it was the church's role to state the overarching moral principles which should govern society, and then leave it to the responsibility of individual Christian citizens to apply these to particular problems. Oldham had not only preferred to speak of "middle axioms", but by the time of the second world war was more concerned that Christian social thinking should *start* with "an understanding of Christianity that has been reached, and could only have been reached, by those who have felt the full pressure of the forces that dominate modern society" and that "it is through contact with actual life that truth acquires a dynamic quality, and the power that will save us will come from a new apprehension of the meaning of the Christian revelation for the actual situation of men to-day".[24] Moreover, while Temple was forceful in stating the responsibility of the Christian laity in society, Oldham believed that laypeople could not be expected to fulfil their vocation as an undifferentiated mass or as isolated individuals, but only as in some way organized as groups or "cells" according to their particular situations of daily life and work.

These differences in emphasis notwithstanding, the fact that Lambeth Palace was now occupied by a primate of such stature and innate sympathy with his

[22] W. Iremonger, *William Temple*, London, Oxford Univ. Press, 1948, p.519.

[23] W. Temple, *Christianity and Social Order*, London, Penguin, 1942.

[24] *Real Life is Meeting*, pp.1f.

aims, and moreover a personal friend, was enormously significant for Oldham. It meant that the concerns driving the Moot and *The Christian News-Letter* now had a potential spokesperson at the highest level in the church and indeed in the nation (in the opinion of many, by now Temple was being listened to by the public with at least as much respect as Winston Churchill). And indeed one result was that Temple supplied a supplement to no. 198 of *The Christian News-Letter*, 29 December 1943, on "What Christians Stand for in the Secular World". It is a powerful, closely argued essay (twelve pages, much longer than a normal supplement). It moves from a careful distinction between the roles of church and state to an affirmation of the church's role of illuminating and guiding society with the qualities deriving from the gospel; to the basic decisions called for, to God and the neighbour; to the purpose of God as the governing reality of history; to the Christian emphasis on association in community as opposed to both impersonal ideologies and post-Cartesian individualism; to the need to distinguish the necessity of organizations and management of power from the duty of love, and yet to relate them together; to Christian commitment to seeking a meaning in history in light of the kingdom of God; and finally to the significance of the church: "What none but utopians can hope for the secular world should be a matter of actual experience in the Church. For the Church is the sphere where the redemptive act of God lifts men into the most intimate relation with Himself and through that with one another."

This was Temple, but not just Temple, speaking. Introducing the supplement in the News-Letter itself, Oldham states that the unusual distinction of the article lies not just in the authority of the writer who has said these things, "but that in saying them he believes, after testing the matter, that he is expressing an 'observable convergence' among those who have given serious thought to the matter", and that "drafts of the paper were at various stages submitted to, and discussed with, persons representing widely different Christian traditions". In fact the originating author was Oldham himself, and the discussions had largely taken place in the Moot. "The Christian Witness in the Present Crisis" was a draft memorandum submitted to the archbishop in September 1943, written by Oldham and twice revised in the light of comments from nearly all the Moot members and a number of others such as J.J. Welch, Oliver Quick, Daniel Jenkins, Alexander Miller and W.G. Symons. Oldham's purpose had clearly been to arrive at, not a brilliantly original piece of individual insight, but an expression of a corporate mind: evidence of something like the "order" he still hankered after. Some time later, in a letter to H.P. van Dusen he said: "The point is not that it is by any means necessarily the statement that we want, but that we shall probably never succeed in arriving at a common mind and *knowing that we have it* unless we are willing somewhat arbitrarily to make it the starting-point of our common thought. In view of the archbishop's position as Chairman of the World Council of Churches, a document by him might be the best starting point."[25]

[25] Letter JHO to H. van Dusen 18 Nov. 1949 [OA].

The main structure of Oldham's paper began with "Fundamental Decisions" – for the transcendent, for history, for sociality, for the duality of the spheres of law and gospel – and moved on to "Commitments": the vindication of man, making power responsible, and healing "the split in consciousness" between "men's ultimate beliefs and basic attitudes and their conscious aims". It closed with a short section on "Practical Objectives" on which the churches might unite. Temple largely reworked the memorandum in writing his supplement, but the main features of Oldham's paper remain clear, especially in the emphasis on a commitment to history and the centrality for Christianity of sociality and the I–Thou interpersonal sphere. At certain points, indeed, the debt to the memorandum is immediate and unmistakeable, as for example when Temple takes up Oldham's point that man is *meant* to have dominion but that a one-sidedly scientific approach to the world proves disastrous. Temple had enabled Oldham and his circle to be heard; and Oldham had enabled Temple to speak with a vocabulary which, even by his rare standards, was enriched.

The supplement did create some interest.[26] One critic, Victor White, felt that Temple – or at least the discussions which he had elicited – had over-stated the nature of transcendence in a dualistic fashion.[27] Had Oldham slightly overstated the degree of "convergence" among Christian minds? The answer is less important than the fact that *The Christian News-Letter* had itself helped to create a sense of fellowship among its readers, in Britain and abroad, who shared the excitement of a common enterprise in search of a new world order based on the biblical faith. This was probably also more important than the fact that his oft-repeated hope to form an "order" had come to nothing, for the readership of the News-Letter had in effect created a kind of order in itself, much more diffuse than the kind he had envisaged but no less significant for that.

## Enter Kathleen Bliss – and peace

In 1940 one of Oldham's helpers in the News-Letter office, an Anglican priest by the name of Rupert Bliss, was summoned to undertake duties elsewhere. He introduced his wife Kathleen to Joe Oldham as a likely substitute for himself. This was the beginning of one of the most important colleagueships and friendships of Oldham's later life, and was to introduce into the ecumenical movement in Britain, and later into the World Council of Churches, one of its most dynamic and creative figures. Kathleen Bliss, then aged 32, was a Cambridge graduate in theology, and had worked for several years in India. Strikingly attractive in appearance and full of energy, she was possessed of

[26] Ronald Preston, at that time an SCM secretary, wrote to Oldham 5 May 1944 [OA] commenting on the feelings in some circles that Temple's supplement had been lessened in effect by his adoption of the "encounter" type theological terminology. In retrospect, Preston believes that the impact was slight by comparison with Temple's *Christianity and Social Order* and the debates surrounding the Beveridge report and "Religion and Life" weeks (letter to author 20 March 1998).

[27] Temple Letter to JHO 17 May 1944 [OA].

*Kathleen Bliss*

unusual organizing ability and, given to decidedly pungent turns of phrase, a brilliant communicator whether by voice or pen. In Oldham's office she found her *métier*, and in her Oldham found an ideal collaborator, the sort of person who not only instantly grasped the importance of an idea but actually made it *happen* by getting people together to work on it. She herself contributed three News-Letter supplements during 1943–44 on "Sex Relations in War-Time", "Families in Future", and "'Teach? Not Likely!'"

Kathleen Bliss was also presently drawn into the Moot, first of all as a guest at the seventeenth meeting in June 1943, and regularly thereafter, being formally elected a member at the twentieth meeting in June 1944. Her first minuted intervention was made at the nineteenth meeting in January 1944 and was typically to the point:

> *Kathleen Bliss* said one of the first jobs must be to convince the Churches about nationalism. Religion and Life weeks still tended to prefer to talk about international hiking parties and bonhomie. They were far away from any sense of *national* vocation, and stood in sharp contrast with, e.g., U.N.R.R.A. with its stress on the responsibility of each nation for its own food supply.

She began to be more vocal at the next meeting, on the relations between town and country in an industrialized society, and on the "manipulation" of housing and the housewife: "The new plans betrayed the "gadget mind" in the structure of the new-fangled house. This would tend to decrease inventiveness and stifle

*A* Christian News-Letter *team meeting, Chipstead,* ca. *1945.*
*From left: Brenda Snook (Secretary), J.H. Oldham, Kathleen Bliss,*
*Kenneth Matthews, Daniel Jenkins.*

the imagination." (The males in the group disagreed, urging that "new methods were necessary if order and neatness were to be possible in the small, confined space of a suburban house or flat", and Karl Mannheim supported this vacuum-cleaner theology, saying that "most intelligent women appreciated the danger involved in getting too dependent on gadgets".)

The war in Europe ended on 8 May 1945. The week following, Oldham penned a News-Letter full of thankfulness for the great deliverance which in 1940 had seemed so remote – and immediately, drawing on George Bell's supplement of some weeks before on "The Churches and European Reconstruction"[28] and on Reinhold Niebuhr's recent *The Children of Light and the Children of Darkness*, also set out the priorities for Christian responsibility in the post-war world and the faith on which these must be built. But he also surprised his readers by announcing his leave-taking of the editorship of the News-Letter which faced "an entirely new situation" in the post-war period. After expressing gratitude for all it had achieved, and appreciation to his collaborators (notably Eleonora Iredale) he named his successor:

[28] *CNL* supplement 225 had reproduced Bell's House of Lords speech on reconstruction.

> There has never been any doubt or hesitation about who should take over the editorship of the News-Letter. The Editorial Board of the News-Letter and the Council of the Christian Frontier, both comprising men and women of widely different outlook and experience, were clear from the first that it must be Kathleen Bliss. I have never known any body of people arrive so quickly and with so little debate at complete certainty about a matter of importance. For one who is still in the thirties, Kathleen Bliss has already an astonishingly wide range of personal contacts. Almost all of those who have helped the News-Letter in the past are her friends . . .[29]

Once more, Oldham demonstrated his belief in the importance of letting go as well as taking up, and nothing could have demonstrated more powerfully his perception that a new era of responsibility had dawned than his handing over the baton to someone less than half his age at this critical moment. Kathleen Bliss maintained the same high editorial standards until 1949 when a new responsibility suddenly came upon her, and *The Christian News-Letter* was, to use her own words, buried in the cradle of her third child.

[29] *CNL* 234, 16 May 1945.

CHAPTER 19

# *Councils of War: The Emergence of the Christian Frontier Council*

THE formation of the Christian Frontier Council in 1942 was, alongside the continuance of the Moot and the production of *The Christian News-Letter*, the third substantial contribution of J.H. Oldham to Christian life and thought in war-time Britain. It was born out of a combination of vision and deep frustration. The vision was Oldham's long-held view that the prime Christian witness in society had to be borne by laypeople, struggling day by day in the secular spheres of work and community, and sharing in those struggles with the increasing numbers of people who stood on the edge of or right outside organized religion. The frustration was due to his innate fear that the moves towards a more organized form of ecumenical life in Britain would inevitably be dominated by ecclesiastical interests, putting the clerics firmly in control at the expense of genuine social concern and marginalizing the contribution of the "best minds" to Christian thinking. This part of the Oldham saga therefore takes us to the tangled path which led to the founding of the British Council of Churches (BCC) in 1942. It was not an entirely happy story, beset as it was by sharp tensions among personalities and several interest groups, Oldham among them. The biographies of two of the other chief figures involved, William Paton and Archie Craig,[1] show that at this distance even the most extensive research does not uncover every step of the way, and the present writer has to confess likewise. The biographer, at the very least, has to beware of a partisan loyalty which would overly justify the stance taken by the hero in question, or even attempt to compensate for the lack of information.

[1] E. Jackson, *Red Tape and the Gospel: A Study of the Significance of the Ecumenical Missionary Struggle of William Paton (1886–1943)*, Birmingham, Phlogiston Press and Selly Oak Colleges, 1980; E. Templeton, *God's February: A Life of Archie Craig 1888–1985*, London, CCBI, 1991.

## Two councils

Following on the Oxford 1937 conference Oldham, as has been seen, sought to create the Council on the Christian Faith and the Common Life (CCFCL). It remained a struggling body, kept financially afloat only by the tireless efforts of Eleanora Iredale. Beyond being able to give a quasi-official endorsement to *The Christian News-Letter* on behalf of a number of the churches and the influential laypeople on its council, it cannot be said to have achieved much, and Oldham knew it. Alongside the CCFCL, there came into existence in 1939 the Commission on International Friendship and Social Responsibility (CIFSR). This was both larger and more representative of the churches than the CCFCL, merging the already-existing English Christian Social Council and the British Christian Council, and consciously intended to follow up both the Life and Work and Faith and Order conferences of 1937. William Temple was its chairman; it produced a bulletin *The Church in the World*, and organized "Religion and Life" weeks up and down the country. Oldham had long known and liked its secretary Archie Craig, a Church of Scotland minister who had in turn, since his student days in Edinburgh before the first world war been a great admirer of Oldham.[2] The two bodies at first shared the same offices in Balcombe Street, London.

Such an arrangement obviously made for cooperation. Members of the councils of both organizations were among Oldham's *Christian News-Letter* collaborators and contributors, and indeed they had over many areas a common agenda. There were also however the seeds of considerable tension. Oldham was clearly wary of a body which belonged much more to the "establishment" of the churches than did the CCFCL. Further, there was an in-built rivalry as far as relations with Geneva were concerned. In setting up the CCFCL Oldham had repeatedly argued that what was intended was a kind of British ancillary to the World Council of Churches: indeed, as he wrote to S.M. Cavert on 23 February 1938: "The line on which we are proceeding in Great Britain is that much of the work [of the WCC] can best be provided for nationally. Our idea is that the new British organization should to a large extent serve the World Council as far as Britain is concerned." Oldham's remarks of course beg the question of who the "we" in Britain were. As events transpired, the "we" represented by the CCFCL was a relatively small group, while the Commission represented a more substantial claim to be the link with Geneva.

This was in large part because the seats of actual power and responsibility in ecumenical leadership were shifting – and, ironically, thanks not least to Oldham himself. In September 1938 Oldham, now aged 64, resigned his secretaryship at the IMC. His tenure had in any case been largely nominal since August 1934, when he agreed to direct the study preparations for Oxford 1937. Oldham's letter of resignation told John Mott of what the older veteran

[2] See Templeton, pp.16f.

knew well enough already – "an increasing absorption in tasks that do not immediately fall within the purview of the International Missionary Council" – yet assured him that he would still be at one with the missionary cause, albeit in other ways.[3] Likewise, Oldham begged Mott that the IMC accede to the invitation for William Paton to give part-time service to the new WCC, since the formation of the WCC was itself a fruit of the early ecumenical vision supplied by the IMC. There can be no doubting the sincerity of Oldham's promotion of Paton's role in the WCC, based as it was on both a long-term, statesmanlike view and a real perception of Paton's qualities.[4]

Paton thus became part-time joint secretary of the WCC, working from his IMC office in London. Oldham, from the time of his resignation, no longer had any official, paid position within any church or ecumenical agency, beyond the CCFCL which he had himself set up; whereas Paton was now both secretary of the IMC and an executive official of the WCC in London. Oldham was still the vice-chairman of the study commission of the WCC, a post inherited from the Life and Work preparations for Oxford 1937, and was a member of the WCC Provisional Committee. He still had the authority of his unrivalled reputation and the means of working creatively in his chosen enterprises, but greater weight of actual management of the ecumenical scene was now with Paton. The question was, in which direction would he use it?

Between Paton and Oldham, as seen earlier, there had already been irritations at times. Paton found tiresome what he saw as Oldham's manipulativeness, as in the Leslie Hunter episode, and was hurt at being excluded from the Moot. But major differences were also emerging in their approaches to ecumenical organization. Paton held firmly to the view that whatever body was set up should be clearly representative of the churches and accountable to them. Oldham was equally firm that such was the way to a dull mediocrity and ecclesiastical sclerosis of the ecumenical movement: the way must be held open for lay initiative and the challenge of "the best minds". Paton was convinced, from early on in the war, that a single ecumenical organization must be created in Britain. Oldham was far from convinced if it meant a structure on Paton's terms. It was above all the link with Geneva that was breeding frustration. Visser 't Hooft was at times unsure just which body, the Commission or "Joe's Council" (as the CCFCL was known behind Oldham's back), or certain other bodies, he was meant to be dealing with.

Paton had been a co-opted member of the CIFSR from its inception, and in terms of effectiveness clearly had more regard for it than for the CCFCL. Moreover he found Eleanora Iredale a difficult person to deal with. But according to Eleanor Jackson, Paton's biggest strategic problem was Oldham himself, who seemed to be wilfully obstructive of all attempts or proposals to create a single new council of churches,[5] and hindered communication between

[3] JHO letter to Mott 20 Sept. 1938 [OA].

[4] It is quite possible that Oldham felt more able to advocate Paton as a part-time secretary for the WCC once he knew that Visser 't Hooft's position as general secretary was secure.

[5] Jackson, p.272.

Geneva and others than himself. As early as September 1939 Paton had a long talk with Oldham and Iredale, arguing that "without their deserting their profounder work with scholars, they ought to become a regular consulting group of the British churches",[6] that is, having a very specific function within a single, inclusive council of churches for Britain. Neither Oldham nor Iredale could be persuaded. It is indeed one of the sadder episodes in British ecumenical history that between Oldham and Paton, to whom the story owes so much and who moreover owed much to each other, so much trust should have broken down. Eric Fenn did his best to mediate but to little avail.

Indeed neither Fenn nor Kathleen Bliss, such close co-workers and devotees of Oldham, can be counted on to defend or even explain Oldham's obduracy: "Kathleen Bliss's only explanation for Oldham's behaviour is that he was continually ill during this period, and secondly, that he could never understand that it was not possible to form the BCC simply by getting the general secretaries of the main denominations together for a cosy chat with Temple. He could not understand that the BCC would not be an ecumenical 'club' with the members proposing others for membership and deciding the rules."[7] The heart of the matter, however, probably lies still deeper, in two factors. First, it was what the proposed council would actually be *for* that most exercised Oldham. Ever since the preparations for Oxford 1937 he had been fixated on *study* as the over-riding purpose of any ecumenical body. That applied in his view to both the World Council of Churches and any body proposed for Britain – as seen in the CCFCL. A key to the passion with which he resisted for so long Paton's efforts to create the British Council of Churches may well be that he felt the battle was not just about a British Council but about the World Council too. As he had said to Cavert in 1938, his belief was that the work of the WCC should essentially be done in national bodies. To have conceded the point about the priority of study in London would have been to concede it in Geneva – and everywhere else – as well.

Second, it is clear – to this writer at least – that another reason for Oldham's holding on to "his" precious Council as an autonomous instrument was his continual longing for that elusive "order" or "body of people" which might emerge as the agency of faith-inspired change in society, and his hope that the CCFCL (in concert with the Moot) might be the catalyst for this. Oldham, yet again, set this out as a project for the CCFCL in a memorandum to Council members on 23 April 1941: "The immediate necessity is the definition of a common purpose and an effort to unite as many as possible in a whole-hearted commitment to its realisation. The crucial question is whether the Council can contribute to the growth of a body of people animated by these common convictions and consciously holding them in common." The matter was also discussed with Archie Craig.

[6] Paton letter to Visser 't Hooft, cited in Jackson, p.272.
[7] Jackson, p.273.

## A defeat . . . and a new advance

However, within a matter of weeks, his patience evidently exhausted, Paton struck. Eleanor Jackson's words do not exactly do him the highest credit: "In 1941 Paton engineered a crisis, forcing Iredale to resign after he had systematically gathered her financial responsibilities into his hands, and persuading Oldham to retire."[8] The actual date of Oldham's resignation was 29 July. Paton took over the secretaryship of the CCFCL. The way was now clear for the formation of the British Council of Churches (BCC), which was eventually inaugurated in September 1942 with Archie Craig as its first secretary and William Temple (who else?) as chairman.

A brief account of this episode and its background, written by Oldham himself in a letter to Mott several months later, in one sense tells us very little:

> Partly owing to the coming of the war, we were never able to obtain the resources in personnel that we aimed at when the new organisation was set up in Britain after the Oxford Conference. It became plain to me a year ago [spring 1941] that we could not continue living in hope, and that there was no use my attempting to edit the Christian News-Letter, and carry out the pioneer work of building bridges between organised religion and life outside, and at the same time act as secretary of an official Council of the Churches. I therefore resigned from the latter office last summer.[9]

If this letter conceals the fact that he had lost a battle with Paton, it also shows a marked absence of rancour. In any case, what might have been simply a bitter and humiliating blow for Oldham was in fact turned to good account in his next creative venture. Having failed to stem the tide, he determined that at least a vessel of his own choosing should ride with it. The BCC, which among other bodies would merge the CCFCL and the CIFSR, was to have five commissions. These would include the social and international agendas, and with that Oldham had no problem. But he still feared for the cause of lay witness in secular life. During the latter months of 1941 he therefore reflected on whether a group promoting this cause might be formed, associated with and endorsed by the BCC yet acting in its own right. This was the genesis of the Christian Frontier.

Oldham's thinking was, as always, strategic. It was now clear that there would be a British Council of *Churches*, in which the church leadership would exercise the decisive control. Despite some assertions to the contrary there is little sign that, once it was clear that this was to be the way ahead, Oldham attempted to obstruct it. Rather, he argued for a *complementary* policy: in his own phrase, "tunnelling from the other end", that is, from the secular world in which laypeople spent most of their lives. By the end of 1941 his scheme was fairly clear. The body would have as its main functions:

[8] *Ibid.*, p.273.
[9] JHO letter to Mott 16 March 1942 [OA].

(a) To provide opportunities for the discussion of Christian thought and action with those who are not Christians and in contexts other than those of organised religion;
(b) To arrive through consultation at a judgment which of the tendencies and changes in modern society (administration, education, etc.) are making in a Christian direction, and how far the efforts by various groups to influence these changes are consistent with, or contrary to, the Christian view;
(c) To bring individuals and groups in contact with one another and so to promote the cross-fertilisation of thought and experience;
(d) To promote a more empirical approach by Christians to the problems of society.[10]

There would be a council of not more than twenty-four. Oldham was firm that these should if possible all be laypeople. The new body would also take over responsibility for *The Christian News-Letter*. It was quite late in the day before the name of the organization was decided upon. Oldham at first suggested simply "The Frontier", redolent as it was of the sense of pioneering into regions unknown as in the wild west. Some thought that the term rather suggested "sitting on the fence". It seems that the name which stuck, "The Christian Frontier" was decided upon at the meeting of the CCFCL on 24 February 1942, which was convened specially to bring the new body into being.

Oldham's deft strategy here was that the CCFCL should both approve the formation of the Frontier and appoint its first Council, and transfer to it the running of *The Christian News-Letter*. The Frontier would thus come into being well in advance of the formation of the BCC, and approved by one of the bodies which was to be constitutive of the new Council. The BCC would therefore inherit the legitimacy of the Frontier on the same basis, that is, approving of it yet recognizing its autonomy.

The meeting of the CCFCL on 24 February unanimously approved these measures and the constitution for the Frontier drawn up by Oldham. It appointed to the Council Walter Moberly, A.D. Lindsay, Edwin Barker of the YMCA, Henry Brooke MP, Melville Chaning-Pearce, T.S. Eliot, Lord Hambledon, H.G. Juss, Walter Oakeshott, Mary Stocks (Westfield College), J.F. Wolfenden, Lady Cripps, H.C. Dent (of *The Times*), A.W. Garrett (Ministry of Labour), F.H. Ogilvie, Reginald Pugh, Clifton Robbins (Ministry of Information), Dorothy Sayers, Ivor Thomas MP, Barbara Ward, H.W. Willink MP and George Woodcock. All were laypeople. Oldham and his young, very able assistant F.C. Maxwell of the SCM would be the officers.

Oldham wrote a number of memoranda during the summer of 1942 on the purpose of the Christian Frontier and attempted to state an underlying theology for it. The basic rationale was clear: to build bridges between those in the churches and those outside who were concerned for a Christian ordering of society. As in his Moot memorandum to William Temple the following year he believed that within all the confusions both of religious thought and political ideology a certain creative stream of convergent thinking was discernible, summed up in "the recognition of God and community as the ultimate realities

[10] "Draft Resolution" 26 Feb. 1942 [OA].

of man's existence". This for Oldham indicated a role for the Frontier as a new fusion between social engagement and communication of the gospel itself:

> The need for a body like the Frontier as an auxiliary to the Council of the Churches arises from the fact that the divergence between the doctrine which the Church proclaims and the actual practice of contemporary society has become so wide and deep, that as a result of this divorce of teaching from life and experience the things which Christian language tries to express have become for many people quite unreal. When that happens – when words become depreciated in meaning – you cannot put things right by words alone. The pulpit ... is at the disadvantage that the words which are its tools have become blunted. The word God, for example, which is the foundation of everything, has for many people ceased to have an intelligible meaning and lost the power to evoke any emotional response. The only way in which the words used in the pulpit can regain their depth and richness of meaning is that they should be re-enforced by actions in the practical sphere informed by the truths which Christianity asserts ... You will not get very far in changing ideas unless you are at the same time changing the practice inspired by them. Some of these practical activities have no obvious or immediate religious reference, though they do in fact presuppose a perverted or restricted view of the purpose of human life. That is why some of the movements in the various spheres of the common life, though they may seem on the surface to have a purely secular character, may in fact be contributing in important ways to the growth of a more Christian society.[11]

Much of what Oldham is saying here comes very close to what Dietrich Bonhoeffer was soon to be writing in his prison letters about the need for a new form of Christian understanding in a "religionless" world where the old words, and indeed words as such, have lost their power to communicate.[12] For his part, Oldham saw the Frontier as having the potential to make a real, if modest, contribution to "a body composed of those responsible for the conduct of practical affairs who will devote themselves to the special task of discovering, stimulating and encouraging those actions in the political, industrial and educational fields which will give a fresh, living content to the truths which Christianity affirms." The Frontier would work by personal contacts, group meetings and some publications – at first *The Christian News-Letter* was naturally one of its main organs. Soon its lunch meetings were to become popular with its members. William Temple came to one in 1943 to speak about his News-Letter supplement.

Before long it became evident that the Christian Frontier, for all its relative modesty, was at least as creative and influential as the CCFCL had ever been. Within months of its formation the Frontier had groups working on the management movement, industrial relations, planning of industry, the revitalization of political machinery, the local community, and education. The new British Council of Churches in the autumn of 1942 willingly took over its sponsorship, and indeed for a time there were joint meetings of the staffs of the

[11] Oldham, "Memorandum on Christian Frontier 18–20 July 1942" [OA], p.11.
[12] D. Bonhoeffer, *Letters and Papers from Prison,* London, SCM, 1971, pp.279f.

BCC and the Frontier – and chaired by William Paton. There was in fact quite a need for coordination to avoid overlapping and duplication with, for example, the "Religion and Life" movement which the BCC had inherited from the CIFSR. But there was a distinct difference in emphasis between the two movements, "Religion and Life" having "primarily a definite evangelistic purpose".[13] Relations between Oldham on the one hand, and Archie Craig, secretary to the BCC, and also with Paton were now evidently sound. Education was emerging as *the* major topic. All seemed set fair when in late December F.C. Maxwell suddenly and quite unexpectedly died. For the better part of the following year the Frontier survived on the narrowest of organizational margins, until in November 1943 when Kathleen Bliss left the BCC where she had been working on a half-time basis to devote all her energies to the Frontier and *The Christian News-Letter*. Daniel Jenkins, then a young Congregational scholar with several publications already to his name, moved from his post as SCM representative at Birmingham University to join the Frontier staff in 1945. Like Bliss, he had contributed several times to *The Christian News-Letter* and was starting to attend the Moot.

The Christian Frontier's early emphasis on education was to prove fruitful. Walter Moberly's *The Crisis in the University* (1949) was the outcome of the work of a Frontier group drawn from the teaching staffs of British universities, who met in private conference over a number of years. The book in turn sparked off a lively debate in the university world.[14] Much else could be said about the Christian Frontier, which at the end of the war still had a long and creative history ahead of it.

## Oldham's wartime propaganda

As propagandist for the view of "God and community as the ultimate realities of man's existence" Oldham did not confine himself to *The Christian News-Letter* and its accompanying books, nor to the Moot papers, nor to the Christian Frontier. The radio broadcast to which W.A. Visser 't Hooft tuned in by chance in February 1941 was one of two which Oldham gave on "The Root of Our Troubles"[15] and published the same year in a collection called *The Church Looks Ahead*, along with contributions by Maurice Reckitt, Philip Mairet, Dorothy Sayers, M.C. D'Arcy, Victor Demant and T.S. Eliot. Three years later he broadcast again, on "Christian Humanism", one of a three-part series on humanism shared with Julian Huxley on "Scientific Humanism" and Gilbert Murray on "Classical Humanism". These were also published.[16]

In these talks Oldham reiterates his now familiar view, that post-Renaissance humanism and the modern scientific revolution have brought great benefits,

[13] Minutes of Joint BCC/Christian Frontier staff meeting 2 Dec. 1942 [OA].

[14] See A.R. Vidler, *Christ's Strange Work*, London, SCM, 1963, p.127.

[15] *The Root of Our Troubles*, London, SCM, 1941; *The Church Looks Ahead*, London, Faber & Faber, 1941.

[16] Published first in *The Listener*, and then as *Humanism: Three Broadcast Talks*, London, Watts, 1944.

but that the one-sided emphasis on a "progressive mastery over an external world"[17] is catastrophic. Truly human existence is relational, towards God and with others. Again it is worth noting his call for a new attitude towards earth and nature: "Our schemes for establishing peace on secure foundations and creating a World-State or a Federal Union will achieve nothing, if they only result in greater efficiency of the civilised peoples in exhausting the resources of the earth on which the life of mankind depends. The lack of a humble, understanding, reverent attitude to nature is a religious failing, and it is plain that this *religious* error may have the most far-reaching consequences in the *economic* sphere."[18]

In retrospect, such words alone would justify the recognition of Oldham as a prophet. Of course his was not the only prophetic voice at that time; what is undeniable is that he was at the heart of one of the most remarkable wellsprings of Christian social and theological thinking. Indeed the years 1942-44, the sadly short time of William Temple's primacy, saw a flowering of such thought which, arguably, for Britain was unprecedented at the time and unequalled since in its intensity, its fertility and in the public interest it generated. As well as the Moot, *The Christian News-Letter* and the Christian Frontier, it saw the full maturity of Temple's own writing on public issues in *Christianity and Social Order*, the Sword and the Spirit movement, the formation of the British Council of Churches, George Bell's courageous speeches in the House of Lords, the "Religion and Life" weeks and the work of the Peace Aims group, while in Scotland the Baillie Commission was hard at work. It was also a time of tragic departures. Not only did Oldham lose Fred Maxwell, his right-hand man in starting the Christian Frontier, but William Paton died suddenly in August 1943 at the age of 57. Whatever the tensions that had arisen between them, Oldham knew it was a blow to the ecumenical cause not only in Britain but in the wider world, especially the nascent WCC. Then in October 1944 came of all losses the most bitter, with the death of William Temple.

In face of such human losses, confidence in the future of an ecumenical Christianity engaged with the world required even more of a leap of faith. Perhaps that is why, penned inside the cover of Oldham's pocket-diary for 1945, the year of "victory", we find the words of James Graham, the ill-fated 1st Marquess of Montrose:

> He either fears his fate too much,
> Or his deserts are small,
> That puts it not unto the touch
> To win or lose it all.

[17] *Humanism*, p.18.
[18] *The Root of Our Troubles*, p.15.

PART VI

# STILL "A PERFECTLY MAD ADVENTURE"

CHAPTER 20

# *From Utrecht to Amsterdam: Oldham and the Inauguration of the World Council of Churches*

THE Utrecht conference of May 1938 had set out the constitution for the World Council of Churches, and in that process J.H. Oldham had taken a leading hand. Ten years, six of them at war, were to elapse before the WCC was fully constituted at its first assembly in Amsterdam. This long gestation period, largely caused by the world conflict, was not to prove a time only of waiting and frustration, however. Provisional and Administration Committees had been set up, W.A. Visser 't Hooft was installed as General Secretary in Geneva (along with Hans Schönfeld and Nils Ehrenström in the research department inherited from Life and Work), and by 1939 William Paton in London and Henry Smith Leiper in New York were appointed as associate secretaries. This skeletal machinery, far from being kept idle, was put to maximum use, and it can truly be said that if the second world war delayed the full coming to birth of the WCC it also intensified ecumenical thinking and activity to an unprecedented degree. The delegates who eventually gathered at Amsterdam in August 1948 met not only with hopes for a new beginning for worldwide Christianity, but with a rich store of experience gained in the past few years. They had been shown dramatically the need and possibilities of interchurch cooperation in a number of fields, from shared visions of a new world order, to assistance to those resisting Nazism, to relief work for refugees and to reconstruction of a physically and morally shattered Europe.

Writing of one of his war-time visits to London in the autumn of 1944, W.A. Visser 't Hooft commented: "The three men in Great Britain who had been foundation pillars of the World Council were Archbishop William Temple, Dr William Paton and Bishop George Bell."[1] This should not be interpreted as

[1] Visser 't Hooft, *Memoirs*, p.184.

implying any depreciation of Oldham's role.[2] Temple, Paton and Bell were indeed the foremost British figures in the public leadership and advocacy of the World Council in its formative stages. But if they were the pillars, Oldham was one of the chief engineers behind the scenes (as has been seen, it was largely he, for example, who had put the Paton pillar in position – not to mention Visser 't Hooft himself). Oldham was of course a member of the Provisional and Administrative Committees, but his main role in these formative years was that of guide and counsellor to those most directly concerned in shaping the future structure and policy of the World Council, and none valued him more for this than Visser 't Hooft himself.

In fact Oldham's evolving thinking in relation to the World Council during 1938–48 forms one of the most fascinating strands in his whole life's work. It is, moreover, of much more than purely biographical or historical interest. Many of the issues which Oldham raised continue to be highly pertinent to ecumenical life today and will, one suspects, return again and again in the 21st century. They cluster around the elemental questions: what are the real tasks of a council bringing together the churches on a world level, and what, therefore, is the most appropriate structure for such a body?

This part of the Oldham pilgrimage may be treated in four chronological stages: the pre-war period from Utrecht, 1938–39; the war itself, 1939–45; the post-war period of preparation for the Amsterdam assembly, 1945–48; and the assembly itself and its immediate aftermath.

## 1. From Utrecht May 1938 to the outbreak of war September 1939

Oldham considered that a prime need following Utrecht, and in the longer-term follow-up to Oxford 1937, was the establishment of a British ecumenical body which would in effect represent the aims and activities of the World Council in Britain itself. As has been seen, this is how he conceived the Council on the Christian Faith and the Common Life (CCFCL). He also told Niels Ehrenström that his Moot was intended to be in close harmony with the work of the research department,[3] and supplied him with a number of the Moot papers. Major problems, it has been noted, beset the CCFCL from the start and eventually in 1941 Oldham had to concede defeat at the hands of William Paton and with the formation of the British Council of Churches. What Oldham did not concede, however, was a principle which he was to make explicit and argue even more strongly right up to the Amsterdam assembly and beyond: that the real work of the World Council had to be done on national levels. It was this principle which, if implicit, was already axiomatic for him in this pre-war period. With the formation of the Commission on International Friendship and Social responsibility in 1939 the British ecumenical scene became

[2] Cf. also Visser 't Hooft, *The Genesis and Formation of the World Council of Churches*, Geneva, WCC, 1982, esp. ch. 8, "Oldham takes the lead".

[3] JHO letter to Ehrenström 17 Oct. 1938 [OA].

more complicated and fraught with tensions, but up until the outbreak of war Oldham advocated strongly the claims of his CCFCL with Geneva and with a number of his American colleagues, and from those quarters – initially at any rate – elicited a good deal of interest and support for his work. Visser 't Hooft, for example, urged that the CCFCL take up a much more self-critical British approach to the geo-political background to the question of rearmament.[4]

In addition, however, Oldham did take seriously the new structures of the nascent World Council itself, and it would have been surprising if he had done otherwise, given that they were largely of his designing. In fact, as was his wont, no sooner had he seen his design accepted than he was anxious lest the full and proper use might not be made of it. At Utrecht Oldham was proposed as chairman of a small temporary commission to plan the study programme of the World Council. He refused, believing that it was now time for new leadership to be encouraged, but agreed to act as vice-chairman if Henry van Dusen could be appointed to the chair. Immediately after Utrecht he wrote to van Dusen encouraging him to accept (citing William Paton's strong backing) and, no less significantly, urging that younger people be brought into WCC work "in addition to the venerable elder statesmen who continue to direct its activities".[5] He returns to the theme later in the letter:

> When I think that the men who are remaking Germany are, for the most part, still in the forties, and when I look through the recent additions to the British Cabinet and find that the new appointments are for the most part people under fifty and in the case of Malcolm Macdonald well under forty, it seems to me absurd beyond words that the Church should try to manage its affairs through groups whose *average* age is probably nearer seventy than sixty.

Oldham's proposal for the chairing of the commission was followed. In the same letter, Oldham argues for a new strategy for ecumenical study: "starting with a statement of *one* carefully worked out point of view and discovering on this basis the points of disagreement and the reasons for them [rather] than by starting off with half a dozen different statements". Whenever the latter plan is adopted, Oldham believes, it is hard for the real differences to be disentangled from accidental and personal, idiosyncratic differences and differing perspectives. Clearly, the architect of the preparatory work for Oxford 1937 is reflecting soberly on the lessons of that approach. Shaping a study programme for the World Council as a whole was also, patently, to be a somewhat more complex matter than even for such a wide-ranging body as Life and Work. Once again the sensitivities of the Faith and Order constituency had to be acknowledged, and in correspondence with Leonard Hodgson in the spring of 1939 the anxieties about a central bureaucracy "dictating" the programme had to be teased out – and assuredly denied.[6] The circulation of correspondence

[4] Visser 't Hooft to JHO 1 March 1939, JHO reply 7 March 1939 [OA].

[5] JHO letter to van Dusen 20 May 1938 [OA].

[6] JHO letter to Hodgson 29 April 1939, Hodgson to JHO 30 April 1939, JHO to Hodgson 3 May 1939. WCC Archives, Geneva, hereafter designated [G].

between Oldham, Hodgson, William Temple, Oliver Tomkins, Hans Schönfeld and Niels Ehrenström during the last months of peace shows just how seriously, notwithstanding his desire to play second fiddle to van Dusen, Oldham took this and other concerns for the future work of the World Council.

The last eight months of peace saw a series of crucial ecumenical meetings at international level. In January the second full meeting of the Provisional Committee of the World Council met in St Germain, Paris, and set 1941 as the date for the first assembly. Oldham was not present. Not until January 1946 was the full committee to meet again. In July a conference took place in Geneva of the World Council and the World Alliance for Promoting International Friendship through the Churches, one of the outcomes of which was the setting up, largely under William Paton's leadership, of the Peace Aims Group based in London. Soon after, the WCC Administration Committee met in Clarens, Switzerland. By now Oldham was more than fully occupied in his own preparations for war and begged Visser 't Hooft to excuse his absence due to pressure of work.[7] At the end of July the world conference of Christian youth was held in Amsterdam, and in due course was to prove significant in having helped to fulfil Oldham's wish for a new generation to be brought into ecumenical leadership. The churches were far better prepared to face war in September 1939 than they had been in August 1914.

## 2. The war years, September 1939 to May 1945

It has to be said again that for Oldham much of his work, especially with *The Christian News-Letter* and the CCFCL, was conceived of as representative of the WCC in Britain. Note has already been taken of the keen interest which Visser 't Hooft took in the News-Letter, and his efforts to transmit it to occupied Europe and the resistance circles in Nazi Germany, and of Oldham's eagerness in turn to secure Visser 't Hooft's contributions. The war was just over three weeks old when Visser 't Hooft wrote to Oldham to express his delight on hearing from William Paton that the CCFCL hoped to use the present emergency to press on with ecumenical work.[8] Visser 't Hooft put three points to Oldham: the need for study of a just peace; study on the ethical function of the church: and a request for Oldham's views on specific practical services in wartime such as the Red Cross and the YMCA. Oldham's reply was enthusiastic, but mainly about his plans for *The Christian News-Letter* and its programme, and he dealt with Visser 't Hooft's enquiry on practical topics by simply promising to pass them on to Archie Craig.[9] Nevertheless he looked forward to collaborating with his Geneva colleague.

During the war, the WCC in formation was inevitably personified in Visser 't Hooft himself, and his *Memoirs* gives a vivid account of the role which Geneva,

[7] JHO letter to Visser 't Hooft 20 June 1939 [G].
[8] Visser 't Hooft letter to JHO 26 Sept. 1939 [G].
[9] JHO letter to Visser 't Hooft 5 Oct. 1939 [G].

in neutral Switzerland but literally on the doorstep of Nazi-occupied France and not much further from the border with Germany itself, played as a communications centre between the resistance circles in Germany and occupied Europe on the one hand, and Britain and the other allied countries on the other; not to mention the work of reconstruction and refugee relief. The WCC office in Geneva had a dramatic if often covert role in all this, but it was also a lonely one. Switzerland always felt on the brink of being the next country to be invaded. The Gestapo had plans to infiltrate the WCC office. For Visser 't Hooft, a Dutchman, the sense of isolation was especially acute after the invasion and occupation of Holland in May 1940. Travel in and out of Switzerland was always possible both for allies and neutrals, but became particularly difficult after the German occupation of the whole of France in late 1942.

As far as mediating with the German resistance circles was concerned, Visser 't Hooft's prime contact in London was William Paton through whom communication with the Peace Aims Group could be maintained until his death in August 1943. But it is significant that Visser 't Hooft on occasion seems deliberately to have chosen Oldham as his contact, and not only in transmitting material for *The Christian News-Letter*. This may in part have simply been due to the reciprocity of a deep and genuine friendship. Oldham's wartime epistles to Visser 't Hooft frequently go beyond functional and theological prose to expressions of deep personal concern for the Dutchman's unenviable position. On 12 May 1940 Oldham began his letter: "The storm has broken with full fury on your country . . . I have wondered with much anxiety whether your family are with you in Geneva or whether they are in Holland . . . I remember you in this time of trial." Only then does the letter go on to deal with exchange of material for the News-Letter. On Visser 't Hooft's side the confidence stemmed not least from the sense that Oldham would make effective judicious use of material or information sent to him: not only about Adam von Trott, but also about pacifists in France,[10] the views of a "consultative group" of diplomats in Geneva,[11] and a perspective from a Nazi sympathizer of Slav origin.[12] A good deal of such material went to London in the diplomatic bag from the British consulate in Geneva.

Oldham was also important to Visser 't Hooft at a very practical level. Visser 't Hooft managed to visit Britain five times during the war: in October 1939, in early 1940, in the spring of 1942, in October 1944 and in April 1945. On at least three of these visits Oldham, at Visser 't Hooft's request, assisted in seeing to the diplomatic formalities and arranging contacts for meetings in London. Particularly significant was his visit of April–May 1942 when, in addition to Oldham, Temple, Bell and Paton, he was able to meet with Henry Leiper and William Adams Brown who had come from the USA for William Temple's enthronement at Canterbury.[13] It was virtually a rump Provisional Committee.

[10] JHO letter to Visser 't Hooft 1 Dec. 1939, Visser 't Hooft reply 20 Dec. 1939 [OA].
[11] Visser 't Hooft letter to JHO 3 May 1940 [OA].
[12] Visser 't Hooft letter to JHO 4 March 1942 [OA].
[13] Visser 't Hooft, *Memoirs*, p.133.

More poignant was the visit of October 1944, for during it occurred the death of William Temple, the greatest of Visser 't Hooft's ecumenical pillars. Oldham, more than anyone, knew what this meant to Visser 't Hooft and wrote to him at his London hotel: "You have been hardly out of my thoughts since the news came yesterday. There is almost no one whose work is so hit by this terrible blow as yours. We can talk things over during the weekend."[14] Visser 't Hooft spent the following weekend with the Oldhams at Chipstead.

By now an allied victory was virtually certain and the war in Europe had barely six more months to run. Visser 't Hooft had not only been able to travel via France but had also called in on the liberated pocket of his native Holland. The ecumenical machinery was already getting into gear for post-war work. Under Oldham's aegis, enough ecumenical representatives were called together in London for a (provisional!) meeting of the Provisional Committee. They included Arnold Warnshuis from the USA, Oldham's colleague in the early days of the IMC. Geoffrey Fisher, bishop of London and soon to be nominated as Temple's successor to Canterbury, had been invited and unexpectedly turned up at the last moment, whereupon Oldham invited him to open the meeting with prayer, thus thoroughly inducting him into his first ecumenical experience at this level: he could scarcely have dreamed that within four years he would be presiding at the Amsterdam assembly. It was an encouraging meeting, Oldham thought, the best thing about it being the appointment of Oliver Tomkins as associate secretary to succeed William Paton (he was also appointed as assistant secretary to the Continuation Committee of Faith and Order). But to Oldham an unsatisfactory element was the speech by Warnshuis which, so far as it penetrated through Oldham's deafness and judging by the comments of others afterwards, seemed to typify an American attitude "leagues away from the tragedy of Europe" and did not, he thought, bode well for ecumenical relations after the war.[15] And again, Oldham was solicitous for Visser 't Hooft's own well-being in an area which was still full of tensions: "Hitherto responsibility in the ecumenical movement has been to some extent shared, e.g. Mott, the Archbishop of Canterbury, Adams Brown, Bill Paton, etc. For the moment an intolerable weight is being allowed to rest on your sole shoulders."[16] However, Oldham sounds a warning note as well and suggests that "it is important not to allow antagonisms to develop in secondary matters where these can be avoided". The implication is that Visser 't Hooft's continental (i.e. Barthian) bias in theology – and that of Hendrik Kraemer about whom Oldham also counsels caution – should not be "foisted" on the ecumenical movement as a whole. Oldham seems, once more, to be reflecting on the lessons of the experience of Oxford 1937.

A decisive contribution of Oldham to the emergent World Council during the second world war was therefore his unswerving friendship and wise counsel

[14] JHO to Visser 't Hooft 27 Oct. 1944 [G].
[15] JHO letters to Visser 't Hooft 7 and 13 Nov. 1944 [G].
[16] Letter 7 Nov. 1944.

for its young general secretary. Like others, however, as the war drew to its close he was giving thought to the actual structure of the World Council. Just before Visser 't Hooft left London in April 1945 to fly with George Bell and others to the USA Oldham wrote to Visser 't Hooft on the matter of membership of the Council, arguing against admitting any more churches to membership than those who had supported the decisions of Oxford and Edinburgh in 1937, at least until the Council had fully met in its assembly. There was a danger in too great a size, he suggested, and there might well be a need for the "larger churches" to confer together in a way analogous to what was being proposed in the Bretton Woods conference of the United Nations. Clearly he senses a danger in the Council being governed purely by a numerical democracy:

> It is obviously desirable that a World Council of Churches should be in close touch with all living branches of the Church throughout the world. It is true at the same time that unless the big denominational families are actively interested in the undertaking, there will be no real World Council at all . . . Moreover, whenever a question arises, the decision of which in a particular way would lead to large bodies like the Orthodox Churches or the Lutherans or the Anglican Communion going out of the World Council (or even to the evoking in their constituency of such strong opposition that the leaders would be compelled to adopt a lukewarm attitude) it is impossible that it should be decided by the vote of a majority in an assembly in which many of its members do not grasp the real issues. An understanding has to be reached with the leaders of the large denominations concerned and a decision reached by a relatively small group of far-sighted men, whether the World Council can continue if the defection takes place; more particularly if the defection of one group leads to coolness towards the World Council on the part of others.[17]

Oldham on the eve of peace was thus trying to look realistically at the problems that might face the fully-fledged Council. However, before long he was to be asking far more radical questions about the make-up of the Council.

### 3. From May 1945 to August 1948: preparing for the Amsterdam assembly

With the ending of the war in Europe the task of fully constituting and putting into action the ecumenical machinery began in earnest. In October 1945 representatives of the ecumenical movement, including George Bell, Hendrik Kraemer, Samuel McCrea Cavert and Alphons Koechlin visited Germany and at Stuttgart listened to leaders of the German Evangelical Church make their famous statement confessing their share in the guilt incurred in the havoc wrought by National Socialism. The ghosts of Versailles were exorcised: the question of 'war-guilt" was not to traumatize ecumenical relations as it did after 1918. In February 1946 the first full and formally constituted meeting of the Provisional Committee to take place since 1939 was held in Geneva. Oldham

[17] JHO letter to Visser 't Hooft 30 April 1945 [G].

could not attend. The first assembly was fixed for August 1948, in Amsterdam. Five presidents were appointed: Marc Boegner (France), John Mott (USA), Archbishop Germanos of Thyateira, Geoffrey Fisher (Archbishop of Canterbury) and Archbishop Erling Eidem (Church of Sweden). Another major step was the approval of plans for the opening of the Ecumenical Institute at Bossey near Geneva, made possible by a donation from John Rockefeller, Jr. In the summer the Churches' Commission on International Affairs (CCIA) was set up. In 1947 the first preparatory meeting for the Amsterdam assembly was held at Bossey. In the autumn the Provisional Committee issued a call to the churches on the assembly, and early in 1948 a second preparatory meeting took place in London.

During all this period 1945–48 Oldham was never as directly concerned in the WCC decision-making as others, or he himself, would have wished. Owing to the pressure of work for the Christian Frontier, he had to excuse himself from most of the Provisional and Administration Committee meetings. He pleaded to have Kathleen Bliss admitted as his alternate – and complained about the woefully inadequate representation of women on these committees. But his commitment to the Council was evident even before it was officially constituted, and remarkable for someone now in his seventies. His interest was shown no less at a number of other points, as when he took up Visser 't Hooft's concern over the apparent exclusion of the World Council from the activities of UNESCO, a body which under the influence of Julian Huxley was apparently moving in an overtly secularist direction.[18]

Nevertheless, as a member of the Provisional Committee, and technically still vice-chairman of the commission on study appointed at Utrecht in 1938, Oldham was deeply concerned for the assembly preparations. His most vital contributions found expression in his correspondence with Visser 't Hooft and others. Four issues in particular concerned him: the membership and representative nature of the World Council; the method of working and concomitant structures of the Council; the theme of the first assembly; and the style of working of the assembly, especially the matter of making "pronouncements".

As has been noted, even before the end of the war Oldham was advising caution to Visser 't Hooft on admitting more churches into membership of the WCC before its first assembly had met and its constitution had been definitively decided upon. A few months later, in January 1946, he was raising a much more far-reaching issue, in part borne out of his positive experience of the work being done by the British Council of Churches' Commission on Atomic Power.[19] Oldham confessed to Visser 't Hooft that he had never been entirely at ease about the 1938 Utrecht decision for membership of the WCC to be made up of individual churches. The experience of the International Missionary

[18] See letters Visser 't Hooft to JHO 25 Oct. 1946, JHO to Visser 't Hooft 28 Oct. 1946, Visser 't Hooft to JHO 12 Nov. 1946 [G].

[19] JHO letter to Visser 't Hooft 22 Jan. 1946 [OA].

Council had indicated the value of national ecumenical bodies, not churches or individual agencies, being the constituents of international bodies. Moreover, whenever a conflict had arisen between a national body and the international organization, the national body had usually won the day by virtue of the weight of authority it carried as the on-the-spot body. Oldham was moved to say this by a feeling of surprise and annoyance that Archie Craig, Secretary of the BCC, had not as expected been invited to attend the Provisional Committee of the World Council to take place in February 1946, even though "he had been asked at Archbishop Temple's request to act as secretary for the British members of the Provisional Committee". Oldham expressed the hope that the constitution of the WCC might on this score be open to revision at some stage. He sent a copy of his letter to Samuel McCrea Cavert in the USA, who replied sympathetically but suggested some kind of "working arrangement" between the national councils and the WCC rather than attempting to amend the WCC constitution.[20] Oldham was prompted to suggest that Oliver Tomkins, now the associate secretary of the WCC based in London, might be made an officer of the BCC for ecumenical work in Britain, and in turn Craig "ought to be in the intimate counsels of the World Council".[21]

Oldham continued to worry over the question for a year or more. At the end of May 1947 he set out his final conclusions to Visser 't Hooft.[22] It was a persuasive letter, arguing that to allot the places on the assembly to individual churches would inevitably mean delegations comprising the officials and safe committee people, at the expense of the really able and imaginative. The only way to get the latter category would be to allot more places to each church but that would make the assembly unworkably large. The problem would become still more acute in the case of the smaller churches which would inevitably fill their one or two positions with their leading ecclesiastics. "The result is that the general cast of the Assembly becomes much too official. The Church, most emphatically, is not the machine, and yet you get an Assembly, the complexion of which implies that it is. This is a spiritual disaster."

Visser 't Hooft himself had mooted the idea of an unofficial ecumenical conference alongside the official assembly. Oldham felt the same problem would arise. The root difficulty, he felt, went back to a wrong decision taken at Utrecht in 1938. "The only way out of the difficulty that I can see is that you should adopt the constitutional basis of the International Missionary Council and base the World Council of Churches on the national organizations . . . There is no guide in these matters but experience and so far as I can judge experience is making it plain that an attempt to base the World Council of Churches on individual churches is not really practicable."[23]

Oldham must have thought that he had delivered into Visser 't Hooft's court an unanswerable lob. Back from Geneva came a crashing return. For one thing,

[20] Cavert letter to JHO 31 April 1946 [OA].

[21] JHO letter to Cavert 5 Feb. 1946 [OA].

[22] JHO letter to Visser 't Hooft 23 May 1947 [OA].

[23] *Ibid.*

Visser 't Hooft felt, "National Councils are no more composed of prophets and pioneers than national church synods. In fact I am afraid that National Councils could bring in a further type of bureaucracy and not help us at all to get the laymen and prophets whom we need so badly."[24] For another, only as the WCC had direct contact with the church leaders themselves, and not indirectly via the national bodies, could it hope to bring pressure on the churches to find the right kind of people. Further – the touch of top-spin, one might say – Visser 't Hooft was emphatic that "there is not the slightest chance of keeping up the interest in the World Council if our relation should become an indirect one". National councils were rightly concerned with their own affairs and just could not give equal attention to those of the World Council. "Our already insoluble problem in making the World Council and its work known to the individual parishes would be even more insoluble if you put the national councils in between ourselves and the churches." Visser 't Hooft himself, no less than Oldham, was emphatically concerned to keep the WCC open "for the prophetic visions" – but this could only be done by acting directly on the churches.

Rarely in his life was Oldham left standing as he was by this riposte, and he conceded the point instantly, completely and with good grace.[25] His only qualification was that his particular experience of the BCC had perhaps made him over-sanguine about the role of national bodies vis-à-vis the World Council, and such a body might have a role in suggesting to the national churches the kinds of people who would be appropriate as delegates. But he did not dare to raise the basic point again.

Oldham was more tenacious, and perhaps more persuasive even if not entirely successful at the end, on the matter of the proper tasks of the World Council and therewith its appropriate structures and staffing, especially in relation to study. Again, the issue was linked with his advocacy of the role of national bodies. Early in 1946 Oldham expressed doubts to Visser 't Hooft on the proposal to set up "a department of international affairs" at the WCC (what eventuated as the Churches' Commission on International Affairs), at least before the assembly itself had met. The dilemma was: "Either you become involved in a disproportionate and unjustifiable expenditure both of funds and of the time of busy people, to make the department really representative, or it remains a small group that in no way represents the real interests of the major Churches, and the risk is always present that its conclusions cut across crystallisations of opinion that are taking place in the larger national bodies."[26] Again, behind Oldham's argument lay his high estimation of the work being done by the BCC on, for example, atomic warfare. For the same reason, he proceeds to be critical of the envisaged future of the study department. Such work cannot really be done effectively at an international level, taking the

[24] Visser 't Hooft letter to JHO 28 May 1947 [OA].
[25] JHO letter to Visser 't Hooft 2 June 1947 [OA].
[26] JHO letter to Visser 't Hooft 22 Jan. 1946 [OA].

leading thinkers in the churches from their work for long periods. The true role of the WCC should be "to do a lot of preliminary thinking", and build on the work of national bodies. For this, not a department but "a first-class secretary" is required who would collate the material and keep in close personal touch with the departments of the national councils. "I see a real danger that you may make the World Council of Churches top-heavy at the start, in a world in which there will for a long time be a stringency of finance, and overwhelming demands on the leading men in all the Churches." In another letter dated the same day and marked "Private", Oldham confessed that in his view Hans Schönfeld, for all the debt owed him for his past work, was not quite the person for this task in the new era, and suggested Stephen Neill as an alternative.

In the early summer of 1946 Oldham was asked by Nils Ehrenström to comment on the proposed procedure for the commissions to be set up for the forthcoming assembly, and used his reply as an occasion for another attack on the conventional policy – a prime feature of Oxford 1937 in fact – of eliciting a variety of papers which were then critiqued by other writers.[27] Too often, Oldham maintained, such criticism was superficial and perfunctory. He repeated his earlier suggestion of a single approach based on a sense of the underlying convergence among Christian thinkers in general. Oldham enlarged on these concerns on new year's day 1948, in a long letter to Ehrenström and Schönfeld, commenting on a draft report on the future policy of the study department. There was, he felt, insufficient sense of the crisis facing the church in the challenge of engaging secular society, and insufficient recognition of the need for the most thorough study before proposals could be recommended for action. Again, he returns to his familiar theme that such study cannot be done effectively at international level and requires the national bodies to carry it out in relation to their particular contexts. The study department has to avoid "the promotion of study merely for the sake of study. The only justification of study in the present crisis is that it is indispensable to action . . .". Oldham proceeds to challenge the assumption that "in order to secure cooperation the study must usually lead up to an international conference". Not always, he argues. Collaboration can take other forms, and the prime role of the study department should not be the promotion of its own programmes, but to serve the churches as a "general staff". And if there is one task that above all others needs undertaking by the World Council, "it is to help the Churches in this time of present crisis to understand its crucial spiritual meaning" with the aid of the most prophetic minds. Oldham confesses to a kind of "hunch" that there were half a dozen people in different countries and of differing traditions and outlook, who if one of their number were to write a paper would probably find themselves in substantial agreement. This could then be circulated to a wider circle for criticism:

[27] JHO letter to Ehrenström 27 May 1946 [OA].

> It is highly probable that in a wider circle there may be acute disagreements, but, of course, what has to be avoided at all cost is the counting of votes. To accept that course is to kill the spirit of prophecy. Prophets have generally been stoned until after they are dead. But if it should be found that there is a consensus of view among some leading minds that deserve our trust about what is really crucial in the situation, then every means should be employed to gain for this the attention of the churches. If there are opposed views they also can be presented. The main thing, however, is to gain the insight of prophetic minds, even if it does not meet with universal acceptance at the start, brought to the serious attention of the churches.

The disinterested reader might well wish to react by noting how, once again, there is an assumption that it is as evident to everyone else, as to Oldham himself, as to who the "leading" or "prophetic" minds actually are, in a world loud with many voices, in the churches no less than elsewhere. But the architect of Oxford 1937 was also raising a serious question about "ecumenical research". It was his own previous methodology which he was now questioning so rigorously, just when it had come to be widely regarded as the assured ecumenical orthodoxy. The challenge is no less pertinent today, and it is worth quoting what Oldham says towards the end of his epistle: "The kind of motto I would like to see inscribed over the portals of the office of the World Council is the Pauline saying, 'This one thing I do'."

Oldham repeated his call for *concentration* to be applied both to the assembly and the ongoing work of the study department, in a letter to Henry P. van Dusen just three months before the assembly met.[28] The study department, he repeated, should not attempt to *direct* the study at an international level but, perhaps assisted by the new Ecumenical Institute under Hendrik Kraemer's guidance, encourage a study, at national levels, of basic problems of society with which Christian faith needs to address itself – rather than beginning with the endless discussion of the Christian principles and then how to apply them.

The third main issue with which Oldham was concerned was the actual theme of the assembly. It went without saying that the context of a world trying to pick itself up out of the debris of war would be determinative, but the angle of theological approach was far from clear. Late in 1945 Visser 't Hooft wrote to Oldham saying that the most likely date being canvassed for the assembly among ecumenical leaders was 1948 – but that Oldham's help was urgently needed on selection of the main theme. Visser 't Hooft's own strong feeling was that the central thought of the assembly should be "justice"[29] and gave three reasons: all humanity was suffering from a desperate sense of arbitrariness without any "objective order"; "justice" was the term with which the biblical revelation hit secular society; and the subject would allow treatment of the great contemporary issues of international anarchy and of social relationships. Slightly tongue in cheek, Visser 't Hooft urged Oldham "as the

[28] JHO letter to van Dusen 28 May 1948 [OD].
[29] Visser 't Hooft letter to JHO 21 Nov. 1945 [G].

éminence grise and auctor intellectualis of Oxford [1937]", to take his rightful place in the planning of the conference.

Oldham's long reply[30] is a prime example of his skill at advancing the discussion without giving a direct answer to the question or proposal. He first invites Visser 't Hooft to *visualize* what *kind* of gathering the assembly will be: largely of ecclesiastics, and middle-aged, for whom "justice" is likely to be engaged with in an abstract way divorced from the actual struggle in society. What can realistically be expected from a few days of such a meeting? One should build upon what is already being thought and done constructively in the churches, and not place too much value on any "pronouncements" the assembly might make. Ought not the assembly concentrate on the over-riding task which *does* face the churches, that of understanding what it will mean to be an ecumenical fellowship in the post-war world? Further, Oldham argues, the assumption should be challenged that "the institutional agency from which the church will seek to exert an influence on social and political life is the church as at present ecclesiastically organised". When clergy discuss the social and political sphere they inevitably, and understandably, "look at everything from their particular standpoint and habits of life." The Christian Frontier was trying a different approach. New forms must be created alongside the existing ecclesiastical institution. Ought not, then, the assembly face squarely this problem of how Christian faith engages with secular society? Oldham warns, however, that if this is to be so, "a great deal of preparatory work and preparatory education will have to be done, or most of the members of the Assembly will not understand what is meant." In almost his concluding paragraph Oldham sums up his own post-Oxford-1937 thinking:

> In some ways the largest issue which the church will have to face in the coming decades is the inevitable tendency towards socialisation. Irresistible technical forces are making in this direction, and most of all the release of atomic energy, which is a potential force far too powerful to be controlled otherwise than by the State, will strongly reinforce these tendencies. What is going to be the condition of the church under the new totalitarianism? In what ways – possibly in quite new ways – can it function? How, under the new conditions, are freedom and elementary human rights to be conserved? These questions raise an issue which might conceivably be the dominating one for the Assembly to face. But perhaps the churches are not yet ready for facing it. The situation may not yet be close enough to America for the church there to grasp its significance. It may be the right thing however to get it tackled and to get work done on it begun in the decade following the meeting of the Assembly.

If ever an ecumenical prophecy is to be located in a single paragraph, it is surely here. More than even he perhaps dared to hope, these words did express the agenda for the next decade of ecumenical work. Visser 't Hooft in turn was much impressed, and took up Oldham's comments in preparing for a meeting of the Administration Committee in February 1946, in preparation for the

[30] JHO letter to Visser 't Hooft 28 Nov. 1945 [G].

assembly.[31] The theme eventually chosen for the assembly was "Man's Disorder and God's Design". Four sub-themes were selected and commissions appointed to prepare for each. Oldham was assigned to work on commission III, "The Church and the Disorder of Society" – essentially a continuation of the Life and Work agenda – and produced a lengthy memorandum for its work. This involvement brought him an opportunity to focus his long-term emphasis on the communal, relational nature of society in Christian perspective. It was in this process that, almost incidentally, he coined a term which was to become the key phrase for that long-term ecumenical agenda outlined to Visser 't Hooft in the paragraph quoted above. Significantly, it is Visser 't Hooft himself who remarks that he first heard the phrase "responsible society" from Oldham's own lips in London where a preparatory meeting was held early in 1948:

> As I walked with J. H. Oldham from the Athenaeum to the place of meeting he asked me whether we could not find an expression to indicate briefly and clearly what a right ordering of society would mean from a Christian point of view. Could we use "The Humane Society"? Or rather "Responsible Society?" I said that the second was just what we needed. At the meeting Oldham proposed both phrases, but I argued that "humane" could not be adequately translated and so it became "The Responsible Society". Not for a moment did we think that for the next twenty years this phrase would continue to serve as a key-concept in ecumenical thinking about social problems.[32]

The earliest use of the term in writing by Oldham himself appears to be in a letter to Henry P. van Dusen of 28 May 1948.

Finally, Oldham dealt persistently and trenchantly with the issue of making "pronouncements". In the first place he was highly critical of any tendency of the Provisional Committee to make statements on public issues, on subjects requiring wide knowledge and much expertise, and claiming to make these on behalf of the church while in fact the Committee was such a small body of limited representativeness.[33] Yet again, he feels that the national bodies are the more appropriate agencies here. But he was no less alarmed at the prospect of even the assembly – for all its wider representation – "speaking" at all either to the churches or the world. To concentrate on a "message" is to divert attention from things of vastly greater importance for the sake of "the cheap and easy way of speech rather than the costly way of action". What is wanted from such a gathering of leading church figures?

> Do you not want them to ask themselves with the deepest earnestness throughout the days of meeting, stimulated by and drawing to the full upon the intellectual and spiritual resources of the whole ecumenical body, what *action* in this crisis they are called by God to take in their respective Churches and within the field of their personal responsibility? Let those who attend the Conference go away from it with committed heart and soul to the realisation of whatever vision and call it may please

[31] Visser 't Hooft letter to JHO 14 Dec. 1945 [OA].
[32] Visser 't Hooft, *Memoirs*, p.205.
[33] JHO letter to Visser 't Hooft 22 Jan. 1946 [OA].

God to send through this drawing together of members of the separated elements of the body of Christ, and forces will be set in motion in the different churches of vastly greater power than anything that can be achieved by a formulated statement, which by its inevitable brevity and the wide range of topics on which it must touch must inevitably consist of generalisations that make relatively little abiding impression on the mind. Who really remembers the vast roll of pronouncements that have emanated from a succession of conferences in the past?

Reverse the order. Let the commitments come first. Let the members of the Conference decide what they are prepared and intend to do in their respective Churches, whether it be little or much does not greatly matter – God can use either – so long as it represents genuine purpose, and is sincere and honest. Let the message of the Assembly be the simple record of such decisions. Then it will have power, because it tells of what hundreds of people are committed to do. What is said in it will be spread through widening circles by their living energies. In carrying out these commitments they will treasure it as a reminder of the vision which came to them in the experience of ecumenical fellowship.[34]

Visser 't Hooft countered by saying that it was a message to the churches themselves that he had in mind, although he was at one with Oldham's view of the limited value of "pronouncements". Oldham returned to the attack from a theological and psychological angle. If one permits the formulation of a message to bulk large, "you have insinuated into the mind of those attending the Assembly that everything is alright with themselves and that their main task is to transmit what they have to other people. Once this idea is adopted, everything is lost. People have withdrawn *themselves* from the judgment of God and in the Christian view it is only when men face that judgment that anything important happens."[35]

What alternative was there? Oldham admitted to being unsure, but suggested that if he were planning the assembly he would in effect put to the leaders of each communion or confession the question: "What do you intend to do in your own Church in response to this demand which has come to us from God?" He was equally uncertain whether this was feasible but continued somewhat tartly:

I have already said that all this is on the very large assumption that the Assembly *is* really confronted with God's demand in the contemporary situation. That this should come about is about as difficult to hope for as the other. It certainly will not come about by the presentation of thirty essays, making up to four volumes, the great majority of which will not be markedly superior in spiritual insight or intellectual force to various articles that have appeared from time to time in different reviews and journals.

Oldham still held out the hope that one or more of the commissions might, by some miracle of grace, be able to speak of this demand to the assembly – or a section of it – in some overpowering and decisive way. He was characteristically diffident about his own work for commission III. Oldham in fact

[34] JHO letter to Visser 't Hooft 19 Feb. 1947 [OA].
[35] JHO letter to Visser 't Hooft 8 April 1947 [OA].

wrote two chapters for the preparatory volume of commission III *The Church and the Disorder of Society*:[36] II, "Technics and Civilisation", and X, "A Responsible Society". Together they make up by far the largest contribution from a single author to the report – or to any of the four preparatory volumes for the assembly. "Technics and Society" is a survey of both the good and ill brought by the "machine age". In face of all the dangers that human persons are being reduced to objects in the present climate, and in spite of all the undoubted benefits being brought by science, he again proclaims his gospel of the interpersonal realm as the hope of humanity:

> There can be no remedy for the present disorder of society unless the present absorption of interest in the technical mastery of things gives place to a new wholeness of thought and living which includes a true understanding of the relations of persons and of human groups. The Christian faith that the greatest thing in the world is love, remote as it may appear from all present realities, is at once the damning judgment of current practice and the clue that can lead mankind out of its present predicament.

The second piece, "A Responsible Society", is not only longer but is virtually a *summa* of Oldham's social philosophy. It faces the fact of the "radical revolution" whereby humankind has taken its future into its own hands. What does faith mean for "Promethean" humankind? Not the denial of power, but the recognition that power is given by the Creator, and therefore to be used for the Creator's purposes. Again the fateful concentration on "mastery over things" at the expense of human personhood itself is criticized as the root of the cultural crisis. Again, Buber, Berdyaev, Brunner and Middleton Murry are among the host of thinkers cited. A Christian doctrine of work is called for, to be worked out less by academic theologians than by those who actually work in secular society, which will restore an element of creativity to labour. People as yet can see little connection between "Christian morality" and the problems with which they have to deal in their daily life. And forms of *collective* morality are called for to guide the actions of groups and communities in relation to one another.

Perhaps the most interesting parts of the essay, in view of its contemporary context and the debates which took place at Amsterdam, are those dealing with the confrontation between the Western democracies and Soviet communism. Oldham is in no doubt that this is the dominant political issue of the day. But the church "cannot identify itself unequivocally with either side in the dispute". No earthly society can claim to be an embodiment of the kingdom of God or evade its judgment. A distinction is to be made between communism as a political and economic system (from which much may be learnt) and as a totalitarian system with which Christians "can make no compromise". Communism originated as a genuine human response to undeniable injustices and with a vision of the liberation of humankind, which owed elements to the

[36] *The Church and the Disorder of Society*, vol. III of ecumenical study volumes preparatory to WCC assembly 1948, London, SCM, 1948.

Judaeo-Christian tradition. The error of its totalitarian form lies in its offering a complete scheme of salvation in which God is denied – and therewith it is not the only guilty party since Western liberalism has also generated atheism. Along with this goes the denial of freedom, freedom to obey God as the highest authority. The crux of Oldham's argument is that:

> ... to obey God men must be free to seek after the truth, to speak the truth and to educate one another through a common search for the truth. Only through the freedom of its members to expose error, to criticise existing institutions and to express fresh creative ideas can society advance to fresh levels of life. In order that this may be possible, there must be free access to sources of information, freedom of expression in speech and writing to criticise authority.

Political freedom, says Oldham, is not the *source* of all freedom, which lies in God's gift of faith. But political freedom is the basis of all other freedoms in society. This is a vision of freedom, not for the individual as such but for the sake of true community, and Oldham argues cogently that it must be pressed in the Western societies, with all their tendencies to mass manipulation and subtle coercion towards uniformity, no less than against the Eastern totalitarianism. Strong echoes are also heard here of the long Moot discussions on the relation between planning and freedom. Much excitement was to be raised at the Amsterdam assembly itself by the sharply opposing speeches of American John Foster Dulles and the Prague theologian Josef Hromadka on the proper Christian response to the new Cold War divide. Oldham's essay, however, had already laid a solid foundation for a measured consideration of the issues.

It had also set out much of the framework for the continuing ecumenical reflection on the "responsible society". W.L. Martin helpfully summarizes Oldham's definition of the responsible society in terms of eight principles (or, one might almost say, "middle axioms"): "the freedom of man to obey God and his conscience; the freedom to seek the truth; the religious respect for man as man; the greater importance of personal relationships than collective relationships; the restraint of irresponsible power; maximum independence for cultural activities; the equitable distribution of material rewards; and political freedom."[37] It would be an interesting exercise to compare this agenda with the actual priorities of churches and ecumenical bodies in the following twenty years or so. That it had a marked influence in ecumenical study is undeniable.

## 4. The assembly[38]

The 351 delegates from 147 churches and forty-four countries, together with hundreds more participants of various kinds, Joe Oldham among them (listed

[37] W.L. Martin, "Joseph Houldsworth Oldham: His Thought and Its Development", Ph.D. thesis, University of St Andrews, 1967, p.602.

[38] For the official report, see W.A. Visser 't Hooft, ed., *The First Assembly of the World Council of Churches*, London, SCM, 1949.

*Amsterdam 1948: 1st Assembly of the World Council of Churches*

as a delegate of the Church of England), gathered for the opening of the first assembly in the Nieuwe Kerk in Amsterdam on Sunday, 22 August 1948. The congregation rose to sing the 100th Psalm, "All people that on earth do dwell". John Mott climbed the pulpit steps and delivered yet again his lifelong message of the decisive call to unite in taking the gospel to all the earth and listed the cloud of witnesses who had brought them thus far. The veteran was followed by the young D.T. Niles of Ceylon, only a 2-year-old infant at the time of Edinburgh 1910 and now representative of the new generation of ecumenical leadership in the world church. Soon the plenaries and sectional meetings were under way. Karl Barth proclaimed the majesty and sovereignty of God in face of which all efforts to build the kingdom of God were futile. John Foster Dulles and Josef Hromadka had their cold-war clash. At times the assembly reflected its theme in witnessing to man's disorder rather than to God's design. Oldham made no intervention in the plenaries. Lesslie Newbigin recalls Oldham himself deeply unhappy at one stage, about the turn the assembly was taking, evidently under the mighty American influence: "I had a glimpse of it when I met Oldham coming out of one of the meetings in utter despair. His vision of what the WCC might be had been shattered."[39] Newbigin believes it was, precisely, his view of the WCC as being a small centre of coordinating local and national work which was being bypassed.

Yet, Oldham by his own account seems to have emerged from Amsterdam on the whole satisfied. The "responsible society" was taken seriously and found a significant paragraph for itself in the final report.[40] Visser 't Hooft judges that Oldham's term was not only adopted but became an ecumenical milestone at Amsterdam. Oldham's strictures against a "message" notwithstanding, a notable and memorable message was in fact adopted – after much tortuous drafting and re-drafting in a succession of committees. Ironically, the phrase which stood out above all others – "We intend to stay together" – was penned by none other than Oldham's protégé Kathleen Bliss. The value of such a simple epigram was undeniable in capturing the spirit of the occasion.

Indeed, Oldham wrote to Visser 't Hooft two months after Amsterdam:

> ... I left the Assembly with feelings of deep thankfulness. The momentous step has been taken, and so far as I can judge it has been taken without any constraint that would compromise the future. The way is quite open for progressive evolution in the light of growing experience. The bringing of the whole affair to this happy conclusion was an astonishing achievement. I know no one who could have carried the undertaking through except yourself. You have my very sincere and warm congratulations. Having had an almost lifelong experience of ecumenical work, I know in living experience and "on my pulses" the innumerable difficulties that have to be surmounted, and I am able to appreciate more than most the remarkable nature of what you were able to accomplish.[41]

[39] Newbigin, *Unfinished Agenda*, p.122.
[40] Visser 't Hooft, *The First Assembly*, p.000.
[41] JHO letter to Visser 't Hooft 5 Nov. 1948 [OA].

Towards the end of the assembly, Oldham had several conversations with Ambrose Reeves on the future of the World Council, and later set out his thoughts on paper in a letter to him.[42] The Amsterdam experience had further consolidated his conversion to Visser 't Hooft's view that the World Council must indeed be a council of *churches*, and therefore the central committee must comprise those who carry weight in their own church constituencies. This also, in his view, put a high premium on the need for regularity of meetings and adequate contact between meetings. At the same time he reiterated his strictures against too much promotion of work by the Council itself at international level (though Faith and Order work might justify exception to this). The letter is a summary of Oldham's whole thinking on the WCC at its birth.

Oldham had now reached the age of 74. The journey from Edinburgh 1910 to Amsterdam 1948 was indeed the fulfilling of a dream, enough for one lifetime. But he had other dreams also, and considerably more lifetime.

[42] JHO letter to Reeves 25 Oct. 1948 [OA].

CHAPTER 21

# *The Post-War Veteran 1945–59*

JOE OLDHAM, in his 71st year when the war ended, had done the work of several normal life-times and would have been more than justified in slipping into gentle retirement, occupied with nothing more than his favourite pursuits of reading, walking, gardening and following the cricket scores. He was ever more conscious of failing physical powers, especially with his still-advancing deafness. This increasingly led him to invite people home to Chipstead for interviews rather than subject them, and himself, to the embarrassment of meetings in more public places which at times had to resemble shouting matches rather than serious conversations. Nevertheless, the immediate post-war years, in addition to his work for the infant World Council of Churches, saw him continuingly active in a number of directions, both at the behest of others and on his own initiative. He was still ready for adventure, still alert to the next frontier.

This chapter will briefly survey these activities of his veteran years 1945–59.

## The era of atomic power

If the start of the second world war had not come as a shock to anyone, the same was not true of the abrupt end of the conflict with the dropping of the atomic bombs on Japan in August 1945. Three months earlier, with the defeat of Nazi Germany, Oldham had spoken of a new era and new challenges but even he could not have envisaged the mind-blowing impact of the vast potentialities of modern science now revealed at Hiroshima and Nagasaki. It belongs to the credit of the British Council of Churches, and to its secretary Archie Craig in particular, to have instantly seen that the proper Christian response was not that of goggle-eyed incredulity, but of sober reflection on the ethical implications of it all. Within two months the executive of the BCC had decided to set up a commission to study and report on the issues. Credit must also go to the new archbishop of Canterbury, Geoffrey Fisher, who received a deputation of influential Anglicans urging that a commission should be set up. Fisher insisted it should be ecumenical. Craig invited Joe Oldham to chair the group. Oldham was at first hesitant – "I still think that it would be better if you could get someone who is less of a lame dog than myself to help you"[1] – but the attractions of the work soon got the better of him, not to mention the fact that having been made a vice-president of the BCC two years earlier he felt duty-bound to offer the Council some specific service.

The commission was to comprise about twelve people. There was quite some controversy in deciding its membership, especially the Church of England representation, and Oldham was concerned to get scientific experts who could speak with authority. The eventual recruits were, in addition to Oldham: John Baillie, R. Birley, E.C. Hudson, Donald Mackinnon, Walter Moberly, Dennis Routh, Mrs J.C. Stocks, M.E. Aubrey, R. Newton Flew, Kenneth Grubb, Archie Craig, George Bell, Norman Goodall, A.D. Ritchie, Kathleen Bliss, and J.D. McCaughey who acted as secretary. Oldham was also eager to liaise with the American churches on the issue, through Samuel McCrea Cavert.[2]

Oldham, characteristically, approached the subject of atomic power with an insistence on the need to recognize an unprecedented crisis of catastrophic dimensions, which could be met only in a deep faith in God yet at the same time the strategic harnessing of the best intellectual resources. "The first word to be spoken about the work of the Commission", he wrote to its members, "must be an acknowledgment that we are facing a situation beyond human and rational control, and that if we are to do anything about it we are utterly dependant on grace and aid from beyond ourselves."[3] This combined with a hard political realism – "the fundamental question transcending all others is that of the relations between the Anglo-Saxon world and Russia". And as always, the agenda which Oldham proposed to the commission was as much theological as political and scientific: God, the nature of man, science, time, power, and Christians and the use of means. On this basis he prepared a memorandum as a starting point for the commission's work.

The commission met first 4–7 January 1946 at College Hall, Malet Street in London.[4] In many ways it was much like a Moot discussion (and of course several of the participants were also in the Moot), winding its way through power and democracy, Christian engagement with and Christian disengagement from society, and there was more talk about Christianity than about the atomic bomb. A few days later Oldham reported to the executive of the BCC and encountered some scepticism as to what would eventuate in clear guidance or concrete proposals from the commission. It was not his best performance.

[1] JHO letter to Craig 19 Oct. 1945 [OA].
[2] JHO letters to Cavert 29 Oct. 1945, 5 Nov. 1945, 14 Nov. 1945 [OA].
[3] JHO letter to members of the commission 14 Nov. 1945 [OA].
[4] Minutes of the commission meetings are in OA.

Repeatedly talking of the contribution hoped for from "the best minds", as Kathleen Bliss told him afterwards, would no longer carry much weight in the post-war world. And he confessed to Archie Craig that his deafness prevented his grasping the real point of questions – "I often wonder whether this infirmity ought not to be a complete bar to my taking any responsible part in debate."[5] A few days later he had a happier time with a sub-group of John Baillie's commission in Edinburgh.[6]

The commission met again on 2–3 March. Drafts of various sections of a possible report were to hand and discussed. The report consisted of eight chapters: "Atomic Power"; "Hiroshima and After"; "The Choice before Society"; "Power and Law"; "Power and the International Community"; "Modern Warfare": "Science and Society"; and "Wholeness of Living". It took no simple doctrinaire stance against the atomic bomb, but put severe questions about the use of the weapon against Japan in a war being waged against "a brutal tyranny and ruthless nihilism": "It is difficult to see how the destruction of Hiroshima and Nagasaki can escape the charge of wantonness." More information on the military and political considerations which led to the decision were called for from the government. The restraints implied in the concept of a "just war" were disappearing fast.

Oldham's hand is particularly to be seen in the final chapter:

> The course that has been followed [in western science-based history] has . . . now brought us to the discovery of the atomic bomb, which may destroy the whole of the civilisation which [man] has created. The time has plainly come, therefore, to ask whether the assumption on which the development has proceeded is not, at least in part, mistaken. Man is certainly explorer; the success that has attended his efforts is convincing evidence. The universe is plainly so constituted that its secrets are discoverable by man's intelligence and he has been endowed with powers which enable him to penetrate those secrets. But the question is whether he is only, or primarily, explorer, or also something else; and whether that something else may not be more fundamental and more important than his capacity to explore.[7]

There follows the by now familiar Oldhamesque exposition of human life as essentially relational, of being fulfilled in encounter, and therefore of power and science to be dedicated to the interhuman realm and not to become pursuits for their own sakes.

The report, *The Era of Atomic Power*, was presented to the BCC council meeting 30 April–2 May 1946, commended to the churches for comment and response, and published by SCM. Oldham basically considered that the commission's work was done, though he was prepared to keep it in being to handle the responses from the churches. The only substantial response was from the Church of England which produced its own report in 1948.[8] The

[5] JHO letter to Craig 28 Jan. 1946 [OA].
[6] JHO letter to Craig 21 Jan. 1946 [OA].
[7] Commission draft report [OA], p.6.
[8] *The Church and the Atom: A Study of the Moral and Theological Aspects of Peace and War*, London, Church Assembly, 1948.

commission was still technically in being in 1948, and R.D. Say, secretary of the BCC, was anxious to keep the report before the churches[9] and to await further responses to be brought back to the Council. Oldham thought it practically impossible to re-convene the commission and clearly thought there was little more to be said than had already been said in the report. In the autumn of 1948, Oldham was also seeing the issues from another angle: "The fact is that atomic warfare opens up into all the questions of our present society, which were the concerns of Commissions III and IV at Amsterdam, involves all the major theological issues which divide the Churches from one another and still more conflicting schools of thought within each individual Church, and raises questions relating to the Churches themselves and their competence to deal with questions that contain a large technical element."[10] In other words, there was a danger of a specific disorder blocking out consideration of a generic condition. The BCC should rather first make some fundamental policy decisions on the use of the precious time available to its council meetings.

Nevertheless Oldham remained keenly interested in the atomic issue, though increasingly disenchanted with the BCC's propensity, like so many churchly bodies, to indulge in moralizing pronouncements. In April 1950 the BCC met in Cardiff, and a statement on the hydrogen bomb was on the agenda. Oldham was sent by Say a carbon copy of the draft. Among other things, it urged the government to declare that in any conflict it would not be the first to use the bomb. Oldham could not attend the meeting but sent back to Say a lengthy comment which was perhaps one of his sharpest interventions ever.[11] To Oldham the proposed statement committed just about every sin associated with ecclesiastical verbiage, above all its assumption that the BCC was in a position to tell the government how to govern, alternating with truisms such as that if policies cease to conflict, no bombs will be dropped, which seemed rather like saying "that if everyone were good the world would be a better place". "If the Churches had nothing to say with a more cutting edge," snapped Oldham, "it is better that they should remain silent." Oldham made clear his personal position – that if Britain were involved in war, he would want it to abstain from the use of weapons of mass destruction whatever the cost. But it was a very different thing to ask a government to make such a public pledge, not least in the state of present public (and indeed Christian) opinion. And neither was it clear whether such a policy declaration would actually make war less, rather than more, likely. "The truth as I see it", concluded Oldham, "is that, in the awful dilemma in which we find ourselves, Christians, no more than any other people, are able to see a real way out. If that is so, the beginning of any fruitful action is to have the humility to acknowledge the fact, and not to pretend that because we are Christians we have useful advice to give to Governments."

[9] Say letter to Oldham 9 June 1948 [OA].
[10] JHO letter to Say 10 Oct. 1948 [OA].
[11] JHO letter to Say 10 April 1950 [OA].

The old man might have become hard of hearing, but not of seeing. The statement that did come to the Cardiff meeting of the BCC, and was unanimously passed, was a good deal more modest than the original, concentrating on an encouragement to the government to seek to break the deadlock in international negotiations.

### The Christian Frontier

The continuation and development of the Christian Frontier was probably the most creative use of Oldham's remaining energies during these years, and most certainly the one which gave him most satisfaction, focusing as it did his whole theology of world-oriented mission and his philosophy of life as encounter, in a single, practical and realizable project. The Council continued its monthly dinners, its lunch-time discussions and residential conferences for laypeople and for specialist groups working on social and public issues, and the publication of its journal *Frontier*. It used the services of Kathleen Bliss in her *Christian News-Letter* office, and from 1945 to 1948 Daniel Jenkins was also employed.

In 1948 Oldham, consciously wishing to hand over more of the reins to younger leadership, persuaded Alec Vidler to head the staff. Vidler had of course long been a collaborator with Oldham as a member of the Moot and as co-editor of *The Christian News-Letter*, and in fact in 1946 Oldham tried to persuade Vidler and Lesslie Newbigin into becoming joint secretaries of the BCC in succession to Archie Craig. Vidler, enjoying the rural setting of Hawarden for most of each week, was highly averse to living and working wholly in London, but in 1948 received an offer he could hardly refuse, of a canonry at St George's, Windsor.[12] This combined all the advantages of ready access to London with all the benefits of a relatively secluded environment conducive to editing *Theology*, and enabled him to become executive officer of the Frontier.

Oldham had officially retired from directing the Frontier in late 1947 though, as Vidler puts it slightly mischievously, "like the high priest Annas he remained an influential figure behind the scenes". In late 1949 it was decided, under Vidler's direction, to launch a monthly journal, *Frontier*, which made its first appearance in January 1950, edited by Vidler and Philip Mairet. In 1951 yet another figure, already widely experienced in Russian affairs and in the future to become still more illustrious, joined the Frontier staff: John Lawrence.

Oldham remained the quiet but keen adviser and counsellor of the movement. In June 1956, after a silence of five years, he gave a paper at a Council meeting, "The Sway of Battle". It was, essentially, a restatement of his long-held view that science must be recognized and valued yet kept in place within a spiritual, relational concept of human existence – Eberhard Grisebach

[12] Vidler, *Scenes from a Clerical Life*, pp.132f.

makes a reappearance. The battle remained one of holding to a true understanding of humanity.

## The British Council of Churches – in concert

Oldham's involvement with the BCC during these years was neither purely nominal as one of its vice-presidents, nor confined to the commission on atomic power. Moreover, for Oldham the BCC was but one, perhaps the most inclusive, ecumenical group intimately overlapping with several others, and all reinforcing one another. The tensions that had accompanied the formation of the BCC in the war years were largely replaced by a sense of mutual complementarity, certainly between the BCC and the Christian Frontier. Not that the relation between the two bodies lacked its sensitivities. In the summer of 1947 George Grieve of the BCC secretariat invited the Christian Frontier Council to appoint an official representative on the BCC social responsibility department. Oldham declined the move, because the Frontier did not "want to become an organisation"[13] and suggested instead co-opting an individual who was also a member of the Frontier Council.

However, in November of that year Oldham, on his own initiative, took up another and much more substantial issue with the BCC secretary, R.D. Say: the actual constitution of the BCC. Harking back to the Council on the Christian Faith and the Common Life (CCFCL), Oldham suggested that what that earlier body had facilitated, and what the present BCC lacked, was "a small meeting of the responsible leaders of the larger denominations".[14] In his view, the way in which, in forming the BCC, one half of the CCFCL had become the Christian Frontier Council and the other half allowed to lapse "was probably a mistake". The executive of the BCC did not meet the need he had in mind, and while the move in the direction Oldham was suggesting could perhaps best be started informally (in conversation with the archbishop of Canterbury, for example), the possibility of an eventual amendment of the BCC constitution to include such a group might be considered. Nothing evidently came of the proposal. Oldham was not, as has been suggested, seeking to "undermine" the BCC.[15] Rather, for all his misgivings about ecclesiastical authorities, he can be seen as already aware of a problem which has continually re-emerged in the life of so many ecumenical organizations: the tendency for them to develop trajectories of their own, diverging from the lives of their constituent bodies and failing to provide a point of actual meeting among them.

What is striking about Oldham's ecumenical activities in these immediate post-war years is their underlying assumption that there is *one* ecumenical

[13] JHO letter to Grieve 15 Aug. 1947 [OA].
[14] JHO letter to Say 25 Nov. 1947 [OA].
[15] E. Jackson, *Red Tape and the Gospel*, p.273, states of Oldham that "as late as 1949 he was trying to undermine the BCC and expressing his disapproval".

movement to be served in a variety of interlocking, complementary and mutually dependent ways: BCC, Christian Frontier, *The Christian News-Letter*, the American ecumenical bodies, the WCC, all were essentially playing in the same concert. For a while in the period just before and just after the end of the war, Oldham gathered yet another Moot-type cell together, called the St Julian's Group on account of its favoured meeting-place for discussions on "the present situation" in church and society. As well as several Moot regulars (Baillie, Mackinnon, Bliss, Fenn, Hodges, Vidler, Hetherington) it drew in Archie Craig of the BCC and a number of younger people from the SCM and higher education circles such as Marjorie Reeves, Kenneth Grayston and Roy Niblett.[16] Oldham also shared enthusiastically with Clifford Cleal of the BCC social responsibility department, and others, in the programme on "The Christian Doctrine of Work".[17]

## After Amsterdam: the World Council of Churches

If the World Council of Churches was indeed, in part, one of Oldham's children then it was only to be expected that he would take a continuing interest in its affairs once it was off his hands, so to speak, after the Amsterdam assembly in 1948. Joe Oldham was never the indulgent parent, however, and his correspondence with Geneva was rarely uncritical. From 1949 he took part in the development of the early programme on Christianity and secular society, centred on the Ecumenical Institute at Bossey. He became somewhat incensed at the initial omission of the subject of "work" from the study, and drew from Visser 't Hooft the admission: "Your letter shows that you continue to be so passionately concerned about our work, and its possibilities and obligations, that you feel forced to speak out frankly, rather than register acquiescence in what we are trying to do. I appreciate that."[18] The upshot was that the subject was readmitted to the study, and Oldham himself wrote the notable booklet *Work in Modern Society*, in which his major perennial concerns for a theology of the laity, a relational view of society, and the church's proper relation to secular life were underlined: ". . . [W]hile the Gospel is, in the first instance, a call away from the world and from immersion in temporal concerns, it is at the same time a call back into the world where alone in this earthly life God is to be served."[19]

Oldham was enthusiastic about the Toronto Statement made in 1950 by the WCC central committee on the relation between the churches and the World

[16] Cf. papers in Selly Oak Library. The "present situation" theme was taken up within the Frontier movement by the higher education group and others, and a conference was held in Oxford in 1952, in which both Christians and agnostics participated.

[17] C.H. Cleal letter to author 6 Nov. 1990. Cleal also, as a staff person of the BCC, at no time suggests that Oldham was anything but the keenest supporter of the work the BCC was actually doing: but he was always trying to enrich its possibilities by creating new relationships and alliances. Letters from JHO to Cleal 28 Jan. 1950 and 20 May 1950 in possession of author.

[18] Visser 't Hooft letter to Oldham 3 June 1949 [OA].

[19] Oldham, *Work in Modern Society*, London, SCM for Study Department of WCC, 1950, p.44.

Council, and wrote a short piece on it for *The Ecumenical Review.*[20] But he was still troubled by major questions:

> ... *What kind* of instrument have we got in the World Council? For what purpose is it adapted, and for what purposes is it not adapted? What auxiliary machinery (Departments, etc) is required to enable it to fulfil the purpose it is capable of serving? It is generally taken for granted that we know the answers to these questions. I do not think that we know them at all. The conviction goes back to the days when I was actively serving the ecumenical movement that unless we can arrive at much better answers than exist at present, there is likely to be a wasteful misdirection of energy into relatively unfruitful channels and that the great thing that the World Council is called to do may be altogether missed.[21]

In the spring of 1951 these general concerns became painfully focused in a way which, while he might not openly admit it, was for Oldham inextricably linked with a deeply personal issue. Visser 't Hooft had invited Kathleen Bliss, who was now working for the British Broadcasting Corporation, to come to Geneva as an associate secretary of the WCC. After a day spent discussing the matter with Oldham, she and her husband Rupert came to the conclusion that she ought to refuse, and cabled Visser 't Hooft accordingly. It was clearly a difficult decision for her to make. She had already made an outstanding contribution to the WCC at the Amsterdam assembly and elsewhere, and would have relished the responsibility of overseeing the women's and youth departments at Geneva. Oldham knew that Visser 't Hooft would be deeply disappointed and, most likely, would suspect Oldham's hand in her decision. He therefore wrote Visser 't Hooft a ten-page letter admitting that "the considerations I put forward may have influenced in some way her decision", and seeking to explain what these considerations were.[22] The crux of his argument is stated early on:

> I am completely convinced about the need for a World Council of Churches. I believe also that it is essential that it should have at headquarters a small central staff of able officers who can maintain personal touch with the leaders of the Churches in intervals between meetings of the Council and of its Central Committee. At Amsterdam your plan for a small group of Associated secretaries strongly commended itself to me.
>
> On the other hand I am sceptical about the Departments on Study, Youth, Laymen and Women. As Departments they seem to me *nonsensical* in the sense that if you effected a merger and combined them, it would be nonsensical to have a Department on the population of the World. They cease to be nonsensical only if out of the thousand potential activities in each field one or two are isolated and reduced to a concrete proposition ...

Such a concrete proposition, in each case, would involve very limited and measurable goals in a specified time. So the pages roll on, with ever sharper

[20] *The Ecumenical Review*, April 1951, pp.248–50.
[21] JHO letter to Visser 't Hooft 11 Jan. 1951 [OA].
[22] JHO letter to Visser 't Hooft 7 April 1951 [G].

rehearsal of his well-known earlier arguments against international work at the expense of what should be done by national bodies. Moreover, he felt, there was not a real job to be done in the Women's Department for someone with Kathleen Bliss's gifts:

> Of course I agree that the place of women in the Church is a question of the first importance, as is also the man and woman relationship in the Church. But I have long known that there is all the difference in the world between a matter being of supreme importance, and the decision that there is something practical that, within the limits of available resources, can be done about it. It is a besetting weakness of the ecumenical movement (as of people in general) to leap without thought from the first proposition to the second, and because a subject seems important, to set up a department or appoint a secretary to deal with it. Why cannot we learn a little sense from the children of this world, i.e. from business men, who, before they invest a vast amount of effort in an undertaking (however important and alluring the results which it promises), undertake at considerable cost of time and money a preliminary investigation to find out whether the enterprise is really water-tight, and whether they will not encounter, sooner or later, insurmountable obstacles.

The best service the WCC could do in relation to women, urges Oldham, would be to set an example by appointing a woman to do the same kind of work as is done by a man – "I know that this is your own view, and was your intention, and that you found the way unexpectedly blocked". Despite admitting that Visser 't Hooft wanted Bliss for purposes not confined to the women's department, Oldham continues to vent his opposition. Clearly, the Bliss predicament had unleashed, as never before, all his fears about the centralizing programmatic tendencies of Geneva. But was that all there was here? As the ten pages of argument roll on, one suspects that at least part of Oldham's agenda was not the future of the WCC, but the need, at all costs, to keep Kathleen Bliss, his most cherished collaborator, alongside him in London. Oldham also protested: "It is hardly fair to ask Kathleen to decide within three days."

Visser 't Hooft's reply[23] was a conciliatory, but firm, statement of the case that if – as Oldham had accepted in their notable exchange in 1947 – the WCC was to be a council of the churches themselves, it could hardly help reflecting the specific forms in which their own constituencies exist as women, youth etc. But on the matter of Kathleen Bliss's decision, he confessed to feeling "explosive". Oldham's implication of undue pressure being brought upon her for a speedy decision had hit him "like a ton of bricks". The discussions with her, said Visser 't Hooft, had begun a whole year previously and the first official letter sent to her the previous autumn had not been replied to. Some British members on the WCC executive committee had in fact surprised Visser 't Hooft by their reactions when he had suggested her as an associate secretary. He did not know what they had in mind but by now, he confessed, he was not

[23] Visser 't Hooft letter to JHO 11 April 1951 [G].

sure if he could work with someone who "keeps you so completely in the dark".

Oldham wrote Visser 't Hooft a reply in still more conciliatory tone,[24] admitting he had not known all the circumstances of the affair, disavowing any intention of "criticism" of the WCC and not wishing (now, at any rate) to accuse him of unfair pressure on Bliss. This may not have been a completely satisfactory explanation of his earlier letter, but both regarded the matter as now closed and this, their sharpest exchange ever, was not allowed to injure for long a friendship which was deeply cherished on both sides – and on Kathleen Bliss's side. Soon after, Oldham retired from the WCC study committee. His last official link with the World Council now untied, the Central Committee sent him a warm message of gratitude for his "inspiring and challenging leadership" from Edinburgh 1910 onwards. In particular, the message acknowledged "a special debt of gratitude for his outstanding contribution to Christian thinking on racial, educational, and international problems, on the place of the layman, and on the whole missionary task and function of the Church in modern society.[25] John Mott, who had ventured yet again across the Atlantic to attend the meeting, was one of those who endorsed the resolution with fervour. Visser 't Hooft added a personal note: "I am convinced that this breaking of the official tie will not and must not mean the breaking of the very strong personal ties which have been built up during the years. I for one hope that you will continue to send us as often as possible your very vigorous letters which always help us to rethink our work in the light of basic Christian convictions."

Those "vigorous letters" certainly continued, to Visser 't Hooft and other Geneva staff, on a variety of topics: the role of laypeople;[26] matters of historical detail on the early part of the ecumenical story[27] and the consultation on "The Meaning of the Secular".[28] In 1957, on the 20th anniversary of the Oxford conference, the Central Committee again sent him a warm greeting, and Oldham was equally warm in reply: "One cannot but be profoundly thankful to God for the dimensions to which the tree which some of us took part in planting twenty years ago has grown."[29]

## Africa re-visited: the Capricorn Society

It is often said that one should not go back, whether to one's old school, or place of work to which a farewell was taken years before. Life moves on, and the space one used to occupy is simply no longer there, which can be discomforting. In the 1950s Oldham did attempt a mental return to the scene

[24] JHO letter to Visser 't Hooft 14 April 1951 [G].
[25] Visser 't Hooft letter to JHO 26 Sept. 1951 [OA].
[26] JHO letter to Walz 14 Jan. 1952 [OA].
[27] JHO letters to Visser 't Hooft 17 Sept. 1952, 20 Sept. 1952, 16 March 1954 [OA].
[28] JHO letter to C. West 28 Aug. 1949 [OA].
[29] JHO letter to Visser 't Hooft 1 Aug. 1957 [OA].

of perhaps his most impressive and fruitful labours a quarter of a century earlier. There are many of his admirers who could wish that he had not tried to do so, at any rate not quite in the form which his attempt took.

The Capricorn Africa Society was the brainchild of David Stirling. As an army officer in the North African campaign during the second world war, Stirling had achieved fame for his daring commando raids deep behind enemy lines, and for his founding of the elite Special Air Service. After the war he made his home in Africa, dividing his time between Rhodesia (as it then was) and Kenya. A Roman Catholic and an idealist, one might say in the best British public school tradition, he was gripped by a vision of Africa from the Limpopo to the Sahara becoming a racially integrated society in an atmosphere of understanding, tolerance and equality regardless of colour and under a common citizenship. To this end, in 1949 in Salisbury (now Harare) he formed with a group of like-minded people, white and black, the Capricorn Africa Society (CAS). Stirling brought to everything he did, including the CAS, an "almost manic drive and determination in pursuit of that which he thought worth fighting for".[30] For several years the CAS had high ideals and, in Stirling himself, great vision and determination, but little else. It needed an administrative base both in British colonial Africa and in London if it was to gain significant support from politicians, influential figures and public opinion; and of course it needed money.

Oldham knew virtually nothing about Stirling himself or the CAS, until Stirling came to visit the Oldhams for Easter weekend in 1954. Oldham had evidently been commended to Stirling as an adept at enlisting significant figures and advisory experts in support of a cause, and in this case Stirling was concerned to locate those with expertise in the constitutional and technical questions which the CAS would have to tackle. Joe and Mary Oldham instantly took to Stirling: the daring raider behind enemy lines, now hazarding all for a great and idealistic cause, immediately rang true to Joe's sense that commitment and adventure were the very life of the human soul. And his own love of Africa was rekindled. The Oldhams had by now moved to Dunford in Sussex, and Joe Oldham felt that he had sufficient leisure from other commitments to be of use to Stirling.

The CAS became Oldham's chief preoccupation for the next two years. It provided him with a number of new acquaintances whom he and Mary came to admire greatly. In particular, as well as David Stirling himself, there was Jeanine Scott who acted as secretary for the cause in London and who became a great favourite in the Oldham home, and Laurens van der Post who also visited Dunford. Oldham quickly decided that the CAS had two prime and urgent needs: the building up of solid support, including financial, at the London end, and a more clearly defined goal and strategy. He tried to help with the former requirement with a stream of correspondence, a number of visits to London and several weekend meetings with invited guests at Dunford,

[30] Obituary, *The Guardian*, 7 Nov. 1990.

and (of course) a memorandum. To one of the main London supporters, Sir John Slessor, he commended his own services with some qualification but genuine commitment: "I am precluded by the handicaps of years, deafness and remoteness from London from taking any initiative the results of which depend on myself. But I have leisure, a certain capacity for understanding other people and gaining their confidence, a small gift, perhaps, of seeing the essentials of a problem and a fairly long experience in getting people of different views to work together."[31] In fact during 1955 full-time administrative staff were obtained for Salisbury and Nairobi. In London, however, politicians of both main political parties remained wary. For example Patrick Gordon Walker was, thought Oldham, very supportive but "does not want to be committed publicly".[32] He set great store by such as Philip Mason who over lunch "poured out helpful and constructive comments on the memorandum". But concrete support was slow in coming.

It soon became evident to Oldham that the handicaps he had listed to Slessor were indeed real factors inhibiting his contribution at the organizational level. Gone were the days of weekly, or daily, conspiratorial têtes-à-têtes at Edinburgh House or in the Athenaeum, and the regular support of an office and its staff. What he was still able to do, however, was to think and to write. His letters to the CAS collaborators often became sermonettes on the significance of the CAS cause: it represented the one hope for Africa, and the future of Africa was one of the major problems in the life of mankind today. Another key CAS advocate was Sir Geoffrey Vickers: decorated with the Victoria Cross in 1915, a director in the department of economic warfare 1944–45 and now on the Medical Research Council. Much occupied with religious and philosophical ideas, he was to write *The Undirected Society* (1959). Oldham both stimulated and strongly supported Vickers' thesis that the key plank in CAS advocacy must be that of education for Africans. He wrote to David Stirling:

> . . .. you must have an *awareness* that a rapid advance in African education is a necessity if the non-racial Society is to become a reality. Unless the number of Africans who can pull their weight in positions of *management* is *rapidly* increased, the whole idea of a non-racial society becomes a deception.[33]

He expanded further on this in another letter to Stirling:

> The basic fact which governs the whole African situation is the contact between what we call western civilization and the life of peoples still in a primitive stage of development. Every one will admit this, but few, if any, have seen its *cruciality* in the way you have done. That insight is expressed in the basic understanding between the white and the coloured members of the Capricorn Society . . . [T]his means that we are confronted with an inexorable choice. *Either* Africans must be given the opportunity of realizing their ineradicable and irrepressible desire for nationhood

[31] JHO letter to Slessor 13 Nov. 1954 [OA].
[32] JHO letter to F. Clarke 18 Sept. 1954 [OA].
[33] JHO letter to Stirling 20 Dec. 1954 [OA].

> and self-government within a framework of western civilization *or* they will seek the fulfilment of these over-mastering passions in an exclusive nationalism and racialism, which can lead only to conflict so disastrous that it may be impossible to rebuild.[34]

Oldham eventually decided that his most effective contribution to the CAS would be to write a book expounding its importance, its vision and its strategy. It would, he told Stirling, "express *your* view, not mine", while working out a fuller and more developed view of the Capricorn movement than Stirling had had leisure to undertake.[35] Stirling spent a week with the Oldhams at Dunford in the spring of 1955 thrashing out the structure and content of the book. One major point which Oldham felt Stirling had not sufficiently appreciated was the question of power. Stirling, in Oldham's view, had the rather romantic conception that, provided a constitution was adopted stating full equality of citizenship regardless of colour, with a common electoral roll, the multi-racial society would be assured. "The reality", said Oldham, "on which all will hinge is how quickly enough Africans will become capable of being *real* partners in the growth of an inter-racial society."[36] Hence the key lay in education, and the CAS began to make plans, for example, for scholarships for Africans in higher education.

Oldham spent the summer of 1955 writing what was published later in the year as *New Hope in Africa*.[37] It reads as a full-blooded call to the CAS cause as opening up a fundamentally new approach to the African problem. Nationalism in Africa is a "volcanic force" which must be put to "constructive ends". Africa has hitherto been faced with a stark choice between white domination and African nationalism. The former was both morally wrong and lacking feasibility. The latter was impracticable since African advancement required a colossal expansion of health, agricultural and educational services which for the time being had to be supplied from outside Africa itself. A third way, however, was that advocated by the CAS: an inter-racial, integrated society in which the different races cooperate without regard to colour, for the common good and the spiritual enrichment of all.

Oldham proceeds to expound the problem of Africa as that of reconciling modern technical civilization with traditional life. He deals with the questions of race and equality in a thoroughly progressive way, supported by recent UNESCO studies. He repeats his view, expressed in earlier correspondence with Stirling, that Africans will either find their fulfilment within the framework of Western civilization or be driven to an exclusive, and ultimately destructive, African nationalism. The need for self-government is affirmed, and therewith the need for Africans to be brought to a level of education and managerial ability where they can be true partners in government. It will be a long process, but throughout the world the tide is running in the multi-racial direction, as

[34] JHO letter to Stirling 18 Feb. 1955 [OA].
[35] JHO letter to Stirling 20 Dec. 1954 [OA].
[36] JHO letter to Stirling 18 Feb. 1955 [OA].
[37] London, Longman, Green & Co., 1955.

shown for example by the statements from the Evanston Assembly of the WCC (1954) and the judgment against racial segregation in schools passed by the US Supreme Court. As would be expected there is some theological anthropology in the argument, with an underlining of human fulfilment as lying in relationships with others.

*New Hope in Africa* was an able and worthy manifesto, but in the long run it did not save the Capricorn movement which ran out into the sand by about 1960, overtaken by other moods for political change and independence in British colonial Africa. In retrospect it is relatively easy to see where the weaknesses of the movement lay. Its goal of the multi-racial ideal and common electoral roll was stated a little too clearly for the cautious mandarins in the Colonial Office, but at the same time it seems to have made little real contact with the African nationalists themselves. Oldham was right to recognize the issue of power, but seems himself to have thought of "power" in terms of individual human capacity, and hence the stress on education. That was not in itself wrong. Most post-colonial African leaders have owed, and acknowledged, a large debt to their Western-based education (not least through Christian missions). But the crucial political issue for Africa was that of *collective* power, and this was not really addressed. Most glaringly suspect of all, perhaps, was Oldham's own conviction that it was only in the framework of Western civilization that Africans could hope to find their fulfilment, and that therefore the opportunities had to be opened up for them to enter this particular promised land. There can be no doubt whatever that Oldham, who in 1923 had established the principle of the "paramountcy" of African interests in Kenya, and who was crucial in the Hilton Young commission's rejection of federation as inimical to Africans' interests, believed deeply in the multi-racial society and political equality. But to make "western civilisation" such an unquestionable absolute in the African scene proved in fact to play right into the hands of white supremacists, as shown by the avowals of Prime Minister Ian Smith, when Rhodesia unilaterally declared independence in 1965, to preserve the country in perpetuity for "civilisation".

## Mission: "a perfectly mad adventure"

In 1949 Oldham addressed the conference of the Church Missionary Society at High Leigh on *The Missionary and the National State*.[38] It was the time when, early in the Cold War, there was much talk of the communist menace. Oldham, still with the memory of the Amsterdam assembly fresh in this mind, again warns his hearers against sheer and self-righteous dismissal of communism. There are elements in communism "quite incompatible" with the Christian view of the meaning of human existence but as a revolutionary force it may, like Cyrus, "be fulfilling a purpose which God can turn to good". The challenge

[38] Oldham, *The Missionary and the National State*, London, CMS, 1949. Following quotes from pp.4, 6.

laid before Christians is not to evade this force, and other attitudes assuming human powers and mastery, but rather to Christianize the Promethean archetype. Humankind's powers are real, but are to be seen as gifts from God, to be used in partnership with God in creating a genuine society where freedom is located in community. But pulsing through this entire paper is, yet again, a call for the church to escape from its religious shell and meet the life of the world where God is already at work:

> When we contrast our preaching, which so easily degenerates into mere talk, which is cheap and easy, and our tendency to lay down high-sounding abstract principles with the work of men who as scientists, or engineers, or skilled workers or administrators, take huge burdens on their shoulders and save human lives and make life better and happier for multitudes, are we not sometimes reminded of the parable of the two brothers who were bidden to work in the vineyard, and of Christ's searching comparison between them?

But the church, whenever it starts to talk about the world, almost invariably does so not from the perspective of those who work in and for it, but from the clerical, ecclesiastical sphere. A vast reorientation is called for and if the CMS is prepared to embark on it there may be even greater days in its future than in its great past. His (almost) concluding words sum up a lifetime's attitude to Christian mission: "I know that the task to which I have been pointing is utterly beyond our human resources. But the missionary enterprise has always been a perfectly mad adventure." An interesting comparison can be made with his address to the same body eighteen years earlier, in which "adventure" had featured just as prominently.[39]

"Old men ought to be explorers": did T.S. Eliot have Joe Oldham in mind?[40] Nothing is more striking than the way in which, in these late years, Oldham's sense of Christian life and thought being an adventure of exploration and commitment, far from declining, if anything grew stronger. It was that which appealed to him in David Stirling. It also drew his admiration of another figure and moved him to write her life, the only biography among the many he could have produced in a career rich in fascinating encounters.

## Florence Allshorn

Florence Allshorn (1887–1950) founded and led the St Julian's Community, based first at Oakenrough and then at Barns Green in Sussex. It was primarily a centre for retreat and spiritual development for missionaries on furlough. The Moot had met there a number of times and Joe and Mary Oldham got to know her well. She had herself served with the Church Missionary Society in Uganda from 1920 to 1924. Returning to England because of ill health, for several years she was in charge of the training of women missionaries at St

[39] *The CMS and the Adventure of Today.* See above, pp.263f.

[40] T.S. Eliot, "East Coker", in *Four Quartets: The Complete Works of T.S. Eliot,* London, Faber & Faber, 1969, p.182.

*Florence Allshorn*

Andrew's Hostel. In Uganda, particularly due to a difficult relationship with a senior colleague, she had passed through a painful time of self-discovery and a realization that, devout missionary though she might be, she had to enter into a still deeper understanding of the love of God and how this had to be manifested in personal relationships. Back in England, she came to the conclusion that her own case was typical of most missionary recruits: that the training provided before leaving for the mission field could only be the merest beginning, and that there was need for a place where missionaries, after their first years of service, could find themselves, God and Christian love all over again. She managed to convince the CMS, and the St Julian's venture was born.

Florence Allshorn was one of those rare individuals in whom contrasts are woven into a creative whole. To use the language of traditional mysticism, she seemed to combine the affirmative and negative ways. Sharply and finely featured herself, and with an infectious gaiety, she had a love of beauty in all things, whether nature, music, poetry, good food or well-cut clothes. Being a missionary was no excuse for dowdiness. Yet she had an intense spirituality. More than one guest at St Julian's used to say that on entering her room one had an almost magical sense of her presence, but left it with an overpowering sense of God. The turning point in her own spiritual journey had been an incident in Uganda: "Her colleague . . . was in one of her furious tempers. She had hurled at Florence bitter and hurtful words. Florence remained silent. 'O God', she prayed inwardly, 'help me to be *sorry* – to love her.' She clung desperately to the thought of God's infinite pity. Suddenly the angry words ceased, and the older woman said, 'You will never know what you have done for me,' and went quietly to her room."

Joe Oldham saw embodied in Florence Allshorn the exemplar of human existence in its wholeness: an openness to all life and to the world in its beauty and tragedy, a deep compassion for the afflicted born out of her own experiences, a daily life suffused with and taken up into prayer, a sense of the presence of God inextricably bound up with personal relationships in community – and all held together in an unswerving, visionary commitment. Early in 1950 he was staying at St Julian's when she showed him the first draft of a small book about the community and its story, and asked him for help in getting it into shape. Before they could meet again to work together on the project, her last illness began. After her death her colleagues asked Oldham to complete the work, and it was agreed that he should incorporate what she had written into a biography of her. Oldham wrote to a mutual friend for advice on how to assess her spirituality in the light of the mystical tradition, and in the course of his letter remarked: "She was the kind of person that I would fain to be and miserably am not. She combined an extraordinary singleness of aim and complete devotion to Christ in every thought and act with a life lived in a real sense in the world, even though outwardly it was in the main the world of Evangelical piety."[41] It was above all in her voluminous letters that Oldham believed to find the essence of her soul.

*Florence Allshorn and the Story of St Julian's* was published by SCM in 1951. Typically, Oldham presented her not as a role-model for conventional piety within the evangelical fold, but as a figure of much wider significance for the time:

> The love of Christ was the ruling passion of her life, but the expression of it was in no way conventional. She had in her lifetime the art of making friends with all sorts of people professing a diversity of beliefs. If this book finds readers among those who do not call themselves Christians, some of them, perhaps, in spite of differences of outlook and language, will recognize in her life an adventure of the human spirit that is directly related to major decisions to-day which confront mankind as a whole, and which are the common concern of all who care about its future.

## Life is commitment: a biographical theology

In one sense, it is not exactly true to say that Florence Allshorn was Oldham's only biographical subject, for *Life Is Commitment*, his last major work, is nothing if not a kind of spiritual autobiography. In fact, it does contain his only published account of his career, albeit compressed.[42] It is a theological

[41] JHO letter to "George" 20 Nov. 1950 [OA].
[42] London, SCM, 1953, pp.11f.

*summa* wrought out of his lifelong spiritual journey, and virtually every page testifies to his personal experience of life as exploration, responsibility and relationships with others. The book originated as lectures given at the London School of Religion in early 1952 and appeared in 1953. Oldham's intention was consciously apologetic, with two classes of readers in mind: "The first is those who are as yet uncommitted to any form of Christian belief, but have an open mind whether it may not contain truth and value which they have not yet perceived; the second is those (of whom I know a good many) who are, or would like to be, Christians but who find it difficult to relate their faith to the realities of existence in present-day society."[43] His approach was likewise undergirded with two strong convictions: that if Christian faith was to have a meaning for ordinary people it must prove itself as a faith by which they could live in their daily tasks in industry and society; and that if there was to be a fruitful discussion of the contemporary meaning of Christianity it had to be opened to the current debates about the fundamental nature of human existence and knowledge.

Much of the argument would have been familiar to those knowing Oldham's numerous earlier writings, but doubtless new to most of those who heard the original lectures and to many of the readers. It opens with a chapter on "Fact and Decision": science has led to brilliant advances in knowledge and mastery of the world, but the world as such, of which the scientist *qua* human being is also a part, remains a mystery requiring a fundamental decision for its interpretation. Science describes only one aspect of life. The self cannot be objectified. It remains open to demands, moral imperatives, calls for *decision* and responsibility. In the last resort a basic choice is required on what is believed to be the nature of being a human person. As to be expected, Oldham advocates the claims of the interpersonal, relational nature of human existence as presented by such as Buber and Grisebach. The title of the book might be taken to mean that "meeting", popularized in his famous war-time slogan "Real Life is Meeting", might now be in process of being soft-pedalled, but in a nice little autobiographical aside he explains:

> *Real* life, [Buber] says, is *meeting.* I adopted the assertion in a small book of essays which I published a few years ago. But since then I have rather refrained from using it. I was influenced, perhaps, by the fact that Mr Christopher Dawson once remarked to me that he wasn't sure that he liked the phrase because it suggested such an awful thought, if you put "s" at the end of it. This is only one way of expressing the fact that the thought can be so easily trivialized, as though what Buber was talking about was a social gathering or a tea-party.[44]

This in no way lessens the force and eloquence of Oldham's exposition that human life *is* that of community, inter-relationship, as opposed to both individualism and collectivism.

[43] *Ibid.*, p.10.
[44] *Ibid.*, pp.27f. Dawson, it should be said, had a reputation as something of a recluse.

From there Oldham moves to the question of God, looking full in the face the claims of modern atheism that "God" is either an irrelevant and unnecessary hypothesis for a world now explained by science, or a denial of human adulthood and capacities. Oldham's answer is, once again, to look into what it means to be human: is there not, precisely when we are invited to shoulder our responsibilities, a sense of a claim being laid upon us which comes from an infinite and unqualified realm beyond us? Why is it that love, for example, comes to us as a call for total and complete surrender? Such happens in taking the marriage vow, but also sometimes in answering the need of a complete stranger. Imagine for example a young man of brilliant promise standing on a pier, who throws himself into the water, at the risk and maybe at the cost of his own life, to rescue an old man who has squandered his years in dissipation. There can be no "rational" justification for such an act, "and yet we feel intuitively that humanity would somehow be a poorer, meaner affair if such things were not done".[45] Sacrifice, even if not of such dramatic proportions, is in fact the stuff of daily life for countless people.

Oldham does not say so, but in fact in using the illustration of the young man risking his life for another in the water, he was re-using almost the exact story he was wont to use fifty years earlier in addresses to student gatherings. Then, he had used it in a fairly conventional evangelical way in an effort to show the quality of the saving love of Christ, and the way in which that love can inspire a similar quality in the Christian. Now, the story is used to illustrate a basal feature of human existence as indicative of an infinite, transcendental realm bearing in upon us: "You can make an unlimited response, and absolute self-surrender, only to what is itself unlimited and unconditional. May not the truth be that when we give ourselves in complete surrender to another person or other persons, we are responding not merely to them in their finitude but to something greater of which they are the embodiment?" Is it not in pondering the implications of love that we are given the clue to the fundamental nature of the universe, of reality? Oldham does not flinch from the assertion that, along this line, one cannot be an atheist. People either believe in God or invent gods.

The rest of the book is an exposition of Christ as the one in whom the infinite offer and claim of God's love comes upon us (with an interesting discussion of the current situation of understanding the "historical Jesus"), of the church (in all its positive and negative features) as the place where this is lived out as community, and the world as the place where faith seeks to realize the inter-relational life in secular responsibilities. The book as published concludes with a lecture given at the "Present Question Conference" at Oxford in 1952 on "Man and Truth". Its final two paragraphs sum up the whole, and the whole of Oldham's spiritual journey:

> I am not attempting here to discuss the difficulties attaching to Christian belief. I know that they are real and manifold. I am only pointing out that those who have encountered Christ and made a wholehearted response to that encounter have found

[45] *Ibid.*, p.55.

an answer to the problem of man and truth. They have been given a faith which they do not have to carry, but which carries them. It is the testimony of Christians that amid all the uncertainties of relativism they have discovered that to which they may surrender themselves in complete trust. They have encountered a reality which gives them confidence that the universe is trustworthy. What they have known and experienced of love is something that they believe will hold firm in all the stresses and tests of life and prove stronger than death itself.

That is one answer to the problem of man and truth. I do not myself know of any other answer in which my mind can rest. But it is inherent in that answer, as I understand it, that the answer must vindicate itself in open and free discussion, that all formulations of the answer made by fallible men are necessarily defective and incomplete and are in constant need of correction and enrichment by the contribution of the experience of all sincere seekers after truth.[46]

In these words, there is both continuity and development in relation to the young undergraduate who on a November night in 1892 in Oxford had answered D.L. Moody's call to give himself "definitely to Jesus Christ". The continuity lies in the commitment to the person of Christ, and the sense of ceaseless adventure to which that surrender and commitment leads, as it had led through a life-time's wealth of experiences and responsibilities. The development is seen in the vast range of human issues which that commitment confronted, and the theological and philosophical resources he now drew upon in his explication of life as the great adventure, and faith as the greatest venture of all. Compressed into *Life Is Commitment* is an extraordinary variety of contemporary reading. Not only are his stalwarts such as Buber, Grisebach, Brunner, Barth, Heim, Tillich, Maritain, Marcel and Berdyaev much in evidence. From outside the Christian fold we meet Albert Camus, Alex Comfort and Charles Sherrington. More recently appearing names feature: Karl Popper, Michael Polanyi, Eugen Rosenstock-Heussy (for whom he had developed a marked enthusiasm and friendship), C.F. von Weizsäcker among them. Dr Samuel Johnson once remarked that a man should keep his friendships in repair, by which he meant not only the maintenance of old friendships but the readiness to make new ones. At 78, Oldham was certainly keeping his intellectual friendships in repair. Dietrich Bonhoeffer's prison letters were drawn upon, even before their appearance in English. Oldham had always had an immense regard for the young German he had known in London and in Life and Work in the 1930s, and now in death one of the century's great witnesses to truth. (In 1953, Eberhard Bethge, Bonhoeffer's close friend and recipient of the prison letters, came to London as pastor of the German congregation where Bonhoeffer had ministered twenty years before. His wife Renate was Bonhoeffer's niece. At their first Christmas in London a large hamper arrived for the Bethges and their three children – from the Oldhams.)[47]

[46] *Ibid.*, p.130.
[47] Information from R. and E. Bethge.

## Partings . . . and new encounters

The repair of friendships was taking on a greater importance with the continual departure of long-standing friends and colleagues. John Mott died on 31 January 1955, in his ninetieth year. Oldham wrote an appreciation of his comrade for *The Ecumenical Review*,[48] recollecting how their long association had grown since that day more than sixty years ago when they had met at the station in Oxford. It was not one-sided eulogy: "He was entirely unversed in theology or philosophy. His judgments on these matters were often naive. In this respect the differences between him and William Temple could not have been wider." None the less Mott was the unquestioned leader of movements which included church leaders and academics. "The explanation is ... that in any practical situation he saw with great clearness and with unrivalled intensity the things that chiefly mattered". It was this unsurpassed gift of leadership, devoid of self-seeking, which Oldham saw as his hallmark. "A great life has reached its end; seen in retrospect, its dimensions seem even larger than in his life-time."

Oldham's continual refurbishment of his friendships, theological and otherwise, was not confined to his reading only. He carried on a lively correspondence in these years with those whose minds he found original and stimulating, not least among the younger generation. John Wren-Lewis, for example, a crystallographer by profession, a lay theologian of radical tendencies and growing repute through his writings, attracted him greatly even in disagreement. Wren-Lewis, Oldham felt, allowed the "scientific world view" to determine in an unqualified way a "modern" approach to reality at the cost of a transcendent dimension, and hence the reality of God. Bultmann's famous remark that it was "impossible" to believe the New Testament "mythological" world-view in an age of science begged the question of complementary interpretations of reality.[49] More constructive, Oldham felt, was Michael Polanyi's *Personal Knowledge* (1958) which he hailed in a letter to the author as "a major heuristic achievement" – "Of all the books I have read in recent years none has taken so powerful a hold on me" – "the book seems to me to have potentially . . . momentous, and I am tempted to say, epochal significance":[50] none of which inhibited Oldham from then offering several pages of critical questions and comments. (Oldham had in fact already read a first draft of the book in manuscript, and persuaded Polanyi to re-write the final chapter, much to the relief of his assistant Marjorie Grene.[51]) A contrasting, but equally attractive, contact for him was Donald MacKay, then a young pioneer in the field of cybernetics which was also intriguing Oldham greatly. The fact that MacKay was by conviction more evangelical than Wren-Lewis made no difference as far as Oldham was concerned: here was someone else tackling a

[48] Oldham, "John R. Mott", *The Ecumenical Review*, vol. VII, no. 3, April 1955, pp.256–259.
[49] Correspondence between JHO and Wren-Lewis 1956–62 [OA].
[50] JHO letter to Polanyi 11 May 1957 [OA].
[51] M. Grene letter to JHO 12 May 1958 [OA].

vital frontier. In any case, that friendship provided yet another chance for Joe and Mary Oldham to indulge their love of small children, even to the point of going on all fours on the lawn to find and blow dandelion-clocks for the MacKays' infant son.[52]

With advancing years the Oldhams had to rearrange their domestic scene. They celebrated their golden wedding in October 1948 at Chipstead, their much-loved home for over twenty years, which had welcomed guests as diverse as Sadhu Sundar Singh and Karl Barth, and was now collecting the affections of a new generation of visitors. "I remember", says Deborah Cassidi, daughter of Kathleen Bliss, "tall bookcases, panama hats, papers lying on a table near an open window, the room with its polished floor dark by comparison with the sunlight outside. I recall two white Scottish terriers and Mary on a brambled walk, but mostly the garden where aubretia sparkled between the flagstones . . . Grown-ups sat in the sun and a kind man later known to me as Joe explained to me the shadow on the sundial and traced the movements with his fine fingers."[53]

Not long after their golden wedding, Joe and Mary left the cherished Dial House for Worcester Park, slightly nearer London. Then in October 1952 they moved again, to Dunford House, a centre for residential study formerly owned by the YMCA, at Midhurst in Sussex. It provided an ideal setting for receiving friends and hosting small weekend discussion groups, while walking the rolling Sussex downland was one of the chief extra-mural attractions.

It was pleasant to be in such relative seclusion, yet to be kept in touch with the wider world. His most official public recognition had come when he was awarded a CBE (Commander of the British Empire) in the King's Birthday Honours list of June 1951 "for service to educational and religious organisations". What probably meant at least as much to him was the occasion in October 1954 when he reached his eightieth birthday. "They gave us a very good day here," Joe told his brother Jack. "At breakfast the household, including the two gardeners, marched in singing, and bringing a gift. Dinner in the evening was an amazing affair. The flower decorations on the table were simple and lovely. The cake had eight candles, while alongside was a candle with a mighty girth, suggesting – I imagine – that you multiply the eight candles by ten."[54] The post brought greetings from many countries, some from old friends, some from people he had never met. "But", he concluded, "life is pretty full these days."

[52] Letter D. MacKay to K. Bliss 17 Aug. 1981 [OA]. MacKay became professor of communications and neuroscience at the University of Keele.

[53] Letter D. Cassidi to author 8 May 1998.

[54] Letter JHO to Jack Oldham 22 Oct. 1954 [OA].

CHAPTER 22

# *The Last Frontier 1960–69*

IN late 1959, a year following their diamond wedding, Joe and Mary Oldham moved from Dunford House to a home shared with several other elderly residents, The Briars at St Leonards-on-Sea. It was to be their last home. It is worth remarking on, that for all the worldwide scope of his thought and activities, Joe Oldham had physically travelled relatively little given that he lived so long. True, there had been his Indian experiences, his visits to continental Europe and North America, his two African tours and one circumnavigation of the world which briefly included China. But compared with, for example, John Mott's restless globe-trotting, Oldham's existence had been markedly desk-bound in London, especially since the mid-1930s. His most important travels had been through reading and personal encounters, and his most adventurous frontier-crossings had been in the worlds of ideas and awareness and personal encounters. In this sense, for a while at least, he still continued to travel while ever more confined physically at The Briars.

So on 25–27 March 1960 there met yet again, though for the last time, a "St Julians Group" convened by Oldham to look at the contemporary religious situation in the light of science. Michael Polanyi, John McIntyre and Geoffrey Vickers were in the small group, and a chief stimulus in calling the group was provided by the presence in England of Davis McCaughey, a younger friend whom Oldham valued greatly and who was now teaching in the University of Melbourne, Australia. As well as chairing the group, Oldham himself prepared a long memorandum on the self and God, drawing upon yet another new-found source, Hengstenberg's *Philosophische Anthropologie.* This burst of energy was his last such effort. He confessed a few weeks later to a friend that trying to organize and lead such a meeting had in fact been a breach of a resolution some five years earlier when he realized that his powers were failing. "The effort seems rather to have taken it out of me, and I have not been very active since, and am able to read a good deal less widely than formerly. My mind is still fairly alert, but I cannot keep it going at full pressure for any long stretch of time."[1] Other groups however were meeting on not dissimilar themes and welcomed his written contributions, notably the WCC consultation on the meaning of the secular, held at Bossey that same year, and for the preparations of which Oldham submitted a paper, gratefully acknowledged by the director of the programme, Charles West.[2]

His reading might have declined in volume, but he was still turning more pages, and more critically, than most people half his age. Lesslie and Helen Newbigin recall visiting him on one occasion when he was confined to bed, propped up and surrounded by books helping him to wrestle with the question of how much one could know of the historical Jesus.[3] He confesses to finding Alasdair McIntyre's *Difficulties in Christian Belief* disappointing. Of the philosophers it was Michael Polanyi who now stood highest for him, closely followed by John Macmurray, and among theologians "Paul Tillich is almost the only one who rings bells with me".[4]

Oldham had been given what is not bestowed on all creative people, time and length of years to see certain fruits of his labours flourishing. In 1960 came the 50th anniversary of the Edinburgh missionary conference, and Oldham mused thankfully on how it had proved "the turning point in the history of the ecumenical movement",[5] stimulating in turn both the Life and Work and Faith and Order movements. But length of years also gave him time to see some disappointments, and his scepticism towards what he perceived as centralizing tendencies in Geneva seemed to grow each year. "The WCC", he lamented to Lesslie and Helen Newbigin, " – only the grace of God can save it." The world scene gave him little comfort: "The outlook with regard to the African situation seems to me about as dismal as it could be. My sympathies are wholly with African nationalism; but it does not in the least follow that, because the Japanese brought it off, the Africans are capable of any similar achievement."[6] Equally, he felt, it was very difficult not to be despondent about the West: "I grew up in a world in which the ascendancy of the West seemed hardly open to question. What a revolution has occurred within a single generation when the possibility can be envisaged that the western world may, in the not too distant future, become a few minor planets revolving round a world-communist civilisation."[7] Not, he hastened to add, that such a civilization need necessarily be worse than preceding ones, "but it *may* be a terrible state of things in which the higher human values are lost for generations".

Oldham's closest intellectual companion was now Geoffrey Vickers who was pursuing his own liberal theological quest and shared many of his thoughts

[1] JHO letter to "Harold" 28 Aug. 1960 [OA].
[2] JHO letter to C. West 2 April 1960 [OA].
[3] Interview with L. Newbigin March 1991.
[4] See note 1.
[5] Oldham, "Reflections on Edinburgh 1910", *Religion in Life*, vol. XXIX, summer 1960, pp.329–38.
[6] See note 1.
[7] *Ibid.*

*With Bishop Lesslie Newbigin,* ca. *1960*

and questions with Oldham in their frequent correspondence. In the spring of 1961 Vickers asked Oldham for his thoughts on life beyond death. Oldham, perhaps not surprisingly, said that he had been "increasingly sensible of its centrality in the religious view"[8] and granted that, on a scientifically-based naturalistic view, it was hard to attach any sense or meaning to it, most of all when couched in the language of golden gates and harps. He continued:

> The idea begins to have meaning only in relation to belief in God. The most convincing argument to me is the saying of Jesus that God is not the God of the dead, but of the living. What I believe (with many doubts and uncertainties) to be God's relation to me in this earthly existence (and to others, some of whom may be unconscious of it) seems to have inherently an enduring quality. Trust in God means confidence that He will not fail me in any way. I feel at times the same deathless quality about human love and trust. I cannot imagine what recognition in an after life might mean, but since love in its nature implies personhood, it seems not irrational that what is essential in it will in some form endure. The universe as we now know it contains so many wonders that were unimaginable to earlier generations that I am ready to believe that many astonishing surprises may be in store for us. I find in myself a peace and confidence about the wholly unknown future of which Tennyson's "faintly trust the larger hope" is too feeble an expression.

With life closing in about him, conscious of physical and mental energies fading, living in a communal home where possibilities of entertaining were very limited, such few close friendships as could be maintained were doubly

[8] JHO letter to Vickers 10 April 1961 [OA].

*"Old men ought to be explorers"*

precious. Joe Oldham had had many friends in the sense of colleagues and collaborators held in mutual affection. He had outlived many of them. In fact after his Oxford student days his very intimate friendships were few. Not that there was a vacuum in his life at this point, for there was one great, enduring and infinitely precious friendship in his life, that of Mary. Throughout their marriage she had been truly his constant companion, helper and adviser, sharing many of his travels, assisting him (not just as typist) in the preparation of his writings and the thinking that went into them, not to mention creating the welcoming atmosphere and hospitality for the many visitors and guests at Chipstead, Worcester Park and Dunford. Joe Oldham's life and work were unthinkable without her. It was therefore a blow that fell on them both when in the summer of 1961 she suffered a severe stroke. The recovery was slow and only partial.

Joe Oldham's mind, however, still strained forward. In 1963 he wrote a piece for *Frontier*, typically titled, "Frontiers Still Unexplored", rehearsing as vigorously as ever the arguments for lay-centred, world-oriented engagement of the churches with contemporary issues: "An effort on the heroic scale is needed to reverse what appears to be the increasing tendency towards the church-centredness of the Christian witness in the world today. The need to make some really new beginning seems as urgent as it did twenty-five years ago

– even, perhaps, more urgent."[9] These were his last words ever to appear in print.

In 1962–63, with the encouragement of the publishers Hodder & Stoughton, he largely occupied himself with attempting a rewrite of *Life Is Commitment*, but finally gave it up. If this was a disappointment, it was partly offset by the appearance in the spring of 1963 of *Honest to God*, the best-selling paperback by John Robinson, Bishop of Woolwich, which created one of the greatest sensations in Christian theology at a popular level in Britain this century. In some ways *Life Is Commitment*, ten years earlier, had anticipated *Honest to God*. Reading in the press that the bishop was already inundated with mail, Oldham thought it would be kinder to write two appreciative letters to the editor of SCM Press, David Edwards – who promptly forwarded them to Robinson. Robinson in turn was touched that Oldham had taken the trouble to read the book so carefully, and wrote back accordingly. Three years later still, Oldham was positive about Ronald Gregor Smith's *Secular Christianity*, though he disliked the title: he thought it misleading for a book which, in contrast to the more slick and brash writings appearing in the genre of "secular theology", essayed a new apprehension of transcendence at the heart of human, historical existence.[10]

It is one of the shadowed mysteries of life that, often, those who have laboured so long, instead of enjoying sheer rest towards the end seem compelled to toil even harder along the last mile. Yet despite increasing physical distress for Mary and himself, and for all his ceaseless questioning about the ultimate issues and the nature of Christian faith, Joe Oldham seems to have preserved a core of certitude. At the same time he knew that there was still risk and danger. In October 1963 Geoffrey Vickers went through a bout of severe depression. Oldham wrote to his friend:

> I sympathise with you in your state of mental disturbance and distress. I know what the condition is like as I sometimes am subject myself to such attacks. I am at present enjoying a state of peace of mind and joy at all the good things life has given me. While I remain without any satisfying defence of traditional Christianity I have a peaceful *trust* in some of the values which have found expression in traditional Christianity. But I know that this state of mind is a gift that, if it is withdrawn, as it sometimes has been, darker forces may take possession.[11]

Soon after, Joe Oldham fell ill with jaundice which left him still further, and permanently, weakened. Sometimes his own changes in mood took place within the writing of a single letter. He wrote to Kathleen Bliss lamenting that the

[9] JHO, "Frontiers Still Unexplored", *Frontier*, vol. 6, spring 1963, pp.33-40.

[10] Information from Mrs K. Gregor Smith. Gregor Smith died at the early age of 55 in 1968. Oldham had long appreciated Gregor Smith as a writer and publisher for SCM Press (not least as the first translator of Buber into English), and had regretted his move to the chair in divinity at Glasgow University in 1956, having hoped that Gregor Smith might follow his own path of pursuing theology in the "Frontier" mode. On this and other contacts between Oldham and Gregor Smith, see K.W. Clements, *The Theology of Ronald Gregor Smith*, Leiden, E.J. Brill, 1986.

[11] JHO letter to Vickers 3 Oct. 1963 [OA].

smallest physical effort, fetching a book or writing a page, was exhausting. That did not stop him venting a new concern: why had the church never really faced the fact that Jesus and the apostles fully expected the kingdom of God to come immediately? Twenty centuries have gone – and now "every feature of our lives is not the kingdom of God but secularism".[12] He continues somewhat bitterly:

> To believe that the relatively small handful of people who meet at Geneva or the Vatican make any serious difference to what happens in history is to read the *Listener* or the Sunday papers with your eyes shut . . . I could get rid of the problem by evading it and reserving it for another book to be published *next century*. But in actual fact it meets me at almost every turn. And now you will see why I don't want to write letters and what a muddle I get into when I try to do so.

Next day he continues the letter apologizing for his previous mood and outburst. Life is full of kindness, he insists, even without much congenial company or inclination to read.

By spring 1964 neither Joe nor Mary – whose memory had largely gone – could walk a few steps without assistance. The letters were getting still fewer, the handwriting more shaky and spidery. Yet the thoughts in them remain grateful, compassionate and startlingly clear. At Christmas 1964 he penned six long pages to Geoffrey Vickers. In the midst of exchange of news he still found room for posing the question which had "haunted" him for years, whether our deepest commitments are self-chosen or "whether in making the choice we are responding to (or turning away from) a reality other and greater than ourselves".[13] Then comes the sharing of his delight at a Christmas card bearing a picture of the holy family. Inside, instead of the customary seasonal greetings were the simple words "Be of good cheer – NATUS EST." The psychological effect, says Oldham, was immense. The trembling handwriting continues:

> I have no satisfying Christology, and never have had. But it seems to me that even from a humanistic standpoint, it is a fact almost as miraculous and incredible as the orthodox interpretation that a man of peasant origin in an obscure corner of the world without any assets whatever beyond his bare personality, should have so lived for one year (or certainly at the most not more than three years) of public ministry that the whole world has come to reckon time by the date of his birth. Whoever writes the figures 1965 is making a tremendous theological assertion, whatever content he may choose to give or not to give to it.

It was indeed a narrow path to walk now. But letters to and from Geoffrey Vickers on cognition and belief still passed in 1965. Then on 26 December 1965, Mary died. Joe Oldham's ties to this world were now at their most tenuous, and one can only guess at his thoughts for much of his four remaining years. But if he felt increasingly isolated from the world, many in that world still felt attached to him. In 1961 the WCC assembly at New Delhi had made him an

[12] JHO letter to K. Bliss 20 April 1963 [OA].
[13] JHO letter to Vickers 23 Dec. 1964 [OA].

honorary president of the Council. Three months after Mary's death Oldham felt so useless he wanted to resign. Visser 't Hooft wrote urging him not to do so – the assembly had specially wished to show its recognition, though not expecting him to attend meetings, since the World Council "was so very largely your own achievement".[14] It was their last correspondence.

On 16 May 1969, Joe Oldham crossed his last frontier.

The funeral was a quiet family affair. Some weeks later a memorial service was held in the University Church in London, attended by a large congregation representing countries and churches from all over the world. The address was given by Wim Visser 't Hooft, who said what had to be said: "Ecumenical history is full of examples of new developments which he started, but which others carried to their conclusion. I have no hesitation in saying that the ecumenical movement owes more to him than to any other of its pioneers." Some of Oldham's friends thought it not the most well-organized service but "it was a great gathering!"[15] The one who had taught a generation that "real life is meeting" would have been well satisfied.

[14] Visser 't Hooft letter to JHO 3 Sept. 1965 [OA].
[15] R. Bliss letter to author 7 March 1998.

*The Oldham Sundial, Ecumenical Centre, Geneva*

EPILOGUE

# *A Return to the Sundial*

IT is time to return to the sundial in Geneva, still silently marking the passage of the hours, and briefly contemplate the significance of the life which has been recorded. Missionary Statesman, Foremost Pioneer of WCC, Friend of Africa: the account, one trusts, has amply justified those titles, and moreover, has shown that given space many more could have been inscribed. Joe Oldham was important to many people and causes in his day. In what ways is he important for today and tomorrow?

The world does not stand still. Close by the sundial there now stands a striking symbol of the passing not only of the hours, but of years and decades, in the form of a piece of the Berlin Wall. That contrivance of the Cold War was built when Joe Oldham still had eight years to live. We have recalled his musings during those years, that while he had grown up ingrained with the assumption of Western dominance of the world, he could now envisage a world in which the West would be a marginal appendix to the global communist realm. That the Berlin Wall, with the Soviet system it represented, has itself been dismembered into scattered relics of the past is testimony to how history indeed flows on, often more swiftly than anticipated. Oldham's times can now seem even further removed from our own, and soon we shall be into the third millennium.

If it is asked, "Why remember Oldham?" then one immediate answer is obvious. If responsible existence requires memory, if a sense of its history is important to every movement, community or organization, then such a life as this must be remembered and retrieved. Oldham's own story and that of the ecumenical movement in the 20th century are inseparable. But to this plain truth two riders must be added. First, while the stories are inseparable, they must not be made identical. Oldham must not be reduced to providing a biographical, illustrative gloss on the history as a whole, least of all a one-sided and triumphalistic version of the story. For not only did he serve that movement, not only was he instrumental in many of its most outstanding developments, but while standing within it he also challenged it. He repeatedly asked of it searching and critical questions, some of which still await answers. Second, his activities ranged well beyond the ecclesiastical realm altogether. It does violence to his commitment to a frontier existence, and to encouraging lay witness in the secular world, simply to wish to memorialize him as a churchly figure. Forty years before "Let the world write the agenda" became a fashionable slogan in ecumenical circles during the 1960s, he was looking for that agenda as it was being written in race relations in India, Africa and elsewhere. In fact, it is a comment on Christian memory that Oldham's name today is probably known at least as well among students of colonial education and African affairs as among the churches at large. To Christians and non-Christians alike, he will always offer a fascinating case study in methods of attempting to bring ethical considerations to bear on complex political matters where everything depends on detail and "the next step".

On any count, Oldham's long career was extraordinarily creative. Not many lives can include so many episodes which gave a discernible push and redirection to history. Within the total picture his finest hours were surely: the consolidation of the Continuation Committee after Edinburgh 1910 and the founding of the *International Review of Missions*; the preservation of German missions during and after the first world war; the formation of the International Missionary Council; his identification of race as the crucial issue for Christian world mission and his writing of *Christianity and the Race Problem*; his engagement with East and Central African issues, both in terms of colonial policy and the setting up of the International Institute of African Languages and Cultures; his organizing of the study programme for the Oxford 1937 conference; his laying out the ground-plan for the World Council of Churches; and, during the second world war, his production of *The Christian News-Letter* and founding of the Christian Frontier Council. At all these points, on stages of varying width, Oldham conspicuously "made a difference"; and probably, no greater effect did he have than his inspirational example and encouragement, through writing and speaking, for countless others to take up his fundamental concerns in their own place and their own way.

Underlying such an impressive catalogue, however, is to be found another history, that of fundamental shifts in perception of the nature of the world and of the vocation of churches and Christians within it. Oldham is significant for the way in which he registered these shifts so early, and helped to communicate them so widely. Edinburgh 1910 is almost universally acknowledged as the great birth-event of the modern ecumenical movement. It might equally be described as the last great expression of the old paradigm of mission summed up in the Student Volunteer Watchword, "the evangelization of the world in this generation". Oldham, it has been shown in this study, was already subverting that paradigm before Edinburgh 1910. The first world war led him towards a concept of mission as evangelization for the sake of a more truly Christian social order. By the later 1920s, it was clearly recognized that this in turn had to be based upon a new Christian conception of human existence which could engage with the threatening ideologies. It was the battle over the nature and purpose of being human, Oldham recognized, which was at stake in the Christian confrontation with totalitarianism in the 1930s – and equally, with the deep confusion and anxiety in the Western capitalistic "democracies". With the post-war world came a universal sense of the need for reconstruction, of power to be made accountable to the requirements of human dignity, justice and freedom, and once again Oldham provided the paradigm for this in the notion of the "responsible society". Oldham was able to read, and read beyond, each successive meta-narrative, a critical necessity for renewal of life and mission.

Joe Oldham, this study can claim to have shown, was one of the most creative people, in any field, to have lived and worked in the 20th-century West. He discerned future agendas when many people (even in some cases, as we have seen, John Mott) were still dealing with yesterday's. He made so much happen. The reasons for his effectiveness and influence, however, are not quite so obvious. He was certainly a remarkable thinker, but not a notably original one nor did he ever claim to be. He was not a Reinhold Niebuhr or a Martin Buber, a Jacques Maritain or even a John Baillie, though he could (and did) engage all such in discussion and more than hold his own. He was extraordinarily wide-read, possibly more so than any other Christian thinker of his generation in Britain. This in itself would not have been significantly fruitful, if he not also had an unusual capacity for quickly distilling a writer's thought to its essentials, relating it to other trains of thought and identifying where inter-connections could be made and syntheses created. Where he did generate a new language for Christian social thought and ethics, as in the key-terms "middle axioms" and "the responsible society", it was precisely through this ability to focus and concentrate on essentials – a very different matter from merely "simplifying". Above all, it was the *interdisciplinary* nature of his study which was crucial. Science (especially biology and genetics), social, cultural and historical studies, political analysis, were as much grist to the Oldham mill as was biblical theology. *Christianity and the Race Problem* is the epitome of Oldham's interdisciplinary method, concomitant with his belief that there can be no Christian theology without an anthropology. "Real life is meeting" was not just a slogan, but a method. He brought people together who would not normally have dreamed of meeting, and encouraged them to generate ideas which they could never have conceived individually. The Moot was a special, but not the only, expression of this approach. In a world which likes to call itself "post-modern" on account of its indulgence in the diverse, the pluralistic and the fragmentary, Oldham's search for a "consensus" might seem suspicious and unreal. But if at the end of the day there is to be one world where at least the many worlds can live together, there will have to be *meeting* precisely in order for the "otherness" to be understood. Oldham therefore has a question waiting to be answered somewhere along the post-modernist road.

If Oldham was not as original as the major thinkers he studied, neither was he simply a popularizer of them. His particular gift was not even just that of recognizing the light which they shed on contemporary human issues, but rather that of seeing what particular lines of action and organization were required for the application of their insights. It was this fusion of the theological and philosophical with the concrete, of the theoretical with the pragmatic, of the vision with the realizable line of action, which was the hallmark of Oldham.

"Prophetic" is a word that has often been used to describe Joe Oldham. It is a just description, provided that it is not always meant to conjure up a picture of flamboyant, rhetorical denunciations from the public platform of moral righteousness. Oldham was indeed prepared to campaign against social wrongs, especially in the international sphere, and in relation to race and Africa in particular: "Christianity is not primarily a philosophy but a crusade." But Oldham the quiet self-effacing one, who for much of his life had to endure the silent world of his deafness, demonstrates that to be prophetic means to think, work and speak at a deeper level than the grand dramatic gesture. More than once Oldham cites a passage from the letters of William James, with the strong implication that they come close to his own personal *credo* of action:

> As for me, my bed is made. I am against bigness and greatness in all their forms, and with the invisible molecular moral forces that work from individual to individual, stealing in through the crannies of the world like so many soft rootlets, or like the capillary oozing of water, and yet rending the hardest monuments of man's pride, if you give them time. The bigger the unit you deal with, the hollower, the more brutal, the more mendacious is the life displayed. So I am against all big organizations as such, national ones first and foremost; and in favour of the eternal forces of truth which always work in the individual and immediately unsuccessful way, under-dogs always, till history comes, often after they are long dead, and puts them on the top.

Oldham was prophetic precisely when working quietly at his desk in Edinburgh House, when studiously examining all aspects of a situation, when conversing in the Athenaeum, when leading discussions in the Moot and when carefully constructing his lengthy memoranda whether to church leaders or to the staff of the Colonial Office. Prophecy is fundamentally a matter of discernment. Oldham was at his most prophetic when discerning how the world scene was shifting and was calling for new responses from the churches, from politicians and educators and from all people with any sort of influence in public affairs and secular life.

He was, moreover, prophetic because he wanted always to be on the frontier, and always trying to discern where the *next* frontier of responsibility lay. His prophetic career began in embryo when he was the young YMCA worker in Lahore, and quickly recognized that Christian missions had no future in India unless there was a new empathy of Western missionaries with Indian aspirations and a new partnership with Indians right down to the personal level of genuine friendship, mutually respectful of dignity. It continued right into his old age with his call to face wholly and squarely the challenge of the era of atomic power. His development of a new kind of missionary consciousness after Edinburgh 1910, his struggles with colonial policy in Africa, his leadership towards a new kind of corporate Christian witness in face of the totalitarian threat centred around the Oxford 1937 conference, his engagement with a search for a new Christian social order during the second world war, his repeated summons to a Christian witness beginning with the secular world and lay responsibility within it: all these and other ventures were manifestations of his frontier mentality. Much of the normal effort of organized religion consists in adaptation to the familiar, immediate world and therefore of preserving the structure of that familiar habitat at all costs. The horizon is regarded as the boundary of safety, the sign of a threat to be denied or avoided if at all possible. For such as Oldham, it is precisely on the frontier that faith must stand, looking into the advent of the new and unfamiliar challenges, if it is to live and grow. Authentic mission will always be a "perfectly mad adventure". That is why the retrieval of his example, like that of other pioneers, is vital. It will always be an antidote to complacency, timidity and introversion. Nor do all the frontiers which he identified even many years ago yet lie behind us, least of all that of race.

Oldham lived long but even he proved mortal, and had other human limitations as well. Having decided what he wanted, and *who* he wanted for a particular project, he could be brilliantly successful at engaging recruits for his causes, not least because he was prepared to put in endless time and effort in personal encounter. It has been amply shown that at certain stages in the ecumenical story this patient effort, the concrete application of his relational understanding of God and humanity, was crucial. But as often the case with strong-willed people, the line between firmness and obduracy can wear very thin. On occasion his persistence, as experienced by those whom he sought such as Leslie Hunter, could be experienced as downright manipulative with scant regard for the personal aspirations or circumstances of his quarry. Most of his contemporaries seem to have been prepared to forgive this as an indulgence of one who never in fact asked of anyone more than he was giving of himself.

More serious, certainly in retrospect from a more avowedly egalitarian age, is the charge against Oldham of "elitism". Even in his own later years, his habitual refrain of needing to secure the service of "the best minds" began to irritate as well as amuse. Today, the very notion of "the best minds" is liable to dismissal on account of ignoring the conditioning of thought and intellectual outlook by cultural context and the interests of social class and gender. The problem with Oldham's approach may lie even deeper than that. For much of his life at least, his ruling assumption seems to have been that the first priority is to identify the correct *ideas*, for which sufficiently wide acceptance is then to be gained by those with social and political influence, so that they may then be applied in practice. Perhaps, in this sense, he was always the Oxford Greats man, ingrained with the ideals of Plato's *Republic* whose society was to be run by philosophers; or maybe, as George Bennett has suggested, the Victorian with a grand belief in the liberating power of education itself. There were undoubtedly great strengths in seeing the need for an underlying social philosophy, and among Christian social ethicists who know their history this will always be Oldham's single most important contribution: to push the church into the contemporary public scene in order to develop a coherent social vision. But during the early years of the second world war it also led him into the vain hope for an "order" of Christian social idealists who would somehow pull the levers of social change for the good of the people at large – a notion which had its inbuilt contradictions if it was meant to counteract the forces making for an overly planned, if not actually totalitarian, society. The attempt at an "order", for a variety of reasons, led into an impasse.

Oldham found his way out of that particular dead-end through his recognition that a society in which faith is at home must be one in which freedom operates, not the spurious freedom of individualism but the freedom which operates through mutual responsibility: the responsible society. And rather than the select "order" of the people who themselves knew what was best for society came the Frontier movement, a fellowship of people in, on the edge of or outside organized Christianity who engaged in a shared search for answers to the problems of secular responsibility. It may still be objected that even such a project remained essentially one of the educated, middle-class professionals. That may be so, but it was nevertheless a movement concerned with the whole of society and its range of issues. It was neither trivial nor self-seeking.

The danger with elites may well lie less in their domination of others (which requires power, not necessarily an attribute they possess), but in their lack of awareness that they themselves may well be subject to manipulation by those even more elite, or at any rate with more power. That will always be a question – and which may require yet more research for an answer – concerning some aspects of Oldham's role with the Colonial Office on African affairs. To conceive of education as a sphere in which government and missions could be in partnership was a bold and imaginative step, and Oldham's contribution to its practical outworking was brilliant. But it did run the risk of drawing missions into ever closer identification with government just when that began to prove problematic in the eyes of the rising nationalism. Oldham's virtual identification of mission with education (though, note, he was always careful to insist on the importance of the specifically religious element in sound education) perhaps went right back to the influence on him of Gustav Warneck as well as W.E. Hocking. But if Oldham's understanding of mission in relation to imperial government, even at its most benign, is thought to be suspect at this point, let this be taken as a warning for today at least as much as a judgment upon him. The issue of collaboration between Western-based governments and church-related organizations working in the south did not die with the end of colonialism and "missions". For example, not dissimilar questions as have been put to the missions-government educational partnership of the past, can be put to today's aid agencies and their relationships to the governments in their home-bases back in the north who are increasingly providing their funding.

"Prophets", it has often been said, tend to view matters with exaggerated sharpness, ruthlessly hewing issues into "either-or" choices rather than carefully sculpturing them into "both-and" affairs. Oldham in fact does not fall neatly into either category. On occasion, he does in retrospect seem to have foretold doom a little prematurely. British society did not, as he feared, totally collapse, materially or morally, in face of the totalitarian threat from 1938 onwards, nor did it actually become totalitarian itself. But he was surely right to raise the question about what deeper values it was meant to be standing for. He did see issues with sharp clarity, but equally saw the need for careful strategy if prophecy was to be more than rhetoric. Habitually, he not only asked "What is wrong?" but also "What will help actually to improve this situation?" That is what governed his approach to Africa. It also gave him a masterly sense of timing in the fraught issue of the maltreatment of German missions during the first world war, when as few others he knew that a reconciliation was called for but had to await the right moment when personal contact once again became possible. And, as in *Christianity and the Race Problem*, he saw that moral discernment and fervour should not bypass scientific rigour, but studiously face it, learn from it and use it as an ally. Oldham's example transcends in significance and relevance his particular context, and must be archetypal for all Christian and ecumenical social engagement which wishes to avoid degenerating into sheer rhetoric and fashionable slogans.

In all this, it should not be forgotten that over the years, probably more than anything else he produced, what placed so many people in conscious debt to Oldham was his little *Devotional Diary*, born out of his own discipline of prayer and wide spiritual reading. "Spirituality" has in our own generation become a vogue word. It can convey a sense of searching for a purely private self-fulfilment, rather precious and artificially cultivated. For Joe Oldham, each day's *activity* began and ended in prayer. For him faith meant engagement with the world, for it was there that God was to be met, in the maelstrom of human claims and counter-claims, challenges and responsibilities, as taught him by Grisebach and Buber. But the bedrock of all hopes, all efforts at human betterment, was a belief in the *grace* of God. The immediate issues were often a matter of struggle and uncertainty, "a fighting chance", the venture of putting it to the touch "to win or lose it all". The ultimate issue could never be in doubt: the God who had acted supremely in Jesus Christ would finally triumph. For Joe Oldham, faith and spirituality at heart meant remembering and being renewed by that basal evangel, not as an escape from facing the great issues or from shouldering the tedious daily routine, but as an inspiration for tackling them. We will probably not find the *Devotional Diary* serving our purposes today, and by the time of his later years its author himself felt that it had had its day. But the matter of finding a spirituality which is an integrative impulse for life in its complex wholeness will be constantly with us.

Kathleen Bliss aptly calls Joe Oldham "a wily saint", and this account, it is to be hoped, has filled out that description. It was Margery Perham, watching Oldham at first hand as he dealt with the Colonial Office on African issues, who said that he exemplified more clearly than anyone else she knew the meaning of the gospel precept to be as wise as serpents and innocent as doves.

It should be noted that Jesus gave his disciples this command on sending them out on a mission where they would be as unprotected as sheep among wolves. Keeping in view a figure like Joseph Houldsworth Oldham will help to ensure that the ecumenical pilgrimage in mission, caring more for the world than itself, will always be the great adventure.

# *Chronology of the Life of J.H. Oldham*

*1874*

10 October, Joseph Houldsdworth Oldham born Bombay, India.

*1881*

Lt. Col. Oldham and family return permanently to Britain.

*1882*

Oldham family settles in Crieff, Scotland.

*1890*

"Lillah", mother of Joe and his three brothers and sister, dies. Family moves to Edinburgh.

*1891*

Joe's 10-year-old sister Lallah dies.

*1892*

October, JHO enters Trinity College, Oxford. 14 November hears D.L. Moody preach and gives himself "definitely to Jesus Christ". Becomes active in Christian Union life.

*1893*

April, JHO enrols in Student Missionary Volunteer Union with commitment to become a foreign missionary. Summer, Oxford students attend Keswick Convention. JHO and Temple Gairdner make a new spiritual commitment.

*1894*

Early summer, JHO meets J.R. Mott on his first visit to Oxford. Summer, Mott addresses students at Keswick. JHO appointed Secretary of OICCU for 1894–95.

*1896*

January, International Students' Missionary Conference, Liverpool. Summer, JHO graduates from Oxford. Starts year's work as joint general-secretary of Student Volunteers and Inter-Varsity Christian Union, based in London.

*1897*

October, JHO takes up appointment as Scottish YMCA Secretary in Lahore, Punjab. Friendship with S.K. Datta begins.

*1898*

October, wedding in Lahore of JHO and Mary Fraser.

*1900*

Autumn, JHO and Mary Oldham ill with typhoid.

*1901*

April, Oldhams return home for health reasons and settle in Edinburgh. JHO begins theological studies at New College.

*1903*

JHO's *Studies in the Teaching of Jesus* published.

*1904–05*

Oldhams spend year in Halle, Germany, for studies under G. Warneck.

*1905*

Oldhams return to Edinburgh. After completion of New College course, JHO works briefly as assistant in parish in Dundee and then at Free St George's, Edinburgh. Elected chairman of Theological Colleges Department of SCM.

*1906*

December, JHO appointed full-time secretary of Mission Study Council of United Free Church of Scotland.

*1907*

Scotland offers to host World Missionary Conference in Edinburgh.

*1908*

January, SVM Conference, Liverpool: JHO and G. Robson confer with Mott on Edinburgh Conference plan. July, JHO attends international committee on Edinburgh Conference, Oxford, and is appointed secretary.

*1909*

Controversies over statistics and Anglican participation in Edinburgh Conference. March, JHO visits USA for first time.

*1910*

14–23 June, World Missionary Conference, Edinburgh. Continuation Committee set up, with JHO as secretary.

*1911*

May, Continuation Committee meets, Auckland Castle, England.

*1912*

January, first issue of *International Review of Missions.* September, Continuation Committee meets at Lake Mohonk, New York. Mott begins Asian tour.

*1913*

"Kikuyu" controversy and debates on role of Edinburgh Conference in promoting "unity". November, Continuation Committee meets at the Hague, Netherlands.

*1914*

4 August, Britain at war with Germany. 5 August, JHO writes to Mott on immediate and long-term issues. JHO and K. Maclennan begin joint work for Continuation Committee and for CMSBI. First efforts to raise funds for German missions. October, Mott visits Europe. JHO participates in W. Temple's *Papers for War-time* group.

*1915*

Abortive plans by JHO to meet German missions leaders in Switzerland. 7 May, sinking of the *Lusitania.* JHO writes "The Church, the Hope of the Future".

*1916*

July, *The World and The Gospel* published.

*1917*

6 April, USA enters war. Mott participates in US "Root Mission" to Russia. Controversies with Germans on this and British statements. August, condemnation of Mott and others by German missions leaders. October, reply by CMSBI. December, CMSBI delegation to Foreign Office on post-war British policy towards missions involving alien personnel. JHO intervenes to prevent auctioning of Basel Mission property in West Africa.

*1918*

Emergency Committee of Co-operating Missions formed. Continuation Committee headquarters moved to London. 11 November, Armistice signed.

*1919*

18 January, Paris Peace Conference opens. JHO secures exemption of German missions from expropriation, and freedom of missionary work in mandated territories. 13 April, Amritsar massacre, India, provokes correspondence with S.K. Datta and K.T. Paul. November, JHO meets with Basel Mission leaders in Zurich. December, visits USA.

*1920*

April, JHO and others from Britain meet informally with German missions leaders at Oegstgeest, Holland. 16–18 June, JHO enlists CMSBI in campaign on enforced African labour in Kenya. 22–28 June, International Missionary Meeting, Crans, Switzerland, resolves to set up permanent international missionary body, with JHO as secretary. 14 December, delegation to Colonial Secretary on Kenyan Forced Labour.

*1921*

January–March, JHO in USA and Canada, and visits black educational projects in southern states. October, meeting at Lake Mohonk, NY, sets up International Missionary Council. JHO produces paper "The Crisis in Christian Education on the Mission Fields." November, JHO sails for India.

*1922*

January, National Missionary Council, Poona; JHO proposes formation of National Christian Council. Oldhams journey on to Ceylon, then China for national conference of China Continuation Committee 2–11 May, returning via Canada to Britain. July, IMC Committee, Canterbury, England. November, JHO returns to India.

*1923*

January, meeting of Indian National Council at Ranchi confirms new structure, with W. Paton as secretary. JHO returns home in spring and takes up issue of Indian and African rights in East Africa: draft memorandum to Colonial Secretary, 29 May, sets out principle of "paramountcy" of rights of native population. At same time, begins conversations with Ormsby-Gore and others in Colonial Office on Educational Policy in Africa. 6 June, "Derby Day" Conference decides to set up Permanent Advisory Committee on Native Education in Tropical Africa.

*1924*

*Christianity and the Race Problem* published. Report of second Phelps-Stokes Commission on education in Africa. International Institute of African Languages and Cultures formed.

*1925*

January, IMC Committee, Atlantic City, USA. First edition of *A Devotional Diary* published. White Paper *Educational Policy in British Tropical Africa* published.

*1926*

January, JHO starts on first visit to Africa: South Africa, Tanganyika, Kenya. Return to London, May. July, IMC Committee, Rättvik, Sweden, obtains W. Paton's services for IMC. September, international conference on Christian Mission in Africa, Le Zoute, Belgium.

*1927*

June, JHO approached as possible member of Royal ("Hilton Young") Commission on Closer Union in East and Central Africa. Appointment confirmed. December, Oldhams start for Africa.

*1928*

January–May, Hilton Young Commission in East and Central Africa. April, International Missionary Conference, Jerusalem (JHO not attending).

*1929*

January, report of Hilton Young Commission published: opposes "Closer Union". JHO and Lugard campaign in press etc. JHO writes *What Is at Stake in East Africa.* Wilson Commission to East Africa. November, J.C. Smuts gives Rhodes Lectures on Africa and Some World Problems.

*1930*

JHO writes *White and Black in Africa* in reply to Smuts. January, JHO visits Germany and Switzerland preparing for IMC study on the Christian message in the contemporary world. Meets Emil Brunner. June, JHO assists with Karl Barth's first visit to Britain. June, Labour Colonial Secretary (Passfield) decisively rejects Closer Union. Joint Select Committee appointed (likewise confirms this rejection in report October 1931). October, first meeting of continental theologians on "the Message", Basel.

*1931*

*The Remaking of Man in Africa* (with B. Gibson) published. Summer, WSCF meeting on "the Message", Zuylen, Holland. September, report of American "Laymen's Commission of Enquiry" on missions published.

*1932*

May, JHO addresses SCM Conference, Bad Boll, Germany, on "The Dilemma of Western Civilization".

*1933*

January, JHO gives Duff Lectures on missions, Scotland. Advent of Adolf Hitler to power; onset of German Church Struggle. May, informal meeting ("Consultative Group") at Bishopthorpe, York, on future of ecumenical movement.

*1934*

April, Life and Work Conference, Paris, on "The Church and the State of Today". Early August, meeting of "Consultative Group", Paris. 22–28 August, meeting of Council of Life and Work, Fanö, Denmark; JHO appointed chairman of Programme Committee for 1937 Conference on Church, Community and State. End September, JHO visits missions leaders in Germany. October, collaborating closely with Bishop George Bell on coordinating international church effort in protest at Reich policy on church affairs. November, delegation from German missions visits London seeking help.

*1935*

*Church, Community and State: A World Issue* published. May, JHO visits church officials in Berlin and Confessing Church leaders in Hanover. Oldham fully occupied on study programme for Oxford 1937. Informal consultation at Princeton considers formation of overall council for all streams of ecumenical movement.

*1936*

21–25 August, Council of Life and Work, Chamby, Switzerland. November, JHO visits USA.

*1937*

*The Church and Its Function in Society* (with W.A. Visser 't Hooft) published. "Committee of 35" meets Westfield College, London, 8–10 July. 12–26 July Oxford Conference on Church, Community and State. 3–18 August, Faith and Order Conference, Edinburgh. 19 August, Joint Constituent Committee of 14 meets, London, and plans meeting of Provisional Committee for setting up World Council. JHO makes plans for setting up Council on Christian Faith and the Common Life (CCFCL)

*1938*

January, CCFCL set up. 1–4 April, first meeting of the "Moot". 9–13 May, Provisional Conference, Utrecht, Holland: basis for formation of WCC agreed. September, JHO retires from secretaryship of IMC. 5 October, JHO's letter in *The Times* following Munich crisis.

*1939*

3 September, Britain at war with Nazi Germany. 23–24 September, 5th (enlarged) meeting of Moot. 18 October, first *Christian News-Letter* (*CNL*).

*1940*

*The Resurrection of Christendom* published. Kathleen Bliss starts work in *CNL* office.

*1941*

29 July, JHO resigns from secretaryship of CCFCL.

*1942*

*Real Life is Meeting* published. 24 February, Christian Frontier Council formed. September 1942, British Council of Churches (BCC) inaugurated.

*1943*

21 August, William Paton dies.

*1944*

26 October, William Temple dies.

*1945*

8 May, war in Europe ends. JHO retires from editing *CNL.*

*1946*

January–March, BCC Commission on Era of Atomic Power meets; report presented to BCC April/May and published.

*1947*

January, Karl Mannheim dies. JHO retires as Director of Christian Frontier. November, last meeting of Moot.

*1948*

JHO writes on "Technics and Civilisation" and "A Responsible Society" in preparation for WCC Assembly. 22 August–4 September, first Assembly of WCC, Amsterdam. October, Oldhams celebrate golden wedding, and soon after leave Chipstead for Worcester Park.

*1949*

JHO addresses CMS on "The Missionary and the National State".

*1950*

*Work in Modern Society* published.

*1951*

*Florence Allshorn and the Story of St Julian's* published. JHO awarded CBE.

*1952*

Oldhams move from Worcester Park to Dunford House, Sussex.

*1953*

*Life is Commitment* published.

*1954*

JHO becomes involved in Capricorn Africa Society.

*1955*

*New Hope in Africa* published.

*1959*

Oldhams move from Dunford to The Briars, St Leonards-on-Sea.

*1961*

JHO elected an Honorary President of WCC.

*1965*

26 December, Mary Oldham dies.

*1969*

16 May, Joe Oldham dies.

# Bibliography

This bibliography comprises:

I. Books and pamphlets (including books edited) by J.H. Oldham.
II. Articles by J.H. Oldham in journals and books (excluding *The Christian News-Letter*).
III. J.H. Oldham and *The Christian News-Letter*.
IV. A note on reviews by J.H. Oldham.
V. Secondary sources cited in the text.

## I. Books and pamphlets (including books edited) by J.H. Oldham


*Studies in the Teaching of Jesus: As Recorded in the Synoptic Gospels* 1st ed., London, British College Christian Union, 1903; 2nd and subsequent eds, SCM, to 9th ed. 1933.

(ed.) *The World Missionary Conference, Edinburgh 1910*, reports, vols I–IX, London, Oliphant, Anderson & Ferrier 1910; New York, Fleming H. Revell, 1910.

*The Possibilities of Prayer*, London, T.N. Foulis, 1912. Gaelic transl. by M. Macleod, *Comasan Na H-Urnuigh*, London, T.N. Foulis, 1913.

*The Church Missionary Society and the Present Situation*, address delivered at the CMS anniversary, London, 8 May 1913, London, Church Missionary Society, 1913.

*The Progress of the Movement for Co-operation in Missions*, a statement with an appendix on cooperative finance prepared for the Continuation Committee of the Edinburgh conference, London, 1913.

*The Decisive Hour, Is It Lost?*, Papers for War-time, no. 5, London, Oxford Univ. Press, 1914.

*The Church the Hope of the Future*, Papers for War-time, no. 36, London, Oxford Univ. Press, 1915.

*The World and the Gospel*, London, United Council for Missionary Education, 1916.

*Christianity and the Hope of Peace*, The Church and the War, Tracts for Today, no. 10, Edinburgh, United Free Church of Scotland, 1917.

*The Missionary Situation after the War*, notes prepared for the international missionary meeting, Crans, Switzerland, 22–28 June 1929, London, Edinburgh House, 1920.

*International Missionary Organization*, a private and confidential report to the International Missionary Council, Crans, Switzerland, 22–28 June 1929, n.p., 1920.

*The Essential Qualifications of a Missionary in View of Present Conditions in the Mission Field*, paper prepared for the board of study for the preparation of missionaries, London, Edinburgh House, 1922.

(ed.) *Treaties Acts and Regulations Relating to Missionary Freedom*, London, International Missionary Council, 1923.

*Christianity and the Race Problem*, London, SCM, 1924.

*A Devotional Diary*, 1st ed., London, SCM, 1925; 2nd and rev. ed., SCM, 1926; subsequent eds to 1947.

*International Missionary Co-operation*, a statement of fundamental questions of policy for consideration by the committee of the International Missionary Council, 11–25 Jan. 1925, London, 1925.

(with L.A. Weigle) *Religious Education*, London, International Missionary Council, 1927.

*What Is at Stake in East Africa*, London, Edinburgh House, 1929.

*White and Black in Africa: A Critical Examination of the Rhodes Lectures of General Smuts*, London, Longmans, Green, 1930.

*The CMS and the Adventure of Today*, address delivered at the Church Missionary Society Congress, London, 23 Sept. 1930, London, Church Missionary Society, 1930.

(with B.D. Gibson) *The Remaking of Man in Africa*, London, Oxford Univ. Press, 1931.

*Christian Education, Its Meaning and Mission*, paper for discussion at the conference on Christian education at home and overseas, April 1931, under the auspices of the Advisory Council for Christian Education Overseas, London, The Auxiliary Movement, 1931.

*The Christian Message in the Modern World*, statement prepared for the meeting of the International Missionary Council at Herrnhut, June and July 1932, London, International Missionary Council, 1932.

*The Financial Crisis and the Overseas Work of the Church*, address given at the Missionary Council of the Church Assembly, 13 Jan. 1932, London, Press & Publications Board of the Church of England, 1932.

*Church, Community and State: A World Issue*, London, SCM, 1935, with preface by William Adams Brown and introduction by George Bell.

*The Question of the Church in the World of Today*, London, Edinburgh House for IMC, 1936; German ed.: *Kirche, Volk und Staat: Ein ökumenisches Weltproblem*, Berlin, Martin Warneck, 1936; French ed.: *L'Eglise, la nation et l'état*, Geneva, Conseil oecumenique du christianisme pratique, and Paris, Editions "Je sers", 1936.

(with W.A. Visser 't Hooft) *The Church and Its Function in Society*, vol. I of *Church, Community and State*, London, Allen & Unwin, 1937.

*The Churches Survey Their Task: The Report of the Conference at Oxford, July 1937, on Church, Community and State*, London, Allen & Unwin, 1937.

*The Resurrection of Christendom*, Christian News-Letter Books, no. 1, London, Sheldon, 1940.

*The Root of Our Troubles*, London, SCM, 1941.

(with H.A. Hodges and P. Mairet) *Real Life Is Meeting*, Christian News-Letter Books, no. 14, London, Sheldon, 1942.

*The Era of Atomic Power*, London, SCM for British Council of Churches, 1946.

*The Missionary and the National State*, address delivered at the conference of missionaries of the Church Missionary Society, High Leigh, 1949, London, CMS, 1949.

*Work in Modern Society*, London, SCM, 1950; German ed.: *Die Arbeit in der modernen Welt*, Stuttgart, Evangelisches Verlagswerk, 1950.

*Florence Allshorn and the Story of St Julians*, London, SCM, 1951.

*Life Is Commitment*, London, SCM, 1953.

*New Hope in Africa*, London, Longmans, Green, 1955.

## II. Articles by J.H. Oldham in journals and books (excluding *The Christian News-Letter*)

"The Bible Study Department of the College Christian Union", *The College Christian Union*, London, British College Christian Union, 1898, pp.75–79.

"Student Work at Lahore", *Student Movement*, vol. I, 7, April 1899, pp.172f.

(with others) "A Letter from Secretaries of the British Student Movement now in the Foreign Field", *Student Movement*, vol. II, 5, Feb. 1900, pp.113f.

(with B. Livingstone-Learmouth) "Letters from Lahore and Manchuria Read at the London Conference", *Student Movement*, vol. II, 6, March 1900, pp.145f.

"Our Work Abroad", *Quarterly Paper*, new series, 1, April 1900, pp.5–7.

"Our Work Abroad", *Quarterly Paper*, new series, 2, July 1900, pp.5–7.

"Our Work Abroad", *Quarterly Paper*, new series, 3, Oct. 1900, pp.3f.

"Foreignness, a Hindrance to Evangelism", *Student Movement*, vol. III, 4, Jan. 1901, pp.91f.

"Our Work in India", *Quarterly Paper*, new series, 6, July 1901, pp.3f.

"I. Counsels on the Devout Life: Prayer", *Student Movement*, vol. V, 1, Oct. 1902, pp.8–10.

"Farewell Letter from Mr Oldham", *Quarterly Paper*, new series, 9, April 1902, pp.3f.

"Bible Study during the Vacation", *Student Movement*, vol. V, 9, June 1903, pp.214f.

"The Death of Christ. I: The Inexhaustible Significance of the Cross", *Student Movement*, vol. VI, 6, March 1904, pp.130–32.

"The Death of Christ. II: The Cross as the Measure of Life", *Student Movement*, vol. VI, 7, April 1904, pp.151f.

"The Death of Christ. III: The Cross as a Sacrifice for Sins", *Student Movement*, vol. VI, 8, May 1904, pp.174f.

"The Death of Christ. IV: The Necessity of the Cross", *Student Movement*, vol. VI, 9, June 1904, pp.198–200.

"The Organic Relation of the Missionary Command to Jesus' Teachings", *Student Movement*, vol. VII, 1, Oct. 1904, pp.13–16, Bible reading given at Conishead conference, July 1904.

"The Death of Christ", *Student Movement*, vol. VII, 2, Nov. 1904, pp.31–33, address given at Conishead conference, July 1904.

"The Death of Christ", *Student Movement*, vol. VII, 3, Dec. 1904, pp.57–60, conclusion of address given at Conishead conference, July 1904.

"Ulfila, a Study in Missionary Methods", *Missionary Record of the United Free Church of Scotland*, no. 57, Sept. 1905, pp.394–96.

"Reconciliation with God", *Student Movement*, vol. VIII, 1, Oct. 1905, pp.16–19, address given at Conishead conference, 1905.

"Reconciliation with God", *Student Movement*, vol. VIII, 2, Nov. 1905, pp.31–34, conclusion of address given at Conishead conference, 1905.

"The Student Christian Movement", *Preparation for the Christian Ministry in View of Present-Day Conditions*, ed. executive committee of the Theological Department of the Student Christian Movement of Great Britain and Ireland, London, SCM, 1906, pp.225–50.

"Christianity and Asia", *Student Movement*, vol. VIII, 4, Jan. 1906, pp.75–78.

"Christianity and Asia, II", *Student Movement*, vol. III, 5, Feb. 1906, pp.104–107.

"The Comprehensiveness of the Evangelistic Aim of the Student Christian Movement", *Student Movement*, vol. IX, 1, Oct. 1906, pp.15–18.

"The Study of Foreign Missions", *Hoc Deus Vult*, London, Student Volunteer Missionary Union 1908, pp.111–21, address given at Student Missionary Conference, Liverpool, Jan. 1908.

"Missionary Study in the Colleges", *Student Movement*, vol. IX, 1, Oct. 1908, pp.10f.

"The World Missionary Conference", *The East and the West*, vol. VII, 28, Oct. 1909, pp.409–20.

"The World Missionary Conference and the Student Christian Movement", *Student Movement*, vol. XII, 4, Jan. 1910, pp.85f.

"The Claim of the Non-Christian World", *Student Movement*, vol. XIII, 4, June 1911, pp.208f., address given at Baslow, July 1910.

"Dr Robson's Work in Connection with the World Missionary Conference", *Missionary Record of the United Free Church of Scotland*, no. 129, Sept. 1911, pp.390f.

"The Liverpool Conference", *Student Movement*, vol. XIV, 3, Dec. 1911, pp.50f.

"Woman and the Church in Scotland Today", in J.G. Stewart [Marquis of Tullibardine], D. Butler and J.H. Oldham, *Woman and the Church in Scotland*, Edinburgh, Macniven and Wallace 1912, pp.37–51, addresses given to wives of ministers of the Church of Scotland and the United Free Church of Scotland, Edinburgh, May 1912.

"The Editor's Notes", *International Review of Missions* [*IRM*], vol. I, 1, Jan. 1912, pp.1–14.

"Daily Converse with God", *Student Movement*, vol. XV, 1, Oct. 1912, p.5.

"The Will of Christ Regarding the Evangelisation of the World", in W. Paton, ed., *The Missionary Motive*, London, SCM, 1913, pp.12–34.

"A Missionary Survey of the Year 1912", *IRM*, vol. II, 5, Jan. 1913, pp.1–82.

"Noteworthy Articles in Recent Periodicals", *IRM*, vol. II, 6, April 1913, pp.356–72.

"Noteworthy Articles in Recent Periodicals", *IRM*, vol. II, 7, July 1913, pp.569–79.

"Noteworthy Articles in Recent Periodicals", *IRM*, vol. II, 8, Oct. 1913, pp.775–84.

"The Position of the Continuation Committee", letter to *The Times*, 1 Jan. 1914.

"A Missionary Survey of the Year 1913", *IRM*, vol. III, 9, Jan. 1914, pp.3–83.

"The Missionary and His Task. I: Conditions and Demands of the Task", *IRM*, vol. III, 10, April 1914, pp.284–96.

"The Missionary and his Task. II: Problems of the Church in the Mission Field", *IRM*, vol. III, 11, July 1914, pp.506–28.

"The War and Missions", *IRM*, vol. III, 12, Oct. 1914, pp.625–38.

"A Missionary Survey of the Year 1915", *IRM*, vol. V, 17, Jan. 1916, pp.3–73.

(with G.A. Gollock) "A Missionary Survey of the Year 1916", *IRM*, vol. VI, 21, Jan. 1917, pp.3–61.

"The Question of a Conscience Clause in India", *IRM*, vol. VI, 21, Jan. 1917, pp.126–41.

(with G.A. Gollock) "A Missionary Survey of the Year 1917", *IRM*, vol. VII, 25, Jan. 1918, pp.3–58.

"Hollis B. Frissell and Hampton", *The Constructive Quarterly*, vol. VI, Sept. 1918, pp.569–76.

"Introductory Note", *IRM*, vol. III, 29, Jan. 1919, pp.3–6.

"Co-operation – its Necessity and Cost", *IRM*, vol. VIII, 30, April 1919, pp.173–92.

"German Missions", *IRM*, vol. VIII, 32, Oct. 1919, pp.459–78.

"Christian Education", *IRM*, vol. IX, 33, Jan. 1920, pp.3–18.

"The Interchurch World Movement, its Possibilities and Problems", *IRM*, vol. IX, 34, April 1920, pp.182–99.

"Nationality and Missions", *IRM*, vol. IX, 35, July 1920, pp.372–83.

"A New Beginning of International Missionary Co-operation", *IRM*, vol. IX, 36, Oct. 1920, pp.481–94.

"International Co-operation in Missions", in F.P. Turner, ed., *Foreign Missions Conference of North America*, New York, Foreign Missions Conference 1920, pp.75–81; and "Governmental Attitudes and How to Meet Them", *ibid.*, pp.140–44, addresses given at Foreign Missions Convention, New Haven, Connecticut, Jan. 1920.

"The Indian Outlook", letter to *The Times*, 11 Dec. 1920, p.6.

"Christian Missions and African Labour", *IRM*, vol. X, 38, April 1921, pp.183–95.

"The Crisis in Christian Education in the Mission Fields", in *Papers on Educational Problems in Mission Fields*, London, IMC, 1921, pp.46–71.

"International Missionary Co-operation", in F.P. Turner, *Foreign Missions Conference of North America*, New York, Foreign Missions Conference, 1921, pp.84–92, address given to committee of reference and counsel, Feb. 1921.

"God the Supreme Reality", in *Christ and Human Need*, London, SCM, 1921, pp.127–40, address given at conference on international and missionary questions, Glasgow, Jan. 1921.

"New Spiritual Adventures in the Mission Field", *IRM*, vol. XI, 44, Oct. 1922, pp.526–50.

"Five Conferences in India", *IRM*, vol. XII, 46, April 1923, pp.262–76.

"The Western Contribution to Education in Asia and Africa", in *Christian Education in Africa and the East*, London, SCM, 1924, pp.1–11; and "Christian Education in Africa", *ibid.*, pp.82–96.

"Religious Education in the Mission Field", *IRM*, vol. XIII, 52, Oct. 1924, pp.500–17.

"India in the Twentieth Century", in *The World Task of the Christian Church*, London, SCM, 1925, pp.41–55; and "The Problem of Race", *ibid.*, pp.91–104, addresses given at a student conference on international and missionary questions, Manchester, Jan. 1925.

"His Message to Nations and Races", in F.P. Turner and F.K. Sanders, *The Foreign Missions Convention at Washington 1925*, New York, Foreign Missions Conference of North America and Fleming H. Revell, 1925, pp.46–52; "Christian Education in Relation to Government Developments", *ibid.*, pp.116–18; and "Notes of a Conference", *ibid.*, pp.361f., addresses given to foreign missions convention, Washington DC, Jan.–Feb. 1925.

"The World's Student Christian Federation Past and Future", *Student World*, vol. XVIII, 4, Oct. 1925, pp.167–72.

"Christ's View of Nations and Races", *Missionary Review of the World*, vol. XXXVIII, new series, July 1925, pp.533–36.

"The World Mission of the Church", *The Intercollegian*, June 1925, pp.279–81.

"Missions", *Encyclopaedia Britannica*, 11th edition, supplement to vol. II, 1925, pp.933f.

"Africa", *The Laymen's Bulletin*, no. 36, Jan. 1926, pp.686–90, address given at the Cambridge conference, July 1925.

"Population and Health in Africa", *IRM*, vol. XV, 59, July 1926, pp.146–48.

"Kenya and Its Problems: A Recent Visit. I: Native Health and Education", letter to *The Times*, 9 June 1926, pp.17f.

"Kenya and Its Problems. II: Dual Policy – The Importance of Research", letter to *The Times*, 10 June 1926, pp.17f.

"The Relation of Christian Missions to the New Forces that are Reshaping African Life", in E.W. Smith, ed., *The Christian Mission in Africa*, London, IMC, 1926, pp.162–72, address given at international conference, Le Zoute, Belgium, Sept. 1926.

"The Christian Mission in Africa", *IRM*, vol. XVI, 61, Jan. 1927, pp.24–35.

"Editorial Changes", *IRM*, vol. XVI, 61, Jan. 1927, p.127.

"Educational Problems in Africa", *Scottish Educational Journal*, vol. X, 6, 11 Feb. 1927, pp.144f.

"The Meeting of the International Missionary Council at Jerusalem in 1928", *The Review of the Churches*, vol. V, new series, 1, Jan. 1928, pp.81–87.

"The Future of Christian Missions", *The World Tomorrow*, vol. XI, Jan. 1928, pp.26–28.

"The Call to Missionary Service", in E. Shillito, ed., *The Purpose of God in the Life of the World*, London, SCM, 1929, pp.147–64, address given at a conference on international and missionary questions, Liverpool, Jan. 1929.

"Preface", in J.W.C. Dougall, *Religious Education in Africa*, London, IMC, 1929, pp.5f.

"The New Christian Adventure", *National Christian Council Review*, vol. XLIX, new series, 10, Oct. 1929, pp.512–21.

"Future of East Africa", letter to *The Times*, 7 Nov. 1929, p.10.

"Education in Africa", letter to *The Times*, 27 March 1930, p.10.

"Devotional Service", in L.B. Moss and M.H. Brown, eds, *Foreign Missions Conference of North America 1931*, New York, Foreign Missions Conference of North America 1931, pp.97–100, prayer of intercession delivered at conference of foreign mission bodies, Atlantic City, Jan. 1931; and "The Challenge of the World Situation for Christian Living", *ibid.*, pp.250–60.

"The Spiritual Hungers of Men", *Far Horizons*, vol. XI, 7, April 1931, pp.3–6.

"Christian Education, Its Meaning and Mission – I", *National Christian Council Review*, vol. LI, new series, 5, May 1931, pp.245–52.

"Christian Education, Its Meaning and Mission – II", *National Christian Council Review*, vol. LI, new series, 6, June 1931, pp.287–95.

"Christian Education, Its Meaning and Mission – III", *National Christian Council Review*, vol. LI, new series, 7, July 1931, pp.345–49.

"When 'Race Problem' Is a Misnomer", *Asia*, vol. XXXI, 10, Oct. 1931, pp.662, 670–72.

"The Devotional Life. I: The Morning Watch", *Student Movement*, vol. XXXIV, 1, Oct. 1931, pp.6f.

"The Devotional Life. II: Listening for the Word of God", *Student Movement*, vol. XXXIV, 2, Nov. 1931, pp.32f.

"The Devotional Life. III: The Practice of Prayer", *Student Movement*, vol. XXXIV, 3, Dec. 1931, pp.50f.

"The Devotional Life. IV: The Daily Round", *Student Movement*, XXXIV, 4, Jan. 1932, pp.74f.

"The Dilemma of Western Civilization", *Student World*, vol. XXV, 3, 3rd quarter 1932, pp.186–96, address given at European leaders' conference, Bad Boll, Whitsuntide, 1932.

"Faith in God and Faith in Man, or, the Dimensions of Human Life", *The Christian Faith Today*, London, SCM, 1933, pp.54–75, address given at a conference on international and missionary questions, Edinburgh, Jan. 1933.

"The Future of Kenya", letter to *The Times*, 22 April 1933, p.6.

"The Meaning of Life", letter to *The Times*, 8 Oct. 1933, p.13.

"The Educational Work of Missionary Societies", *Africa*, vol. VII, 1, Jan. 1934, pp.47–59.

"Education for an International World", *Religion in Education*, vol. I, 3, July 1934, pp.123–26.

"The New Conflict between Church and State", *The News-Letter*, vol. VI, 6, 8 Dec. 1934, pp.88–90.

"Die Kirche und der Staat", in P. Althaus *et al.*, *Die Kirche und das Staatsproblem in der Gegenwart*, Geneva, Forschungabsteilung des Ökumenisches Rates fur Praktisches Christentum, 1935, pp.214–16.

"Introduction", *The Modern Missionary*, London, SCM, 1935, pp.7–13.

"Education, Politics, Religion", *The New Era in Home and School*, vol. XVI, Jan. 1935, pp.297–313.

"Basic Issues Underlying the Christian Attitude to the State", *Student World*, vol. XXVIII, 1, 1st quarter 1935, pp.65–68.

"The South African Protectorates", letter to *The Times*, 24 May 1935, p.12.

"The International Review of Missions after Twenty-Five Years", *IRM*, vol. XXIV, 9, July 1935, pp.297–313.

"The Christian World Community", *World's Youth*, vol. XI, 3, Oct. 1935, pp.196–210.

"The Christian World Community", *Student World*, vol. XXVIII, 4, 4th quarter 1935, pp.374–89, address given at international student conference on missions, Basel, Aug.–Sept. 1935.

"An Open Letter from Dr J.H. Oldham on the Oxford Conference", *Student World*, vol. XXX, 2, 2nd quarter 1937, pp.109–11.

"Christians in Conference", letter to *The Times*, 4 Aug. 1937, p.8.

"Some Concluding Reflections", in *Church, Community and State in Relation to Education*. vol. VI of *Church, Community and State*, London, Allen & Unwin 1938, pp.211–34, Oxford conference preparatory reports.

"Lessons of the Crisis", letter to *The Times*, 5 Oct. 1938, p.15.

"The Church in War Time", *The Listener*, vol. XXII, 559, 28 Sept. 1939, pp.623f.

"How Far Will This Take Us?", *The Listener*, vol. XXVIII, 724, 26 Nov. 1942, p.690.

"The Future of British Imperialism", *Christian Century*, vol. LX, 3 Feb. 1943, pp.129–31.

"William Paton", *IRM*, vol. XXXII, 128, Oct. 1943, pp.462f.

"A Choice – with Everything at Stake", *The Listener*, vol. XXX, 780, 23 Dec. 1943, pp.711f.

"Introductory Chapter", in A.M. Chirgwin, *Coming Together the Churches Co-operate*, London, Edinburgh House, 1944, pp.5–10.

"Christian Humanism", in J. Huxley, G. Murray and J.H. Oldham, *Humanism: Three Broadcast Talks*, London, Watts, 1944, pp.15–20.

"Technics and Civilisation", in *The Church and the Disorder of Society*, vol. III of *Man's Disorder and God's Design*, London, SCM, 1948, pp.29–49; and "A Responsible Society", *ibid.*, pp.120–54, preparatory volume for WCC assembly, Amsterdam, 1948.

"A Responsible Society", *Christendom*, vol. XIII, 3, summer 1948, pp.284–316.

"The Two Orders in which We Live", *The Frontier*, vol. I, 12, Dec. 1950, pp.458–65, address given at annual conference of Christian Frontier Council, autumn 1950.

"A Faith that Rebels", *The Frontier*, vol. II, 4, April 1951, pp.140–57, address given at Frontier lunch, London, 21 Feb. 1951.

"Comments on the "The Church, the Churches and the World Council of Churches", *The Ecumenical Review*, vol. III, 3, April 1951, pp.248–50.

"Personal Existence in a Period of Cultural Disintegration", *Student Movement*, vol. LIV, 1, Oct. 1951, pp.13–16, address given at study conference, Swanwick, 1951.

"Personal Existence in a Period of Cultural Disintegration", *Student Movement*, vol. LIV, 2, Nov.–Dec. 1951, pp.11–15, concluding the address given at study conference, Swanwick, 1951.

"Man and Truth", *Question*, vol. 5, 1, winter 1952, pp.85–107.

"Kenneth Maclennan", *IRM*, vol. XLI, 163, July 1952, pp.351f.

"John R. Mott", *The Ecumenical Review*, vol. VII, 3, April 1955, pp.256–59.

"The Frontier Idea", *Frontier*, vol. III, winter 1960, pp.247–52.

"Reflections on Edinburgh 1910", *Religion in Life*, vol. XXIX, summer 1960, pp.329–38.

"Fifty Years After", *IRM*, vol. XLIX, 195, July 1960, pp.257–72.

"A Great Anniversary 1910–1960", *Student Movement*, vol. LXII, 5, summer 1960, pp.32f.

"Frontiers Still Unexplored", *Frontier*, vol. VI, spring 1963, pp.33–40.

## III. J.H. Oldham and *The Christian News-Letter*

*The Christian News-Letter*, from no. 0, 18 Oct. 1939 and no. 1, 1 Nov. 1939, thence generally weekly to no. 178, 24 March 1943, and from then fortnightly to no. 234, 16 May 1945, appeared over the name of J.H. Oldham. His signature was likewise given to nos 241, 22 Aug. 1945; 242, 5 Sept. 1945; 260, 15 May 1946; 268, 4 Sept. 1946; 269, 18 Sept. 1946; 274, 27 Nov. 1946; 275, 11 Dec. 1946; 276, 25 Dec. 1946; 318, 18 Aug. 1948; 340, 22 June 1949.

J.H. Oldham was author of the following supplements to *The Christian News-Letter:*

"What is a Christian News-Letter?", no. 0, 18 Oct. 1939.

"What Is God Doing?", no. 1, 1 Nov. 1939.

"Evacuation – a Social Landmark", no. 3, 15 Nov. 1939.

"Preliminaries to the Consideration of Peace Aims", no. 5, 29 Nov. 1939.

"The Way Out", no. 45, 4 Sept. 1940.

"Youth, the War and the Future", no. 47, 18 Sept. 1940.

"The Demand for a Christian Lead", no. 57, 27 Nov. 1940.

"Predicament and Salvation", no. 59, 11 Dec. 1940.

"Predicament", no. 70, 26 Feb. 1941.

"Christianity and Manhood", no. 72, 12 March 1941.

"The Predicament of Society and the Way Out", no. 86, 18 June 1941.

"The Predicament of Society and the Way Out", no. 88, 1 July 1941.

"The Need for a Fresh Approach to Christian Education", no. 108, 19 Nov. 1941.

"The Growth of Co-operation between the Churches", no. 136, 3 June 1942.

"Christmas 1942", no. 164, 16 Dec. 1942.

"Christians and the Beveridge report", no. 178, 24 March 1943.

"The Church in Europe", no. 181, 5 May 1943.

"Belief in the Resurrection", no. 192, 6 Oct. 1943.

"Christianity and Power", no. 212, 12 July 1944.

"The Church in Germany", no. 241, 22 Aug. 1945.

"The Control of Atomic Energy", no. 269, 18 Sept. 1946.

"Christians and Modern War", no. 325, 24 Nov. 1948.

## IV. A note on reviews by J.H. Oldham

From 1906 onwards, J.H. Oldham was a prolific writer of reviews of works in theology, missiology, philosophy, education, colonial policy and many other contemporary issues. For reasons of space these are not listed here, but the bibliography in W.L. Martin's unpublished Ph.D. thesis (see Bibliography of Secondary Sources below) gives what must be the closest to a complete list attainable. The relevant journals are *Student Movement, International Review of Missions, The Christian News-Letter, Frontier,* and *The Plain View.*

## V. Secondary sources cited in the text

*A. On J.H. Oldham*

BENNETT, G., "Paramountcy to Partnership: J.H. Oldham and Africa", *Africa*, vol. XXX, 4, Oct. 1960, pp.356–61.

BLISS, K., "The Legacy of J.H. Oldham", *International Bulletin of Missionary Research*, Jan. 1984, pp.18–24.

——, "Oldham, Joseph Houldsworth", in E.T. Williams and C.S. Nicholls, eds, *Dictionary of National Biography 1961–1970*, Oxford, Oxford Univ. Press, 1981, pp.806–808.

——, "Oldham, Joseph Houldsworth", in N. Lossky *et al.*, eds, *Dictionary of the Ecumenical Movement*, Geneva, WCC, 1991, pp.746f.

CELL, J.W., ed., *By Kenya Possessed: The Correspondence of Norman Leys and J.H. Oldham 1918–1926*, Chicago, Univ. of Chicago Press, 1976.

MARTIN, W.L., "Joseph Houldsworth Oldham: His Thought and Its Development", unpublished Ph.D. thesis, University of St Andrews, 1967.

*B. On related topics*

BEBBINGTON, D.W., *Evangelicalism in Modern Britain: A History from the 1730s to the 1980s*, London, Unwin Hyman, 1989.

BELL, G.K.A., *Randall Davidson*, vols. I and II, Oxford, Oxford Univ. Press, 1935.

BETHGE, E., *Dietrich Bonhoeffer*, London, Collins, 1970.

BHATIA, S., *Social Change and Politics in the Punjab 1848–1910*, New Delhi, Entry Publications, 1987.

BONHOEFFER, D., *Letters and Papers from Prison*, London, SCM, 1971.

BOYENS, A., *Kirchenkampf und Ökumene 1933–1939: Darstellung und Dockumentation*, Munich, Chr. Kaiser, 1969.

BRUNNER, E., *Der Mittler*, Tübingen, J.C.B. Mohr, 1927. English transl. by Olive Wyon, *The Mediator*, London, Lutterworth, 1946.

BRUNNER, R., *Das Gebot und die Ordnungen*, Tübingen, J.C.B. Mohr, 1937. English transl. *The Divine Imperative: A Study in Christian Ethics*, London, Lutterworth, 1937.

BUSCH, E., *Karl Barth: His Life from Letters and Autobiographical Texts*, London, SCM, 1975.

CARPENTER, E., *Archbishop Fisher – His Life and Times*, Norwich, Canterbury, 1991.

CHURCH ASSEMBLY, *The Church and the Atom: A Study of the Moral and Theological Arguments of War and Peace*, London, Church Assembly, 1948.

CLARK, A., ed., *The Colleges of Oxford*, London, Methuen, 1891.

CLATWORTHY, F.J., *The Formulation of British Colonial Education Policy, 1923–1948*, Michigan, Univ. of Michigan School of Education, 1971.

CLEMENTS, K.W., "Baptists and the Outbreak of the First World War", *Baptist Quarterly*, vol. XXVI, April 1975.

——, *The Theology of Ronald Gregor Smith*, Leiden, E.J. Brill, 1986.

——, "John Baillie and the Moot", in D. Ferguson, ed., *Christ, Church and Society: Essays on John Baillie and Donald Baillie*, Edinburgh, T. & T. Clark, 1993.

——, "Oldham and Baillie. A Creative Relationship", in A.R. Morton, ed., *God's Will in a Time of Crisis: A Colloquium Celebrating the 50th Anniversary of the Baillie Commission*, Edinburgh, Centre for Theology and Public Issues, New College, 1994.

CONWAY, J.S., *The Nazi Persecution of the Churches*, London, Weidenfeld & Nicolson, 1968.

ELIOT, T.S., *The Complete Works of T.S. Eliot*, London, Faber & Faber, 1969.

FINDLAY, J.F., Jr, *Dwight L. Moody: American Evangelist 1837–1899*, Chicago, Univ. of Chicago Press, 1969.

GAIRDNER, W.H.T., *"Edinburgh 1910": An Account and Interpretation of the World Missionary Conference*, Edinburgh and London, Oliphant, Anderson & Ferrier, 1910.

GANN, L.H. and P. DUIGNAN, eds, *Colonialism in Africa 1870–1960. Vol. 2: The History and Problems of Colonialism 1924–1960*, Cambridge, Cambridge Univ. Press, 1970.

GREEN, V.H.H., *Religion at Oxford and Cambridge*, London, SCM, 1964.

HAMPSON, D., "The British Responses to the German Church Struggle 1933–1939", unpublished D.Phil thesis, Oxford, 1973.

HASTINGS, A., *A History of English Christianity 1920–1985*, London, Collins, 1986.

HASTINGS, A., *The Church in Africa 1450–1950*, Oxford, Oxford Univ. Press, 1994.

HEADLAM, C., *The Story of Oxford*, London, J.M. Dent, 1907.

HINSLEY, F.H., ed., *The New Cambridge Modern History*, vol. XI, Cambridge, Cambridge Univ. Press, 1967.

HOCKING, W.E., *Human Nature and Its Remaking*, 2nd ed., New Haven, Yale Univ. Press, 1923.

HOGG, W.R., *Ecumenical Foundations: A History of the International Missionary Council and its Nineteenth Century Background*, New York, Harper, 1952.

HOPKINS, C.H., *John R. Mott 1865–1955*, Geneva, WCC, and Grand Rapids, Eerdmans, 1979.

IREMONGER, F.A., *William Temple: Archbishop of Canterbury*, Oxford, Oxford Univ. Press, 1948.

JACKSON, E., *Red Tape and the Gospel: A Study of the Significance of the Ecumenical Missionary Struggle of William Paton (1886–1943)*, Birmingham, Phlogiston Press and Selly Oak Colleges, 1980.

JASPER, R.C.D., *George Bell: Bishop of Chichester*, London, Oxford Univ. Press, 1967.

JONES, R.F., "Secular Civilization and the Christian Task", in *The Christian Life and Message in Relation to Non-Christian Systems*, vol. I of report of the Jerusalem meeting of the International Missionary Council, 24 March – 9 April 1928, London, Oxford Univ. Press, 1928.

KENT, J.H.S., *Holding the Fort: Studies in Victorian Revivalism*, London, Epworth, 1978.

KETTLER, D., V. MEJA and N. STEHR, *Karl Mannheim*, London, Tavistock, 1984.

KOJECKY, R., *T.S. Eliot's Social Criticism*, London, Faber & Faber, 1971.

LENWOOD, F., "The International Missionary Council at Lake Mohonk", *IRM*, vol. XI, 41, Jan. 1922, pp.30–42.

LUGARD, E., *The Dual Mandate in Tropical Africa*, Edinburgh, William Blackwood, 1922.

MEHTA, V., *The New Theologian*, London, Penguin, 1965.

MOTT, J.R., *The Decisive Hour of Christian Missions*, London, Student Volunteer Union, 1910.

MÜLLER, K. *et al.*, *Mission Theology: An Introduction*, Nettertal, Steyler, 1987.

NEWBIGIN, L., *Unfinished Agenda*, Edinburgh, St Andrew Press, 1993.

OLDHAM, H.W., *Lt-Col. G.W. Oldham R.E.: A Memoir*, London, Morgan & Scott, 1927.

OLIVER, R., *The Missionary Factor in East Africa*, 2nd ed., London, Longman, 1970.

PADWICKE, C. E., *Temple Gairdner of Cairo*, London, SPCK, 1929.

PERHAM, M., *Lugard: The Years of Authority 1898–1945*, 2nd part of life, London, Collins, 1960.

REEVES, M., ed., *Christian Thinking and Social Order*, London, Cassell, 1999.

REYNOLDS, J.S., *Canon Christopher of St Aldate's, Oxford*, Abingdon, Abbey, 1967.

ROBBINS, K., "Church and Politics, Dorothy Buxton and the German Church Struggle", in D. Baker, ed., *Church, Society and Politics*, Oxford, Blackwell, 1975, pp.419–33.

——, "Free Churchmen and the Twenty Years' Crisis", *Baptist Quarterly*, vol. XXVII, 8, Oct. 1978, pp.346–57.

ROBINSON, K., *The Dilemmas of Trusteeship: Aspects of British Colonial Policy Between the Wars*, London, Oxford Univ. Press, 1965.

ROUSE, R., *The World's Student Christian Federation*, London, SCM, 1948.

—— and S. NEILL, eds, *A History of the Ecumenical Movement 1517–1948*, London, SPCK, 1967.

SCHOLDER, K., *The Churches in the Third Reich*, vol. I, London, SCM, 1987; and vol. II, London, SCM, 1988.

SMITH, H.M., *Frank, Bishop of Zanzibar: Life of Frank Weston 1871–1924*, London, SPCK, 1926.

SMUTS, J.C., *Africa and Some World Problems*, Oxford, Clarendon, 1930.

STEWARD, I.R.G., *Dynamic: Paget Wilkes of Japan*, London, Marshall, Morgan & Scott, 1957.

STUDENT VOLUNTEER MISSIONARY UNION, *"Make Jesus King": The Report of the International Students' Missionary Conference, Liverpool, 1–5 Jan. 1896*, London, Student Volunteer Missionary Union, 1896.

SYMONDS, R., *Oxford and Empire: The Last Lost Cause?*, London, Macmillan, 1986.

TATLOW, T., *The Story of the Student Christian Movement of Great Britain and Ireland*, London, SCM, 1933.

TAYLOR, W., "Education and the Moot", in R. Aldrich, ed., *History and Education: Essays in Honour of Peter Gordon*, London, Woburn, 1996.

TEMPLE, W., *Christianity and Social Order*, London, Penguin, 1942.

TEMPLETON, E., *God's February*, London, CCBI, 1991.

TIGNON, R.L., *The Colonial Transformation of Africa*, Princeton, Princeton Univ. Press, 1976.

VIDLER, A.R., *Christ's Strange Work*, London, SCM, 1963.

——, *Scenes from a Clerical Life*, London, Collins, 1977.

VISSER 'T HOOFT, W.A., ed., *The First Assembly of the World Council of Churches*, London, SCM, 1949.

——, *Memoirs*, London, SCM, 1973; 2nd ed. Geneva, WCC, 1987.

——, *The Genesis and Formation of the World Council of Churches*, Geneva, WCC, 1982.

WARNECK, G., *Modern Missions and Culture: Their Mutual Relations*, Edinburgh, James Gemmell, 1888, transl. from German by T. Smith.

——, *Outline of a History of Protestant Missions from the Reformation to the Present Time*, Edinburgh, Oliphant, Anderson & Ferrier, 1901, transl. from German by G. Robson.

WATT, H., *New College Edinburgh: A Centenary History*, Edinburgh, Oliver & Boyd, 1946.

WEBER, H.-R., *Asia and the Ecumenical Movement 1895–1961*, London, SCM, 1966.

WILKINSON, T., *Two Monsoons*, London, Duckworth, 1976.

WOLPERT, S., *A New History of India*, 3rd ed., Oxford, Oxford Univ. Press, 1989.

WORLD COUNCIL OF CHURCHES, *The Church and the Disorder of Society*, vol. III of ecumenical study volumes preparatory to WCC assembly 1948, London, SCM, 1948.

# *The Moot Attendance Record*

| | April '38 | Sept. '38 | Jan. '39 | April '39 | Sept. '39 | | Feb. '40 | April '40 | July '40 |
|---|---|---|---|---|---|---|---|---|---|
| * Baillie, J. | ✓ | ✓ | ✓ | ✓ | ✓ | | | | |
| * Bliss, K. | | | | | | | | | |
| Chaning Pearce, M. | | | | | | | | | |
| * Clarke, F. | | | | | | | ✓ | ✓ | ✓ |
| * Dawson, C. | ✓ | | | | | | | | |
| * Eliot, T.S. | ✓ | ✓ | ✓ | ✓ | ✓ | | | ✓ | ✓ |
| * Farmer, H.H. | ✓ | | | | ✓ | | | | |
| * Fenn, E. | ✓ | ✓ | ✓ | ✓ | ✓ | | ✓ | | ✓ |
| Hall, N.F. | | | | ✓ | | | | | |
| * Hetherington, H. | | | | | | | | | |
| * Hodges, H.A. | ✓ | ✓ | ✓ | ✓ | ✓ | | | ✓ | ✓ |
| * Iredale, E. | ✓ | ✓ | ✓ | ✓ | ✓ | | | ✓ | ✓ |
| * Jenkins, D. | | | | | | | | | |
| Lampert, E. | | | | | | | | | |
| * Löwe, A. | ✓ | ✓ | ✓ | | ✓ | | ✓ | ✓ | |
| * MacKinnon, D. | | | | | | | | | |
| Mairet, P. | | | | | | | | | |
| * Mannheim, K. | | ✓ | ✓ | ✓ | ✓ | | ✓ | ✓ | ✓ |
| Miller, A. | | | | | | | | | |
| * Moberly, W. | ✓ | ✓ | ✓ | ✓ | ✓ | | ✓ | ✓ | ✓ |
| * Murry, J.M. | ✓ | ✓ | ✓ | | ✓ | | ✓ | ✓ | ✓ |
| Newbigin, L. | | ✓ | | | | | | | |
| Niebuhr, R. | | | | | ✓ | | | | |
| * Oakshott, W. | | ✓ | | | | | | ✓ | ✓ |
| * Oldham, J.H. | ✓ | ✓ | ✓ | ✓ | ✓ | | ✓ | ✓ | ✓ |
| * Oldham, M. | ✓ | ✓ | ✓ | ✓ | ✓ | | ✓ | ✓ | ✓ |
| Pakenham, F. | | | | | | | | | |
| Paton, W. | | ✓ | | | | | | | |
| * Polanyi, M. | | | | | | | | | |
| Russell, G. | | | | | | | | | |
| * Shaw, G. | | ✓ | ✓ | ✓ | ✓ | | ✓ | ✓ | |
| Symons, W.G. | | | | | | | | | |
| Tomkins, O. | | | ✓ | ✓ | ✓ | | | | |
| Vickers, G. | | | | | | | | ✓ | |
| * Vidler, A.R. | | ✓ | ✓ | ✓ | ✓ | | ✓ | ✓ | ✓ |
| * Actual Moot members. | 1. High Leigh | 2. Westfield | 3. Elfinsward | 4. Jordans | 5. Annandale | 6. | 7. Jordans | 8. Jordans | 9. Jordans |

| Meeting | | | | | | | | | | | | | | | | | | | | | | | | | | | | | | | | | | | | Date |
|---|---|---|---|---|---|---|---|---|---|---|---|---|---|---|---|---|---|---|---|---|---|---|---|---|---|---|---|---|---|---|---|---|---|---|---|---|
| 10. Cold Ash | √ | | | | √ | | | | | | √ | √ | | | | √ | | √ | √ | | | | | √ | √ | √ | | √ | | √ | √ | | | | | Jan. '41 |
| 11. Cold Ash | √ | | | | √ | √ | | | | √ | √ | | | | √ | √ | | √ | | | | | | √ | √ | √ | | | | | | √ | | | | April '41 |
| 12. Oxford | √ | | | | √ | | | | | | √ | √ | | | | √ | | √ | | | | | | | √ | | | √ | | √ | √ | √ | | | √ | Aug. '41 |
| 13. Oxford | | | | | √ | | | | | √ | √ | √ | | | √ | √ | | √ | | | | | | √ | √ | | | √ | | √ | | √ | √ | | √ | Dec. '41 |
| 14. Oxford | √ | | | | √ | | | | | | √ | | | | | √ | | √ | | | | | | √ | √ | | | √ | | | | √ | √ | | √ | Mar. '42 |
| 15. Jordans | √ | | | | | | | | | √ | √ | | | | √ | √ | | √ | | | | | | √ | √ | √ | | | | √ | | | | | √ | Sept. '42 |
| 16. Jordans | √ | | | | √ | | | | √ | | √ | | | | | √ | | √ | | | | | | √ | √ | √ | | √ | | | | | | | √ | Jan. '43 |
| 17. Oakenrough | √ | | | | | | | | | √ | √ | | √ | | | | √ | √ | | | | | | √ | √ | √ | | √ | | √ | | | | √ | | June '43 |
| 18. St Julians | √ | | | | √ | | | | | √ | √ | | | | | | √ | √ | | | | | √ | | √ | | | √ | | | | √ | | √ | | Nov. '43 |
| 19. St Julians | √ | | | √ | √ | | | | | √ | √ | | | | | √ | √ | √ | | | | | √ | | √ | | | √ | | | | √ | | √ | | Jan. '44 |
| 20. St Julians | √ | | | | | | √ | | | √ | √ | | | | | √ | √ | √ | √ | | | | | | √ | | | √ | | | | | | √ | √ | June '44 |
| 21. St Julians | √ | | | | | | √ | | | √ | √ | | | | | √ | √ | √ | | √ | | | | | √ | | | | | | | √ | | √ | √ | Dec. '44 |

# Index